Introduction to Cruising	2
Preparing to Cruise	20
Bon Voyage!	46
Cruise Lines and Cruise Ships	65
Top Ships	66
A Cruise Ship Directory	92
Destinations	139
North America	140
Bermuda	160
The Bahamas	162
Caribbean	166
Central/South America	178
Antarctica	192
Northern Europe	196
Mediterranean	210
Indian Ocean	234
Hawaiian Islands	240
South Pacific	244
New Zealand	250
Australia	254
Asia	260
Index	280

First Edition ©1997 by
ACCESS®PRESS. All rights
reserved. No portion of
this publication may be
reproduced or transmitted in
any form or manner by any
means, including, but not
limited to, graphic, electronic,
and mechanical methods,
photocopying, recording,
taping, or any informational
storage and retrieval systems
without explicit permission
from the publisher. ACCESS®
is a registered trademark of
HarperCollins Publishers Inc.

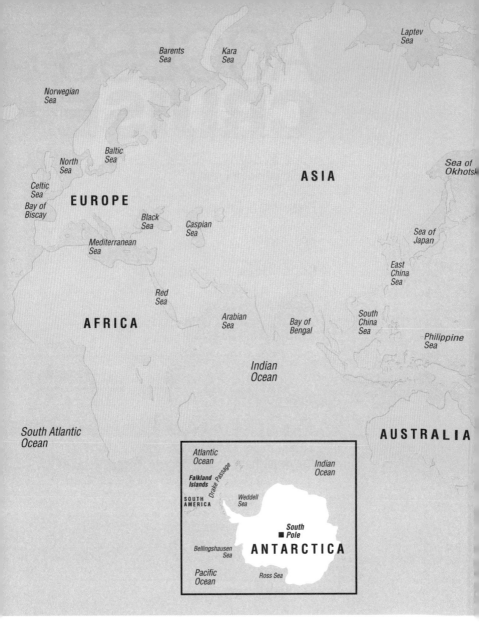

Introduction to Cruising

Many people dream of sailing away on a luxury cruise ship, setting a course for exotic ports and unforgettable adventures. Today making that fantasy a reality is easier than ever: Cruise lines offer wider price ranges, greater flexibility in ship size and voyage length, and an ever-increasing number of ports—nearly 500 in 100 countries. Every year about five million Americans board ships—not just for transportation or commerce as they did in yesteryear, but for pleasure.

Worlds of oceans, seas, rivers, canals, and fjords await discovery by the cruise traveler. For sun-and-fun cruisers, there's **Bermuda**, the **Caribbean**, **Mexico**, and **Hawaii.** Those voyagers more interested in history and culture can choose destinations ranging from the **Baltics** to the **British Isles,** the **Mediterranean** to **Madagascar, South America** to **Southeast Asia.**

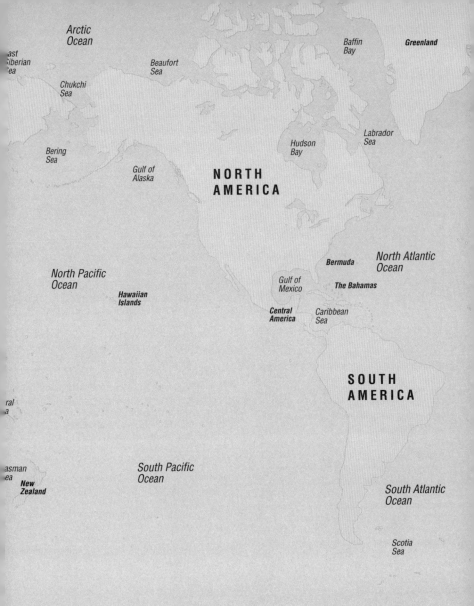

Aficionados of natural beauty are particularly drawn to the **South Pacific**, as well as to **New England/Canada**, the **Norwegian** fjords, and **Alaska.** For those looking for surreal landscapes, the possibilities extend to **Iceland** and **Antarctica.**

Seagoing vacations are gaining popularity. Gone is the notion that cruises are only for wealthy retirees. In fact, research by the Cruise Lines International Association (CLIA), a New York–based trade group, shows that every year the average cruiser is younger and of more modest means. And in keeping with the trend of travelers of all ages and interests to take briefer, more frequent vacations, cruise companies now offer shorter itineraries.

But whatever your age or income, your choice of destinations, style of vessel, or length of cruise, a host of ships awaits to whisk you away across the open seas to boundless pleasures.

History of Cruising

The modern cruise vacation has its origins in the passenger lines of the past. In 1840 Samuel Cunard established regular steamship service between **North America** and Liverpool. Its main purpose, however, was to carry mail—people were an afterthought. Charles Dickens, a passenger on the 1842 transatlantic crossing of **Cunard**'s *Britannia*, graphically described the ordeal in his *American Notes*. He complained that his quarters were cramped and flooded, the food miserable, and the nausea never-ending. **Cunard** survived the bad press simply because there was no other way to cross the **Atlantic** in those days.

Through much of the 1800s ships were viewed solely as a means of transportation, not as pleasure boats. Traffic flowed freely in both directions across the Atlantic: Wealthy Americans sailed to **Europe** to take the "Grand Tour"; for their part, Europeans (many not affluent at all) boarded ships to emigrate to the **United States.** On rare occasions, ships were pressed into leisure service, calling at multiple ports in voyages that were precursors of the modern-day cruise. In 1844 essayist William M. Thackeray sailed to **Malta, Greece, Constantinople,** the **Holy Land,** and **Egypt** on several **P&O Cruises** ships. His *From Cornhill to Grand Cairo* is an account of his experiences. And two **Orient Lines** ships started offering seasonal cruises in the Norwegian fjords in 1889.

Twain hilariously describes "a pleasure voyage" to Europe and the Holy Land in his 1869 book, *The Innocents Abroad or The New Pilgrims Progress.* With characteristic wit and irony, he chronicles the adventures and misadventures of a ship of Americans as they encounter the Old World. His focus is on the ports visited, with descriptions of the steamship *Quaker City* confined to a few pages on the cabins ("room to turn around in, but not to swing a cat in") and such shipboard pastimes as prayer sessions and dancing the Virginia reel.

MICHAEL STORRINGS

In the late 1800s, trade between the US and Europe boomed, and the Atlantic grew into the world's busiest commercial sea route. Companies competed by building bigger, better, and faster ships, and crossings became races for the coveted Blue Ribband, a prize earned by the speediest transatlantic vessel. The trip took about six days at that time.

After the turn of the century, such liners as the famous **Cunard** sisters—*Mauretania, Lusitania,* and *Aquitania*—were launched, boasting such elegant features as mahogany paneling, an unusually high number of private bathrooms, and first-class dining rooms. Rival **White Star**'s trio of giants, *Olympic, Titanic,* and *Britannic* were described as "floating palaces."

The Germans, jealous guardians of the Blue Ribband in the 1930s, had their own magnificent ships, including **Hamburg-Amerika Line**'s *Amerika, Vaterland, Imperator,* and *Bremen,* with the *Imperator* setting a record—5,000-plus people on a crossing. The transatlantic passenger business even survived such horrific maritime disasters as the 1912 collision of the "unsinkable" *Titanic* with a North Atlantic iceberg.

World War I interrupted transatlantic traffic but did not strike a fatal blow. In 1915 Germany and Britain were at war when German submarines torpedoed the British **Cunard** liner *Lusitania* off the Irish coast. Hundreds of Americans were aboard, and the incident is often credited with drawing the US into the conflict. (See "The Cruise that Changed History" on page 15.)

In the postwar era of the 1920s, sea travel boomed. One of the epoch's famous shipping companies was France's **Compagnie Générale Transatlantique,** which operated the stylish *Paris* and *Ile de France.* In the 1930s the French launched *Normandie,* the nation's pride. A contemporary was **Cunard**'s *Queen Mary.* At the same time, passenger ships were plying the **Pacific** and other oceans.

Traffic halted abruptly during World War II, when passenger ships became troop carriers, but the liner business bounced back when peace resumed. And though airplane travel was also growing in popularity, the vessels retained their cachet, as when Grace Kelly chose a ship to whisk her wedding entourage off to **Monaco** for her 1956 marriage to Prince Rainier. As in decades past, Hollywood stars, society figures, politicians, and royalty continued lending social prestige to crossing.

In 1957, postwar liner travel peaked as more than one million passengers took to the high seas aboard some 70 steamers. Then everything changed. As marine historian Walter Lord wrote in his forward to John Maxtone-Graham's *The Only Way to Cross,* "On October 26, 1958, the first American commercial jet took off for Paris, and a whole new era was born. With flight time cut from 12 to less than seven hours, the lure was irresistible."

By 1960 jet planes had cornered 70 percent of the traffic, and before the decade ended only a fraction of travelers went to Europe by sea. But then a new concept—cruising—was born: Rather than using a ship as a means of getting from one place to another, the vessel became a floating hotel that stopped at various ports.

MICHAEL STORRINGS

In 1966 Miamian Ted Arison and Norwegian shipping magnate Knut Utstein Kloster teamed up and turned Kloster's *Sunward*—previously a car/passenger ferry—into a Caribbean cruise ship. From the start, the over-800-passenger ship, outfitted with such luxuries as private toilets, sailed full. The Arison-Kloster partnership is considered the start of the modern cruising industry. The pair eventually split, with Arison going on to form **Carnival Cruise Lines** and Kloster setting up **Norwegian Caribbean Line** (later changed to **Norwegian Cruise Line**). Both companies continue to operate today.

Today's Ships

Dickens, Thackeray, and Twain would be surprised to see how cruise ships have evolved. Modern cruise liners are marvels of beauty, design ingenuity, and comfort. They range from towering to sleek, enormous to yachtlike, twin-hulled to sail-powered. All come equipped with stabilizers—large, retractable fins that steady a vessel in the event of rough seas.

Contemporary vessels feature multistory atriums; fountains; fold-out marinas where passengers may swim at sea when the ship is anchored; sprawling fitness centers and lavish spas; galleries of boutiques; and show lounges with sunken orchestra pits, the latest sound systems, dazzling costumes, and special effects rivaling Las Vegas. They come with libraries, miniature golf courses, teen centers, and children's playrooms. Dining choices include 24-hour

MICHAEL STORRINGS

pizzerias and cafes; patisseries; Chinese, Japanese, and Italian restaurants; and of course the traditional main dining rooms serving international fare.

Cabins are roomier and more comfortable than ever, some with queen- or even king-size beds, mini-bars, marble baths, walk-in closets, and private verandas. Many have VCRs as well as televisions, radios, and telephones that link passengers to the world via satellite communications systems.

Further ingenious technological innovations include interactive television that's making its appearance on some liners. Through the TV screen it's possible to order room service and gift-shop items and book shore excursions. And you can even check the balance of your shipboard account. In the not-too-distant future, passengers will probably be able to settle their bills this way, too.

Why Cruise?

People choose cruises over land vacations for a variety of reasons. In a CLIA poll, 9 out of 10 cruisers proclaimed seagoing holidays as good or better than other vacations. Their top five reasons were:

To Escape and Relax

A cruise is the perfect choice for people looking to unwind. It offers long days of idle relaxation, sleeping late, breakfasting in bed, sunbathing by the pool, sipping tropical drinks, and catching up on reading.

To Be Pampered

Cruisers get the royal treatment on board. In the cabin a steward performs a variety of tasks, including tidying up several times a day, replenishing ice and towels, fluffing pillows, and providing fresh fruit. In the dining room waiters quickly learn passengers' likes and dislikes, and on deck, stewards on some ships spritz loungers with Evian water. Bartenders remember if your martini should have an olive or onion, and when you waltz into the piano bar, the pianist strikes up your favorite tune.

To Visit Several Destinations

Cruise travelers can sample a wide variety of places without the hassles of packing and unpacking, checking in and out of hotels, and shuttling back and forth to airports. You can wake up in a new port every day without doing a thing to get there.

To Enjoy a Good Value

The transportation (air and ship), transfers, accommodations, shipboard activities, fitness center, library, lectures, dining (including room service), and entertainment are *generally* all part of the cruise package. Passengers know what they're paying, up front, because virtually everything is included.

Other items not included: Tips for service personnel, such as cabin stewards, waiters, and buspeople; laundry, dry cleaning, wine, bar drinks, purchases at on-board boutiques, beauty and spa treatments, casino play, doctor visits, shore excursions, phone calls, and trip cancellation insurance. Some companies list port charges (governmental fees and other expenses related to a ship's visit in port) separately from the fare. Check the brochure pricing tables or ask your travel agent.

Exceptions exist. Some very upscale cruise lines include gratuities, wine, and drinks in the cruise fare; a few include port charges. A couple of lines offer a complimentary shore excursion for all passengers. Some nature-cruise companies include all shore tours in their fares; one even offers complimentary laundry service, reasoning that passengers trekking through Central America's rain forests on bird watching and nature hikes need frequent changes of clothing.

And keep in mind that practically *nobody* pays the brochure price. Because of all the new ships out there, it truly is a buyer's market. As a result, there are dozens of discounts floating around. The scoop on cruise discounts and how to get the best deal on a cruise are discussed at length in "Getting the Best Value" (see page 26).

To Experience Diverse Activities

A cruise offers the chance to enjoy an active vacation with sight-seeing and shopping in every port and, on board, such pastimes as dance classes, wine tastings, films, lectures, sports contests, games, parties, and shows.

MICHAEL STORRINGS

Passengers are free to do everything—or nothing at all. Be active in the morning and kick back in the afternoon; stay up all night and sleep all day.

Who Are Today's Cruisers?

Here are some broad descriptions of "types" of passengers and how cruise ships are accommodating them:

Singles

According to CLIA research, one in four cruise passengers is a single person. That doesn't always mean they travel alone; more often they sail with friends or, in the case of single parents, with children.

Activities for singles, such as cocktail parties or relaxed get-togethers, are long-standing shipboard traditions. Cruise lines that regularly attract more single women than men feature "gentlemen hosts" who socialize and dance with the women—without being Don Juans or playing favorites. (See "Perfect Gentlemen" on page 121.) The cruise staff can usually be counted on to include singles in the daily activities and, in the dining room, the maître d' looks to seat singles with other guests.

Very few ships feature single cabins and, as cruise pricing is generally based on two people occupying a room, singles usually have to pay a supplement. Some lines that attract a high percentage of singles, however, adjust their rates to give singles who book double cabins a better deal. Most lines will also, on request, arrange shares with a same-sex passenger, of smoking or no-smoking preference.

Families

With the explosion in family travel, cruise ships are welcoming a growing number of passengers with children by offering supervised activity areas for different age groups, trained counselors, and even shore tours designed specifically for kids. Some ships feature "family cabins" with more room and extra beds, while many others have at least some connecting cabins for those parents and youngsters who want their own space.

More dining options and special kiddie menus let both children and adults order the food they enjoy in comfortable settings. And baby-sitters and adults-only areas allow parents a breather.

Short cruises combined with a few days at **Walt Disney World** or other family attractions are a popular choice. These are packaged in easy-to-buy, one-week programs with everything included.

Groups

Nearly all cruise lines welcome groups—often at reduced rates, depending on how many people are involved. A group can be of just about any affinity—extended families, reunions, clubs, office colleagues, church or museum groups, alumni, fraternal organizations, military, or whatever. Ships will set aside lounges or other public rooms for meetings and, usually for a reasonable charge, will staff and cater social gatherings.

Most ships can provide audiovisual equipment, computers, printers, copiers, and fax machines for corporate groups. New ships offer dedicated meeting facilities and can set up for break-out rooms. Some are equipped for video conferencing, and a few offer secretarial services.

Honeymooners

A cruise is the ultimate romantic vacation—made to order with moonlight, superb dining, excellent service, fun entertainment options, and exciting ports to explore together. A pampering cruise is the ideal way to relax and enjoy each other after the hectic weeks before the wedding. Aboard ship, honeymooners are considered VIPs; cruise lines indulge newlyweds with such honors as a cocktail party with the captain, a cake in the dining room, and, often, a special souvenir—perhaps Champagne glasses or a framed photograph. Some lines feature romantic honeymoon packages that may include sensuous treats like a couples' massage, Champagne, and an in-suite dessert.

But one of the best reasons for a honeymoon cruise is the romantic places ships visit: seductive Hawaii, sophisticated but sporty Bermuda, the exotic South Pacific, the alluring Caribbean islands, the fun-loving **Mexican Riviera,** the wonders of the great European capitals, the pleasures of the **Greek Isles.** Couples getting married in autumn might enjoy the novelty of a New England/Canada cruise when the trees' colors are at their height.

And what about tying the knot on board? Contrary to popular belief, the captain is not authorized to marry couples, but a growing number of cruise lines are happy to arrange for weddings on board before the ship sails or, depending on the itinerary, in some ports of call. For details, see "Getting Hitched at Sea" on page 108.

Gays and Lesbians

Cruises have long been an attractive vacation choice for gay and lesbian travelers. And with the explosion of specialized, gay-oriented travel companies in recent years, the cruise option has blossomed.

Such companies now package programs on cruise ships to the Caribbean, Alaska, the Mediterranean, and other destinations. Sometimes they charter small ships for all-men or all-women sailings.

In addition, cruise lines like **Windjammer Barefoot Cruises** sometimes offer their own gay and/or lesbian theme sailings.

Seniors

An ever-increasing number of seniors are traveling, and many find cruises a secure, comfortable, and economical way to visit exciting venues. For those who relish remote places, today's cruises offer such tour options as African safaris, bird watching in **Costa Rica,**

and hot-air ballooning in Europe. And more and more grandparents are taking along their grandchildren to share the cultural and educational experiences offered by some destinations. A ship is the ideal setting for cross-generational travelers because people of all ages can find an activity they enjoy.

Seniors with low-salt, low-fat, or other diets, exercise regimes, or medical needs find that cruises accommodate with a range of special menus, fitness facilities, and a qualified doctor and nurse always on call at the on-board medical center.

Physically Challenged Travelers

Although most cruise lines make an effort to accommodate passengers in wheelchairs, the reality is that few ships offer special facilities. Most cruise ships are not registered in the United States, so they are technically not (at press time) required to comply with the Americans With Disabilities Act. Many new liners, however, come equipped with at least a few "wheelchair accessible" cabins. This usually means more room, wider doors, no raised lip between the cabin and the bathroom, and handrails near the toilet.

Usually, the newer and bigger the vessel, the more likely it is to have wide passageways and plenty of space for wheelchair users to comfortably navigate public areas. Most ships are equipped with elevators, with the exception of some sail-cruisers and small, expedition-style vessels. In the dining room and in show lounges, some ships reserve space for wheelchair users.

Crew members normally don't mind assisting at the gangway, but wheelchair travelers could find it difficult—if not impossible—to get ashore in ports where the ship anchors, and a tender service shuttles passengers back and forth. Consider selecting an itinerary that has only docking ports and/or traveling with a companion.

Be sure to work with a travel agent who is experienced in making bookings for wheelchair travelers and who thoroughly understands your specific needs. For more information, see "Making A Reservation" on page 34.

In general, travelers with impaired sight or hearing should be able get along well if they have a companion. Notify the cruise line in advance if you are bringing a service animal on board and if you will need special assistance in an emergency situation.

Silversea Cruise is affliliated with Le Cordon Bleu, the renowned French culinary academy. On selected voyages, Silversea chefs de cuisine join Le Cordon Bleu master chefs in hosting cooking presentations, wine tastings, and culinary tours.

People with Special Interests

Folks with hobbies or special interests can find extra fun and camaraderie on a theme cruise. Every year, scores of theme sailings are offered, featuring guest lecturers, workshops, social events, and shore excursions built around a particular topic or pursuit.

Quilting, beauty tips, photography, snow skiing, antique collecting, food and wine, whale watching, Hollywood films, classical music, murder mysteries, Mediterranean history, square dancing, gardening, and jazz are just some of the many specialized cruises offered. For more information, see "Special-interest Sailing: Selecting a Theme Cruise" on page 33.

MICHAEL STORRINGS

Cruising Styles

There are cruise ships to cover every prospective passenger's need: megaships, traditional vessels, and specialty ships (which include small ships, ultraluxury liners, sail-cruisers, riverboats, and boats focusing on nature or adventure programs). In addition, European-style vessels, including those of **P&O Cruises** and **Norwegian Coastal Voyages,** offer a different cultural flavor.

Megaships

These modern, superlarge ships (1,750 passengers plus) emphasize a variety of activities, fun, value for money, and, when it comes to dining and entertainment, mainstream tastes. The onboard atmosphere is relaxed. Daytime dress is casual, though a couple of nights are formal, and passengers always have the option of dressing up—many do. Formalwear includes not only tuxedos and full-length gowns, but dark suits, cocktail dresses, and fancy pantsuits. Such cruises are offered year-round from ports including **Miami, Fort Lauderdale,** and **New Orleans** to such sun-and-fun destinations as the **Bahamas,** the Caribbean, and the Mexican Riviera.

Similar style cruises sail to **Baja California** and the Mexican Riviera from **Los Angeles,** through the **Panama Canal** from both coasts and, in the summer only, to Alaska from **Vancouver, British Columbia.**

Companies that cater to this broad market include **Carnival Cruise Lines, Celebrity Cruises, Costa Cruise Lines, Disney Cruise Line** (debuting in 1998)**, Norwegian Cruise Line, Princess Cruises**, and **Royal Caribbean International**.

Traditional Cruising

Medium- and large-size liners (about 500 passengers to no more than 1,700) are considered traditional ships. They may be older than the megaships and offer a more elegant style, international flavor, and broader itineraries. They tend to sail to seasonal destinations, but a few cruise year-round.

Traditional ships are part of such companies as **American Hawaii, Celebrity Cruises, Costa Cruise Lines, Crystal Cruises, Cunard, Disney Cruise Line** (starting in 1998)**, Holland America Line,** most of the **Norwegian** fleet, **Premier,** some of the **Princess** fleet, **Orient Lines,** some of the **Royal Caribbean International** fleet, and **Royal Olympic Cruises** (composed of **Epirotiki** and **Sun Line).**

But just because they are called "traditional" doesn't mean that they aren't innovative. **Disney** and **Premier,** for example, focus on family cruising. **Celebrity** introduced banks of video screens into the public rooms of its newest ships, and the **Costa** fleet weighs in as the only line offering "Cruising Italian Style"— fresh pasta is served at lunch and dinner, Caribbean theme nights include "Toga Night," and other touches. But traditional certainly describes the graceful, vintage ships of **American Hawaii, Dolphin,** and **Royal Olympic,** as well as **Cunard**'s elegant *Vistafjord* and *Queen Elizabeth 2,* and **Norwegian Cruise Line**'s *Norway* (formerly the ocean liner *France*).

And all these vessels fulfill the expectations of those cruisers who are drawn to the time-honored, seagoing pleasures: a relaxed tempo, varied entertainment, fine dining, good service, and opportunities to dress to the nines on gala nights.

Small Ships

Sailing on a small ship is a whole different experience from a voyage on a towering liner. Travelers seeking intimacy (the ships' capacity ranges from only several dozen to 500), personal service, and a sense of camaraderie with their fellow passengers prefer this style of cruising.

With their shallow drafts, small ships provide access to smaller, more exotic, and off-the-beaten-path ports of call. Some can be powered by sail, adding an adventurous, romantic flair, and can come with reinforced hulls that let them roam polar waters. Small ships can comb canals and rivers, probe secluded inlets teeming with wildlife, and cruise thrillingly close—but not *too* close—to icebergs, reefs, and coastlines. Their voyages connect passengers more intimately with the environment.

Small ships, of course, have some drawbacks. Variety is sacrificed: A small vessel can't offer the enormous range of public rooms and entertainment options available on larger liners. Social activities are more limited, too, as are dining choices, exercise facilities, and other amenities. Some may lack such facilities as swimming pools, casinos, children's playrooms, and perhaps even elevators.

Consider, too, that small ships are indeed small and so are affected more by high seas than are larger vessels. This doesn't mean the ride on an intimate vessel is always rough; that depends on the cruising ground, season, and other factors. But someone who tends toward motion discomfort should not choose a yachtlike vessel for a late autumn transatlantic voyage.

Small ships offer a range of cruising styles:

Adventure/Expedition/ Nature Cruises

An adventure cruise can be many things, from a voyage to the icy realm of penguins in Antarctica to whale watching off the sun-drenched coast of Baja California. It can be searching for puffins off the misty coves of northern **Scotland** or probing Alaskan wilderness to glimpse grizzlies and bald eagles.

If the geographic scope is huge, so is the choice of ships—from riverboats to Russian icebreakers. There's the plucky, expeditionary feel of a vessel like **Abercrombie & Kent**'s 100-passenger *Explorer*. A Yankee spirit and small-country-inn ambience characterizes the cozy ships of **Clipper Cruise Line**, while plush is the only way to describe the marble baths and European butler service of **Radisson Seven Seas**' 170-guest *Hanseatic*.

Still, an adventure cruise isn't a floating resort, glitz and glitter, black-tie galas, gambling, discos, or shopping. The focus is not the ship. It's the destination.

Most passengers who opt for an expedition have an intense interest in the places they visit and so want to spend a lot of time in port, learning, observing, and mingling with the local people. They want to bring home knowledge—not a

MICHAEL STORRINGS

tan or a suitcase full of souvenirs. Dress is generally casual.

Education and personal enrichment are emphasized. The small ships may sail with a coterie of guest lecturers who are experts in their fields, and shoreside tours stress nature, history, and culture. Ships offering such cruises usually boast well-stocked libraries and come equipped with gear like rubber Zodiac rafts for wildlife watching or shore landings in ecologically sensitive areas.

The far-flung itineraries may include such remote spots as Antarctica, **Tierra del Fuego,** the **Northwest Passage,** and Costa Rica. But the destinations aren't necessarily distant; they could be as close to home as Mexico's **Sea of Cortés,** Alaska's **Glacier Bay,** or the less frequented islands of the Caribbean.

Expedition cruises usually run more than seven days, giving passengers an in-depth experience. Because the itinerary is longer and the destination often more remote, these voyages tend to be pricier than a routine sailing.

In addition to **Abercrombie & Kent**, **Clipper**, and **Radisson Seven Seas**, companies offering the adventure-oriented, small-ship experience include **Alaska Sightseeing/Cruise West**, **American Canadian Caribbean Line**, **Bergen Line**'s **Norwegian Coastal Voyages** (see "Cruising the Coast of Norway" on page 209), **Society Expeditions, Special Expeditions, Swan Hellenic Cruises** and **Temptress**. (Note: **World Explorer Cruises** also features nature-oriented voyages, but its ship, the 739-passenger *Universe Explorer*, is relatively large.)

Barge and River Cruises

When it comes to cruising, most people think of the open sea, but passenger ships also ply the world's rivers. River cruises range from the trio of comfortable paddlewheel steamers of New Orleans–based **Delta Queen Steamboat Co.**—which roam the **Mississippi** and other rivers in America's heartland, imparting a strong flavor of Americana—to the small, deluxe barges traveling the canals of **France, The Netherlands, Sweden,** and other European lands, which lavish guests with regional gourmet fare.

River cruises in South America explore **Venezuela**'s **Orinoco,** Brazil's **Amazon,** and Amazon tributaries in **Ecuador.** River boats designed for Western travelers sail Egypt's **Nile, China**'s **Yangtze,** and even the remote waterways of **Siberia.**

Passengers booking river cruises usually want a close look at the region they're visiting. They're focused on the scenery and the ports along the way rather than the ship. Whenever possible, they like to meet the locals.

River voyages appeal to sophisticated travelers who yearn to experience a region in as intimate a way as possible while still enjoying the ease and comfort of cruising. For more information, see "Rollin' on the River" on page 147, "Plying the Exotic Rivers of the World" on page 130, and "Barging Through Europe" on page 83.

A Legendary Liner

In an earlier life, **Norwegian Cruise Line**'s flagship *Norway* was a famous transatlantic liner, **French Line**'s *France*, christened in 1960 by Yvonne de Gaulle (wife of Charles). The height of elegance in her day, the Art Deco *France* carried such famous passengers as Princess Grace and Prince Rainier of Monaco, Audrey Hepburn, Salvador Dalí, Marc Chagall, Burt Lancaster, Joe DiMaggio, Betty Grable, Alfred Hitchcock, and even the famed *Mona Lisa*, on her way from the **Louvre** to an American museum.

The *France* completed 377 transatlantic crossings and 93 cruises, including two circumnavigations, before falling on hard times. Jets began taking over transatlantic traffic in the 1960s and, with the quadrupling of oil prices in the early 1970s, the ship became too costly to operate efficiently. The French government eventually decided to discontinue the

annual subsidy used to operate the liner. The *France* languished in Le Havre until **Norwegian Caribbean Lines** (later **Norwegian Cruise Line**) bought her for $18 million in 1979. Renamed the *Norway*, the ship underwent a $100-million transformation from which she emerged a Caribbean cruise liner.

The *Norway*'s 1980 introduction in Miami caused a sensation; she was by far the largest cruise ship afloat at the time (and she held that title for almost a decade). Still based year-round in Miami, *Norway* has subsequently undergone several major refurbishments, including a $40-million refit in 1990 that increased her tonnage from 70,202 to 75,000 and added a lavish Roman spa and a top deck of suites and penthouse cabins. Subsequent renovations have increased the ship's tonnage to 76,042.

COURTESY OF NORWEIGIAN CRUISE LINES

Sail Cruises

Some small cruise ships sprout sails. While also equipped with engines and able to operate under power if necessary, when conditions are right, these vessels unfurl the sails and let the wind do the work.

The range of sail-cruise options includes **Windstar Cruises**' sleek, upscale trio with their computer-controlled rigging; the active and sporty **Club Med 1** and **2;** the authentic clipper ships of the **Star Clippers** fleet; the elegant *Sea Cloud*, built as the private yacht of Marjorie Merriweather Post; the romantic schooner *Sir Francis Drake;* and the fun-loving ships that comprise **Windjammer Barefoot Cruises**.

On some ships, guests are encouraged to hoist a sail if they're so inclined; on others, nobody outside the crew lifts a finger. Whatever their style, sail-cruise vessels are more casual and decidedly more relaxed about activities than are conventional cruise ships. They have fewer entertainment facilities and scheduled activities; for the most part, passengers do as they please.

But unscheduled doesn't mean dull. Sailing cruise ships offer water-sports equipment, and passengers can fill an entire day while the ship is in port or at anchor with snorkeling, diving, windsurfing, and

sailing. Reading, games, in-cabin videos, and music and dancing round out the entertainment.

In this relaxed atmosphere, sail-cruise passengers dress informally. Depending on the ship, changing for dinner might mean slipping on a clean T-shirt or donning comfortable resortwear. Dining might be family-style or open seating, where passengers don't have an assigned table, but dine wherever and with whomever they choose.

Some sail-cruise companies follow strict itineraries, cruising into and out of port exactly according to schedule. Others map out only a general route, giving the captain the freedom to duck into an enticing cove or make an unscheduled stop at a secluded beach for an impromptu cookout. The smaller, more informal sail-cruisers may occasionally put itinerary choices to a passenger vote.

Sail-cruise ships usually frequent balmy, island-studded regions like the South Pacific, the Caribbean, and the Mediterranean, where they glide into small, chic ports seldom visited by big, conventional liners.

Passengers with some sail-cruise lines may be younger in years than the average cruiser on a traditional ship or simply younger at heart. They may be refugees from the big vessels who are seeking more offbeat ports. A good number describe themselves as "romantics."

Fares vary. The chicest sail-cruise options can be as costly as the most glamorous traditional cruise ship, but mid-range and budget choices are there for the less affluent.

Ultraluxury Cruises

Catering to the sybarite, everything on these small-ship voyages is top drawer. That translates to spacious, elegantly appointed cabins or ocean-view suites, a high crew-to-passenger ratio, white-glove service, such extra personnel as butlers and concierges, true gourmet dining, a wide choice of vintage wines and fine liquors—all while voyaging to the world's most exotic ports.

Passengers pay a premium for this level of luxury. But once guests are on board, they seldom have to pull out their money clips. Virtually every nicety is included in the cruise fare. Depending on the line, that can mean bar drinks or an in-cabin bar stocked with the passenger's preferred brands, as well as gratuities, tours, and possibly port charges.

Although most (but not all) ultradeluxe vessels are like yachts, the staterooms are ample. Suites, many with private balconies and marble baths, are the norm. A stateroom on an ultradeluxe ship may be double the size—or more—of a standard line. Bathrooms come with tubs and often whirlpools. Storage room is ample and includes walk-in closets. Appointments and amenities are as fine as the space. Every detail is perfect, down to the brand of sheets and towels, even the soap.

The staff on ultraluxury ships often come from top European hotels. They're trained not only to respond to guests' needs but to anticipate them. Service is discreet and efficient.

Another hallmark of ultradeluxe cruises is the made-to-order gourmet cuisine. Some lines appoint internationally known chefs as consultants. **Silversea Cruises**, for example, is affiliated with France's Le Cordon Bleu culinary academy. Dining is flexible, too. All the small luxury ships offer single-seating dining, meaning that guests can arrive and dine at their leisure, wherever and with whomever they choose.

Predictably, onboard atmosphere is formal. People dress for dinner every night and linger for hours over meals accompanied by fine wines. Those who wish to dine *en suite* may order from the dining room menu and, on some lines, a waiter serves guests in their cabin course by course.

Shipboard life on the ultraluxury lines leans toward education and enrichment, not solely entertainment. Guest lecturers speak on subjects ranging from food and wine to antiques, art history, personal finance, and world affairs. Usually the enrichment programs correspond to the itinerary, so that passengers learn about Australian wines while cruising Australia, Oriental antiques when visiting China, and czarist history while plying the Black Sea.

MICHAEL STORRINGS

The shoreside programs are as carefully elegant as the onboard experience. Itineraries focus on history, culture, and style. Clients who select such a cruise are generally sophisticated, discerning travelers, so the ports they visit have to be unusual and compelling. These ships offer cruises to such exotic realms as the South Pacific, Asia, **East Africa** and the **Seychelles,** the Baltic, and the more glamorous ports in the Mediterranean. Because such places are far-flung, itineraries tend to be longer—usually at least 10 days. Sometimes shorter cruises are offered.

Companies like **Seabourn Cruise Line** go to great lengths to plan unforgettable shore excursions. While calling at **Russia,** for example, **Seabourn** passengers may be treated to a private dinner and concert at a palace or visit a ballet school and mingle with the dancers and instructors.

Passengers who can afford the good life at sea are affluent and tend to be older. But most sailings carry some successful young professionals and, increasingly, grandparents are traveling with their grandchildren.

Besides **Seabourn** and **Silversea**, top-of-the-line companies operating at least some small ships include the **Radisson Seven Seas** fleet, **Renaissance Cruises**, and **Sea Goddess** (part of **Cunard** line). (**Crystal Cruises** also belongs in the ultradeluxe category, but its two ships, carrying 960 passengers each, cannot be classified as small. Also, **Crystal** guests dine in two sittings, unlike passengers on small luxury vessels.)

For bubbly fans: No fewer than 37 labels of Champagne are stocked in the wine cellar of Cunard's *Queen Elizabeth 2*.

European-style Cruising

Americans are not the only nationality that likes to cruise. The British, Germans, Swiss, Scandinavians, French, Spaniards, Italians, and others are avid seafarers.

Sophisticated American travelers looking for a different cruise experience might consider sampling European ships. Some options: British **P&O Cruises,** *Oriana*, marketed in the United States by Los Angeles-based **Princess Cruises**, the fleet of **Norwegian Coastal Voyages**, marketed stateside by New York's **Bergen Line,** and the host of continental ships represented by **EuroCruises** in New York.

On such vessels, Americans may be in the minority, and dining and entertainment are geared to European tastes. Since many Europeans speak English, language isn't generally a barrier. On ships that routinely host a variety of nationalities, the announcements and programs are delivered in several languages, usually including English. Some entertainment is multilingual, too. You may not understand the comedian but, chances are, the movies are from Hollywood or subtitled.

Depending on the vessel and itinerary, the onboard atmosphere could be more formal or more casual than a similar cruise where Americans predominate. For example, European cruises to the **Canary Islands** and the Greek Isles often attract young crowds looking for an affordable sun-and-fun getaway. But passengers on a transatlantic sailing might be more mature and enjoy dressing smartly for dinner.

Before you sign on, recognize that differences in cruising European style may go beyond food and language. Smoking policies, for example. If you don't smoke, accept that you could well be in the minority. Even if you're seated at a no-smoking table, your neighbors could still be puffing away.

The upshot: For flexible, open-minded passengers, cruising to a different cultural beat can be a delightful, broadening experience.

When to Cruise

Cruise ships generally follow the sun. That means they either sail year-round to such perennially warm destinations as the Caribbean and the South Pacific, or they reposition to seasonal areas like Alaska and the Mediterranean during sunny periods.

Every cruise area, including year-round destinations, has high or peak seasons, as well as low or value seasons. Basically, this translates to periods of high and low demand, which affects pricing. For more information on lower fares, see "Cruising Off Peak" on page 13.

Typical Seasons

Africa—Year-round, but mostly May into October for North Africa, November through March for East and South Africa

Alaska/Western Canada—May through September

Antarctica—November to early March

Australia/New Zealand—Year-round but mainly November into April

Bahamas/Caribbean/Mexican Gulf—Year-round

Bermuda—May through October

Black Sea—April through October

Baltic Sea/Scandinavia/Russia—May into October (Note: European cruise-ferry companies operate year-round)

British Isles—May into October

Hawaii/South Pacific—Year-round

Mediterranean—Year-round

Mexican Riviera—Year-round

New England/Eastern Canada—May into October

Norwegian Fjords/North Cape—May into September (Note: The **Coastal Steamers** fleet operates year-round)

Orient—May through October

Panama Canal—September through April

Red Sea—November through March

South America—Year-round for Caribbean countries; November through March for southern portion of the continent

Southeast Asia—Year-round

MICHAEL STORRINGS

Transatlantic—Spring through fall; spring and autumn for repositioning cruises (Caribbean-based ships move to Europe in the spring for the summer season and return to the Caribbean in the fall for winter cruising)

Western Europe—May into October

World Cruises—January through March (Note: most start in January)

Cruising Off Peak

Many passengers are discovering the pleasures of cruising "off peak"—seeing Alaska in early May, Northern Europe in September, or the Mediterranean in February. If you can be flexible and travel outside the periods of high demand—when school's out or the weather is more reliably pleasant—you'll be rewarded in many ways.

First, prices during these times are significantly lower. Scan several cruise catalogs to get an idea of seasonal pricing. Also, be on the lookout for advertised specials or ask your travel agent to keep you posted on any discounts.

Second, fewer people travel in off peak. This means that air connections are less frantic, ships carry fewer passengers, and ports are less crowded. Generally, you'll have a better selection of cabins, more access to the facilities, and probably more attentive and personal service. In port the lines will be short, the places to visit emptier, and the shops stocked more amply.

Third, the weather might actually be more pleasant than during peak periods. Many Americans, for example, choose spring or autumn cruises in sunny climes like the Greek Isles to avoid the summer heat.

A giant bottle of Coca Cola was used to christen American Flag Cruises' *American Adventure.* Unfortunately, cola doesn't seem to be as lucky as Champagne; the company closed in 1994 after operating just over a year.

On a seven-day cruise, the 3,400 guests aboard Carnival Cruise Lines' *Destiny* will consume 26,300 cans of soft drinks, 900 gallons of soda from the bar fountain, 266,300 beers, 1,530 bottles of Champagne, 4,100 bottles of wine, 815 liters of scotch, 600 liters of rye and Canadian whiskey, 825 liters of vodka, 520 liters of gin, 750 liters of rum, 1,350 liters of tequila and vermouth, 100 liters of cordials and liqueurs, and 75 fifths of brandy and cognac. Cheers!

In 1970, an estimated 500,000 people took cruises. In 1996, nearly 10 times that many travelers—4.7 million—went on seagoing vacations.

Sizing Things Up

The unit of measurement that describes the size of a ship is the gross registered ton (grt). Unlike the ton, the gross registered ton indicates not weight, but space. Each grt represents 100 cubic feet of enclosed space within a vessel, not counting certain areas such as the bridge and galleys.

By grt, the 10 largest cruise ships currently sailing or under contract are:

Royal Caribbean International's not-yet-named 130,000-grt vessel, due to be launched in 1999.

Princess Cruises' *Grand Princess* (104,000 grt). Delivery: 1998

Carnival's *Carnival Destiny* and *Carnival Triumph* (101,000 grt). Delivery *(Triumph)*: 1999

Disney Cruise Line's *Disney Magic* and *Disney Wonder* (85,000 grt). Delivery: 1998

Celebrity Cruises' *Galaxy* (77,317)

Princess Cruises' *Sun Princess, Dawn Princess,* and *Sea Princess* (77,000 grt). Delivery *(Sea Princess)*: 1999

For the sake of comparison with the liners of yesteryear, a former record holder was the original *Queen Elizabeth*, **Cunard**'s 83,367-grt liner, built in 1940 and retired in 1968.

The spaciousness of a cruise ship is described by its "passenger-space ratio." This number is calculated by dividing the vessel's gross registered tonnage by the number of passengers (in lower berths). The resulting figure is meaningless on its own but, by comparing the space ratio of various ships, it is possible to get a feel for their relative "densities."

Another term of ship measurement is "Panamax," which refers to the largest beam (or width) acceptable for transiting the **Panama Canal**'s 110-foot-wide locks. A "post-Panamax" ship is too wide to fit through the locks. **Royal Caribbean International**'s 78,491-grt *Rhapsody of the Seas* is said to be the largest passenger ship able to navigate the canal.

As this book went to press, there was just one post-Panamax cruise ship in operation: **Carnival Cruise Lines'** *Carnival Destiny*. **Princess Cruises'** *Grand Princess*, to be launched in 1998, and **Carnival**'s *Carnival Triumph*, due a year after that, also will be post-Panamax. Because they can't squeeze through the canal, this trio of ships will cruise the Caribbean year-round.

What's the Best Cruise Length

Cruises range in length from one day to three months, and how long a voyage you decide to take will be based on three factors: time and funds available, degree of luxury sought, and experience in cruising. The longer the cruise, the more time and money are required, for which you'll get greater diversity and comfort. Novices generally feel more comfortable with a shorter trip.

Standard Cruises

The most popular cruise length is seven days, which fits conveniently into the normal American vacation schedule. And travel agents often recommend a seven-day itinerary for first-time cruisers—it's enough time to get to know the ship and try the facilities, as well as to visit a variety of ports. Seven-day cruises cover a lot of territory: the eastern, western, and southern Caribbean; Alaska; and the Mediterranean. Many ships sail on Saturday or Sunday and return the same day the following week.

MICHAEL STORRINGS

Short Cruises

People who like to cruise but aren't particularly interested in visiting ports have many options. Day cruises, overnight party cruises, and "cruises to nowhere" that sail around without stopping at any destination give a taste of the shipboard experience. Such cruises tend to run on older vessels and, because of their "party-hearty" nature, the public rooms often suffer a lot of wear and tear.

Three- and four-night cruises might be better choices. They present a more realistic sample of a longer cruise and can be ideal for those who only have time for a quick getaway or for those on a tight budget. They're also the perfect length for corporate meeting or incentive cruises.

Mini-cruises used to be a graveyard for aging ships that couldn't compete in the seven-day market. That all changed in 1990 when **Carnival Cruise Lines** and **Royal Caribbean International** introduced the first liners built specifically for three- and four-day cruising. **Carnival's** *Fantasy* and **Royal Caribbean International's** *Nordic Empress* breathed new life into short voyages by offering new cabins and all the facilities passengers could expect on a seven-day ship. Around this time, too, people started favoring shorter vacations.

There's a range of vessels to choose from, and they visit a surprising variety of destinations. Ships leaving from Miami, for example, call at ports in the Bahamas, at **Key West,** and **Cozumel, Mexico.** Mini-cruises from Los Angeles dock at **Catalina Island.** Short cruises also run round-trip from **San Juan, Puerto Rico,** to **St. Thomas, St-Martin/St. Maarten,** and **St. Croix.**

Still other options are America's inland waterways, Asia (leaving from **Singapore** and **Hong Kong**), and the Greek Isles, with departures normally from **Piraeus,** Athens' port city. But it's the rare American who flies all the way to Greece for a three-day cruise.

Three-day cruises usually set sail on Friday evening, returning Monday morning, while four-day cruises often depart Monday evening and come back on Friday morning. Some vary this schedule and offer Thursday afternoon to Sunday morning and Sunday afternoon to Thursday morning departures.

Long Cruises

Cruises of 10, 12, and 14 days—generally departing Friday through Monday—are the most common and leave from ports the world over. The typical European cruise itinerary catering to the traveler from the US is at least 10 days long—most Americans want to spend a fair amount of time on the ship once they've invested all those airplane hours. The same holds true for Asia, the South Pacific, Africa, and other remote cruise venues.

And then there are world cruises, the ultimate experience—three-month voyages to everywhere. Most of these global circumnavigations leave from **New York,** Fort Lauderdale, and Los Angeles, although occasionally other embarkation ports are offered. You'll sail off on a course of adventure to dozens of exotic destinations in distant lands and stand on deck as the ship slips into legendary harbors like **San Francisco, Rio de Janeiro, Capetown, Sydney,** and Hong Kong. You'll explore such wonders as the **Taj Mahal, Istanbul's Topkapi Palace,** and the **Great Wall of China.** You'll snorkel **Australia's Great Barrier Reef,** go on safari in **Kenya,** trek by horseback to the pyramids at **Giza,** and ride an elephant in **Thailand.** You'll cross the **International Dateline, Equator, Tropic of Capricorn,** and **Tropic of Cancer.**

Dancers, singers, and folkloric groups board the ship at many ports to perform, and guest lecturers enrich every stop with their insights into the region's history, culture, and politics.

Cruising Safely

Ship safety is one of the most important factors in cruising today. This touches on not only the ship's physical structure, but on security, health, and sanitation, and onboard medical care.

International Maritime Organization's (IMO) Regulations

A ship's safety is governed by a web of international, national, and local organizations, and governmental bodies. The most important is perhaps the London-based International Maritime Organization (IMO). Today the IMO, with almost 140 member states, oversees all but a fraction of the world's ships. The IMO's Maritime Safety Committee spells out standards in the International Convention for the Safety of Life at Sea—SOLAS for short.

SOLAS regulations cover all aspects of ship safety, from ship design and building materials to crew training to operations. New rules are continually being phased in, with the toughest requirements yet added in 1997. At press time, some of these stipulations included: All passenger ships had to update their fire fighting plans and stock special fire fighting equipment; and all vessels must have installed emergency floor-level lighting to mark escape routes and added smoke detectors in cabins, service areas, corridors, and stairways.

In addition, initial construction modifications must have been made to all ships. These include such things as installing noncombustible materials in certain areas and ensuring that all fire doors can be closed automatically from a central station.

Even older ships have to comply with SOLAS requirements: Ships built before 1980 must install sprinkler systems. Those assembled from 1980 on have until 2005 (or 15 years from their date of construction, whichever is later) to add sprinklers. These ships get an extension because 1974 SOLAS amendments require them to be built with more noncombustible materials, making them less susceptible to fire than pre-1980 ships.

Finally, by 2010, all vessels, including those built before 1980, must be constructed of noncombustible materials.

The tradition of breaking a bottle of Champagne over the bow to christen a ship has its roots in the practice of splashing the blood of sacrificed animals on new ships to invoke the protection of the gods.

Flag State, Port State Rules

Beyond the IMO's edicts, cruise-ship operators must also obey the rules of their flag and port states.

A ship's registry (also called "ship's flag") indicates the country under whose laws the ship and its owners operate. For example, a Norwegian-registered (or Norwegian-flag) ship would follow the laws of Norway when handling such matters as the training, education, wages, and working conditions of the crew. In addition, the ship flies the flag of the country of registry; the name of the country or a city in the flag state is listed on the stern, below the ship's name.

In addition, ships must obey the laws of the lands whose ports they visit. That means that when sailing from Miami, the Norwegian-flag ship is subject to such US rules as Coast Guard regulations and public health inspections.

Security

Like airlines and airports, cruise lines and sea ports have beefed up their security measures in recent years. In place at US ports are such enhanced security procedures as X-raying baggage and carry-on items and having passengers pass through a metal detector as they board the ship.

Cruise lines also enforce similar measures at foreign destinations. It's standard practice for passengers to be required to present their cruise identification cards (issued at embarkation) and, often, a photo ID at the gangway whenever reboarding the vessel. Again, they pass through a metal detector and packages and other hand-carried items are X-rayed.

The Cruise that Changed History

The torpedoing of the British liner *Lusitania* is often described as the event that drew the United States into World War I. But did it really?

Britain and Germany had been warring for nine months when the sleek **Cunard** liner cast off from New York's Pier 54 on 1 May 1915, bound for Liverpool. At the time Germany suspected the *Lusitania* of carrying weapons, and the German Embassy in Washington, DC, had even taken out newspaper advertisements warning Americans that it was risky to travel on British vessels. But that didn't stop 1,959 passengers—including hundreds of Yanks—from boarding.

The *Lusitania* was cruising off Kinsale, Ireland, on 7 May when a German submarine blasted a single torpedo. It made a direct hit, amidships. The *Lusitania* sank in 18 minutes. Only 764 passengers survived.

The world was aghast, but despite public outcry, it would be two more years before the US entered the fray. For the record, *Lusitania* was indeed transporting war materials such as rifle ammunition, shrapnel, and motorcycle parts.

Health and Sanitation

Cruise ships train their personnel to use sanitary techniques when handling food, disposing of waste, and generally keeping the ship and environment clean. The ship's medical personnel routinely test drinking water, as well as water from the swimming pool and hot tubs, for bacteria.

Sanitation inspections of cruise ships calling at US ports are supervised by the US Centers for Disease Control and Prevention, which runs the Vessel Sanitation Program. Water, food preparation and handling, general cleanliness, and repair are checked to minimize the spread of disease. The inspections are unannounced and non-US flag ships participate on a voluntary basis, but the CDC reserves the right to recommend a vessel not sail when potential health risks are present, such as a contaminated drinking-water supply.

Reports on individual vessels or a list of the latest cruise-ship inspection scores (called "Green Sheets") are available by writing to: Chief, Vessel Sanitation Program, National Center for Environmental Health, 1015 North America Way, Room 107, Miami, FL, 33132.

Medical Care at Sea

Onboard medical care is regulated only by a few of the countries that register cruise ships, leading some critics to charge that the cruise industry doesn't apply consistent, universal standards. Concerned, the American Medical Association adopted a resolution urging that criteria be set for the care of passengers sailing to US ports aboard cruise ships. The International Council of Cruise Lines subsequently wrote the guidelines. All of its 17 member lines (83 ships) have agreed to follow them.

Many cruise lines, however, have already set their own high standards, going to great expense to equip shipboard medical facilities with the latest technology and to staff them with highly qualified medical personnel. Depending on the ship size, this usually means at least one physician and two nurses, one of whom is on call 24 hours a day.

Cruise-ship infirmaries are not intended to be full-service hospitals. Instead, they are on hand to stabilize patients and provide safe, expedient transfers to hospitals ashore. Depending on where the ship is and the proximity to high-quality shoreside facilities, gravely ill passengers may remain on board until a port of call or, if the ship is far from land, be airlifted by helicopter to a hospital.

Passengers with medical conditions that could require emergency treatment should discuss their cruise plans with their personal physicians. When booking, too, make sure your travel agent has informed the cruise company of any special equipment—mobility aids, oxygen—you will need to use on board.

Travel insurance covering medical evacuation and emergency treatment in foreign facilities is also recommended. For more information, see "Medical Protection and Emergency Evacuation" on page 41.

Is Cruising Safe for the Environment?

Like cruise-ship safety, marine pollution concerns international, national, and local bodies, as well as consumer environmental groups. In the 1970s international conventions met to negotiate agreements aimed at reducing ship-generated waste that was being dumped into the oceans.

In 1987 the United States joined more than 30 other nations in ratifying MARPOL Annex V, which addresses the disposal of this onboard garbage. Each signatory is supposed to implement Annex V by passing its own law. In 1987, the US passed the Marine Plastic Pollution Research and Control Act.

MARPOL Annex V went into force internationally in 1988 and, since then, mariners have begun to change the way they handle shipboard wastes. For their part in curbing pollution, cruise lines are, among other things, requiring minimal packaging from suppliers and vendors; replacing what items they can with recyclable versions; and sorting and recycling glass bottles, aluminum cans, and plastics. What can't be recycled is burned, sanitized, and flushed, crushed, or stored for off-loading to waste disposal sites ashore.

Royal Caribbean International, Princess Cruises, Carnival Cruise Lines, and others have pushed beyond the minimum antipollution requirements in their campaigns to "go green." They enlist passengers' support—with announcements by the captain and the cruise director, as well as reminders in the ship's daily program—in protecting the marine environment. Signs around the ships prohibit throwing objects overboard, and sometimes recycling bins are placed in public view.

Still, not all cruise lines are doing everything they can to reduce pollution. When considering a cruise, see if the brochure mentions

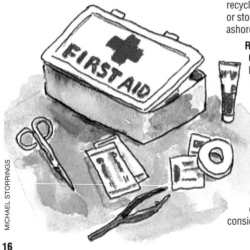

MICHAEL STORRINGS

any policy about environmental issues. Chances are, if a company is environmentally friendly, it will be publicizing its good policies. You might also ask your travel agent how various lines are handling "green" matters.

Air and water are contaminated from fuel and exhaust emissions, and cruise lines are working with shipyards and environmental engineers to develop cleaner, less polluting engines. They report significant strides in this area.

The next big environmental item on the cruise-industry agenda is working with ports to develop shoreside waste-handling facilities and protect

marine habitats. The IMO has pinpointed areas of special concern, including the Baltic, Black, Caribbean, Mediterranean, and Red Seas, and Antarctica.

Inadvertently, cruise ships can cause other damage, too, as when an anchor drags through sensitive coral reefs. At press time, the Caribbean island of **Grand Cayman,** an anchor port, was in the process of installing permanent cruise-ship moorings as a means of protecting its reefs. Ports are also safeguarding the sea environment by limiting cruise-ship calls and building passenger terminals in less environmentally sensitive areas.

A Typical Day on a Caribbean Cruise

First-time cruisers might find it hard to imagine what it's like to spend a vacation aboard an ocean-going vessel. Programs vary from ship to ship; the following gives a general idea of what two days— one at sea and one in port—might be like on a seven-day Caribbean cruise. Remember, though, that cruise-ship passengers have a range of choices and are free to partake of as many or as few as they wish.

Sea Day

It's morning. Early risers are up and about. They've had coffee and rolls on deck and are enjoying a dip in the pool or doing some laps on the jogging track. Some have joined the Walk-a-Mile group for company as they power-walk around the **Promenade Deck.** In the gym, a fitness instructor leads a stretch class. Already, the treadmills, stationary bikes, stair climbers, and rowing machines are whirring away. As they exercise, some passengers wear headphones tuned in to the **CNN** broadcast; others scan the daily program of shipboard events or study the news, sports, and stock market reports, faxed in by a maritime news service such as *The New York Times*. Meanwhile, in the library, some people search the shelves for a new novel, check out puzzles or games, or consult the reference books, getting a head start on the daily quiz.

A full breakfast is served in the dining room for passengers at the main (also called "early" or "first") seating. In an hour or so, the dining room will be open to passengers at the late seating. (On most ships the dining room isn't large enough to accommodate all passengers in a single seating, so they eat in two groups.) Passengers who want to set their own schedule can take advantage of room service or, until mid-morning, enjoy a casual buffet breakfast, available on **Lido Deck.** Some people take their buffet trays to the umbrella-shaded tables poolside.

The ship's well-equipped medical center is open for morning office hours. In the privacy of their own staterooms, a few workaholics have already called the

home office, maybe to discuss faxes they've received or sent.

After breakfast, shipboard activities shift into high gear. In the spa, passengers are arriving for massages, herbal body wraps, and other relaxing treatments. The beauty salon is open for cuts, coloring, sets, manicures, pedicures, and European-style facials. Many guests have scheduled appointments for new styles; tonight is the special Captain's Welcome Aboard Party, a formal affair, so they want to look their best.

At the teen center, some kids are locked into the video games while a counselor organizes a group for a Ping-Pong tournament. Others sort through music in the DJ booth, gearing up for the night's teen disco. In the children's playroom, one counselor is helping a group of youngsters prepare their costumes for a play; others are supervising a painting class and keeping an eye on kids romping in the ball room.

The casino is open, and the slot machines are jangling. At one craps table, a croupier explains the finer points of the game to beginning players. In the card room a bridge instructor offers a lesson in bidding as players form tables. Arts-and-crafts enthusiasts gather with their instructor in another room to work on projects they're preparing for an exhibit later in the cruise.

Up on sports deck, mixed doubles teams are pairing off for a paddle tennis tournament. A golf pro conducts a clinic for duffers as they play in a room where a computer simulator recreates the conditions at some of the world's top courses. In the aerobics room a step class is underway, while in the gym, personal trainers are working with individual passengers.

The winners of a company's sales incentive are gathering in the ship's computer-equipped **Business**

Center where they'll get a briefing on the new spring product lineup.

In the main lounge, dance instructors are leading a class in Western line dance; tomorrow they'll take on the tango. For the single ladies, several gentlemen hosts are available as partners.

In the ship's boutique, a group of women on a family reunion cruise tries on swimsuits and resortwear, while a honeymoon couple samples the perfumes and colognes. In the jewelry shop, a retired man prices necklaces. He wants a surprise for his wife of 40 years; they're celebrating their anniversary on this trip. At the **Photo Shop** passengers are buying pictures of themselves on yesterday's tour, snapped by the ship's professional photographers, and dropping off their own film for processing.

Out on deck the lounge chairs are filling up. At one end of the main pool is a snorkeling demonstration. At the pool bar bartenders are mixing up the day's first Bloody Marys.

A lecture about tomorrow's port is taking place in the theater; the shore excursion manager explains local points of interest, shopping and touring possibilities, and details the range of excursions on sale at the tour desk. The talk is broadcast on cabin television, which also airs movies throughout the day.

Shortly before noon, the cruise staff invites all singles on board to the piano bar for complimentary cocktails or soft drinks and a get-acquainted sing-along; at the same time, former drinkers are having their own Friends of Bill W. get-together in a meeting room.

As with breakfast, lunch offers a choice of eating in the restaurant or at the more casual buffet—the favorite for sunbathers who don't want to dress for the dining room. Burgers, hot dogs, and snacks are also available at the **Pool Grill,** along with slices from the pizzeria.

In the afternoon, the pool deck becomes the most popular spot on the ship as a live band entertains with calypso and reggae tunes. Children are playing in the splash pool; adults are unwinding in the whirlpools, and an energetic bunch is playing a lively game of water volleyball. Sunbathers are sampling the drink of the day, strawberry daiquiris served in souvenir glasses. Passengers seeking quieter surroundings are scattered around the sun decks and in lounge chairs along the shady **Promenade,** reading, chatting, and gazing at the sea.

Around every corner, people are making new friends as they discover fellow passengers with common interests or similar backgrounds. The non–English-speaking passengers are fitting right in, assisted by the multilingual social staff.

Some guests try their hand at shuffleboard; others take part in the golf putting tournament. On sports deck the teens are shooting hoops. In the gym, a

fitness instructor leads a class focusing on abdominal muscles while some passengers work out with free weights or relax in the saunas and steam rooms.

Friends gather in the sports bar for beers around banks of TV screens as they watch the big game, broadcast to the ship by satellite. A backgammon tournament is underway in the card room. Passengers working on needlepoint projects have rendezvoused in a sunny corner of one of the lounges.

On another deck, the chef leads a tour through the galley where guests glimpse the behind-the-scenes operation that turns out thousands of meals a day. Vegetable- and ice-carving demonstrations are presented. Up on the bridge, deck officers give passengers a tour of their realm, explaining the ship's state-of-the-art navigation and safety equipment.

A special guest lecturer, a well-known financial consultant, is giving tips on how individual investors act as their own brokers using the Internet during a computer-illustrated demonstration in the **Business Center.** In the dining room the ship's sommeliers are uncorking bottles for a wine tasting. On deck, kids flock to a make-your-own-ice-cream sundae party.

The afternoon walkers are out in full force, circling the **Promenade** as they tote up miles. Inside, the cruise staff hands out bingo cards; there's a jackpot session today, and the lucky winner could take home hundreds of dollars. But before that, the ship's hostess reads answers to the daily quiz and doles out prizes. In another lounge, white-gloved waiters pour afternoon tea.

As afternoon melts into evening, the rabbi conducts a Sabbath eve service in one of the meeting rooms. (On Sunday morning, the chapel will be used for a nondenominational service.) A pre-dinner concert of classical music is offered in one lounge while, in another, a band plays for dancing.

Passengers at the main (early) seating are turning out for dinner dressed in their finest. For one of the two formal nights of the cruise, the captain is hosting a Welcome Aboard cocktail party in the main lounge and receiving guests as they arrive. Some ladies are dressed in elegant gowns that sweep the floor; their escorts wear tuxedos. Other couples look sharp in dark suits and cocktail dresses.

Some parents with young children have taken the kids for an early dinner at the ship's pizzeria and dropped them off in the children's room for baby-sitting before heading out for a relaxed dinner in the dining room.

After the first-seating guests have gone in to supper, the second seating takes its turn meeting the captain. Later, when the first-seating guests have finished, they pour into the lounges. One features a Broadway-style show with fabulous costumes, intricate choreography, and dazzling special effects. The show is repeated later for guests in the second seating.

Another lounge offers dancing to a live band; in the discotheque, the DJ is cranking up the music while, elsewhere, the teens are rocking at their own disco. The bing-bing-bing sound of the slots forms the background music for gamblers seated around the casino's blackjack tables. In the nightclub, a comedian steps on stage, while the piano bar becomes a karaoke club. Some couples sneak off to the quiet wine-and-caviar bar; others stroll around the deck, gazing at the stars. At midnight, the doors open on the late-night buffet.

Some passengers have long since turned in or are watching movies on cabin television. Others will stay out all night, catching the sun's first rays as they illuminate the horizon.

Port Day

No two port calls are the same. Let's assume the ship is calling at **Montego Bay, Jamaica.** Arrival is scheduled for 8AM.

Many passengers are up early and, having break-fasted, are on deck to see the ship make landfall—one of the most exciting moments in cruising. Others are lounging on their private verandas, snapping pictures, and finishing coffee from their cabin breakfast. Some are dining leisurely on deck at the breakfast buffet, others are into their normal morning fitness routines, and those who had a late night are still snoozing.

After the lines are secured, local officials come on board to examine the ship's documents and clear passengers to go ashore. That doesn't take long. Departures for the first of the day's excursions are being announced on the public address system. Passengers are reminded to take along their tour ticket and, as a security measure, their boarding card, which they'll need to present at the gangway when they return to the ship.

At Montego Bay the ship offers no fewer than 14 tour options (all booked in advance) including river rafting, horseback riding, golf, photography, scuba, sport-fishing, and plantation visits. Some tours last 2.5 hours; others run 6 hours and include lunch ashore.

When the departures are called, those embarking stroll down the gangway onto the dock and through the terminal building where they're met by a crush of taxi drivers, chauffeurs for private cars, and a fleet of buses and minivans, waiting to load the tour members. It's organized chaos. Signs in the bus windows indicate the tour and shore excursions personnel are there to direct passengers.

Tours depart at intervals throughout the morning, minimizing crowding on the gangway. A local guide and, often, an escort from the ship travel with each tour group.

Some of the tours, like diving and sport fishing, are action-oriented. Others involve hiking, climbing, or swimming. Still others blend motorcoach touring with an easy bit of walking and are suited to those who might have difficulty getting around.

Not everybody books a tour. Some passengers have made advance arrangements through the ship's tour desk for rental cars or private cars with drivers. Others hop into waiting taxis, some board the ship's shuttle for the downtown shopping area; it will operate on the hour throughout the day. A few people set off on foot.

And some passengers don't go ashore at all. For them, the staff offers a pared-down program of shipboard activities. The gym, beauty salon, library, lounges, and other public rooms are at their disposal. Only the ship's boutiques and casino are closed in port. Those who stay on board can find books, table games, and sports equipment to use. In the gym, they can take the regular fitness program of stretch and step classes, aerobics, and workouts with the weights, and run as usual. The pianist is in the piano bar.

The dining room schedule changes, though. Because many passengers are ashore, the restaurant is open for a single seating, and guests may sit where they like, instead of at their regular assigned tables. Burgers at the outdoor grill and the poolside buffet are available as on a sea day.

Toward noon, the half-day tours return, and some folks can't wait to don their swim-suits and take a dip in the ship's pool. Others head for the dining room.

In the late afternoon a calypso band entertains on **Lido Deck** as passengers begin to trickle back from ashore. The pizzeria is doing a huge trade. The pool area is bustling.

At 5:30PM, a half-hour before sailing, everyone is back on board. All passengers have returned through the gangway, passing their bags and purses through a metal detector and showing their boarding passes to the security personnel. Some remark that it's good to be back "home."

The ship is preparing to leave. The engines are cranking up. At precisely 6PM, the lines are cast off and the vessel slowly pulls away from the pier. Ashore, a few officials and some children wave at passengers lining the rails. The ship makes a graceful turn and steams out of the harbor. Many passengers linger on the rails as the calypso band plays and the coast of Jamaica fades into the distance.

The show isn't over—the sun is slowly setting in a blaze of colors. Many people find it hard to tear themselves away from the deck as this balmy tropical day fades to evening.

But inside, the ship is gearing up for another busy evening. Tonight, because it was a port day, dress is casual. The gents leave their jackets and ties behind, and the ladies wear pants suits, sun dresses, or other easy-going attire. There's a relaxed and jovial mood on board as new friends swap tales of the day's adventures and anticipate tomorrow's port visit.

Preparing to Cruise

Though a few lines accept direct bookings, most cruises—about 95 percent according to CLIA—are booked by travel agents. From the cruiser's standpoint, reserving through an agent has many bonuses. The agent is experienced in dealing with cruise lines, knows the products, and can find the best deals. In addition, by having an established relationship with the cruise lines, agents can usually arrange things you wouldn't be able to get on your own. And if a problem arises, the agent can act as your advocate. Finally, reserving through an agent doesn't cost extra—the commission is paid by the line.

Although a travel agent may be the best person to contact to help you make a final decision about a cruise, you need to lay some groundwork before talking to the expert: deciding on destinations, reading brochures, examining how cruises are packaged, priced, and sold. You'll also have many decisions to make when you book your cruise—type of cabin, air/sea or cruise only, etc. And then the final and most worrisome preparation—packing.

How to Choose a Cruise

With so many possibilities, how does one choose the right cruise? This section will put you on course—by asking yourself some questions and gathering information on specific ships and itineraries, you can fashion your ideal cruise vacation.

Some Basic Questions

Visiting a travel agency or calling or writing a cruise line for brochures is a good idea—*eventually*. But first, consider your personal likes and dislikes in order to narrow the range of cruise choices. Poring over a pile of brochures without having some clear ideas of what you're seeking can be an exercise in confusion.

- What is your vacation budget?
- How much time do you have?
- Will you cruise alone, as a couple, with children, or with friends?
- Where would you like to go?
- When would you like to go? Are you flexible on departure dates if it means a better price?
- Where have you vacationed in the past?
- When you travel, do you seek relaxation? Nightlife? Education/personal enrichment? Adventure? Is any one of these far more important than the others?
- What are your special interests? (Golf? Gambling? Shopping? Nature?)
- What have you most enjoyed about previous vacations?
- What have you disliked about previous trips?
- What kind of hotels do you favor? (HoJo's? Hyatt? Four Seasons?)
- Do you want a small, medium, or large ship? If you aren't sure, consider whether you prefer large resorts with plenty of dining, nightlife, and recreational facilities, medium-sized hotels that aren't too overwhelming but have ample facilities, or small inns that may offer a narrow range of facilities but the most personal service.

- Is dining a priority? Are you happy with plain cooking or do you crave gourmet cuisine? Any special dietary requirements?
- Do you like dressing up, or are you strictly a T-shirt and jeans type?
- Do you enjoy meeting a variety of people, or do you prefer to stick with your own age group or professional level? Would you object to a ship with many children on board?

Take a good look at your answers. They should be revealing. Keep your findings in mind when gathering information about cruises from this book, newspaper and magazine articles, newsletters, the Internet, Cruise Nights, and friends. You might also wish to take your answers to a travel agency to see which cruise lines or specific ships or itineraries it recommends. For advice on finding a good agent, see page 32.

An agent can provide brochures or cruise-line videos for you to take home and study. Otherwise, you can phone or write to cruise lines for brochures.

Resources

Publications

After you read the "Ships" chapters in this book, you can learn more about various vessels and their itineraries by looking through travel magazines and the Sunday travel section of your local newspaper. If you live in a small town where cruise stories are not regularly featured, go to the library and look for the Sunday travel sections of major newspapers in cities like Atlanta, Boston, Chicago, Dallas, Fort Lauderdale, Houston, Los Angeles, Miami, New Orleans, New York, Orlando, San Francisco, and Seattle. Published in these port cities or top cruise markets, such papers offer regular cruise coverage and their twice-a-year (spring and fall) cruise issues contain a bonanza of information.

Besides reading the stories, study the ads for an idea of pricing. Don't believe everything you read; only a few cabins may be available at the rock-bottom lead prices mentioned, but ads do clue you in on price ranges. Cruise pricing will be discussed later in this guide.

Porthole and *Cruise Travel* are glossy magazines devoted exclusively to cruising. They highlight ship and port reviews and give tips on tours, shopping, and industry trends. Both are sold on newsstands, as well as by subscription.

The World Ocean and Cruise Liner Society publishes a monthly newsletter, *Ocean & Cruise News*. It is full of cruise-line updates and examines in detail a "Ship of the Month." From time to time, society members receive hot-off-the-presses brochures and get special discounts on selected sailings. For more information, call 203/329.2787.

MICHAEL STORRINGS

Cruise Lines International Association (CLIA)

Established in 1975, CLIA is a trade group aimed at raising public awareness about cruising. More than two dozen cruise lines are members, and the association has nearly 23,000 travel agency affiliates. CLIA's booklet, *Cruising—Answers to Your Questions,* explains where cruises go, how to book, and how to prepare for a cruise. Included are charts and tables showing where CLIA members' ships travel and what types of amenities are available to children, honeymooners, active adults, and singles. To get a free copy, send a stamped (55¢), self-addressed business envelope to **Cruise Lines International Association** (Dept. S, 500 Fifth Ave, Suite 1407, New York, NY, 10110).

CLIA also operates a home page on the World Wide Web at http://www.ten-io.com/clia/, which includes information on cruising, links to the home pages of individual cruise lines, and a "travel agency locator" that directs potential cruisers to their nearest CLIA-affiliated travel agency.

Internet

Many cruise lines have their own Web sites that detail their fleets, itineraries, costs, onboard activities, and shore excursions. But they stop short of taking bookings, a process that Web browsers still must do themselves through travel agencies. Many of the sites help by providing lists of agencies convenient to the consumer.

Here are addresses:

American Hawaii Cruises:
http://www.cruisehawaii.com

Carnival Cruise Lines: http://www.carnival.com

Celebrity Cruises:
 http://www.celebritycruises.com

Cunard Lines: http//www.cunardline.com

Delta Queen Steamboat Co.:
http://www.deltaqueen.com

Dolphin Cruise Line: http://www.dolphincruise.com

Holland America Line:
http://www.hollandamerica.com

Majesty Cruise Line: http://www.majestycruise.com

Norwegian Cruise Line: http://www.ncl.com/ncl

Premier Cruise Lines: http://www.bigredboat.com

Regal Cruises: http://www.regalcruises.com

Royal Caribbean International:
http://www.royalcaribbean.com

Windstar Cruises: http://www.windstarcruises.com

For the addresses of other cruise-line Web sites, contact CLIA.

America Online (AOL) subscribers can tap into a wealth of information at "Cruise Critic," which features candid reviews of more than 100 ships worldwide plus an interactive "Cruise Selector" that helps consumers find the cruises best suited to their interests and lifestyles. "Cruise Critic" recommends some ships and provides reviews, too.

AOL members can add their own reviews and share opinions on a host of topics ranging from tips for first-time cruisers to the inside scoop on shore excursions. Other features include a comprehensive rundown of family-cruise details and "News & Bargains," with the hottest cruise deals.

Personal computer owners can obtain a free trial of "Cruise Critic" and America Online by calling 800/418.0707.

Travel Agency Newsletters

Some larger travel agencies publish their own informative newsletters. Since these are sales tools, the material they contain may be biased. Still, agency newsletters can be a wonderful source for cruise news and special deals.

One example is The Cruise Line, Inc.'s *World of Cruising.* Published three times a year, the newsletter contains feature stories about new ships and itineraries, as well as cruise line advertisements and lists of discounted sailings available from this North Miami Beach, Florida, agency. For a free subscription, call 800/777.0707.

Check with agencies in your area to see if they offer newsletters. If they do, most will be pleased to send you a copy.

Cruise Nights

Sponsored by travel agencies, these events are advertised in the local newspaper or by direct mail. They mingle socializing with information and are usually held at the agencies or in country clubs. Cruise line representatives may be on hand to give short presentations and show videos. Brochures will be available. Sometimes refreshments are served and prizes awarded, or there may be a drawing or raffle for a free cruise. There's a sign-up sheet for further information.

Friends and Associates

It may seem obvious, but it's always a good idea to consult experienced cruisers—especially friends, business associates, or others who share common lifestyles and interests.

How to Read A Brochure

Brochures are a cruise line's most important advertising and sales tool. Some companies publish one fat brochure that includes all their programs in a one- or two-year period. Others print booklets for individual regions, such as **Europe** or **Alaska,** different seasons of the year, or even individual ships.

From time to time, cruise lines may revise their itineraries and issue updated brochures reflecting the changes. Before reading a catalog seriously, be sure you have the latest version.

Here are some tips on how to wade through the ocean of brochures and come out with a few that might be right for you.

Look Closely at the Covers

You can tell a lot about a cruise line just from the cover of its brochure. Study it carefully, asking yourself the following questions:

What size ship is pictured? Will it have access to smaller, lesser-known ports? Is it a classic or a new vessel? A luxury liner or a sailing ship?

If a scene is shown, is it a sun-and-fun theme, a dramatic destination, or an adventure setting?

Are the passengers (usually models) the age group you're looking to spend time with? Do they look sophisticated? Families? Couples? Singles?

Does the cover copy mention discounts? The type of cruise? Destinations visited?

When you've selected a few brochures with appealing covers, take an equally critical look at what's inside.

Study the Pictures

The models—in rare cases, actual passengers—are carefully chosen to represent the cruise line's perceived clients. With this in mind, notice what ages are represented. Are there lots of young couples? Children? Seniors? Folks of different colors? Anyone in a wheelchair? Does this appear to be an all-American or an international crowd? Are they dressed casually? Formally? Can you picture yourself as one of these passengers?

As you scan the photos, keep in mind that you're seeing things at their best. If something looks shabby in the brochure, it's not going to appear better in person.

What kinds of activities are pictured? Dining? Sports? Gambling? Dancing? Shopping? Touring? Are they things that appeal to you?

Is food emphasized? Are there pictures of burgers and pizza or of gourmet food presentations? Are the dining room tables set simply or loaded with bone china, crystal, and silver? Which is your style?

Do the cabins look comfortable and inviting? Spacious enough for the time you'll be spending there? (If it's a short cruise or you aren't the type to entertain or spend a lot of time in your room, size may not matter so much.) Are there choices of staterooms with portholes, large windows, or

MICHAEL STORRINGS

private verandas? Single-, double- or queen-size beds? Upper and lower berths? Just beds or sitting area? Does it look like there's ample closet space and drawers? Would you feel at home in this room?

Read the Text

Now that you have some ideas about a particular cruise line, read the text in the front of the book. (You can pore over the terms and conditions and other fine print at the back later.) Chances are, everything will sound wonderful. But be aware that these seductive words are promotional copy designed to sell. Most cruises are pleasant and rewarding, but look out for inflated claims. For example, if the text promises "gourmet dining," is that represented in the cuisine that's pictured, the table settings, and the general feeling of the ship that the photos suggest? If the cruise line says it's "perfect for families," is that backed up by pictures of family facilities and activities?

Does the text emphasize things that are important to you? Do destinations matter more than the ship? If so, are the ports discussed at length or just brushed over? Does the cruise line tout its tour programs?

If you're an active type who adheres to a fitness regime, does this cruise line highlight its sports facilities? Its "healthy choice" options in the dining room?

If you're into personal enrichment, does the text mention a superb guest lecturer program, a well-stocked library, or activities in your area of interest? Are any of the lecturers named? Are they people whose ideas and opinions spark your curiosity? Does the text accompany pictures of passengers engaged in thoughtful pursuits?

Does the brochure highlight enough games, contests, parties, and entertainment to keep fun-seekers' spirits high?

What about the level of formality? Are words like "elegant," "sophisticated," and "discerning" used and, if so, is that what you seek?

What specific amenities are promised? Terry bathrobes, *The New York Times* news summary delivered to your door, fresh flowers on your bedside table, French milled soap, butler service? Are these things you simply *must* have to feel comfortable, or are they luxuries you can do without?

When the brochure mentions service, are the adjectives "friendly," "attentive," or "exquisitely trained?" Which type suits you, and what are you prepared to pay for?

Analyze the Itineraries

Assuming you've already decided on a region you want to cover in your cruise, this is the place in the brochure to look at specific stops.

Is the proportion of port days to sea days satisfactory? More sea days might be desirable in a region such as Alaska that is noted for its breathtaking vistas, as well as interesting cities and towns.

Is the departure date convenient? Does the itinerary coincide with a holiday? (If so, holiday festivities might add to the voyage or they might detract if, for example, a holiday means the ship would be extra full or shops in port would be closed.)

A skilled travel agent is a great resource when it comes to comparing cruise lines, ships, and itineraries. See "Choosing a Travel Agency" on page 32 for tips on how to find a good agent.

Compare the Brochure Fares

Unfortunately for consumers, brochures don't provide a very accurate idea of what a cruise actually costs—these fares are the usually the highest rates. Practically nobody pays the brochure rate because most cruises are discounted—sometimes heavily. For more information on the wide array of discounts available and how to get the best deal, see "Cruise Discounts" on page 27.

Fare tables are based on double occupancy, and detail various seasons and types of accommodations. Study the ship's deck plan (see "Examine the Deck Plans," below) to find out where various cabins are located, and look at the pictures of several categories for further guidance. (See "Choosing the Right Cabin" on page 34 for more information on selecting the best stateroom.)

Check if the fares listed are air/sea packages or cruise only. The fare table will also tell you the cost of having a third or fourth person or an infant in the cabin, single occupancy tariffs, port charges and taxes (which are sometimes extra), amount of deposit required, and the optional cancellation protection plan.

There are also Fly/Cruise pages, which explain details and options such as the cost of flying in a few days before the cruise (or staying on after) and stopping at a hotel at the embarkation (or debarkation) point or the service charge for deviating from the cruise line's standard air schedules.

Examine the Deck Plans

Price is based on cabin category. These may range from a handful of types on smaller vessels to more than a dozen on bigger ships. Some factors that differentiate categories are: location on the ship, dimensions, outside (ocean-view, with a porthole or window) or inside (no window), quality of view (unobstructed/partially obstructed/obstructed), private balcony or veranda, type of beds (king/queen/double/twin/upper and lower berths), bathroom (shower only/with tub/tub with whirlpool), and furniture configuration. Ask your travel agent to get information from the cruise line about specific cabin dimensions.

Cruise brochures include deck plans of the ships, showing where all the public rooms and staterooms are located. At this point, focus on categories instead of specific staterooms. The objective is to select a few types of cabins that will suit your needs. When you're ready to book a cruise, your travel agent will request a particular sailing date and cabin category. The cruise line will come back with a selection of specific staterooms that are available in that category. If every cabin is already reserved in your first-choice category, you'll need to try a second or third choice, choose another sailing on the same ship, or another ship altogether. You can also add your name to a wait list.

The earlier you book, the wider the choice of cabins will be. If you're planning to travel at peak seasons—Alaska or Europe mid-June through mid-August, for example—chances are you'll have to book nine months ahead to get your top choice or at least six to seven months ahead for a good selection. In the Caribbean, which is a year-round destination, allow about five months for your preferred cabin.

Read the Fine Print

Now turn to the back of the book. The last pages of any cruise brochure contain a wealth of general information: how to make reservations, the requirements for deposits and final payments, cancellation policies, documents, details on the cruise line's air/sea program, suggested dress on board, and just about everything else you'll need to know.

The back of the book also usually includes information on land programs or hotel stays that can be added on to a cruise for a complete land-tour package.

How Cruises are Priced and Packaged

Many factors affect cruise pricing, including the number of people in a cabin, seasonality, air/sea packages, the costs of the cruising locale, and the price of flying to and from the ship. Being aware of these is an important first step in comparing discounts and getting the best deal on a cruise, subjects covered in upcoming sections.

MICHAEL STORRINGS

By Number of People in Cabin

Two or More

Cruise fares are priced per person, based on double occupancy of a cabin. The standard cabin configuration is two beds—in cruising jargon, "lower berths." When every lower berth is booked, the ship is said to be sailing at 100 percent occupancy.

It's possible for a ship to sail at more than 100 percent occupancy. That's because some cabins come with more than two berths, allowing children or a third or fourth adult to occupy the same cabin—usually at a sharply reduced price. The extra berths are called "uppers" because they're located on top of the lowers, folding out from the wall to form a bunk bed.

Singles

Only a few older ships offer single (one-person occupancy) staterooms, and they're a hot commodity. Singles who want sole occupancy of a double cabin must pay a supplement. Depending on the line and the cruise, that's usually anywhere from 150 percent during periods of low demand to 200 percent (the double occupancy rate) for peak times. Sometimes supplements vary according to cabin category, with higher supplements charged for deluxe cabins and suites. Some companies routinely court single travelers with attractive supplements; **Orient Lines**, for example, charges 125 percent for all categories except A (the top) and suites.

Some lines offer alternatives to paying a single supplement, such as a "guaranteed single rate." This is a set rate (for example, **Royal Caribbean International** charges the equivalent of the lowest category, inside cabin rate). There is no choice of categories; the cruise line assigns a cabin at its discretion. But singles are assured that whatever cabin they get is theirs alone.

Another choice, offered by most cruise lines, is called a "guaranteed share." Single travelers agree to share a stateroom with a guest of the same sex and same smoking preference and pay only the per-person double occupancy rate. Usually the line charges a set rate, and passengers get no choice of category; they must take what the line offers. If the cruise line doesn't find a roommate for you, you have the cabin to yourself at the one-person price. Some lines limit their guaranteed share options to certain categories.

The CLIA booklet *Cruising—Answers to Your Questions* includes a table listing the ships with single cabins, member cruise lines' singles supplements, and other information. (See page 21 for details on ordering this free booklet.)

By Seasonality

By now you know that seasonality plays a key role in the cost of a cruise—it's a matter of supply and demand. One reason the **Bahamas,** the **Caribbean,** and the **Mexican Riviera** are among the most affordable cruise choices is that they're year-round destinations, which spreads out demand over a 12-month period. This doesn't mean that all Caribbean cruises are inexpensive or priced the same year-round. Even this balmy region has its peak periods.

When it comes to destinations like Alaska, **Bermuda, New England/Canada,** and Europe, the seasons are limited, concentrating demand and forcing prices up. Be aware, however, that those seasons still contain periods of lesser and greater demand. In Alaska, for example, the earliest and latest weeks of the summer are more affordably priced.

The same is true of Europe and other seasonal spots, although brochure fares don't always reflect this because sometimes cruise lines price seasonal programs uniformly in the hopes that high demand will move everything at good price. If that doesn't happen, the cruises at the fringes of the season are often the first to be discounted.

In the autumn, when the weather is cooling down, the kids are back in school, and business cycles are often in high gear, demand for cruises hits its lowest ebb. Called the "shoulder season," this is the most discount-packed time of the year.

After New Year's, when the winter doldrums set in for those in cold climes, cruising experiences a surge. If blizzards strike, a flurry of cruise bookings is sure to follow. This parallels peak season in the Caribbean, but it doesn't necessarily mean that cruise prices are peaking. Supply in the region is high; many ships that spent the summer in Alaska and Europe are now back in the warm Caribbean waters, so deals can be found even now.

Retirees and others with flexible schedules find that they can enjoy significant savings by cruising off-peak. Other pluses are less crowded destinations and ships. This can mean better onboard service, shorter lines at the buffets, better seats in the show lounges, and less waiting for everything from beauty salon appointments to your turn on the paddle tennis court.

Choosing a low-season sailing could also net you a free cabin upgrade. Sometimes when a ship is not sold out, the cruise line decides to reassign guests to higher category cabins. If space is available, why not move cruisers into better accommodations? It's a people-pleaser that costs a company little or nothing.

Seasonal price swings are already written into the brochures of the big cruise lines whose bread-and-butter is year-round Caribbean itineraries or other extended series. Seasons fall under labels like "peak," "standard," and "value" or "economy" and "budget."

The cost of doing business in a region also affects cruise pricing. European cruises are more costly than Caribbean voyages because prices are higher in Europe.

Also, in any distant cruise destination—Europe, **Asia, China, Africa, Australia/New Zealand**—the cost of air travel to and from the ship is a significant portion of a cruise vacation.

MICHAEL STORRINGS

Air/Sea Packages

Many cruises are sold as air/sea (sometimes called fly/cruise) packages, meaning they include the cost of air travel to and from the ship. And some cruise lines that include air in their advertised pricing bill it as "free air." This, of course, is a gimmick; you're paying even when the air is woven into the package.

But no matter how it's advertised or presented in the cruise brochure, you're probably paying a lot less by buying the cruise company's air/sea package than you would if you arranged your own flights. That's because cruise lines, as regular, high-volume customers for airlines, snap up big blocks of seats at discounted prices.

Some cruises—especially those in exotic climes—do not operate round-trip from a port. That means you fly into one port to board the ship and fly home from another port. A round-trip air ticket is normally more economical than two one-way flights. In cases like this it's advantageous to use the cruise line's air/sea package because the line can usually get a better price than an individual.

If you choose to go with the package, you'll have little say in the departure times, routing, and choice of carrier. About all you get to do is select the most convenient gateway from among the cities provided by the cruise line. Sometimes, if you live in a very remote area, none of the gateways will be very convenient. You may have the option of paying a supplement to the cruise line to arrange a flight from a closer city, or you may decide to arrange and pay for your own air travel.

Since the cruise line normally doesn't issue passengers their air tickets until a few weeks before departure, you may not know how you're going to be routed until the last minute; by then it's too late to arrange something better on your own. Furthermore, some airlines don't let you claim mileage for air tickets in an air/sea package (if so, a notice will be included with your ticket packet). And most cruise companies book passengers in coach, unless there's a special promotion—usually offered only by upscale lines on long-haul flights. Of course, you can pay extra and upgrade to business or first class.

Passengers who buy the cruise line's air/sea package but who choose to deviate from the line's standard routing can request changes via their travel agent. Normally they pay a set service fee to the airline for arranging such flight "deviations."

The cruise line's service charge for arranging air upgrades and routing and date deviations is listed in the back of the brochure. Depending on the company, the charge ranges from about $35 to $50.

A travel agent skilled at booking cruises can advise you about all the air options and guide you to the best alternative for your needs.

When you purchase an air/sea package, the cruise line takes the responsibility of getting you and your luggage from the airport to the ship and back again. You mark your bags with the cruise-line tags sent with your final documents. The representatives who meet your flight pull all the tagged bags directly from the aircraft or from the luggage carousel, load them onto a bus, and whisk them to the port. You don't see them until you board, when porters deliver them to your cabin.

You, meanwhile, are met at the arrival gate or in the luggage area by a representative who leads you to a motorcoach that drops you at the ship. Sometimes, if your flight arrives early in the day and the ship sails late, the cruise line arranges a complimentary day room at a hotel where early arrivals can store carry-on items and freshen up. A bus takes early arrivals from the hotel to the pier when the ship is ready for boarding. All these ground transfers are included in the cost of your air/sea package.

Cruise Only

If you arrange your own air, you're called a "cruise only" passenger. Cruise lines that list air/sea prices in their brochures include a "Cruise-Only Travel Allowance" on the fare pages. That could be a standard amount, such as $250 for a range of cruises, or it could vary from cruise to cruise. You subtract the amount from the air/sea rate to get the price you pay for the cruise alone.

If you don't buy the air/sea package, you'll have to arrange your own ground transportation from the airport to the ship, and back again after the cruise, and handle your own luggage all the way. Some lines, however, allow cruise-only passengers to purchase a post-cruise ticket for the ship-to-airport transfer; others let independents join a bus to the airport if seats are available.

Another important consideration for "cruise-only" passengers: Should there be any delay, disruption, or cancellation in your air schedule, you're on your own. The risk, of course, is that you might miss the ship's departure and be saddled with the additional hassle and cost of trying to fly to the next port of call for boarding. As many cruises depart on the weekend, it could be tough for a stranded passenger to get in touch with his or her travel agent to iron out the problem. In such a situation, the cruise line may be able to assist you—but it's not obligated to do so.

Also, in the very rare event of a change in the ship's schedule, a cruise line has no way of contacting passengers who are traveling independently unless you've provided the company with your itinerary.

Cruise lines, on the other hand, are responsible for those on air-sea programs. If a flight carrying a number of passengers is delayed, a cruise line may instruct the ship to hold sailing until everyone arrives, or it will arrange for guests to be flown to the next port for boarding. Any hotel arrangements would be handled—and paid for—by the company. If a flight is canceled, the line automatically rebooks passengers on an alternate route.

Getting the Best Value

Cruises are one of the few vacation alternatives that have held the line on pricing over the past few years. One reason is that the cruise industry has been building so many ships that supply sometimes outpaces demand.

It's a buyer's market, where consumers find themselves with a great selection of cruises on modern, well-equipped ships—at very good prices. The only drawback is the time and effort it takes to compare the various deals. See "Cruise Discounts" on page 27 for more information.

When pricing cruises, think in terms of getting the best *value,* rather than the best price. Think about factors like the number of ports versus the number of sea days in an itinerary. Some people are looking for a destination-intensive experience; how many ports they visit is a quantitative measurement of "how good" the cruise is. If they're flying all the way to the **Baltic Sea** for a cruise, a 12-day itinerary offering seven cities sounds like a much better deal than a cruise hitting only three or four capitals. The amount of time in port may represent value, as well. A voyage overnighting in **St. Petersburg** might be worth more than one offering just a day stop.

But for some people, especially those who choose a very luxurious ship, the sea days are equally—if not more—enjoyable and "valuable." People who are paying a premium for gourmet dining, white-glove service, and "free" Champagne and caviar want to be sure they have enough sea days to fully appreciate these amenities. If they're in port every day, it doesn't seem like they're "getting their money's worth."

If you've narrowed your search to a few choices, check itineraries to find out the number of hours in port compared to the number of sea days. Then, depending on what's important to you, assign a value.

What else matters most to you? Do you want alternative dining choices, low-fat menu options, extensive children's facilities, jogging track, golf program, bathrooms with tubs, large casino, ballroom dancing and gentlemen hosts, or a casual dress code? Once you have a list of, say, 10 or so vital features, use cruise-line brochures to compare the facilities and amenities offered by the various ships.

To hone in on a cruise line's "added value," comb brochures for the details that would enhance your cruise experience. These things, though not, perhaps, personal "requirements," are factors that contribute to the general ambience. Include only what matters to *you*. Perhaps you really enjoy fresh flowers, bathrobes, full-menu room service, in-cabin VCR, and hair dryer in the bathroom. Is it worth it to pay more for a cruise offering these "extras?" Or can you do without?

When comparing a standard cruise with the "free" features of a more all-inclusive line that charges a higher fare up front, assign a monetary value to tangibles and services that you're sure you would use and that, on a standard cruise line, would cost extra. These could include shore excursions, wine and cocktails, butler service, gratuities, and port charges.

Another consideration: Is it a better value to book the least expensive cabin on the most expensive ship, or the most expensive cabin on the least expensive ship? Passengers who choose a low-category cabin on a luxurious ship point out that they indulge in the same fine dining, entertainment, amenities, and ambience of the people occupying the upper-deck suites. The size and location of the cabin don't matter to them because they spend the greater part of the day in the public areas or ashore.

Others use the reverse logic, signing up for the priciest staterooms or suites on the least expensive ships. This, they explain, nets them all the perks and perceived prestige that come with occupying a top cabin, while paying less than they might spend on lower-category accommodations aboard a more elegant ship.

Cruise Discounts

An almost dizzying array of discounts is available, and they seem to come and go with lightning speed. Discounts may be widely and heavily promoted or advertised only in limited markets. Travel agents often are the best source for current discounts because they're continuously updated on specials through their computer reservations systems, the Internet, and their office fax lines. It's their business to know about the deals.

MICHAEL STORRINGS

Discounts, however, are not always what they seem. It pays to compare and make an educated decision based on all the facts. Always do the math to uncover the better deal.

Early-booking Discounts

In retailing terms, a cruise is a perishable item. If a ship sails with empty cabins, that inventory and the potential revenue it could generate evaporates.

As a way to avoid this, many cruise lines reward the earliest bookers with the best prices—nearly all companies offer an enticing early-booking or "early bird" discount. Booking early usually means at least six months before sailing. But check brochures; for some lines, three months out constitutes "early." Nowadays some major cruise lines have added a new twist to the equation.

When a company announces a cruise, it advertises a fare that's a certain percentage less than the brochure rate (also called the "rack rate," "base rate," or "market rate").

Royal Caribbean International's **Breakthrough Rate Program,** for example, discounts brochure rates by 30 percent or more and pledges that "the greatest savings are given to those passengers who book earliest; fares often increase as sailing dates approach." **Princess Cruises** offers **Love Boat Savers** promising 50 percent off second passenger fares for early bookers, and **Carnival Cruise Lines** touts **Super Savers** with up to $1,200 off per stateroom on a seven-day cruise. Other lines pitch similar deals.

For Full Payment in Advance

Several upscale lines give discounts for paying in full at least six months before sailing. Examples: **Crystal Cruises** shaves 5 percent off; **Silversea Cruises**, 15 percent. **Seabourn Cruise Line**'s **WorldFare** program promises the best rates to guests who prepurchase blocks of cruise days that can be used within a 36-month period.

Mileage Programs

Passengers enrolled in frequent flyer programs have earned mileage from cruises booked with **Norwegian Cruise Line** (10,000 miles for a standard inside or outside cabin; 25,000 miles—enough to earn a domestic round-trip coach travel award—for a suite).

From time to time, members of frequent flyer programs are invited to redeem their mileage for discounts on cruises. These offers are advertised in promotional mailings from the airlines.

Cruise Combos

Some cruise lines give discounts to guests who combine one or more consecutive sailings. While many ships repeat itineraries, traveling the same circuit week after week, some do not. Some, for example, alternate a western Caribbean route with an eastern Caribbean route, so a passenger could stay on board for two cruises totaling 14 days and repeat only the port of embarkation—at a discounted price. The idea also works with ships that don't operate circuits but that offer long cruises. For example, most around-the-world voyages are broken into shorter segments; passengers more than one consecutive segment are rewarded with a discount.

Two-for-Ones

Although the idea of two passengers traveling for the price of one may sound like a terrific deal, airfare for the second passenger is not normally included. Say a four-day cruise costs $1,200 per person, with air. When figuring the per-couple price on a two-for-one, find out the cost of air for the second person and factor it in. In this example, the air for the second passenger is $400, so the air/sea package price for the couple equals $1,600.

Compare this with the cruise line's standard 30 percent early bird discount: $2,400 (the brochure cost for two, including air) less 30 percent (early bird discount) = $1,680, including air.

In this example, the couple saves $80 by waiting until the cruise line announces the two-for-one sale. But one drawback is convenience: separate air arrangements will have to be made for the person who's traveling free, and there's no guarantee the pair will be able to hop the same flight to the ship and back. Second, because the two-for-one was a last-minute discount, the cabin selection, preferred dining room seating, and other early-booking perks may have been forfeited. It may not be worth the $80 savings.

For Second Passenger

In this scenario, the first passenger pays the brochure tariff; the second gets a certain percentage discount (for example, 50 percent). Airfare is usually included (unlike two-for-one discounts).

What might seem like a juicy discount in the above case is actually the same as 25 percent off per person. That could work out to less than the line's standard early-booking discount.

Children or Third/Fourth Passenger Go Free

Some cabins come with more than two berths, allowing children or a third or fourth adult to occupy the same room—usually at a reduced price. Third/fourth rates seldom include air, so don't overlook that when considering discounts applied to third and fourth passengers in a cabin.

Free or Reduced Air/ Air Upgrades

The incentive for booking is a reduced price for the air add-on, which is sometimes applicable only to certain gateway cities. A variation on the theme is a free or reduced-price upgrade to business class. Such upgrades are usually offered in connection with cruises in Europe or other long-haul destinations.

Flat Rates

From time to time, a few lines set a flat rate for nearly all cabins on a ship. Passengers booking first get the best categories.

Free Days

"Cruise 10 days for the price of seven! Three free days!" Sounds enticing, right? But say that the price of the 10-day cruise is $2,000, or $200 a day. With three free days, the price drops to $1,400.

Compare this to the brochure-listed early-booking discount, which happens to be 40 percent (a standard early-bird rate). Forty percent of $2,000 is $800, so the early bird rate works out to $1,200, making it a better deal than the free days.

Credit Card Perks

Some cruise lines, including **Carnival**, **Majesty**, and **Norwegian**, issue their own credit cards (in

MICHAEL STORRINGS

conjunction with companies like Visa) where purchases charged on the card translate into points towards cabin upgrades, discounts, and free cruises. Some credit card companies also promote discounted cruises to cardholders.

Group Rates

Most lines offer reduced rates for groups booking a minimum number of cabins. This could be an option for large families, family reunions, friends, corporate groups, clubs, and other parties traveling together. If the group reserves enough cabins, the cruise line usually throws in a free berth for the leader, on top of the group discount.

Policies vary from line to line, but travel agents are skilled at negotiating attractive group rates.

Organization Discounts

Such large organizations as university alumni, the World Wildlife Fund, the Smithsonian Institution, AARP, and savings and loan associations have travel clubs that offer discounts on cruises. Check the publications of groups to which you belong for details.

Annual Promotions

The first National Cruise Vacation Month was instituted by CLIA in 1990, and it's become an annual event. Every February, CLIA goes on a promotional binge, and individual cruise lines try to attract business with a range of special offers: cabin upgrades, shipboard credits, 10 percent off deals, and others. That makes the month of February a good time to shop for a cruise.

Sail-a-bration, like National Cruise Vacation Month, is the brainchild of CLIA, introduced in 1994 to spark bookings in autumn, the industry's slow or "shoulder" season. September is the month for this annual event; look for special deals, particularly last-minute savings on fall and holiday sailings and early-bird discounts for the coming year.

Introductory Discounts

The first cruise of a new ship is known as the inaugural; sometimes behind the scenes, it's referred to as a "shakedown." When a vessel enters service, she may still have a few kinks to work out; on rare occasions, a ship isn't completely finished, and workers on board might be discreetly adding last-minute touches.

Some cruise aficionados don't worry about this and make a practice of booking inaugural sailings; they relish being on the first sailing. In fact, inaugurals are usually festivity-filled sellouts. Nevertheless, first cruises may be priced lower than subsequent sailings.

Contract bridge, a variation of the game of auction bridge, was invented in 1925 by railroad heir Harold S. Vanderbilt while he was on a Caribbean cruise.

The same may be true for an inaugural itinerary or even the entire season of new itinerary. The reason is twofold: to boost market awareness of the new program and to compensate, in advance, for any possible first-time glitches.

In the early 1990s, after the collapse of the Soviet Union, new Baltic ports were open to Western cruise ships for the first time in decades. Some of the pioneering vessels into the region offered low "introductory season" fares at this time. The following summer, when the region was solidly on the cruise charts, prices climbed.

Stateroom Upgrades

Offering passengers higher-category cabins at no extra charge is a very common practice. Some lines upgrade their repeat clientele whenever possible. If a sailing is very "soft" (few passengers have booked), it's not unheard of for everybody on board to get bumped up a category or two—sometimes more.

Often upgrades are not advertised by cruise lines but are offered as a sales incentive for travel agents to use when enticing clients. The upgrades apply only to certain sailings.

Sometimes, if the category you request on a particular sailing is sold out, the cruise line will guarantee you space on an alternative sailing in the same category cabin you booked or higher. You pay the fare for the cruise you wanted (minus any applicable discounts), and the line accommodates you to the best of its ability.

Paid upgrades are another possibility. Request these through your travel agent shortly before sailing or when you board. Provided the ship has space in a higher category and you or your agent ask for the best available rate, you might get upgraded at a discounted price.

But don't go on board expecting a free upgrade. It does no good to tell the ship's purser that your travel agent promised it. The fact is, if your agent has been able to arrange this courtesy through the cruise line, he or she will get an advance confirmation and will advise you prior to sailing.

Last-minute Discounts

Rather than sail with empty cabins, some companies "top off" their ships by steeply discounting fares shortly before the departure date. These discounts are usually advertised in Sunday newspaper travel sections and appear only in select markets, specifically, cruise port cities or states like Florida, under the heading "Florida Residents' Discounts." The theory is that locals can hop in a car and drive to the port, without having to tangle with last-minute air tickets.

While last-minute discounts can be the best deals around, they come with tradeoffs. First, if you live far enough away that you'll have to fly to the port of embarkation, it can be tough to get convenient and/or reasonably priced air tickets at the last minute. Second, there's little or no choice of cabins. And, finally, you may not get your preferred dining room seating.

One premium line regularly offers Florida residents a seven-day Caribbean cruise starting at under $100 a day per person during the months of January, February, and March. Similarly, Seattle residents might find last-minute discounts on Alaska cruises—they only have to drive to Vancouver, BC, where most sailings start, or pick up the cruise line's motorcoach transfer from Seattle to Vancouver.

Standby Rates

These deeply discounted programs are usually advertised only in local markets and do not include air. A cruise line lists specific itineraries and sailing dates; passengers rank their choices and send them, plus a deposit, to the company. If space opens up, the cruise line notifies your travel agent at least 30 days in advance. If you get your first choice, your deposit is nonrefundable.

Singles' Discounts

Single supplements of as low as 110 percent are offered on selected sailings. Upscale lines featuring longer itineraries, including **Crystal Cruises**, **Seabourn Cruise Line**, and **Silversea Cruises,** seem more generous than others with singles' discounts, probably because they have a high percentage of loyal single clientele. Singles' discounts are usually mentioned in the cruise-line brochure.

Seniors' Discounts

Cruise lines know that most seniors have more flexible schedules than the general population and can travel at off-peak times and at short notice. That's why seniors' discounts usually crop up in newspaper ads around the autumn shoulder season and a few months or weeks before the departure date of cruises that are selling slowly. The amount of the discount and the restrictions vary but usually the line requires at least one person in a cabin to be 55 or older.

Value-added Discounts

With this discount, you pay the full fare but get credit toward purchases during your cruise. For example, you may be offered a free hotel night in port before or after the sailing or such onboard perks as free shore excursions.

A very common value-added discount is giving you a credit to your shipboard account. Here's how it works: If you're offered a $200 per person shipboard credit, you and your traveling partner receive a total of $400 on your onboard account to use for any purchases, such as drinks, wine in the dining room, beauty and spa treatments, tours, or photographs.

Onboard Booking Discounts

Some lines, such as **Crystal Cruises**, take bookings on board for future sailings and dole out savings to those who make deposits. These usually can be combined with discounts for full payment in advance and with alumni discounts (see below).

As a courtesy to the passenger's travel agent, the cruise line will transfer any onboard booking to the agent of record. Some lines offer the choice of letting you designate a different agent to receive the commission if you aren't happy with the one who arranged the cruise you're on.

Alumni Discounts

These are offered to passengers who have cruised previously with the line. They may come in a special mailing or in the alumni newsletter. Such discounts are not always cash off the fare; they might be a cabin upgrade or on-board credit. See "Perks for Cruise Line Alumni" on page 31.

Special or Offbeat Promotions

From time to time, companies feature offbeat promotions. For example, in a past offer, **Delta Queen Steamboat Co.** awarded grandparents booking one cabin at full fare a second cabin, free, for two children 18 years and younger. **Club Med** has given couples a 1 percent discount for each year of their marriage. Other lines have also featured creative deals, especially to commemorate such events as anniversaries or to mark the inauguration of a new itinerary.

Rebates

These are unadvertised and little-known (to the public) discounts that come out of an agent's own pocket. Cruise lines pay a commission, usually 10 percent, to travel agents when they make a sale. But they also give them additional commissions, known as "overrides," as an incentive to sell their product, a reward to top-producing agents, or a way of defraying marketing costs. Sometimes agents will then rebate all or part of the bonus to a customer by reducing the cruise fare.

Most travel agents say they disdain the practice of rebating, but many do it if it clinches the sale, especially with a first-time client.

In recent years, a handful of agencies have tried a new tack. They charge a set fee for making a cruise booking, then rebate their entire commission to the client. Whether this is a good deal or not depends on the cost of the cruise and the commission level the agent is earning.

One note of caution: Such agencies are not the "hand-holding" type. They make their money in volume and are not likely to devote hours of time to counseling clients on the pros and cons of various cruises.

> "Life on board a pleasure steamer violates every moral and physical condition of healthy life except fresh air. . . it is a guzzling, lounging, gambling, dog's life. The only alternative to excitement is irritability."
>
> George Bernard Shaw, while on a Mediterranean cruise aboard the *Lusitania* in 1899

Perks for Cruise Line Alumni

A dozen long-stemmed red roses in a crystal vase, a personal note of thanks, an invitation to another rendezvous.

The attentions of an ardent suitor? In a way, yes. Gestures like these—as well as newsletters, cocktail parties, exclusive activities, and other forms of special treatment—are extended to passengers by many cruise lines as a way of forging customer loyalty. Usually all it takes is one cruise to be inducted into the ranks of cruise line alumni. After their first sailing on a particular line, passengers are either automatically included in the company's alumni organization at no charge or may join for a nominal fee.

Alumni organizations with names like the "Venetian Society" (**Silversea Cruises**), "Captain's Circle" (**Princess Cruises**), "Society of Master Mariners" (**Holland America**), and "Crystal Society" (**Crystal Cruises**) send out newsletters or magazines with tips on upcoming cruises, new ports, and company developments. Some of these publications, including **Carnival's** *Currents* and **Seabourn's** *Seabourn Club Herald,* feature travel stories by top writers as well as stunning photographs. Valuable coupons or certificates may be included. **Royal Caribbean International's** *Crown & Anchor* magazine, for example, occasionally offers savings certificates for selected sailings and onboard amenities.

Once they come back for another cruise, repeat passengers may be presented with gifts or invited to a special cocktail party hosted by the captain. **Crystal Cruises** greets all returning passengers with gifts in their staterooms. A few cruise lines reward every alum; others single out those who have logged the most cruises or days aboard ship. But everyone—whether it's their second or 102nd sailing—is made to feel part of an inner circle, distinct from the novice cruisers on board.

Besides giveaways like luggage tags, tote bags, and visors, some companies reward their best customers with presents ranging from flowers and wine to clocks and brandy snifters. Others offer collectable pins or medals designating the number of voyages sailed. Additional means of recognition might include priority boarding and debarkation, separate airport transfers, preferred dining room seating, shipboard credits, and cabin upgrades.

Some cruise companies, such as **Holland America** and **Crystal**, offer alumni discounts on all sailings; other lines designate specific dates. Members of **Cunard's** "Cunard World Club" may redeem points earned for miles sailed for upgrades and free cruises, while **Seabourn** offers three levels of discounts based on the number of days sailed.

Many lines also promote alumni reunion cruises hosted by company executives or celebrities. Passengers on these voyages are lavished with goodies like parties, presents, and special lectures, tours, and other activities. For many "alumni," this is a chance to meet old friends, and for that reason alone, reunion cruises can prove very rewarding.

MICHAEL STORRINGS

How Cruises are Sold

Many people think—quite logically—that if they want to book a cruise, they call a cruise line. Actually, most cruise lines avoid taking direct bookings. There's a more efficient means of distribution: travel agencies. In addition, wholesalers often sell cruises directly to the public.

Travel Agencies

About 40,000 travel agency locations are spread across the United States. This kind of sales network would be far beyond the means and resources of individual cruise lines. So agents sell cruises, earning commissions from the line. If you called a cruise line and tried to make your own booking, chances are that the company would most likely steer you to a travel agent; and if you don't have one, it might offer to help you find an agency in your area.

It's not that cruise lines *can't* take your reservation; usually they *won't* because they don't wish to alienate the travel agency community. And from a practical standpoint, most cruise lines don't have the staffing to handle consumer calls. Working through travel agents is more efficient for them.

Also, because the cruise line pays the commission, it doesn't cost a consumer extra to use an agent (a small percentage of agencies do, however, charge set service fees that are presented to clients up front).

This system offers many benefits to the consumer:

1. The agent is a travel and cruise expert and your advocate. An agent works to match you to the right cruise—s/he deals with cruise operators on a regular basis, and many possess first-hand knowledge of the individual ships. Agents can work to ensure that your requests for a specific type of cabin, dining room seating, or air tickets, are properly handled and that you receive all travel documents in a timely manner. In addition, should anything go wrong, the agent is in the best position to correct the problem.

2. Travel agents have the deals. Cruise lines keep agents well informed of special discounts, so they, more than anybody, are a good source for the latest deals. And as discussed above, some agencies also offer their own discounts and booking incentives on top of what the cruise line is advertising.

3. As an agent learns your needs, s/he can keep you apprised of cruises that might be of interest. Once you've taken one cruise, your record is on file, which speeds future bookings. Good agents keep in touch with clients, informing them of new itineraries, new ships, and new discounts.

One possible drawback to using a travel agent: They can't know everything about all of the dozens of cruise lines, so many specialize in selling a handful of companies, known as their "preferred suppliers." Usually they earn bonus commissions whenever they sell those brands. In theory, that could motivate an agent to push a cruise line that isn't exactly right for you. In practice, it seldom happens because agents would have unhappy customers and never get repeat bookings.

When you first contact an agency, ask who their preferred suppliers are. Later, if you aren't confident you're getting unbiased recommendations, take your business to another agency.

Choosing a Travel Agency

Ask friends or associates who have cruised. Check the Sunday travel section of your local newspaper for cruise advertisements that are sponsored by particular agencies. Keep an eye out for "Cruise Nights."

When seeking a capable counselor within an agency, look for any degrees or titles that indicate the person has made an effort to hone professional skills beyond the minimum requirements. For example, the initials "CTC" on a business card indicate the agent has earned the designation Certified Travel Counselor after completing a course run by the Institute of Certified Travel Agents (ICTA). Such titles don't guarantee expertise in the cruise arena, but they do indicate overall proficiency.

The following are some other things to consider when researching agencies:

CLIA-Affiliated Agencies

Look for one of the nearly 23,000 CLIA-affiliated agencies nationwide, identified by the blue CLIA seal in the window and/or telephone directory. CLIA trains and certifies agents as "Accredited Cruise Counselors" and more advanced "Master Cruise Counselors." When contacting a CLIA agency, ask to speak with the person who has earned such certifications. To find a CLIA-affiliated agency near you via the Internet, access the CLIA directory by typing http://www.ten-io.com/clia.

Cruise-only Agencies

Some agencies specialize in planning cruise vacations and are listed as "cruise-only" in the Yellow Pages. The National Association of Cruise Only Agencies (NACOA) is an affiliation of 850 travel agencies selling cruise vacations exclusively. All members must be affiliated with CLIA. NACOA members are identified by the decal in their window, which they may also use in advertising. To find out if an agency is a NACOA member or for a list of NACOA agencies near you, send a stamped, self-addressed envelope to **NACOA** (7600 Red Rd, Suite 128, South Miami, FL, 33143, 305/663.5626).

Independents vs. Networks

Some travel agencies are locally owned and independent. Others are franchises or affiliated with big international chains like American Express or Thomas Cook and may or may not be locally owned.

Sometimes you'll get more personal service from a small, local agency—especially if the owner is on the premises. The local mom-and-pop agency thrives on reputation and word of mouth so it's compelled to serve the community.

Other times the more polished national affiliates are more service-minded because they may attract more accomplished employees and operate more professional staff training programs.

Very often, bigger companies have the pricing edge because, as part of a huge network, they have more negotiating clout with cruise lines. On the other hand, small agencies can join forces with other companies through national consortia that act on their members' behalf in securing better sales support and commissions from the cruise operators.

Wholesalers

Other parties who sell cruises are wholesalers. They secure an option to buy, at a steep discount, high volumes of cabins from cruise lines. Then they sell the cabins through retailers (travel agents), paying them a commission. Or because they don't have to pay a commission, wholesalers in most cases sell directly to consumers.

Wholesalers are often among the largest advertisers in Sunday newspaper travel sections. If you see a cruise advertised, call the 800 number listed, and if you find that you're talking with a company half-way across the country (very often in a cruise-port state like Florida), you could be chatting with a wholesaler.

Not all cruise lines deal with wholesalers, so the choice may be somewhat limited. Wholesalers tend to sell big companies that have a lot of inventory to move. Such lines usually operate in the Caribbean and Alaska but not in more exotic venues.

Wholesalers handle your cruise booking just as a local travel agent would, but they usually give less personal attention. Since they handle large volumes of cabins every year and conduct a major chunk of their business by phone, it's less likely they'll invest as much energy as a local travel agent would. If you're a person who demands a high level of personal service or if you prefer face-to-face transactions when making a major purchase like a cruise, a wholesaler may not be for you. But if you're shopping largely for price, wholesalers usually offer very attractive deals.

"The pure pleasure of it was unimaginable. For days on end, we took to our pews in the Smoke Room, lazily moving from one romantic place to another."

H.L. Mencken, about a 1920s-era world cruise

Special-interest Sailing: Selecting a Theme Cruise

Whether your passion is gourmet cooking or gardening, cigar smoking or the cinema, murder mysteries or rhythm and blues, there's a theme cruise for you. These sailings revolve around a specific topic, offering passengers special activities, extra goodies, and the chance to travel with people who share common interests.

The theme-cruise concept probably originated with the "Music Festival at Sea" on **Paquet**'s *Mermoz* (now operated by **Costa Cruise Lines**). First held in 1968, this annual event has become the world's longest-running theme cruise. During the voyage, classical music lovers are privy to rehearsals, attend lectures and concerts, and rub elbows with big-name artists over cocktails.

In three decades since the first "Music Festival at Sea," cruise lines have offered seagoing vacations focused on everything from antiques to auto racing. Even a few eyebrow-raising topics have cropped up—witness the popular "O.J. Trial of the Century" voyage marketed on a ship sailing from **Los Angeles**. Quite possibly the hottest theme cruises, believe it or not, are nude cruises. Perennial sell-outs, they're marketed by a nudist travel company and are held on an assortment of ships.

For prospective cruisers, deciding on a special-interest voyage can help narrow the overwhelming field of ships and itineraries from which to choose. For both novice and experienced sailors, selecting a theme trip helps ensure that shipboard activities will be appealing and other passengers simpatico.

Another bonus of theme cruises are the extras—the chance to sip rare vintages on a wine-tasting cruise, to be pampered with an expert make-over on a beauty cruise, or to consult with top authorities in an area of particular interest (anything from golf to the stock market). Some theme sailings even give you the chance to meet your heroes, whether they're athletes, politicians, economists, astronomers, movie stars, authors, or bandleaders.

Most all lines offer theme cruises from time to time. Check with your agent to see what's on tap. Here's an idea of the possibilities:

Cunard is noted for its themes, particularly on transatlantic cruises aboard the *Queen Elizabeth 2*. Past voyages have focused on golf, gardening, gastronomy, art, vintage automobiles, and Hollywood (with Richard Dreyfuss, Rita Moreno, Cliff Robertson, James Earl Jones, and other movie stars on board).

Norwegian Cruise Line's annual "Floating Jazz Festival" is well into its second decade, and the line has hosted cruises celebrating other types of music (country, big band, 1950s and 1960s) as well. However, **NCL** is especially known for its comprehensive "Sports Afloat" program featuring professional baseball, hockey, football, and basketball stars as well as Olympic gold medalists. Activities include clinics, workshops, question-and-answer sessions with the athletes, autograph signing sessions, and passenger competitions.

A cruise focusing on antiques, with seminars by appraisers, has been offered by **Commodore Cruise Line.** The company has also advertised wackier themes such as a "multiples" trip honoring twins and triplets, and a voyage especially for people named Smith or Jones (it featured genealogy lectures and films like *Mr. Smith Goes to Washington* and the Indiana Jones series).

American Hawaii cruises have focused on everything from whale watching, photography, and big band music to the anniversary of the attack on Pearl Harbor. The line's annual "Aloha Festivals" celebrate the islands' heritage. **Delta Queen Steamboat Co.** highlights the Civil War, Mark Twain, the Kentucky Derby, and a host of other American themes.

Seabourn Cruise Line's theme cruises delve into the worlds of politics, business, and finance with presentations by accomplished journalists and authors. Oktoberfest, the Superbowl, and comedy have been **Holland America Line** themes, while **Radisson Seven Seas Cruise Line's** *Radisson Diamond* has been the setting for a murder mystery cruise in which passengers joined actors in unraveling "who dun it."

Making a Reservation

A competent agent will steer you through all the intricacies when s/he makes your reservation. The agent will take down all the specifics and make the booking in your presence, either phoning the line's reservations department or using a computer to access the cruise line's inventory directly.

Not all cruise lines offer their inventory on computer reservation systems (CRS). **Royal Caribbean International** was the first to do so, in the early 1990s, developing its own system. **Princess Cruises, Norwegian Cruise Line, Radisson Seven Seas Cruise Line**, and others followed suit, choosing a joint system developed in conjunction with an airline CRS. Agents using such a computer system are able to get reservations confirmed immediately. Those who book by phone may receive written confirmation by fax, following a short delay.

The following are things you'll need to know (or choices you'll need to make) when booking your cruise:

- The cruise line, the itinerary, the ship, and preferred sailing date(s).
- Preferred cabin type (or category) and alternate choices.
- Will you buy the cruise line's air/sea program or arrange your own air? Will you request an air deviation or upgrade?
- Preferred dining room seating (early or late, size/location of table).
- Any special dietary requests?
- Any requests for travelers with special needs (the physically challenged, those with infants or small children, honeymooners)?
- Pre-book any shore excursions?

- Pre-/post-cruise packages?
- Celebrating any special occasion (birthday, anniversary) on board?
- Deposit and final payment schedule, form of payment.
- Will you purchase trip cancellation and/or baggage insurance?
- What identification is required? Will you need a passport and/or visas? What about inoculations?
- When will travel documents be delivered?

Choosing the Right Cabin

After you've selected the ship and itinerary, one of the most important decisions you'll make about your cruise is choosing the cabin you would prefer. Rather than having your heart set on a specific stateroom or staterooms, think in terms of categories and keep an open mind. Most often it's budget that determines your choices.

For most folks a mid-range cabin provides a pleasing balance of comfort and economy. But, interestingly, the least expensive and most expensive staterooms are the first to sell out on any ship. So if you're thinking of splurging on the owner's suite or a penthouse or, if you're of the opposite mind and willing to forego the niceties in favor of nabbing the most economic room of all, you'll have to book as far ahead as possible.

Aside from cost, a predetermined factor, how do you narrow down the choices and find the cabin that's right for you?

Here are the basic considerations:

Number of People in the Cabin

Doubles

The most plentiful cabins are designed for two people and come with two berths (usually side by side but, occasionally, upper and lower) or a double or queen bed.

Compare the cabin layouts (also called "configurations") by looking at brochure deck plans, which usually offer a page picturing sample cabin categories. These show whether your stateroom comes with uppers and lowers (usually the least expensive) or with lower twins. During the day, one of the lower berths often doubles as a sofa.

Newer ships have twin beds that convert to queen- and even king-size beds, a big plus for honeymooners, tall people, and couples used to sleeping side by side. On the most luxurious ships, queen-size beds are standard.

A word of caution: bed size may vary from cabin to cabin, ship to ship, and line to line. Don't expect a king at sea to be as large as the one in your bedroom at home. If you need a lot of

MICHAEL STORRINGS

space when you sleep, have your agent ask the cruise line about the measurement of the bed in the cabin you're considering.

Singles

Single-berth cabins are rarities, and they are mostly on older ships. If you're traveling alone on a ship with no single cabins, you'll need to weigh the options covered earlier in this book (see page 6).

Triples/Quads

The availability of cabins sleeping more than two people is limited on most ships, so parents traveling with children or parties of more than two will need to book early, especially in peak seasons in markets that draw families, such as summer Caribbean cruises.

Of course, another option for parties of more than two traveling together is booking more than one cabin. In the interest of more space and comfort, some families choose this option, especially if the children are teenagers. Parents who wish to be close to their children might choose "connecting cabins." These side-by-side accommodations have a door that links the two rooms.

More and more contemporary vessels are advertising what they call "family cabins." These not only have more berths, they're also roomier and may provide kid-pleasing features, including toiletries of cartoon characters or two televisions. Lines such as **Carnival, Disney,** and **Royal Caribbean International** are among those promoting such accommodations.

Physically Challenged Passengers

Those requiring wheelchair-accessible accommodations will find a larger selection, in a range of categories, on newer ships. The features of such cabins were discussed on page 7.

Older ships and such specialized vessels as sail-cruisers, expedition vessels, and river barges may offer few or no wheelchair-accessible rooms.

Ocean-view or Inside?

Inside cabins have no windows and usually are the most economical choice. Cruise lines design and decorate inside cabins to give the illusion of light and space; some are more successful than others. Inside cabins on contemporary ships are very seldom claustrophobic or depressing. If you're on a budget and don't intend to spend a great deal of time in your cabin, an inside cabin might be the way to go.

But if you don't want to have to go on deck to enjoy a sea view, if you plan on spending a lot of time in your cabin, or if you're celebrating your honeymoon, anniversary, or other special or romantic occasion, spending extra on an ocean-view cabin is probably worth it.

Some smaller, luxury lines, including **Radisson Seven Seas, Renaissance, Seabourn, Sea Goddess, Silversea,** and **Windstar** offer only ocean-view cabins. Nearly all the staterooms of **Crystal Cruises'** *Crystal Harmony* and *Crystal Symphony* are outside.

Outside cabins come with portholes or windows; most new ships feature large windows. Usually, the pricier a cabin, the bigger the views. The less expensive categories may come with a small window or a porthole. Note: Portholes on modern ships are sealed shut.

Standard or Deluxe?

Cruise lines often distinguish the pricier cabins from the more economical staterooms by using the broad terms "deluxe" and "standard." The exact meaning of these words is hard to pin down because it varies so much from company to company. But basically the considerations are cabin size, amenities, and location on the ship.

For most people, budget is the deciding factor. But other variables may also be considered.

When it comes to your vacation, the cheapest may not be the best choice. That's especially true if you're marking your honeymoon, anniversary, or another special occasion. If so, you may wish to go deluxe. This level of accommodation comes not only with more space and more lavish amenities but often with such perks as butler service, an invitation to a cocktail party with the captain or another senior officer, or even a seat at the captain's table in the dining room.

The opposite theory is: Why spend a lot of money on a cabin when you'll probably spend so little time there? Some frequent cruisers, even very wealthy ones, select inside or lower-category cabins, pouring their money instead into sailing on more upscale ships or ones with longer itineraries, or taking more frequent sea-going holidays. After all, they reason, today's ships provide one-class service, and everyone's entitled to the same dining, entertainment, and public facilities. (An exception is **Cunard's** *Queen Elizabeth 2*, where dining is determined by the class of accommodation booked).

So deciding whether to go standard or deluxe is a matter not only of budget, but of philosophy and life style.

Cabin size varies from line to line, with more ample dimensions usually found on pricier ships. But that's not always true. **Carnival Cruise Lines**, for example, is considered a mass market company, but its standard outside cabins average about 185 square feet. That outsizes some of its swankier competitors.

Older ships offer cabins of varying shapes and sizes. The rooms also tend to be bigger than on modern ships because cruises of yesteryear spent more time at sea and less in port. Also, people entertained more in their cabins, especially on longer sailings, when hosting a cocktail party in your stateroom was a social ritual.

Cabins on new ships may be smaller and more standardized, but they offer other comforts. Amenities that once appeared in only the most upscale rooms now show up at many levels. These include toiletries baskets, hair dryers, in-cabin safes, refrigerators, and even private balconies.

If the cruise line brochure doesn't specify cabin dimensions—and most don't—ask your travel agent. And be aware that cabins with private balconies usually incorporate the balcony size into the overall dimensions.

When choosing a cabin, don't overlook the bathroom. Some categories come with shower only; others come with shower and tub. Deluxe categories may offer tubs with whirlpools; suites almost always do.

Suite Dreams

Suite categories range from junior or mini to penthouse or owner's and come with a range of amenities. Some standard features include separate seating and sleeping areas, VCRs, complimentary bars, mini-refrigerators, walk-in closets, and tubs and whirlpools. Suites almost always come with their own private verandas or at least extra-large windows. Passengers will also find fresh flower arrangements, personalized stationery, bathrobes, and other niceties.

Distinctive features range from the Oriental art collections in the owner's suites on **Orient Lines'** *Marco Polo* to the white baby grand pianos in the top suite of the newest liners of the **Royal Caribbean International** fleet to butler service and cocktail-hour hot hors d'eouvres in **Crystal Cruises'** *Crystal Harmony* and *Crystal Symphony*.

Besides the lavish accommodations, suite-dwellers are showered with such small courtesies as choice dining-room seating, often at a table hosted by a ship's officer, invitations to a cocktail party with the captain (commonly held in his quarters), and a private visit to the bridge.

Private Balconies

One of the hottest new design features of contemporary ships is the private veranda or balcony. They're great spots to enjoy cabin breakfasts, snoozing, reading, sunbathing, and cocktails. And what could be more romantic than watching the ship glide into and out of port from this superb perch? Itineraries rich in scenic wonders, such as Alaska, may be all the more enjoyable with a private view available around the clock.

The private balconies are currently in such demand that more and more ships offer them. Once found only in the owners' or penthouse suites, today they're available in a broad range of categories.

Be forewarned: sometimes private balconies use space that would otherwise be part of the interior cabin, so rooms with a veranda may be smaller than those without. Also, balcony size varies according to cabin category, from ship to ship, and line to line. Some verandas are so cramped they hold only a couple of deck chairs; others are more spacious and better furnished.

Location

When booking, you'll instruct your travel agent which category or categories you prefer. The agent sends that information to the cruise line in a request for space availability. The line normally responds with several specific cabin choices.

Say you're offered two options in Category D and three in Category F. Their size and configurations are nearly identical. How do you choose?

Two key factors are location of a particular deck and where on it the cabin is found: The more expensive cabins and suites are usually located on higher decks and often facing forward just above or below the bridge.

The view from such perches may be spectacular. But otherwise, high and forward is not always the best place to be because motion at sea is much more noticeable. In calm waters, it's smooth sailing but in high seas, passengers prone to seasickness might be very uncomfortable. If that's the case for you, choose a stateroom on a lower deck.

Selecting a lower deck doesn't mean you're stuck with a less desirable cabin. While upper-deck rooms traditionally carry a certain cachet, that prestige is diminishing as cruise lines scatter their suites throughout various levels. For example, veranda suites, the top accommodations on **Carnival's** newest "Fantasy Class" liners, are located midship on **Level Three** of these 10-deck ships.

Cabins in the forward tip of the vessel, even on low decks, can also sustain more movement in heavy seas. And some passengers in low forward locations may be disturbed by the sound of waves breaking against the bow and the rattle of the anchor being raised and lowered.

MICHAEL STORRINGS

Aft cabins (those in the rear) on low decks may vibrate with the ship's propellers. Sometimes jokingly referred to as "propeller suites," they may be noisier than other rooms.

So where's the best place to be? Cabins that are low and midship (near the center of the vessel) are usually quiet and the least subject to motion, making them the choice of experienced cruisers.

How well a ship takes the waves depends on its design. The old oceangoing liners with their sleek profiles and thick iron sides were built to withstand the bashing seas sometimes encountered on Atlantic crossings. Modern ships follow the sun and normally avoid bad weather. They also come with retractable stabilizers that steady a ship in rocky situations.

On contemporary liners internal noise—more than motion—can be an issue. To avoid being roused from your sleep by late-night disco music, early morning joggers, or the first aerobics class of the day, study the deck plan carefully and choose a cabin that's not directly beneath the disco, the jogging track, or the gym.

You might also want to stay away from banks of elevators, which are used by passengers around the clock, unless you have trouble walking or are in a wheelchair and find it convenient to be near the lifts. In fact, most of today's cruise ships purposely position their wheelchair-accessible cabins near elevators.

To find a good view, check the deck plan for potential obstacles like lifeboats. When in doubt, ask. Most cruise lines indicate in their brochures which cabins have obstructed or partially obstructed views, and the prices of such rooms are adjusted accordingly.

Also, if you're looking at a cabin situated on a walk-around promenade deck, will you have to keep your curtains closed for privacy? Often, windows on such decks are specially treated so you can see out but nobody can see in.

Air/Sea or Cruise-only?

The pros and cons of choosing the cruise line's air/sea package or of buying the cruise only and arranging your own air were discussed on page 25. You may want to refer to that section again before you visit your travel agent.

Air Deviations

If you purchase an air/sea package but decide you want to deviate from the standard routing or upgrade to business or first class, inform your travel agent when making your booking. Most cruise lines require a written request for deviation and payment no later than 60 days prior to departure. The sooner you make your request, the better the cruise line will be able to accommodate you.

Dining-room Seating

Another decision to make when you book is dining room seating (or "sitting"). More exclusive lines with smaller ships, such as **Radisson Seven Seas,**

Renaissance Cruises, Seabourn, Sea Goddess, Silversea Cruises, and **Windstar,** offer single-seating dining—all passengers are served at one time. Under this pleasant system, meals are more leisurely because the waiters aren't rushing to serve the first group, get them out, reset the tables, and take care of the second.

Many of the above lines also offer an "open seating" policy, inviting their guests to choose where and with whom they dine rather than assigning them to set tables.

But big-ship lines don't have the space to serve 2,000 passengers at once, so they divide their guests into two seatings: early (also called "main" or "first") and late (also called "second"). Schedules vary, but here's a sample:

Breakfast (in port): 6:45AM (early) and 8AM (late)

Breakfast (at sea): 7:45AM (early) and 9AM (late)

Lunch: Noon (early) and 1:30PM (late)

Dinner: 6PM (early) and 8PM (late)

Select the first option if you're the early-to-bed, early-to-rise type or if you're traveling with young children. But select second if you're a night owl, if you like to spend long afternoons on deck or enjoy long cocktail hours without having to dash off to the dining room, if you're disabled and need a little more time to eat, or if you can't stand being rushed and prefer to linger over your meals. Late-seating folks who tarry too long may miss the start of the show or preshow dancing.

When you make your booking, ask to be seated with friends or family. You may also ask for a table for two by the window, a round table for eight, a table hosted by a ship's officer, or some such preference. If your request can't be honored in advance, go see the maître d' as soon as you board the ship. But realize that he is trying to accommodate hundreds of passengers, and you may not always get exactly what you want.

A window table may sound romantic, but keep in mind that at night there isn't much to see after the sun goes down, and the curtains will probably be closed. Also be aware that very few are available.

Many experienced cruisers say that a highlight of their voyage is the new friends they meet at their dining room table. In addition, if you're new to sailing and don't know anyone on board, it's probably best to try for a large table where you'll have a better chance of meeting someone you like (although if you're really unhappy you can ask the maitre d' for a new table assignment).

The 1997 Broadway musical *The Titanic* follows the story of several survivors of the 1912 sinking of the legendary luxury liner. It is the second Broadway musical to feature the famous ship. The title character of *The Unsinkable Molly Brown* is also a *Titanic* survivor.

Special Diets

Booking is also the time to let your travel agent know about any special dietary requirements. Today many cruise lines include vegetarian and/or heart-healthy, spa or low-fat, and low-salt selections on their standard menus. Some lines offer these choices (and others) on special request only. Be aware that only a few ships are able to offer kosher food.

Have your agent check the line's policy about special diets; often you must submit a request in writing at least several weeks ahead of your sailing date. It's probably better to do that at the time of booking and reconfirm with your agent several weeks before departure.

Some folks with special dietary requirements find it pleasant to dine at the luncheon buffets rather than in the dining room because they can select what they like in the quantity they prefer. Today's chefs know that more and more passengers are demanding fresher, lighter, and healthier buffet items, and salad bars and hot and cold vegetarian entreés have become standard on many ships.

Travelers with Special Needs

Travelers with special needs should notify the cruise line *at the time of booking.* Be sure your travel agent thoroughly understands all your requirements; s/he is the person who will communicate your requests to the cruise line.

Physically Challenged Passengers

You must notify the line of your health condition and any special medical equipment or devices that you intend to bring aboard ship. For example, will you need to use a wheelchair (most cruise lines usually require passengers to bring their own chairs)? Oxygen? Will you bring your own attendant? A service animal?

For information on wheelchair-accessible cabins, see page 7.

If you plan to use a wheelchair in the dining room, be sure your agent notifies the cruise line that you will need a large table in an easily reached location.

Specific Medical Requirements

If you have a medical condition, make sure your travel agent conveys information about such special needs as mobility aids, oxygen, or ADA equipment to the ship prior to your cruise.

Consider travel insurance. Coverage should include medical evacuation and emergency treatment in foreign facilities.

A Harley-Davidson motorcycle goes to the jackpot winner in the casino on Carnival Cruise Lines' *Inspiration*. The lucky passenger can ride the new "hog" off the ship, or Carnival will deliver an identical model to the winner's hometown Harley dealer.

Travelers with Infants/ Young Children

Double-check about children's menus and baby-sitting services, and ask about the availability of equipment such as a high chair in the dining room, a crib to use in the cabin, and a kiddie-size life jacket.

Be sure you also have proper documentation for youngsters if you're boarding or debarking your cruise ship outside the United States. Your travel agent can advise you.

Honeymooners

One important matter to have your travel agent confirm at the time of booking is to be sure you're getting a stateroom with a double bed. Many older ships are equipped only with twins that are bolted to the floor. Most new vessels, however, offer twins that convert to doubles, and sometimes even queens and kings.

Honeymooners should be sure the ship is informed, in advance, of their special status. Most lines honor newlyweds with perks like flowers, an invitation to a cocktail party with the captain, a commemorative certificate, a complimentary photo, souvenir Champagne glasses, wine, or a cake.

For more information, see "A Checklist for Honeymooners" on page 42.

Pre-booking Shore Excursions

Usually only the very upscale companies and/or smaller ships offer pre-booking of excursions. Some passengers find it convenient to reserve and pay for tours in advance; others like to wait until they get on board to hear the shore excursion lectures, plan port activities with new friends, or just wait until the last minute to see how they feel about that full-day horseback riding trek.

Ask your travel agent for the cruise line's booklet of shore excursion options. If it's not available, inquire whether you'll receive it when your cruise documents arrive (usually a few weeks before sailing) or if you'll have to wait until you're aboard ship. Many people—whether they book tours in advance or not—enjoy at least looking over the choices to get an idea of what they can look forward to seeing and doing ashore.

If you do plan to pre-book tours, be sure to check the cut-off date for payment, as well as the refund policy. If you change your mind, will all or just part of your money be returned? And when?

For certain cruise programs, pre-booking tours is strongly urged. Such itineraries are built around big events like Mardi Gras in **New Orleans**, Carnival in **Rio de Janeiro**, the **America's Cup** competition, or a special exhibition at the **State Hermitage Museum** in St. Petersburg. Because demand is so high, the cruise line must make arrangements far in advance and, to be assured of space, passengers usually have to buy tickets well before sailing.

Another type of land program for which you'll often need advance reservations is anything rare, costly, or complicated to arrange. For example, **Seabourn Cruise Line** requires pre-cruise booking (and payment) for hot-air balloon rides in Europe. Wildlife safaris and other overland tours where you leave the ship for a few days on an organized excursion and rejoin at another port are usually also bookable in advance.

Pre-/Post-cruise Packages

Many passengers choose to combine their cruise vacation with a stay on land. To accommodate them, most cruise lines offer convenient and attractively priced pre- or post-cruise hotel or resort programs, often with optional tours available.

For an idea of the vast range of choices, check out the back-of-the-book pages of cruise-line brochures. Depending on the destination, you'll see possibilities ranging from the two- or three-day tours in exotic places like **Bali, Bangkok**, and **Singapore** in connection with **Orient Lines' Indonesia and Java Sea Program** to the one- to four-night packages in **Orlando, Miami Beach, Hollywood, Las Vegas**, and other cities offered by **Carnival Cruise Lines**.

Holland America Line and **Princess Cruises**, both Alaska veterans, have built up extensive resort facilities in the 49th state and offer fully escorted rail and motorcoach programs that are very popular with passengers. And such companies as **Disney Cruise Line** and **Premier** are among several that feature family-oriented land packages at Orlando theme parks.

Post-cruise packages are particularly enticing in connection with cruises to Alaska, Europe, and the **Far East,** where passengers crave a deeper look at nature and wildlife or want additional exploring and shopping time in the great cities. Also, travelers taking long-haul flights to join a cruise starting from, for example, **Hong Kong** or **Sydney**, often choose a pre-cruise hotel stay to rest up and overcome their jet lag prior to boarding the ship. Alternatively, some vessels act as floating hotels, staying in far-flung embarkation ports for a night or two before setting sail.

The details and prices of pre- and post-cruise hotel stays and tour programs are outlined in cruise brochures. Usually such packages are offered only immediately before or after the cruise and must be booked in advance.

It's usually not necessary to reserve land packages at the same time you book your cruise, but keep in mind that such programs affect your air schedule and making arrangements as far ahead as possible always guarantees better availability.

Commemorating a Special Date

Be sure to inform your travel agent if you or anyone in your party will be celebrating a birthday or wedding anniversary during the cruise. Most companies surprise celebrants with a cake or other treat on their special day.

If you want to plan an onboard soiree, ask your travel agent if preparations should be made in advance. Usually you can visit the food and beverage manager or bar manager to plan a catered party in a lounge or other public room once you're on board ship. For in-cabin parties, ask your steward about arrangements.

Payment

Cruise-line brochures outline the payment schedule, as well as acceptable forms of compensation. Most companies accept major credit cards; some accept personal checks. Savvy travelers protect themselves by paying for the cruise with a credit card. This offers the security of being able to cancel payment in the event of a problem.

Some consumer advocates recommend that passengers ask to have their credit-card charge run through the cruise line account, rather than the travel agency's. That avoids the possibility of a financially troubled agency using your money for paying debts rather than forwarding it to the cruise line. If that happened, and the agency collapsed, you would be liable.

However, if you've selected an agency you know well or one that's established or associated with a big, solid travel company such as **American Express, Carlson**, or **AAA**, or if an unfamiliar agency checks out with the Better Business Bureau, you're probably quite safe running your card on the agency account.

Deposit

This is a partial payment of the cruise fare—usually a certain percent or a flat rate—required at the time of booking to secure a cabin. Many lines call for a 10 percent deposit of the total cruise vacation package price within seven days of booking. Variations include a

MICHAEL STORRINGS

different payment schedule based on the number of cruise days.

Final Payment

Payment of the remaining cruise fare plus any necessary or agreed extras, such as taxes and airfare add-ons, is usually due no later than 60 days prior to departure and must be received before travel documents are issued. But individual lines' policies vary, so check the brochure for specifics.

Option

The cruise line informs a prospective passenger that the desired cabin will be reserved for a designated period. If the customer decides to take the cruise, s/he must make a deposit or final payment before the option expires. If not, the cabin becomes available for sale to another client.

Wait List

When a cruise is sold out, would-be passengers may place their names on a list and pay a deposit that is applied to the fare (the amount is specified in the brochure) to do so. If a cabin becomes available, these people are accommodated on a first-come, first-served basis. If no space opens, or if the customers decide not to accept the available stateroom, the deposit is refunded.

Cancellations

Cancellation policies vary from line to line and are spelled out in the brochure. Most companies require notification in writing at least 60 days before the sailing date or the air/sea program departure date. Some may require more time, perhaps double that, so be sure to read the brochure closely.

Passengers who cancel after the cutoff date for any reason, including medical and family, are subject to cancellation fees that vary based on the length of the cruise or the cruise fare and the number of days remaining before sailing.

Normally, cruise lines have a deadline after which they grant no refunds. Depending on company policy, that could be as close as 7 days prior to sailing or as many as 29 days or more. In addition, most cruise lines refuse to give refunds to passengers who terminate midway through their cruises or cruise/land packages, to those lacking proper documentation, and to "no shows." (A "no show" is usually defined as failure to check in at least 30 minutes prior to sailing.)

Note: If you cancel, and the cruise line is able to resell your cabin, that usually doesn't change the company's refund policy.

Refunds are normally made through travel agents; direct all inquiries to them. In addition, agencies may also assess their own cancellation fees. Be sure to clarify all these points with your agent before booking. You may also wish to inquire about trip cancellation insurance (see below).

Insurance

You may want to buy à la carte policies for trip cancellation, medical and emergency evacuation, and baggage protection, or you may choose to be extra safe and purchase a comprehensive policy.

When weighing any policy, be sure it's clear when coverage starts: At the time of deposit? Final payment? At the airport? The moment the ship sails? Insurance agencies, travel agents, and cruise lines sell cruise insurance. Mutual of Omaha Companies, American Express, and The Travelers are among the big companies offering cruise policies. Your travel agency may have its own program.

As for the cruise lines themselves, most feature comprehensive, "customized" policies underwritten by major insurance companies. Examples include Love Boat Care, **(Princess Cruises), Cunard**Care, Cruise Care **(Royal Caribbean International),** and **Carnival**'s Cruise Vacation Protection Plan. Such policies offer a range of coverage, including trip cancellation and interruption, medical protection and emergency evacuation, and baggage protection. Usually they also throw in such extra features as emergency cash transfers, lost document replacement, and 24-hour emergency assistance anywhere in the world.

Prices vary but, as an example, **Carnival's** Cruise Vacation Protection Program ranges from $39 to $199, depending on the voyage length.

Buy these policies through your travel agent at the time of booking or directly from the cruise line. Usually no paperwork or enrollment form is necessary, and coverage begins when the cruise line receives payment for the insurance.

Some lines automatically include their own comprehensive insurance policy on your invoice. Should you choose not to accept it, you subtract the premium from your payment. Check the cruise brochure for information.

Trip Cancellation and Interruption Insurance

This reimburses your nonrefundable, prepaid trip costs when you must cancel or cut short your cruise due to a personal medical problem or a family emergency. Most travel agents recommend it for their cruise clients, because the cost is negligible compared to the price tag of the vacation. The majority of policies specify death, injury, and illness; some allow notice of jury duty, a court order, flood or natural disaster at home, an accident en route to the airport, hijacking, etc. It's a rare policy that allows cancellation for any reason, so check out the fine print. Try to negotiate as much coverage as you can.

Some cruise policies feature a benefit for those with pre-existing medical conditions—credits for a future sailing. To receive the credit, you may have to make a new booking within a specified period, say, within a year of the original departure date.

In the Touch of Class piano bar on Carnival Cruise Lines' *Sensation*, patrons sit on barstools shaped like giant hands with red polished fingernails.

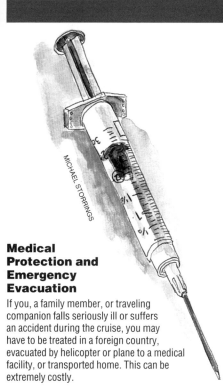

MICHAEL STORRINGS

Medical Protection and Emergency Evacuation

If you, a family member, or traveling companion falls seriously ill or suffers an accident during the cruise, you may have to be treated in a foreign country, evacuated by helicopter or plane to a medical facility, or transported home. This can be extremely costly.

Check to see if your existing health insurance policy or HMO covers medical treatment overseas. If not, you may choose to purchase supplemental insurance. Emergency evacuation is not always routinely covered. Medicare and many group health insurance policies often do not reimburse patients for emergency evacuation overseas.

Any passenger may consider medical and emergency evacuation insurance, but agents highly recommend it for elderly clients and those with pre-existing medical conditions.

Identification Papers

Passengers traveling outside the United States will need proper identification, both to board the ship and to visit foreign ports of call. Requirements vary from country to country and depend on whether you are a US citizen or a foreign resident. Your travel agent can advise you on all these matters.

Some countries—Bahamas and **Mexico**—may accept a cruise passenger's birth certificate, voter's registration card, or other identification in lieu of a passport. But in general, if you're going abroad, a passport is required.

Passport

If you don't have a passport and will be needing one for your cruise, be sure to apply immediately, as the process can take weeks or longer, depending on demand. Obtain an application form from your local post office.

Check the expiration date if you already have a passport. Some countries in Africa and **South America,** for example, require that your passport be

valid for at least six months beyond the date of your visit.

Visas

Your travel agent will advise you if you'll need visas for visiting any foreign ports of call. Caribbean islands and most Western European countries don't require a visa for US citizens who are visiting as tourists. Even some countries that ask for visas may exempt passengers who are visiting for a limited period, say, less than 24 hours, and staying on a cruise ship.

On cruises where you plan to debark in port and travel overland for a few days before rejoining the ship, a visa may be obligatory. This would be the case if you're a US citizen on a China cruise, and you leave the vessel, travel overland to **Beijing,** then reboard the ship a few days later. Again, your travel agent can tell you the requirements.

Be sure to apply for visas well ahead of the departure date. Your travel agent can guide you on how and where to do this, as well as provide names of companies that specialize in obtaining such documents on short notice, for a fee.

Many countries require proof of onward travel, such as an air or cruise ticket. Since you aren't likely to receive your travel documents from the cruise line until about 30 days before departure, this sounds like a problem. Here, again, your travel agent can assist. For example, s/he might be able to arrange for the cruise line to send a letter certifying that you have purchased a cruise ticket for onward travel.

Inoculations

Check with your travel agent or doctor about any inoculations that may be required. Officials in some countries may demand proof of vaccination.

Travel Documents

Included among these papers are your cruise ticket with the passage contract, which details the cruise line's terms of responsibility and accountability; your air ticket (if you've purchased an air/sea package); a passenger registration form; immigration forms for foreign ports of call; baggage tags; and a brochure or information sheet about the cruise, outlining the time and location of check-in, the itinerary, suggested dress code (to guide you when packing), and other helpful tips, such as the shipboard telephone and fax numbers where you can be reached in an emergency. (Note: Be aware that although most cabins have ship-to-shore hookups, the rates are steep for outgoing calls.)

Some companies also enclose a booklet detailing shore excursions offered during the cruise, instructions for ordering such bon voyage gifts as flowers, hors d'oeuvres, and Champagne or wine for yourself or friends, and perhaps even information about onboard tuxedo rental for formal nights.

When booking your cruise, always ask the agent when your travel documents will be delivered. Normally they'll arrive about 30 days prior to departure, but this varies from company to company. If you haven't received them two weeks before your sailing date, call your travel agent. If you booked at the last minute, documents may come just a few days before departure.

Be sure to read all documents as soon as they arrive to check for any errors in your cabin assignment, flight schedule, or other part of the trip. Call your travel agent if anything is amiss.

Complete your passenger registration form and any immigration documents before leaving home. Keep all these materials together with your passport or other identification and carry them with you. *Do not pack these items in checked luggage.* You will need to present identification and documents to check in for the cruise when you arrive at the pier.

Also be sure to write your name, cabin number, ship, sailing date, and other relevant information on the baggage tags you've received. You should securely attach a tag to each item of luggage. This is *very* important—especially if you're part of an air/sea program—and will help ensure that your suitcases are delivered to the right ship and cabin.

Finally, it's a good idea to carry along phone numbers for your travel agent and the cruise line, just in case you run into a problem en route to the ship. If your ship sails on a weekend, and your travel agency or the cruise line will be closed, try to get an after-hours contact number.

A Checklist for Honeymooners

Because it's a once-in-a-lifetime trip (theoretically, anyway!) a honeymoon cruise may require a little extra thought and planning. For example, don't assume that all ships offer double beds. They don't. (This has come as an unpleasant surprise to more than one newlywed couple.) To help you avoid overlooking any such important details, here's a list of questions to go over with your travel agent:

♡ What's included in the cruise fare? How much should we budget for extras like shore excursions?

♡ If coach-class airline tickets are part of the cruise package, how much does it cost to upgrade to business or first class?

♡ Is the transfer from the airport to the ship included? Can we make special arrangements, such as hiring a limo to take us from the airport to the ship?

♡ How much of a deposit is required? When is final payment due? What is the refund policy if it becomes necessary to cancel? Is cancellation insurance offered?

♡ Where is our cabin located on the ship? Is it inside or ocean-view? Will we have a porthole or a window? Can we get a private veranda?

♡ Are we confirmed in a cabin with a double/queen/king bed?

♡ Does our bathroom have a tub with a shower or just a shower? What about a Jacuzzi?

♡ Does our cabin come with a VCR? A refrigerator or a wet bar?

♡ May we request a certain type of dining room seating (e.g., a table for two by the window)? Will our request be confirmed or must we check with the maître d' upon boarding? How do we arrange special dietary requests? Is room service available? Does that mean breakfast only, snacks, or a full menu? Is there a charge?

♡ How many formal-dress nights are there? Does formal mean a dark suit or a tuxedo? How many casual nights? Is there a costume night? Are men required to wear jackets and ties to dinner?

♡ What kinds of activities are there that we can enjoy as a couple? Will there be other couples our age on board?

♡ Is it possible to pre-book shore excursions? Can we exchange our tickets for a different tour or get a full refund if we change our minds?

♡ Are pre- and post-cruise land packages available? What's included?

♡ Will we need passports or another type of identification? What about visas for any port calls?

♡ What is the cruise line's tipping policy? Whom should we tip and when?

♡ Is the line notified that we are honeymooners? What special amenities are we entitled to? Are these included or must we pay extra?

Packing for a Cruise

This can be the most exciting—and nerve-wracking—part of preparing for a cruise. Not only do you have to think about bringing the "right" clothing, but it's also important not to forget such essential items as prescription medication, sunglasses, and money. The following are some general packing tips.

Clothing

First, you'll want to check out the weather for the area you're cruising. Sometimes average temperatures are listed in the cruise brochure or in information included with your cruise documents. You might also consult travel guidebooks, the **Weather Channel,** the Internet, or international temperatures listed in the newspaper. Your travel agent can also be a good resource.

MICHAEL STORRINGS

The Bahamas, Mexico, and the Caribbean are warm year-round, but it's always wise to be prepared for the occasional cool night or rain showers. In areas like Alaska and **Northern Europe,** the weather is changeable. You might be baking in the midday sun of **Skagway** or **Stockholm** but by late afternoon, you're wishing for a sweater and long pants. The best way to deal with temperature swings is by bringing clothing to layer.

Plan to travel light for your own convenience but keep in mind that most people find they change clothes several times a day on a cruise as they move from pool or beachwear to sight-seeing to dinner dress. Almost all cruise ships offer self-service laundry facilities, as well as professional laundering, pressing, and dry-cleaning (for a fee). Some ships' washers and dryers require coins; others are free, along with the detergent.

Cruise lines generally have no luggage size and weight restrictions, usually permitting what the brochures somewhat nebulously call "a reasonable amount of clothing and personal effects." What's important are airline requirements. Check with your travel agent or the carrier.

Most cruises are casual by day—aboard ship or shoreside. Comfortable, flat-soled walking shoes, sneakers, sandals, T- or polo shirts, slacks, shorts, skirts, and sundresses are appropriate. For steamy climes, choose cool, breathable natural fabrics like cottons rather than synthetics.

At breakfast and lunch, dress is relaxed—but that doesn't mean swimsuits or bare chests. Sun worshipers who don't care to change for the dining room can take advantage of the poolside buffets or burger bars available on most ships.

When you're on deck, sunglasses and sunscreen are musts. Many people also find a hat that shades the eyes is a welcome accessory in tropical zones. Along with a swimsuit, bring a coverup and beach bag to take with you from your cabin to the pool or to the beach ashore. Towels are normally provided at the pool; a few lines even offer towels (which must be returned) to use at the beach. Otherwise, pack your own light beach towel or buy one on board in the ship's shop.

When planning your wardrobe for touring ashore, remember that very short shorts, skimpy halters, tube tops, and other daring fashions are frowned upon in more conservative countries. This is especially true if your sight-seeing includes churches and monasteries. And if you plan to visit museums or other indoor spots that might be over–air-conditioned, think about taking a light jacket or sweater. It's also a good idea for women to pack a light wrap for evenings on the ship.

Passengers booked on an expedition cruise or who plan to go hiking, mountain-biking, or pursuing other active excursions should take proper footwear and gear, including a light backpack, binoculars, a rain poncho, and insect repellent.

If you're an avid tennis player or a golfer who plans to be on the course in every port, by all means take your own racquet, clubs, and balls. Be sure to check with your travel agent or the airline about how to pack these items.

MICHAEL STORRINGS

Fitness-minded cruisers shouldn't forget suitable clothing for paddle tennis, basketball, workouts in the weight room, and aerobics and step classes. Most ships require gym users to wear proper athletic footwear. And don't forget a jogging suit or coverup.

It never hurts to tuck in a collapsible umbrella or light raincoat.

While all cruise ships have a relaxed dress code by day, the tone may rise as the sun goes down. Suggested evening dress is usually outlined in the back of the cruise brochure and included in the materials that come with your travel documents. If in doubt, ask your travel agent for guidance.

A man won't go wrong packing slacks and a sport coat or blazer. Slacks, skirts, and dresses are fine for women. Some ships have casual nights where jackets are unnecessary, and open-necked shirts are fine. Many men wear jackets and ties on informal nights, but some ships never require ties.

On formal nights, a dark suit is appropriate for men, and a cocktail dress or dressy pantsuit works for women. Some passengers choose to go all-out, wearing dinner jackets or tuxedos and evening gowns. A few lines rent tuxedos on board; if so, information about this service will be included in your travel documents.

Each cruise usually features at least one formal night, even on three- or four-night sailings. That's normally the Captain's Gala or Welcome Aboard Party, traditionally held on the second night of the voyage (the first night is almost always casual). A weeklong cruise may have a second formal night, the Captain's Farewell. That's often the second-to-the-last night; the last night, when folks are packing, is usually casual. On long cruises, count on about two formal nights per week.

The evening dress code—applicable from about 6PM on—is advertised in the daily program.

At the other end of the formality spectrum, most expedition or adventure cruises and many sail and river cruises don't require formal attire. If you're wearing parkas, waterproof gear, and rubber boots by day to frolic with the penguins, you generally don't have to worry about dressing like a penguin for dinner. Sail-cruise and river-cruise ships vary in formality: on most, "casual elegance" (resortwear) is appropriate in the evenings. For a laid-back line such as **Windjammer Barefoot Cruises**, dressing for dinner can be as uncomplicated as changing into a clean T-shirt.

Miscellaneous

There are myriad items besides clothes to take along on a cruise: sunscreen and sunburn cream, an extra pair of contacts, eyeglasses, sunglasses, a travel alarm clock, contraceptives, and

toiletries (many ships provide basics like shampoo and lotion in your cabin; the swankier the line, the more complete and lavish the amenities). If you forget something, most shipboard boutiques stock the basics, including toothpaste and razors. You'll want to take plenty of film and camera batteries; most ships sell them, and you can buy them ashore, but at a high price.

Check the cruise brochure, information that came with your travel documents, or with your travel agent about such electrical items as hair dryers, razors, and travel irons. Most cruise ships marketed to Americans equip staterooms with 100-volt AC current and standard US plug fittings, so any appliances you use at home should work just fine on board.

Today, more and more ships provide hair dryers in each cabin, and those that don't usually have a few to loan at the reception desk. Check the brochure to be sure.

Other optional items: a diary or notebook for recording your impressions, stationery and envelopes (although most ships furnish writing paper and postcards or sell them in the gift shop), a personal stereo and tapes or CDs, and magazines or books.

Some passengers also like to take along a travel guidebook covering the region they'll be cruising, a pocket-size language phrase book, and maps. If you don't want to pack travel reference materials, you can glean port information from the ship's newspaper, the shore excursions' office, and the onboard library. Otherwise, find out from the reception desk where the local tourism offices are located and plan to make them your first stop in port.

It might also be helpful to take along an extra, collapsible tote for visits to the pool and beach and for carrying gifts and souvenirs home after the trip.

Medication

Passengers with medical conditions should be sure to carry an ample supply of prescription drugs and medications, along with a list of them and their dosages, in their carry-on luggage. If you are at risk for a medical emergency, tell your doctor about your cruise plans, and take along your medical records (heart patients should have the most recent EKG). Be sure to carry your personal physician's phone number with you.

MICHAEL STORRINGS

You may also want to include seasick remedies and, for touring, moistened towelettes or a packet of tissues and a water bottle.

Money

A money belt, or leg, around-the-neck, or under-the-shirt pouch—sold in most luggage stores—are the best ways to conceal money and credit cards when you're touring in port. Fanny packs are not nearly as secure.

One of the conveniences of cruising is that most everything—at least transportation, meals, and entertainment—is paid for upfront. That makes budgeting easier. Most of what you don't pay in advance may be charged to your shipboard account. When making such purchases on board as bar drinks, tours, or items at the boutique, passengers present their cruise identification card and sign a receipt. About the only time they pay cash on board is in the casino.

Passengers establish credit for their shipboard account at the start of the cruise. For more information, see page 48. At the cruise's end, passengers pay accounts before debarking, using credit cards, cash, traveler's checks, or sometimes (when authorized in advance) personal checks. Forms of acceptable payment are specified in the cruise brochure.

Onboard ATMs have recently been introduced to the cruise industry. **Carnival Cruise Lines** was the first to offer them on several ships in its fleet.

You will need to have some cash for tipping at the end of the cruise. Plan to have small denominations: ones, fives, tens, and twenties. You can always get change at the purser's desk, but it's advisable to plan ahead and avoid possible lines at the end of the cruise.

For port calls, you will, of course, need spending money. Figure on souvenirs and gifts, any tours that you haven't booked on board through the ship's shore excursions' office, taxi and bus fares, refreshments or meals, entrance fees to museums and attractions, tips to local guides, and such incidentals as postcards and stamps.

If the ship is visiting a lot of countries, you might want to have a bit of local currency in advance. It's usually possible to exchange money in an international airport en route to the ship, but keep an eye on the transaction fees. It's probably better to wait until you arrive at each port and exchange money at a local bank. Check with your travel agent or home bank for advice.

More and more places abroad accept credit cards and traveler's checks but, if you're visiting very remote ports, you might need to pay cash. Your travel agent can advise, or consult a guidebook.

Whenever you travel, it's safer to carry credit cards or traveler's checks instead of large quantities of cash. While on the cruise, stow valuables in your in-cabin safe or in a safe-deposit box at the reception desk. In port, plan to carry only small amounts of cash. It's a good idea to conceal cash and credit cards in a money belt or an under-the-shirt pouch.

Bests

Phyllis Diller
Entertainer

In **San Juan, Puerto Rico,** in the refurbished old **San Juan Hotel** there is a **Champagne Bar** just inside the entrance. Once when I gazelled through the door there was a string quartet off to one side nestled amongst the verdant fernery playing classical music. The hotel is resplendent with dark mahogany the likes of which there'll be no more.

Blackbeard's Castle in **St. Thomas** is a gem high up in the hills with a magnificent view and fine food. There's open-air eating and at night a pianist. This is off the beaten path; a rewarding little side trip. You just have to know about this place. It's very "in!"

Karen Murphy
President, Murphy/O'Brien Communications

When my partner, Brett O'Brien, and I set sail on the *Crystal Harmony*, neither of us knew what was in store! We set sail on the **Mediterranean** with the wind at our backs and no fax machine in sight!

The beauty of the *Crystal* for the first-time cruiser is simple. There is so much to do both on and off the ship that there is no time for boredom. Some of our favorite aspects included:

Private late seat dining for two in the main dining room and Japanese restaurant, **Kyoto.**

Bingo at 4:30PM—promptly—daily!

We both love to gamble and the **Caesar's Palace** casino kept us busy nightly!

The wine selection was impeccable.

The cuisine was superb.

The health club was great—we are both workout fanatics.

Everyone left us alone!

On Shore:

There's a great local restaurant in **Florence** called **Il Martini.** Only the cabbies know where it is. No need to order—they do it for you! Best ravioli I've ever had.

If you've been to **Cannes** as many times as I have, it's great to rent a car and explore **St-Paul.** The restaurant, **Colombe d'Or,** is one of the best in the **South of France.** Make sure you have a reservation, though, as we had to bribe our way in.

If you have been recently proposed to (Brett proposed to me in the **Vista Lounge** at sea!), then Ghent is the port for you! We hailed a cab to the nearby town of **Antwerp,** the diamond capital of the world. After pouring over hundreds of diamonds, we found the perfect one!

We married in April of 1995 and are anxiously awaiting our second cruise experience aboard the *Crystal Symphony.*

Bon Voyage!

The big day has arrived. Your luggage is packed and tagged, and your carry-on bag holds your travel documents, including cruise and air tickets, and your completed embarkation documents, passport or other identification, and contact numbers for your travel agent and the cruise line.

After arriving at the ship, you'll check in and be given an orientation to your cabin. Now comes the fun part—watching the ship leave the port and then getting acclimated to life on board.

You'll learn all about activities—both on the ship and on shore—and start to make new friends. Before you know it, the cruise will be over and you'll have to leave. But rest assured that you'll have wonderful memories of the places you visited, people you met, and things you did on your floating pleasure palace.

MICHAEL STORRINGS

Getting to the Ship

Cruisers who fly independently or drive to the port are responsible for getting to the ship at embarkation time, which is noted in the pre-cruise documents. Be sure to arrive there *no later than* a half-hour before the ship sails. Most ships sail in the late afternoon or evening.

If you bought the cruise line's air/sea package, a cruise line representative in uniform will meet your flight at the gate or baggage claim area. Some lines have their personnel pick up all luggage with the cruise line tag on it, but for most ships, you'll have to claim your own luggage, and then follow the cruise line representative's instructions. Normally, bags are gathered in a central area for collection by the cruise line transfer staff. Passengers simply board the waiting bus or minivan and head off to the port.

Sometimes, especially in foreign cities, the cruise line might include a quick city tour or offer a hotel day room if flights arrive before the ship is ready to embark. If this is the case, when packing your carry-on bag, don't forget to toss in a clothing change or whatever items you need for sight-seeing or relaxing during the day before you board the ship. It's a good idea to plan for climate changes. If you're coming from a New York winter to the balmy Caribbean, wear layers you can peel off or pack a suitable change of attire, including comfortable footwear. Don't forget sunglasses.

When you arrive at the port, the cruise line representative will guide you through the check-in process. Your luggage will be transferred directly to your cabin.

Checking In

There are desks or check-in stations inside the terminal building that are divided according to the letters of passengers' last names. Here you will present your documents and identification. Some cruise lines will also ask at this time if you'd like to use a credit card to set up your shipboard credit account.

Other cruise lines will suggest stopping by the purser's desk on board at your leisure to initiate your account. If you don't provide a credit card, some will ask for a deposit in cash or traveler's checks. A few accept personal checks but these normally must be authorized in advance.

Here you'll also receive your boarding pass or passenger identification card or cabin keys; procedures vary from line to line. And you'll either proceed directly on board via the ship's gangway or you'll relax in a terminal lounge until the vessel is ready for boarding.

Sorry, No Visitors

Due to increased security measures, cruise ships seldom allow visitors on board. A few vessels do make available a limited number of visitor passes, but these must be applied for well in advance, and usually in writing. Check with your travel agent. In any case, your guests will have to provide photo identification at the gangway and will be allowed on board only for a specified time.

Cole Porter wrote "Begin the Beguine" during a 1935 world cruise aboard the *Franconia*.

Welcome Aboard!

As you board the ship you'll be welcomed by the staff, a photographer may take your picture to mark the occasion (you may choose to buy it or not, later, at the photo shop on board), and then you'll be escorted or directed to your cabin.

In the Cabin

Here you'll find your cabin keys and passenger identification card, if you haven't already received them. Chances are, you will *not* find your luggage. This is no reason for panic. Remember that hundreds or thousands of suitcases are being brought on board at the same time; it can take anywhere from a few minutes to a few hours for your bags to show up. Most cruise lines suggest allowing two hours after the ship's sailing before contacting your cabin steward or the purser's desk. Here again is reason to plan carefully when packing your carry-on bag.

The person who escorted you to your cabin might give you a quick briefing of stateroom facilities, including the location of your cabin keys, the light switches, and the air-conditioning and television controls. Or this person may leave the "grand tour" up to your personal cabin steward, who should be making an appearance sometime to introduce her/himself and show you the ropes. Usually you'll find a card or a piece of paper with

MICHAEL STORRINGS

your steward's name and, possibly, telephone or beeper number. Don't worry if the steward doesn't make an instant appearance. Remember that s/he may be responsible for 20 other cabins and is likely to be bustling about on embarkation day.

Look around your cabin. Be sure it's what you expected. If you paid for a stateroom with a large window, queen-size bed, and refrigerator, are they all there? If your cabin should have two lower berths, but it looks like there's only one double bed and a sofa, understand that the sofa will be converted into a bed every evening by the steward. In cabins with upper and lower berths, sometimes the upper berth is stowed, Pullman-style, into the wall during the day.

If you've been given the wrong type of cabin, this is the time to correct the situation. Go to the reception desk or the purser's office. If your problem is not resolved, ask to see the hotel manager. Be calm but firm. Shipboard personnel want satisfied passengers, and most will do their utmost to assist you.

In the rare event that you find your cabin simply won't do—it's what you booked, all right, but it's not what you expected—this is also the time to request a paid upgrade. Go to the reception desk or purser's office and ask if a better category stateroom is available and say you're willing to pay for an upgrade. If there's space, you might get a better cabin at a discounted rate.

Note that this is an exception, not a standard procedure. You shouldn't count on being upgraded, much less being upgraded at a discount rate. But it does happen from time to time because cruise lines strive to make their passengers happy.

When checking out your stateroom, be sure you understand how to work all the controls. For some reason, temperature controls are often mystifying. Sometimes they also seem unresponsive. Be patient; it may take awhile for a cold cabin to heat up or a hot cabin to cool down. Sometimes cabin temperatures are a little abnormal during embarkation. On the other hand, if it's frigid or boiling for hours on end, the system may need repairs; report it to your steward.

Test the temperature and volume control of the bathroom faucets so you don't scald yourself. Also, note that the toilet is probably a little different than those at home. On most modern ships, these are vacuum-operated and sometimes make an alarming whoosh sound when flushed. A sign will instruct you to close the lid before flushing and warn of the havoc that will be wreaked to the ship's plumbing system if you toss anything bulky, like a diaper, into the bowl.

Your cabin should also contain glasses, an ice bucket and, if you've booked a pricier category of cabin or cruise line, you may find a wet bar, mini-refrigerator, or even a stocked bar. Before cracking open the bottled water, realize it's probably not free. Look for a piece of paper indicating that this will be charged to your shipboard account. Water on cruise ships is safe to drink, but since many people today prefer bottled water, cabin stewards make it available, for a charge. Just because bottled water is there doesn't mean the tap water is unsafe.

Check to see that everything in the stateroom works properly. Are there enough hangers in the closet? Is the promised hair dryer found in the bathroom or tucked away in a drawer? If you like to sleep with an extra pillow or blanket, is one stowed in the closet? Are order forms for cabin breakfast available, or will your steward provide those each evening? What about laundry bags?

There should be a guide to ship's services and/or an information sheet or ship's newspaper. Many ships also provide a pocket map or deck plan. Take a look at the cabin television; often there's an information channel.

Are the lifejackets stowed in a closet, compartment, or under the bed? Are there enough for everyone in the cabin and are they in good repair?

A sign will give details on safety information and the number and location of your lifeboat. Be sure you know how to get to your lifeboat from your cabin, via the nearest staircase. In the event of a fire or emergency, elevators may be shut off.

If you're disabled and need assistance or if you are audio impaired and can't hear a fire alarm, be sure to inform your cabin steward and/or the purser's office so you'll be cared for in the event of an emergency. Also, if you're cruising with small children, you'll want to contact your steward about obtaining child-size life preservers.

Finding Your Way Around the Ship

Once you've had a good look around your cabin, take some time and explore the ship. Many contemporary liners are enormous, stretching the length of three football fields and towering a dozen decks high. Although it might seem overwhelming at first, in a day or two you'll feel quite at home on board.

Here are a few hints for getting around: Ships post deck plans at elevator banks and stairwells. It helps to orient yourself by establishing your deck name and number and its relation to such major ship "landmarks" as the reception desk, dining room, and pool deck, as well as to determine the direction of the front or bow of the ship and the back or stern. Other helpful markers are starboard, the right-hand side of the ship *as you face forward*, and port, the left-hand side.

Starboardside cabins are usually odd-numbered; portside cabins, even. The low numbers traditionally begin at the bow and increase as you head aft. On a small vessel, all the numbers in the 100 series may be located on the lowest—or highest—accommodation deck; all the 200 series are on the next—above or below—deck and so on. But big ships have more than 100 cabins per deck; therefore, Cabins 103 and 207 may well be on the same level.

To make things *sound* even more complicated, some ships number their cabins with the first letter of the deck name (U for **Upper**, M for **Mediterranean**) followed by a number.

About the only incontrovertible cabin numbering pattern is this: If you're wandering along a corridor where the cabins numbers are, for example, 214, then 212, then 210, it's a good bet you're moving forward on the port side of the ship.

Getting a little lost is part of the ship discovery game. Don't be afraid to ask crew members; they're there to help.

Dining Arrangements

If you didn't receive a confirmation with your travel documents or a card in your cabin notifying you of the name of your dining room (some ships have more than one) and table number, visit the maître d' to verify your dining arrangements. Also see the maître d' if you aren't happy with your seating or table assignment—usually he will do everything possible to satisfy your preference.

And keep in mind that you can always see him after your first meal or meals. Sometimes it takes a day or two to feel comfortable with your dining room companions. But if you really don't like them, your table location, or your waiters, don't suffer through the cruise. See the maître d' early on about a change that will make you happy.

Shipboard Credit Line

It's a good idea to establish your shipboard credit as soon as convenient after boarding (if you didn't do so when checking in) so that you can enjoy the freedom of signing for purchases.

Today's cruise ships function as "cashless societies." Every time you buy anything—from a bar drink to a shore excursion to a facial in the beauty salon—you'll be asked to present your ship's identification card and sign a receipt. (One possible exception is in the casino, where you'll probably need cash to buy chips.)

All charges are billed to your account at the purser's desk. Be sure to save your receipts for purchases made on board, and check them for accuracy as you go. Sometimes this can spare an end-of-cruise headache.

The night before the end of the cruise, a statement will be delivered to your cabin. You will need to settle this before leaving the ship. (See "Account Settlement" on page 62.)

For more information on what needs to be done to establish credit, see "Checking In" on page 46.

According to a recent study conducted for Cruise Lines International Association (CLIA):

- More than 74 million Americans 25 and older with annual incomes of $20,000 or more want to go on a cruise.

- The fastest growing segment of cruisers is the 25 to 35 age group.

- Most recent cruisers (84 percent) say they would take another cruise.

Setting Sail

The moment has arrived—the ship is preparing to sail! As the engines crank up, announcements are made for all visitors and officials to proceed ashore. Don't miss this magical moment. Go out on deck when the ship sails. You'll find everyone in a festive mood, and you'll want to be a part of the fun.

Perhaps you'll spot the captain and the pilot standing out on the bridge wing, walkie-talkies in hand, barking orders. Usually a band plays on deck, and sometimes cruise staff dole out streamers. Smiling waiters dole out drinks.

A few lines treat their guests to a complimentary toast of bon voyage Champagne. But more likely you'll have to sign for any tall, fancy tropical drinks in souvenir glasses, so don't be surprised when that smiling waiter hands you a bill to sign.

Lean on the rails to see the gangways being pulled and the mooring lines being cast off. As the ship gradually, almost imperceptibly, slips away from the pier, note the looks of wonder and envy on the faces of family, friends, and strangers ashore.

The ship gracefully maneuvers sideways from the pier. The crowd on shore waves frantically and shouts "Bon voyage!" Finally, the vessel picks up steam and heads out toward open sea.

Fire/Lifeboat Drill

International maritime law requires cruise passengers to participate in a fire and lifeboat drill within 24 hours of embarking on an international voyage. Cruise ships take this matter seriously, and passengers should, too. The drill's purpose is to ensure the safety of everyone on board in the event of an emergency. Attendance is mandatory.

Procedures vary from line to line. Some companies hold it while still in port, shortly before the ship sets sail. Others conduct the drill just after the ship departs. Some have it after breakfast the next morning. You'll be informed of the drill by announcements over the ship's public address system, notices in the cabin, and notes in the daily program.

Some minutes before the drill, the captain or another ship's officer will let passengers know that the ship's emergency signal will be sounded and that everyone should get their lifejackets from their cabins, put them on, and proceed to the muster station or lifeboat indicated on a notice posted in each cabin (usually on the door). Signs in the corridors indicate the location of the muster stations and the lifeboats, and crew will be posted to direct passengers.

At the drill, which normally lasts about a half-hour, crew members will explain emergency procedures, including the proper way to wear a lifejacket, what to do if you smell smoke or spot a fire, how to behave, and where to go in the event of an emergency. They will explain the location and operation of the vessel's lifeboats, and a boat or two may even be lowered so passengers can look inside.

Once the drill is complete, you'll return the lifejackets to their cabins for storage.

Making the Most of Your Cruise

It's important to know that the cruise experience belongs to *you*. There may be a hundred activities offered every day, but you don't have to participate unless you choose to. That's why "making the most" doesn't necessarily mean "doing the most."

For some people, the pleasure of cruising lies not in the whirlwind of parties, games, and activities, but in

MICHAEL STORRINGS

kicking back and really relaxing. It means a deck chair in a restful corner, the deck steward at your beck and call, massages in the spa, room service, and hanging the "Do Not Disturb" sign on the cabin door.

Alternatively, if you're seeking a more active schedule, or even gearing up to try everything at least once—from playing in a bridge tournament to touring the navigational bridge—you can be sure your participation will be welcomed by the cruise staff and your fellow passengers.

Whatever your style, this section provides some hints for enjoying your cruise to the fullest.

The Daily Program

How do you keep track of what's happening on board? Every cruise ship publishes a daily program of activities. Here you'll find a schedule of events offered from before breakfast until long after the midnight buffet.

The daily program is normally distributed to cabins the night before so that passengers have the opportunity to plan ahead. Be sure to read it thoroughly so you don't miss anything of interest. Although the cruise director may announce major events over the ship's public address system, the daily program is the most comprehensive source of all the ship's activities.

In addition, the daily program may list such items as ship arrival and sailing times, the name and location of the pier, meal and bar hours, tour departure times, plus information about tour sale deadlines, phoning and faxing ship-to-shore, customs regulations, and bios of the captain, other crew members, and entertainers. You may also find such information provided in a reference folder in your cabin.

Many passengers tuck the daily program in their pocket, purse, or beach bag for handy reference. Some even take a copy ashore to remind themselves when the ship sails and the schedule of mealtimes in port.

Shipboard Activities

The cruise staff plans programs designed to appeal to the majority of passengers on board. Of course, that can vary widely depending on the type of ship, itinerary, and duration of the voyage.

Big ships sailing in such sun-and-fun destinations as the Caribbean might emphasize pool games, sports, and contests, while an expedition ship sailing to Antarctica is likely to focus on educational films and lectures.

Don't be afraid to participate. Contests, tournaments, and sports aboard ship are meant to be fun rather than competitive. Classes and lectures are a great way to investigate new interests and make friends.

Whether it's sports, wine, bridge, art, dancing, or some other interest, a cruise is sure to offer plenty of options in a relaxed, friendly environment. Keep an eye on the daily program for subjects that attract you, but remain open to trying new things as well.

Cruise ships often mimic the type of amusements found at shoreside resorts. But to experience the special qualities of vacationing at sea, don't overlook activities that are unique to the ship. Galley and bridge tours, for example. Almost every ship schedules one or two passenger visits to these interesting and important areas.

A tour of the bridge usually includes a briefing by one of the deck officers or a member of the cruise staff. From the captain's perch in the front of the ship you'll have a wide, magnificent view of the sea. Even if the captain isn't there, you'll at least see the duty watch, composed of the officers who plot the course and steer the vessel. Don't be alarmed if it appears that nobody is actually steering the ship! Chances are, the helm is on autopilot.

MICHAEL STORRINGS

You'll also get a look at the navigational equipment, including the system that uses satellites to pinpoint the ship's location down to an incredibly minute margin of error. You'll see the radar, fire safety plan, and a panel indicating the network of watertight doors that can be opened and closed automatically from the bridge.

Some small ships allow passengers 24-hour access to the bridge; take advantage of this privilege if you're on one of these vessels. If not, keep an eye on the daily program for the scheduled bridge visits. Note: tours of the ship's engine room are not usually allowed for safety and insurance reasons.

The galley, however, is another behind-the-scenes place open to passengers on scheduled tours. Every ship is different, but some pull out all the stops when showing off their galley, treating visitors to demonstrations of ice carving or pastry decorating and sometimes even offering glasses of Champagne or small snacks.

The chef, food and beverage manager, or a member of the cruise staff guides passengers through the dining room and into the galley—of course only during one of the rare periods when meals are not being served. That means the atmosphere is much cooler and calmer than during the hustle, bustle, and heat of cooks preparing dishes for impatient waiters to whisk off to hungry diners.

But a galley visit is still fascinating. You'll be led around the various food preparation stations, through such areas as the hot galley where meats, fish, and other main dishes are prepared, to the cold galley where salads are chopped and assembled, to the bakery with its colossal ovens, to the pastry area where immense helpings of calories are being whipped into fancy cakes, cookies, and desserts.

You'll probably stroll through the dishwashing area, where huge, industrial-strength machines provide the elbow grease, and you might catch a glimpse of recently prepared foods on trays in cold storage areas that are really just big refrigerators. Keep an eye out for the chef's office, where s/he is busy orchestrating menus and ordering provisions—tasks that almost always are done by computer.

Dining

Even if you're meticulous about your figure, expect to spend a good deal of time eating during your cruise. That's because dining aboard ship becomes a social activity and very often even an event. If you're so inclined, one of the luxuries of cruising is sitting back, being served, eating well, and savoring conversations with dining companions. (Also see "Making Friends on Board" on page 58.)

Range of Meals

Most cruises offer about a dozen opportunities to feast and snack every day. Here's a typical roster:

- Early risers' coffee and rolls
- Breakfast buffet
- Dining room breakfast

MICHAEL STORRINGS

- Mid-morning bouillon or snacks
- Lunch buffet
- Dining room lunch
- Burgers, hot dogs, fries, and the like at the pool grill
- Slices at the pizzeria
- Afternoon tea with finger sandwiches and pastries
- Ice cream and cookies
- Cocktail hour, with hot and cold hors d'oeuvres
- Dinner in the dining room
- Dinner in an alternative restaurant
- Midnight buffet
- 24-hour room service

Of course, you don't have to eat. Plenty of people cruise nowadays without putting on extra pounds. Cruise lines have updated their menus to feature healthier, lighter options, and many ships routinely offer low-cal, low-fat, and vegetarian choices. For some ships, you'll need to send a written request for a special diet well ahead of your sailing date. Discuss any special dietary requirements with your travel agent when you making your booking. (Also see "Keeping Fit Afloat" on page 190.)

Hours

Dining hours are listed in the daily program; be sure to consult it every day because mealtimes vary. If you have chosen a ship with two seatings, it's polite to arrive at your table in good time. Most people like to wait until everyone has arrived before they order; it's disruptive to saunter in halfway through dinner. And if you know you won't be coming to the dining room for a particular meal, inform your waiter and table companions in advance.

On ships with single-seating dining, courtesy dictates being at the table no later than a half-hour after service begins. Should your restaurant feature open seating, in which passengers are not assigned a table but may dine where and with whom they please, don't be shy about joining a partially filled table (it's a great way to meet new friends), or if you prefer, start your own. The maître d' or headwaiter is available to guide you.

Captain's Table

Despite their reputation, captains' tables aren't always stuffy. It largely depends on the captain's personality, and many love to spin yarns. Even if you aren't guaranteed sparkling conversation, you are assured of sparkling wines, great food, and wonderful service. That should be the case at every table in the dining room, but captains somehow usually luck out, scoring the tastiest morsels, the choicest wines, and the best, most experienced waiters.

Wines and Cocktails

A wine list is available from your waiter or the sommelier and may also be posted outside the restaurant. Some people like to consult the list ahead of time, placing their wine order for dinner at lunchtime. This ensures that the bottle will be properly chilled, and, if uncorked immediately when you arrive, it will have ample time to breathe. But more often, passengers place their wine order when they order their meal.

Many ships now serve selected wines by the glass. Check the menu or ask the sommelier. If not, on some cruise lines, waiters will save the rest of your bottle for the next meal.

The sommelier will present a bill at the end of the meal, and like other shipboard purchases, it's added to your account. Many lines automatically add in a 15 percent tip; write in a different amount if you wish.

You might want to attend any wine tastings offered by the ship to learn more about the wines served in the dining room. These are usually fun but educational sessions where you can sample different vintages and jot down the names of ones you like.

Some passengers enjoy a cocktail or after-dinner drink in the dining room. That's usually served by a bar waiter, not the sommelier. If you want to order a drink, ask your waiter to summon the proper person. You'll pay by signing a receipt.

MICHAEL STORRINGS

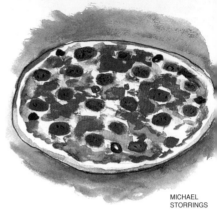

MICHAEL STORRINGS

Alternative Dining

Today more and more cruise ships offer alternatives to the main restaurant. Depending on the line, that could be a venue specializing in Japanese, Chinese, or Italian food. Or it could be a pizzeria or an international restaurant that's open 24 hours a day.

Some ships require advance reservations, and a per person service charge of, say, $5 is suggested. Others operate on a first-come, first-served basis, and the tip is up to you.

Alternative restaurants are the place to go when you want to sample a specialized cuisine, dine with friends, or share an intimate evening with somebody wonderful. Some alternative dining spots are elegant; others are casual. A few offer music or entertainment.

On some ships, notably **Crystal Cruises**' *Crystal Harmony* and *Crystal Symphony*, the alternative restaurants are in such big demand that passengers must make reservations upon embarking or at least very early in the cruise. See the maître d' for guidance.

Smoking

When making cruise reservations, your travel agent will ask if you prefer a smoking or nonsmoking table in the dining room. A few ships also offer smoke-free cabins.

More and more cruise lines are listening to the growing ranks of nonsmokers and forbid lighting up in the dining room. Cruise companies with no-smoking policies in the restaurant include **Carnival Cruise Lines, Clipper Cruise Line, Delta Queen Steamboat Co., Epirotiki Lines, Majesty Cruise Line**, and **World Explorer Cruises.** Other ships designate smoking areas in a separate wing or along one side of the dining room.

Some cruise lines also maintain a smoke-free main lounge or enforce a no-smoking policy during shows. More often, though, one side of the lounge is for smokers, and the other is smoke-free.

Pipes and cigars are absolutely forbidden in most dining rooms and lounges. However, some ships designate special rooms for cigar and pipe aficionados.

Shipboard Etiquette

Cruise lines request that passengers refrain from saving seats in the lounges and deck chairs around the pool. These are available purely on a first-come, first-served basis. It's impolite and annoying when people start placing jackets and purses on a row of seats in an attempt to save them for late-comers, and arguments have erupted over this issue. Better to plan ahead and be on time.

Similarly, unauthorized videotaping of shows is prohibited on most ships. That's because the big production shows are copyrighted. Also, most passengers consider it a distraction and annoyance to have their view blocked by a bank of video camera people.

Another area where unpleasantness sometimes erupts is about the use of sports facilities and equipment. The solution, in most cases: sign-up sheets for everything. That way everyone gets a turn, and play or use of equipment is limited to the suggested time posted.

Going Ashore

Preparing

To get the most from days in port, it's always a good idea to do some advance research. You may have brought books or maps from home. If not, try the ship's library; often there will be reference materials about the cruising area.

When weighing what to do in port, it's a good idea to attend the shore excursion lectures. The main objective of these talks is to sell the ship's tours but very often the shore excursions' manager provides a lot of useful information, such as local dining specialties, the currency exchange rate, how much it costs to take a taxi into town, any safety precautions, and other tips.

If you have trouble walking, pay close attention to the lecturer's comments about cobblestones, uneven pavement, climbing, or stairs. Sometimes tours are designated "easy walking," "moderate walking," or whatever, in the brochure. When in doubt, ask the shore excursions' office exactly what's involved.

Passengers using wheelchairs may find very limited options. In progressive countries like **Denmark, Norway,** and **Sweden,** it's probably possible to arrange a wheelchair van. Don't wait until you're on board ship to find out; discuss any special needs with your travel agent when you book the cruise.

Organized or Independent Tour?

The shore excursion booklet that you receive with your travel documents or at the start of the cruise informs you about the ship's organized tours. Some people balk at taking these, saying they don't want to move around in a large group of passengers or adhere to a regimented tour. Also, some people think the ship's tours are overpriced.

Keep in mind that not all programs involve busloads of passengers. If you choose a more offbeat option, such as a walking or biking tour, you're certain to be part of a small group. Passengers buying the ship tours can be reasonably certain of getting decent transportation and guides—and, sometimes, excellent ones. Also you can be sure that if you're on an organized ship excursion, the vessel will not sail without you. Finally, although the ship's tours may cost more than you might pay independently, they include insurance that covers you while you're on tour.

All these advantages don't mean that a ship tour is always the right choice. A private car and driver, which can usually be arranged through the ship's tour office, might be advised if you prefer to travel as a family or with friends, or if you have trouble walking or don't like to be rushed. It also may be the best option if you're pursuing a special interest, such as shopping for antiques or adding to your chess-set collection.

If you're on a tight budget, or you're the type who likes to strike out from the crowd, consider your own walking tour, taking public transportation, or bargaining with a taxi driver on the pier to show you around. Just be sure you know where you're going, that you'll be back to the ship in good time, and that you agree on the price, in advance.

Most passengers choose several organized tours during the cruise, especially if they're visiting very remote or unfamiliar places. A group tour of **Beijing**'s **Forbidden City** is probably more reassuring for travelers on their first trip to **China.**

When ariving at a large foreign city for the first time, many passengers choose an organized half-day tour in the morning, which gives them a good overview of the major sights and shopping opportunities. In the afternoon, they're free to explore on their own, going back to places of interest that they only glimpsed earlier in the day.

Taking a Shore Excursion

At the shore excursion lectures, most cruise lines try to give passengers objective information. On more upscale ships, you can be fairly confident you're getting solid recommendations. Unfortunately, some

MICHAEL STORRINGS

cruise lines persist in hiring shore excursion lecturers who have financial agreements with various shops ashore. They send business to the shop; they get a cut of the sales.

In their defense, such cruise lines say the "approved" shops have been screened for quality and service; if there's a problem with purchases, passengers can exchange items or get refunds with no hassles.

That may or may not be true, but this practice seems to have more to do with lining the pockets of the companies supplying the lecturers than promoting better business practices and protecting the passenger as consumer.

At any rate, at the shore excursion lecture you'll be briefed on tour options and given a deadline for signing up. Whenever possible, sign up early because some programs sell out.

If a much-desired tour is full, ask the shore excursion office about putting your name on a wait list. Very often you'll be told to simply show up on the pier or at the bus ready to roll; if somebody cancels, you're in.

Before booking, be sure you understand the tour cancellation policy. If you're a no-show due to sleeping late, a cold, or rainy weather in port, you may not be eligible for a refund. That's because the ship has had to reserve and pay for a certain number of buses, tour guides, and lunches in advance. If you back out too late, and the ship can't sell your spot, the cruise line eats the cost.

To buy a tour ticket, stop by the shore excursion office and sign up, or fill out a request form that's delivered to your cabin and drop it off at the shore excursion office. Your shipboard account is billed, and tickets are slipped under your cabin door. Always check that you've received tickets for the proper tours.

Before arriving at port, be sure you know your tour departure time. This may be listed on the ticket, in the daily program, or on your cabin television's information channel. Also, double-check the time and place of departure and listen for announcements upon arrival in port; sometimes departure times and places change.

You may also take along the shore excursion booklet or a copy of your itinerary so you'll know the schedule. Occasionally, too, some tour guides "forget" to stop at certain attractions, or refreshments are not served as promised. If something mysteriously drops from the itinerary, call the guide's attention to the printed schedule.

Active Tours

In recent years, more and more cruise lines have introduced active tours. Now passengers can go scuba diving or sportfishing in the **Caribbean,** mountain biking in **Alaska,** kayaking along the coast of **Maui** in the **Hawaiian Islands,** whitewater rafting in **Fiji,** and hot air ballooning in **Kenya.** When booking such programs through the ships, travelers can feel confident about the quality of the equipment they'll be using.

Children's Excursions

Holland America Line was the first company to design shore excursions exclusively for kids on its Alaska cruises. Canoe rides, jet boat rides, treasure hunts, crafts sessions, and hiking through a rain forest are among the programs designed for youngsters in two age groups: 6 to 12 years of age and teens. A youth coordinator or naturalist accompanies each group, leaving parents free to pursue their own on-shore interests.

All Ashore!

Upon arrival at ports of call, the ship must be cleared by local officials before passengers are free to debark. This usually takes anywhere from a half-hour after arrival to an hour or so. Don't crowd the gangway area while waiting, as this only delays officials trying to go back and forth. Relax in your cabin or a public room until you hear the announcement that the ship has been cleared.

If you've booked a shore excursion, be sure you know when and where to meet. If you aren't on a scheduled tour, try waiting about a half-hour until the initial crowd of passengers has gone ashore. This is a particularly good idea if the ship is at anchor and has a tender service.

Tenders usually operate continuously on arrival at port, allowing a maximum number of passengers to get ashore quickly. Then, after an hour or two, tenders either depart as filled or on a regular schedule, say every half-hour. This information is announced or listed in the daily program.

MICHAEL STORRINGS

Some very big ships, to alleviate crowding and ensure an orderly debarkation, issue tickets for the first few tenders. Normally these tickets are available, prior to arrival, at the reception desk or the shore excursions' office. Usually tickets are used only for the first hour or two of tender departures, until the stream of passengers dwindles.

Be sure to carry the ship's identification card when going ashore. You will need to present it when reboarding at the gangway or, in anchor ports, at the tender embarkation site. Some ships also require a photo ID, such as a driver's license.

MICHAEL STORRINGS

Many passengers carry a copy of the daily program or a postcard of the ship, noting the name and location of the terminal and the time of sailing. If you're in a country like China where you don't know the language, and few people speak English, you can ask a local tour guide, a taxi driver, or an official in the terminal building to write the name of the pier on the card in the local language. This can be a big help if you go sight-seeing independently, lose your way back to the ship, and can't find anyone who speaks English.

Before going ashore, be sure you know the time you must be back on board for departure. Ships normally ask that passengers return at least a half-hour before the scheduled sailing time. If the ship is at anchor and you have to ride a tender back to the vessel, note the time of the last tender departure from shore to ship (usually at least one hour before sailing) and make certain you arrive in good time.

Should you be delayed for any reason, don't expect the ship to wait. You will be left behind, possibly without your passport, and it will be your responsibility to make your way to the next port.

Dress comfortably and conservatively, wearing good walking shoes, and, if it's sunny, a hat. Some cruisers like to carry a small bag to hold camera, bottled water, suntan lotion, tissues, bug spray, and other notions. Don't forget extra film and batteries, a calculator if you need help figuring exchange rates, and a notepad to record your impressions, jot down directions, or note prices when comparison shopping.

Safety on Shore

Follow the advice of the shore excursion office and any tips published in the daily program. No matter where you are, it's best to exercise caution; don't wear flashy jewelry or sport too many valuables. That Rolex may be a fake but it could be awfully tempting to a street urchin in an impoverished country. Better safe than sorry.

Try to have a look at a city map and familiarize yourself with the port before you head off on your own. If you can't get a map ahead of time, you can take a taxi from the pier to the nearest tourist information office. Ask there about any areas that are unsafe and should be avoided.

When on your own in an unfamiliar place, stick to well-trafficked areas. Don't accept rides in unmarked "taxis" and, if you use public transportation or stroll through crowded markets, watch out for pickpockets. When walking around, don't dangle purses and cameras or leave a fat wallet bulging in your back pocket.

It's much safer to carry credit cards and money in an under-the-shirt neck pouch or a money belt. You can tuck a few bills into a pocket for easy access when making small purchases or taking taxis.

It's a good idea to familiarize yourself with the local currency and the exchange rate (consult a travel guidebook or the ship's daily program or ask at the tour or reception desk). Don't assume that US dollars, traveler's checks, and credit cards are accepted everywhere.

Before hopping into a taxi, ask the driver if there's a meter and if it works. In some very touristy areas, taxi drivers may carry a list of set fares to various destinations. If you have to negotiate on a price, be sure you agree in advance on the cost *per person* or *per carload*, in *local currency* or *US dollars*.

Respecting Other Cultures

When traveling abroad, try to keep an open mind about different cultures and customs. It's sometimes easy for cruise passengers, especially in well-trafficked areas like the Caribbean, to forget that they are guests in another country.

Go with a spirit of adventure and curiosity, but remember to respect the local people and their traditions. Try reading up on the destination before your cruise. The more you know, the richer your encounters are likely to be. It's also fun to learn a word or two in the local language: even saying "please" and "thank you" can bring smiles and open doors.

For tips on how to be a responsible traveler, contact the **Center for Responsible Tourism,** PO Box 827, San Anselmo, CA, 94901 (415/258.6594; fax 415/454.2493). The center publishes a "Code of Ethics for Tourists." The first three items are:

- Travel in a spirit of humility and with a genuine desire to meet and talk with local people.
- Be aware of the feelings of the local people; prevent what might be offensive behavior. Photography, particularly, must respect persons.
- Realize that other people may have concepts of time and thought patterns which are different from yours—not inferior, only different.

Exercise special courtesy when visiting churches, temples, and sacred places. In some countries, it's disrespectful to enter a temple wearing shorts (for both sexes), mini-skirts, or tank tops. Sometimes, places that attract large numbers of international tourists have modest dress, such as a long, wrap-around skirt or robe, for loan or rent. Accept it gracefully.

When traveling in ecologically fragile areas, think about how your actions might disturb wildlife or damage delicate flora. Go gently. Keep a distance from animals; when hiking in protected areas, stick to the trails. Never remove objects. Do not litter.

Shopping

One of the delights of cruising is shopping in ports. Many passengers enjoy buying gifts and souvenirs. In your pre-trip research, try to learn about the local specialties of the areas you'll visit. Aboard ship, the shore excursion staff should be able to advise you.

These days, shops in the most frequented ports seem to present a disappointingly similar range of duty-free, designer-name brand clothing and watches, cosmetics, and liquors. It might take a little effort to find more original, hand-crafted or locally manu-factured items that truly evoke the place. Markets, shops that lie on back streets, crafts cooperatives, and even local supermarkets can reward intrepid shoppers with interesting, distinctive goods.

In certain cultures, bargaining is expected, so don't be shy. But the Society for Responsible Tourism cautions that the poorest merchant will give up a profit rather than his or her personal dignity. Don't feel driven to knock pennies off the price, no matter what.

Here are a few guidelines, especially relevant when shopping in developing countries: never acquire sacred items, goods necessary for daily life, or items manufactured from endangered species. While some such products can be sold legally, that doesn't mean it's legal (or ethical) to bring them home. Importing fresh produce, meats, or agricultural products is forbidden.

Finally, when making major purchases abroad, be prudent. Carefully check the quality of every item and pay, if possible, with a credit card. Some stores offer "guarantees" that may evaporate when you're 3,000 miles away. It's also a wise idea to keep an eye on items as they are being wrapped or packaged; in rare cases, purchases have been switched for inferior goods.

Savvy travelers recommend personally carrying purchases to the ship rather than having the seller ship them to home. Sometimes, shipped goods arrive damaged or not at all, despite the best of intentions. If you must have an item shipped, be sure you're dealing with a reputable merchant (the ship's shore excursion staff may be able to advise you) and insist on paying by credit card. Also, be clear about how the item will be forwarded: By air? Freighter? Can you expect to receive your purchase in six days, six weeks, or six months? It's always a good idea to have valuables insured.

Eating and Drinking Ashore

This can be a delightful adventure; tasting the distinctive flavors of a region is a great way to get to know a place and eating in local restaurants provides a wonderful opportunity to go native. To avoid upset stomachs and serious troubles like cholera and hepatitis, educate yourself before you go about what's usually safe and what's not.

It's generally advisable to steer clear of food at market stalls in developing countries, where proper hygiene may not be possible. Tasting food that's been improperly cooked, unrefrigerated, or sitting out in the tropical sun can be risky. In some places, you should eat only vegetables and fruits that can be peeled. In developing countries, water and ice cubes are frequently the purveyors of bacteria. They should be avoided in favor of bottled or boiled drinks.

Raw seafood and shellfish can be especially dangerous; don't risk dishes like raw oysters that may have been harvested from water polluted by raw sewage.

Deck the Decks: Passengers may buy real Christmas trees for their cabins on Holland America's Christmastime cruises.

Delta Queen Steamboat Co.'s *American Queen* had a spicy send-off. Instead of the traditional Champagne, the largest steamboat ever built was christened with the world's largest bottle of Tabasco sauce.

The first ship to be fitted with stabilizers was P&O Cruises' *Chusan*, built in 1949.

Sailor Speak: A Guide to Shipboard Lingo

Ships have a language all their own. To sound like a savvy sailor (and to understand what the crew is talking about), bone up on the following nautical terms:

Aft Near the stern (rear) of the ship. Example: The dining room is aft on **Deck 6.**

Alleyway A passageway or corridor.

Amidships or **Midships** In or toward the middle of the ship or, more technically, the longitudinal center portion of the vessel. Example: The purser's office is located on **Deck 5**, midships.

Berths Beds. Most cabins are meant to accommodate two passengers and come with two lower berths ("lowers"). But staterooms known as "triples" or "quads" have additional bunks that pull out of the wall, Pullman-style, and are referred to as "uppers."

Bow The front or forward portion of the ship. (Landlubbers, that's the pointy end!)

Bridge The raised, transverse platform from which the vessel is steered. Usually the bridge is off-limits to passengers, except during bridge tours, which give seafarers the chance to learn about the navigation and safety equipment. A few cruise lines feature an "open bridge" policy, meaning passengers are free to visit the bridge any time they please.

Brig A place for temporary confinement of miscreants (a shipboard jail).

Cabin or **Stateroom** A room used as living quarters by passengers or crew. An outside cabin is one with an ocean or sea view through a porthole or window. An inside cabin has no window.

Deck Floor. Hotels have floors; ships have decks. Example: My cabin is on **Deck 8.**

Draft The measurement, in feet, from the waterline to the lowest point of the ship's keel (the longitudinal spine that extends the length of the bottom of the ship). Ships with shallow drafts can sail closer to shore with less danger of running aground.

Even keel Describes the ship when it is steady in a vertical position.

Forward Toward the bow (front) of the ship. Example: My cabin is located forward on **Deck 9.**

Funnel and **Stack** Two names for a ship's "chimney." "Stack" is short for "smokestack."

Galley The ship's kitchen.

Gangway The opening in the hull and the ramp by which passengers board and leave the vessel.

Hull The frame and body of the ship, exclusive of the masts, superstructure, and rigging.

Knot Unit of measure for ship speed, equal to one nautical mile per hour. Note: It's redundant to say "knots per hour."

Latitude Imaginary lines running parallel to the equator, numbered from 0° to 90°. Latitude and longitude (see below) are part of a grid system by which a ship's location can be pinpointed.

Leeward (rhymes with "steward") Away from the wind; in the direction opposite from the way the wind is blowing.

Longitude Imaginary lines running through both the North and South Poles and numbered from 0° to 180°. Longitude and latitude (see above) are part of a grid system by which a ship's location can be pinpointed.

Manifest A list or invoice of passengers, crew, and cargo. Before a ship is cleared to enter a port, and passengers can go ashore, local officials come on board to examine the manifest to make sure everything's on the up and up.

Moor To secure a ship to a fixed place using hawsers, cable, or anchor.

Nautical Mile Unit of measure for distance at sea. One nautical mile equals 6,080.2 feet.

Pitch The rise and fall of the ship's bow.

Port The left side of the ship when facing forward, toward the bow.

Roll The side-to-side sway of a ship.

Running Lights International law requires that these shipboard lights be turned on between sunset and sunrise while a vessel is in motion. Three running lights are necessary: green on the starboard side, red on the port side, and white at the top of the mast.

Screw The ship's propeller. "Twin screw" means two propellers.

Starboard The right side of the ship, when facing forward.

Stern The rear of the ship.

Superstructure The structural part of the ship above the main deck. Thanks to the use of lighter building materials, today's ships have larger (some would say boxier) superstructures than the sleek liners of yesteryear. A big superstructure can hold more and bigger public rooms and allows for dramatic design features like multistory atria.

Tender A small vessel, sometimes a lifeboat, that's used to transport passengers to and from shore when the ship anchors away from port. Depending on the size of the cruise ship and the time of day, "tender service" is offered continuously or at set intervals such as every half hour. Passengers who aim to hop the first tender from ship to shore will probably get stalled in a long line; those who miss the last tender from shore to ship will find themselves heading to the next port by airplane—at their own expense.

Windward Toward the wind; in the direction from which the wind blows.

Making Friends on Board

Sometimes passengers—especially singles—are apprehensive or shy about making friends on board. But there's no need to worry—a more sociable environment than a cruise ship was never invented. Everyone lives together, dines together, plays together. Everyone shares the adventure of being aboard ship, discovering new wonders at sea and new ports of call.

Meeting other passengers is easy. First, you'll get to know the folks who share your dining room table. Second, you might want to eat more meals at the buffet or alternative restaurant. While waiting in the buffet line or at the pizzeria, talk to other passengers. Take your tray to an occupied table and ask to join the people already seated.

There's no shortage of conversational topics—from the weather to last night's show, this afternoon's movie, or plans for the port visit tomorrow; all are ice-breakers.

If you're a single, contemplating entering the dining room alone can sometimes make you a little nervous. But a skilled maître d' or headwaiter is trained to look out for singles, making them feel at ease by greeting them or personally escorting them to the table. On a ship with an open-seating dining policy, the maître d' may guide singles to tables hosted by a ship's officer or a member of the cruise staff.

Don't be afraid to approach other passengers in the library, chat with people in the neighboring deck chairs, in the pool, in the gym. Join an aerobics class and invite new friends to the juice bar afterwards. Sign up for a sports tournament where you'll be paired with a partner or placed on a team.

Be sure to attend the singles' events on board. These are not intended to be matchmaking affairs but are a fun way for guests traveling alone to meet other singles. On some ships, there's one singles' cocktail party at the beginning of the cruise; other ships offer more singles' get-togethers.

Don't be shy about stopping at a bar or lounge on your own for a drink. Join the crowd at the piano bar or hop on a barstool and chat with the bartender. Entering a bar on a ship unaccompanied is perfectly acceptable and a natural way to socialize with other passengers.

Host your own informal cocktail party if you want to firm up some friendships. You can reserve a table in a lounge or see the ship's bar manager to arrange a private room or service in your cabin. Hot or cold snacks can be ordered as well. Invite friends you meet on tour, in the dining room, wherever. And don't be surprised when they return the invitation, in time-honored ship tradition, by hosting their own get-together.

As you move around the vessel, greet the officers, the staff, and the crew. It's the social staff's job to get to know you and, if you're a woman traveling alone, expect the gentlemen hosts to seek you out for dancing, cocktails, and socializing (for more about these folks, see "Perfect Gentlemen" on page 121). Don't feel embarrassed by the attention; you're entitled to enjoy as active a social life as everyone else on board.

Most hosts are retired gentlemen of means who normally are not compensated for their duties. They travel free, in exchange for dancing with the single ladies at classes and in lounges during the evening and, sometimes, escorting shore excursions or assisting with other activities.

Hosts are carefully screened. They aren't hired to be Romeos; in fact, they have strict orders not to get involved with passengers. They must be gentlemen at all times, as well as talented dancers and good conversationalists.

Passengers also are invited to hobnob with staff members such as the cruise director and hostess, as well as with the ship's officers. It's perfectly fine to join an officer, the cruise director, host, or hostess at a show, for a dance, or a drink in any of the ship's public areas.

MICHAEL STORRINGS

Teens and Children

How can the younger set make friends on board? A ship that's kid-friendly will have a youth counselor, as well as a full program of activities. If not, ask the cruise staff about improvising a few.

Most cruise ships tailor programs for different age groups, so the little ones can play with their contemporaries, while the older kids and teens hang out in separate, supervised groups. For details on family cruises, see "Child's Play" on page 248.

Shy children might stick with parents for the first couple days on board. Once they've gained confidence in their new surroundings, they may be comfortable participating in the kids' program.

Unfortunately, they could also become glued to their folks for the entire voyage. Avoid this problem by planning ahead. Long before the cruise, start telling children how much fun they're going to have with the other kids on the ship and how they'll get to play with lots of new toys and games in a special room for children only. In the same enthusiastic spirit, introduce them to the kiddie program on the first day of the cruise.

MICHAEL STORRINGS

Teens usually have no problem making friends and fitting in aboard ship. A cruise feels like freedom to them, and in fact, they're free to enjoy everything but the casino and some lounges (for example, ships with teen discos discourage teens from patronizing the adult disco). Also, underage drinking is strictly forbidden.

Besides joining organized activities, teens can strike up new friendships by hanging out at the pool, the burger bar, the pizzeria, or the ice cream parlor. Some ships offer video arcades that are magnets for teens. Another trick: check out a backgammon set or another game from the library, take it to a table on deck, and ask others if they'd like to play.

The same technique works with such sports equipment as Ping-Pong paddles, basketballs, and deck tennis racquets. Check them out from the cruise staff or sports director, go to the sports deck, and challenge other kids to a game.

With the Crew

Socializing with waiters, cabin stewards, and bar staff is not encouraged because they are banned from the ship's public areas when they're off duty and out of uniform. Crew members are not allowed to join passengers for a drink at a bar or in their cabins.

If you're invited to a crew party, show your respect for the staff's privacy by not going. You may think you're welcome because one person says so, but few crew members are pleased when a passenger crashes a crew party. And those staff who take passengers to "crew only" areas risk a reprimand, even dismissal.

Enjoying Life at Sea

With cruise ships growing bigger and more like floating resorts, it's almost possible to overlook your larger surroundings. On a megaship, you may seldom feel it or smell it, but the ocean is all around. Revel in its beauty and changeability.

Imagine yourself as not just a passenger but a sailor. Plot the voyage; most ships post a chart in the reception area showing the course and distance traveled. Often the captain delivers a noontime update from the bridge, reporting the course, bearing, speed, ocean and air temperatures, and the weather forecast. On cruises offering great scenic variety, the captain may give regular updates on points of interest.

Sip early riser's coffee on deck as the sun appears. Go for a pre-breakfast swim. Walk the promenade at all hours of the day.

The first ship to offer private bathrooms in cabins was Cunard's Campania, built in 1893.

Actually heard during a Pacific crossing: "Where can I get today's *New York Times*?"

MICHAEL STORRINGS

Study the ocean from every angle. Stand all the way forward and let the wind blow through your hair. Lean over the rail to watch the waves break against the bow. Hear the splashing, rushing sound of the water kissing the hull and falling away. From the stern, gaze at the ship's churning wake. Are seagulls gliding on the air currents? What shapes do the clouds resemble?

Look for flying fish and schools of dolphins. Scan the horizon for ships.

At sunset, take in the constantly changing colors of the sea and sky. Before turning in, climb to an upper deck, away from the lights, to marvel at the brilliance of the stars. If it's a moonlit night, notice how the moon's reflection in the water is so bright you feel you could walk on it.

Is something glittering like diamonds in the black ocean? That's phosphorescent algae.

Go on deck as your ship glides into port. Observe the rituals of arrival: a motorboat brings the pilot alongside, he jumps aboard through a hatch and heads to the bridge to assist the captain. Notice how skillfully the big ship swings into the harbor and how delicately it inches up to the dock. See the sailors toss lines to the longshoremen who tie up the ship.

Don't miss sail-away. The engines start to purr, the lines are cast, the ship slips out into the channel, building up speed until it meets the wide ocean and the port melts into the distance.

Many passengers say that being attuned to the ship and the ocean is an enriching experience. Some report that their most memorable hours were spent hugging the rails, gazing at sunsets, and admiring ocean.

Troubleshooting

Cruising is the most people-pleasing vacation around, if the findings of several travel-industry surveys are to be believed. But what happens in the rare event that you have a problem aboard ship?

For example, your neighbors bang their doors and drawers at all hours of the night, or your cabin vibrates so much that your teeth chatter. The waiter is showering your teenage daughter with unwelcome attention or dining room service is unbearably slow. Yesterday's tour was a disaster: the guide didn't speak English, and the bus broke down.

Any of the above problems, and others like them, can be resolved by the ship's personnel. It's best to clear things up immediately so that you can enjoy the rest of your trip. (See "Who's Who on Board" on page 253, which outlines the responsibilities of various officers and staff.) If you're unsure who's in charge of what, inquire at the reception desk.

If the problem concerns your cabin, first talk with your cabin steward or the housekeeper. If it's an issue these people can't correct, as with unbearably noisy neighbors or excessive vibration, go to the reception desk and make an appointment with the chief purser. Scheduling a meeting allows the officer to make time to give your discussion his or her full attention. It also impresses upon the officer that the matter is one of gravity for you.

At the meeting, explain that you're enjoying your cruise and hope to give the line future business, but the noisy cabin issue is souring your experience. The purser, at his or her discretion, might offer to speak to your noisy neighbors or, in the case of the vibration problem, to move you to a different cabin.

Unfortunately, there aren't always empty cabins available because some ships routinely sail at 100 percent occupancy. If that's the case, ask the purser how you can cope for the rest of the cruise. You could learn, for example, that your cabin vibrates only when the ship's engines are revving up to leave port. In other words, the problem is only intermittent, and you can probably learn to live with it.

Should you encounter indifference on the part of the chief purser, call the reception desk to make an appointment with the hotel manager. He or she is the highest ranking officer in the hotel department, overseeing all issues pertaining to accommodations and service. If this person can't solve your problem, no one can.

In situations involving the dining room, take your concern to the headwaiter or maître d'. It's probably a good idea to schedule an appointment outside of service hours, when you have their full attention.

Calmly explain the situation. In the case of your daughter, the headwaiter or maître d' should offer to take the lovestruck waiter aside with instructions to be more professional—or the supervisor could offer to move you or reassign the waiter.

When the complaint is about slow service, the headwaiter might offer to assist the waiter during meal service to speed things up, or he could offer to move you to a new table. Perhaps it's not the waiter's fault; the problem could lie in the galley, or maybe the waiter has been assigned too many diners to care for properly. The supervisor may ask for a day to correct the problem or may offer to move you immediately to a different table.

Once again, should you encounter indifference, call the reception desk and make an appointment to see the hotel manager. Meanwhile, you may opt for room service or try the alternative dining area.

If you have had a disappointing shore excursion, don't buttonhole the shore excursion staff in the next port while they're on the pier, supervising the loading of 20 buses, and also don't wait until the cruise is over. Make haste to the tour director's office and calmly explain what happened or call the office and ask for an appointment at a convenient time. Chances are the tour director already knows of an incident like a flat tire and, if the breakdown left you stranded for hours, miles from anywhere, your shipboard account may already have been credited.

Unfortunately a guide's poor command of English is probably not grounds for a refund. But discuss your discontent with the tour director and most likely you'll come to a satisfactory conclusion. You might try using the additional leverage of mentioning that you have bought or plan to buy a number of other tours.

If you can't reach a happy conclusion with the tour director after paying for an excursion that proved essentially worthless, make an appointment with the chief purser or the hotel manager.

Most cruise-ship personnel are hard-working and eager to please. If approached in a calm, reasonable manner, they will do their utmost to make you happy. On a ship, observing the chain of command is important. But it's always best to start with the super-visor closest to the situation, then work your way up.

If, after trying the above suggestions, you don't get any satisfaction, be sure to make note of the problem on your end-of-cruise comment card. These cards are forwarded to the cruise-line headquarters ashore where the staff takes them seriously.

Also, inform your travel agent of any unresolved problem when you return home. Provide detailed information about what happened and when and to whom you spoke. Also write a letter outlining the circumstances that your agent can forward to the cruise line's customer service department.

Your action calls the cruise line's attention to a problem it needs to fix for the benefit of future passengers.

All Good Things Must Come to an End

As the cruise draws to a close, besides thinking about packing and how much to tip the crew, passengers must go through several formalities that are detailed in a debarkation talk, although some ships provide a summary of debarkation information in the daily program, in a notice delivered to your cabin, and/or on your stateroom television. If you have any questions, ask the reception desk.

Tipping

Formerly a discretionary matter based on the quality of service, tipping is now expected on most ships, although cruise lines handle the practice in a variety of ways. Some include gratuities in the fare; **Seabourn** goes so far as to say "tips are neither solicited nor accepted"; **Holland America Line** and **Windstar Cruises** use the slogan "tipping not required"; and Greek companies such as **Royal Olympic Cruises** traditionally pool tips, distributing them to all service personnel on board.

Tipping may cause some anxiety for the first-time cruiser, but rest assured that the cruise ship will do its utmost to inform you in a range of subtle—and sometimes not so subtle—ways about the "appropriate" amounts. This information is often provided in the cruise brochure, included in your travel documents, noted in the shipboard newspaper, distributed to your cabin in the form of a flier, and passed along by the cruise director at the end-of-cruise debarkation briefing.

Tips should be given in US currency (cash), although on a few lines you can add the tip to your credit card and give each person a gratuity card.

Here's a general guide:

Most cruise lines suggest approximately $3 per person, per day, for the cabin steward; $3 per person, per day, for the dining room waiter; and $1.50 per person, per day, for the assistant waiter or busperson.

You might also want to tip other people—maître d' or headwaiter and the concierge—who have performed a special service. The amount is at your discretion, based on the service rendered. For example, if a headwaiter prepares a special dish for your table, $5 might be an appropriate thank you. If a concierge arranges private cars and front-row theater tickets in every port, a larger amount is certainly warranted.

More and more ships seem to be encouraging passengers to tip the maître d' and headwaiter as a matter of course. The **Celebrity Cruises** brochure, for example, suggests giving a one-time tip of $5 per person for cruises of 8 nights or fewer and $7.50 per person for 11-night sailings. **Celebrity** even suggests that the chief housekeeper be tipped: $3.50 per person for cruises of 8 nights or fewer and $5 per person for 11-night voyages.

Nearly all ships add a 15-percent service charge to bar bills and to wine bills in the dining room. For other personnel, such as beauticians and massage therapists, tips may be added to the bill at your discretion.

Handing out tips is normally done on the last night of the cruise. Cruise lines often provide envelopes in your stateroom for this purpose; if not, ask for them at the reception desk. On very long cruises—those lasting more than a couple of weeks—passengers normally tip every week or, at least, halfway through the voyage.

Debarkation Talk

This will be announced in your daily program and on the ship's public address system. At least one family member is urged to attend this important talk, which normally lasts about a half-hour.

The cruise director or another member of the ship's staff will explain procedures for leaving the ship, including how to settle shipboard accounts, where to obtain luggage tags, customs and immigration formalities, the order of debarkation, transfers to the airport or hotels, and other matters.

First-time cruisers are often baffled by the seemingly complex procedures that come with the end of the voyage. The debarkation talk should make things clear and answer any of your questions.

Account Settlement

Settling your shipboard charges is, nowadays, mostly a painless process, provided you left a signed credit-card imprint with the purser or reception desk sometime during the cruise.

If you did, a statement listing all your charges will be delivered to your cabin sometime during the late night or early morning before debarkation. Look it over. If everything tallies, you don't need to do a

thing. The company already has your credit card slip. Just keep your statement to check your next credit card bill.

If, however, you find an error, go to the purser or the reception desk (wherever final account settlement is being handled). Take along the receipts you've accumulated during the cruise and show them to the staff. If you're right, they'll adjust your account and that's that.

Should you have a difference of opinion that you can't seem to resolve, ask to see the purser or, only as a final resort, the hotel manager. It's best to straighten any account problem while still on board, but if you can't seem to get satisfaction, you still have three options: call your travel agent on your return home, write to the cruise line, or contact your credit card company.

Passengers who opt to settle their accounts with cash, traveler's checks, or—if allowed—personal checks, may have received either a statement under their cabin door or a note asking them to go to the purser's desk to get their statement and settle their account. Depending on the size of the ship, the number of passengers paying with cash or checks, and the efficiency of the purser's desk, this can be quick and easy or time-consuming and maddening. For those who detest waiting in lines, the credit-card route is the way to go.

At press time, a few new ships were planning to introduce account settlement via interactive in-cabin television. So far, passengers can only check their account balance whenever they wish, via their TV screen.

Passenger Questionnaires/ Comment Cards

Most cruise lines seek passenger comments and suggestions through comment cards that are handed out at the end of the cruise. Usually your steward leaves a card in your cabin for you to complete.

You'll be asked about a variety of areas, including dining, entertainment, service, the itinerary, and the comfort and cleanliness of your cabin.

MICHAEL STORRINGS

Cruise executives take comment cards very seriously. They take action on poor ratings for particular ports, tours, entertainment acts, or personnel. By the same token, staff or crew singled out for praise are rewarded with a pat on the back from their supervisors or, sometimes, a promotion, bonus, or award.

Drop your completed comment card in the box at the reception area or mail it to the cruise line in the envelope provided. Some companies, as an incentive for passengers to fill out the cards, hold a drawing. If your card is selected, you win a prize.

Customs/Immigration Forms

Depending on the country where you're debarking and your citizenship, you may have to complete customs and immigration forms. The debarkation talk covers this matter, and the reception desk can help if you have any questions. Be sure these forms are filled out and signed before debarkation. Keep them handy for inspectors.

On some cruise ships, passengers are asked to surrender their passports to the purser for the duration of the cruise. The reason for this is so that documents can be prepared for officials in the various ports.

You will be informed when and where to claim your passport before leaving the ship. Sometimes you don't get this document until after seeing immigration inspectors on board ship the day of debarkation.

Procedures vary from ship to ship and country to country.

Packing Up

It's helpful to place gifts and purchases together in one bag. That will ease customs inspection when you leave the ship. Also, keep receipts together and handy. In addition, be sure not to pack valuables, breakables, medications, and travel documents in your luggage. Keep these items with you in your carry-on luggage.

Upon arrival in port, air/sea passengers who have early flights go straight to the airport—oftren on the same bus as their bags. Those with later flights can turn their luggage over to cruise-line personnel who transfer it to the airport later in the day. Passengers are then free to shop or sightsee without worrying about their luggage and are transported to the airport in time for their flight. It's a good idea keep a carry-on bag for items needed during the day—bathing suit, comfortable walking shoes—and a change of clothes or a sweater or jacket for the plane. In addition, some lines arrange a day room at a hotel for those who have very late flights, so they can freshen up before flying out.

Baggage

Place your tagged bags outside your cabin door before retiring. Check the ship's newspaper for the deadline to have luggage out. If you plan to make the most of your last night on board and close down the

MICHAEL STORRINGS

bar or disco, consider packing and placing your bags outside your door before heading off to dinner.

Don't forget to leave aside pajamas, toiletries, a change of clothes for the next day, valuables, breakables, medication, and documents including passport and air tickets.

Debarkation

It's the morning of debarkation. Suddenly a vacation that seemed so leisurely has cranked into overdrive. This is not a day to sleep late. Be aware that most ships do not offer room service or cabin breakfast on this last morning because the ship's staff is extremely busy. (After you debark, the ship must be cleaned, provisioned, and otherwise readied—in the space of just a few short hours—for the new group of passengers boarding for their cruise.)

Instead, buffet and dining room breakfast are served at an earlier hour than usual. Times will be listed in the ship's program.

There's a general hustle and bustle on this morning as passengers prepare to leave. But before anyone can get off the ship, all accounts must be settled. All baggage must be off-loaded. And port officials must clear the vessel, after examining the passenger list and, depending on the country, checking passports.

US citizens debarking at US ports normally do not have to present themselves to immigration officials. But Americans getting off at a foreign port may have to see the immigration officials of that country, who usually come aboard and station themselves in a lounge. Ship's personnel will advise you of the procedures.

If you are a non-US citizen debarking at a US port, you probably will have to go to through a US immigration inspection. Listen for announcements and go promptly when called.

It normally takes two or three hours to complete these formalities. Meanwhile, passengers are asked to vacate cabins at their earliest convenience so stewards can clean and prepare them for the next group of guests. Before leaving your stateroom, have a last look around for any stray items you might have forgotten to pack, and make sure you've emptied the safe and left it unlocked. Leave your cabin keys or key card on the desk.

Take your carry-on items and relax on deck or in a public room, along with a book or crossword puzzle to while away the time. Some ships show films or offer entertainment in the main lounge.

The ship's staff will inform passengers when the vessel has been cleared and the first group (usually identified by baggage-tag color) can proceed ashore. As soon as they're on their way, the next group is called, until everyone has left. To ensure an orderly debarkation, don't head to the gangway until your group has been called. Passengers who crowd the gangway area only delay the process. Generally, those on the earliest flights leave the ship first, the next-earliest flights leave second, and so forth.

Claim your luggage, which has been grouped according to tag color or some other system, in the terminal building. Porters are usually on hand to assist.

After collecting your bags, you'll pass through customs. Hand the inspector your completed customs declaration. If you're within the duty-free limit, you'll probably be waved through. Otherwise, you may have to show your purchases.

If you've exceeded your duty-free limit, you'll most likely have to pay duty. Depending on the country, that's assessed using a standard scale or at the discretion of the customs inspector. Some countries accept credit cards; most demand cash. Be sure you get a receipt for what you pay.

Once you've cleared customs, proceed out of the terminal where you'll usually find a taxi stand and buses waiting to take you to the airport. If you bought the cruise line's air/sea program, your bags will be loaded onto a bus and taken to the airport. Some cruise lines now provide onboard or at-port airline check-in, so you may already have your flight boarding passes. You'll be directed to the proper bus. When it's filled, you'll head to the airport.

Usually the cruise line handles luggage check-in here, and you won't see your bags again until you arrive at your home airport. If you've already received a boarding pass on the ship or at the pier, simply proceed to your gate. Otherwise, you'll need to check in with the airline. The ship's air/sea personnel will be on hand to guide you.

As you stepped off the gangway, you probably felt a tinge of sadness at leaving your floating home. That's only natural, but now is the time to start planning your next voyage.

May each one be as enjoyable as the first.

MICHAEL STORRINGS

Cruise Lines and Cruise Ships

In many ways, planning a cruise is a snap compared to planning other kinds of vacations. Once you've settled on a ship, most of the work is done—your accommodations, meals, activities, and entertainment are pretty much taken care of. A cruise is not only a means of transporting you to a sunny isle, an exotic port, or a legendary city—the ship is a hotel, restaurant, nightclub, theater, resort, casino, fitness center, spa, bar, disco, shopping center, and more, all rolled into one seagoing package. Which makes selecting the right ship all the more important.

Many factors can affect passengers' overall shipboard experience. Some are obvious (size, type of ship, itinerary, type of facilities), and others are more subtle (the age and interests of other passengers, the level of personal service, the emphasis placed on certain activities). In addition, each ship has its own distinct personality and style, born of myriad elements, from the decor of the public rooms to the officers' nationalities. The following section presents all the information you need to select that special ship—the one that will be the most enjoyable for you.

This section is divided into two chapters. In the first, "Top Ships," we single out our picks of the best cruise ships currently sailing. Among them are vessels that outshine all the rest, each in its own way (and that we've awarded six stars), as well as ships that are the best choices in their respective size and price categories (these we've awarded five stars). The second chapter, "A Cruise Ship Directory," is a comprehensive list of the world's most popular cruise ships, all of which promise an enjoyable cruise and a good value for your vacation dollar. Rated from one to four stars, the ships in this section represent all size, price, and style categories.

In both chapters, the ships are listed alphabetically by cruise line; identical "sister ships" are covered in a single entry. (All ships are also listed individually by name in the index.) Since the size and type of ship are perhaps the two most important factors to consider when planning a cruise, you can see these two factors at a glance. The color of each entry denotes the ship's size, and a symbol represents the type of vessel (see "How to Read this Guide," on the inside front cover).

All entries include facts such as the year the ship was built and when it was last refurbished, the number of passengers it holds, its size in gross registered tons (grt), the number and types of cabins, the ship's country of registration, the nationalities of the officers and crew, the ship's smoking and tipping policies, its usual itinerary, and the cruise line's telephone number. (Since all bookings are made through travel agents, the telephone numbers are provided solely for the purpose of obtaining brochures and information.) Each entry also has a "snapshot" of the ship, which points out its most important characteristics, as well as a description of the kind of travelers who favor it, and first-hand reports on the ambience and decor, cabins, sports and fitness facilities, activities, entertainment, food, and dining rooms. The result is a comprehensive portrait of each vessel.

Note: New ships due to be launched by the end of 1998 are listed under the appropriate cruise line with whatever details were available at the time of this writing. In addition, details on new ships from the cruise industry's newest company are provided in "Disney Cruises: Magic and Wonder at Sea" on page 109. Finally, keep in mind that the cruise industry is an extremely volatile one. New ships are being built at a rapid rate, and ships and entire cruise lines are changing hands with increasing frequency. This book includes the most up-to-date information available at press time.

Top Ships

Here they are—the best ships at sea. In this section we recognize (and recommend) our favorites, six- and five-star ships that are the finest vessels afloat, providing passengers the ultimate in cruise vacations.

The 11 ships that we've awarded six stars are the crème de la crème of cruising, extraordinary luxury vessels that are in a class by themselves. Lest the six-star ships prove too expensive for your dream cruise, our list of "Top Ships" also includes 15 five-star vessels that are tops in their respective size and price categories: megaships, "traditional" cruise liners, budget ships, and small sailing ships.

No matter which of these ships you choose, cruising doesn't get any better than this.

Celebrity Cruises

800/437.3111 or 800/327.9501

Century/Galaxy
$$$★★★★★

Built: 1995/1996

Passengers: 1,750/1,870

Size: 70,606 grt/77,317 grt

Cabins: 875/935

Outside: 569 (61 with verandas)/639 (220 with verandas)

Inside: 306

Suites: 52 (including 2 penthouse suites)/50 (including 2 penthouse suites)

Wheelchair Accessible: 8

Registry: Liberian

Officers/Crew: Greek

Tipping Policy: About $9 per passenger per day suggested

Smoking Policy: Prohibited in dining rooms and entertainment lounges; restricted to designated smoking sections in all other public areas

Snapshot You need to see these $320-million futuristic cyberships to believe them. They debuted as the second-largest cruise ships in the world (after the 77,000-ton *Sun Princess*), and immediately joined the upper echelon of megaships in the mid-price category. An excellent value, they offer innovative electronic systems, fine food, exemplary service, and all the comforts of floating five-star hotels.

(At press time, the *Mercury*, sister to the *Century* and *Galaxy*, was scheduled to be launched in late 1997.)

Itinerary The *Century* sails the eastern and western Caribbean on seven-day trips from Ft. Lauderdale. In winter, *Galaxy* plies the western Caribbean on seven-day cruises, departing from San Juan. In summer

she sails through the Panama Canal and on to Alaska, where she offers 7- and 10-day cruises out of Vancouver.

Typical Passengers Most are part of the **Celebrity** crowd—repeat passengers who like to sample all the ships of this stylish line. The mix of ages runs from 30 on up. The ships cater to families, but are nonetheless comfortable for couples and singles.

Ambience & Decor Nearly identical (the *Galaxy* is a little bigger, with more deck and interior space), these megaships are space-age splashy, with an interactive Sony communications and entertainment system in each stateroom. The system allows passengers to shop, watch movies, order room service, make spa appointments, play casino-style games, and more, all with a click of their television remote controls. Other high-tech features include a video bar and a two-deck theater with a 48-screen video wall, a revolving stage, lasers, an advanced sound and light system, and a hydraulic lift for the orchestra. A faux sky moves in time from dawn to dusk on the domed ceiling above each ship's spectacular **Grand Foyer.**

The ships have a sleek, modern decor that melds futuristic, high-tech elements (neon, video screens) with more traditional features such as cherry woodwork, etched glass, and expensive furnishings and artwork. The overamplified music might prove a little harsh for some ears, but modernists, Generation-Xers, and kids love these techno-liners.

Life on board is high-energy and active, and folks dress accordingly during the day. Casual elegance is the rule on informal evenings; on formal nights, men tend to wear dark suits (only a few don tuxedos) and women's outfits range from simple to smashing.

The service is usually superb. With one staff member for every two passengers, it should be.

Cabins The standard staterooms on each ship are well equipped and fairly commodious—each is about 172 square feet and offers a double bed, bathroom with shower, three closets and ample bureau space, a radio, mini-bar, safe, telephone, and a TV with remote control access to everything from the ship shops to the wine list.

Each ship also has several **Royal Suites** (8 on the *Century*, 10 on the *Galaxy*) measuring 637 square feet and featuring a living room, dining area, marble bath with whirlpool, and private veranda. **Sky Suites** are smaller versions of the same; there are 20 on the *Century*, 24 on the *Galaxy*. Each of the penthouse suites (two per ship) has 1,515 square feet of living space, leather furniture, cherry-wood floors, a stereo and video system, walk-in closets, a dining room with a well-stocked pantry and bar, a marble bath with whirlpool, a large private veranda, and a butler.

Sports & Fitness Now here's a real spa! The 9,340-square-foot **AquaSpa** offers exotic seaweed/seawater therapies designed specifically for **Celebrity** passengers, as well as other salubrious treatments in a serene, Japanese-inspired environment. The centerpiece of the spa is a hydro-pool for which passengers may buy an all-day "soaking pass." There are also steam and sauna baths. Spa packages may be purchased in advance (recommended) or on board.

Folks looking to work off all those extra calories will find more than enough weight and exercise machines to get their muscles burning and their hearts pounding. Super exercise classes led by experienced instructors are held regularly, and personal trainers are available.

Passengers can also get their exercise jogging on the track, swimming in one of the three pools (the **Oasis Pool** features a retractable glass roof), hitting balls in the golf simulator, or just walking around the 62,000 square feet of outside deck space.

Activities & Entertainment Just romping around these Goliath techno-craft can be fun. For those who prefer them, though, plenty of organized activities are available. One day's schedule might include shuffleboard, volleyball, and bridge tournaments; arts-and-crafts classes; presentations on bartending and jewelry; an art auction; a couples' massage lesson; golf competitions; wine tasting; movies; and more.

The Las Vegas–like, 7,460 square-foot **Fortunes Casino** provides passengers with lots of chances to try their luck, while the library and card rooms are comfortable venues for quieter pursuits. Shoppers will want to browse through the lavish boutiques of the **Boulevard** shopping gallery; those with advanced eye-hand coordination can play every video game known to modern technology in **Images**, a sports-and-video bar with a half-dozen big-screen TV sets and a whole wall lined with Sony video games. Cigar lovers can head to **Michael's Club** to puff on stogies hand-rolled by a resident cigar maker. Passengers can also watch pay-for-view movies in their cabins.

For kids, the **Fun Factory** has computer terminals set up with CD-ROM games and educational programs. The children's TV room, video library, ball court, and reading area also keep kids busy, along with a fully supervised program of activities.

At night lavish Broadway-style shows fill the stage in the sensational **Celebrity Theater,** a two-deck room with cantilevered balconies, unobstructed views, and one of the most technologically advanced sound systems on any cruise ship. The Art Deco **Crystal Room** nightclub, where cabaret performances are staged, is a more intimate spot.

Each ship offers about a dozen bar/lounges. A sun-lit vantage point by day, at night **The Hemisphere** observation lounge is both a futuristic disco and a planetarium, with telescopes conveniently placed around the room. On the *Galaxy*, the Casablanca-inspired **Savoy Night Club** creates a romantic setting for dancing, while its **Martini Bar** offers a menu of variations on the classic cocktail that would horrify Agent 007.

Cuisine Celebrity has been credited with raising the culinary consciousness of large cruise ships, and deservedly so. Chef Michel Roux (of London's three-Michelin-star **Le Gavroche**) created the menu of innovative French-American fare served fleetwide, and the food is about the best you'll find on any ship this size. Menu highlights include a rack of veal (almost unheard of on megaships), duck confit linguine, lamb curry, and salmon baked in the traditional Alaskan style with brown sugar, mustard, and garlic.

The ships' main dining rooms, the *Galaxy*'s **Orion Restaurant** and the *Century*'s **Grand Restaurant,** differ only in name and in a few embellishments (for example, the **Orion** features a bronze sculpture of the eponymous constellation, accented by more than 200 fiber-optic stars). Both rooms provide the perfect showcase for Roux's cuisine, with sweeping stairways, brass columns, extravagant chandeliers, wide picture windows, fresh flowers, and plush carpeting. Dinner is served in two seatings.

In addition to meals in the main dining room, four buffets are offered throughout the day in the **Islands Cafe,** and two grills by the pool serve up hot dogs and burgers along with one or two daily specials. Twice each cruise, a special "gourmet bites" spread is set up at midnight. This tasting buffet allows passengers to sample exotic and international foods—chimichangas, vegetable and fish tempura, pizza with wild mushrooms and fennel, and finger sandwiches, to a name a few—as well as yummy desserts. Another nice extra on each ship is the **Tastings** coffee bar; conveniently situated under the **Grand Foyer** dome near the boutiques, it's a favorite rest stop for shoppers. Room service is available around the clock, but only passengers in suites may order full meals; the menu is limited for all other cabins.

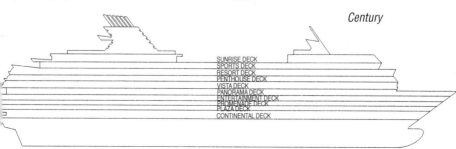

Century

SUNRISE DECK
SPORTS DECK
RESORT DECK
PENTHOUSE DECK
VISTA DECK
PANORAMA DECK
ENTERTAINMENT DECK
PROMENADE DECK
PLAZA DECK
CONTINENTAL DECK

Costa Cruise Lines

800/462.6782

CostaClassica/
CostaRomantica/
CostaVictoria

$$★★★★★

Built: 1992/1993/1996

Passengers: 1,300/1,356/1,950

Size: 54,000 grt/54,000 grt/76,000 grt

Cabins: 654/678/964

Outside: 438/462/573

Inside: 216/216/391

Suites: 10/34/20

Wheelchair Accessible: 6

Registry: Liberian

Officers/Crew: Italian/International

Tipping Policy: About $8 per passenger per day suggested

Smoking Policy: Restricted to designated smoking sections in dining rooms and lounges (the policy is not strictly enforced)

Snapshot These European-style cruise liners are not superluxurious, but they sure are fun and comfortable, with a continental ambience and great entertainment. The best of the big budget ships, they offer a first-rate cruise vacation for a reasonable price.

(The *CostaOlympia*, a larger twin of the *CostaVictoria*, is due to debut in 1998. Weighing in at 78,000 grt and carrying 2,100 passengers, she will take over **Costa**'s heavyweight title.)

Itinerary All three ships roam the Mediterranean in summer and the Caribbean in winter.

Typical Passengers Many passengers are **Costa** alumni—the line has a coterie of loyal fans who refuse to sail on any other type of ship. The group on board is likely to be international, and the age range varies with the seasons, with younger folks during the summer and older travelers the rest of the year.

Ambience & Decor The style and atmosphere are very European. The captains and officers and crew are Italian, the fare is continental/Italian, and European customs are observed (for example, the second dinner seating may be as late as 9PM). "Cruising Italian Style" is the **Costa** slogan, and it is their European air that make these ships particularly appealing.

The hallmarks of these ships are comfort, attractive decor, and a lively atmosphere. They are similar in ambience and appearance, although the *CostaVictoria*, the newest of the three, is considerably bigger. The interiors are decorated with a pleasing amount of marble, brass, tile, and wood, accented with art and sculpture. Among the nicest features are the spacious teak decks and the wonderful wicker chairs on the top deck—perfect perches for gazing at the sea.

These cruises are best for active types. Passengers tend to be vivacious and sociable, and although nobody is forced to take part in the ship's activities, everybody usually does get into the act .

There are usually two formal nights per week-long cruise, and passengers favor their fanciest duds (tuxedos for men, evening gowns for women) for these occasions. On informal evenings, no jackets are required for men, and people appear in anything from blue jeans to designer outfits. Daytime wear is very casual, but shorts are never worn in the dining room.

The service, from the conscientious cabin staffers to the able dining room servers, is excellent.

Cabins Standard cabins are plain and seem smaller than their 200 square feet, but they are nicely appointed. Each has twin beds that can convert to a double or queen-size, a TV, telephone, large porthole, and a smallish bathroom with shower, good storage space, a hair dryer, and basic toiletries (soap, shampoo, and moisturizer). On the *CostaVictoria*, each cabin is also equipped with a refrigerator and mini-bar.

Mini-suites and suites are plusher than the standard units, offering such extras as floor-to-ceiling windows, a sitting room with a sofa and desk, a queen-size bed, and a bathroom with a Jacuzzi, separate shower, and twin sink. All suites are attended by a steward and butler who—if they're anything like the *Romantica*'s Swedish-born Leena— go out of their way to meet passengers' needs.

Sports & Fitness A small gym provides Stairmasters and free weights, but no treadmills, and exercise classes are held in the disco daily. In addition, the spa/salon has a coed steam room, separate men's

Costa Classica

Cortina
Ravello
Capri
Portofino
Florence
Rome
Genoa
Amalfi
Pisa
Venice

and women's saunas, and rooms for facials, massages, and other pampering treatments. The two pools are surprisingly small for such large ships, but have lots of terry cloth–covered chaises for lounging. (The *CostaVictoria* also has an indoor pool.) An outdoor jogging track completes the fitness facilities.

Activities & Entertainment More fun seems to go on aboard these ships than than on just about any other cruise liner around. On a recent *Romantica* cruise, Nick Weir (the most beloved cruise director at sea, who may jump ships to the new *CostaVictoria*) kept passengers entertained day and night with his Monty Pythonesque humor and antics. The shows are also among the cruise industry's best, with much passenger participation and great performances by the *CostaRomantica* orchestra and singer/dancer Peppe, another **Costa** favorite. During the day, passengers may choose from a full schedule of organized activities, which might include cooking and dance classes, Ping-Pong and bridge tournaments, pool games, grandparents' "brag sessions," and more.

The highlight of every cruise is the toga party, held on the last night on board. Just about every passenger dons a toga and wreath (provided by the cruise line) and parades around the ship from dinnertime until show time—where a standing-room-only crowd enjoys one last evening with Nick Weir.

In keeping with the festive atmosphere, each ship boasts a total of eight bars and lounges. The **Piazza Navona** (on the *Classica*), the **Piazza Italia** (*Romantica),* and the **Concord Plaza** (*Victoria*) are the popular pre-dinner gathering spots. The ships' glassed-in **Observation Decks,** lookout points during the day, become lively discos at night. Another hot spot on each ship is the bar adjacent to the dining room, which tends to be quite noisy. In fact, the ships have a shortage of small, quiet bars, but this doesn't seem to bother most **Costa** passengers a bit.

Also on board are a small casino, a library, and a handful of shops selling everything from casual cruisewear to perfume and jewelry. **Costa** also offers a well-run children's program, although these really aren't child-oriented ships.

Cuisine Continental/Italian dishes are served with flair in the dining rooms, fairly ordinary-looking spots made extraordinary by strolling musicians, lovely table settings and superlative service.

Best menu offerings are the shipboard-made pastas and other Italian dishes, particularly the osso buco. Headwaiters prepare the Caesar salad and other special dishes at the tables.

At last sampling the daily luncheon buffets proved unappealing, but the breakfast buffet and freshly prepared omelettes served on deck in the morning were worth getting up for, and the coffee was excellent. For night owls, snacks are served at 11:30PM, but don't expect anything lavish.

Full room service is available in suites only; passengers in other cabins may have beverages delivered, but there is a charge. Complimentary continental breakfast is provided daily in all cabins, but it's minimal. Those who enjoy a hearty morning meal are better off going to the dining room or deck buffet.

Cruise Ship Superlatives

Are you cruising with the kids or seeking a romantic getaway for two? Eager to plunge into the sea or to sink into a luxurious herbal bath? The following lists will help you find ships that excel in areas important to you.

Best Fitness Programs and Facilities

Nautica Spas, Carnival Cruise Lines

Century and *Galaxy* spas, **Celebrity Cruises**

Spa and fitness program, **Crystal Cruises**

Golden Door at Sea program, *Sea Goddess I&II* and *Vistafjord,* **Cunard**

QEII spa, **Cunard**

Roman spas, **Norwegian Cruise Line**

Cruisercize program, **Princess Cruises**

Sun Princess and *Dawn Princess* spas, **Princess Cruises**

Stella Solaris spa, **Royal Olympic Cruises**

Best Children's Programs

Carnival Cruise Lines

Crystal Cruises

Disney Cruise Line

Princess Cruises

Best Water Sports

Princess Cruises

Sea Goddess I & II, **Cunard**

Seabourn Cruise Line

Silversea Cruises

Best Food

Celebrity Cruises

Crystal Cruises

Sea Goddess I & II, **Cunard**

Radisson Diamond and *Song of Flower,* **Radisson Seven Seas Cruise Line**

Seabourn Cruise Line

Silversea Cruises

Most Romantic

Silversea Cruises

SeaGoddess I & II, **Cunard**

Crystal Cruises

Best Entertainment

Carnival Cruise Lines megaships

Costa Cruise Lines

Crystal Cruises

Princess Cruises

Crystal Cruises

800/446.6620

**Crystal Harmony/
Crystal Symphony**

$$$$★★★★★★

Built: 1990/1995

Passengers: 960

Size: 49,400 grt/51,004 grt

Cabins: 480/480

Outside: 461 (260 with verandas)/480 (342 with verandas)

Inside: 19/0

Suites: 62/64 (all with verandas)

Wheelchair Accessible: 4/7

Registry: Bahamian

Officers/Crew: Norwegian & Japanese/International

Tipping Policy: $8 to $9 per passenger per day suggested; an additional tip is suggested for **Penthouse Deck** butlers

Smoking Policy: Prohibited in dining rooms and entertainment lounges; restricted to designated smoking sections in all other public areas

Snapshot Exceptional style and elegance, impeccable service, uncommon comfort, and outstanding food place these six-star ships in the upper echelon of cruise liners. For overall excellence, they are simply the best mid-size ships afloat.

Itinerary Both ships have worldwide itineraries, cruising in Africa, Alaska, Australia, the Caribbean, the Far East, Hawaii, the Mediterranean, Mexico, the Panama Canal, South America, and the South Pacific.

In addition, the *Symphony* offers a number of 10- to 16-day round-trip cruises from Ft. Lauderdale or San Juan to Acapulco between May and December, and makes an annual world cruise from Los Angeles. The world voyages feature a special **Computer University at Sea** program.

Typical Passengers Most of the folks on board are of middle age or older (with a few in their late twenties and thirties). Once they've sailed on either ship, many travelers stick steadfastly to **Crystal**; 70 percent of the line's clientele are repeat passengers.

Ambience & Decor Comfortable luxury combined with a warm, accommodating atmosphere—cruising just doesn't get much better than this, particularly on ships this large.

The ships are elegant from bow to stern. The attractive public rooms and lounges feature silk damask, marble floors, Murano glass, and cherry-wood furnishings. The lavish lobby has a grand "crystal" piano (it's made of clear lucite), bronze sculptures, cascading waterfalls, and Tivoli lights. Classical music fills the air, thanks to harpists and pianists.

These aren't stuffy ships, but passengers do tend to dress rather nicely. Tasteful designer casuals are the norm by day; women slip on exquisite evening outfits after dark, while men wear suits or jackets and ties. (Nearly all the men wear tuxedos on the formal evenings.)

The highly trained, 500-member staff take the company's "never say no to a passenger" policy seriously. As in the early days of transatlantic cruises, passengers are treated like royalty. Tips are well deserved on these two ships (although it would be more convenient if gratuities were included in the fare).

Cabins Staterooms and suites are exceptional, offering lovely blue or pink color schemes, attractive furnishings, Frette linens, lots of special amenities, and the ultimate in comfort. Only the accommodations on smaller, all-suite luxury liners compare.

Standard staterooms measure a quite comfortable 246 square feet (including veranda). Each has a separate sitting area, twin beds that convert to a double or queen-size, a TV and VCR, a telephone, makeup mirror, and hair dryer. There's a bit more storage space on the *Symphony*, but both ships have enough to keep wardrobes and belongings neatly stowed. The Italian marble bathrooms have tub-and-shower combinations and are stocked with toiletries and plush terry robes and slippers.

More than half of the staterooms and suites have private balconies overlooking the sea, offering passengers an ideal spot to enjoy a peaceful breakfast, sip cocktails or afternoon tea, or catch a glimpse of playful dolphins that often swim alongside the ships.

An entire deck is devoted to lavish penthouses and penthouse suites. Penthouse suites range from 360 to 395 square feet on the *Harmony* and from 367 to 491 square feet on the *Symphony* and are equipped with such niceties as Jacuzzis. Two palatial **Crystal Penthouses** offer 948 square feet *(Harmony)* and 982 square feet *(Symphony)* of space and a long list of luxuries, but at about $1,400 per person per day they're out of range for most budgets. All **Penthouse Deck** guests are accorded special privileges such as butler service, an unlimited supply of caviar, a full bar setup, and first dibs on restaurant reservations.

But cabin category is irrelevant when it comes to service. All staterooms are meticulously cared for by stewardesses who keep passengers' clothing carefully folded and hung and everything else tidy and spotless. Any request is happily accommodated. Feel like having a favorite snack or drink at the same time each day? No problem, it appears like clockwork. Arriving back at their cabins at the end of an evening, passengers find their nightclothes artistically arranged on their beds, along with the next day's program of activities, a breakfast menu and order form, and a special treat.

Sports & Fitness The fitness centers, located on each ship's upper deck, could be bigger considering the large number of passengers who use them. They're equipped with treadmills, Stairmasters, stationary bicycles, free weights, and weight machines. Both ships offer exercise classes led by first-rate instructors. Adjacent to the workout area is the omnipresent **Steiner** spa and beauty salon (a staple concession on cruise ships) offering the full array of high-priced head-to-toe treatments along with complimentary saunas and steam baths. Each ship also has two pools and two adjacent Jacuzzis. The larger pools are among the biggest at sea, nearly 40 feet in length; the smaller pools can be sheltered beneath retractable roofs. There's a nicely padded jogging track, golf driving range, paddle-tennis court (heavily used), skeet shooting, shuffleboard, Ping-Pong, and acres of deck space for lounging.

Activities & Entertainment There's more than enough to keep cruisers amused aboard these ships. The exquisite, horseshoe-shaped **Galaxy Lounge** is the site of first-rate entertainment—razzle-dazzle floor shows, cabaret acts, classical music concerts, and other performances are staged here. Passengers can take in a recent movie in the **Hollywood Theater,** sample wine by the glass in the **Bistro,** sign up for dance or bridge lessons, or try their luck at the ships' **Caesar's Palace Casinos At Sea,** staffed with dealers and croupiers from the Las Vegas and Lake Tahoe resorts, and offering gaming tables and lots of slots. (Gamblers note: At 4,400 square feet, *Symphony*'s casino is twice as large as her sister's.) Assorted audience-participation "game shows" are also popular. Shoppers can head for the Rodeo Drive–like **Avenue of the Stars,** where shops are stocked with fine jewelry, upscale clothing, perfume, and souvenirs, while more intellectual sorts can attend lectures and educational seminars. Each ship also has a well-stocked library providing books, magazines, videotapes, and a quiet place to read. (The *Symphony*'s library also has a business center.)

Both vessels have seven bars and lounges; the **Avenue Saloon,** an old-style spot with dark wood, comfortable leather chairs, and a friendly piano player, is a passenger favorite. Seats at the bustling bar are choice spots before and just after dinner.

Crystal caters to the youngest cruisers too. The children's program keeps them entertained with games, pizza parties, and dances while their parents are off doing "adult" things.

Crystal ships are the only vessels this size to provide complimentary transportation to the center of town in most ports. On a more mudane note, the ships are equipped with self-service launderettes, offering all the laundry-day basics free of charge.

Cuisine The fare is continental and American, with low-calorie and vegetarian selections, and it has been consistently excellent during several samplings—even on the *Symphony*'s maiden voyage in May 1995. (Inaugurals are a real test of a ship's quality, and this one passed with flying colors.)

The biggest drawback on these ships is the two-seating system in the main dining rooms (one-seating dining being a hallmark of luxury cruising). But two alternate restaurants on each ship provide some dinnertime flexibility. The *Harmony* has a Japanese eatery and an Italian spot; the *Symphony* has Chinese and Italian restaurants.

The main dining rooms are sensational; the low-ceilinged, circular rooms are embellished with crystal chandeliers, plush carpeting, wood paneling, fresh flowers and plants, and tables set with Frette linen, Limoges china, and crystal glasses. The waiters are attentive but unobtrusive.

Unlike many ships this size, the *Harmony* and *Symphony* also offer full meals in all cabins and suites (orders are limited to the dining room menu during regular mealtimes). An intimate stateroom dinner is an experience not to be missed. Breakfast on the veranda is another treat. Everything from eggs Benedict to Nova Scotia lox and bagels is available. Try the whole wheat and walnut pancakes—they're good enough to eat every day.

Each ship also offers deck buffets; the casual **Lido Cafe** for breakfast and lunch; a pizzeria; a bistro for snacks, specialty coffees, or wine; and a popular ice cream/frozen yogurt bar on deck (attended on a recent *Harmony* cruise by one of the nicest servers at sea). Afternoon tea is also special. It's served on the ships' top decks and can be a light supper for those with small appetites.

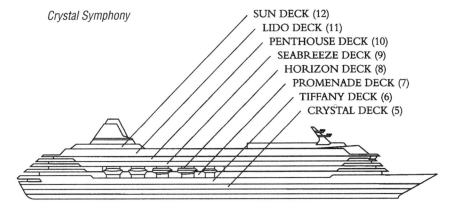

Crystal Symphony

SUN DECK (12)
LIDO DECK (11)
PENTHOUSE DECK (10)
SEABREEZE DECK (9)
HORIZON DECK (8)
PROMENADE DECK (7)
TIFFANY DECK (6)
CRYSTAL DECK (5)

Cunard

800/221.4770

CUNARD

 Royal Viking Sun
$$$$★★★★★★

Built: 1988

Refurbished: 1995

Passengers: 760

Size: 37,845 grt

Cabins: 384

Outside: 359 (141 with verandas)

Inside: 25

Suites: 19

Wheelchair Accessible: 4

Registry: Bahamas

Officers/Crew: Norwegian/International

Tipping Policy: Gratuities included in fare and a 15 percent service charge added to bar and spa tabs; no additional tips expected

Smoking Policy: Restricted to designated smoking sections in dining rooms and all other public areas; there is a cigar- and pipe-smoking lounge

Snapshot When she belonged to the **Royal Viking Line,** this classy luxury liner was one of the most acclaimed and copied afloat. The ship was constantly filled with repeat clientele, and the service was so exceptional it became the standard to which competing cruise lines aspired. **Cunard,** which acquired the stylish vessel in 1994, has endeavored to preserve the high standards **Royal Viking** was known for—and for the most part has succeeded.

Itinerary She literally covers the globe, starting the year with an around-the-world cruise that takes in the Orient, India, Africa, and South America; then crossing the Atlantic and spending the summer and fall sailing the Mediterranean, the North Cape, the Baltic Sea, and around Ireland and Scotland; and finishing the year with a cruise that includes Southeast Asia, Australia, Polynesia, and Hawaii.

Typical Passengers The *Sun* is the choice of well-traveled, well-heeled seniors, both couples and widows. About 60 to 70 percent of the travelers on any given cruise are repeat passengers (most die-hard **Royal Viking** devotees). European cruises attract a wide range of nationalities, with Americans making up about 40 percent of the total.

Large ships (more than 1,000 passengers): Blue

Mid-size ships (500-1,000 passengers): Green

Small ships (fewer than 500 passengers): Red

Ambience & Decor Understated elegance is the hallmark of this ship, with little in the way of opulence or glitz. The color scheme features soft blues, mauves, and pastels, and the walls are adorned with simple pieces of art or tapestry. Wall mirrors, shiny brass fixtures, and large vases filled with fresh flowers brighten up the public areas. Music enhances the understated setting; there are at least three pianos, all attended at various times during the day and night.

This ship is not for the action-seeker. The mood is subdued and refined, which suits most passengers just fine. Though distinctly upscale, the ambience is not stuffy—passengers are usually eager to mingle with fellow travelers. Shipboard attire is traditional—neatly casual by day and dressy at night. Men are asked to wear jackets on informal nights.

The service is efficient and sophisticated. Crew members are cordial but not noticeably friendly, in keeping with the conservative atmosphere.

Probably the main contender to "top cruise ship" title, which is now held jointly by **Crystal Cruises'** two vessels, the *Sun* falls a bit short in a just a couple areas. The food is not consistently as excellent and the service is just a notch below the level found on the **Crystal** ships. For example, waiters in the self-service cafe on *Crystal Harmony* and *Crystal Symphony* always carry passengers' trays to their tables; not so on the *Sun*. And poolside tables are not as efficiently bussed on the *Sun*. But these are small flaws on an otherwise outstanding ship.

Cabins Cabins range in size from 190 to 342 square feet (there are a few 138-square-foot cabins recommended for singles). More than one-third feature private verandas with teak decks. Standard staterooms are quite comfortable and appealing, with teak furniture and a muted peach and mauve color scheme. Each offers two twin beds that convert to one queen-size, adequate storage, a walk-in closet, a TV and VCR, telephone, mini-refrigerator, a desk and/or vanity with a makeup mirror, two bureaus, a leather sofa, and a large table for in-room dining.

Penthouse suites are a very commodious 606 square feet; they offer everything standard cabins have, plus a larger walk-in closet, lots of storage space, and a separate living area with two sofas. The marble bathroom has a tub and shower, two sinks, and a separate toilet area. Other penthouse perks include complimentary liters of liquor, a mini-refrigerator, and a butler who will serve breakfast in bed and otherwise make life more pleasant. It's easy to acquire a taste for such luxury, especially if your butler is Joseph, who was properly efficient during a recent cruise. Scandinavian stewardesses keep all the staterooms and suites immaculate.

Sports & Fitness The **Golden Door Spa at Sea** is the best afloat when the fitness instructors from the famous California health spa are on hand. When offered, aerobics, calisthenics, and step sessions are guaranteed to keep you shipshape. However, a recent cruise had a noticeable dearth of classes, possibly because the ship spent more days in port than cruising. In general, three to four classes are offered each day.

Those who prefer to follow their own exercise routine can head for the well-equipped fitness center, home to two rowing machines, four treadmills, six Stairmasters, free weights, and a jungle gym–like Hoist weight system. An outdoor lap pool is adjacent to the gym, and a full-service beauty salon offers the gamut of face, hair, and body treatments.

Up on the top deck is a smaller pool, a Jacuzzi, a Ping-Pong table, and a paddle-tennis court. The ship has a lot to offer golf enthusiasts—a driving range, a putting green, and a golf simulator, which offers "play" at many of the world's top courses. There's even a golf pro to help you with your swing.

Activities & Entertainment Daytime amusements include the standard shipboard activities (bingo, bridge, shuffleboard) and special programs such as cooking demonstrations, wine tasting, and dance lessons. A smallish cinema, a well-stocked library, and port lectures provide other diversions. Shoppers, however, will be disappointed by the **Royal Arcade,** which consists of only two duty-free shops. There's also lots of space to do nothing, with plenty of lounge chairs and deck stewards to fetch beverages. Other conveniences: a self-service launderette and (in certain ports) complimentary shuttle buses to the center of the city.

The evening variety shows feature the usual assortment of singers, dancers, comics, magicians, and ventriloquists. They are well done (on a recent cruise a musical tribute to Bob Fosse proved very entertaining), but don't expect Broadway- or Las Vegas–caliber productions. Unlike larger ships, which stage two performances each night to accommodate two dinner seatings, the *Sun* has one show at 10:15 (a schedule that many of the older passengers appreciate).

The casino, of modest size, offers blackjack, craps, and roulette, and a wall lined with slot machines.

The ship's "nightlife," such as it is, takes place in the five pleasant lounges. The inviting rose-colored **Norway Lounge** is the venue for the evening shows and also hosts before- and after-dinner dancing. A musical trio plays old-time melodies throughout the day and into the night in the **Midnight Sun Lounge,** while the handsome **Oak Room,** with its red marble fireplace and brown leather chairs and sofas, is an intimate spot for gathering with shipmates over drinks or simply relaxing with a good book. A giant globe stands in the middle of the compact **Compass Rose Room,** another quiet spot for relaxing in a big leather chair. During the day the **Stella Polaris Room** provides a 360° view of the ocean; at night it turns into a romantic, star-lit cocktail lounge where a

harpist adds to the ethereal ambience. Each of the lounges attracts its share of passengers for before- and after-dinner socializing and dancing. The mood is always subdued, however—this is not the ship for all-night partying or noisy revelry.

Cuisine Meals are served in a civilized one seating, allowing passengers to dine when they want (during set hours) at assigned tables. The **Royal Viking Dining Room** is made up of three separate sections; some areas feel cut off from the action, but attentive waiters keep things moving efficiently. Floor-to-ceiling windows, burgundy carpeting and upholstery, fine Norwegian china, Italian silver, and crystal glasses all complement the elegant dining experience.

An Austrian chef creates continental dishes that are pleasingly presented and usually exceptional. (As on most ships, the galley can slip up once in a while, but if something is not to your taste, your waiter will replace it without hesitation.) A typical dinner menu might include salad of quail breast, cream of chicken soup with truffles and pistachios, and Caesar salad for appetizers; Peking-style duck, veal medallions, and steak for entrées; and a selection of desserts, such as chocolate mousse cake, German apple pie, or fresh fruit.

The dishes tend to be rich (the barley soup was more like a bowl of cream), but lighter alternatives are always available. The **Golden Door** menu features creative reduced-calorie dishes.

The airy **Garden Cafe,** with its floor-to-ceiling windows, pink tile tables, and pretty baskets filled with plants and flowers, is open daily for self-service breakfast and lunch. The buffets are lovely to look at and might include made-to-order omelettes, salads, and hot entrées. For light lunches, an outdoor grill serves up burgers, hot dogs, fish fingers, and fries. The **Bistro Cafe** (an adjunct to the **Garden Cafe**) is open in the evening for salads and light suppers.

On all but formal evenings, **Venezia,** an Italian restaurant, serves as another alternative to the main dining room. The plush, burgundy room with crystal chandeliers and wide windows is a romantic setting for a multicourse, traditional Italian meal. The wine list offers Italian vino by the glass or bottle and 15 types of grappa. Reservations are required for dinner at **Venezia,** but there is no extra charge. The small room, which seats 60, is always filled to capacity.

For between-meal hunger pangs, tea, sandwiches, and sweets are served every afternoon, while a snack buffet of cold meat, salads, and more desserts is set out nightly from 11:30PM to 12:30AM. Room service is always available.

Royal Viking Sun

Cunard

800/221.4770

Sea Goddess I & II
$$$$★★★★★★

Built: 1984/1985

Refurbished: 1995 *(Sea Goddess I)*

Passengers: 116

Size: 4,250 grt

Cabins: 58

Outside: 58

Inside: 0

Suites: 58

Wheelchair Accessible: 0

Registry: Norwegian

Officers/Crew: European & American

Tipping Policy: Gratuities included in fare; no additional tips expected

Smoking Policy: Restricted to designated smoking sections in dining rooms and all other public areas; cigar smoking is allowed out on deck only; cigarettes available free of charge at bars

Snapshot With an average cost of $700 to $1,000 per passenger per day, these luxury ships are not for everybody. But it's almost worth refinancing the house to experience the phenomenal food, exceptional facilities, and unparalleled pampering afforded passengers on these stylish ships. It is truly difficult to go back to the "real world" after a sojourn aboard a *Sea Goddess*.

Itinerary The ships circle the globe, sailing European waters in fall, Africa and the Orient in spring, Alaska in summer, and the Caribbean and the Greek Isles in winter. Among the exotic ports added to their itineraries in 1997: the Seychelles, Comoros Islands; Mombasa, Kenya; Madagascar; Zanzibar, Tanzania; and Hokkaido, Japan.

Typical Passengers People with Champagne taste—and pocketbooks to match—are the target audience here. The shipboard population is usually dominated by well-traveled, affluent, and urbane couples, including many retired captains of industry. Ages vary, but the majority of passengers are 60 or

older. (A recent Caribbean cruise proved the exception, when a group of 25- to 30-year-olds livened things up.) These ships are not recommended for young children.

Ambience & Decor The gifts of the *Goddesses* are many. Travel documents arrive in a fine leather wallet ensconced in a red velvet box, along with a "Personal Preference Request" card that allows prospective passengers to order specific reading materials for their cabins and the library, state what types of ship and shore activities they prefer, specify which beverages they want stocked in their mini-refrigerators, schedule hair or beauty treatments, and indicate what special occasion they might be celebrating during the cruise.

The ships look and feel like private yachts, with Scandinavian-style furnishings made of light wood and natural fabrics and fine art work in public rooms and hallways. To preserve their intimate, noncommercial atmosphere, public announcements are made only to inform guests of port arrivals or shore excursions. They are also among the most spotless vessels afloat.

These are sophisticated, somewhat sedate ships; the prevailing attitude is one of luxury and ease. Most cruisers stay out on deck during the day soaking in the rays, chatting with fellow wayfarers, sipping Champagne (or beer, or piña coladas, or. . .), and consuming large quantities of caviar and shrimp. Many passengers indulge in all of the above while luxuriating in the Jacuzzi or in one of the soft cushioned lounge chairs. All beverages are complimentary, and deck stewards are always on the lookout for thirsty sun worshipers.

In fact, the 89 staff and crew members endeavor to fill passengers' every request, from delivering a private dinner right to a deck chair to fetching whatever a passenger might desire, be it an extra towel, sunscreen, a book, or a bottle of Champagne. These myriad small, special services make a cruise extraordinary; for example, when passengers return to the ship after a day in port, they're greeted with a cold washcloth and a cool drink.

Cabins Had these ships been built later than the early 1980s, they would probably offer private verandas (a 1990s luxury that has become *the* most desirable cabin feature). Nonetheless, the overall *Sea Goddess* experience more than makes up for this deficit. (And besides, the outside decks are so inviting, most people don't spend much time in their suites anyway.)

Sea Goddess I and II

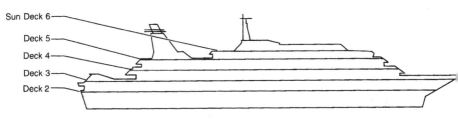

Sun Deck 6

Deck 5

Deck 4

Deck 3

Deck 2

Most suites measure 205 square feet, with shiny oak furniture. There's a long desk/dresser with three drawers on either side and shelves above; a long, narrow vanity with a makeup mirror and drawers to store cosmetics; mirrored closets with a set of shelves; two twin beds that can convert to one queen-size; and a separate sitting area with a large sofa, coffee table that converts to a full dining table, and mini-refrigerator stocked with the soft drinks and alcoholic beverages of your choice. A nice touch is a wall clock, which only a handful of other ships offer. Each suite also has a TV with VCR, two telephones, a hair dryer, terry robes, and fresh flowers. Bathrooms are somewhat small, with a tub and shower, one sink vanity, and a great assortment of Smith & Vandiver toiletries—hydrating spritzers, body cream, and bath gels as well as the usual shampoo and conditioner. Passengers also receive personalized stationery and all the postcards they desire. Friendly, efficient stewardesses keep suites spotless, bars well-stocked, robes fresh, and clothes neatly folded or hung.

Note: Four suites on **Deck Five** are less desirable than the rest, measuring only 167 square feet and offering limited closet and drawer space.

Sports & Fitness For sea lovers, the ships' best feature are their retractable marinas, which enable passengers to dive directly into the water or go jet skiing, windsurfing, waterskiing, or snorkeling (all equipment provided free). The platforms are usually available in the afternoons when the ships are anchored offshore in calm, clear waters.

For fitness buffs, the **Golden Door Spa at Sea** program is the ships' star attraction. Trained instructors from the famous Escondido, California, health resort lead a variety of exercise classes, from morning stretch and toning to afternoon aerobics and step sessions—all guaranteed to ward off avoirdupois. A nice gym (whose low ceiling was not designed with tall folks in mind) offers treadmills, Stairmasters, stationary bicycles, and weight machines as well as a lovely sauna with a one-way window that affords bathers a view of the sea (without allowing others to look in!). Massages, facials, hairstyling, and nail care are available in a tiny salon for a fee. On the lowest outside deck there's a 19-foot-long salt-water pool and a very popular Jacuzzi.

Activities & Entertainment Most *Sea Goddess* cruises are port intensive, so the focus is on landside activities and excursions. (One shore excursion, either to a beach area or historical site, is included in the fare.)

Aboard ship, you won't find bingo, skeet shooting, or any of the other usual big ship activities. Passengers are looking to relax, and that's what they do—in comfy, cushioned chaises on one of three attractive outside decks, up in the lovely **Observation Lounge,** or in their suites. During the day, the deck bar is the most popular gathering spot; it stays open as long as there are customers to serve (and there is always a tray of sandwiches to nosh on).

The library offers a good collection of books, magazines, videos, and table games, and there's a "gift shop" in the reception lobby (it's actually a group of display cases housing Gucci and Swatch watches, jewelry, perfume, Polo shirts, ties and cummerbunds, and the like).

Evening diversions are intentionally low-key, limited to dancing in the main salon and performances by cabaret-style singers or musical trios. There's also small casino with blackjack tables and slot machines. Passengers tend to gather after dinner in the lovely **Piano Bar,** furnished with marble-topped tables and adorned with whimsical artwork.

Each Caribbean cruise ends with an extra-special beach party that's far superior to the usual last night Baked Alaska shindig. The evening begins with caviar and Champagne served in the surf (waiters wade out to you); later still more drinks arrive, followed by a scrumptious barbecue. Everybody joins in the fun, playing volleyball, windsurfing, jet skiing, and snorkeling.

Cuisine The food is simply sensational, among the best served at sea. (It's tied with the first-rate fare offered on the newer **Silversea** ships.) Passengers may eat virtually anything they like (providing the raw materials are available), just about whenever and wherever they like. Hungry by the pool? No problem, a steward will bring you caviar, shrimp cocktail, a cheeseburger, pizza, a sandwich—whatever. If you want to have dinner out on deck or in your stateroom, the crew will oblige.

The fare is gourmet, artistically presented, light (no heavy sauces), and as tasty as can be. Fresh fish, the tenderest filet mignon and steaks, luscious lobster tails, jumbo shrimp, perfect pasta, great cookies and pastries, and other divine desserts such as pecan and walnut tarts and profiteroles are all available. **Golden Door Spa** cuisine is also offered on all menus.

On these ships, the dining "salons," attractive and comfortable with low ceilings and soothing colors, seem almost like an extra amenity (an additional restaurant) since passengers tend to take their meals all over the ship. Dining room hours are posted but there are no table assignments (although the maître d' tends to seat passengers in the same spot each night). One small complaint—there are only four tables for two.

Breakfast and lunch spreads are set out in an attractive area of **Deck Five** that features a waterfall along one wall. The morning buffet includes a variety of fresh fruits and juices, cereals, breads, yogurts, and nuts, but it's possible to order anything from eggs Benedict to pancakes. The luncheon buffet is similarly abundant, with salads, special dishes of the day (chicken fajitas, lasagna), and more. Passengers can also order from a menu that changes daily or put in a special request. Deck stewards will carry your plates anywhere on ship you like, or (in a whole new spin on the buffet concept) you can simply sit down somewhere and ask to be served. Ahh, the seafaring life.

Large ships (more than 1,000 passengers): Blue
Mid-size ships (500-1,000 passengers): Green
Small ships (fewer than 500 passengers): Red

Princess Cruises

800/PRINCESS

Crown Princess/ Regal Princess

$$$★★★★★

Built: 1990/1991

Passengers: 1,590

Size: 70,000 grt

Cabins: 795

Outside: 564 (134 with private verandas)

Inside: 171

Suites: 14 suites and 36 mini-suites with private verandas

Wheelchair Accessible: 10

Registry: Liberian

Officers/Crew: English/International

Tipping Policy: $7 to $8 per passenger per day suggested

Smoking Policy: Prohibited in dining rooms and entertainment lounges

Snapshot Despite their large size, these "Love Boats" have a congenial, intimate atmosphere. In fact, they are two of the friendliest, prettiest, and most extravagantly produced large ships afloat.

Itinerary The *Crown Princess* offers Alaskan cruises in summer and 10- and 15-day Caribbean trips from Ft. Lauderdale the rest of the year. The *Regal Princess* makes 10- and 11-day Panama Canal cruises between San Juan and Acapulco, but joins her sister in Alaska in summer.

Typical Passengers For the most part, passengers are **Princess** loyalists, age 40 and older, although there are some twenty- and thirty-somethings and children on board in the summer.

Ambience & Decor The ships have an unusual hump-back profile (said to be inspired by the silhouette of a dolphin) forward and pencil-thin smokestacks aft. They feature wide, open decks, spacious public rooms, and luxurious materials. Designed by Italian architect Renzo Piano, the interiors are decorated in restful colors and feature Burma teak, Carrara marble, granite, burlwood paneling, stainless steel, fine leather, and expensive fabrics. The walls are graced with an impressive $1-million contemporary art collection, which includes

works by such notable artists as David Hockney, Frank Stella, Robert Motherwell, and Richard Diebenkorn. The centerpiece of each ship is a gorgeous three-story atrium dominated by a grand staircase and a shopping arcade with stores selling jewelry, clothing, perfume, and sundries.

The English captains and officers and the international crew of more than 600 exude good humor, helping to promote a light-hearted mood throughout these stylish, albeit over-size, ships. A traditional cruise ship dress code—casual by day, dressy at night—prevails.

Cabins Even the lowest-priced cabins are a roomy 190 square feet, with 36 mini-suites measuring 360 square feet and 14 veranda suites a practically palatial 587 square feet.

Best choices are the standard staterooms with verandas and the mini-suites (which also have verandas). Accommodations in both categories feature two lower beds that can be converted into one large bed, a TV, mini-refrigerator, lots of drawers, a walk-in closet, dresser, and bathroom with tub and shower, supplied with a full complement of toiletries (shampoo, conditioner, body lotion, bath gel) and a hair dryer and terry robes to use on board.

If money is no object, opt for a suite. They're pure luxury, with lots of space, two TV sets (one in the bedroom, the other in the living room), two bathrooms (a marble master bath with tub and shower and a guest bath with toilet only), a mini-refrigerator stocked with complimentary beverages, and a spacious private veranda.

Sports & Fitness Princess's **Cruisercize** program is outstanding, with able-bodied instructors leading aerobics, step, and body-toning classes that work off extra calories acquired at the ice cream shop or midnight buffets. The **Images** health and fitness center on each ship features a large aerobics floor and an adjacent weight room where exercise bikes, treadmills, and weight equipment are kept. Although the gym is situated in the bowels of the ships (a less scenic setting than on most vessels), if you take the stairs (about 99 steps from the top deck) your hips and thighs will thank you for it. Other sports and fitness facilities include a one-sixth-mile tractioned outdoor jogging track, two outdoor pools, and a netted game court where basketball, volleyball, and tennis are played. For every organized exercise activity passengers participate in, they receive coupons that are redeemable for logo merchandise.

Less ambitious passengers may want to take advantage of the ships' four Jacuzzis and acres of deck space dotted with comfy lounge chairs (don't forget to bring a beach towel from your cabin). The very attractive **Steiner** spa has steam baths and saunas and offers an array of beauty treatments.

For ocean lovers, **Princess**'s excellent **New Waves** shore excursion option (truly the best around) offers passengers hassle-free snorkeling and scuba diving trips in appropriate ports. Gear, instruction, and safety equipment are included. In addition, passengers may earn scuba certification during a **Princess** cruise through an instructional program

Crown Princess/Regal Princess

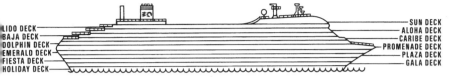

run in conjunction with the **Professional Association of Diving Instructors (PADI)**.

Activities & Entertainment When it comes to keeping passengers happily occupied and amused, few cruise lines do as well as **Princess**. Lavish productions, with singers, comedians, and other talented performers, are staged in each ship's dynamite, two-level **International Show Lounge**, while the **Princess Theaters** on both vessels show recent movies on a big screen. Each ship also has an attractive, bustling casino; a library; a card and game room; and a full schedule of activities.

In addition, pianists and singers perform throughout the day and night in the ships' inviting bars and lounges. Favorite haunts include the **Chianti** *(Crown)* and **Bacchus** *(Regal)* wine bars, where wine, Champagne, and caviar are served; **Kipling's** *(Crown)* and the **Bengal Bar** *(Regal)*, midship lounges with mirrored bars and leather and rattan furniture; **Intermezzo** *(Crown)* and **Adagio** *(Regal)*, cozy piano bars; and **Jammers**, the very-late-night disco on the *Crown*.

Thanks to **Princess Cruises**' exceptional **Love Boat Kids** program, these ships are a good choice for families. The program is divided into two categories: **Princess Pelicans** for children ages 2 to 12 and the **Princess Teen Club (PTC)** for youths 13 to 16. "Pelicans" are entertained with arts and crafts, scavenger hunts, deck parties, videos, and afternoon ice cream socials, while teens enjoy pizza parties, play murder-mystery games, compete in shipboard Olympics, and bop at the disco.

Cuisine The food varies from cruise to cruise, but it's essentially good, especially the fresh pasta, just about any beef dish (steak, filet mignon, hamburger), and all the desserts and pastries. An exceptional "Healthy Choice" menu offers appealing low-cholesterol, fat- and sodium-reduced dishes such as broiled eggplant with pistachio-mint salsa, Moroccan vegetable ragoût, and caramelized bananas flambé.

The attractive, two-level main dining rooms are light, airy, and festive, and the charming dining crew is always a delight. Although they have 844 mouths to feed at each seating (there are two per meal), the well-trained waiters manage to do so with style.

Other restaurants include the supercasual **Lido Deck Cafe Cabana** *(Crown)* and **Cafe del Sol** *(Regal)*, offering massive breakfast and lunch buffets, and the poolside pizzerias, which serve slices most of the day. Yet more calories can be consumed at the **Patisserie** on the ships' **Plaza Decks,** where complimentary coffee and pastries are available all day long (espresso and cappuccino cost extra). And, although the ships do not promote or encourage the practice, it is possible to have full meals delivered to staterooms when the dining room is open. At other times of day, passengers may order from a simple room-service menu of sandwiches and snacks. Complimentary continental breakfast is also offered in cabins.

The Godmother

Seafaring tradition requires that ships be christened by a woman sponsor or "godmother." At the christening ceremony, this woman cracks a bottle against the bow (Champagne is traditional, but giant bottles of everything from Coca Cola to Tabasco sauce have been used) while saying something like "I name this ship MS *Albatross*. Bless her and all who sail on her."

Godmothers are generally members of ship-owning families or royalty, politicians, dignitaries or—a recent trend—entertainers. At least one was a cartoon character (Minnie Mouse).

Godmothers are not paid, but receive tokens of gratitude from the cruise line and the shipyard. Some sail as regular guests of the line or appear at charitable benefits staged aboard ship.

Over the years, many famous females have broken bottles of bubbly over cruise ship hulls. Here are a few:

Lauren Bacall—**Royal Caribbean International's** *Monarch of the Seas*

Barbara Bush—**Norwegian Cruise Line's** *Windward*

Diana, Princess of Wales—**Princess Cruises'** *Royal Princess*

Gloria Estefan—**Royal Caribbean International's** *Nordic Empress*

Whoopi Goldberg—**Royal Caribbean International's** *Viking Serenade*

Audrey Hepburn—**Princess Cruises'** *Star Princess*

Angela Lansbury—**Crystal Cruises'** *Crystal Symphony*

Sophia Loren—**Princess Cruises'** *Crown Princess*

Mary Tyler Moore—**Crystal Cruises'** *Crystal Harmony*

Debbie Reynolds—**Holland America Line's** *Veendam*

Beverly Sills—**Royal Caribbean International's** *Song of America*

Shirley Temple—**Seaborn Cruise Line's** *Seabourn Pride*

Princess Cruises

800/PRINCESS

Dawn Princess/ Sun Princess

$$★★★★★

Built: 1995/1996

Passengers: 1,950

Size: 77,000 grt

Cabins: 975

Outside: 603 (410 with balconies)

Inside: 372

Suites: 6 (with private balconies); 32 mini-suites (with private balconies)

Wheelchair Accessible: 19

Registry: Liberian

Officers/Crew: English/International

Tipping Policy: About $8 per passenger per day suggested

Smoking Policy: Prohibited in dining rooms and entertainment lounges; permitted in most other public areas

Snapshot Towering 14 decks high and measuring almost three football fields long, these are two bodacious boats. The *Sun Princess* was the biggest ship afloat for a few months after she was launched in December 1995; the *Dawn Princess* made her debut in May 1997. More like a sea-going hotels than ships, with the same amenities, they're smart-looking vessels with lots to offer, from dazzling art collections to an amazing amount of deck space.

(A third sister ship, the 77,000-grt, 1,950-passenger *Sea Princess,* is scheduled to be launched in 1999.)

Itinerary Between October and May, the *Dawn* offers seven-day southern Caribbean cruises from San Juan, while the *Sun* makes seven-day western Caribbean trips from Ft. Lauderdale. Both ships cruise Alaskan waters in summer.

Typical Passengers Typical **Princess** clients are found on board. The group is predominantly American and usually on the older side (fifties and up), with an occasional sprinkling of passengers in their thirties and forties. Some children are brought along during the summer.

Note: These ships are not the best choices for anyone who has trouble walking. They're so big that long treks are required to reach the dining room and other public areas. In addition, wheelchairs are difficult to navigate in the narrow hallways, especially during the hours when cabin stewards are cleaning cabins and have their carts in the halls.

Ambience & Decor Spacious and sprawling, the ships may prove *too* big for comfort for some, while others truly enjoy all the extra room, which is more evident outdoors than in.

The twins are identical, differing only in color schemes. Public spaces are decorated with $2.5-million art collections—each work a commissioned, one-of-a-kind piece. The ships' focal points are their stunning, four-story **Grand Plaza** atriums, which feature lovely circular marble foyers accessible by two glass-and-brass elevators or a circular marble staircase. The pianos in the atriums keep music in the air.

The ships are big but friendly, though for the most part the mood is on the quiet and reserved side (things sometimes get lively in the bustling **Wheel House Bar**). Dress is very casual by day, casual chic most nights. On formal nights (there are two per seven-day cruise), many men opt for dark suits over tuxes while women's attire ranges from plain to glitzy.

The service is a cut above that found on other megaships. In fact, on two recent cruises on the *Sun Princess,* the level of service was higher than that generally found on **Princess** ships—the crew was more attentive than usual and quite eager to please.

Cabins At 135 to 173 square feet, standard state-rooms are on the small side for such a large ship. But they are comfortably appointed, and mirrors hung behind the beds and over the desk make them seem roomier. Each cabin has two twin beds that can convert to one queen-size, plenty of closet and drawer space, and a dresser, TV, safe, mini-refrigerator, and telephone. Bathrooms are small, with a single sink and shower, but they are supplied with terry robes and a full complement of toiletries.

The best accommodations are the 536- to 754-square-foot suites and the 374- to 536-square-foot mini-suites, which offer such extras as a private balcony, Jacuzzi and separate shower, a desk/vanity, and a sitting room decorated with a leather sofa, table and chairs, and original artwork. **Suite 748** is probably the best on board each ship. Situated at the stern, with a big balcony overlooking the wake, it's ideal for newlyweds. The interior is done in marble

Sun Princess

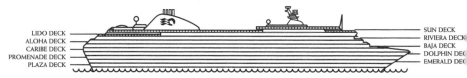

LIDO DECK
ALOHA DECK
CARIBE DECK
PROMENADE DECK
PLAZA DECK

SUN DECK
RIVIERA DECK
BAJA DECK
DOLPHIN DECK
EMERALD DECK

and mahogany, and the mini-bar is replenished daily with soft drinks and mini-bottles of liquor.

All the cabins are kept pristine by the predominantly Filipino crew, and each deck features a convenient self-service laundry.

Sports & Fitness Princess offers **Cruisercize,** one of the best supervised fitness programs at sea. Based in the ships' gymnasiums—located on the upper deck, with wide windows looking out to sea—it offers aerobic, step, stretch, and assorted body toning classes throughout the cruise. Passengers also can do their own thing in the fully equipped exercise room, which has plenty of treadmills and stationary bicycles as well as free weights and weight machines. The omnipresent **Steiner** salon provides high-priced pampering in any of 11 attractive treatment rooms. Passengers can also take complimentary steam baths or saunas at the spa, or can step just outside the gym into one of two Jacuzzis or a small, round swimming pool suspended between two decks. Just be sure to remember to bring the beach towels from your cabin; you won't find any on deck or at the spa (unless you've booked a treatment). On a recent trip aboard the *Sun Princess,* a helpful deck steward got towels for us; at the spa, an attendant refused to supply any when we went to take a steam and realized too late we forgot to bring towels.

Out on deck there are five pools and whirlpools, a paddle-tennis court, a computerized golf center, basketball and badminton courts, and a one-sixth-mile jogging track.

Princess's **New Waves** program makes it easy for passengers to go snorkeling and/or scuba diving in appropriate ports. Gear, instruction, and safety equipment are all included in the price. In addition, **Princess** offers a **New Waves** program run in conjunction with the **Professional Association of Diving Instructors (PADI).** It enables passengers to obtain scuba certification during a cruise.

Activities & Entertainment Most passengers spend the daylight hours out on the spacious decks, which have lots of chaises and plenty of deck stewards to fetch beverages. There's also a band stand, the **Island Bar,** and an ice cream kiosk.

Indoors, there's a large library and a full-scale shopping arcade with seven shops carrying everything from sundries and souvenirs to fine leather goods and evening attire.

The list of organized activities fills a full page of the ship's newsletter (in small type) and includes everything from bridge tours and port talks to trivia competitions and line dance classes.

For nightime entertainment, passengers head for the exquisite, double-deck **Princess Theater,** whose Art Deco decor provides a backdrop for lavish musical productions. At the other end of the **Promenade Deck,** the **Vista Lounge** offers cabaret-style performances as well as a cozy bar, a large dance floor (after the show is over), and ocean views through floor-to-ceiling windows. Shows are generally excellent and attract large crowds (tickets are often handed out at the second dinner seating to ensure that first-seating passengers don't sneak in for an encore performance). The alluring casino, with every imaginable gambling option, draws an after-show crowd.

Numerous bars and lounges are scattered around the ship. The lively **Wheel House Bar**—a handsome, library-like room decorated with mahogany wood paneling, brass fixtures, and replicas of vintage ships—attracts a crowd before and after dinner. There's dancing in the **Atrium Lounge,** where big bay windows overlook the atrium. For younger folk, the disco/nightclub (called **Jammer's** on the *Dawn Princess* and **Shooting Stars** on the *Sun Princess*) is the popular place to be after 11PM. Both have a celestial theme, with a dramatic star-studded ceiling and tiny lights embedded in the carpeting. Video screens and a dance floor illuminated by neon enhance the flashy effect.

Princess Cruises operates an exceptional **Love Boat Kids** program that's divided into two sections: **Princess Pelicans** for ages 2 to 12 and the **Princess Teen Club (PTC)** for teenagers 13 to 16. For "pelicans" there are scavenger hunts, deck parties, galley and backstage tours, and slumber parties. **PTC** activities include shipboard Olympics, murder-mystery games, karaoke, and theme parties; the teen center has a video disco, refreshment bar, and video games. There's also a toddler's **Fun Zone,** which features a splash pool, theater, doll's house, castle, and ice cream kiosk.

Cuisine The food is quite good for a ship this size, particularly the pizza and pasta, which are prepared to perfection. As on other **Princess** ships, the fare is continental/American, with some Italian and English touches. On a recent cruise the lobster, steaks, and fresh fish proved superb, and desserts (including cherries jubilee and flaming baked Alaska) were delicious.

Each ship has two identical dining rooms and two dinner seatings, generally 6:15 and 8:30. The dining rooms are divided into separate dining coves, creating a unique asymmetrical layout. Each of the coves has dramatic etched-glass and granite entryways and ceilings with Art Nouveau designs. Muted lighting provided by decorative sconces contributes to the intimate atmosphere.

Among the other shipboard eateries is the **Horizon Court** restaurant, a rustic-looking room where granite, marble, and ceramics mingle pleasantly, and buffet tables hold soups and salads, hot and cold entrées, cheese, fruits, desserts, and more. The ships' pizzerias (**LaScala** on the *Dawn,* **Verdi's** on the *Sun*) have a Roman theme and are decorated with marble, stainless steel, and whimsical art. For a special snack, both ships have a wine-and-caviar bar, which is usually fairly quiet (in contrast to the pizzerias, which draw a lively crowd from the moment they open). Other options for a quick bite include a hamburger and hot dog grill, an ice cream parlor, and a patisserie.

Since the **Horizon Court** is open nonstop, no midnight buffet is offered. Room service is also available around the clock in all cabin categories.

Radisson Seven Seas Cruise Line

800/333.3333

RADISSON SEVEN SEAS
C R U I S E S

 Radisson Diamond
$$$$★★★★★

Built: 1992

Passengers: 354

Size: 20,295 grt

Cabins: 177

Outside: 177 (123 with verandas, 54 with large bay windows)

Inside: 0

Suites: 2

Wheelchair Accessible: 2

Registry: Finnish

Officers/Crew: European & American/International

Tipping Policy: Gratuities included in fare; no additional tips expected

Smoking Policy: Restricted to designated smoking sections

Snapshot The *Radisson Diamond* is both the largest twin-hull ship ever constructed and the first luxury cruise ship to employ semisubmersible-craft technology. The $125-million vessel has struts attached to a pair of submerged hulls that lift the vessel above the water, resulting in greater seagoing stability and less pitching, rolling, and heaving than conventional hulls.

When the catamaran-style luxury liner debuted in 1992 it was marketed as an "all-inclusive" ship, with cruise packages priced at about $1,000 per person per day. Although the unique sailing machine had a lot going for it, the tab proved too high for most potential passengers. So fares were slashed, but (to the line's credit) the quality of the food and service weren't. Today the ship rates five-star status for its excellent food, efficient and attentive service, and incredibly smooth ride.

Itinerary She sails the Mediterranean in summer and makes transcanal and Caribbean voyages in winter. Most cruises are from 10 to 15 days, although shorter voyages are sometimes offered.

Typical Passengers Savvy seafarers with a taste for the good life set sail aboard the *Diamond*. Most

are American, and most are in their forties and fifties, although shorter cruises attract more passengers in their thirties. The ship is occupied by meeting and convention groups for about one-third of each year.

Ambience & Decor Unusual because of its catamaran hull, this ship also has some architectural quirks. One uncommon aspect is its single deck, which actually works quite well because the ship is very roomy—the passenger-to-space ratio (57:9) is one of the highest of any cruise liner. Other features are somewhat unattractive; for example, the stairs leading down to the marina at the stern pass crates of provisions, which are only partially concealed behind canvas curtains.

The public rooms, clustered around a central atrium, are large and simply decorated. The atrium, with its glass elevators, is the most lavish space aboard ship, but it pales in comparison to the glitzy lobbies of most other vessels.

The mood on board is similarly understated and low-key. Dress is relaxed and casual by day, a bit more formal at night. Ties and jackets are suggested for men on informal nights, while tuxedos or dark suits are de rigueur for formal evenings, when women wear either gowns or cocktail dresses. While passengers adhere to the suggested dress codes, they tend to wear simple, elegant attire as opposed to the flashy sequins and spangles frequently found on larger cruise ships.

Finnish officers oversee an exceptional international crew of 191. The passenger-to-crew ratio is one of the best in the business; for every two passengers there is more than one crew member to tend to their needs.

Cabins The standard staterooms are comfortable, measuring a spacious 246 square feet. Most have balconies (the others have picture windows), and some have walk-in closets (the others offer minimal hanging space but plenty of drawers). Each has two twin beds or one queen-size bed, a telephone, TV and VCR, vanity with lighted mirror, a safe, a mini-bar stocked with complimentary soft drinks and water (replenished daily), and a one-time bar set-up of four fifths of liquor. Bathrooms have tubs and showers and are supplied with hair dryers, somewhat worn terry robes, and lovely Lord & Mayfair almond soap, shampoo, conditioner, bath gel, and body lotion. Some larger staterooms are furnished with a sofa and table; others have separate sitting areas. Cabin stewardesses (mostly Austrian) keep everything spotless.

Sports & Fitness Here's where the *Diamond* misses the boat. The rather compact spa and fitness center is minimally equipped with free weights, three Stairmasters, a few other machines, and one much-coveted treadmill (we were told a second was on order). While waiting their turn on the treadmill (there's a sign-up sheet), passengers can jog or walk on the outside track (13 circuits equal one mile).

The adjacent **Steiner** spa has saunas, steam rooms, and a full-range of overpriced beauty treatments.

Radisson Diamond

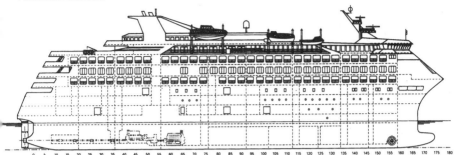

The one pool is only about four feet deep and a couple of swim strokes long, and there's one Jacuzzi, but there are lots of deck chairs and ample space to spread out.

A popular retractable marina/diving platform/swimming cage is lowered when the ship is at anchor, so passengers can swim, snorkel, windsurf, jet-ski, and water-ski in the ocean without having to go ashore. It is used mostly in the Mediterranean, weather permitting. Jet skis, Windsurfers, and water skis are available at no charge, but there's a rental fee for snorkel gear.

Activities & Entertainment Three bar/lounges are the focus of this ship's social scene—there are none of the organized games, activities, or classes found on large cruise liners here. **Windows Lounge,** a big, somewhat awkwardly arranged room (chairs are lined in rows on the balcony and in front of the stage), offers great ocean views during the day, when it is the setting for afternoon tea. After dark it serves as the entertainment lounge, with nightly musical revues staged by a very talented repertory cast. This is also where the captain holds his "welcome aboard" party, and cocktails are served here well into the early morning hours. The **Splash Bar** is unusual for a ship's poolside bar in that it stays open after dark (in this case, until the last person leaves); **The Club,** a small, intimate bar with comfortable brown leather chairs, also remains open until the last customer calls it a night.

In addition, **Chip's Casino** draws the gambling crowd with slot machines offering "possible $10,000 jackpot payoffs" and the usual table games. A fancy boutique carries brand-name watches, high-end jewelry, and the usual assortment of T-shirts and nautical souvenirs.

Cuisine The food—an eclectic mix of expertly prepared traditional dishes (beef Wellington, steaks, lobster tails)—is exceptional. The menu is extensive, and everything, be it lamb, steak, pasta, fish, or chicken, is prepared to order. (Sauces tend to be heavy—passengers watching their diets may want to ask for them on the side.) Complimentary house wines are poured at lunch and dinner.

The gorgeous Art Deco **Grand Dining Room** is as unique as the ship itself, with floor-to-ceiling

windows draped in sheer fabric, ornate gold-leaf pillars, and glass, gold, copper, and brass trim. Beautifully set with Villeroy & Boch china and Schott-Zwiesel crystal, the tables spread out from a center room into side areas that have still more windows. The European dining room waitresses (mostly Austrian) are quite efficient. (Strangely enough, this is the only major cruise ship to have female dining room staff members.)

Casual meals are offered in **The Grill,** site of wonderful lunch and breakfast buffets (among the best at sea). The well-arranged buffets feature food stations strategically placed to avoid having passengers wait in line.

There's also **Don Vito's,** a festive Italian restaurant. It offers an authentic multicourse Italian meal complete with red-and-white checkered tablecloths and Italian waiters who serenade diners between courses. While a menu is provided, there are no choices; the food just keeps on coming. Dinner might begin with wild mushrooms in a puff pastry and continue with shrimp risotto, pasta of the day, filet mignon, salad, and more. The experience is definitely worth enjoying more than once; reservations—and a hearty appetite—are required.

There's no midnight buffet, but afternoon snacks and tea are offered daily, and room service (including full meals) is remarkably prompt and always available.

> "After dinner I stretched out on a deck chair. It suddenly came to me that there was nothing, absolutely nothing, that I had to do … A self-conscious peace descended upon me as I lay there looking up at the stars."
>
> Noel Coward, during a 1930s-era world cruise

Radisson Seven Seas Cruise Line

800/333.3333

 Song of Flower
$$$$★★★★★★

Built: 1986
Refurbished: 1989
Passengers: 172
Size: 8,282 grt
Cabins: 100
Outside: 100
Inside: 0
Suites: 20 (10 with verandas)
Wheelchair Accessible: 0
Registry: Norway
Officers/Crew: Norwegian & Japanese/European
Tipping Policy: Gratuities included in fare; no additional tips expected
Smoking Policy: Restricted to designated smoking sections

Snapshot This tiny pearl of a vessel (formerly the *Explorer Starship*) packs elegance and fun into one exceptional, highly rated package. The service is impeccable, with European waiters and friendly but extremely efficient cabin stewardesses. Nearly everything is included in the fare—airfare, transfers, gratuities, shore excursions, and beverages (alcoholic and otherwise); port charges are extra.

Itinerary *Song of Flower* explores Europe and the Mediterranean in summer, Asia and Australia in winter.

Typical Passengers It's an upscale group, a mix of yuppies, baby boomers, and well-to-do older couples who enjoy romantic, luxury sailing that feels like yachting. The ship is not recommended for small children.

Ambience & Decor Comfortably elegant, this yacht-like vessel is decorated with marble and polished wood with walls and fabrics in subtle shades.

Exceptional service is the hallmark here. The tone is set the minute passengers step on board—a crew member greets each guest with a broad smile and a glass of Champagne. With an impressive passenger/space ratio of 48:2 and 144 young but well-trained crew members, passengers enjoy lots of room and plenty of attention. The European waiters and the cheerful Scandinavian cabin stewardesses are among the most efficient at sea. The Norwegian and Japanese officers welcome visitors on the bridge at all times.

The small number of passengers results in a convivial shipboard spirit, with friendships forming quickly. Traditional cruisewear is the norm. A nice plus: Formalwear can be rented on board.

Cabins Most staterooms are a quite comfortable 200 square feet (those on **Galaxy Deck** are a slightly smaller 198 square feet). Pretty in pink and other pastels, standard cabins have light wood furnishings, either portholes or windows, a choice of two lower beds or one queen-size bed, and spacious closets. Bathrooms are equipped with tubs or "half-tubs" (a short, deep tub with a shower). Upper-deck cabins have private verandas and full-size tubs. Nice extras include a mini-refrigerator stocked with complimentary soft drinks and liquor (refilled regularly), slippers and terry robes to use during the cruise, and complimentary logo caps. Stewardesses keep everything neat and tidy.

Sports & Fitness Most passengers enjoy the water sports (swimming, snorkeling, scuba diving, windsurfing, jet skiing) made available by the retractable diving platform at the stern, which offers easy access to the sea when the ship's at anchor. Also popular are excursions on the *Tiny Flower,* a little explorer vessel that can pull up right on the beach, allowing passengers to spend a day sunning, swimming, snorkeling (gear is provided), or shell hunting. Other facilities include a surprisingly large two-tier sundeck with a medium-size pool and Jacuzzi and a compact fitness room with a sauna. Massages are available for an additional fee. The small beauty salon completes the facilities.

Activities & Entertainment Life on board is unregimented, with no organized activities. Passengers tend to spend the daylight hours engaged in active pursuits (see above). But for those in search of more sedentary pastimes, there's a lovely library stocked with nearly 1,000 books and hundreds of videos that may be viewed in the comfort of the staterooms. Bargain hunters may want to peruse the **Royal Flower** boutique, one of the few seagoing shops offering real savings, especially on perfumes. The small casino is adequate, with a few slot machines and roulette and blackjack tables, but hardly ever used.

Otherwise, fellow shipmates tend to gather for drinks and conversation in the **Observation Lounge,** a cozy spot with lush leather chairs and floor-to-ceiling windows overlooking the sea. After dark, singers or musicians perform in the intimate cabaret-style nightclub.

Cuisine Everyone who's been on this ship raves about the food, a mix of contemporary California and continental cuisine. Mealtimes are flexible, with open seating allowing passengers the freedom to dine when and with whom they like. Complimentary wines are poured with lunch and dinner.

Dinner is served in the inviting **Galaxy Dining Room**, where tables are adorned with fresh flowers, linen tablecloths and napkins, and beautiful china, flatware, and crystal. Elegant waiters are Old World–attentive, pulling out chairs, folding napkins whenever someone leaves the table, and, while never intrusive, always on hand the moment they're needed.

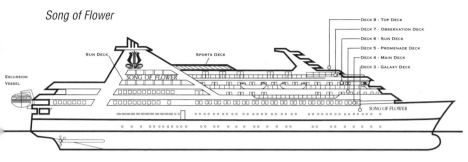

Song of Flower

The breakfast and luncheon buffets, served in the **Cafe** on the **Pool Deck,** are a special treat. Passengers may start the day off with freshly squeezed juice and the morning entrée of their choice—eggs, pancakes, French toast, omelettes, and so on—cooked to order. Lunch offerings run from hamburgers and hot dogs to crab or lobster caught at the last port. Room service is available around the clock.

Barging Through Europe

At one time, traveling through Europe on a barge meant roughing it. But no more. Today, scores of comfortable—even luxurious—barges sail the canals and rivers of **England, Belgium, France,** and **Holland.**

There are two types of barge cruises: self-skippered rentals and charters. On self-skippered barge vacations (which are wildly popular with Europeans but just catching on with Americans), you and your traveling companions do the driving, bring the provisions, and make the meals. On chartered barges, the sailing is handled by a captain and crew, and the most important person on the entire boat is the cook. On self-skippered barges, you travel with family or friends; on charters you join a group of strangers (who often become friends).

Barges accommodate from to 2 to 28 passengers and anywhere from three to eight crew members. Most have private cabins but shared bathrooms. Barges are always comfortable, but slow, cruising in a week the distance that a car could cover in a couple hours. But the leisurely pace is the raison d'être of the cruises, for passengers are able to see a small section of a foreign country with an intimacy impossible using any other means of conveyance. Passengers can wander through villages, read, take leisurely bike rides along the towpath, visit historic sites, or make half-day or day trips arranged by the captain. A typical barge trip lasts one week and includes all meals, some excursions, and the use of bicycles. Dining is a highlight on chartered barge tours—most serve up superb foods, wines, and liquors.

Favorite itineraries in England include the **Avon River,** from **Stratford-upon-Avon** to **Tewksbury;** the **Thames,** from **Oxford** to **Windsor;** and the **Norfolk Broads,** through John Constable country. Belgian cruises usually focus on the **Flanders** region, with **Bruges** and **Ghent** the most frequented stops. Popular French routes cover the canals and rivers of **Burgundy,** the **Canal du Midi** in the Mediterranean province of **Languedoc,** and the canals and rivers of **Brittany** and **Alsace.** In the **Netherlands,** cruises generally begin at **Rotterdam** and proceed through the canals to **Gouda** and **Delft.** Some barge journeys are built around themes such as gourmet cooking, tulip time in Holland, or antiques-shopping in England.

The following are just a few of the companies that arrange European barge cruises:

Crown Blue Line offers self-skippered barge vacations in England and France. The US reservations number is 800/355.9394.

French Country Waterways features six-night cruises through Burgundy on four well-appointed hotel barges carrying eight to 18 guests. Some ships are equipped with a fitness studio and sauna. Every sailing features an elegant dinner ashore at a three-star restaurant. For details, call 800/222.1236.

Continental Waterways, a three-decades-old French company, operates a fleet of 28 barges ranging from the very comfortable (and equipped with a captain and crew) to more basic, family-sized, sail-your-own-type vessels. They offer cruises in France, Holland, and England. In the US, call 516/746.6061.

M. BLUM

Seabourn Cruise Line

415/391.7444

 **Seabourn Pride/
Seabourn Spirit/
Seabourn Legend**

$$$$★★★★★★

Built: 1987/1991/1992
Passengers: 204
Size: 10,000 grt
Cabins: 106
Outside: 106
Inside: 0
Suites: 106
Wheelchair Accessible: 4
Registry: Norwegian
Officers/Crew: Norwegian/International
Tipping Policy: Gratuities included in fare; no additional tips expected
Smoking Policy: Restricted to designated smoking sections

Snapshot To experience cruising at its finest, book a voyage aboard one of these luxury ships. Everything about them is exceptional—the divine food, impeccable service, spacious suites, and more.

The *Seabourn Legend,* the newest ship in the fleet, was purchased for $55 million from the now-defunct **Royal Cruise Line** in January 1996. Previously named the *Royal Viking Queen* and the *Queen Odyssey,* she is identical to **Seabourn's** other ships. **Seabourn Cruise Line,** founded by Norwegian industrialist Atle Brynestad in 1987, is now jointly owned by Brynestad and the **Carnival Corporation** (which owns **Carnival Cruise Lines**).

Itinerary The three sisters pretty much cover the globe throughout the year, cruising Alaska, the Amazon, the Arabian Sea, the Atlantic, the Baltic Sea, the British Isles, Cape Horn, the Caribbean, China, East Africa, the Indian Ocean, Japan, the Mediterranean, the Mexican Riviera, the Norwegian fjords, the Panama Canal, the Red Sea, the east and west coasts of South America, and Southeast Asia.

Typical Passengers Not only are they jet-setters, many own their own planes. Retired captains of industry, CEOs, and socialites are frequently found aboard these ships. The majority of passengers are 60 and older, although there is often a small sprinkling of people in their fifties.

Ambience & Decor A hint of the pampering to come arrives in the form of a handsome leather case carrying travel documents; a complete itinerary with everything from air transportation, transfers, and pre- or post-cruise hotel arrangements spelled out in detail; and tips on packing, information on how to dress on the ship and in port, and just about everything else you need to know before you go.

The ships' decor is as elegantly understated as that fine leather case, with rich woods and plush mauve, rose, and light blue upholstery and carpeting. Public rooms are circular and are connected with spiral staircases with brass and glass railings. (There are also well-used elevators.)

The mood is distinctively clubby, friendly despite the elite clientele. Passengers mingle easily, and many become fast friends, often making plans to sail on future cruises together.

Dress is informal for breakfast and lunch and dressy at night. Jackets and ties seem to be the preferred uniform for men in the evening, even if the suggested dress code is "casual." On formal nights, nearly every man wears a tuxedo while women dress smartly in cocktail dresses and gowns.

The predominantly European staff is exceptional, with an honest-to-goodness "never say no" approach. Cases in point: the maître d' who went ashore to fetch not only a preferred brand of coffee, but a special pressed-coffee pot, for a couple of fussy java drinkers, and the chef who ordered ground turkey meat to please a passenger concerned about cholesterol.

Cabins The only thing these ships lack are veranda suites such as you find on **Silversea** and **Royal Viking** vessels. But all suites have huge picture windows and window sills large enough to accommodate two people seated on some pillows. "A" category suites (which make up most of the ship) measure 277 square feet and are furnished with two comfortable beds that convert to one queen-size, a sofa, table, desk/vanity, TV with VCR, walk-in closet, telephones in both the bedroom and bath, and a bathroom with tub and hand-held shower (a separate shower would be more appropriate for such a classy ship), twin sinks, big fluffy towels, terry robes, and a complete supply of toiletries and sundries (shampoo, conditioner, cotton balls, Q-tips, bath gel, sewing kit, and a selection of fine soaps). Two glasses of Champagne are delivered by the cabin stewardess upon your arrival at your seagoing home away from home.

 Megaship    **Traditional Cruise Liner**

 Sailing Ship    **Expedition Ship**

 **Ultraluxury Ship**

Large ships (more than 1,000 passengers): Blue
Mid-size ships (500-1,000 passengers): Green
Small ships (fewer than 500 passengers): Red

Special touches include personalized stationery provided in each suite, a self-service laundry, free drinks at the bars and lounges, and two complimentary fifths of liquor or wine and fine crystal glasses in each suite. Electronically operated blackout curtains keep the morning sun from waking travelers too soon. The intentional lack of announcements adds to the serenity of the suites.

Sports & Fitness These are not the most active of ships, except during warm-weather cruises when the sports platform is put down and passengers can swim or snorkel in the sea or climb aboard a jet ski or Zodiac inflatable boat. The small but adequate gym has four treadmills, a Stairmaster, free weights and weight machines, an aerobics floor, and steam and sauna rooms. Exercise classes (stretch, low-impact aerobics, step, body toning) are offered during days at sea. Passengers also can indulge in a massage, facial, manicure, or other beauty treatment at the adjacent salon.

Activities & Entertainment Unlike some large ships, fun is not force-fed here. Passengers are left to themselves to decide whether to read in a deck chair, attend a lecture (topics range from bridge to the upcoming ports), or just sit and smoke a good cigar.

Daytime activities are limited to bridge tournaments and lessons; darts, backgammon, Ping-Pong, chess, and team trivia competitions; sunning; sitting in one of three whirlpools; taking a dip in the tiny pool; or hanging out in the **Sky Bar** on the **Pool Deck,** where you can sit until sunset on a stool, at an umbrella table, or on a lounge chair.

There's also a small boutique with the usual duty-free goods (jewelry, beaded blouses, perfumes, nautical souvenirs, and sundries); a tiny library open around the clock, with books, magazines, and videos to borrow; and a small business center with a computer and a typewriter. When the ships are in port, complimentary transportation to the center of the city is usually provided.

Soft piano music is played in the lounges during the afternoon, with evening entertainment provided by a comedian or singer. These before- and after-dinner variety shows are staged in the main **Amundsen Lounge;** the productions are simple but entertaining nonetheless. The circular, gently tiered room with mauve and rose furnishings and carpeting also provides a nice setting for after-dinner dancing to tunes suitable to the mature clientele (younger passengers shouldn't expect anything too contemporary). The ships' **Movies Under the Stars** program offers another after-dark entertainment option; first-run and classic films are shown on a large screen set up on deck (weather permitting).

The lounges never get too crowded. The **Sky Lounge** on the uppermost deck is probably the least used, but quite pleasant, with a radar screen on a huge globe and cushy chairs. A few more people may be found in **The Club,** a cozy room with a small bar, wide windows, and a sparkling white piano as a centerpiece. The adjacent casino offers roulette, poker, and blackjack along with about a half-dozen slot machines.

Cuisine The food is continental and exceptional; meals may feature lobster right off a Maine fishing boat, halibut from Alaska, the freshest fruits and vegetables, and pastries that seem to have been lifted right off the pages of *Gourmet* magazine. Lighter fare and more ethnic dishes were recently added to the menu. Passengers may eat when and with whomever they like—there are no assigned tables or set dining times. The cozy circular restaurant offers an amiable elegance that could easily rival any five-star, on-land operation. The muted decor of the rest of the ship is continued here, with pastel and rose-colored furnishings and curtains. Tables are set with fine linen, Royal Doulton china, Robbe & Berking flatware, and Hadeland and Schott-Zwiesel crystal. The service is outstanding.

The **Veranda Cafe** on the pool deck aft provides a casual indoor/outdoor setting for the breakfast buffet (which is served until the oh-so-civilized hour of 11:30AM). Almost anything you might want for your morning meal is available: eggs prepared to order, cereal, pancakes, fresh fruit, juices, marvelous breadstuffs, yogurt, perfectly done bacon, and more. The buffet lunch (served until 2PM) is an equally appealing assortment of hot and cold dishes, literally from soup to nuts (cashews, pecans, macadamia nuts, and walnuts to sprinkle on salads or ice cream). Other items that might appear include beef goulash, grilled fish, the finest smoked salmon, freshly prepared pasta dishes, and hamburgers. Except on formal nights, the cafe is also open evenings for casual dining.

Afternoon tea is poured in the **Sky Lounge,** accompanied by finger sandwiches and wonderful pastries (chocolate raspberry torte, rich butter cookies, almond cake, eclairs). There's no buffet at midnight, but no one seems to miss it, especially since room service is always just a phone call away. And all passengers *must* experience room service on these ships at least once, particularly for dinner, which is served in courses by European hotel–trained waiters who go out of their way to accommodate any whim.

Seabourn Spirit

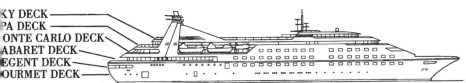

KY DECK
PA DECK
ONTE CARLO DECK
ABARET DECK
EGENT DECK
OURMET DECK

Silversea Cruises

800/722.9955

SILVERSEA

 Silver Cloud/Silver Wind
$$$$★★★★★★

Built: 1994
Passengers: 296
Size: 16,800 grt
Cabins: 148
Outside: 148
Inside: 0
Suites: 148
Wheelchair Accessible: 2 on *Silver Wind*
Registry: Bahamian/Italian
Officers/Crew: Italian/European
Tipping Policy: Gratuities included in fare; no additional tips expected
Smoking Policy: Restricted to designated smoking sections; cigarettes available free of charge at bars

Snapshot Passengers love these ships so much that, without prompting, they launch into paeans during casual conversations on the deck or at the bar. Most are veteran seafarers who have been on **Seabourn** or **Royal Viking** ships, or **Cunard**'s *Sea Goddess I* and *II* and insist these are the simply the best. And we have to agree. For food, service, and style, it doesn't get much better. Everything is included in the fare, including gratuities, port charges, airport transfers, wine, liquor, soft drinks, and one **Silversea Experience** land excursion. A major advantage over their competition (**Seabourn** ships and the *Sea Goddesses*) is the abundance of verandas—about 75 percent of all staterooms offer this popular feature.

Itinerary These twin sister ships cover the globe, offering cruises of different durations on the waters of Africa, the Baltic Sea, Canada, Europe, the Mediterranean Sea, New England, South America, the South Pacific (including Australia and New Zealand), and Southeast Asia throughout the year.

Typical Passengers The shipboard population is composed of sophisticated, very well-traveled, nattily dressed, and usually quite wealthy middle-aged and older couples (and a few singles) from all over the world, particularly England, Germany, and the US. Most are experienced cruisers.

Ambience & Decor "Comfortable elegance" best describes these stylish, all-inclusive, all-suite ships. Sleek on the outside, exquisitely appointed inside, they have teak decks and interiors featuring cherry wood, brass trim, etched-glass doors, fresh floral arrangements, and expensive art.

Shipboard life is relaxed and sociable, and passengers meet and mix with an easy sense of conviviality. Traditional cruise attire is the norm, casual by day, dressy at night. On formal nights, most men wear tuxedos and women don gowns or fancy cocktail dresses.

Italian captains head international staffs composed mostly of career cruise personnel who pride themselves on exceptional service. The waiters, bartenders, and cabin stewardesses have all worked on other luxury liners or in fine hotels and know the proper way to keep guests happy. Charming concierges handle any request, from arranging taxis or limos in port to fulfilling any onboard desire (having dinner, flowers, or videos sent to a cabin, taking care of ironing or laundry, etc., etc., etc.).

As do other cruise lines of this caliber, **Silversea** offers a multitude of services and perks aimed at making their clients feel pampered. The special treatment starts long before the ship sails, when cruise documents arrive in an expensive zippered leather case, complete with a comprehensive booklet outlining everything travelers need to know about their impending journey.

Cabins Cruise ship accommodations don't get much more comfortable than this. All the staterooms are suites measuring a roomy 294 square feet, and three-quarters of the units boast private teak deck verandas with floor-to-ceiling glass doors. Among

Silver Cloud

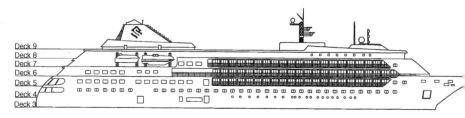

Deck 9
Deck 8
Deck 7
Deck 6
Deck 5
Deck 4
Deck 3

the standard features in each suite are two twin beds than can convert to one queen-size, Frette linen bedsheets and soft Frette terry robes, a large walk-in closet with drawers and plenty of hanging space, a desk supplied with personalized stationery, a separate vanity with makeup mirror, a telephone for direct dialing the outside world (if you're so inclined), TV with VCR, a coffee table that converts to a dining table (on which to enjoy full meals, not just snacks), and a gorgeous marble bathroom with a tub and shower, sink, and medicine cabinet.

You are greeted in your cabin with a chilled bottle of French Champagne, fresh flowers, and canapés. Your mini-refrigerator is stocked with all your favorite beverages—from Diet Coke to Chardonnay—at no extra charge. At your disposal are 24-hour room service and an attentive European stewardess who will bring extra towels or more Champagne, assist with laundry, and in other ways make your cabin more comfortable and your cruise more pleasant. In short, you've found nirvana on the high seas.

Sports & Fitness Each ship has a nice, long pool perfect for lap swimming; a good jogging deck (seven times around equals a mile); a small fitness room equipped with two treadmills (they could use more), five exercise bicycles, one Technogym (for a full-body workout), and free weights; and an exercise floor where well-trained fitness instructors hold excellent aerobics classes. Adjacent to the workout rooms are separate men's and women's locker rooms with steam baths, saunas, and showers (they're also thoughtfully supplied with toiletries and robes for passengers to wear back to their staterooms). A **Steiner** beauty salon offers pricey head-to-toe beauty treatments.

Activities & Entertainment The two ships offer identical diversions and entertainment venues. Daytime offerings include bingo, bridge, board games, audience-participation quiz shows, and a variety of classes and lectures (on a recent cruise, passengers could attend a lecture on "Voodoo Ecstasy and Rastafari Agony," take Italian lessons, and tackle tap dancing all in the same day). There's a small, handsome library with books and videos to borrow and a computer and printer to use, and, for shoppers, **Allders Boutique** carries everything from dress shoes and designer frocks to T-shirts, stuffed animals, costume jewelry, perfume, cosmetics, and cameras—not exactly at bargain prices, but tax- and duty-free. (Most of the moisturizers and face products, for example, were about the same price as on shore, save the sales tax.)

A nice touch is the complimentary launderette stocked with detergent and fabric softeners for passengers who prefer doing their own wash. (For an additional charge, the crew will take care of laundry and dry cleaning for you.)

The hot spot for daytime socializing is the **Pool Bar** on the top deck, where passengers gather for glasses of Champagne, soft drinks, or friendly banter with the amiable barkeep. **The Piano Bar** comes alive during tea time and cocktail hour, when the resident pianist performs.

Later, every stool at **The Bar** is filled with the pre-dinner crowd. The handsome room, with a circular cherry-wood bar, cushy chairs and sofas, and wide windows, is a favorite gathering spot. There's a small band and dance floor, but passengers seem to prefer chatting over fox trotting on these ships. (Gentleman hosts are on board to serve as dance partners or just pleasant company for women traveling alone.)

There is nightly entertainment, but it's nothing flashy—puppet shows, magic acts, or song-and-dance duos are the norm. There's also a very compact casino with roulette and blackjack tables and a handful of slot machines.

Cuisine Whether in the informal **Terrace Cafe,** where wonderful breakfast and luncheon buffets are spread out, and waiters carry passengers' plates to their tables, or in the restaurant, which offers impeccable service and an intimate, candle-lit setting, meals on board these ships are a real treat. The varied menu embraces French, Italian, and American cuisine along with specialties of the part of the world the ship happens to be in at the time. On a recent voyage the food was exceptional, as good as any cruise ship has to offer (**Silversea** ships and the *Sea Goddess I* and *II* are tied in this department). Both the preparation and presentation were worthy of a five-star restaurant on shore.

Menu highlights include marvelous freshly made pasta; pizza as good as Wolfgang Puck can fix; and Italian, French, and German dishes. Meals end with divine desserts (Viennese-style tortes, apple pie, buttery cookies) and/or perfectly aged cheeses with fruit, accompanied by Champagne or wine, cappuccino, espresso, or perhaps an after-dinner drink. (Complimentary wine, drinks, and even cigarettes are always available and frequently offered.)

Except on formal nights, there are also romantic theme dinners held nightly in the **Terrace Cafe.** On a recent cruise, "French Night" began with Champagne and moved on to an incredible duck salad followed by sea bass cooked to perfection, sorbet, tender lamb in a delicate sauce, and, for the finale, white and chocolate mousse, cheeses and wines, and coffee. Reservations are required for the popular theme dinners, and the tables fill up fast.

These are not ships that overwhelm you with food—there are no midnight buffets, pizzerias, or ice cream parlors. But there's always room service for between-meal snacks, and each evening before dinner Scandinavian stewardesses deliver plates of tempting canapés to the suites.

Full meals are also served in the comfort of the suites—course by course, of course. The same Limoges china (Bernardaud and Villeroy & Boch), Frette napkins, Baccarat crystal, and Christofle flatware found in the dining room grace your stateroom table.

Large ships (more than 1,000 passengers): Blue
Mid-size ships (500-1,000 passengers): Green
Small ships (fewer than 500 passengers): Red

Star Clippers

800/442.0551

STAR CLIPPERS

  Star Clipper/Star Flyer

$$★★★★★

Built: 1992/1991

Passengers: 170

Size: 2,298 grt

Cabins: 85

Outside: 81

Inside: 4

Suites: 0

Wheelchair Accessible: 0

Registry: Luxembourg

Officers/Crew: European/International

Tipping Policy: $8 per passenger per day suggested (a bit steep considering most meals are self-service buffets, and there is no food or meal service in cabins). Tips are pooled for the entire crew, with the exception of bar personnel (a 12.5 percent service charge is added to all bar bills)

Smoking Policy: Prohibited in cabins and restricted to designated smoking sections in dining rooms; allowed anywhere on deck

Snapshot Replicas of the rakish vessels that once combed the seas from China to Baltimore, these are four-masted, square-rigged clipper ships. Built in the early 1990s, they were the first passenger sailing vessels to be classified by Lloyds since the early 1900s. The tallest of today's tall ships, they have masts that loom more than 220 feet above the deck. The identical sisters have no entertainment lounges, casinos, beauty salons, gyms, or movie theaters—the thrills they offer come from gliding across the water under full sail and dropping anchor at pristine ports where larger vessels can't go.

Itinerary The *Star Clipper* sails Caribbean waters in winter and the Mediterranean in summer. The *Star Flyer* plies the Aegean during the summer months and the waters of Thailand in the winter.

Typical Passengers Adventuresome and with a passion for sailing, passengers range in age from mid-twenties to mid-sixties and hail from all over the world (although most are from the United States). Note: Because of the steep stairs that lead to the

upper decks and down to the launches that take passengers to shore, these ships are not recommended for the physically challenged or elderly.

Ambience & Decor Unlike their 19th-century ancestors (the clipper-ship era came to an abrupt halt in 1869 with the opening of the Suez Canal), these ships are equipped with stabilizers, electricity, a 1,500-horse-power engine for when the wind won't cooperate, modern sail-handling equipment, power winches to stretch the sails, air conditioning and smoke detectors, and an up-to-date galley. But in spite of these modern amenities, the ships retain the appearance of traditional clippers, with teak, mahogany, brass fixtures, and nautical details throughout.

The mood and attire are both informal. No dressy clothing is required; there are no formal dinners, and casual clothing—even jeans—is acceptable in the evening.

Don't expect the level of service found on bigger cruise ships. There's no room service, and the deck steward doubles as the bartender; if you can catch his eye, he'll fetch you drinks (which, by the way, are reasonably priced). German captains oversee an international (Filipino, German, Turkish, Russian, Swedish) 50-member crew.

Cabins For the seafaring types who pick these ships, cabins are just a place to sleep at night. Nonetheless, the staterooms are comfortable and well-designed, albeit small (about 120 square feet). As is appropriate for clipper-ship accommodations, they have mahogany furnishings and brass lighting fixtures (two lamps placed on either side of the mahogany vanity mirror resemble kerosene lanterns). All but two units have portholes.

Each cabin has twin beds that can convert to a double (in some cases, however, the double bed is flush against the wall, making it difficult for the sleeper on that side to maneuver out of bed easily), a tiny TV, telephone, and just enough storage space to accommodate the casual wardrobe appropriate for these cruises. The bathrooms are small and equipped with showers (no tubs). As a water conservation measure, the faucets in both the shower and sink turn off every 30 seconds, which takes some getting used to. (You have to press a bar for each half-minute of water, although you can do so as many times as needed.) Lighting is dim in both bathrooms and cabins, but there are adequate reading lights over the beds. Cabin stewards are rather elusive, but they do keep things neat and clean.

Sports & Fitness An exercise class is held each morning on the **Tropical Deck,** but nobody showed up during a recent cruise. Most passengers prefer to get their exercise on and in the water—swimming, snorkeling, scuba diving, windsurfing, and boating (banana boats and inflatable Zodiacs are available). These ships offer one of the most extensive water-sports programs of any cruise ship; with the exception of scuba diving, all nautical activities are included in the fare. Trained instructors always accompany passengers on water-sports outings.

Star Clipper

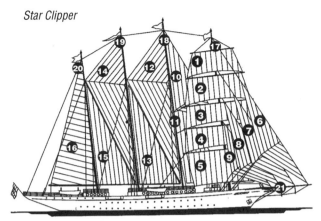

1. Upper Topgallant
2. Lowere Topgallant
3. Upper Topsail
4. Lower Topsail
5. Fore Course
6. Flying Jib
7. Outer Jib
8. Inner Jib
9. Fore Staysail
10. Topgallant Staysail
11. Main Staysail
12. Main Fisherman
13. Mizzen Staysail
14. Mizzen Fisherman
15. Jigger Staysail
16. Spanker
17. Fore Mast
18. Main Mast
19. Mizzen Mast
20. Jigger Mast
21. BowSprit

Both ships are certified by the **Professional Association of Diving Instructors (PADI),** the international regulatory body for scuba diving, as official dive centers. This means passengers can earn official scuba certification during their cruise.

Two tiny swimming pools on deck round out the list of sports facilities.

Activities & Entertainment The main event takes place on the 11,400 square-foot upper deck, when the skipper turns off the engines, and the crew hoists the sails. Passengers are invited to help pull the ropes that set the 36,000 square feet of Dacron aloft—and many join in eagerly. Watching the 226-foot-high canvases billow against the blue sky and feeling the wind propel the ship along the sea is nothing short of exhilarating. Passengers sit back, sip Champagne (even if it is the cheap stuff), and soak in the magical moment.

During the day, most passengers take advantage of the ships' water-sports program (see above). Whenever the ships are docked in port or at anchor near a tropical port, passengers are offered a variety of free snorkel or beach trips, often to the most pristine spots in the area. Sometimes there are wonderful beach barbecues with tasty fish kabobs, chicken, hot dogs, hamburgers, salads, and desserts to fuel folks for an active day of beach volleyball, snorkeling, windsurfing, waterskiing, and swimming. Of course, sunbathing, sitting under a shady tree with a good book, or even napping are certainly allowed. Shore excursions operated by local companies are available for an additional fee.

The ships have no casinos, beauty salons, fitness centers, or movie theaters, but the two friendly bars on each are pleasant spots for relaxing and socializing. The **Piano Bar** and **Tropical Bar** are arranged back-to-back, with the latter facing the outside deck and the former a cozy inside room with mahogany chairs and a glass ceiling that looks into one of the swimming pools.

A handsome library, with a Belle Epoque fireplace, carved mahogany paneling, and paintings of ancient vessels, serves as a quiet reading room with a good assortment of books to borrow. The entrance is guarded by a live parrot. A tiny boutique next to the reception desk carries T-shirts, sarongs, toiletries, hats, and postcards.

There's little in the way of formal shipboard entertainment. A singing piano player makes music throughout the day, and local performers or calypso bands occasionally board when the ships are in port. For the most part, passengers make their own fun.

Cuisine Not particularly noted for their culinary efforts, the galleys do a just-adequate job (most passengers don't mind, since food is not really the focus of these cruises anyway).

The breakfast buffet includes the usual fresh fruits, cereals, bacon and eggs, and the like. The lunch time smorgasbord is pretty standard too, with salads, hot dishes (pasta, chicken curry, veal, fish, sweet-and-sour pork, and lamb seem to be the favorites), and fair pastries.

Dinner alternates between sit-down affairs and buffets and is served in the ships' handsome, nautically themed dining room, burgundy-hued and adorned with mahogany and brass. There's open seating—passengers can arrive any time between 7:30 and 10PM and sit where they please, either by themselves or with fellow shipmates at the big beige leather banquettes or large tables for eight. The food is standard American fare, and there is a small, reasonably priced wine list.

In 1970, Royal Caribbean launched its first ship, *Song of Norway,* which had 724 berths and cost $13 million to build. Fares were $48 a day ($40 a day in the off season). Today, new ships have as many as 2,600 berths and carry price tags of $250 million to $400 million. As for fares, it's possible to get a discounted cruise for $80 a day—if you shop around.

Actually heard on board:

"Does this elevator go to the front of the ship?"

89

Windstar Cruises

800/258.7245

![Ship logo] **Wind Song/
Wind Spirit/
Wind Star**

$$$★★★★★

Built: 1987/1988/1986
Refurbished: 1996/1995/1996
Passengers: 148
Size: 5,350 grt
Cabins: 74
Outside: 74
Inside: 0
Suites: 1
Wheelchair Accessible: 0 (and no elevators)
Registry: Bahamas
Officers/Crew: European/International
Tipping Policy: No tips required, but "rewarding superior service" suggested (and envelopes are put out at the end of the cruise for this purpose)
Smoking Policy: Restricted to designated smoking sections

Snapshot These computer-operated, 440-foot, four-masted sailing ships offer a smooth ride, especially when the captain raises the billowy white sails. A vacation aboard one of these stylish vessels is sure to be a wonderful experience for active types, water buffs, and anyone who enjoys exploring unblemished beaches and remote areas where larger ships cannot navigate. Bring plenty of film.

Itinerary *Wind Song,* which has been cruising around the French Polynesian Islands since July 1987, is scheduled to move in December 1997 to Costa Rica, where it will offer weeklong cruises from November through March. Her sister ships will continue to sail the Mediterranean and the Greek and Turkish Isles in summer and the Caribbean in winter.

Typical Passengers Active, sophisticated travelers who enjoy the good life also enjoy these cruises. They tend to be young or young at heart, with most in their thirties, forties, and fifties. Many are scuba aficionados who choose these ships for the super diving opportunities and watersports. These cruises are not appropriate for small children (not enough to keep them amused) or the physically challenged (no elevators on board).

Ambience & Decor The identical yachtlike ships have a unique layout; on each, the entrance hall/reception area, restaurant, shop, and lounge are all next to each other on **Deck 3,** while staterooms are down below on **Decks 1** and **2.** The decor is nautical, with lots of wood, brass trim, and colorful fabrics. Art adorns the walls and fresh floral arrangements are scattered throughout, including the cabins.

The mood on board is low-key and casual. Particularly nice is the relaxed dress code, which allows cruisers to be as cool and comfortable as they like (most wear tasteful casualwear). Forget your jackets, suits, and tuxedos, men—you won't need them.

The personable British captains keep a high profile and allow passengers open access to the bridge. An accommodating international crew of 88 keep the ships in tiptop shape.

Wind Song

![Side-view schematic of the Wind Song showing the four-masted sailing ship with dimensions 204' height and 440' length]

204'

440'

Cabins The 185-square-foot cabins are surprisingly comfortable for ships this size. Creatively designed, they feature cleverly concealed shelves and storage bins. The bedroom is decorated in white with birch trim; two lively pieces of art hang on the wall, and mirrors give the illusion of added space. Two twin beds that can convert to queen-size are covered in colorful spreads. Each stateroom has two closets (one with drawers), a large vanity console with pull-up mirror and shelves below, a pull-up table, safe, telephone, mini-bar, large TV with VCR, a CD player, and two portholes. Bathrooms are small but ingeniously designed for maximum space efficiency, and the cylindrical double-spray shower offers the best water pressure at sea. There are two large medicine cabinets and lots of shelves. Toiletries (chamomile shampoo, ginseng body lotion, mouthwash, etc.) and terry robes are provided, as is an inefficient hair dryer (bring your own). Accommodating Indonesian stateroom staffers keep cabins clean and tidy and happily tend to any request.

Sports & Fitness Retractable marina platforms, which are open whenever the ships anchor offshore (depending on surf conditions), are the most popular spots for swimmers and aquatic-sports aficionados. Passengers can dive directly into the ocean, windsurf, water-ski, go kayaking, ride a banana boat, or go scuba diving or snorkeling. (The use of all water-sports gear, except scuba equipment, is complimentary.) Other sports facilities include a minuscule pool, a very popular Jacuzzi, and a compact gym with a small collection of exercise machines. Although the top deck circles the ship, it's not ideal for jogging or walking since you have to navigate around tables and passengers. A tiny salon provides basic head-to-toe beauty services (prices are slightly lower than the inflated rates charged by most shipboard salons).

Activities & Entertainment There are no organized daytime activities other than the shore excursions—which just about everybody takes. In tropical ports, launches or Zodiacs often take passengers to local beaches. A well-attended weekly beach party barbecue takes place at some pristine spot on the Caribbean and is usually lots of fun.

The lounge, with its dance floor, bandstand, and cozy bar, is the focal point of each ship and the site of most social events, beginning with the captain's "welcome aboard" Champagne party (there is also an open bar during this fete). Pre-dinner cocktails and complimentary hors d'oeuvres are served in the lounge to musical accompaniment; on some evenings the chef prepares special hors d'oeuvres such as crab cakes and sushi here.

Nightly shows are also staged in the lounge. They differ from ship to ship but usually feature a singer and small band or musical trio. Occasionally local entertainers and dance troupes come on board to perform.

Each ship also offers a popular pool bar that's often open late into the night; a small casino with slot machines and blackjack and poker tables; and a library stocked with a great selection of videos, CDs, and books. About four movies are available at any given time on stateroom TV sets.

Cuisine With menus created by Los Angeles superchef Joachim Splichal, you would expect more consistency in the cuisine. On the contrary, some dishes are outstanding, while others leave something to be desired, although this seems to depend on the chef. Breakfast and lunch are served buffet-style in the glass-enclosed, cylindrical, top-deck verandas; passengers have the choice of eating inside or out on the deck. Breakfast is well presented with wonderful selections of fresh fruits (including papaya, raspberries, pineapple, melon, and mangos), cereals, eggs and omelettes prepared to order, waffles, pancakes, lox and bagels, and more. The lunch buffet has a different ethnic theme (Mexican, Indonesian, Italian, etc.) each day. Afternoon tea features a variety of sandwiches and sweets.

Dinner is in the ships' charming dining rooms with open seating. (Once or twice a cruise a special theme night barbecue is held up on deck.) The dinner menu is heavy on fresh fish (seared ahi tuna, grilled salmon, swordfish, Caribbean white fish, halibut) and shellfish; the seafood strudel of lobster, scallops, mussels, king crab, and shrimp with a lobster/papaya sauce is exceptional. In addition, there's always a meat selection and usually a pasta dish, as well as vegetarian options. A "Sail Light" menu is featured at all meals. Whether you order from the menu or request a special dish, the waiters gladly oblige. The wine list offers excellent choices from all over the world. Full-course meals also will be delivered to cabins during normal dining hours; for between-meal snacks, a limited room service menu is available.

A program called "Cigars under the Stars" allows passengers to purchase an after-dinner cigar and cognac or whiskey on the open pool deck when the ship is under sail.

Bests

Barbara Sloane
Personal Assistant, Writer, Proofreader

Visiting **Bali,** one of the most beautiful places on earth, on the *Golden Princess,* and spending a long afternoon at the **Amandari Resort** in **Ubud.** It's a very private tranquil and magnificent setting overlooking rice fields, about an hour's drive from the sea. And for a price, one can even rent a room for the day.

Ashore in **Singapore**, lunching at the legendary **Raffles Hotel** in the **Tiffin Room** and ordering at least one of the Singapore slings. Afterwards, take a stroll in the hotel's beautiful gardens.

Being totally decadent one evening on board ship—calling room service for a sumptuous meal of Champagne, caviar, and lobster and dining under the stars on your own private balcony, as soft music plays in the background. It doesn't get much more romantic than this!

A Cruise Ship Directory

Though not among the "Top Ships" (see page 66), the following vessels (rated one to four stars) are among the most popular cruise ships in the world. Representing a full range of size and price categories, they offer a variety of shipboard experiences. Together they are largely responsible for the ever-growing popularity of a cruise vacation.

This section makes selecting a ship as simple as ABC. Each entry includes all you need to know about the ship's:

Ambience, which takes into account decor, service, dress code, and the overall shipboard mood;

Basics such as cabins and public spaces, sports and fitness facilities and programs, and entertainment options; and

Cuisine, including the type and quality of food served, the dining room, alternative restaurants and other eateries, buffets, and room service.

Abercrombie & Kent

800/863.9376

 Explorer

$$$$★★★

Built: 1969

Refurbished: 1992

Passengers: 100

Size: 2,398 grt

Cabins: 56

Outside: 56

Inside: 0

Suites: 2

Wheelchair Accessible: 0 (there are no elevators either, making this ship unsuitable for disabled travelers)

Registry: Liberian

Officers/Crew: European/Filipino

Tipping Policy: Gratuities included in the fare; no additional tips expected

Smoking Policy: Prohibited in the dining room and lecture hall

Snapshot This charming little expedition vessel, formerly the *Lindblad Explorer*, was purchased and refurbished by **Abercrombie & Kent** in 1992. Designed to maneuver narrow channels, coves, and backwaters, it specializes in no-frills adventure/ educational cruises for active travelers.

Itinerary True to its name, the *Explorer* heads for remote and exotic shores, including the Antarctic and the Amazon, and offers charter cruises all over the world. Trips are of varying lengths, seven days or longer.

Typical Passengers Well-traveled, affluent adventure seekers choose this ship. Quite a few are repeat passengers who have met before on previous voyages, and most are well past retirement age, although younger folks with a thirst for adventure (and the financial means to quench it) do climb on board from time to time. Sybarites and sun worshipers will feel out of place here—most passengers much prefer attending lectures or exploring ports to sunning by the small onboard swimming pool.

Ambience Posh it's not, but who cares when you're venturing to parts unknown? The decor is nothing special, and the mood is definitely cerebral— educational programs are well attended and the reference library is much used. Dress is always designer-casual (lots of Ralph Lauren and Polo attire). European officers supervise a crew of more than 60, and the service is sublime.

Basics Staterooms are simple. The standard cabins are tiny (about 80 square feet) and have two lower berths, a dresser, two small closets, a long, narrow window, and a compact bathroom with a shower and sink. There are also seven larger cabins and two suites (about 150 square feet) that are worth the splurge (when budget allows). Both offer separate sitting areas, queen-sized beds, small bathrooms with showers, refrigerators, and two double windows.

Public areas are basic as well. In addition to a well-stocked library, there's a bar/lounge (the ship's only gathering spot), a pint-sized health club with a limited amount of equipment, a small sauna, a pool and sunbathing area on deck, and a hair salon.

There are no slot machines or flashy shows— entertainment comes in the form of films on local flora, fauna, geology, and marine life; lectures by noted anthropologists, historians, and environ-mentalists; and excursions to exotic ports. Explora-tions take place aboard inflatable landing craft called Zodiacs. A typical day might be spent gliding past glaciers or walking through a rain forest with an expert guide.

Cuisine The American/continental food is nicely prepared and tasty. Breakfast and lunch are served buffet-style, while dinner is a sit-down, single-seating affair in the simple-but-cheerful dining room. Room service is available during regular meal times.

American Canadian Caribbean Line

800/556.7450

 Caribbean Prince/ Grande Caribe/ Mayan Prince/ Niagara Prince

$★

Built: 1983/1997/1992/1994

Refurbished: 1989 (*Caribbean Prince*)

Passengers: 76/96/92/84

Size: 89/99/99/95 grt

Cabins: 38/48/46/42

Outside: 32/39/44/40

Inside: 6/7/2/2

Suites: 0

Wheelchair Accessible: 0

Registry: American

Officers/Crew: American

Tipping Policy: $10 to $12 per passenger per day suggested

Smoking Policy: None

Snapshot A quartet of yacht-like ships, they offer affordable educational/adventure cruises and fairly funky facilities.

Itinerary Caribbean and Panama Canal cruises are offered in winter; trips on the Great Lakes, Canada, and along the Northeast coast are featured the rest of the year. The *Grande Caribe,* which debuted in 1997, makes coastal cruises to locales ranging from Labrador to the Amazon. Ten-day, 12-day, and longer sailings are available.

Typical Passengers Mature (60 or older) travelers who enjoy offbeat places and don't mind roughing it select these ships. Luxury-seekers look elsewhere.

Ambience The no-frills facilities are simple—comfort is not the top priority here. The atmosphere is friendly, dress is casual, and the service is good.

Basics The stark cabins are small and definitely not for claustrophobes (only 80 square feet). Some have upper and lower berths, and others have two lower beds that can convert to a double. The tiny bathrooms are cramped with the bare essentials: wash basin, shower, and commode. Opt for one of the slightly bigger cabins (about 88 square feet) if possible; they cost $20 or so more per day.

The ships have no fitness centers, pools, casinos, entertainment lounges, or shops. The out-of-the-way ports (in Belize and Honduras, for example) are the main attractions. Swimmers also love the easy accessibility to sea (you can dive right off the bow and paddle around in the ship's dock area).

Cuisine American-style fare is served in one seating in the rather nondescript dining room. No liquor is available on board, but passengers are allowed to bring their own. There's no room service, snack bar, or midnight buffet, but snacks are available 24 hours a day—cookies, fruit, muffins, beverages, and the like are set out in baskets throughout the ship .

American Hawaii Cruises

800/765.7000

 Independence

$★★

Built: 1951

Refurbished: 1994

Passengers: 818

Size: 30,090 grt

Cabins: 421

Outside: 203

Inside: 218

Suites: 37

Wheelchair Accessible: 2

Registry: American

Officers/Crew: American

Tipping Policy: About $9 per passenger per day suggested (which we feel is too high)

Smoking Policy: Prohibited in public rooms; smoking is allowed on deck and in cabins only

Snapshot Built in the 1960s and spruced up for the 1990s, this luxury liner offers a relaxed, hassle-free way to explore four heavenly Hawaiian islands.

Itinerary Three-, four-, and seven-day cruises from Honolulu to Kauai, Maui, and Hawaii (the Big Island) are offered year-round; overnight stays in Kauai and Maui are available.

Typical Passengers The *Independence* attracts first-time visitors to Hawaii and honeymooners of all ages. Most of the passengers are in their thirties or older. A well-run children's program makes it ideal for families.

Ambience Some much-needed refurbishments in 1996 added a real Hawaiian flavor to the ship's decor, with island art and artifacts, vintage Hawaiian travel posters, colorful floral furnishings, and lots of tropical foliage. Don't expect luxury, though, or great service. This is a very casual, friendly, and family-oriented ship.

Basics The lovely solarium cabins and suites are the best choices; they're bigger than the standard staterooms and airier and brighter thanks to good-sized windows. But the standard accommodations are comfortable. Rooms range in size from 95 to 375 square feet and feature just the basics—twin beds and bathrooms with showers.

The assumption is that passengers will spend much of their time on shore, and the ship's design reflects this. There is, however, a nice-sized pool as well as three bars/lounges and a nightclub featuring Hawaiian-style shows performed by local talent. The **Keiki Program** offers organized activities (hula lessons, lei-making, pool parties, scavenger hunts) for children ages 5 to 12; the **Summer Surf Club** features beach volleyball, pool games, disco and karaoke parties, and folk crafts workshops for teenagers.

Cuisine The food is sometimes wonderful, sometimes not, but still greatly improved over what it was only a few years ago. Stick with simple dishes. Dinner is served in the charming and casual dining room; there are two seatings. There are also buffets at lunch and midnight. Room service is limited.

Carnival Cruise Lines
800/327.9501

Carnival Destiny
$$★★★★

Built: 1996

Passengers: 3,400

Size: 101,353 grt

Cabins: 1,321

Outside: 806 outside (418 with verandas)

Inside: 515

Suites: 40 suites and 8 penthouse suites

Wheelchair Accessible: 0

Registry: Panamanian

Officers/Crew: International

Tipping Policy: About $8 per passenger per day suggested

Smoking Policy: Prohibited in dining rooms and entertainment lounges; restricted to designated smoking sections in all other public areas

Snapshot A larger version of **Carnival**'s "Superliner" ships, the $400 million *Destiny* looms 207 feet (55 feet taller than the Statue of Liberty) and is nearly three football fields long. Launched in November 1996, this will be the largest ship afloat until **Princess Cruises'** 1997 launch (scheduled at press time) of its 104,000-ton *Grand Princess*.

(The 101,000-grt, 2,642-passenger *Triumph*, sister ship to the *Destiny*, is scheduled to be launched in 1999.)

Typical Passengers The ship attracts first-time cruisers, young partyers, and a few middle-aged and older folk. Note: Passengers under 21 must be accompanied by someone over 25.

Itinerary Too big to fit through the Panama Canal, the *Destiny* will stay based in Miami, offering seven-day eastern and western Caribbean cruises.

Ambience It's big, but it doesn't feel *too* big. In addition to the obvious—spacious public rooms and cabins, expansive deck space, and variety of bars and entertainment venues—there are plenty of small, intimate spaces as well.

The decor is toned down compared to the interiors architect **Joe Farcus** created for **Carnival**'s "Fantasy Class" vessels, but the *Destiny* is still far from subdued. Farcus used lots of polished stone and shiny metals, as well as more traditional materials such as brass, wood, and glass. Plenty of tiny white lights and an abundance of neon ensure that no room looks *too* traditional.

The ship's mood is similarly exuberant—passengers are active, sociable vacationers looking for fun in the sun and lively nightlife. Attire is casual, but some passengers do break out the tuxes and spangled cocktail dresses on formal nights.

On an inaugural cruise, crew members were friendly and willing, but the service was erratic.

Basics Decked out in pleasing shades of apricot, peach, and mauve, *Destiny*'s staterooms are more plush than the rather spartan ones on older **Carnival** ships. Standard ocean-view staterooms measure a roomy 220 to 260 square feet and feature twin beds that can convert to a double bed, a sofa and table, safe, two closets, a vanity, lots of storage space, a bathroom with a large shower and hair dryer (but no toiletries), and an interactive TV system that enables passengers to order room service, shop, select pay-per-view movies, and more.

About 60 percent of all staterooms have an ocean view, and more than half of the ocean-view cabins have verandas. A nice feature: Balconies have glass front panels that allow for unobstructed views.

Forty full suites (340 square feet) and eight penthouse suites (430 square feet) offer such extras as a separate sitting area, a bar and refrigerator, and a whirlpool. There are also family staterooms (230 square feet), located near the children's facilities.

The main **Lido Deck** pool area is the hot spot during the day, with a lively swim-up bar, the ship's largest pool (still rather small), and two very popular Jacuzzis. The multitiered deck is arranged around a stage where a calypso band plays almost nonstop during the daylight hours. The lounge chairs that line the tiers are usually filled with sun worshipers.

> "It needed a few days after the taking of your departure for a ship's company to shake down into their places, and for the soothing, deep-water ship routine to establish its beneficent sway."
>
> Joseph Conrad, *Mirror of the Sea*

Above the main pool area is a two-deck high, 214-foot spiral water slide, which ends in a "deceleration" area (so that people in the nearby pool and Jacuzzi don't get splashed). The **Lido Deck** aft has another pool, two Jacuzzis, and swim-up bar, and can be covered by a telescoping glass roof in inclement weather.

For those who want to sit outside in peace and quiet, there are open-air promenades with wooden deck chairs on both sides of the ship on **Deck 3,** just 39 feet above the water.

Another popular place is the **Nautica Spa;** at 15,000 square feet, it's the largest fitness facility on any cruise ship. The facility also features floor-to-ceiling windows, 36 exercise machines, two whirlpools, an aerobics room, and a juice bar. The adjacent **Steiner** salon has steam rooms and saunas with ocean views and offers a broad range of spa treatments. There's also an outdoor jogging track (10 laps equal one mile).

Other shipboard facilities include three shops, a video arcade (the simulated ski race is a lot of fun), and a library. The schedule of games and activities includes everything from cooking demonstrations to pillow fights.

The ship's children's area includes a small playroom and an outdoor playground with a wading pool. **Camp Carnival** offers activities and social events for four age groups.

The *Destiny* also boasts the largest cruise ship theater; the **Palladium** spans three decks and seats 1,500. Designed to resemble a European opera house, it features gold and beige brocades, brass railings, and a Viennese chandelier.

Shows are Las Vegas–style, but not Las Vegas caliber, although they are crowd-pleasing. There are two performances each night as well as a popular late-night show featuring a comedian, magician, or singer (get there early).

The **Millionaire's Club,** billed as the most enormous casino at sea, is the *Destiny* at its most frenetic, with a dizzying decor and ever-flashing neon. Covering 9,000 square feet, it features 324 slot machines and 23 tables games.

The ship also has nearly a dozen bar/lounges. Among the most popular night spots is the flashy (literally) **Point After** disco, which features 567 video screens, and the **Apollo Lounge,** with a microphone at every table for passengers who want to belt out a tune. Oddly, the decor of the latter is classical—walls are covered with handmade Italian mosaics inspired by ancient Greek vases. The coolest place on board is the **Downbeat Lounge,** a small jazz club decorated with huge musical instruments.

Cuisine The menu is international and varied, but the quality of the fare is inconsistent. Dishes on a recent cruise ranged from quite tasty roast veal to a nearly inedible salmon fillet.

The identical bilevel **Universe** and **Galaxy Dining Rooms** feature wide windows and the most restrained decor on the ship, with an elegant beige

and gold color scheme, brass railings, etched glass, and wood trim. Meals are served at two seatings.

Informal meals and snacks are available day and night at the two-level **Lido Deck Sun & Sea Restaurant.** The restaurant is actually composed of several eateries; in addition to breakfast and lunch buffets it features a 24-hour pizzeria; a grill serving hamburgers, hot dogs, and chicken sandwiches; and two take-out windows, one featuring Chinese stir-fry dishes and the other pasta. The ship also has a patisserie, and a limited room service menu is available around-the-clock.

Celebration/Holiday/Jubilee
$★★★

Built: 1987/1985/1986

Passengers: 1,486/1,452/1,486

Size: 47,262/46,052/47,262 grt

Cabins: 743/720/743

Outside: 453/447/453

Inside: 290/273/290

Suites: 10 each

Wheelchair Accessible: 14/15/14

Registry: Bahamian

Officers/Crew: International

Tipping Policy: $7 to $8 per passenger per day suggested

Smoking Policy: Prohibited in dining rooms and entertainment lounges; restricted to designated smoking sections in all other public areas

Snapshot Floating Las Vegas–style hotels, these liners offer fun cruises for folks of all ages at the most affordable prices in the industry.

Itinerary *Holiday* and *Jubilee* make three-, four-, and seven-day trips to the Mexican Riviera from Los Angeles; the *Celebration* departs for seven-day Caribbean cruises from Miami.

Typical Passengers The fun-seekers are primarily singles and couples in their twenties, but people of all ages will feel comfortable on these ships. If you have children, by all means bring them along. Note: **Carnival** does not accept passengers under 21 unless they are accompanied by someone over 25.

Ambience These razzle-dazzle ships offer a flashy, high-tech, whimsical decor in keeping with their festive atmosphere. Among the fanciful public rooms are a grotto bar under an undulating azure-colored "undersea" tile ceiling, a piano bar that once was a real piano, and a million-dollar entertainment center with virtual-reality video machines.

The prevailing attitude can be stated in six words: party, party, party, fun, fun, fun. Attire is casual, of course, but most passengers dress with flair, with styles ranging from hip to outrageous.

The service in the public rooms and restaurant is efficient, but hardly exceptional, while bothersome deck stewards are constantly trying to sell prepared cocktails (which are overpriced and often watery because of melted ice).

Basics Standard cabins are a comfortable 190 square feet and provide a nice respite from the glitz and nonstop action of the public rooms and decks. They have beds that convert to doubles or queen-size, fairly large windows, good storage space, and bathrooms with showers (suites have bathtubs as well). Television sets offer closed-circuit movies day and night (there's no movie theater on board). These are budget ships, so don't expect frills. All you get are motel-size bars of soap—bring your own robe, shampoo, and toiletries. Cabins are kept spotless.

Active fun is what these ships are all about. During daylight hours, much of the action takes place out on deck, where bikini-clad sun worshipers fill the chaises. Other hot spots include the expansive **Nautica** health spas, which feature state-of-the-art exercise equipment and several well-attended exercise classes daily. Each ship also offers three somewhat small pools, two very popular Jacuzzis (site of testosterone- and beer-fueled mating dances), a "top-optional" sundeck, and a lengthy jogging track. The list of organized activities goes on and on—everything from calypso contests to trap shooting.

For children, **Camp Carnival** offers special performances, behind-the-scenes tours, and plenty of organized activities and supervised social events. But the hands-down kids' favorite is the multimedia entertainment center on the *Holiday*. It offers an ice cream parlor, a teen disco, virtual-reality video games, and lots of futuristic fun.

At night, the grown-ups come out to play and, again, the choices are many. Each ship has a massive entertainment lounge that stages productions combining Broadway style with Las Vegas flash, a grand casino, a disco, late-night cabarets, and lots of bars and lounges. Favorite haunts include: the *Celebration*'s **Trolley Bar; Smuggler's** and **The Speakeasy** on the *Jubilee;* and the Casablanca-themed **Rick's American Cafe** on the *Holiday*.

Cuisine No one will ever go hungry on these ships, each of which offers more than a dozen different eating opportunities throughout the day (including a 24-hour pizzeria). The food is more crowd-pleasing than gourmet, but it's often good, sometimes exceptional, and always plentiful. There are low-calorie and vegetarian meals on each menu.

 Megaship    **Traditional Cruise Liner**

 **Sailing Ship**   **Expedition Ship**

 Ultraluxury Ship

Large ships (more than 1,000 passengers): Blue
Mid-size ships (500-1,000 passengers): Green
Small ships (fewer than 500 passengers): Red

The dining rooms are identical and quite attractive; there are two dinner seatings. Each ship also has a very popular outdoor bar and grill open around the clock. The midnight buffets are popular with younger passengers hungry after a day of intense partying and playing. While continental breakfast is delivered to cabins upon request, it's hardly worth waiting for. The deck buffet or dining room are much better morning choices.

 ### Ecstasy/Fantasy/ Fascination/Sensation
$★★★

Built: 1991/1990/1994/1993

Passengers: 2,040

Size: 70,367 grt

Cabins: 1,020

Outside: 618 (54 with verandas)

Inside: 402

Suites: 28

Wheelchair Accessible: 20

Registry: Liberian (*Ecstasy* and *Fantasy*)/Panamanian (*Fascination* and *Sensation*)

Officers/Crew: International

Tipping Policy: $7 to $8 per passenger per day suggested

Smoking Policy: Prohibited in dining rooms and entertainment lounges; restricted to designated smoking sections in all other public areas

Snapshot The mood is high-energy and light-hearted on these identical megaliners with fun and flashy interiors.

Itinerary The ships make three- and four-day Bahamas cruises and seven-day eastern, western, and southern Caribbean cruises year-round.

Typical Passengers Young merrymakers eager to meet and mingle flock to these ships, which also attract a sprinkling of fun-loving "older" (over 30) folk. In summer the cruises are more family-oriented, with 30 to 40 percent of the passengers accompanied by children. Note: **Carnival** does not accept passengers under 21 unless they are accompanied by someone over 25.

Ambience It's all bright lights, noisy revelry, and fantasy on board these modern megaliners. Noted ship designer **Joe Farcus** sets the mood with such head-spinning touches as a Rolls Royce in a cocktail lounge and Marilyn Monroe and James Dean mannequins perched on counter stools in a 1950s-style diner.

Attire, like the atmosphere, is easygoing. Only a few men sport tuxes at the formal dinner—most wear business suits, while the women show up in cocktail dresses, some glittering with sequins and spangles. Most nights, men don jackets and women wear cocktail dresses ranging from chic and simple to outrageous minis or micro-minis. Daytime wear is very casual.

Basics When compared to the ships' glittery public areas, cabins are almost plain. (The no-frills decor is a reminder that these are, in fact, budget ships.) Measuring a comfortable 185 square feet, the standard cabin has two beds that can be moved together, two big closets, a fair amount of storage space, a TV with VCR (videos may be rented for a fee), and a small bathroom with a shower and no extras other than small bars of soap.

If your budget can handle it, spring for one of the 28 suites. At roughly 420 square feet, each has about triple the space of a standard cabin and features a private veranda; a separate sitting area with comfortable furniture, a mini-refrigerator and bar, and a TV with VCR; a bedroom with twin beds that convert to queen-size; and a big bathroom with whirlpool tub (but still no complimentary toiletries).

Onboard diversions are many and varied. There are plenty of organized activities, **Carnival**'s **Nautica Spas** boast 12,000 square feet of fitness and pampering space, and **Steiner** salons offer outrageously overpriced face and body treatments. Sun worshiping is also a popular pastime on these ships, with lots of deck space and lounge chairs on which to pursue it, including an adults-only topless sundeck. Each ship also has three pools. Also on board each are a trio of shops, a library, and a coin-operated laundry.

The ships stage Vegas-style shows nightly, with spectacular costumes and talented performers who rank among the best at sea. The lively casinos and dance clubs pulsate until the wee hours. Each ship has five bar/lounges with different fantasy themes. For example, **Cleopatra's Bar** on the *Fantasy* has a stone floor, hieroglyphics on the walls, and ancient Egyptian–style sarcophagi and statues of Egyptian gods and goddesses.

Camp Carnival amuses the youngest cruisers with tours, classes, movies, parties, and other fun stuff.

Cuisine The bountiful, crowd-pleasing fare is simple, but often quite tasty. The huge dining rooms have big portholes, low ceilings, and restrained decor (compared to the other public areas). There are two dinner seatings. The breakfast and lunch buffets are appetizingly presented and better than average for ships in this price range. In addition to a main dining room, each of the ships has a **Lido Deck** bar and grill that's open 24 hours a day, an ice cream parlor, a pastry shop, and assorted buffets available through midnight. Room service is provided around-the-clock, but since menus are somewhat limited, the dining room or the 24-hour bar and grill are better choices.

Elation/Paradise

These 70,000-grt, 2,600-passenger "Fantasy Class" ships, sisters to Ecstasy, Fantasy, Fascination, *and* Sensation *(see above) and* Imagination and Inspiration *(see below) are slated to hit the high seas in February and November 1998.*

Imagination/ Inspiration
$★★★★

Built: 1995/1996

Passengers: 2,040

Size: 70,367 grt

Cabins: 1,020

Outside: 618 (54 with verandas)

Inside: 402

Suites: 28

Wheelchair Accessible: 20

Registry: Bahamian and Panamanian

Officers/Crew: International

Tipping Policy: $7 to $8 per passenger per day suggested

Smoking Policy: Prohibited in dining rooms and entertainment lounges; restricted to designated smoking sections in all other public areas

Snapshot The fifth and sixth in **Carnival**'s series of "Fantasy Class" megaships, they're a step—and a star rating—above the rest, boasting a more elegant, classy ambience than their flashy older sisters (*Ecstasy, Fantasy, Fascination,* and *Sensation*). They offer exceptional value and a downright festive shipboard atmosphere.

Itinerary The *Imagination* makes three- and four-day Bahamas cruises and seven-day eastern and western Caribbean cruises year-round. The *Inspiration* offers seven-day southern Caribbean trips from San Juan year-round.

Typical Passengers Dominated by fun-loving, twenty-something singles, these lively ships also appeal to energetic "older" (30-plus) vacationers and families. Note: **Carnival** does not accept passengers under 21 unless they are accompanied by someone over 25.

Ambience Although the first six "Fantasy Class" ships are structurally identical and all were designed by noted ship architect **Joe Farcus**, each has its own distinct personality and style. While the older members of the Fantasy fleet are awash in neon and glitter, *Imagination* and *Inspiration* have a toned-down glamour, albeit with offbeat and humorous touches.

The *Imagination*'s public rooms have an Art Deco decor, with mosaics, Venetian glass, gold leaf, and revolving glass columns. Although as whimsical as the *Imagination*, the *Inspiration* has a slightly more sophisticated feel. Decorated in Art Nouveau style, it has etched glass, carved wood, and marble floors, modernized with pastel neon lights. As on all Fantasy fleet ships, the centerpiece of both ships is a seven-story **Grand Atrium.**

Fun is the name of the game on **Carnival** ships, and these are no exception. Most passengers party hard, stay up late, and hang out by the pool or on one of the three upper decks during the day.

In keeping with the mood, casual attire is the norm. Even on formal nights, a business suit is as dressed up as most of the men get, while the majority of women wear simple cocktail dresses (you will see the occasional outrageous mini).

Basics In contrast to the opulence of the public rooms, the cabins have a simple, toned-down look (almost too simple—a little panache would be welcome here). Measuring a comfortable 185 square feet, standard staterooms offer two beds that can be moved together, big closets, good storage space, TVs with VCRs (video rentals are available), and a small bathroom with shower. Bring your own shampoo and toiletries; only small bars of soap (like the kind found in a motel) are provided. Pack a robe, too—the ships do not furnish them. These are budget ships, so there aren't a lot of extras.

Nonetheless, the 28 suites are worth the extra fare. While not exactly luxurious, each is decorated with pretty artwork and provides about triple the living space of a standard cabin (roughly 420 square feet) as well as a private veranda. Other extras include a separate sitting area with a comfortable curved sofa, coffee table, two chairs, a mini-refrigerator, a lovely bar equipped with cocktail glasses, and a TV with VCR; a bedroom with two twin beds that convert to one queen-size, and a desk/vanity with lots of drawers; a walk-in closet; a safe; and a big bathroom with a whirlpool tub (but still only those tiny bars of soap).

Carnival's signature **Nautica Spas** provide 12,000 square feet of workout space and feature state-of-the-art exercise equipment. The aerobics classes held on the two ships are so popular that it's often necessary to sign up in advance. The ships' **Steiner** salons offer every salubrious body treatment known to the beauty world, but the services are overpriced (a 55-minute massage is $70, typical for this chain of cruise ship salons, but outrageous for budget ships).

Jogging tracks and paddle-tennis courts round out the list of the ships' sports facilities.

The three pools are the most popular spots during the day, particularly the one with the amazing 114-foot water slide, which is enjoyed by young and old alike (although it is a bit disruptive for those who just want to swim).

Sun worshiping is a favored pastime on these ships, with plenty of deck space to pursue it (including an adults-only topless sundeck). There are enough lounge chairs to go around, and deck stewards keep everyone supplied with beverages. The Jacuzzis (six per ship) are hot spots; they're often occupied by twenty-something passengers power-drinking piña coladas or big beers and searching for Mr. or Ms. Right.

Each day's schedule of events includes plenty of organized activities and games, including bingo, calypso and limbo contests, skeet shooting, and more. And the ships' colossal casinos, equipped with more than 200 slot machines and roulette, poker, blackjack, and craps tables, are almost always jumping.

But as lively as things are during the day, these ships really jump after dark. Each night brings lavish, Las Vegas-style productions featuring spectacular costumes and some of the most talented performers at sea. The entertainment lounges are themselves spectacular: The *Inspiration*'s **Paris Lounge** sparkles with polished brass, elegant curtains, and deep red carpeting and upholstery, while the *Imagination*'s **Dynasty Lounge** is an elegant, multilevel room with comfortable seats, each with an unobstructed view of the stage.

Each ship boasts a total of five bar/lounges, each of which has a different theme. On the *Inspiration*, the **Rhapsody Piano Bar** sits under a canopy of turquoise sails, the **Violins Bar** is draped in stringed instruments, and the **Chopin Grand Bar** recreates the Renaissance era with Ionic columns, Roman sculptures, and a Raphael-style mural. The **Shangri-La Lounge** is the most interesting of the *Imagination*'s bar/lounges. Contemporary but ethereal, it has graceful Ionic columns, curving aluminum walls, and gold-painted surfaces studded with sparkling "jewels."

Also on board each ship are a library, a trio of shops offering everything from casual cruisewear to perfume, jewelry, and sundries, and self-service coin-operated laundries.

For young cruisers, **Camp Carnival** offers organized activities and supervised social events as well as special performances and behind-the-scenes tours.

Cuisine The food is simple but often quite tasty (it was particularly good during an inaugural season cruise aboard the *Inspiration*), and it is available in ample portions around the clock. In addition to regular meals in the dining rooms, both ships offer at least a dozen different eating options: ice cream parlors, pastry shops, **Lido Deck** bar and grills that serve pizza 24 hours a day, and assorted buffets, which are attractively presented and well done for ships this size.

The dining rooms are big and appealing, with large windows, low ceilings, and understated decor. There are two dinner seatings.

Room service is provided around the clock, but since the menu is somewhat limited, you're better off going to the dining room or the 24-hour bar and grill for snacks or meals. (Especially if you like to start the day with something other than cereal, a roll, canned juice, and weak coffee.)

Royal Olympic Cruises' annual "Maya Equinox Cruise" to Mexico's Yucatán Peninsula is timed to coincide with the first day of spring. The highlight of the cruise is a trip to Chichén Itzá, where passengers watch the "Sun Serpent," the shadow of a snake that appears only on the vernal equinox, move down the facade of an ancient Mayan temple.

Hollywood Sets Sail

From the early days of the silver screen, Hollywood stars set sail on ocean liners, adding glamour and prestige to their chosen ships. In the 1920s, Douglas Fairbanks and Mary Pickford frolicked for photographers on board **White Star Line**'s *Olympic*, sister ship to the *Titanic*. Three decades later, the paparazzi dogged Grace Kelly as she sailed off on the *Constitution* to her fairy-tale wedding in **Monaco.** Cary Grant, Ronald Reagan, Glenn Ford, and Elizabeth Taylor are among the galaxy of stars who have lent a special twinkle to the passenger lists of ships over the years.

But Hollywood doesn't just play on cruise ships; it makes movie magic on board. Here's a survey of films set at sea:

Monkey Business (1931) The Marx Brothers are stowaways aboard a cruise ship, crashing blueblood parties and accidently foiling some thieves.

A Night at the Opera (1935) The Marx Brothers create madness and mayhem —and torment the ever-game Margaret Dumont—on a luxury liner.

Shall We Dance (1937) Fred Astaire and Ginger Rogers do their thing, this time aboard a cruise ship.

History is Made at Night (1937) Having found a new love (Charles Boyer), a divorcee (Jean Arthur) runs into trouble with her ex-husband.

Love Affair (1939) Irene Dunne and Charles Boyer meet on a cruise, fall in love, and then fall prey to tragic circumstances. The movie was remade in 1957 as *An Affair to Remember* with Cary Grant and Deborah Kerr. The *Constitution* and *Independence* (the latter still cruising the **Hawaiian Islands**) garnered roles. A 1994 remake with Warren Beatty and Annette Bening was set aboard a plane.

The Lady Eve (1941) Barbara Stanwyck and Henry Fonda meet aboard a cruise ship, and she sets out to fleece him.

Now, Voyager (1942) Bette Davis plays a repressed New Englander who meets a fascinating, but married, man on a cruise in **South America.**

Across the Pacific (1942) John Huston directed this spy story of an army officer cashiered by secret arrangement on the eve of Pearl Harbor to contact pro-Japanese sympathizers. Part of the film—with Humphrey Bogart, Sidney Greenstreet, and Mary Astor—is set on *noir*-ish freighters and cruise ships.

Journey into Fear (1942) Orson Welles plays a munitions expert threatened by assassins. He is smuggled home from **Istanbul** aboard a ship.

Titanic (1953) Personal dramas unfold aboard the ill-fated liner. Clifton Webb, Barbara Stanwyck, and Robert Wagner star.

The Last Voyage (1960) Robert Stack, George Sanders, and Dorothy Malone star in this tale of a ship that sinks when its boiler room explodes.

The Passenger (1965) A German woman aboard an ocean liner recognizes another passenger as one of the charges she oversaw when she was a concentration camp official.

Ship of Fools (1965) In this drama starring Vivien Leigh, Jose Ferrer, and George Segal, a German liner bound on a transatlantic journey leaves Veracruz in 1933 with an unusual group of passengers.

The Poseidon Adventure (1972) An all-star cast including Gene Hackman, Ernest Borgnine, Shelley Winters, Red Buttons, Leslie Nielson, Roddy McDowall, and Stella Stevens find themselves trapped when a luxury liner capsizes.

Death on the Nile (1978) Agatha Christie's Hercule Poirot (Peter Ustinov) investigates a star-studded cast of suspects (Bette Davis and David Niven among them) in the murder of an heiress. The action takes place on a luxury steamer cruising the **Nile.**

Beyond The Poseidon Adventure (1979) Rescuers reach the capsized liner, and one of them has a devious plan to plunder the vessel. This also has a cast of stars, including Telly Savalas, Karl Malden, Sally Field, Shirley Jones, and Slim Pickens.

And The Ship Sails On (1983) Directed by Federico Fellini, this is the offbeat story of what happens when a luxury liner sets sail from Naples in 1914 to scatter the ashes of an opera singer.

Table for Five (1983) A divorced dad (Jon Voigt) takes his brood on a European holiday, during which he must tell them their mother has been killed in a car accident. Some segments were filmed on **Cunard Line**'s *Vistafjord.*

Bitter Moon (1992) While on a cruise, a mild-mannered man (Hugh Grant) tries to infuse passion into his marriage but instead falls in love with another woman.

Speed 2 (1997) The sequel to the popular 1995 bomb-on-the-bus flick was filmed aboard the *Seabourn Legend.* It features Sandra Bullock.

Titanic (1997) Hollywood's fascination with the 1912 shipwreck continues. A love story starring Kate Winslet and Leonardo DiCaprio, this film may be the most expensive ever made.

Out to Sea (1997) Walter Matthau and Jack Lemmon play "gentlemen hosts" on a luxury liner. Scenes were shot aboard **Holland America Line**'s *Westerdam.*

MICHAEL STORRINGS

99

Celebrity Cruises

800/437.3111 or 800/327.9501

*This Greek-owned cruise line is an industry sleeper that has quietly become a giant in the mass cruise market since it was founded in 1989 by the **Chandris Group**. The company, which sold the Meridian in early 1997 and will launch the Mercury in late 1997, owns five luxury liners.*

Century/Galaxy

$$$★★★★★

These futuristic sister ships are among the best megaships in the mid-price range. See page 66 for a detailed description.

Horizon/Zenith

$$$★★★★

Built: 1990/1992

Passengers: 1,354/1,374

Size: 46,811/47,255 grt

Cabins: 677/687

Outside: 533/541

Inside: 144/146

Suites: 20/22

Wheelchair Accessible: 4

Registry: Liberian

Officers/Crew: Greek/International

Tipping Policy: $8 to $9 per passenger per day suggested

Smoking Policy: Prohibited in dining rooms; restricted to designated smoking sections in all other public areas

Snapshot These shipshape, well-groomed modern cruise liners are for people with Champagne taste and a beer budget. Featuring handsome public rooms, large teak decks, and comfortable cabins, they offer a friendly and affordable cruise experience.

Itinerary The *Horizon*, *Celebrity*'s flagship, offers 10- and 11-day cruises from Ft. Lauderdale to Catalina Island, Barbados, Martinique, Antigua, and St. Thomas in winter. In the summer she makes a series of 11-, 12-, and 14-night Mediterranean, North Cape, Baltic, British Isles, Western Europe, Greek Isles, Holy Land, and Black Sea cruises. In winter the *Zenith* offers seven-night trips from New York to Bermuda; in summer she offers 11-, 12-, and 14-night cruises on the Mediterranean.

Typical Passengers Cruisers of all ages and socioeconomic backgrounds spend their vacations on these ships, including families with children, youngish singles, and middle-aged and older folk.

Ambience The style and grace of these ships—with their imposing main entrances, stunning two-deck lobbies, rich teak decks, and high-gloss brass trim—make cruises aboard them seem more luxurious than the reasonable fares would suggest. The service is superior—crew members go out of their way to be accommodating.

The mood on board both ships is friendly, low-key, and family-oriented. Dress is casual by day, dressy at night.

Basics Standard 176-square-foot cabins have all the necessary creature comforts (twin beds that convert to a double, a TV, lots of closet space, a bathroom with a generous-size shower), while deluxe suites are the lap of luxury with extra space (500 square feet in all), large windows, butler service, private Jacuzzis, and more elegant appointments. The two top suites have 510 square feet to stretch out in, a Jacuzzi to unwind in, and a butler to tend to every need.

The **Olympic Health Club,** located on each ship's upper deck, has all the equipment necessary to keep passengers in shape. It's a pleasure working out in these spacious rooms, where wide windows provide a panoramic view of the sea from the treadmills and bicycles. The **AquaSpa** program of exercise classes offers daily organized workouts while the spa provides pampering in lovely treatment.

There are men and women's saunas but no steam baths. In addition to a full complement of adult activities organized by the cruise director, each ship also offers two pools, Jacuzzis, a jogging track, acres of deck space for sunning or lounging, shops, a library, and an excellent children's program.

The evening shows are standard shipboard fare, with well-produced musicals, magic acts, and comedians sharing stage time. Each ship also has a casino and four bar/lounges. **Harry's Tavern,** a replica of a Greek taverna decorated with whimsical, Mediterranean/Mexican art, is a favorite spot on both ships; also popular is the cabaret-style **Rainbow Room** on the *Zenith.* Youthful passengers like to mingle in the observation lounges on the two ships' uppermost decks.

Cuisine As is true on all **Celebrity** ships, the menu was created by Michel Roux, chef/owner of London's **Le Gavroche** restaurant, which boasts three Michelin stars. The ship chefs do an excellent job translating Roux's French-American recipes, including coquilles St-Jacques, leg of lamb, and pan-seared salmon. There are two dinner seatings in the show-stopping dining room, which has exquisitely set tables.. The popular self-service cafe up on the **Pool Deck** serves tasty dishes at breakfast and lunch. Room service is available around the clock; full meals are available in suites, while standard cabins may order light fare or continental breakfast only.

Days of Wine and Roses: Extras for Newlyweds and Other Happy Couples

All the world loves a lover, the saying goes, and that may partly explain why cruise lines pamper newlyweds with special gifts and courtesies.

Many ships offer Sunday and Monday departures, accommodating weekend weddings, and provide such complimentary goodies as a honeymooners' reception or cocktail party, Champagne, a cake, flowers, a fresh fruit basket, and mementos such as commemorative certificates, photographs, or engraved glasses. Some cruise lines present similar premiums to couples celebrating an anniversary or renewing their wedding vows.

To ensure that they receive these perks, couples should ask their travel agent to inform the cruise line of their special status at the time of booking.

In addition to freebies, special amenities packages designed for newlyweds—or for any couples who wish to treat themselves—are sold by several cruise lines. **Royal Caribbean International**, for example, offers "Crowning Touches," a package consisting of a "welcome aboard" bottle of Dom Pérignon Champagne and canapés, monogrammed terry bathrobes, an invitation to visit the bridge, a formal portrait in an engraved frame, massages or facials, and

MICHAEL STORRINGS

Champagne breakfast in bed. The **Royal Caribbean** "Royal Occasions" package includes a bottle of Moët & Chandon Champagne, a formal framed portrait, dessert served in your cabin, and Champagne breakfast in bed.

Costa Cruise Lines' honeymoon or anniversary package features a bottle of sparkling Italian wine, fresh flowers, a keepsake portrait and a silver frame, a commemorative certificate, a cocktail party with the captain, his and hers robes, and a single red rose.

Most cruise companies offer similar packages or individual gifts that can be ordered in advance by the newlywed or anniversary couple—or their family or friends. Often called "Bon Voyage Gifts," they can be purchased through a travel agent or the cruise line. A wide range of romantic treats are available, including Champagne and caviar for two, a bottle of wine or spirits, a dozen red roses or a tropical floral arrangement, imported chocolates, breakfast in bed, logo bathrobes, a formal portrait, and his and hers massages. It's even possible to purchase casino credit so the happy couple can try their luck at the blackjack tables and slot machines.

(For important questions to ask when planning a seagoing wedding trip, see **A Checklist for Honeymooners**, page 42.)

Mercury

Sister to the Century and Galaxy (see page 66), this 74,000-grt, $300-million high-tech vessel is due to be launched in late 1997. The ship will accommodate 1,870 passengers in 900 cabins (more than 30 percent with private verandas). Her special features will include two atriums and a retractable glass roof over one of three swimming pools, as well as a teen lounge and an indoor/outdoor children's area.

Clipper Cruise Line

800/325.0010

Clipper Adventurer

Scheduled to be launched in spring 1998, this 122-passenger, 4,575-grt ship will explore the Iberian Peninsula, North Africa, Scandinavia, Russia, and the Amazon.

Nantucket Clipper/ Yorktown Clipper

$$$★★★

Built: 1984/1988

Passengers: 100/138

Size: 95/97 grt

Cabins: 51/69

Outside: 51/69

Inside: 0

Suites: 0

Wheelchair Accessible: 0

Registry: American

Officers/Crew: American

Tipping Policy: About $9 per passenger per day suggested

Smoking Policy: Prohibited on board

Snapshot Built with a small, shallow draft designed specifically for coastal and inland cruises, these yacht-size clipper ships sail along some of the more provocative waterways of the Americas. Well-run, laid-back, unconventional cruises are what they're all about.

Itinerary While itineraries are subject to change, the *Nantucket* cruises the US and British Virgin Islands in winter, and Chesapeake Bay, the Great Lakes, New England, and Canada in summer. The *Yorktown* maneuvers the waterways of Alaska in summer, northern California and the Pacific Northwest in fall, and Costa Rica, the Sea of Cortes, the Orinoco River, the Grenadines, and the Caribbean in winter. Both offer cruises of varying lengths of five days or longer.

Typical Passengers These ships are the choice of well-heeled, middle-aged seafarers who like the experience of sailing (although the ships are more often power-driven than under sail).

Ambience The cruises are sophisticated, with an emphasis on nature and culture. You won't find flashy shows, gambling, or discos, but you will enjoy interesting lectures and films; wonderful port tours conducted by onboard naturalists, historians, and other experts; snorkel or scuba excursions; and friendly traveling companions. In keeping with the simple, nautical decor on these sailing ships, dress is natty/casual, with no formalwear required. The young and enthusiastic crew provides good, dependable, friendly service.

Basics Cabins are comfortable enough although they're not luxurious. Standard rooms vary in configuration and size (they're about 121 square feet on average) and are furnished with twin beds, a desk/dresser combo, and a bathroom with shower only. Larger spreads (measuring about 138 square feet) cost about $100 a day more per person.

There's no fitness center or jogging track, but most passengers get their exercise swimming, snorkeling, or scuba diving. They can dive in right from the ship or board inflatable Zodiacs for guided scuba/

snorkeling tours in the coral reefs off Peter Island, Virgin Gorda, Norman Island, or St. John. Golfers should bring their clubs—the ships can arrange entry to top golf courses along their routes.

When not off exploring, guests lounge on the **Sun Deck;** view nature and wildlife films in the dining room-cum-screening room; or gather in the pretty, pastel-colored **Observation Lounge** to play cards, knit, chat, or listen to talks on art, history, local flora and fauna, and the like.

Cuisine The food is remarkable, as most of the chefs are trained at the **Culinary Institute of America.** The menu leans toward light fare, with lots of fresh fish and vegetables cooked to perfection. But (luckily) not everything from the galley is good for you—these ships are known for their delicious fresh-baked chocolate chip cookies, served up every afternoon. Meals are in the inviting dining room, which features large windows and pleasant service. Breakfast and lunch have open seating; tables are assigned at dinner. There's no room service.

Club Med Cruises

800/CLUBMED

Club Med

*Note: As this book went to press, Club Med 1 was sold to **Windstar Cruises.** The ship was to be remodeled and rechristened and was scheduled to begin sailing as part of the **Windstar** fleet in May 1998.*

Club Med 1 & 2

$$$★★★★

Built: 1990/1992

Refurbished: 1995 *(Club Med 1)*

Passengers: 376/386

Size: 14,745/14,983 grt

Cabins: 186/191

Outside: 186/191

Inside: 0

Suites: 2/5

Wheelchair Accessible: 0

Registry: Bahamian/French

Officers/Crew: French

Tipping Policy: Gratuities included in fare; no additional tips expected

Smoking Policy: No overall policy, although there are some no-smoking areas

Snapshot These supersleek, five-masted, computer-operated sailing vessels are owned by the same folks who run **Club Med** villages around the world. With their French food and ambience, they offer a *très merveilleux* way to sail in and out of exotic ports.

Itinerary In winter, *Club Med 1* cruises the Caribbean from her base in Martinique; in summer she sails the Mediterranean. *Club Med 2* circles French Polynesia year-round. Trips are from three to seven nights long.

Typical Passengers The **Club Med** ships are favored by an international (mostly European) assortment of young to middle-aged active, athletic singles and couples who want to play and party hard. It helps to know French, as most of the 63 *gentils organisateurs* (as crew members are called) prefer to speak in their native tongue. These ships are not suitable for the physically challenged or young children.

Ambience Life on board is *très, très* French, from the morning croissants to the nightly pâté de foie gras. Dress is casual but fashionable—itsy-bitsy bikinis (sometimes only the bottoms) during the day and chic resortwear at night. Like onshore **Club Med** villages, the ships emphasize active fun and mixing and mingling (they're somewhat like floating singles' bars). They're a blast for Generation-Xers, yuppies, and anyone who enjoys French-flavored fun. The service is fair to good, but pampering is not the point here.

Basics Cabins are attractively designed, offering beautiful teak bathrooms with showers, built-in storage areas, twin beds that convert to king-size, TV sets, mini-bars, terry robes, and hair dryers. Standard cabins are 188 square feet; suites are 321 square feet on *Club Med 1,* 258 square feet on *Club Med 2.*

The highlights of these vessels are the water-sports marinas, which are lowered when the ships are at anchor and make it possible for passengers to swim, snorkel, windsurf, jet ski, boat, water ski, and scuba dive in the ocean without having to go ashore. Each ship also has two pools, five bars, and organized **Club Med**—style activities (contests, pool and water games, volleyball and other sports) galore.

The variety-Lido-like revues can prove quite entertaining, although if you've ever been to a **Club Med** village the shows will seem familiar. Most of the entertainment is provided by staffers, with occasional guest performances by locals in various ports. There's also a library, a casino, five bar/lounges, and a sundries shop on each ship.

Cuisine The French-influenced buffets and multicourse meals are always good and often superb. Wine accompanies meals at no extra charge. The nicely appointed dining room offers sea views through wide windows. Dinner is served at one seating. There's also a continental restaurant, a casual cafe, a self-service eatery, and an outdoor snack bar. Room service is available for an additional fee.

In recent years, the cruise industry has invested $7 billion into building new ships.

Costa Cruise Lines

800/462.6782

CostaAllegra/ CostaMarina

$$★★★★

Built: 1992/1990

Passengers: 810/772

Size: 30,000/25,000 grt

Cabins: 410/388

Outside: 216/183

Inside: 194/205

Suites: 13/8

Wheelchair Accessible: 8/0

Registry: Liberian

Officers/Crew: Italian/International

Tipping Policy: About $8 per passenger per day suggested

Smoking Policy: Restricted to designated smoking sections in dining rooms (the policy is not strictly enforced)

Snapshot It's cruising Italian style, with a European crew, a spirited personality, and lots of activities. The two ships are nearly identical, except that the *Marina* is a bit smaller and carries 40 fewer passengers.

Itinerary Both ships cruise the Baltic Sea and northern Europe in summer and the southern Caribbean in winter on 7- to 14-day excursions.

Typical Passengers On board you'll find hip, designer-clad, young and middle-aged couples and singles with upscale taste and a penchant for fun. About half the passengers are European.

Ambience The ships and cruises are distinctively European, from the excellence service to the sophisticated decor. The friendly Italian captain and his international crew of 450 add to the ambience, performing their duties with efficiency and a certain continental flourish. Passengers dress casually but with panache.

Basics Standard cabins are a comfortable 155 square feet; each has plenty of storage space, two twin beds that convert to one queen-size, large portholes, and a nice, big bathroom with shower. The suites with private verandas and the **Grand Suites,** with floor-to-ceiling windows, are simply outstanding, offering such special features as hand-sewn bedspreads, whirlpool baths, and mini-bars.

Onboard facilities on both ships include the 3,000-square-foot **Caracalla Spa,** which has an adjacent outdoor pool, whirlpools, an aerobics room, weight machines, free weights, exercise bicycles, Stairmasters, steam rooms, saunas, massage rooms, and a solarium. There are also shops, and passengers may choose from the usual selection of organized shipboard activities.

Among the evening options are amusing shows, a casino, several bars, and a disco. The decadent bacchanalia costume party at the end of every cruise is not to be missed, with toga-draped passengers drinking, dancing, carousing, and otherwise having a grand time. A children's program frees parents for adult pursuits (although these are not really child-oriented ships).

Cuisine Truly excellent Italian/continental meals are served with style in the charming **Restaurant Montmartre,** whose floor-to-ceiling windows offer ocean views. Freshly made pasta and authentic Italian-style pizza are always available at lunch and dinner, along with a substantial selection of other dishes. Dinner is served in two seatings. There's also a casual, buffet-style restaurant open at breakfast and lunch and limited room service.

CostaClassica/ CostaRomantica/ CostaVictoria

$$★★★★★

These ships offer outstanding value—a comfortable, enjoyable, and very European experience at a reasonable price. See page 68 for a detailed description.

CostaOlympia

Due to be launched in 1998, this 78,000-grt, 2,100-passenger ship, sister to the CostaClassica, CostaRomantica, and CostaVictoria, will sail the Caribbean in winter and the Mediterranean in summer.

Mermoz

$$★★★★

Built: 1957

Refurbished: 1987

Passengers: 530

Size: 14,133 grt

Cabins: 270

Outside: 231

Inside: 39

Suites: 4

Wheelchair Accessible: 0

Registry: Bahamian

Officers/Crew: French/Filipino & French

Tipping Policy: $8 per passenger per day suggested

Smoking Policy: Few restrictions; smoking is allowed in most areas of the ship

Snapshot Small and thoroughly French, this ship offers European and Caribbean voyages in a convivial, continental setting. Note: Although owned by **Costa,** *Mermoz* is marketed in Europe by **Costa Crociere** in Italy and **Paquet Cruises** in France.

Itinerary *Mermoz* sails 14-day Caribbean, Australian, and Far East cruises in winter and makes world and European voyages of varying lengths the rest of the year. The annual **Music Festival at Sea,** which takes place during an autumn Mediterranean voyage, is highly recommended; the all-inclusive cruise features performances by top classical musicians along with shore excursions, fine wines, and great food.

Typical Passengers An eclectic collection of voyagers can be found on board: fashionable French couples and singles, a mix of other Europeans, and Americans who enjoy gourmet French food. A wide range of ages—from late twenties to late sixties—is represented.

Ambience The food is French, the crew is French, the style is French (right down to the French maid uniforms on the cabin stewardesses)—the only things missing are the Eiffel Tower and the snooty attitude. Like a sailing Côte d'Azur, this small and cozy ship combines the joie de vivre of St-Tropez with the elegance of Paris. While very casual by day, passengers dress to the nines at night, especially in Europe. The French crew members perform their duties with exquisite efficiency and élan.

Basics Cabins are simply but stylishly appointed, with portholes, large armoires, and bathrooms with showers only. Suites offer such extras as a separate sitting room and two bathrooms with tubs.

The **Grand Salon** is the site of wonderful Folies Bergère–like shows featuring lavish costumes and talented bilingual entertainers. Passengers can also amuse themselves in the casino, shop, nicely equipped fitness center, and four bar/lounges. Up on deck there are two pools (only one large enough to swim in). There's also a volleyball court (the ball's attached by rope so it won't fly overboard); players take the game seriously, often battling it out all afternoon.

Cuisine The food is outstanding and very French in flavor and presentation: salads are tossed at your table, whole grilled fish are presented for your admiration prior to being served, the desserts are divine, and wine is complimentary at lunch and dinner. There are two dining venues, the **Renaissance Grill,** which features large windows and wicker furnishings, and the intimate **Massalia Dining Room.** There is one dinner seating, with assigned seats. A lunchtime buffet is set up on deck (weather permitting), and the ship also offers a civilized version of the midnight buffet, with an array of pâtés, terrines, salads, and pastries.

 Megaship    **Traditional Cruise Liner**

 Sailing Ship  **Expedition Ship**

 Ultraluxury Ship

Large ships (more than 1,000 passengers): Blue

Mid-size ships (500-1,000 passengers): Green

Small ships (fewer than 500 passengers): Red

Crystal Cruises

800/446.6620

Crystal Harmony/ Crystal Symphony

$$$$★★★★★★

These super-stylish sisters are simply the best mid-size cruise ships afloat. See page 70 for a detailed description.

Cunard

800/221.4770

CUNARD

Queen Elizabeth 2 (QE2)

$$$$

★★★★ Grill Class (Q and P Grade)

★★★ Caronia Class (C Grade)

★ Mauretania Class (M Grade)

Built: 1969

Refurbished: 1994

Passengers: 1,500

Size: 70,327 grt

Cabins: 781

Outside: 635 (13 with verandas)

Inside: 146

Suites: 2

Wheelchair Accessible: 96 (4 completely equipped for disabled passengers)

Registry: British

Officers/Crew: British/International

Tipping Policy: Gratuities included in fare; no additional tips expected

Smoking Policy: Restricted to designated smoking sections

Snapshot The *QE2* began her seafaring career in 1969, attracting affluent globe-trotters and travelers who wanted to cross the Atlantic in style. Today the legendary luxury liner still offers old-style cruising. However, the *QE2* has suffered her share of misfortunes in the past few years, including some rocky transatlantic crossings. Despite a much-needed $45 million face-lift in 1994 and additional improvements in 1996, some industry insiders fear for the beleaguered *Queen*'s future.

Itinerary The *Queen* embarks on a three-month-plus around-the-world cruise every January, usually departing from New York. Afterwards she makes six-day transatlantic crossings from New York to Southampton, England, as well as a series of cruises in the Caribbean and Bermuda.

Typical Passengers The *QE2* appeals to an international mix of mostly older (50-plus) travelers,

although younger passengers occasionally can be found on board, usually in the lower-priced cabins.

Ambience This is classic cruising, right down to the archaic three-class system. As a result the ship is sometimes stuffy, especially on the upper decks (off-limits to economy-class passengers). Top cabin passengers don tuxedos and gowns every evening on transatlantic crossings, and suits and ties and cocktail dresses on even "casual nights" on other voyages. The style is a little more informal in the lower-priced cabins.

A nautical theme permeates the *Queen.* The public rooms are decorated with numerous ship models, sailing artifacts, and maritime-theme paintings. A 1994 face-lift resulted in stylishly redesigned public spaces, staterooms, and decks, and more gracious dining rooms and bars. Additional changes in 1996 included the reconfiguring of cabins to eliminate upper beds (and reduce passenger capacity from 1,750 to 1,500) and the remodeling of the **Mauretania** and **Caronia Restaurants.**

The quality of service you enjoy depends on the category of cabin. Not surprisingly, service is excellent in the higher-priced **Grill** cabins; it's good elsewhere.

Basics The accommodations are excellent in top cabins, so-so down below. The best and most expensive staterooms and suites are in the **Grill** category, which is divided into **Queens Grill** (Q Grade, the crème de la crème) and **Princess Grill** and **Britannia Grill** (both P Grade). **Caronia** (C Grade) cabins are the next level down, followed by **Mauretania** (M Grade) cabins.

Queens Grill staterooms range from penthouse suites to ultradeluxe staterooms, all with sitting areas, full bathrooms with tubs and showers, walk-in closets, TVs , and VCRs, and refrigerators. Guests in this category are the only passengers permitted in the **Queens Grill,** the *QE2's* finest restaurant.

The best staterooms below the very top level (and the only ones we recommend unless you can afford the very best) are the **Britannia Grill** and **Princess Grill** cabins. Each has a sitting area, a big bathroom with tub and shower, twin beds that can be moved together, a walk-in closet, TV, VCR, and a refrigerator. **Caronia** cabins are smaller and have TVs, VCRs, and bathrooms with showers. **Mauritania** cabins are quite small, basic, and rather stark; they are not recommended.

The *Queen* truly excels in the area of sports and fitness. The sensational spa and fitness center is one of the best to be found on a cruise ship. Facilities include a spectacular swimming pool, inhalation and steam rooms, saunas, hydrotherapy baths, and an amazing Jacuzzi. Up on deck are shuffleboard courts, two pools, a Jacuzzi, and ample space to run around. A golf instructor is always on board.

Mardi Gras, Carnival Cruise Lines' first ship, grounded on a sandbar as it sailed from the Port of Miami on its maiden voyage on 11 March 1972.

Daytime options for more sedentary types include lectures, book signings, and the usual shipboard fun and games spearheaded by the cruise director. The *Queen* boasts the "largest library afloat," along with a computer-learning center. And then there's shopping—the **Royal Promenade** is filled with fine shops, including a nautical branch of **Harrods.**

Nightfall brings elegant balls and parties in the **Queen's Room,** lavish shows, classical concerts in the **Grand Lounge,** and screenings in the movie theater. Favorite haunts for either day or night are the authentically English **Golden Lion Pub** and the intimate **Chart Room** bar.

Cuisine The food is fair except in the **Queen's Grill,** where the plates are gilded, the cutlery gold-plated, the white-gloved waiters attentive, and the exquisitely presented continental fare always exceptional. Unfortunately, only passengers in Q-grade cabins are afforded this dining paradise.

It's a different story in the other dining rooms, where the fare doesn't deserve mention. However, the **Princess Grill, Britannia Grill, Caronia,** and **Mauretania** restaurants are all truly lovely. Single-seating dining is now offered throughout the ship, and room service is available around the clock.

Royal Viking Sun
$$$$★★★★★★

Offering extraordinary elegance and service to match, this classy luxury liner was in its heyday one of the world's most celebrated and copied cruise ships. See page 72 for a detailed description.

Sea Goddess I & II
$$$$★★★★★★

With an average per diem of $700 to $1,000 a passenger, these luxury liners are not for everyone. But it's almost worth refinancing the house to experience their unparalleled service and style. See page 74 for a detailed description.

Vistafjord
$$$$★★★★

Built: 1973

Refurbished: 1994

Passengers: 677

Size: 24,492 grt

Cabins: 379

Outside: 322

Inside: 57

Suites: 18

Wheelchair Accessible: 4

Registry: Bahamian

Officers/Crew: Norwegian/European

Tipping Policy: Gratuities included in fare; no additional tips expected

Smoking Policy: Few restrictions; cigarette smoking, but not pipe or cigar smoking, is allowed in the dining room

Snapshot A comprehensive refurbishment in 1994 completely transformed this ship, with dramatic changes in cabins and public rooms and the addition of an Italian restaurant. Now she's a standout, offering a traditional cruise ambience and excellent service.

Itinerary The ship cruises the Caribbean, Panama Canal, Hawaii, and Tahiti in winter; the Mediterranean and Black Sea in summer; and Western Europe and the Greek Isles in fall. Trips are 7 or 14 days or longer.

Typical Passengers Most are middle-aged and older; many are retired; all are well-to-do. Both couples and singles (many widowed) choose this ship, and there's usually a fairly even division of Americans and Europeans (most often Germans) on board. Nearly 70 percent of all passengers have sailed the *Vistafjord* more than once before.

Ambience The atmosphere is clubby, with passengers mingling easily. Attire is casual by day, dressy at night. The elegant, understated decor has a Scandinavian accent.

Suave (and quite handsome) Norwegian captains and officers are very sociable, while attentive Northern European crew members pamper guests.

Note: With a large number of European smokers, it's often difficult to find a truly smoke-free area. Otherwise this ship is truly a delight from bow to stern.

Basics Decorated in soft beige tones and nicely appointed, standard staterooms are fairly spacious. Each has two beds that can convert to a double or king-size, plenty of space for storage, a hair dryer, terry robes, a mini-refrigerator, a telephone, a safe, a TV with VCR, and a European marble bathroom (several cabins have tubs, most have showers only). Nordic cabin stewardesses keep cabins spotless and cater to passengers' every need.

The top-of-the-line accommodations are the two dual-level glass-enclosed **Penthouse Suites**. Measuring 872 square feet, each offers such super-luxurious extras as an outdoor hot tub on a private deck and an indoor sauna. But before you pull out your credit card or checkbook, check out the tab—about $1,200 per person per day.

The **Golden Door Spa at Sea** program is the best afloat, with skillful instructors from the posh health resort in Escondido, California, leading workouts throughout the day in the ample gym. There are also treadmills, weights, and other exercise equipment as well as a sauna, Jacuzzi, and indoor pool. Up on the handsome teak decks you'll find a jogging track, outdoor pool, plenty of space to spread out, attentive deck stewards proffering drinks and towels, and the usual organized activities (games, dance lessons, and the like). For passengers eager to enter the cyber age there's a computer center with instructors. The duty-free boutiques and the handsome, wood-paneled library provide other diversions.

Afternoon tea is served in the beautiful, wide-windowed ballroom, which is a favorite spot for socializing throughout the day. At night the dance floor is filled with couples swinging to Big Band–era hits. The gorgeous **Garden Lounge** and the warm and cozy **North Cape Bar** are *the* places for before- and after-dinner drinks. The attractive two-tiered **Club Polaris** nightclub is the hub of nighttime activity, while the lovely entertainment lounge stages amusing cabaret-style acts (but no lavish, Vegas-style shows). There's also a chic casino.

Cuisine Superb continental food is served at the single dinner seating by gracious, white-gloved waiters who quickly learn each guest's personal preferences. The attractive dining room, with its burnished wood and crystal chandeliers, helps showcase the fine food. The menu offers everything from rich German dishes to low-calorie fare. For a change of pace (and no additional charge), passengers may dine at the lovely, intimate **Tivoli** restaurant.

A sumptuous luncheon buffet is set up in the indoor/outdoor **Lido Cafe,** which has wicker furnishings and an airy ambience. Breakfast is served in the cabins, on deck, or in the dining room, and room service is available in all cabin categories around the clock.

Dolphin Cruise Line

800/222.1003

OceanBreeze
$$★★

Built: 1955

Refurbished: 1995

Passengers: 776

Size: 21,486 grt

Cabins: 388

Outside: 238

Inside: 150

Suites: 12

Wheelchair Accessible: 0

Registry: Liberian

Officers/Crew: Greek/International

Tipping Policy: About $9 per passenger per day suggested

Smoking Policy: Restricted to designated smoking sections

Snapshot Christened the *Southern Cross Queen Elizabeth II* in 1955, this gracious, vintage ship later became the *Azure Seas*. She was given her present name when **Dolphin** acquired and refurbished her in 1992. This is the perfect choice for budget travelers who enjoy quick, but stylish, getaways.

Itinerary Three- to four-day cruises from Miami to Nassau and Blue Lagoon Island (a private island), and from Nassau to Key West are offered year-round.

Typical Passengers The passenger manifest usually includes senior citizens, budget-minded first-time cruisers, and families with children.

Ambience Cruises on the *OceanBreeze* are enjoyable—the mood is relaxed, and the staff is friendly and accommodating. Attire is informal during the day, but people dress up a bit at night. The decor is classic cruise ship, from the teak decks to the old-fashioned wooden deck chairs.

Basics Cabins come in a variety of configurations and appointments; some are considerably smaller than others (sizes range from 99 square feet to 400 square feet). They may have either two beds or a double, portholes or windows, a tub or just a shower. Best bets are the suites, which feature bathrooms with both tub and shower, a mini-bar, a separate sitting area, large windows, and other wonderful appointments. Decks provide a good mix of shaded and sun-filled spaces, and a small pool. There's also a spa and beauty salon.

This is a good ship for families. The children's program offers the usual fun and games (treasure hunts, dolphin encounters, sand-castle building), and folks attired as Fred Flintstone, Yogi Bear, and other Hanna-Barbera cartoon characters roam around delighting young cruisers.

Adult amusements include a two-deck casino, a disco, two bar/lounges, and so-so shows. Romantics may have the chance to witness an onboard wedding when the ship is in port.

Cuisine The food is much better than it was when this was the *Azure Seas,* but don't expect gourmet. All meals are in the one dining room; there are two dinner seatings. Room service is available around the clock, but offers sandwiches and snacks only.

Crystal Cruises offers the "Crystal Martini Collection" on board *Crystal Harmony* and *Crystal Symphony*. Among the variations of the classic cocktail that passengers may order (shaken or stirred) are "The 007," "The Cosmopolitan," and "The Czar Pierre Martini."

The 1840 launch of Cunard's *Britannia* established the first regular transatlantic service, a tradition continued today by the Queen Elizabeth 2. The silver "Britannia Cup," presented to Cunard by the city of Boston in 1840 to celebrate the maiden arrival of Cunard's first ship to US shores, is now displayed in the *QE2*'s Britannia Grill.

Getting Hitched at Sea

A shipboard wedding, with the captain presiding, is a notion more grounded in romance than reality. The fact is, ship captains haven't been legally allowed to perform marriage ceremonies at sea since World War II. Nevertheless, couples wishing to tie the knot on a cruise ship can usually do so in certain embarkation ports or ports of call.

Among the cruise lines offering wedding packages are **American Hawaii, Carnival, Dolphin, Holland America, Norwegian,** and **Princess.** In some cases these lines work with wedding consulting companies that handle all the arrangements, including obtaining the required licenses and arranging for a notary public or minister to perform the ceremony.

Perhaps the most exotic shipboard wedding available is offered by **Cruise Tours** (800/248.6542), a travel agency based in Chico, California, which arranges traditional Russian nuptials, including caviar and vodka toasts, on **Volga River** cruises. **Princess Cruises'** *Grand Princess* (debuting in 1998) is equipped with a chapel where married couples may renew their wedding vows.

For security reasons, some cruise lines forbid weddings in certain ports or limit the number of guests (nonpassengers) who may attend the ceremony. Other lines don't permit shipboard weddings at all.

If you're dreaming of a shipboard wedding, it's important to plan ahead. To allow enough time for all the necessary arrangements, make reservations *at least* six months before the sailing date.

(Also see **A Checklist for Honeymooners,** page 42, and **Days of Wine and Roses: Extras for Newlyweds and Other Happy Couples,** page 101.)

SeaBreeze
$$★★

Built: 1958

Refurbished: 1995

Passengers: 840

Size: 21,000 grt

Cabins: 421

Outside: 260

Inside: 161

Suites: 7

Wheelchair Accessible: 0

Registry: Panamanian

Officers/Crew: Greek/International

Tipping Policy: About $9 per passenger per day suggested

Smoking Policy: Restricted to designated smoking sections

Snapshot The best things about a trip aboard this venerable cruise ship are the lively, carefree ambience and the affordable price.

Itinerary Seven-night eastern/western Caribbean cruises depart from Miami.

Typical Passengers A mix of young and not-so-young American first-time cruisers, veteran seafarers, and families are found on board.

Ambience Shipshape from bow to stern, she looks good for having been at sea for nearly 40 years. Energetic passengers and congenial crew members contribute to an upbeat atmosphere. Traditional cruise attire is the norm. The service is good.

Basics Cabins come in a variety of configurations and sizes (from as small as 65 square feet to as large as 258 square feet). With fares as low as these, many people splurge on a suite (available for about $230 per person per day more). Each offers a king-size bed, sitting area, sofa, desk/dresser, and double windows.

The *SeaBreeze* is equipped with all the standard shipboard facilities: outdoor pool, Jacuzzis, fitness center, beauty shop, casino, entertainment lounge, and three other bar/lounges. There's also a children's program.

Cuisine They call it "continental," but "basic banquet" would be more accurate. It's certainly edible, but nothing to rave about. All meals are served in the dining room; there are two dinner seatings. Room service (the menu offers sandwiches and snacks only) is available around the clock.

Royal Caribbean International's *Legend of the Seas* and *Splendour of the Seas* each have top-deck, 18-hole miniature golf courses. Greens fees are $5, but passengers can buy a more economical pass to play multiple rounds.

Disney Cruises: Magic and Wonder at Sea

The **Walt Disney Company** is bringing its wonderful world to the sea. The **Disney Cruise Line,** established in 1995, is scheduled to launch its first two ships, the *Disney Magic* and the *Disney Wonder,* in 1998.

Disney Cruise Line vacation packages will include three- or four-day visits to **Disney World** and a week-long cruise from Port Canaveral, Florida, to the **Bahamas,** with a day-long stop at Castaway Cay, **Disney**'s 1,000-acre private island near the **Abacos.** Fares (including airfare) will be $4,000 to $5,000 for a family of four.

Slated to debut in early 1998, the 85,000-grt *Disney Magic* will accommodate 1,650 passengers in 875 staterooms (73 percent outside, 44 percent with verandas). Standard cabins will be a spacious 220 square feet and will offer such family-friendly features as a split bathroom, with the tub and the toilet in two separate rooms (so that the whole bathroom isn't tied up during bath time). There will be 84 **Family Suites,** 18 one-bedroom suites, two two-bedroom suites, and two **Royal Suites**.

Other features include a three-tier atrium; a 5,500-square-foot shopping area featuring Disney logo shops (of course); a 6,700-square-foot, ocean-view spa/salon/fitness center; three pools; a jogging promenade; and a sports deck with a batting cage, a driving range, table tennis, paddle tennis, shuffleboard, and basketball courts. There will also be a 270-seat cinema and a 1,040-seat theater, which will stage Broadway-style shows.

Dining options on the megaship will include three theme dining rooms and an adults-only restaurant; a pool bar and grill serving pizza, hot dogs, and hamburgers; an ice cream and frozen yogurt bar; and 24-hour room service. There will also be a coffee bar, a sports bar, and numerous lounges—but no casino on this family-oriented vessel.

Among the special child-oriented facilities and services will be the largest children's recreation area on any cruise ship (15,000 square feet), a wading pool, children's counselors, a teen club and game arcade, and baby-sitting.

Although details on the *Disney Wonder,* due out in December 1998, were not yet available at press time, the 85,000-ton, 1,650-passenger vessel will be the *Magic*'s sister ship and will likely have comparable features and facilities.

Holland America Line
800/426.0327

A TRADITION OF EXCELLENCE®

Maasdam/Ryndam/ Statendam/Veendam
$$$★★★★

Built: 1994/1994/1994/1996

Passengers: 1,266

Size: 50,000 grt

Cabins: 633

Outside: 485 (includes 120 deluxe staterooms with verandas)

Inside: 148

Suites: 29 (all with verandas)

Wheelchair Accessible: 6

Registry: Dutch/Bahamian (*Veendam*)

Officers/Crew: Dutch/Indonesian & Filipino

Tipping Policy: No tips required, but rewarding superior service suggested

Smoking Policy: Restricted to designated smoking sections

Snapshot Subdued sailing in elegant surroundings is the specialty of this quartet of sister ships. For travelers who want a smooth ride on a spectacular ship (and who aren't too food-fussy), they are a good choice.

Itinerary The *Maasdam* makes 11- and 12-day voyages, cruising the Mediterranean and northern Europe in summer and the Caribbean in winter, with a few 10-day Panama Canal trips in between. *Statendam, Ryndam,* and *Veendam* sail a series of 7- to 10-day Caribbean cruises from Ft. Lauderdale in winter; 13-day Panama Canal crossings in spring and fall; and 7-day Alaska journeys from Vancouver or Seward in summer. *Statendam* also cruises the waters of Hawaii, offering 10-, 16-, and 29-day trips in March and September.

Typical Passengers There's always a mixed group on board, but most are Americans—generally middle-aged and older and middle-income and higher—who appreciate the ships' relaxed, low-key atmosphere.

Ambience Similar but not identical (the *Maasdam* feels a little homier and warmer, the *Veendam* is newer), the four ships are all large and casually elegant. Their decor is striking, with fabulous faux Tiffany lamps and lots of fresh flowers, mahogany, and brass. In keeping with **Holland America** custom, each is adorned with an impressive $2-million collection of antiques and art as well as an abundance of old-fashioned navigational maps and other nautical artifacts.

The mood on board—low-key, genteel, reserved—reflects the ship's classic cruise style. This is not the ship for hardy partyers. Nonetheless, daytime attire is very casual, with most passengers in shorts or bathing suits while on deck. Traditional cruisewear is the norm in the evenings; on formal nights men are required to wear a jacket and tie (some show up in tuxes).

The service is good but not exceptional. Crew members, while agreeable and friendly, lack sophistication and English-language skills.

Basics Cabins range in size from 120 to 243 square feet. Standard outside staterooms are nicely arranged and larger than average, with a sitting area, two twin beds that convert to one queen-size, a TV set, bathroom with tub, and an adequate amount of drawer and closet space.

If your budget can handle it, spring for one of the 565-square-foot suites. Each has a sitting area with a large sofa, a spacious private veranda, a mini-bar, two telephones, a TV with VCR, lots of closet and drawer space, a marble bathroom with Jacuzzi , and a dressing room with a vanity and sink.

The 1,400-square-foot **Ocean Spa** on each ship is exceptionally well-equipped, with treadmills, Stairmasters, rowers, exercise bicycles, and a circuit of weight machines. There's an exercise floor where aerobics, step, and body-toning classes are held. Each ship also has a **Steiner** spa offering steam rooms, saunas, massage rooms, and a plethora of health and beauty treatments; a juice bar; a beauty salon; and a barber shop.

On deck are two pools (the larger with a retractable roof for use during inclement weather); two Jacuzzis; a jogging track, and a practice tennis court. The **Passport to Fitness** program rewards passengers for their exertions with points redeemable for merchandise.

More sedentary seafarers can try their hands at the traditional deck sports like shuffleboard, Ping-Pong, and quoits, or they can just lounge around—there's lots of deck space. Indoor pursuits include cards and other games, lectures, and arts-and-crafts classes. There's not much for shoppers, though; each ship has just the perfunctory duty-free perfume shop and an arcade with a logo shop and boutique.

The large and comfortable two-level entertainment lounges are the settings for a variety of shows, from performances by "big names' (mostly older entertainers like Rita Moreno or Vic Damone), to comedians like **Holland America** favorite Rick Starr,

to musical productions. While hardly exceptional, the shows are diverting and well attended.

Each vessel has a total of eight attractive bar/lounges including a cozy **Piano Bar;** the action-packed **Ocean Bar,** where Fred Astaire and Ginger Rogers wannabes trip the light fantastic; and the **Crow's Nest,** an observation lounge by day and a disco after dark. A casino, library, and small movie theater round out the list of entertainment venues.

For young passengers, **Holland America**'s Club Hal offers programs for three age groups: 5 to 8, 9 to 12, and 13 to 17. **Club Hal** activities include arts-and-crafts classes;"Olympic" competitions; pizza, karaoke, and dance parties; and kids-only shore excursions.

Cuisine Opinions on the food vary, with the consensus falling somewhere between "above average" and only "so-so." But with more than 1,000 passengers to feed it's hard to fault the chefs, who definitely make an effort to jazz up the mass-produced dishes. Besides, the elegance of the bi-level dining rooms—each with two spiral staircases and a frosted Venetian-glass ceiling—and the friendliness of the Indonesian and Filipino waiters more than make up for any culinary lapses.

The dining room is augmented by numerous buffets, cocktail-hour hors d'oeuvres in the bars and lounges, and several eateries (a taco stand, an ice-cream parlor, and a coffee shop). Gustatory highlights include the exceptional salad bars, the outstanding international-theme midnight buffets, the ice-cream/frozen yogurt parlors, and the weekly "Chocolate Extravaganza" buffets. Room service is available 24 hours a day.

Nieuw Amsterdam/ Noordam
$$★★★

Built: 1983/1984

Passengers: 1,214

Size: 33,930 grt

Cabins: 605

Outside: 411

Inside: 194

Suites: 0

Wheelchair Accessible: 4

Registry: Dutch

Officers/Crew: Dutch/Indonesian & Filipino

Tipping Policy: No tips required, but rewarding superior service suggested

Smoking Policy: Restricted to designated smoking sections

Snapshot Identical cruise liners, they offer genteel voyages at budget rates.

Itinerary Both ships offer seven-day western Caribbean cruises in winter—the *Nieuw Amsterdam* from New Orleans, the *Noordam* out of Tampa (with a stop in Santo Tomas de Castilla, Guatemala). In summer they travel north to Alaska for seven-day trips out of Vancouver or Seward.

Typical Passengers These ships appeal to a middle-aged or older crowd, mostly couples or widowed singles (the latter most often on Alaskan cruises). They are not for children or swinging singles.

Ambience Identical twins with different interiors, these ships have an angular, squared-off design some may find unattractive. The decor on both is understated and approaches elegance, but is not extravagant by any means. The efficient crew provides reliable service.

The mood on board is distinctly quiet and low-key—passengers are looking to relax and enjoy the scenery. Dress is conservative (some older men even don jackets and ties for breakfast!). Evenings are dressy, but not necessarily black tie. Women passengers wear everything from polyester pantsuits to designer silks (more often the former).

Basics Cabins are a comfortable 152 to 295 square feet with good storage space, twin beds that convert to queen-size, and adequate bathrooms (many with tubs).

Each ship has two pools, a Jacuzzi, a fitness center, and a spa offering a selection of beauty treatments. The **Passport to Fitness** program rewards passengers for their efforts with points redeemable for merchandise.

The evening shows suffer from a paucity of talent, but if you're not fussy they can be amusing. There's also a casino, movie theater (with free popcorn during matinees), eight bar/lounges, three shops, a library, a beauty shop, and a coin-operated, self-service laundry. A signature tote bag is presented to all passengers.

Holland America Line's well-run youth program, **Club Hal,** features the usual array of arts and crafts, games, sports, and social events for passengers ages 5 to 8, 9 to 12, and 13 to 17.

Cuisine The fare is international, and it's just fine; there are several theme dinners when ethnic fare (Indonesian, French, Italian) is featured. Dinner is served in two seatings in a pretty, Old World–style dining room. A casual restaurant features buffets at breakfast, lunch, and midnight, and room service is available around the clock.

Webster's dictionary lists the origin of the word "posh" as "unknown." But marine historians like John Maxtone-Graham say that booking agents for passenger ships sailing between England and India used to write POSH (an acronym for "port out, starboard home") on the cabin requests of their favored clients. The initials indicated that the passengers' cabins should be on the port side of the ship during the outgoing voyage and the starboard side on the way back. "It had nothing to do with scenery, only heat," writes Maxtone-Graham in *Liners to the Sun.* "The shaded side of a ship is several degrees cooler than its sunny counterpart."

The Captain's Table

John-Maxtone Graham, in his entertaining *The Only Way to Cross,* describes certain rituals followed on transatlantic liners during the first half of the 20th century. When it came to reserving a seat in the dining room, the author comments, "There were some passengers who, incredibly enough, intimated to the chief steward that they would consider dining with the captain. Such gaucherie betrayed their ignorance of the tradition that a seat at the head table might be refused but never requested."

Though the great ocean liner era has passed, alas, "such gaucherie" is alive and well among some contemporary cruisers.

To be fair, why shouldn't one covet a seat at the captain's table? Imagine the thrill of having all eyes upon you as you sashay into the dining room, the extraordinary service that is usually lavished on the captain and his dinner companions, and the gratification you'll derive from working your elevated status into casual conversation: "As I said to the captain over cherries jubilee last night. . . ."

How *does* one snare a spot at the captain's table? Some possible tacks to take:

- Book the most expensive suite on the ship.

- Be an extraordinarily loyal customer; sail 50 times with one cruise line.

- On the aforementioned 50 sailings, befriend the captain.

- Choose a travel agent who enjoys a longstanding relationship with the cruise line. (Sometimes a special request from him or her will do the trick.)

- Be young, beautiful, rich, and famous. (It can never hurt!)

What probably *won't* work is a special trip—or a tip—to the maître d' once you're aboard. At that point it's probably too late to secure the coveted seat. Most cruise lines send an advance "Commend List" to the ship, notifying personnel of VIPs, celebrities, top alumni, penthouse-suite residents, and other "special" passengers. Names on this list are usually culled for the captain's table well before the ship sets sail.

If you aren't selected as the captain's dining companion, don't be too disappointed. Many veteran cruisers say that sitting at the captain's table isn't all it's cracked up to be.

MICHAEL STORRINGS

Rotterdam VI

Slated to make her debut in late 1997, the Rotterdam VI *will replace the* Rotterdam V, *a grande dame of the high seas retiring after more than 1,000 voyages. The new, 62,000-grt ship will hold 1,320 passengers; around-the-world and transatlantic cruises will be her specialty.*

Although longer and faster than other **Holland America** *ships (she can travel at the nautical speed of 25 knots), the* Rotterdam VI *has the same basic arrangement of public rooms as the company's four* Statendam-*class ships. This vessel will, however, boast a few innovations: an Italian restaurant, an* **Admiral's Lounge** *with a dance floor, and a children's playroom. The ship will also feature a million-dollar collection of specially commissioned artwork and a double-funnel smokestack, which recalls the appearance of the original* Rotterdam.

The ship will have 660 passenger cabins, including 120 deluxe outside cabins with verandas, 36 suites with verandas, and four penthouse suites. Eighteen cabins and two suites will be wheelchair accessible.

Standard cabins will measure 185 to 195 square feet. The suites will range in size from 245 square feet to 565 square feet and offer special amenities such as VCRs, whirlpool tubs, refrigerators, robes, and verandas. Passengers staying in suites will also enjoy a private concierge lounge.

Westerdam

$$★★★

Built: 1986

Refurbished: 1989

Passengers: 1,494

Size: 53,872 grt

Cabins: 747

Outside: 495

Inside: 252

Suites: 6

Wheelchair Accessible: 4

Registry: Dutch

Officers/Crew: Dutch/Indonesian & Filipino

Tipping Policy: No tips required, but rewarding superior service suggested

Smoking Policy: Restricted to designated smoking sections

Snapshot You get more than you pay for on this, the largest ship in the **Holland America** fleet. Originally the *Homeric*, it was acquired by the **Holland America Line** in 1989.

Itinerary The ship makes 8- and 10-day trips along the New England and Canadian coastlines in the late summer and fall and offers 7-day eastern and western Caribbean cruises the rest of the year.

Typical Passengers Middle-aged and older value-seekers find what they're looking for on this ship.

Ambience Big and stretched out, this nine-deck cruise liner isn't exactly luxurious, but she does provide a comfortable and affordable cruise experience. Passengers enjoy good service and an informal atmosphere. Traditional cruisewear is the norm.

Basics Cabins are fairly large (from 160 to 241 square feet); standard accommodations have sitting areas, two lower beds, lots of storage space, and bathrooms with showers. The six suites are highly recommended; with about 425 square feet, they offer a separate sitting area, a king-size bed, and bathrooms with tubs and showers. All of the staterooms are attended to by the efficient Indonesian/Filipino cabin crew. Passengers in all accommodations categories receive a canvas tote bag.

For recreation there's a large outside deck with two pools and a Jacuzzi, a fitness center, a spa, an entertainment lounge offering the usual musical productions and the occasional "big name" entertainer, a casino, more than a dozen bar/lounges, a library, and shops. Onboard conveniences include a beauty salon and a self-service laundry.

As on other **Holland America** ships, **Club Hal** keeps young passengers entertained with activities geared to three age groups: 5 to 8, 9 to 12, and 13 to 17.

Cuisine The meals are typical of the **Holland America Line**—international in flavor, often good, sometimes not. Dinner is served in two seatings in the attractive dining room, which has a domed ceiling, overstuffed chairs, and an abundance of fresh flowers. There's also the casual, self-service **Veranda** restaurant, where live music accompanies lunch and afternoon tea; breakfast and a midnight buffet are also set out here. Room service is available 24 hours a day in all cabin categories.

Cunard's *Queen Elizabeth 2* lists the following transatlantic fares for animals:

Bird: $110

Cat: $250

Dog: $440

Pets aren't allowed to bunk with passengers, though; they have to sleep in the ship's kennel.

 Megaship   **Traditional Cruise Liner**

 Sailing Ship    **Expedition Ship**

 Ultraluxury Ship

Large ships (more than 1,000 passengers): Blue

Mid-size ships (500-1,000 passengers): Green

Small ships (fewer than 500 passengers): Red

Majesty Cruise Line

800/645.8111

*Note: **Majesty Cruises Line's** Crown Majesty and Royal Majesty were acquired by **Norwegian Cruise Line** in March 1997. At press time, **NCL** planned to continue to market the ships under the **Majesty Cruise Line** name. Check with your travel agent for up-to-the-minute information.*

 ## Crown Majesty

$$★★

Built: 1993

Passengers: 800

Size: 20,000 grt

Cabins: 399

Outside: 281

Inside: 118

Suites: 12 Royal Suites and 31 junior suites

Wheelchair Accessible: 4

Registry: Panamanian

Officers/Crew: Greek/International

Tipping Policy: About $12 per passenger per day suggested.

Smoking Policy: Prohibited in the dining room; restricted to designated smoking sections in all other public areas

Snapshot Formerly **Cunard's** *Crown Dynasty*, this mid-size ship offers Hanna-Barbera cartoon characters for the kids and good service for adults.

Itinerary Cruises Alaska in summer, the Panama Canal in fall and winter. Trips are of varying lengths, usually 7 or 14 days.

Typical Passengers Families as well as middle-income travelers of middle age and older choose this ship.

Ambience A lovely vessel, she features gracious public rooms, including a five-deck atrium with a spiral staircase. Passengers follow the traditional cruise dress code—casual by day, dressier at night.

Basics Standard staterooms are 140 square feet and feature TV sets, telephones, and bathrooms with showers. Most have twin beds that can convert doubles.

There's a nice health spa, a good-sized pool, a tiny fitness center, an entertainment lounge, six bars, a casino, and a library. The children's program, along with the costumed cartoon characters, make this ship a favorite with families.

Cuisine Dinner is served in two seatings in the dining room, which offers sweeping views of the sea. Breakfast and lunch buffets are set out in a cafe on deck. There's also a late-night buffet and 24-hour room service.

 ## Royal Majesty

$$★★

Built: 1992

Passengers: 1,056

Size: 32,400 grt

Cabins: 528

Outside: 343

Inside: 185

Suites: 16

Wheelchair Accessible: 4

Registry: Panama

Officers/Crew: Greek/International

Tipping Policy: About $9 per passenger per day suggested

Smoking Policy: Prohibited in the dining room (this was the first ship to introduce a totally nonsmoking dining room); restricted to designated smoking sections in all other public areas. Nonsmoking cabins are available

Snapshot Don't be fooled by the costumed cartoon characters roaming the decks—this is a classy ship with exceptional service.

Itinerary She makes three- and four-day trips from Miami to Bermuda and Key West in winter, seven-night Boston-to-Bermuda cruises in summer.

Typical Passengers Depending on the cruise, the passenger list includes thirty-something women traveling alone and/or middle-aged and older couples. Summer cruises have more children traveling with their parents and younger couples and singles.

Ambience This family-oriented ship has a handsome, nautical decor. Children are delighted when Fred Flintstone and other Hanna-Barbera cartoon characters come to life, while adults enjoy the outstanding service, which begins the moment white-gloved stewards escort passengers to their staterooms. Officers are Greek, and the international crew numbers 500.

Basics Staterooms are a compact 152 square feet, but feature many nice touches, including a choice of bed size (up to queen), a big window, a vanity, hair dryer, logo kimonos, an ironing board, and lots of storage space. Suites offer extra space, a mini-bar, large windows, a queen-size bed, and butler service.

Fitness buffs will love the fully-equipped **Bodywaves Spa** and excellent exercise classes, while runners, joggers, and walkers can wear out their Nikes on the rubberized track that circles theship. Less ambitious types can loll in the sauna or steam baths or indulge in one of the beauty treatments offered in the salon. There are two outdoor pools and two Jacuzzis.

113

Other onboard amusements include browsing and buying in the shops, relaxing and socializing in the three bar/lounges, and risking a few dollars in the casino. The entertainment lounge is the venue for productions put on by a shipboard troupe. The children's program keeps young cruisers happy.

Cuisine Fine continental cuisine is served in the modern **Epicurean Restaurant**; there are two dinner seatings. There's also an outdoor cafe, a pizza/ice cream parlor, a coffee lounge, and a late-night buffet. Room service is available for times when you don't feel like "going out."

Norwegian Cruise Line

800/327.7030

NORWEGIAN®
CRUISE LINE

Dreamward/Windward

$$$★★★

Built: 1992/1993

Passengers: 1,242/1,246

Size: 41,000 grt

Cabins: 621/623

Outside: 529/531 (48 with verandas on both ships)

Inside: 92

Suites: 101

Wheelchair Accessible: 6

Registry: Bahamian

Officers/Crew: Norwegian/International

Tipping Policy: $8 to $9 per passenger per day suggested

Smoking Policy: Restricted to designated smoking sections

Snapshot The smallest—and most popular—ships in the **Norwegian Cruise Line** fleet, these classy cruise liners offer a more sophisticated ambience than that found on the rest of the **NCL** fleet.

Itineraries The *Dreamward* offers weeklong cruises, sailing the western Caribbean from Ft. Lauderdale in winter, to Bermuda from New York in summer, and the coasts of New England and eastern Canada in the fall.

The *Windward* departs from San Juan for seven-day Caribbean cruises in winter and moves northwest to Alaska in summer for a series of seven-day voyages from Vancouver. In addition, the *Dreamward* offers a few repositioning cruises between Ft. Lauderdale and New York, while the *Windward* makes a couple of transcanal cruises to the Pacific.

Typical Passengers Preferred by folks seeking a hint of luxury for less, these ships appeal to young travelers attracted by the exceptional sports facilities and high-energy activities. However, cruisers of all ages may be found on board.

Ambience Creative design tactics make these handsome ships seem much more intimate than their size would suggest. There are no vast atriums or glitzy light fixtures—interiors are decorated in subdued pastels with wood furnishings and trim.

The mood on board both the *Dreamward* and the *Windward* is lively but not overpowering. Passengers can choose from a wide selection of activities, sneak off for a tête-à-tête in a cozy lounge, or just commune with the sea. Traditional cruisewear is the norm.

Each ship has Norwegian officers and an international crew of about 700 who provide passengers with a level of attention that's a cut above the good service offered on other **NCL** ships.

Basics The standard staterooms measure just 160 square feet, but a separate sitting area makes them seem larger. Furnishings are made of real wood and are quite nice, but bathrooms are disappointingly small, with showers (no tubs) and very limited storage space for toiletries (except in the top cabins), so pack accordingly. All cabins have TV sets and either twin or queen-size beds.

Among the 51 suites on each ship are six extra-special (and extra-pricey) 350-square-foot units with such extras as a living room, mini-refrigerator, safe, and bathroom with tub. (Tip: Suites are often available for less than the "official" rate.)

Active passengers love these ships and no wonder: Each has a volleyball/basketball court, a rubberized shuffleboard surface, two pools, a Jacuzzi, and a knockout 6,000-square-foot Roman spa featuring state-of-the-art equipment, luxurious steam rooms and saunas, and a salon offering the full spectrum of body and beauty treatments. Duffers can practice their swing in one of two golf driving cages on each ship. The popular fleet-wide **In Motion on the Ocean** fitness program encourages participation with rewards such as Frisbees, fanny packs, hats, T-shirts, and water bottles. For the indolent, each ship's inviting sunbathing deck provides comfortable lounge chairs situated on a series of terraces.

Each ship offers the same menu of entertainment options. Known for its lavish production shows, **NCL** wows 'em with razzle-dazzle Broadway-style shows staged in the flashy **Stardust Lounge.** Both ships also have a shop, a library, and five bar/lounges (the favorite hangout is the **Sports Bar & Grill,** where fans nosh on hot dogs and down massive quantities of beer). At night, the **Observation Lounge** turns into a disco with a marble dance floor and high-tech lighting. The two-deck-high Las Vegas–style casino is packed with gamblers from the minute the doors open.

The **Kid's Crew** program for children ages 6 to 8, 9 to 12, and 13 to 17 offers scavenger hunts, bridge tours, parties, and autograph sessions with pro athletes. Kids can even learn circus routines and put on a performance for adult passengers. Each ship also has a children's playroom and a teen center.

Cuisine Most passengers rave about the American/continental food, but others say it's just so-so. A nice plus is that passengers may dine around in four different venues: **The Terraces** and **Sun Terrace,** ship-width, two-tiered restaurants with floor-to-ceiling windows looking out to sea; **The Four Seasons,** a romantic room decorated in soft pastels, marble, and brass; and **The Cafe,** open only for tea and special wine-tasting events. There's also a bounteous midnight buffet displayed on a replica of a Viking ship, and limited room service (light fare and beverages).

Leeward
$$★★★

Built: 1992

Refurbished: 1995

Passengers: 950

Size: 25,000 grt

Cabins: 482

Outside: 317 (8 with verandas)

Inside: 165

Suites: 16

Wheelchair Accessible: 6

Registry: Bahamian

Officers/Crew: Norwegian/International

Tipping Policy: $8 to $9 per passenger per day suggested

Smoking Policy: Restricted to designated smoking sections

Snapshot NCL took an Baltic ferry and completely transformed it into an attractive mid-size ship offering brief and affordable cruises to tropical islands.

Itinerary The ship offers three- and four-day round-trip hops from Miami to Key West, Nassau, Cozumel, and Great Stirrup Cay (**NCL**'s private island).

Typical Passengers There are young couples and families as well as some single men and women of various ages.

Ambience This former Scandinavian ferry boat now has a sleek Art Deco decor. The smallest cruise ship currently offering three- and four-day tropical cruises, it feels friendlier and less impersonal than some of the megaships. Fun in the sun is the focus here, and there's a festive, party atmosphere on board. The crew is very congenial, and the service is good. Shipboard attire is casual—as you would expect for folks on a brief island getaway—but men don tuxes or dark suits, and women wear evening gowns and cocktail dresses on the one formal night per cruise.

Basics Standard staterooms range in size from 140 to 180 square feet and have twin beds that can convert to a double, wood furniture and cabinetry,

attractive bathrooms with showers, and very limited drawer space; some also offer a separate sitting area.

Onboard facilities include a fitness center and spa, pool, Jacuzzi, and jogging track. Passenger participation in the comprehensive **In Motion on the Ocean** fitness program is encouraged with rewards such as Frisbees, fanny packs, T-shirts, water bottles, and hats.

Lavish Broadway-style shows keep passengers entertained at night while organized fun and games keep everyone amused during the day. The bustling **Sports Bar & Grill** shows televised athletic events and is a popular gathering spot whenever a big game is on. In addition there are three other bar/lounges as well as a casino, video arcade, beauty salon, library, and shops.

The **Kid's Crew** program offers organized fun for three age groups: 6 to 8, 9 to 12, and 13 to 17. Among the activities offered are scavenger hunts, tours of the bridge, parties, games, and instruction on circus routines. There's also a children's playroom.

Cuisine Nightly theme dinners feature usually tasty ethnic fare (Italian, French, Indonesian, Chinese) served in hefty portions. There's also an appealing spa menu for waist-watchers and—at the other end of the caloric spectrum—**NCL**'s luscious "Chocoholic Bar." The two dining rooms are a manageable size, unlike the vast expanses of tables found on most ships. There are two dinner seatings. For a change of pace, passengers may dine at **Le Bistro** or call room service, which is available 24 hours a day (the menu is limited to sandwiches, snacks, and beverages).

Norway
$$$★★★★

Built: 1962

Refurbished: 1996

Passengers: 2,032

Size: 76,049 grt

Cabins: 1,064

Outside: 670

Inside: 394

Suites: 165 (58 with verandas)

Wheelchair Accessible: 11

Registry: Bahamian

Officers/Crew: Norwegian/International

Tipping Policy: About $9 per passenger per day suggested

Smoking Policy: Restricted to designated smoking sections

Snapshot Perfect for nostalgia buffs, this legendary ship, formerly the *France,* offers old-style cruising in an Art Deco setting. Built in 1962, she was magnificently refurbished in 1993, although she still retains some fixtures and furnishings from her younger days. (Also see "A Legendary Liner" on page 10.)

Itinerary The vessel cruises the eastern Caribbean from Miami, with stops at **NCL**'s private island in the Bahamas. Seven-day trips are offered year-round. The ship occasionally hosts popular "Sports Afloat" theme cruises that give passengers a chance to consult with fitness and beauty experts and mingle with professional football, hockey, and basketball players.

At press time the *Norway* had just begun to offer summer transatlantic crossings, which she will continue if there is sufficient demand.

Typical Passengers This venerable ship attracts older travelers who enjoy the old style of cruising. Many passengers sailed this ship when she was the *France*.

Ambience Topped by two stunning glass-enclosed decks, this sleek, stylish matron has classic cruise-ship lines—she's one of the best-looking liners afloat. The decks are teak, and the plush public rooms have Art Deco decor, with hand-laid mosaics, Art Deco murals, marble statues, and a million-dollar art collection.

In keeping with the older clientele, the mood on board is somewhat subdued and restrained. Traditional cruise attire—casual by day, smart on informal nights, very dressy on formal nights—is the norm.

A Norwegian captain and officers oversee a competent international crew of about 900.

Basics There's a wide variety of staterooms in different designs and configurations—the ship's brochure lists more than 20 different categories. On average, cabins measure 150 square feet, and all feature two lower beds, a mini-refrigerator, portholes, and a bathroom with shower. Some cabins retain some elements—such as old-fashioned heated towel racks—from when the ship was the *France*.

Junior suites are a good deal. They cost only $100 to $200 more per passenger per week than a "superior" outside stateroom, and the extra cash buys a sitting area with sofa, two lower beds that convert to a queen- or king-size bed, floor-to-ceiling windows or a large picture window, a vanity, mini-refrigerator, bathroom with tub and shower, and the services of a concierge. There are also penthouse and deluxe penthouse suites, equipped with all of the above plus private balconies, and the **Owner's Suite,** which has a wraparound veranda, a huge bathroom with Roman tub, hot tub, dressing room, living room, and more.

The 6,000-square-foot Roman spa offers cardiovascular equipment, an aquacise pool, and supervised workouts. There's also a health and fitness center that takes up 4,000 square feet of the **Olympic Deck** and offers aerobics, the latest in fitness equipment, and floor-to-ceiling windows from which to watch the sea. If that's not enough, run on the quarter-mile jogging track, shoot hoops on the basketball court, practice your golf swing at the driving range, play volleyball, shoot skeet, or swim in one of the two pools. The popular fleet-wide

In Motion on the Ocean fitness program awards prizes (T-shirts, hats, etc.) based on the number of laps swum, miles run, aerobics classes sweated through, and so on.

There's plenty of deck space for lounging or sunning. Helpful deck stewards fetch fluffy beach towels and lounge chairs, and even proffer iced towels and cool water spritzes. For a more sociable experience, ease into one of the Jacuzzis, which are always filled with people chatting and ordering drinks. The **Sunspots Bar** or the **Pool Bar** are also popular daytime gathering spots. Meanwhile, gamblers flock to the **Monte Carlo Casino,** and shoppers head for the shops and boutiques on the **Promenade Deck.**

For evening entertainment, it's hard to beat the Broadway shows and high-style productions performed in the stunning **Saga Theater.** For pre-dinner drinks and dancing, passengers head for **Checkers Cabaret** or the smaller **North Cape Lounge.** A more intimate aperitif or after-dinner rendezvous spot is the **Windjammer Bar,** which features piano music. Later, the young and young at heart dance the night away in **A Club Called Dazzles.** The ship also boasts one of the plushest nightclubs to sail the seas, the deluxe **Club Internationale.**

For the kids there is the **Trolland** playroom as well the **Kid's Crew** program of organized activities for three age groups: 6 to 8, 9 to 12, and 13 to 17.

Cuisine The American/continental fare—everything from hot dogs and hamburgers to lobster thermidor—is varied enough to please all tastes and appetites. There are assorted theme cuisine nights as well.

Dinner is served in two seatings in the brown and beige **Windward** and **Leeward Dining Rooms,** where attentive but sometimes harried waiters and waitresses do a commendable job. Passengers also may dine at **Le Bistro,** a relaxed, intimate eatery with an Italian/continental menu, open seating, flexible hours, and attentive service. Breakfast, lunch, and snacks are also available in the **Great Outdoor Restaurant** while **Svenn's Ice Cream Parlor** dishes out yummy sundaes, cones, and frozen yogurt. If that's not enough try the "Chocoholic Bar," a scrumptious dessert buffet. Room service is available around the clock.

Norwegian Cruise Line destroys diets with a tempting once-a-cruise "Chocoholic Bar." The buffet features three dozen goodies, including Black Forest cake, brownies, eclairs, chocolate sundaes, biscotti, white chocolate–dipped cream puffs, chocolate whiskey torte, and a calorie-laden concoction called "chunky monkey." The thoughtful NCL chefs also whip up a few sugar-free confections.

Norwegian Crown
$$$★★★★

Built: 1988

Passengers: 1,052

Size: 34,250 grt

Cabins: 526

Outside: 412

Inside: 114

Suites: 90 suites (including 16 penthouses and 4 Owner's Suites)

Wheelchair Accessible: 4

Registry: Bahamian

Officers/Crew: Norwegian/International

Tipping Policy: About $9 per passenger per day suggested

Smoking Policy: Restricted to designated smoking sections

Snapshot Formerly the *Crown Odyssey* of the now-defunct **Royal Cruise Line,** this pretty, contemporary ship was acquired by **Norwegian Cruise Line** in 1996.

Itinerary Seven-day western Caribbean cruises depart from Ft. Lauderdale and Miami in winter. In summer she offers 12-day trips to Scandinavia, the North Cape, the British Isles, and the Canary Islands.

Typical Passengers Passengers include everyone from thirtysomethings to retirees; there are loyal **NCL** followers as well as people who sailed on this ship when she was the *Crown Odyssey.*

Ambience The ship has appealing Art Deco decor, with comfortable furniture, warm woods, and brass, glass, and marble accents.

Shipboard attire is traditional: casual by day and dressy at night. The service is typical of **NCL**—both friendly and efficient.

Basics Standard staterooms (the line calls them "superior deluxe") are about 165 square feet, with two lower beds (most cannot be moved together to makes a double bed), a bathroom with shower, good storage space, and windows. Nice touches include hardwood furniture and cabinetry, a full vanity, two mirrored closets, and a tie and shoe rack.

The sixteen 450- to 550-square-foot penthouse suites are exceptional, with private verandas, hand-crafted cherry furniture, and contemporary art. And the 1,000-square-foot **Owners' Suites** have every convenience and luxury (for a price).

Like all the other **NCL** ships, the *Crown* has a full range of facilities. The Roman-style fitness center and spa includes a fully equipped gym, exercise classes, a sauna, an indoor pool with whirlpools, a juice bar, and a complete menu of beauty treatments. **NCL**'s **In Motion on the Ocean** fitness program provides further incentives to active passengers, who earn souvenirs by exercising. Also on board are a pool, Jacuzzis, a shopping arcade, and a movie theater.

Evening entertainment venues include the show room, site of **NCL**'s signature Broadway-style productions; the casino; and 11 bar/lounges, including a sports bar with a large-screen TV and the **Top of the Crown** lounge, which has 360° views and is a favorite spot for dancing.

The **Kid's Crew** program, offered during the ship's western Caribbean sailings, features contests, ship tours, parties, games—even classes on juggling and other circus routines—for children ages 6 to 8, 9 to 12, and 13 to 17.

Cuisine As on other **NCL** ships, the American/continental fare is varied and tasty, although not outstanding. There are two dinner seatings in the main dining room. For more casual meals, **Le Bistro** offers open-seating, an Italian/continental menu, and a relaxed ambience. There's also a cafe where breakfast and lunch buffets and an afternoon snack are set out. Dining "in" is another option; room service is always available. And don't miss **NCL**'s famed "Chocoholic Bar," a decadent dessert spread offered one evening during each cruise.

Norwegian Star

*This 848-passenger, 28,000-grt ship was added to the **NCL** fleet in spring 1997. It sails from Houston to Cozumel and Calica in Mexico and Roatan in Honduras's Bay Islands.*

Oceanic Cruises

800/545.5778

Oceanic Grace
$$$$★★★★

Built: 1989

Passengers: 120

Size: 5,025 grt

Cabins: 60

Outside: 60 (8 with verandas)

Inside: 0

Suites: 0

Wheelchair Accessible: 1

Registry: Japanese

Officers/Crew: Japanese/International

Tipping Policy: Gratuities included in fare; no additional tips expected

Smoking Policy: Restricted to designated smoking sections

Snapshot This superluxurious, yacht-like sailing ship is a look-alike of **Cunard**'s *Sea Goddesses,* which was the intention of the Japanese mogul who owns it. It offers Asian-style cruising, with stiff bar and wine prices but everything else included.

Few Americans have experienced this ship, which offers an ideal, hassle-free (albeit costly) way to see the coastline and cultural offerings of Asia.

Itinerary The *Grace* offers cruises of varying lengths (from 3 to 58 nights) year-round, visiting China, Guam, Japan, Korea, the Philippines, Singapore, Taiwan, and Russia.

Typical Passengers Just as you'd expect given the price tag and such exotic ports, passengers are older, well-traveled, and urbane. Many are from the top echelon of corporations in Japan and around the world; most are over 40.

Ambience The story goes that after the Japanese owner/founder of **Oceanic Cruises** sailed on the *Sea Goddess*, he decided to build a near-replica for use in the waters of his home turf. The result is this luxurious yacht-size look-alike.

Dress is formal in the evening, with most Asian women draped in kimonos, western women in spiffy designer ensembles, and men in suits on informal nights and tuxedos on formal occasions.

Basics Standard cabins are neatly laid out on 185 square feet of space. Appointments include twin or queen-size beds, sofa, desk/dresser, vanity, TV with VCR, mini-bar and mini-refrigerator, robes, toiletries, safe, and a marble-trimmed bathroom with recessed Japanese tub. Eight suites have private balconies.

The cruises are light on entertainment, heavy on culture and sightseeing. There is no casino or show room, but a dance band plays in a lovely lounge.

The nice-sized gym has all the necessary equipment for a thorough workout; a personal trainer is available. The retractable water-sports platform at the stern allows passengers to dive directly into the sea, hop on a jet ski, water ski, or scuba dive. A jogging track, small outdoor pool, Jacuzzi, and beauty salon round out the list of health and fitness facilities.

Cuisine Wonderful Japanese delicacies from sashimi and sushi to teriyaki as well as equally tempting continental fare (from steaks to lobster) are perfectly prepared by chefs trained in the top restaurants of Tokyo. Meals are served at a single seating with no table assignments.

 Megaship  **Traditional Cruise Liner**

Sailing Ship  **Expedition Ship**

 Ultraluxury Ship

Large ships (more than 1,000 passengers): Blue
Mid-size ships (500-1,000 passengers): Green
Small ships (fewer than 500 passengers): Red

Orient Lines

800/333.7300

ORIENT LINES®
THE DESTINATION CRUISE SPECIALISTS

 Marco Polo
$$$★★★★

Built: 1965
Refurbished: 1993
Passengers: 850
Size: 22,080 grt
Cabins: 425
Outside: 292
Inside: 133
Suites: 6
Wheelchair Accessible: 2
Registry: Bahamian
Officers/Crew: Scandinavian/Filipino
Tipping Policy: About $8 per passenger per day suggested
Smoking Policy: Restricted to designated smoking sections

Snapshot An expedition vessel, *Marco Polo* offers excellent food and service and fascinating ports of call. Founded in 1993 by British entrepreneur/adventurer Gerry Herrod, this one-ship cruise line is ideal for adventurous types who enjoy a little luxury with their explorations.

Itinerary She just about covers the world in various 10- to 20-day cruises: the Antarctic Peninsula in December and January, New Zealand and Australia in February, Southeast Asia in March, Egypt and Africa in April, and the Greek Isles and the Mediterranean from May through October.

Typical Passengers They are globetrotters, mostly couples in their forties, fifties, and older. Many are retired executives from the US and England; all are more interested in the educational programs and exotic destinations than shipboard life.

Ambience As one passenger put it, "It just feels the way a ship should feel." Stylish without going overboard, the *Marco Polo* features an impressive collection of Oriental art and antiques. The mood on board is convivial, and attire is traditional cruisewear. Sea-savvy Scandinavian officers and cheerful Filipino crew members provide service that's simply superb.

Basics Standard staterooms are suitable if not overly spacious (most measure only 120 square feet). Each offers cleverly constructed closet space, twin beds or a double, a desk/vanity, a dresser, and a compact bathroom with built-in hair dryer and a shower or tub. Accommodations aren't the strong suit of this ship, but most passengers use their cabins mainly to dress and sleep.

Shore excursions are the vessel's raison d'être, and they're exceptionally well run. When in port, Zodiacs and high-speed tenders shuttle passengers to remote spots, accompanied by naturalists, anthropologists, and other experts. Also first-rate are the lectures offered on board.

Although this is a "destination" vessel, with an ice-breaker bow and an emphasis on exploration, shipboard amenities are ample. A big nod of approval goes to the fabulous fitness center, where treadmills, bicycles, and Stairmasters are situated in front of wide windows looking out to sea. Effective, but not exhausting, exercise classes are held daily. Arranged around the fitness/beauty center are saunas, steam baths, a juice bar, and a salon offering the usual beauty treatments. Three outdoor decks offer plenty of space, as well as a smallish pool, three very popular Jacuzzis, and a walking track that circles the entire ship.

After the day's expedition, many passengers adjourn to the pretty **Palm Lounge,** the perfect setting for afternoon tea or cocktails. At night, an onboard troupe stages variety shows or local singers and dancers perform. The most popular evening pastimes are ballroom dancing and sitting on a green stool at the granite bar in the Art Deco **Polo Lounge** listening to entertainer David Perry play the piano, tell jokes, and belt out a repertoire of tunes.

Rounding out the list of shipboard facilities are a small casino (it's hardly ever used); a library; and three boutiques.

Cuisine The inventive California/continental menu, created in part by designer-pizza king Wolfgang Puck (of LA's **Spago** fame), is quite pleasing. In addition to the main dining room, which has assigned seats and two dinner seatings, **Raffles** restaurant serves as a casual dinner spot. It features specialties of whatever region the ship is located at the time and offers substantial self-service breakfast and lunch buffets. Room service is available.

"There is *nothing*—absolutely nothing—half so much worth doing as simply messing about in boats. In or out of 'em, it doesn't matter. Nothing seems really to matter, that's the charm of it. Whether you get away or whether you don't; whether you arrive at your destination or whether you reach somewhere else, or whether you never get anywhere at all, you're always busy, and you never do anything in particular; and when you've done it there's always something else to do, and you can do it if you like, but you'd much better not."

Rat, in *The Wind in the Willows,* by Kenneth Grahame

Talk About a Water Hazard!: Golf on the High Seas

The link between golfing and cruising is an unlikely one. Golf, after all, is played on wide expanses of grassy land, and cruises, well, they take place on *water.* Cruise lines, nonetheless, have done everything in their power to lure duffers to sea, offering not only golf excursions in port, but an array of golf-related facilities and programs aboard ship. These include putting greens, mini-golf courses, driving cages, virtual-reality courses, golf-theme sailings, and workshops with pros.

When **Royal Caribbean** introduced *Legend of the Seas* in 1995, it boasted a seagoing first: a top-deck mini-golf course, complete with little waterfalls, lakes, and bridges. The 6,000-square-foot "Legend of the Links" proved so popular that the company built a similar course, dubbed "Splendour of the Greens," on *Splendour of the Seas,* launched in 1996. Not coincidentally, **Royal Caribbean** is the official cruise line of the **Professional Golfers' Association of America,** the **PGA Tour,** the **Senior PGA Tour,** and the **Ladies Professional Golf Association Tour.**

Aboard **Princess Cruises'** *Sun Princess,* an indoor golf simulator challenges players with six virtual-reality championship courses. **Cunard's** *Royal Viking Sun* is equipped with both a simulator and an outdoor putting green, while the *Queen Elizabeth 2* is one of several liners to build theme sailings around golf, featuring lectures and workshops with big-name pros. **Crystal Cruises** takes pride in its resident pros, who are available on most cruises to help passengers brush up on their strokes. And **Radisson Seven Seas** is one of the many lines that arrange golf outings in ports, including transportation. That means golfers can play several courses in one vacation.

Other cruise ships offer driving practice from the deck into the sea. Passengers need not fret about filling up the ocean with golf balls—most are specially manufactured to decompose in salt water.

Fore!

Premier Cruise Lines

800/327.7113

*Note: **Premier Cruise Line** and its ship, the* Oceanic, *were sold in March 1997 to Cruise Holdings, Ltd. At press time there were no plans to change the* Oceanic*'s itinerary. The new owner also indicated that it would continue to use the **Premier Cruise Line/The Big Red Boat** name. Check with your travel agent for up-to-the minute information.*

Star/Ship Oceanic

$$★★

Built: 1965

Refurbished: 1993

Passengers: 1,800

Size: 38,772 grt

Cabins: 558

Outside: 252

Inside: 306

Suites: 8

Wheelchair Accessible: 1

Registry: Bahamian

Officers/Crew: Greek/International

Tipping Policy: About $9 per passenger per day suggested

Smoking Policy: Restricted to designated smoking sections

Snapshot The Big Red Boat promises (and delivers) affordable fun for the whole family. Although now known for cruise packages that include pre- and post-cruise stops to **Disney World, Premier** may abandon this program when **Disney Cruises** introduces its new *Disney Magic* supership in 1998.

Itinerary Three and four-day cruises to Nassau and Port Lucaya in the Bahamas depart from Port Canaveral year-round.

Typical Passengers The ship is filled with young couples and their children and older couples and their grandchildren. There's a small smattering of singles.

Ambience The red-hulled vessel features multilevel teak decks and a bright, cheery, contemporary decor.

The exuberance of the young passengers rubs off on all aboard this modern megaliner. Everybody's happy and excited, so things can get a little loud and chaotic at times. Attire is a little more casual here than on other cruise ships. Shorts and T-shirts are de rigueur for all ages during the day; adults dress up a bit at night. Service is good.

Basics Tailor-made for kids, the *Oceanic* features a huge playroom, a children's pool, and a super teen center complete with video game arcade, movie theater, and assorted other fun stuff. Adults can amuse themselves at two grown-ups' pools (covered by a retractable roof), on the jogging track, in the gym and weight room, or in the casino, entertainment lounge, pub, disco, and shops.

Cabins average 200 square feet, with upper berths and bathrooms with tubs. Suites offer additional space (475 square feet), separate sitting areas, and twin or queen-size beds.

Cuisine If your tastes tend to hamburgers, hot dogs, and apple pie, this ship's for you. These and other home-style American choices are served in the ship's dining room. There are two dinner seatings. Room service is not available.

Princess Cruises

800/PRINCESS

Crown Princess/ Regal Princess

$$$★★★★★

*Despite their size (1,590 passengers, 70,000 tons), these pretty, extravagantly equipped ships have a friendly, intimate feeling. They're among the best **Princess** has to offer. See page 76 for a detailed description.*

Dawn Princess/ Sun Princess

$$★★★★

Towering 14 decks high and measuring almost three football fields long, they're smart-looking sister megaships with lots to offer. See page 78 for a detailed description.

Grand Princess

*When she is launched 1998, this 105,000-grt, 2,600-passenger ship will be the largest luxury liner in the world. Like **Princess**'s other "Grand Class" ships (the Sun Princess and Dawn Princess), she will offer numerous public rooms, hundreds of cabins with private balconies, several dining options, and a wrap-around promenade deck.*

Island Princess/ Pacific Princess

$$$★★★★

Built: 1971/1972

Refurbished: 1993/1993

Passengers: 640

Size: 20,000 grt

Cabins: 305

Outside: 238

Inside: 67

Suites: 13

Wheelchair Accessible: 4

Registry: British

Officers/Crew: British/International

Tipping Policy: About $8 per passenger per day suggested

Smoking Policy: Prohibited in dining rooms and some entertainment lounges; allowed in most other public areas

Snapshot The original "Love Boats," on which many scenes from the eponymous television series were filmed, are now the runts of **Princess Cruises'** flourishing fleet. After 25 years of service, these extremely well-preserved twins are still charmers, offering comfortable cabins, outstanding service, first-rate shows—and a classic cruising experience.

Itinerary The *Pacific Princess* sails the Mediterranean and Europe in the summer and fall and Africa in winter. The *Island Princess* is based in the Mediterranean in summer and Asia, India, and Australia in winter. Both ships generally make 12- to 18-day voyages.

Typical Passengers Most of the folks on board are middle-aged or older and fairly well-to-do. Many are long-time *Princess* fans who refuse to sail on any other cruise line.

Ambience In a sea of overly commercial cruise ships, these two offer a refreshing change of pace. You won't find glitzy public rooms, cabins with verandas, or truly lavish suites, but you will encounter a cozy, understated decor; friendly fellow travelers; and the warm, pampering atmosphere of an old-style cruise.

Charming British officers, skilled stewards, attentive Italian waiters, and the rest of each ship's topnotch international crew of 350 cater to passengers, many of whom are familiar regulars. Daytime wear is casual, but pack your nicest evening clothes—you'll feel like dressing up at night.

Basics Standard cabins range in size from 126 square feet to a much roomier 275 square feet. All are comfortable and are equipped with twin beds and baths with showers. Suites are 443 square feet and offer separate sitting areas, twin beds that convert to doubles, mini-refrigerators, and baths with showers. Terry robes are provided in all cabins for use as bathrobes or cover-ups at the pool.

Cabin stewards and/or stewardesses keep everything tidy and spotless, bring breakfast, and otherwise serve passengers well. Most get to know their charges' habits quickly and are soon delivering a favorite beverage at exactly the right time every day and cleaning the rooms when it is most convenient for their occupants.

Each of the ships also has a small fitness center, a spa, two pools, three bar/lounges, a casino, and a host of organized activities. The shows are among the best at sea.

Cuisine Perhaps because there are fewer mouths to feed on these than on other *Princess* ships, the finely tuned dining rooms turn out some of the best food in the fleet. The fare is a mix of continental/Italian and American; the pizza and pasta are particularly noteworthy. For the diet-conscious, there's the enticing "Healthy Choice" menu offering creative low-cholesterol and fat- and sodium-reduced dishes.

The dining rooms are more intimate than those on most ships, and the service is excellent. There are two dinner seatings. In warm weather, breakfast and lunch buffets are set up on deck. Room service is available 24 hours a day.

Perfect Gentlemen

Who are those dashing dancers, those suave and sophisticated seagoing gents, who prowl the lounges of cruise liners seeking the company of unattached ladies?

Maritime mashers? Cruise ship Casanovas?

No. They're "gentlemen hosts," and they're perfectly aboveboard.

Because some cruises attract larger numbers of single women than single men—which can make it awkward for ladies who love to dance—companies sign up carefully screened "hosts" to serve as dancing, dining, and social partners. Most are accomplished, retired or semiretired fellows who share their social graces aboard ship in exchange for traveling the world in style. They have strict orders: no favoritism, no tips, and no hanky-panky!

Gentlemen hosts must be experts at breaking the ice as well as impeccable dancers. **Cunard** ships feature "guest hosts," while **Crystal Cruises'** **Ambassador Host Program** promises at least four gentlemen hosts on each sailing. **Silversea Cruises** have multitalented hosts whose duties range from dancing the bossa nova to playing bridge.

Holland America Line provides hosts on selected sailings, usually cruises of at least 10 days. The line even promises that, time allowing, hosts will accompany singles on shore excursions.

Cruising European Waterways

River cruising in **Europe** is scenery-rich, with breathtaking views of medieval castles towering high above forested riverbanks, towers and church steeples stretching for the sky, and island fortresses perched precariously in midstream. As the continent's great cities float by, passengers relax on the spacious open decks of an intimate riverboat, savor regional cuisine in dining rooms with panoramic windows, or even take a dip in a glass-domed pool.

Popular for years with Europeans, river cruising on the continent is catching on like wildfire with Americans. Unlike barges, which are smaller and usually less luxurious (see "Barging Through Europe," page 248), riverboats are more like small cruise ships, with multiple decks and cabins with private baths. A wide range of journeys is offered by numerous cruise lines. Here are a few:

KD River Cruises is Europe's largest river cruise operator, with a fleet of nearly a dozen boats offering 38 itineraries and a total of almost 450 departures. **KD** ships cruise the waterways of **Austria, France, Germany, the Netherlands, Switzerland, the Czech Republic, Hungary,** and **Slovakia.** All cabins have river views, every dining room is glass-walled, and a few boats are

equipped with swimming pools. For information, call 800/346.6525 from the Eastern US, 800/858.8587 from the West.

Peter Deilmann EuropAmerica Cruises offers more than 150 sailings on a fleet of small, graciously appointed ships plying the **Danube, Rhine, Moselle, Rhone, Saône,** and **Elbe Rivers,** as well as the **Rhine-Main-Danube Canal.** These vessels boast comfortable lounges and bars, libraries, beauty salons, and plenty of open deck space. Some even have heated swimming pools. Seven-, 10- and 11-night cruises are offered from March into November. For information, call 800/348.8287.

Sea Cloud Kreuzfahrten, the German company that operates the historic sailing ship *Sea Cloud,* has built a new vessel, the 98-passenger *River Cloud,* which cruises the Rhine, Main, Danube, Moselle, and other rivers from April to mid-October. For details, call 800/825.0826.

EuroCruises offers trips aboard vintage steamers that ply **Sweden**'s **Göta Canal,** which links Göteborg on the west coast with **Stockholm** on the east. The journey entails navigating through 65 locks, past fortress ruins, medieval cloisters, thick forests, and picturesque hamlets. Fresh gravlax and other Swedish specialties grace the table. Call 800/688.3876.

MICHAEL STORRINGS

Oriana
$$$★★★

Built: 1996

Passengers: 1,800

Size: 69,153 grt

Cabins: 914

Outside: 594 (118 with verandas)

Inside: 320

Suites: 8

Wheelchair Accessible: 8

Registry: British

Officers/Crew: British/International

Tipping Policy: About $8 per passenger per day suggested

Smoking Policy: Prohibited in dining and entertainment lounges; allowed in most other public areas

Snapshot This megaship debuted in January 1996 with a world cruise. While the *Oriana* is already

heavily marketed in England, **Princess Cruises** recently decided to promote her more extensively in the US.

Itinerary The ship circles the globe, departing from Southampton, England; travelers may sail on 17-, 20-, 22-, 27-, and 90-day cruises.

Typical Passengers At present, Englishmen and -women of varied ages, many with families, take these cruises. A major North American marketing blitz by **Princess** should attract more Americans.

Ambience Everything is very British, from afternoon tea to the Monty Pythonesque entertainers. The mood is lively, and the public areas are bright and cheerful, blending modern and traditional styles. Public rooms display an extensive collection of works by British artists, including sculptures, watercolors, limited edition prints, specially commissioned murals, and trompe l'oeil paintings. The crew is able and efficient.

Basics Staterooms vary from splendid suites to four-berth affairs. They range in size from 151-square-foot cabins to 501-square-foot suites. All offer twin beds that can convert to a double; higher-priced units have bathtubs. Standard staterooms are comfortable enough, with wide windows, wood furnishings, and good storage space, but if you can afford to splurge, suites are the way to go. They offer added space, lots of storage room, a mini-refrigerator, a separate sitting room, and a large glass door that opens onto a private veranda.

Features include a big **Champney's** health spa (one of the very few cruise ship spas not run by **Steiner**), three pools, five Jacuzzis, acres of deck space, and a wide wraparound promenade deck. The usual organized activities are available.

Families' needs are well-served by the ship's extensive youth program. An entire deck is dedicated to kids, with a pool, a spacious lounge, a video gameroom, and a large disco for teens. Activities include games, arts and crafts, dances, and pizza parties. Other nice touches include baby-listening facilities in each cabin, and a night nursery for tots ages 2 to 5. There's even a children's tea every afternoon.

For nighttime entertainment there are nightly shows, six lounges, nine bars, three dance floors (with music provided by live musicians), a disco, and a casino.

Cuisine The menu is extensive; offerings might include pâté and smoked salmon appetizers, sole Veronique or prime rib as entrées, and cherries jubilee and French pastries for dessert. But the emphasis is on traditional English favorites such as kippers, kidney pie, black pudding, fried bread, pheasant, game stews, shepherd's pie, and the like. Lots of potatoes and farmhouse cheeses are served, but there's nary a pasta or green salad in sight.

Meals are served in two seatings in two nicely appointed dining rooms. Passengers also have the option of enjoying lavish buffets (breakfast, lunch, and dinner) in the **Conservatory.** Room service is available around the clock.

⚓ Royal Princess
$$$★★★★

Built: 1984

Refurbished: 1995

Passengers: 1,200

Size: 45,000 grt

Cabins: 600

Outside: 600 (150 with verandas)

Inside: 0

Suites: 14 and 52 mini suites (all with verandas)

Wheelchair Accessible: 6

Registry: British

Officers/Crew: British/International

Tipping Policy: About $8 per passenger per day suggested

Smoking Policy: Prohibited in the dining rooms and entertainment lounges; allowed in most other public areas

Snapshot When **Princess Cruises** inaugurated this sleek ship in 1984 she was the largest and most luxurious of the fleet and the first to offer all outside staterooms and private verandas in several cabins (a trend that caught on fast among competing cruise lines). While she's no longer the biggest, the *Royal* is as lovely as ever and still one of **Princess**'s best.

Itinerary She sails the New England and Canadian coasts in the fall, South America and Africa in the spring and summer, and the Mediterranean in the winter. Cruises vary in length; most are 10 or 14 days.

Typical Passengers Both **Princess** loyalists and first-time **Princess** cruisers mount the gangway—people who enjoy big luxury liner cruising like this ship. The typical passenger is middle-aged, but it's not unusual to encounter twenty- and thirty-somethings along with a few seniors.

Ambience Lovely to look at, the *Royal Princess* features sensuous curving stairways along five exquisitely designed decks embellished with fine art, plants, murals, tapestries, and top-quality appointments throughout. A beautiful blend of classic luxury liner and contemporary cruise ship, she offers an atmosphere of comfortable, understated elegance.

Pack a spiffy evening wardrobe—on formal nights most men wear tuxedos (although dark suits are acceptable) and women show up in their dressiest evening gowns. Casual resortwear is perfect for day.

The British captain and officers oversee a friendly international crew of 520. Everyone from the deck crew and the stateroom stewards on up to the captain provides excellent, attentive service.

Basics Every stateroom is a winner, with the exception of a few on the lower decks that have windows obstructed by lifeboats. Standard staterooms (168 square feet) are quite comfortable, with twin beds that can convert to one queen-size, ample storage space, picture windows, a TV set, a mini-refrigerator, vanity, and original lithographs on the walls. The big bathrooms have tubs and showers and are furnished with such nice extras as a hair dryer, terry robes, and toiletries.

Staterooms on the **Aloha Deck** have private verandas and are well worth the extra cost. Or, if your budget can handle it, go for a mini-suite with a private veranda, floor-to-ceiling windows, and much more space (231 square feet). Big spenders will want to splurge on an 800-square-foot **Royal** or **Princess Suite,** which have all of the above and more (whirlpool bath, Oriental rugs, and other extras). Whatever the cabin category, the stateroom attendants keep everything clean and orderly and cheerfully respond to any request.

Fitness facilities include three pools on the large **Lido Deck,** a large lap pool, two deck Jacuzzis, a jogger's dream track that wraps around the **Promenade Deck,** a fully equipped gym with wide windows that look out to sea, and a spa/salon offering everything from hair styling to massage and aromatherapy. **Princess**'s

Cruisercize program provides exercise classes by ace instructors; participation is rewarded with coupons redeemable for logo merchandise. There are also the usual shipboard activities for adults (dance classes, language lessons, bingo, skeet shooting) and a children's program.

The gorgeous entertainment lounge is the site of lavish shows with flashy costumes (many the creations of noted Hollywood designer Bob Mackie). There's also the bustling **Crown** casino, which fills up with hopefuls after the shows; the **Horizon Lounge,** which doubles as a disco (and usually is filled with more officers than passengers); and several cozy lounges to snuggle up for pre- or post-prandial drinks. Also on board is a pretty movie theater and the usual duty-free shops.

Cuisine As on all **Princess** ships, the food is continental with English and Italian influences, but it's just a bit better here than on most other ships in the fleet—possibly because the *Royal* is smaller than the others. Few ships do a better beef Wellington and baked Alaska, and the fresh pasta is always a winning choice. This is a ship that still breaks out the caviar (osetra and sevruga) on occasion. An excellent "Healthy Choice" menu offers low-cholesterol, low-fat, and reduced-sodium dishes.

Meals are served in the inviting and elegant dining room, which has two dinner seatings. Other eateries include the 24-hour **Lido Cafe**, where breakfast and lunch are served buffet-style, and a pizzeria. Room service delivers breakfast, lunch, and dinner to staterooms during regular meal times, snacks and beverages around the clock.

Sky Princess

$$$★★★★

Built: 1984

Refurbished: 1992

Passengers: 1,200

Size: 46,000 grt

Cabins: 600

Outside: 347

Inside: 215

Suites: 10 (with verandas), 28 mini suites

Wheelchair Accessible: 6

Registry: British

Officers/Crew: British/International

Tipping Policy: About $8 per passenger per day suggested

Smoking Policy: Prohibited in the dining rooms and entertainment lounges; allowed in most other public areas

Snapshot In the past she was the *Fairsky,* operated by **Sitmar Cruises** (which was acquired by **Princess**). With the arrival of **Princess Cruises'** "Grand Class" megaliners, the *Sky* was moved into the cruise line's "Exotic Adventures" series and sent to Southeast Asia.

Itinerary Exotic ports are a specialty: Bangkok to Sydney, Osaka to Hong Kong, Sydney to Tahiti and the South Pacific. During the summer she makes a series of Alaskan cruises from San Francisco, and one voyage from Vancouver to Osaka and back. Cruises are seven to 11 days or longer.

Typical Passengers Repeat cruisers from the days when she was the popular *Fairsky* are often found aboard the *Sky*. Passengers tend to be middle-aged and older, although there are couples with children as well.

Ambience A 1995 refurbishment brought some nice touches to the ship's aging interior. The decor now features marble floors, plush carpeting, Venetian-glass light fixtures, silk-covered walls, lots of brass, leather chairs and sofas, and plants.

The ship has a comfortable, quietly festive air. Passengers dress casually during the day and elegantly in the evening; many men wear tuxedos on the formal nights. The quality of service is excellent.

Basics Quite the charmer, the *Sky* offers spacious staterooms measuring 170 to 520 square feet. The standard cabins have twin beds that convert to doubles, bathrooms with showers, and good closet space.

There's a plethora of shipboard amenities. Broadway-style shows, a bustling casino, and a lively disco provide evening entertainment, while during the day an always-energetic cruise director keeps passengers busy with everything from Trivial Pursuit games to dance lessons to grandmothers' bragging sessions. **Princess's Cruisercize** program plus a well-equipped gym fill the bill for fitness enthusiasts. There are also acres of deck space, two nice-sized pools, a Jacuzzi, the usual cluster of duty-free shops, a library, cinema, lots of lounges and cozy bars, and plenty of pleasant nooks and crannies to steal off to for a quiet moment.

Cuisine The continental food is typical of **Princess** ships; every edible from hot dogs and hamburgers to beef Wellington and caviar is served. The two bright, attractive dining rooms are staffed with charming waiters. Dinner is served in two seatings. There are breakfast and lunch buffets, and room service is available around the clock.

Star Princess

As this book went to press, the Star *had been renamed the* Arcadia *and repositioned in England, where she will operate under the aegis of* **P&O Cruises,** *another branch of the company that owns* **Princess Cruises***.*

Actually heard on board:

Passenger: Is the pool filled with fresh water or salt water?

Steward: Salt water, ma'am.

Passenger: Oh, that's why it's so rough.

Radisson Seven Seas Cruise Line

800/333.3333

RADISSON SEVEN SEAS
C R U I S E S

Hanseatic

$$$$★★★★

Built: 1993

Passengers: 188

Size: 9,000 grt

Cabins: 90

Outside: 90

Inside: 0

Suites: 4

Wheelchair Accessible: 2

Registry: Bahamian

Officers/Crew: European/International

Tipping Policy: Gratuities included in fare; no additional tips expected

Smoking Policy: Restricted to designated smoking sections (the policy is not strictly enforced)

Snapshot Indisputably the classiest of the expedition ships—it's not unusual for a harpist to play while you sail past fjords and icebergs. With a special "1-A-1 Super" ice classification, she can travel through frigid seas.

Itinerary The *Hanseatic* cruises Scandinavia, Spitsbergen, Iceland, and Greenland in summer, the Caribbean and South America in fall.

Typical Passengers On board you'll find curious explorers of all ages. These cruises are not suitable for small children and can pose some problems for the disabled (particularly getting in and out of the Zodiac landing craft).

Ambience The mood is distinctively adventurous and cerebral—passengers select this ship for its excursions to remote locations and take a lively interest in each area's history, culture, flora and fauna, and topography. Nonetheless, the setting is smart and stylish, with lots of rich wood and expensive appointments.

Dress is informal, although men do wear jackets and ties at dinnertime (no tuxes required). Parkas and rubber boots are provided for Arctic and Antarctic shore excursions.

The European officers run an excellent ship, and the international crew of 134 garners rave reviews from past passengers. There is one crew member for every four passengers.

Basics Measuring 236 square feet, each stateroom is nicely appointed with wood-toned paneling, marble bath with tub and shower, hair dryer, lots of closet space, convertible twin beds, a separate sitting area, TV with VCR, and mini-refrigerator stocked with soft drinks. Cabins in the top three categories have picture windows; others have large portholes.

Four deluxe suites are a roomy 475 square feet; they also offer such extras as a walk-in closet, large living area, and the services of a personal butler (also provided to passengers in the **Bridge Deck** staterooms).

Most of the fun occurs when passengers, accompanied by expert guides, are taken ashore in one of the ship's 14 Zodiacs. There they may catch a glimpse of a rare masked booby or get up close to penguins. (There is no charge for shore excursions.) Lectures by biologists and naturalists further enhance the onshore expeditions.

Back on board, passengers can get a 180° view from large windows of the **Observation Lounge**—a great place for a close look at the fjords or even a glimpse of a family of polar bears perched on the ice. Amateur mariners can head for the special **Passenger Bridge** to read the ship's chart or check out the radar monitor. Passengers are also welcome on the **Navigational Bridge,** where the captain or officers are always willing to chat (providing they're not busy with some intricate maneuver).

A small but well-equipped fitness center meets the needs of exercise enthusiasts while a pool and glass-enclosed Jacuzzi provide a pleasant outlet for hedonists. Saunas, massage, and hair styling also are available.

There's little in the way of formal nighttime entertainment save for a small band playing dance music in the **Observation Lounge,** which also doubles as a movie theater. There's a library, a small boutique, and a couple of bar/lounges, but no casino.

Cuisine Austrian chefs prepare commendable comestibles—not extraordinary, but sufficient to fuel the intrepid travelers on board. Meals are served in the charming **Marco Polo Restaurant**, which has open seating. The **Columbus Lounge** provides a casual setting for breakfast and luncheon buffets, while there's English-style tea each afternoon in the **Observation Lounge.** Meals, snacks, or beverages are available in the cabins around the clock.

Paul Gauguin

Scheduled to be launched as this book went to press, this 18,800-ton, 320-passenger luxury liner will offer seven-night cruises year-round in French Polynesia (Tahiti, Bora Bora, and other Society Islands, as well as Rangiroa in the Tuamotu Archipelago).

The ship will feature 160 staterooms ranging in size from 249 to 299 square feet; all will have ocean views and half will have verandas. The seven suites will measure

from 300 to 457 square feet and boast large verandas. Stateroom amenities will include two twin beds that convert to one queen-size, a marble bathroom with shower and full-size tub, TV with VCR, and a stocked mini-refrigerator.

The cruises will focus on shore excursions; lectures on Polynesian culture and the island's natural environment will be offered. Among the onboard facilities will be a spa and fully equipped fitness center, an outdoor pool, a retractable marina, and an alfresco restaurant in addition to the main dining room. A casino, lounge, and night-club will provide evening entertainment.

Radisson Diamond
$$$$★★★★★

This twin-hulled catamaran-style luxury liner rates all-star status for the food, efficient and attentive service, and incredible smoothness of ride. See page 80 for a detailed description.

Song of Flower
$$$$★★★★★★

A tiny gem, she packs elegance, entertainment, and outstanding service into one exceptional all-inclusive package. This ship is so special, past passengers keep on coming back for more. See page 82 for a detailed description.

Renaissance Cruises

800/525.5350

R1/R2

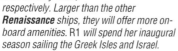

These new 690-passenger ships are scheduled to be launched in August 1998 and February 1999, respectively. Larger than the other *Renaissance* ships, they will offer more on-board amenities. R1 *will spend her inaugural season sailing the Greek Isles and Israel.*

Renaissance V, VI, VII & VIII
$$$★★★

Built: 1989

Passengers: 114

Size: 4,280 grt

Cabins: 57

Outside: 57 suite-like staterooms (12 with verandas)

Inside: 0

Suites: 0

Wheelchair Accessible: 0

Registry: Liberian

Officers/Crew: Italian/International

Tipping Policy: $15-plus per passenger per day suggested

Smoking Policy: Prohibited in all public rooms

Snapshot Four small, identical all-suite ships travel to interesting ports and offer passengers the thrill of sailing on what feels like a private yacht.

Itinerary With a variety of 11- and 13-day voyages, the fleet pretty much covers the world: the Seychelles, Indonesia, the Baltic Sea, Northern Europe, the Mediterranean, the Greek Isles, and Africa (where land safaris are offered). Most of the cruises include before and after land packages.

Typical Passengers The **Renaissance** "type" is a quite congenial, very well-traveled, educated, and experienced cruiser who's partial to small ships. Many people on these ships are repeat passengers who return with friends they met on previous **Renaissance** cruises. Ages vary, but the majority are well into their sixties; there are a few 40-and 50-year-olds and the occasional family. (But there really aren't enough activities to entertain young children.)

Ambience The overall look is very yacht-like, with lots of shiny wood, brass trim, and mirrors, and the mood is warm, relaxed, and convivial. Passengers mingle easily, and many friendships are struck up. (The downside is that with so few passengers, everyone seems to know everyone else's business.)

Dress is nautical casual, with jackets and ties and cocktail dresses suggested, but not required, only on the one or two formal nights. Walking shorts and polo shirts or the like are fine during the day, with resort casualwear the norm most evenings.

The service is always good, and sometimes outstanding.

Basics The all-outside staterooms, which this line calls "suites," really do give passengers the sense of sailing on a private yacht. Although large by industry standards (210 to 287 square feet), they feel smaller. Each one is laid out a little differently but all have twin beds that convert to queen-size, mini-refrigerators, sofas and chairs, TV/VCRs, and desk/vanities. Bathrooms are small and have showers only; they come equipped with toiletries and robes. Be sure to pack lightly—storage space is severely limited (probably the reason for the relaxed dress code).

There are none of the organized activities or entertainment found on larger ships, which suits the typical *Renaissance* passenger just fine. Guests are welcomed on board with Champagne cocktails, then pretty much left on their own to enjoy the yacht-like cruise experience and shore excursions.

The only forms of formal entertainment are the piano player and small band that play during tea and cocktail hours, and an occasional appearance by local performers, such as folk dancers, during some port calls. There is a staff/passenger talent show once a week, and the cruise director gives informative port talks.

The ships' facilities are also minimal. There are no gyms or spas; what they call "pools" are actually tiny saltwater dunking tubs; and the ships' Jacuzzis have been put out of commission due to health concerns. But each vessel boasts a retractable marina that allows easy access to the sea for swimming, snorkeling, jet skiing, or diving (it more than makes up for the ships' other deficiencies).

Each ship also offers a shoebox-size casino, a small boutique, a beauty salon, a library well stocked with both books and videos, and two bars: **The Lounge,** a popular pre-dinner gathering spot where a trio or piano player provides background music, and **The Club,** where afternoon tea is served, and drinks are poured at night.

Cuisine The entire fleet dishes out identical menus of basic American fare. The quality is inconsistent, but few passengers complain; nobody's on board for gourmet meals. It's best to avoid dishes that sound too fancy and stick with simple choices.

The breakfast and lunch buffets are not exactly lavish, but afternoon tea, late-night snacks, and room service fill in the gaps. The dining room is attractive and quiet, with tables that accommodate large parties or couples. There are no assigned seats, and passengers are free to dine when they like within certain time frames. Waiters are extremely attentive and go out of their way to please. By the second day most call passengers by name.

Room service delivers full lunches and dinners to cabins during normal meal hours; a limited room service menu is offered at other times from breakfast until 11PM.

Royal Caribbean International

800/327.6700

Enchantment

Launched just as this book went to press, this 73,000-grt, 1,950-passenger megaship will offer seven-night eastern Caribbean voyages from Miami year-round.

Grandeur of the Seas

$$★★★★

Built: 1996

Passengers: 1,950

Size: 74,000

Cabins: 975

Outside: 576 (212 with verandas)

Inside: 399

Suites: 82 (with verandas); 4 family suites; 5 owner's suites; 1 royal suite

Wheelchair Accessible: 14

Registry: Liberian

Officers/Crew: Scandinavian/International

Tipping Policy: About $8 per passenger per day suggested

Smoking Policy: Prohibited in entertainment lounge; restricted to designated smoking sections in all other public areas

Snapshot The newest addition to **Royal Caribbean's** fleet (launched in December 1996), this ship has something for almost everyone, from great children's facilities to a lively disco to a Las Vegas–style casino.

Itinerary *Grandeur of the Seas* makes seven-night eastern Caribbean cruises year-round from Miami.

Typical Passengers Couples and singles age 30 and older, both first-time cruisers and loyal **Royal Caribbean** fans, are found on board year-round. In the summer, younger parents and their children liven up the mix.

Ambience This megaship is big and beautiful without being overwhelming or ostentatious. The understated decor is accented with a 2,000-piece, multimillion-dollar art collection with a theatrical theme. Among the noteworthy works is "Aeolus," a 28-by-8-foot starlike sculpture of brass tubes and gold-colored mesh by Norwegian artist Knut Steen. It hangs from the dome ceiling of the **Centrum,** the ship's dramatic six-deck atrium.

The ship has a congenial atmosphere, comfortable for families, couples, and singles alike. The efficient and helpful crew contributes to the pleasant ambience. Dress is casual by day, semi-formal at night.

Basics Standard cabins are 165 square feet, although creative storage space makes them more comfortable than their size would suggest. Each has two twin beds that can convert to one queen-size, and a desk/vanity, telephone, TV, safe, hairdryer (on request), sofa or chair, glass table, and bathroom with shower and a medicine cabinet with lots of shelves. Bring your own toiletries—only small bars of soap and tiny packages of shampoo are provided. Suites are larger (366 square feet) and offer a separate sitting area and veranda.

Passengers looking for lots more space and a bit of luxury (and willing to pay an extra couple thousand dollars per person for it) might opt for one of the **Owner's Suites** (495 square feet) or **Family Suites** (463 square feet), or even the **Royal Suite** (1,033 square feet). They all offer such extras as a Jacuzzi, an entertainment center, a veranda, and mini-bar.

There are two large pools—one with a retractable roof—four Jacuzzis, and lots of lounge chairs and deck space. A calypso band keeps things lively on deck, where waiters dance with passengers,

passengers dance with passengers, and just about everyone gets into the act.

Fitness facilities include an aerobics room and a fully equipped, but too small, workout center (it's almost impossible to get on one of the four treadmills, and the room can get awfully crowded). The **Steiner** spa offers a full menu of overpriced massages, facials, and other treatments.

The daily diet of diversions ranges from bingo to belly flop competitions to (believe it or not) napkin folding demonstrations. Passengers can also pass the time in the handsome library and seven boutiques.

At night, most folks head for the **Palladium,** site of lavish Las Vegas–style productions featuring scantily clad showgirls. The stunning beige and gold theater offers a state-of-the-art sound system, a 14-person orchestra pit, and unobstructed views of the stage.

The ship also has seven bar/lounges for sipping and socializing. The most popular is the **Champagne Bar,** where passengers congregate before and after dinner. Located in the reception and lounge area of the **Centrum,** it has a raised marble piano platform and marble staircase. Things are more lively in the top-deck disco, which pulsates into the early hours of the morning. The **Casino Royale** also jumps day and night.

Royal Caribbean runs an exceptional children's program. Activities are well supervised and include games, pizza parties, arts-and-crafts sessions, and a masquerade parade. Teenagers can hang out in the **Fanta-SEAS Teen Center,** which is equipped with a dance floor, a big-screen TV, and a video arcade, while younger children play in **Club Ocean,** which has a submarine theme and a winding slide.

Cuisine For the most part, the fare is basic and the menu fairly predictable—from hot dogs and hamburgers to filet mignon and lobster tails. Occasionally, however, the chef does wax creative, concocting (for example) a tasty veal dumpling appetizer, a portobello mushroom sandwich, or a luscious cappuccino chocolate cake. A healthy "Shipshape" menu offers vegetarian and low-fat fare.

Meals are served in two seatings in the two-tier **Great Gatsby Dining Room,** a nicely decorated space with wide windows, stunning scalloped balconies, turquoise-colored chairs and carpeting, and a soothing waterfall with onyx panels. The large and comfortable **Windjammer Cafe** offers standard breakfast and lunch buffets. The midnight buffets are also fairly routine, with the exception of the special "gala" spreads, which feature lobster and other delicacies as well as lots of pastry. Room service is available around the clock; passengers may order from the dining room menu during regular mealtimes.

Completed in 1927, the *Ile de France* was the first luxury cruise liner with Art Deco decor.

Legend of the Seas/ Splendour of the Seas
$$$★★★★

Built: 1995/1996

Passengers: 1,804

Size: 69,130 grt

Cabins: 902

Outside: 575 outside (231 with verandas)

Inside: 327

Suites: 231

Wheelchair Accessible: 17

Registry: Liberian/Norwegian

Officers/Crew: Norwegian/International

Tipping Policy: About $8 per passenger per day suggested

Smoking Policy: Prohibited in entertainment lounge; restricted to designated smoking sections in all other public areas

Snapshot The first of six **Royal Caribbean** megaliners, the *Legend* made her maiden voyage in May of 1995, offering traditional, big-ship style cruises. She was followed in March 1996 by her semi-twin sister, the *Splendour of the Seas.* One of the fastest ships at sea, with a cruising speed of 24 knots, *Splendour of the Seas* is slightly different than her twin. She has more windows than any other ship—a full two acres of glass. An exceptional value, these passenger-friendly ships offer a lot for a reasonable price.

Itinerary The *Legend* makes a variety of 7-, 10- and 11-night voyages, cruising Alaska during the summer, through the Panama Canal in winter, and Hawaii in the spring and fall. *Splendour of the Seas* offers 12-night cruises in the Mediterranean, Scandinavia, Russia, the Norwegian fjords, and the British Isles in summer, 7-night southern Caribbean cruises from San Juan in winter.

Typical Passengers Middle-income forty-something couples and singles (mostly women) choose these ships. Both first-time cruisers and repeat **Royal Caribbean** customers climb aboard.

Ambience The decor is upscale and extravagant, with million-dollar art collections and expensive appointments. Among the unique features are stunning seven-deck atriums with glass elevators, marble terraces, boutiques, and a popular Champagne bar. The shipboard atmosphere is serene, congenial, and casual. Crew members are both amiable and able.

Basics Standard staterooms range from 145 to 199 square feet; nearly one out every four has a balcony, and all feature separate sitting areas. Each also has twin beds that can convert to queen-size, one and a half closets, and a bathroom with shower. If your budget can handle it splurge on a suite. Family suites offer two bedrooms and both a sofa and Pullman bed and can house up to seven people each. They also have a living room, veranda, mini-refrigerator, and two bathrooms (one with a tub, the other, a shower). If you really want to go top cabin, book the **Royal Suite**—1,148 square feet of luxury with a baby grand piano in the living room, a separate bedroom with a king-size bed, and a marble bathroom with an oval Jacuzzi, separate shower, and twin sinks. It's $650 or so a day (and worth every penny!).

Sports and fitness are areas in which **Royal Caribbean** excels. The fitness centers are outstanding, with good weight equipment, first-rate workout sessions, saunas, steam baths, a lovely solarium, indoor and outdoor pools, and a lavish, Roman baths–style pool area with Jacuzzis, marble flooring, and a Plexiglas retractable canopy roof. Each ship also has plenty of deck space, a jogging track, and an 18-hole miniature golf course (the first at sea).

A casino, several duty-free shops, and lots of bars and lounges offer still more places to while away the hours at sea. The usual shipboard activities are available, and there are youth centers for both teens and tots.

Lavish, attention-grabbing shows are staged in the ships' state-of-the-art lounges, snazzy spots with gold marble floors and crystal chandeliers. They offer big orchestra pits, large video screens, and high-tech projection systems that enable entertainers to interact with televised images. Better still, every seat has a clear view of the stage. In addition, a DJ spins discs in the lounge on the ships' topmost decks, while couples glide across the dance floor in a 1930s-style ballroom.

Cuisine The food, provided by an independent caterer, is fine and plentiful, but don't expect haute cuisine. Buffets, which are offered at breakfast, lunch, and midnight, are the galleys' strong suit. The ships' attractive, two-level dining rooms feature glass walls, a stunning staircase, and comfortable, uncrowded table arrangements. There are two dinner seatings. Dining room staffers do their best to please, but with so many mouths to feed, the service is sometimes slow. Room service is available around the clock.

Majesty of the Seas/ Monarch of the Seas
$$★★★

Built: 1992/1991

Refurbished: 1995/1994

Passengers: 2,354

Size: 73,941 grt

Cabins: 1,177

Outside: 732 outside (62 with verandas)

Inside: 445

Suites: 62

Wheelchair Accessible: 9

Registry: Norwegian

Officers/Crew: Norwegian/International

Tipping Policy: About $8 per passenger per day suggested

Smoking Policy: Prohibited in entertainment lounge; restricted to designated smoking sections in all other public areas

Snapshot Identical sister ships, they offer lively but not boisterous cruises at a moderate price.

Itinerary The *Majesty* sails year-round on seven-day trips from Miami to the western Caribbean, while the *Monarch* makes seven-day southern Caribbean cruises from San Juan.

Typical Passengers Families with children and couples and singles representing just about every age group from mid-twenties on up to senior citizens choose these ships.

Ambience These ships feel as big as they look, with lavish public areas and dazzling interior designs. The centerpiece of each is a seven-story atrium, accessible by glass elevators. The atmosphere is lively but not loud; although there's a lot of activity, there are also plenty of spots in which to spend some quiet time alone. Dress is shipboard-casual by day, semi-formal by night.

Basics On these ships, more emphasis was placed on the decor and amenities *outside* the cabins, many of which are too close together for comfort. A standard stateroom (160 square feet) has two lower beds that can convert to a double, a TV, sufficient closet space, and an adequate bathroom with shower.

Each ship offers the usual complement of onboard amusements: a Las Vegas–style casino, nightly "feathers-and-flash" musical productions, two pools, a big, well-equipped fitness center, spa/salon, movie theater, library, shops, and a children's program and playroom.

Cuisine Crowd-pleasing ethnic fare is served in each ship's twin dining rooms; there are two dinner seatings. Breakfast, lunch, and midnight buffets are set out in the **Windjammer Cafe**, and there is 24-hour room service.

Royal Caribbean International operates Crown & Anchor Clubs in downtown Charlotte Amalie on St. Thomas and in San Juan, Puerto Rico. The clubs provide a place for passengers to pick up tourist information, call home, and relax over refreshments. More are planned in other ports.

 Megaship　　🚢 **Traditional Cruise Liner**

 Sailing Ship　　 **Expedition Ship**

🛶 **Ultraluxury Ship**

Large ships (more than 1,000 passengers): Blue

Mid-size ships (500-1,000 passengers): Green

Small ships (fewer than 500 passengers): Red

Plying the Exotic Rivers of the World

Amazon, Orinoco, Nile, Yangtze, Irrawaddy, Volga—the very names conjure up a multitude of exotic images. Now it's possible to explore these wondrous waterways on a surprising variety of cruise ships and riverboats.

Stretching 4,000 miles, the Amazon begins as a trickle high in the Peruvian Andes and, fed by hundreds of tributaries, grows into a mighty force as it flows through the rain forest, out to the sea. Several cruise lines, including **Abercrombie & Kent, Royal Olympic,** and **Silversea,** and the Miami-based tour operator **Amazon Tours & Cruises** (800/423.2791) run expeditions along this great river system. Highlights of Amazon river cruises include wildlife tours that use rubber Zodiac boats, visits to coastal villages, and stops at cities such as **Manaus** where a plush opera house stands as a monument to the wealth of the rubber barons.

Nature-minded travelers can explore the **Aguarico River** in **Ecuador**'s Amazon region on board the 48-passenger *Flotel Orellana.* It's marketed in the US by Dallas-based **Adventure Associates** (800/527.2500).

Trips on **Venezuela**'s wildlife-rich Orinoco River are regularly offered by companies including **Clipper Cruise Line** and **Royal Olympic Cruises;** other lines visit occasionally. An optional flightseeing excursion to **Angel Falls,** the world's highest waterfall, is a cruise highlight. Orinoco sailings are usually paired with visits to islands in the **Southern Caribbean.**

On the other side of the globe, the Nile beckons as a treasure-trove of antiquity. More than 200 small ships—most operated by big hotel chains such as **Hilton, Sonesta,** and **Sheraton**—take passengers on excursions between **Aswan** and **Luxor,** gateway to the dazzling temples and tombs in the Valley of the Kings. **Abercrombie & Kent** and **Swan Hellenic** also offer Nile cruises.

As they sail along the Nile, passengers spy date palms fringing the shore, water buffaloes wallowing in the mud, and veiled women scrubbing the family laundry. (To get in the mood, read Agatha Christie's *Death on the Nile.*) Cruises generally last three to five nights and depart from both Aswan and Luxor.

Very different, but equally exotic, the Yangtze River slices through the heart of **China,** meandering between **Tibet** and the **East China Sea.** A spectacular 125-mile stretch known as **Three Gorges** is plied by fleets of small riverboats holding tourists from all over the world. Two companies, **Regal China Cruises** and **Victoria Cruises,** boast new ships with Western-style amenities and have offices in New York City and Woodside, NY, respectively. Cruises of four or five nights are standard. The Chinese government plans to build a controversial dam amid the gorges over the next two decades, spurring many visitors to visit the region now.

In little-known **Myanmar, Abercrombie & Kent**'s *Road to Mandalay* sails the Irrawaddy River between **Mandalay** and **Bagan,** the site of 2,000 pagodas.

New York City's **EuroCruises** and **Classical Tours and Cruises,** and **OdessAmerica,** based in Mineola, NY, offer cruises on the waterways of the former Soviet Union. The tours showcase the region's intriguing history and culture: Passengers are treated to local music and dancing and get the chance to sample traditional dishes (though international cuisine is the mainstay). Some of the riverboats that make the trips once catered to high-ranking Soviet officials and thus seem the perfect places to enjoy **Black Sea** caviar washed down with Russian vodka or Champagne.

Perhaps the most popular route covers the Volga River, lakes, and canals linking **St. Petersburg** and **Moscow.** Another favorite itinerary, **Kiev** to **Odessa,** follows the **Dnieper River** as it winds through **Russia, Belarus,** and **Ukraine.** Even Siberian rivers offer cruise opportunities—but only during the height of summer.

MICHAEL STORRINGS

Nordic Empress

$$$★★★

Built: 1990

Refurbished: 1993

Passengers: 1,600

Size: 48,563 grt

Cabins: 800

Outside: 471 outside (69 with verandas)

Inside: 329

Suites: 69

Wheelchair Accessible: 4

Registry: Liberian

Officers/Crew: Norwegian/International

Tipping Policy: About $8 per passenger per day suggested

Smoking Policy: Prohibited in entertainment lounge; restricted to designated smoking sections in all other public areas

Snapshot This is the first ship of its size to be built specifically for short cruises. Brief tropical excursions and a lovely shipboard environment are its main attractions.

Itinerary This ship cruises the Bahamas on three- and four-day trips out of Port Canaveral from June through August; offers three- and four-night Caribbean cruises from San Juan in winter.

Typical Passengers The *Nordic Empress* is often the choice of young first-time cruisers and older folks who enjoy shorter voyages.

Ambience Simply stunning, the ship has a contemporary decor highlighted by a nine-deck atrium with a cascading waterfall, a white marble stairway, a sensational silver-and-crystal sculpture of a ship's prow, and glass elevators that offer a bird's-eye view of it all. Shipboard atmosphere and attire are both casual. Crew members are very attentive, offering good, personalized service.

Basics Standard cabins are a narcissist's dream, with lots of preening space in the bathroom and a vanity with a makeup mirror. Decorated in pretty pastels, the rooms offer a good amount of storage space, twin beds that can convert to one queen-size, and a TV set.

Up on deck you'll find two pools, four Jacuzzis, a fitness center, a spa, and lots of open space. Most activity takes place on the pool deck—there are fun and games during the day and dancing under the stars at night.

The entertainment options are many, with lavish shows, an amazing tri-level casino, half a dozen bar/lounges, plenty of deck diversions, and several shops. For children there's a great program of organized activities as well as the **Kids Connection Playroom,** site of all manner of amusements.

Cuisine If only the food was as good as the decor and ambience. . . . Still, you won't go hungry. Crowd-pleasing dishes (pasta, roast beef, hamburgers, fried fish) are served in the two-story dining room. There are two dinner seatings. Breakfast, lunch, and midnight buffets are set up in the **Windjammer Cafe**; room service is available day and night.

Rhapsody of the Seas

Scheduled to be launched at press time, this megaship (75,000 grt, 2,000 passengers) will begin her inaugural year with a series of Alaskan cruises.

Song of America

$$★★★

Built: 1982

Refurbished: 1994

Passengers: 1,402

Size: 37,584 grt

Cabins: 701

Outside: 406

Inside: 295

Suites: 21

Wheelchair Accessible: 0

Registry: Norwegian

Officers/Crew: Norwegian/International

Tipping Policy: About $8 per passenger per day suggested

Smoking Policy: Prohibited in entertainment lounge; restricted to designated smoking sections in all other public areas

Snapshot The pick of discerning bargain-seekers, *Song of America* is the only luxury liner left in the Mexican Riviera. She offers a lot of activities, a friendly ambience, simple accommodations, and fine service—all for a good price.

Itinerary She makes seven-night southern Caribbean and Mexican Riviera cruises in winter, and weeklong Bermuda trips in summer.

Typical Passengers This ship draws a mix of young, middle-aged, and older vacationers seeking a traditional-style cruise at a reasonable price.

Ambience This modern ship has a sleek design, spacious decks and public rooms and contemporary decor that's bright and a tad busy. The pleasant, friendly atmosphere is enhanced by the excellent service. Traditional cruisewear, more casual than formal, is the typical mode of dress.

Basics Standard cabins can be cramped, with only 110 square feet in which to fit two twin beds, a TV, two bureaus, and a dressing table (not to mention two passengers). But there's plenty of action to keep you out of your cabin. There are two pools, a fitness center, a casino, shops, and a beauty salon. At night passengers can take in Las Vegas–style shows or kick back in one of the other seven bars and lounges. The children's program keeps young cruisers amused.

Cuisine Ample amounts of above-average but rather unimaginative American fare is served in the lovely **Madame Butterfly Dining Room,** where there are two dinner seatings. For a change of pace, head to the **Windjammer Cafe** for breakfast, lunch, or midnight buffets, or order room service—it's available any time.

Sovereign of the Seas

$$★★★

Built: 1988

Refurbished: 1996

Passengers: 2,276

Size: 73,193 grt

Cabins: 1138

Outside: 722

Inside: 416

Suites: 12

Wheelchair Accessible: 6

Registry: Norwegian

Officers/Crew: Norwegian/International

Tipping Policy: About $8 per passenger per day suggested

Smoking Policy: Prohibited in entertainment lounge; restricted to designated smoking sections in all other public areas

Snapshot Short tropical vacations and a lively ambience are the *Sovereign*'s hallmarks.

Itinerary She makes three- to four-night Bahamas cruises out of Miami year-round.

Typical Passengers On board you'll find **Royal Caribbean** loyalists and the usual Miami-Caribbean crowd of sun worshipers and sybarites. In general, most passengers are middle-aged, although the group is somewhat younger in summer.

Ambience An amazing floating hotel, this ship rises 14 decks above the water. Big, bright, and shiny, it features striking public rooms, including **The Centrum,** a five-story atrium with glass elevators and marble walls. Your fellow travelers are likely to be an energetic, sociable lot, while the crew is both affable and efficient. Traditional cruisewear is the norm.

Basics While everything else about this ship is big and glitzy, the cabins are surprisingly small (about 120 square feet), albeit nicely arranged. A standard cabin features twin beds, a bathroom with shower, and limited storage space.

On the plus side, **Royal Caribbean** has put a lot of effort into making the public rooms and deck activities truly outstanding. The many places to enjoy range from the show-stopping **Casino Royale** gaming parlor to the high-tech disco, as well as lots of lounges, a Champagne bar, twin movie theaters, eight boutiques, a library, and extravagant shows.

And that's just inside. The massive deck boasts two pools, two whirlpools, two bars, a jogging track, and basketball and shuffleboard courts. With **Royal**

Caribbean's outstanding **ShipShape** fitness program and well-equipped fitness center at your disposal, it's hard to come up with an excuse for not working out. There's also a fabulous children's program, so don't hesitate to bring the kids.

Cuisine The "theme" fare (Italian, French, Caribbean, and so on) changes nightly; it's sometimes wonderful, sometimes not. Dinner is served in two sittings in both the **Gigi** and **Kismet Dining Rooms.** The **Windjammer Cafe** offers breakfast, lunch, and midnight buffets, and 24-hour room service is available.

Vision of the Seas

A 75,000-grt, 2,000-passenger luxury liner, she is expected to make her appearance in the fall of 1998.

Royal Olympic Cruises

800/972.6400

Royal Olympic Cruises

*In 1995 the Keusseoglou family, owners of **Sun Line Cruises,** and the Potamianos family of **Epirotiki** merged their two cruise lines, creating a new company, **Royal Olympic Cruises.** Sun Line Cruises and Epirotiki are now brand names under the **Royal Olympic Cruises** umbrella. The company uses the colors of the Greek flag to differentiate between the two lines. **Royal Olympic** "Blue Ships" are **Sun Line** ships, which offer a more elegant, traditional cruise experience; **Royal Olympic** "White Ships" are **Epirotiki** ships, which offer a more relaxed, festive atmosphere.*

The "Blue Ships":

Odysseus

$$★★

Built: 1962

Refurbished: 1995

Passengers: 400 passengers

Size: 12,000 grt

Cabins: 224

Outside: 183

Inside: 43

Suites: 14

Wheelchair Accessible: 0

Registry: Greek

Officers/Crew: Greek/International

Tipping Policy: About $8 per passenger per day suggested; tips are presented to the chief steward at end of cruise and divided among the entire crew. No tips on bar bills

Smoking Policy: Restricted to designated smoking sections

Snapshot A vintage ship, which went into service in 1962 and was completely overhauled in 1987, she specializes in short Aegean and South American cruises.

Itinerary The *Odysseus* makes 3- and 4-day round-trip cruises from Piraeus to the Greek Isles in spring and fall; 10-, 12-, and 14-day voyages in the western Mediterranean, northern Europe, and the Baltic Sea in summer; and South American cruises of varying lengths from Rio de Janeiro to Buenos Aires in winter.

Typical Passengers Most of the passengers are in their sixties and older and European, although a few adventurous Americans are on board as well.

Ambience Warm and attractive, the ship has nice public rooms decorated with Mediterranean flair. Shipboard life also has a lively, sociable Mediterranean spirit. Dress is the usual shipboard wear, generally casual, with fancier attire seen on the couple formal nights.

The Greek officers and crew are affable, and the service is pretty good all around, although it falters at times.

Basics Staterooms are compact (100 to 120 square feet) but nicely furnished, with twin or double beds and bathrooms with showers. The suites aren't really worth the extra investment.

Shipboard facilities include a fitness center, pool and Jacuzzis, spa and beauty salon, a nice entertainment lounge, casino, shop, library, and four bar/lounges. The most popular gathering place is the **Taverna,** an authentic Greek saloon.

Cuisine The food is Greek—and great. Dinner is served in two seatings in the charming dining room. Other food options include deck buffets at breakfast and lunch, and limited room service, available around the clock.

Stella Oceanis
$$★

Built: 1965

Refurbished: 1994

Passengers: 300

Size: 6,000 grt

Cabins: 159

Outside: 113

Inside: 46

Suites: 10

Wheelchair Accessible: 0

Registry: Greek

Officers/Crew: Greek

Tipping Policy: $8 to $9 per passenger per day suggested; tips are presented to the chief steward at end of cruise and divided among the entire crew. No tips on bar bills

Smoking Policy: Restricted to designated smoking sections

Snapshot A pleasant little vintage vessel, she offers convivial sailing in an intimate setting.

Itinerary In spring and fall *Stella Oceanis* makes seven-day round-trip cruises from Piraeus to ports in Greece, Turkey, Israel, and Egypt. During the winter she sails the Red Sea on seven-day round-trip cruises from Eilat, Israel, stopping in Jordan and Sharm El Sheikh, Egypt. In summer she makes 12-day trips in the western Mediterranean, from Piraeus to Rome.

Typical Passengers Europeans of middle age and older make up most of the passenger list, although it usually includes a handful of bargain-seeking Americans who prefer smaller ships.

Ambience Well preserved, the ship features a rich wood interior. While passengers tend to be older and low-key, the Greek crew members foster a taverna-like atmosphere that's fun without being raucous. Passengers wear casual duds during the day and dress up a bit at night. The officers and crew competently see to passengers' needs.

Basics Standard cabins range from 96 to 208 square feet and have twin beds (they can't be pushed together to make a double bed), small bathrooms with showers, and limited storage space.

This is not a good choice for luxury seekers. You won't find a casino, an entertainment lounge, beauty salon, or a Jacuzzi. What you *do* get are great ports of call, an attractive sundeck with a nice pool, good food and service, and the chance to take Greek language lessons from native speakers.

Cuisine The galley consistently turns out tasty Greek dishes. In addition to meals in the elegant dining room, breakfast, lunch, and midnight buffets are served and 24-hour room service is available (with a limited menu). Meals are served in two seatings.

Stella Solaris
$$$★★★

Built: 1953

Rebuilt: 1973

Refurbished: 1996

Passengers: 620

Size: 18,000 grt

Cabins: 329

Outside: 185

Inside: 144

Suites: 66

Wheelchair Accessible: 0

Registry: Greek

Officers/Crew: Greek

Tipping Policy: $8 to $9 per passenger per day suggested; tips are presented to the chief steward at end of cruise and divided among the entire crew. No tips on bar bills

Smoking Policy: Restricted to designated smoking sections

Snapshot Another aging lady of the sea, born in 1953, she's kept her sleek, tidy look (thanks to a few nips and tucks, including a full face-lift in 1996). She offers sedate voyages in an understated setting.

Itinerary Seven-day round-trip Mediterranean cruises from Piraeus to the islands of Greece and ports of Turkey and the Black Sea are offered in spring, summer, and fall; in winter she sails from Ft. Lauderdale to the Amazon and back, then makes Panama Canal cruises from Galveston, Texas, with a stop on the Yucatán Peninsula.

Typical Passengers *Stella Solaris* is a favorite of well-to-do middle-aged and older folk, many repeat passengers, who enjoy a taste of luxury on a smaller ship.

Ambience Although not elegant, this ship—with its decor of rich wood, deep colors, and fresh floral arrangements—has a touch of class. She's not as overtly Greek in ambience as the **Royal Olympic** "White Ships," but the flavor is still there, thanks to the Greek officers and crew of 300 (who provide good service). Life on board is generally calm and a bit quiet. Traditional cruisewear is the norm.

Basics Cabins, which were given new furnishings, carpeting, and drapes in 1996, range from a quite compact 96 square feet to a more comfortable 225 square feet. They feature portholes, two lower beds (that cannot be pushed together to make a double bed), TVs, built-in desks, and bathrooms with both tub and shower. The 34 suites on the top deck offer such extras as a large sitting area, a separate bedroom with two beds that can convert to one queen-size or double, a big walk-in closet, and roomy bathroom with tub and shower.

Also new is the impressive 2,600-square-foot **Daphne Spa.** Under the direction of Gianni Zecchino, co-founder of the **Beauty Physiotherapy Institute** of Florence, the spa aims to provide the ultimate in pampering, offering massages, facials, and exotic treatments. Fitness classes are available, as is weight-training equipment. Other shipboard amenities include two outdoor pools, an entertainment lounge, a library, a beauty salon, a casino, shops, and four bar/lounges.

Favorite evening haunts are the cozy **Grill Room Bar;** the **Solaris Lounge,** where piano music sets the mood for drinking and dancing; and the **Piano Bar,** with more music at tea time and cocktail hour.

Cuisine Best dishes are Greek, but other continental choices can be tasty. There's a spa cuisine menu as well. Dinner is served in two seatings in the pleasantly elegant dining rooms. There are breakfast, lunch, and midnight buffets and a limited room service menu, available any time.

The "White Ships":

Olympic
$$★★

Built: 1956
Refurbished: 1994
Passengers: 900
Size: 31,500 grt
Cabins: 488

Outside: 221
Inside: 267
Suites: 5
Wheelchair Accessible: 0
Registry: Greek
Officers/Crew: Greek
Tipping Policy: $8 to $9 per passenger per day suggested at end of cruise; tips are presented to the chief steward and divided among the entire crew. No tips on bar bills expected
Smoking Policy: Prohibited in dining room; restricted to designated smoking sections in all other public areas

Snapshot This legend of the sea first set sail in 1956, and she's still going strong, now specializing in brief Aegean jaunts.

Itinerary She makes three- and four-day trips from Piraeus to Patmos, Kusadasi, and Rhodes, with stops at Mykonos, Heraklion, and Santorini on alternating trips.

Typical Passengers The ship has a loyal crowd of repeat passengers, most of whom are retirees.

Ambience The decor of teak, brass, and bright colors is attractive, but this is not exactly the most luxuriously appointed ship afloat. The atmosphere is relaxing and serene; the service is good.

Basics Standard cabins are comfortably spacious at about 200 square feet, but offer few amenities (not even TV sets) beyond the basic two twin beds that can be pushed together to make a double, a bathroom with shower, and a desk/dresser.

There's also a lot of deck space as well as indoor and outdoor pools, a Jacuzzi, a fitness center, a beauty salon, five bar/lounges, an entertainment lounge, a casino, a shop, and a children's program.

Cuisine Basic Greek fare is served in a pleasant dining room with big windows and a soft color scheme. There are two dinner seatings. Breakfast and lunch buffets are occasionally set up on deck, and there's tea in the intimate **Piano Lounge** in the afternoon. Room service is available around the clock, although the menu is limited.

Orpheus
$$★★

Built: 1952
Refurbished: 1993
Passengers: 250
Size: 5,092 grt
Cabins: 152
Outside: 118
Inside: 34
Suites: 0
Wheelchair Accessible: 0 (and no elevators)
Registry: Greek

Officers/Crew: Greek

Tipping Policy: $8 to $9 per passenger per day suggested; tips are given to the chief steward at end of cruise and divided among the entire crew

Smoking Policy: Prohibited in dining room; restricted to designated smoking sections in all other public areas

Snapshot Another vintage vessel, this one began sailing in 1952.

Itinerary Seven-day Greek Isle, Aegean, and Ionian cruises are offered.

Typical Passengers They're a mix of Europeans and some Americans, most middle-aged or older.

Ambience Well maintained throughout the years, the handsome ship has a nice teak deck and pleasant public rooms. Shipboard life is casual and low-key, with an emphasis on things cerebral, with guest lecturers attracting good-sized crowds. The officers and crew of 190 are Greek, and the service is good.

Basics Standard cabins are 140 square feet and simple, with two twin beds (that cannot be moved together to make a double), a bathroom with shower, and basic furnishings.

On board you'll find three bar/lounges and a casino, shop, library, pool, beauty salon, and children's program. There is no spa or fitness center, but the deck offers enough square feet for a good walk or run. Simple shows are staged at night.

Cuisine The food is Greek and well prepared. There are two dinner seatings in the pleasant but undistinguished dining room. A limited room service menu is available around the clock.

Triton
$$★★

Built: 1971

Refurbished: 1994

Passengers: 620

Size: 14,000 grt

Cabins: 377

Outside: 249

Inside: 128

Suites: 0

Wheelchair Accessible: 0

Registry: Greek

Officers/Crew: Greek

Tipping Policy: $8 to $9 per passenger per day suggested; tips are presented to the chief steward at end of cruise and divided among the entire crew. No tips on bar bills expected

Smoking Policy: Prohibited in dining room; restricted to designated smoking sections in all other public areas

Snapshot The youngest and sleekest of the line, she specializes in Aegean voyages.

Itinerary This ship sails from Piraeus on seven-day cruises stopping at Greek and Turkish ports.

Typical Passengers A mixed bag of Europeans, middle-aged and older, select this ship.

Ambience The *Triton* is well groomed and decorated with bright colors; the public rooms are cozy and comfortable. All is graciously and authentically Greek—the food, officers and 285 crew members, and especially the "Greek Night" celebrations, when the ship turns into a floating taverna, and everybody dances the Sytaki. The mood is generally subdued, and the service ranges from good to wonderful.

Basics Cabins are from 118 to 132 square feet—not exactly large, but comfortable. Each has two lower beds that can be moved together to make a double bed, a dresser/desk combo, limited storage space, and a bathroom with shower. Suites are not really worth the extra money.

An attractive oval-shaped pool is situated on a large teak sundeck, and a **Promenade Deck** circles the entire ship. Inside is a casino, library, shop, entertainment lounge, fitness center, and beauty salon. Favorite watering holes include the **Nine Muses Nightclub,** which offers a panoramic view of the sea, and the **Nefeli Bar** on the covered upper deck. The children's program caters to the underage crowd.

Cuisine The Greek fare is good and served in two seatings in the cheerful dining room. The room service menu is limited, but it's available any time.

Seabourn Cruise Line
800/929.9595

Seabourn Legend/ Seabourn Pride/ Seabourn Spirit
$$$$★★★★★★

Take a trip on one of these luxury ships to experience cruising at its finest. See page 84 for a detailed description.

Sea Cloud, Inc.
888/SEACLOUD (general information only) or 800/683.6767

Sea Cloud
$$$$★★★★

Built: 1931

Refurbished: 1993

Passengers: 69

Size: 2,523 grt

Cabins: 34

Outside: 34

Inside: 0

Suites: 2

Wheelchair Accessible: 0

SEA CLOUD
CRUISES

Registry: Maltese

Officers/Crew: International

Tipping Policy: About $7 per passenger per day suggested

Smoking Policy: Allowed only on deck

Snapshot Built for cereal heiress Marjorie Merriweather Post by her husband, E.F. Hutton, in the 1920s, this striking, four-masted sailing yacht has hosted the Duke and Duchess of Windsor, King Gustav V of Sweden, and numerous other celebrities and blue bloods. Also once the property of Latin American dictator Rafael Trujillo (Post traded it to him in return for a prop jet), the ship is now owned by a German consortium, which charters her out to various operators. A dazzling beauty, she specializes in luxurious cruises to interesting locations. Just seeing her at anchor is exciting; to experience her at full sail is nothing short of exhilarating.

Itinerary She sails (most of) the seven seas, from the Caribbean to the Mediterranean, on a variety of 9- and 12-day cruises.

Typical Passengers They are older, wiser, wealthier folks with a love of exploration and a penchant for elegant digs.

Ambience Given the *Sea Cloud*'s pedigree, you can probably guess what she looks like: handsomely appointed and shipshape, with lots of polished teak and burnished brass trim. The public rooms are adorned with carved oak paneling, Italian marble, and antiques. An art gallery features original oil paintings of vintage vessels. While the yacht-like setting is decidedly upscale, dress is casual and comfortable. The international crew provides excellent service.

Basics Staterooms range from 90 to 140 square feet and feature double beds, safes, and telephones as well as luxurious bathrooms with tubs, Carrara marble appointments, and gold fixtures. Top-of-the-line accommodations include Merriweather Post's 422-square-foot marble-and-gold suite, which boasts a canopy bed and satin brocade ottomans, and her husband's handsome pine-paneled quarters (375 square feet), which features Chippendale furniture and a Carrara marble fireplace.

There is no entertainment lounge or casino—and the clientele likes it that way. Lectures and port talks are the shipboard activities of choice during the day, and there are two beautiful bars for drinking and socializing at night. The sports and fitness options are nonexistent as well, although there's a nice sundeck with comfortable chaises (but no pool or Jacuzzi). On days in port passengers can swim in the sea or avail themselves of the water sports (snorkeling, scuba diving) and complimentary shore excursions. On the latter, naturalists and historians lead walks through rain forests, wildlife sanctuaries, and other interesting locales.

Cuisine The food is generally quite good, mostly continental in style. Breakfast and lunch are buffets, while dinner is a civilized sit-down affair, served at a single seating in the elegant, candle-lit dining room. Complimentary wines are poured at lunch and dinner. The only thing missing is room service, which should be available on such a fancy ship.

Silversea Cruises

800/722.9955

*At press time, this cruise line was planning to add two new 390-passenger, 22,000-grt ships to its fleet by the end of 1998. The still-to-be-named luxury liners will be slightly larger than the company's other two ships (Silver Cloud and Silver Wind) and will feature verandas in 75 percent of the staterooms. Like **Silversea**'s other ships, they will offer all-inclusive cruises.*

Silver Cloud/ Silver Wind

$$$$★★★★★★

Sail on one of these two small vessels for the finest all-around cruise experience available. For food, service, style, class, elegance, and comfort, luxury liners don't get much better than these all-inclusive, all-suite ships. See page 86 for a detailed description.

Special Expeditions

800/348.2358

SVEN·OLOF LINDBLAD'S

SPECIAL EXPEDITIONS

Polaris

$$$$★★

Built: 1960

Refurbished: 1982

Passengers: 80

Size: 2,214 grt

Cabins: 41

Outside: 41

Inside: 0

Suites: 1

Wheelchair Accessible: 0

Registry: Bahamian

Officers/Crew: Swedish/Filipino

Tipping Policy: About $7 per passenger per day suggested

Smoking Policy: Restricted to designated smoking sections

Snapshot Education and exploration are the operative words on this supercasual expedition ship.

Itinerary This ship sails the waters of Central America in winter, then spends the rest of the year in the Galapagos.

Typical Passengers Due in large part to the high fares, this ship attracts a well-heeled clientele of mostly middle-aged and older travelers, many retired and avid explorers.

Ambience Once a Scandinavian ferry, this comfortable ship has a simple decor with lots of wood trim. Shipboard life is similarly simple. You won't need a tuxedo, tie, or cocktail dress, and you won't find a casino, shows, fitness center, or pool, but you will visit some exotic ports and learn something new about the world. Good service is provided by the friendly crew.

Basics Cabins are comfortable, range in size from 106 to 230 square feet, and have windows, twin beds, desk/bureaus, telephones (but no TVs), and bathrooms with showers. The one suite is spacious; it comes complete with two double beds, a sitting area, and two windows and costs considerably more than a standard stateroom.

The ship facilities are basic: three little shops, a library, and self-service laundry. Lectures and films on local history, geology, and flora and fauna are the main forms of shipboard entertainment. Excursions are the focus of these cruises, and the ship carries Zodiac landing craft and a glass-bottom boat for in-depth exploration.

Cuisine While hardly *haute*, the cuisine is healthful, fresh, and plentiful. All meals are served in single seatings in the dining room, which has views of the sea through wide picture windows.

Sea Bird/Sea Lion
$$$★★

Built: 1982/1981

Passengers: 70

Size: 99.7 grt

Cabins: 37

Outside: 37

Inside: 0

Suites: 0

Wheelchair Accessible: 0

Registry: United States

Officers/Crew: American/American

Tipping Policy: About $7 per passenger per day suggested

Smoking Policy: Restricted to designated smoking sections

Snapshot These ships cater to those who enjoy educational experiences more than sybaritic pleasures. A shallow eight-foot draft allows these sturdy craft access to small ports and uninhabited islands where larger vessels can't maneuver.

Itinerary Both offer Mexican trips (whale watching in Baja, cruises on the Sea of Cortés) in winter; sail the coastal waterways of Alaska in summer; and explore the Pacific Northwest, departing from Portland, in spring and fall.

Typical Passengers Wealthy and older explorers interested in learning more about the world and its ecosystems select these ships.

Ambience Sturdy and simple in appearance, these ships offer no-frills cruising with minimal appointments. The voyages are casual and have a strong emphasis on education. The service is adequate, but passenger pampering is not the point here.

Basics Cabins are cramped (84 to 110 square feet), with twin beds, big windows, tiny bathrooms with showers, and little else. Larger accommodations with sitting areas and a touch more comfort are available for a price, but there are no suites.

Each ship has a bar, shop, and library, but no casino, fitness center, spa or salon, or entertainment lounge. Highlights of the cruises are naturalist-led excursions aboard Zodiac landing craft; shipboard lectures also popular passenger pastimes.

Cuisine Good and good-for-you American fare is served in single seatings in the nondescript dining room.

Star Clippers
800/442.0551

Star Clipper/Star Flyer
$$★★★★★

These identical four-masted vessels, authentic replicas of 19th-century clipper ships, offer passengers the rare experience of actually helping to hoist the sails. See page 88 for a detailed description.

Swan Hellenic Cruises
800/252.7745

Minerva
$$$★★★

Built: 1995

Passengers: 300

Size: 12,000 grt

Cabins: 164

Outside: 117

Inside: 47

Suites: 10

Wheelchair Accessible: 2

Registry: Bermuda

Officers/Crew: British/International

Tipping Policy: Gratuities included in fare; no additional tips expected

Smoking Policy: Restricted to designated smoking sections (the policy is not strictly enforced)

Snapshot All-inclusive cruises to compelling ports are this sleek, new mid-size luxury liner's forte. The fares include round-trip flights to London; only alcoholic beverages are extra.

Itinerary Cruises of various durations in the eastern and western Mediterranean, the Orient, Vietnam, and India are offered.

Typical Passengers It's too soon to tell for sure—the *Minerva* has only been sailing since April 1996—but **Swan Hellenic** ships tend to attract British travelers, along with a small number of Americans.

Ambience The atmosphere is so warm and welcoming, you feel as though you're sailing on a friend's very large yacht. The staterooms exude elegance and comfort, with Oriental carpets, hardwood floors, wood paneled walls, and cushy couches and chairs. Walls are adorned with original art.

Voyages aboard this vessel have a cultural bent, and include a program of scholarly lecturers and seminars on art, history, botany, astronomy, music, and archaeology, combined with educational shore excursions. Dress is casual by day, and semi-casual in the evening, with one formal night. The crew and service are first-rate.

Basics Accommodations range from standard cabins (142 to 164 square feet) with two beds to suites (229 to 248 square feet) with twin beds or doubles. All cabins have TVs, telephones, and fax machines; all but the lowest-priced cabins have bathtubs.

Shipboard amenities include an outdoor pool, a small but fairly well-equipped fitness center, a library, auditorium, card room, smoking room, gift shop, and launderette. This is one of only a handful of cruise ships without a casino, and there is no formal entertainment. Evenings find passengers mingling in the two lounges and the bar.

Cuisine The cheerful main dining room offers open-seating service, while a cafe provides indoor/outdoor dining. International fare is served. Room service is available around the clock.

Windjammer Barefoot Cruises

800/327.2600

Fantome/Flying Cloud/ Mandalay/Polynesia/ Yankee Clipper

$★★

Built: 1927/1935/1923/1938/1927

Refurbished: 1995/1992/1994/1993/1992

Passengers: 128/74/72/126/64

Size: 676/400/420/430/327 grt

Cabins: 42/33/36/57/32

Outside: 20/10/36/15/32

Inside: 22/23/0/42/0

Suites: 24/1/8/2/12

Wheelchair Accessible: 0

Registry: Equatorial Guinean

Officers/Crew: British/West Indian & American

Tipping Policy: About $8 per passenger per day suggested at end of cruise

Smoking Policy: Allowed on deck only

Snapshot **Windjammer**'s small sailing ships are simply equipped, but they offer a relaxed environment and cruises that focus on exploration and the pleasures of sea, sun, and sand.

Itinerary Captains' choice: The skippers decide which islands they're going to explore from their home ports of Cancun *(Fantome),* Tortola *(Flying Cloud),* Grenada and Antigua *(Mandalay),* Sint Maarten *(Polynesia),* and Grenada *(Yankee Clipper).*

Typical Passengers Passengers range in age from the mid-twenties on up. A few singles and lots of honeymooners, anniversary celebrants, and old married folks choose these ships.

Ambience One of the most appealing aspects of the "barefoot" cruises aboard these ships is their casual, carefree atmosphere. No dressy clothes are necessary—in fact, shoes actually are optional.

All the vessels have the nautical decor you'd expect on a sailing ship, and all offer exemplary service.

Basics Cabins are very small (54 to 84 square feet), but fairly comfortable nonetheless. They're equipped with upper and lower berths, mini-refrigerators, picture windows, and bathrooms with showers.

Although they differ in size, the ships have (and don't have) the same facilities. None has a pool, Jacuzzi, fitness center, beauty shop, casino, or entertainment lounge. Passengers drink at the bar(s), read in the library, explore lovely ports on well-run excursions, and swim, snorkel, and scuba dive off pristine beaches. During days at sea, crew members give informal sailing lessons and invite passengers to assist in the operation of the ship.

Cuisine The continental cuisine is fair to good; dinner is served in two seatings in attractive wood-paneled dining rooms. Breakfast and lunch are served buffet-style. There's no room service.

Windstar Cruises

800/258.7245

Wind Song/Wind Spirit/ Wind Star

$$$★★★★★

These computer-operated, 440-foot, four-masted sailing ships travel to remote areas where larger ships cannot navigate. For a detailed description of these vessels, see page 90.

Destinations

It's likely that there's a cruise ship docking at a port in almost every corner of the world at some time during the year. With an increasing number of sleek new ships launched to meet consumers' growing interest in seaboard vacations, cruise lines are constantly changing and expanding their itineraries, always looking for fresh ports of call, something to set them apart from the competition.

These pleasure boats glide across every ocean, from the **Indian** to the **Atlantic**, and sail every sea, from the **Caribbean** to the **Coral**. When it comes to rivers, passenger vessels roam inland waterways from the **Mississippi** to the **Yangtze**. And canals, such as the **Panama**, are regularly transversed by cruise ships.

If it's fjords that spark your wanderlust, choose cruises to **Norway**, southern **Chile**, and **New Zealand**. Ice aficionados can seek out penguins in **Antarctica** or crunch through the frosty **Northwest Passage.**

But it's the sun worshipers who have the broadest range of destinations from which to choose. Sailing from the **Bahamas** to **Mauritius**, the majority of vessels plying the waters today are seeking the balmiest beaches, bays, and coves the world has to offer.

In recent years the changing international political scene has opened new destinations to Western cruise ships, spicing up itineraries with such exotic names as **Ho Chi Minh City** in **Vietnam, Yangon** in **Myanmar** (formerly **Burma**), **St. Petersburg** in **Russia**, and **Tallinn** in **Estonia**.

What follows is a sampling of nearly 200 of the most popular ports of call worldwide, chosen on the basis of current conditions and accessibility at press time. The geography, history, and culture of each destination is briefly described, followed by its top ten "must-sees." Note that some destinations are followed by port names in parentheses. In all, it's our abridged introduction to the world. Read on...

PATRICIA KEELIN

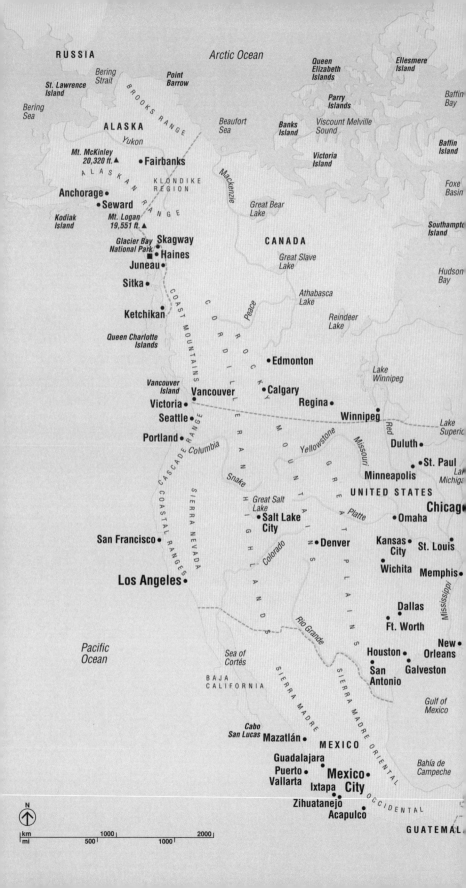

North America

Steeped in history, tradition, and rugged beauty, North America's coasts offer cruise itineraries for all seasons. The northeastern part of the continent was first discovered by Vikings and later colonized by the British and French. The **Atlantic** coast of **Eastern Canada** and the United States's **New England** feature European-style charm, crisp air, colonial towns trimmed in autumn's burgundy and gold, and scenic harbors filled with wooden boats guarded by long-standing lighthouses. In contrast to this bucolic landscape is **New York**—the city that never sleeps—where slipping past the **Statue of Liberty** at dawn or dusk remains an intensely emotional, peaceful experience.

On the other side of the continent, the US's **Pacific Northwest**, namely **Alaska**, offers immense, primeval beauty—towering snow-capped mountains, pristine pine forests, enormous ancient glaciers, and seemingly endless waterways. Bordered by the **Arctic Ocean,** the **Bering Strait** and **Sea,** the 49th state's rugged coastline stretches for about 40,000 miles, including some 15,000 square miles of fjords and inlets. Alaska is the habitat of an astounding array of marine mammals, birds, and other wildlife, as well as being home to one segment of another quickly vanishing population—Native American peoples.

Farther south, **Mexico**'s lush tropical shorelines, washed by both major oceans, are a steamy Spanish-influenced contrast to their northern neighbors.

Sexism at Sea? Only one cruise ship, the *Radisson Diamond*, has dining room waitresses. On all other ships, dining room servers are male.

Canada

Halifax, Nova Scotia

This part of Canada has always been a center of maritime activity, from its original settlement by the Micmac Indians as a summer fishing village to today's lively seaport of Halifax. Established as a military outpost in 1749 to counter the French fort on **Cape Breton Island,** Halifax was also a British staging area in its conquest of Canada. During the American Revolution the British were headquartered here, and 25,000 loyalists flocked to Halifax after the mother country's defeat. The town also served as an important base during the War of 1812. World War I initially brought prosperity and growth to Halifax, but in 1917 the *Mont Blanc*—a French munitions boat—collided with another ship in the harbor, causing a devastating explosion that leveled the northern part of the city. Swiftly reconstructed, Halifax soon reassumed its position as a center of Canada's maritime industry.

Today a city of about 300,000 people of English, French, Scottish, Irish, and German descent, Halifax is the commercial and financial center for Canada's eastern provinces, as well as the country's **Atlantic** naval base. It is also one of the continent's major ports, and **Bedford Basin** is the world's second-largest natural harbor. Resident Haligonians consider it a very liveable city, with tree-lined streets, beautiful parks, and fine old buildings.

Fish and seafood feature prominently in the local cuisine. A local favorite is deep-fried fish (or scallops or clams) and potatoes. Halifax's many native craftspeople produce a wide range of goods, including jewelry, ceramics, rugs, quilts, woodwork, and dolls.

- **Halifax Citadel National Historic Park**
- **St. Paul's Church**
- **Province House**
- **Historic Properties**
- **Maritime Museum of the Atlantic**
- **Fisherman's Market**
- **Bluenose II**
- **Nova Scotia Museum of Natural History**
- **Peggy's Cove**
- **Public Gardens**

Montreal, Quebec

While sailing up the **St. Lawrence River**—which today provides the crucial navigable link between the **Great Lakes** and the **Atlantic Ocean**—in 1535 in search of a shortcut to the Orient, French explorer Jacques Cartier found an Iroquois village named **Hochelaga.** It was located on the slopes of a mountain he called **Mont Réal** (Mount Royal) in honor of King Francis I. Samuel de Champlain arrived here in 1611, explored the area with the idea of starting a settlement, and established a temporary trading post. Some 30 years later a devout group of French colonists, priests, and nuns set up a missionary outpost called **Ville Marie de Montréal,** braving harsh winters and Indian raids in an effort to convert the inhabitants. This settlement at the head of **Lachine Rapids** became a major trading center, especially in furs, as the churning waters beyond the island made further navigation impossible. The French surrendered Montreal to the English under the 1763 Treaty of Paris, and during the American Revolution, American colonists led by Benedict Arnold and Benjamin Franklin occupied the city for

Notre Dame Basilica, Montreal

M. BLUM

seven months. A new wave of predominantly Irish and Scottish immigrants arrived in the city in the 19th century. Although the French-speaking population continued to grow, a feeling of exclusion from business and government dealings spurred some French Canadians to work for a separatist movement. Today the separatist issue remains alive and controversial.

Built on an anvil-shaped island 32 miles long and 10 miles wide in the middle of the St. Lawrence River, today Montreal is Canada's second-largest city. After Paris, it is the world's biggest French-speaking metropolis, with two-thirds of its more than three million inhabitants of French origin. Visitors will have little doubt about this sprawling, modern city's primary tongue, although most of its residents also speak English.

Montreal's complete midtown facelift in the 1960s sparked a renovation that gained momentum during **Expo '67,** continued throughout the early 1970s, and reached a peak in 1976 when it hosted the **Summer Olympic Games.** The city's past is well preserved in **Vieux Montréal,** a 95-acre repository of 17th–19th-century buildings, cobblestone streets, fascinating museums and monuments, beautiful boutiques, and some of Montreal's best French restaurants, bistros, and outdoor cafes.

- ■ Pointe-à-Callière Museum of Archaeology and History
- ■ Montreal Museum of Fine Arts
- ■ Montreal Botanical Garden
- ■ Place Jacques-Cartier
- ■ Place d'Armes and Notre-Dame Basilica
- ■ Château de Ramezay
- ■ Olympic Park Observatory
- ■ Rue St-Paul and Notre-Dame-de-Bonsecours Chapel
- ■ Parc du Mont-Royal
- ■ Ile Ste-Hélène and Old Fort

Quebec City, Quebec

The 18th-century sandstone wall of Quebec, the only fortified city north of Mexico, surrounds an area crammed with one of the continent's largest collection of 17th- and 18th-century structures. Museums, warehouses, churches, military installations, homes, and other architectural treasures have all been painstakingly restored, earning the city the distinction of being named a UNESCO World Heritage Site in 1985. Quebec is capital of Canada's largest province of the same name and is an important military, educational, and administrative center.

In the 1930s, US residents partied on overnight "booze cruises," which sailed out of US territory—and beyond the reach of Prohibition.

French explorer Jacques Cartier spent the winter here in 1535, but it wasn't until 1608 that fellow countryman Samuel de Champlain established the settlement of **Kebec,** an Algonquin word meaning "narrowing of the waters." For more than a century the French were harassed by both the English and the Iroquois, a dispute that culminated in a battle at the **Plains of Abraham,** which in a mere 15 minutes in 1759 ended France's dreams of a North American empire.

A perfectly preserved piece of France, Quebec City is all that is antique and elegant in the grandest of Old World styles. The city is divided into two parts: **Upper Town**—built high on **Cap-Diamant**'s cliff and crowned by the turreted **Château Frontenac;** and **Lower Town,** which spreads up the **St. Lawrence River.** The two sections are connected by a road and the aptly named **Escalier Casse-Cou** (Breakneck Stairway). **Vieux Québec** is a wonderful place to wander, with its meandering cobblestoned streets, panoramic views, unexpected courtyards, and cozy little cafes where French cuisine is served with an emphasis on game and seafood. A *calèche* (horse-drawn buggy) ride is a charming way to take in the sights, while shoppers would be advised to investigate the antiques shops along **Rue St-Paul** and craft boutiques on **Rue du Petit-Champlain,** full of interesting artifacts.

- ■ Château Frontenac and Dufferin Terrace
- ■ Place d'Armes and the Musée du Fort
- ■ Basilique-Cathédrale Notre-Dame-de-Québec
- ■ La Citadelle (The Citadel)
- ■ Promenade des Gouverneurs (Governors' Promenade)
- ■ Parc des Champs-de-Bataille (Battlefield Park) and Museé du Québec
- ■ Place-Royale, Eglise Notre-Dame des Victoires (Church of Our Lady of Victory)
- ■ Rues du Trésor and St-Louis
- ■ Quartier Petit Champlain (Little Champlain Quarter) and Maison Louis-Jolliet (Jolliet's House)
- ■ Musée de la Civilisation

Vancouver, British Columbia

Canada's third-largest city (about 1.8 million residents), Vancouver is a spirited cosmopolitan place rich in culture and exotic cuisine. Located amid a stunning backdrop of forested mountains laced with rivers and inlets, Vancouver sits on a peninsula between the **Fraser River** and **Burrard Inlet** (cruise ships dock here at **Canada Place**'s billowing sail terminal).

The Vancouver area was originally inhabited by Coast Salish Indians. Spanish explorers found the **Strait of Georgia,** west of the peninsula in 1790, and the next year British Captain George Vancouver was sent to explore, chart, and claim the coast of what is now British Columbia for the crown. It was another 70 years until permanent European settlements were established. Sawmills created growth centered around an area named for motor-mouth saloon owner "Gassy Jack" Deighton. Although a vicious fire razed the city shortly after it was incorporated in 1886, tenacious citizens rebuilt in time for the arrival of the first **Canadian Pacific Railway** transcontinental passenger train the next year. The Japanese and Chinese laborers who helped build the railway stayed, adding an Asian flavor to an otherwise Anglo-Saxon history.

Local cuisine centers around seafood and fish. Pacific salmon, grilled with a lemon-butter sauce or smoked, is highly coveted. The Chinese food found here is among the best on the continent. Trading posts have given way to shopping malls, but the colorful, striped Hudson Bay blankets are still coveted. Native American handicrafts—whose authenticity is guaranteed by a Department of Indian Affairs label—include baskets; carvings in soapstone, onyx, bone, and ivory; mukluks (fur and sealskin boots); totem poles; jewelry from black argillite; hand-woven rugs; and wall hangings. Cowichan sweaters are waterproof woolens with eagle and whale designs originally knit by 19th-century Scottish settlers. **Chinatown** is a great spot to pick up such items as porcelain, cookware, jade, woodcarvings, and lacquered pottery.

- **Grouse Mountain and Tram**
- **Robson Square**
- **Vancouver Art Gallery**
- **Chinatown**
- **Gastown**
- **Stanley Park**
- **University of British Columbia Anthropology Museum**
- **Vancouver Museum**
- **Queen Elizabeth Park and Bloedel Conservatory**
- **Lynn Canyon**

Victoria, British Columbia

The densely forested and rugged **Vancouver Island,** at 282 miles long, is the biggest island off the west coast of North America. Its largest city, Victoria, is on the island's southeast tip. Founded in 1843 as a Hudson Bay Company trading post, Victoria was named after the British queen and became a British Crown Colony in 1848. That year the gold rush hit the **Fraser River** in Cariboo country, and 25,000 American miners came through town. Victoria became the capital of the province of British Columbia in 1871.

Timber—spruce, fir, and cedar—is big business on this heavily forested island, along with fishing and mining. Home to over a quarter of a million people, Victoria is an affluent, groomed garden city with a sunny mild climate that attracts many retirees. Many reminders of the British Empire remain, from Tudor architecture to Victorian-era streetlights decked with hanging flower baskets to elegant afternoon tea. The **Inner Harbour** is full of pleasure boats.

Pacific salmon—sockeye, coho, pink, chum, spring, and steelhead in descending order of delicacy—is abundant here, and smoked whole salmon makes a succulent souvenir. Similar to the Boston variety, clam chowder is a specialty. Native American handicrafts and Hudson Bay blankets are found locally, and **Antique Row** on **Fort Street** offers such heirlooms as British china, glassware, and silver.

- **Parliament**
- **Royal British Columbia Museum**
- **Thunderbird Park**
- **Beacon Hill Park**
- **Afternoon tea at the Empress Hotel**
- **Craigdarroch Castle**
- **Maritime Museum**
- **Butchart Gardens**
- **Art Gallery**
- **Undersea Gardens**

Mexico

Acapulco

A 22-mile gorgeous crescent on the **Pacific Ocean** that boasts 23 beaches is what has brought Hollywood's rich and famous here since Cuba became off-limits in 1960. The largest city on the **Mexican Riviera,** Acapulco is a glamorous, hectic place, teeming with fashionable clubs, restaurants, crowded markets, and cruise-ship passengers.

The Spanish discovered the **Bahía de Acapulco** (Acapulco Bay) in 1512 and subsequently used the village as a home base for Spain's trade route to the Pacific. Pirates often plied Acapulco's waters looking to confiscate the goods arriving from Asia, and a fortress was built high in the hills in the 17th century to defend the port against raids. After Mexico was granted independence in 1821, and Acapulco lost its military importance, it became a relatively obscure port until a paved road from Mexico City was constructed in 1927. Even then another 30 years passed until a burst of development along the bay's central coast turned Acapulco from a small town to a big city jammed with towering condos and palatial mansions.

The Franciscan missionaries forced Catholicism on the Aztec, and the Aztec introduced the Spaniards to such foods as avocado, chocolate, peanuts, sweet potatoes, tomatoes, and turkey. Here, as in other parts of modern Mexico, meat, chicken, or bean enchiladas, tacos, and tamales are culinary favorites. The local seafood delicacies are ceviche and *huachinango a la veracruzana* (red snapper baked in a wine sauce with tomato, onion, garlic, peppers, and spices). Leather goods, hand-painted pottery, glassware, onyx, Taxco silver, woven cotton blankets, and resortwear can be found at any of the many handicraft markets and souvenir stands. Be sure to bargain vigorously. Tequila, practically the national drink, and the coffee liqueur Kahlúa are also popular purchases.

- ■ **Puerto Marqués**
- ■ **Zócalo (Main Plaza)**
- ■ **Fuerte de San Diego (Fort San Diego)**
- ■ **Carretera Escénica**
- ■ **Pie de La Cuesta Beach**
- ■ **Clavadistas de La Quebrada (Cliff divers at La Quebrada)**
- ■ **Laguna de Coyuca (Coyuca Lagoon)**
- ■ **Playa Condesa (Countess Beach)**
- ■ **Playa Hornos (Oven Beach)**
- ■ **Isla de La Roqueta**

Cabo San Lucas

At the southernmost tip of the **Baja California Peninsula,** Cabo San Lucas juts between the **Pacific Ocean** and the **Sea of Cortés** at **Land's End.** Here the **Sierra de la Laguna** mountain range becomes an isolated, cactus-dotted lunar landscape that descends into the water in a series of imposing rock formations of arches and peaks. Two jagged pinnacles rise 291 feet above water while the underwater shelf drops off steeply, complete with sandfalls. Whales, sailfish, and dolphins play in these waters. Gray whales migrate from the Bering Strait to the Pacific coast of Baja from December to April, congregating to calve in several bays and lagoons along the southern coast.

Conquerors, colonizers, and developers usually passed up the rugged terrain of Baja California for more hospitable lands, although the Spanish established a pirate-free port for their galleons en route from the Philippines here. Until the 1970s Cabo San Lucas was a sleepy village known for sports fishing and frequented by the likes of Ernest Hemingway. Today it's an international resort and one of the fastest growing in Mexico.

The catch of the day here is prepared with tomatillo and *guajillo* chili sauces. The area is known for dark

ironwood carvings of marlins, dolphins, and whales; Talavera pottery from Puebla; lacquered trays from Michoacán; and silver jewelry.

- ■ **Los Arcos (The Arches)**
- ■ **Los Frailes (The Friars)**
- ■ **Roca Pelicano (Pelican Rock)**
- ■ **Cerro La Vigía**
- ■ **Zócalo (Plaza)**
- ■ **Playa del Amor (Love Beach)**
- ■ **Playa El Médano (Dune Beach)**
- ■ **Playa Solmar**
- ■ **Deep sea fishing**
- ■ **Snorkeling**

Cancún/Cozumel

The mighty Maya enjoyed an advanced civilization on the **Yucatán Peninsula** a millennium before Columbus set sail. Their legacy is widespread in the state of **Quintana Roo**—well-preserved ruins stand in mute testament to the Maya's once-powerful empire. **Chichén Itzá,** the largest and most famous, boasts a 365-step pyramid, which is actually an astronomical clock designed to mark seasonal solstices and equinoxes. Perched on a rocky cliff overlooking the **Caribbean,** the ancient walled city was once a local trade center and one of the first Maya communities to be seen by Europeans (who discovered it in 1519).

Twenty-five years ago Cancún was a tiny fishing village, home to a few families. Because of its perfect weather, Maya ruins, white sandy beaches, and accessibility to North America, the government slotted it for development as a premier resort destination. Today it has a population of nearly a quarter-million. It is 10 miles long, and in the shape of a seven—the top portion faces the calm waters of the **Bahía de Mujeres,** and the bottom, the Caribbean. Cancún boasts the second-longest reef system in the world; water visibility here is more than 100 feet.

Pyramid of Kulkulkan, Chichén Itzá

J. DEL GAIZO

The name Cozumel is derived from the Maya word *Cuzamil* (Land of Swallows). It was an important Maya trading and pilgrimage center. The Spaniards first stepped foot on the island in 1518, but left two years later, after destroying most of the Maya shrines. Cozumel is a flat jungle island fringed with beaches of white sand, and famous for its reefs—especially **Palancar.** The main town, **San Miguel,** on the sheltered western coast, still has some small shops and traditional eateries, but is slowly catching up to its more glamorous sister city across the water in an attempt to cater to the cruise-ship crowd.

Local cuisine includes *conchinita pibil* (marinated pork steamed in banana leaves) and *puco-chuc* (seasoned, grilled pork chops). Shoppers will find ceramics, brass, wood carvings, blankets, onyx, silver jewelry, hammocks, and Maya artifact reproductions.

- Tulum
- Chichén Itzá
- Xel-Ha
- Sian Ka'an Biosphere Reserve
- Isla Mujeres and Parque Garrafón Nacional
- Xcaret
- Parque Nacional Chankanaab
- Cozumel Archaeological Park
- Museo de la Isla de Cozumel
- San Gervasio

Mazatlán

Mexico's largest **Pacific** port, Mazatlán is located at the foot of the **Sierra Madre** on the **Bahía del Puerto Viejo** at the mouth of the **Sea of Cortés.** Nearly a half-million people make their home in this commercial and industrial center that is the base for the country's largest shrimp fleet. Its waters teem year-round with sailfish and marlin, making it a prime sportfishing center.

Mazatlán was established in the 1820s, and today is the northernmost city on the **Mexican Riviera.** The old part of town is wrapped around **Plazuela Machado.** Most tourist facilities and palm-fringed beaches, however, are in the **Zona Dorada** (Gold Zone) in the northern part of the city. Lagoons and mangroves surrounding this city on a peninsula are home to egrets, flamingoes, pelicans, cranes, and herons. Deer continue to roam the Sierra Madre above town to the north, reflecting the accuracy of the name the Aztec bestowed on the city—Mazatlán means "Place of the Deer" in Nahuatl. Be sure to look out for two-legged wanderers—boisterous bands of brass-blowing, drum-beating musicians who travel around the city day and night.

The fish is fresh here and the shrimp, of course, is succulent. Shoppers usually head for the **Centro de Artesanías** for such well-priced products as blankets, pottery, lace, silver jewelry, and shell items, and a chance to watch artisans at work.

- El Faro (Lighthouse)
- Malecón (Seaside Promenade)
- Plaza de la República (Republic Square)
- Mercado Municipal (Municipal Market)
- Playa Olas Altas (Beach of the High Waves)
- Copala and Concordia
- Iglesia Mazatlán (Mazatlán Cathedral)
- Teatro Angela Peralta (Angela Peralta Theater)
- Cerro del Crestón (Summit Hill)
- Playa Brujas

Puerto Vallarta

Richard Burton and Elizabeth Taylor fell in love while he and Deborah Kerr were filming John Huston's classic, *The Night of the Iguana,* at this seaside resort in the heart of the **Mexican Riviera.** Tucked between the tropical jungles of the **Sierra Madre** and the **Pacific** coast waters of crescent-shaped **Bahía de las Banderas,** Puerto Vallarta has drawn visitors in droves since that famous film was shot here in 1964. Its clear, deep-blue waters attract underwater visitors as well: fish, dolphins, sea turtles, and migrating whales. Divers discover nirvana at **Los Arcos** (The Arches) rock formations. The **Rio Cuale** divides Puerto Vallarta in two, with most of the city located on the northern side. Puerto Vallarta boasts a Mediterranean flavor—whitewashed houses and red-tile roofs crawl up cobblestone streets into the hills of **Viejo Vallarta** (Old Town). But the sandy white beaches that stretch north and south for 25 miles are the city's main attraction.

Although Spaniard Don Pedro de Alvarado sighted its shores in 1541, the village of **Las Peñas** was left untouched by Europeans until 1851 when Guadalupe Sanchez settled along the Rio Cuale to farm. The name was changed to Puerto Vallarta in 1918, after Ignacio Luis Vallarta, a prominent Mexican statesman. Today most of the city's approximately 300,000 residents earn their living from tourism.

Local dishes include *sopa de tortilla* (tortilla soup), made from tomato stock seasoned with coriander and poured over fried tortillas; gazpacho; and ceviche. Puerto Vallarta's peddlers are almost as famous as its beaches. Woven blankets, silver jewelry, straw hats, painted pottery, leather goods, and embroidered textiles are just some of the items they offer. Don't forget to bargain.

- Marina Vallarta
- Malecón (Promenade)
- Iglesia de Nuestra Señora de Guadalupe (Our Lady of Guadalupe Shrine)
- Plaza de Armas (Main Square)
- Casa Kimberly
- Mercado Municipal (Municipal Market)
- Isla Río Cuale (Cuale River Island)
- Playa Quimixto (Quimixto Beach)
- Snorkeling at Los Arcos
- Mismaloya

Rollin' on the River

Ever since Mark Twain's day, folks have been fascinated with river travel. More than 100 years after Samuel Clemens sailed the **Mississippi**, it's still possible to hop aboard an authentic paddle wheeler (or a small motor ship or catamaran) to explore **North America**'s inland waterways. The following is just a sampling of the many American river journeys available. For more ideas, see your travel agent.

Since 1890, the **Delta Queen Steamboat Co.** has kept alive America's great steamboating legacy. The line's trio of steam-powered paddle wheelers plies the rivers of Middle America, with departures from **New Orleans,** Memphis, St. Louis, Cincinnati, Louisville, Chattanooga, Pittsburgh, and a host of other cities. As the big red paddle wheel churns, the steam calliope pipes its distinctive tune, heralding a voyage with old-fashioned treats like sing-alongs, kite-flying, down-home cooking, and tales of yesteryear from the ship's own "Riverlorian."

The intimate ships of the **American Canadian Caribbean Line** cruise the **Great Lakes** and sail down the **Chicago, Illinois, Des Plaines, Mississippi, Ohio, Mobile,** and **Tombigbee Rivers.** ACCL vessels also journey from **New England** to **Florida** on the **Intracoastal Waterway,** passing marshes, sand dunes, forests, ponds, and villages as the salty scent of the nearby **Atlantic** wafts in on the breeze.

On the West Coast, **Alaska Sightseeing/Cruise West** combs **California**'s rivers, offering tours to the **Napa Valley** and **Sonoma** wine country. The company's trips on Oregon's **Columbia** and **Snake Rivers** feature the scenic beauty of the **Columbia River Gorge** and other natural wonders. The sternwheeler *Queen of the West*, operated by

American West Steamboat Co., also cruises the Columbia and Snake, as well as the **Willamette**. And **Great Rivers Cruises & Tours** offers day and overnight catamaran cruises on the Columbia and Willamette Rivers, with overnight accommodations in hotels ashore.

Up north there's the **American Canadian Caribbean Line,** which has been sailing the **Erie Canal** and the **St. Lawrence Seaway** since 1966. Its small ships inch close to little villages lining the canal and meander around some of the **Thousand Islands** of **Lake Ontario** en route to the seaway. Some voyages sail up **Canada**'s fjordlike **Saguenay River;** the line's fall foliage trips are especially popular for their dazzling scenery.

From May through October, Ontario-based **St. Lawrence Cruise Lines Inc.** runs excursions on Canada's **St. Lawrence** and **Ottawa Rivers** aboard the 66-passenger *Canadian Empress*.

Clipper Cruise Line offers a wide array of inland voyages, from cruises on waterways of **Northern California** to trips on the St. Lawrence and Saguenay. This small-ship company staffs its vessels with historians and/or naturalists, who provide insight into the regions visited. (Also see page 101.)

MICHAEL STORRINGS

Zihuatanejo/Ixtapa

This rugged part of Mexico 150 miles northwest of Acapulco was left untouched by colonists and developers until the late 1970s when Mexico's National Fund for Tourism Development picked this pair of sleepy, swampy villages to lure sun-seeking tourists to their beautiful beaches. Zihuatanejo, which means "place of women" in the ancient Nahuatl tongue, has remained a quiet cobblestoned town of 80,000 despite being freshened up for tourists. It sits on a C-shaped bay lined with beaches and blue and white wooden boats belonging to fishermen who make a living from the sea. In contrast, sister city Ixtapa ("where there are salt lakes") five miles to the north was developed into an unabashed resort, with a series of international luxury hotels along its 14 beaches.

Ceviche, quesadillas with cheese and *huitlacoche* (a mushroomlike fungus cultivated on corn husks), and *chilaquiles* (corn tortillas in broth) are some of the culinary delights found in the two cities. Both places boast their share of handicraft outlets and markets, offering a broad selection of Oaxaca crafts, hand-loomed woolen rugs, wood carvings and masks, hand-painted pottery, ceramics, weavings, and leather goods. Ixtapa's malls sell designer clothing and accessories.

Zihuatanejo

- Playa Las Gatas (Cats' Beach)
- Paseo del Pescador (Fisherman's Promenade)
- Museo Arqueológico de la Costa Grande (Archaeology Museum of The Big Coast)

- Plaza de Toros (Plaza of the Bulls)
- Mercado Artesanal (Artisan's Market)
- Mercado Municipal (Municipal Market)
- Catedral (Cathedral)

Ixtapa

- Isla Ixtapa (Ixtapa Island)
- El Morro de Los Pericos
- Mercado Artesanal (Artisan's Market)

United States

Anchorage, Alaska

Founded in 1914 as a tent city for the nearly 2,000 **Alaska Railroad** workers who came to build the railway, Anchorage is situated at the head of the 220-mile **Cook Inlet**, between two arms—**Knik** and **Turnagain.** The latter was named by Captain James Cook who, on his search for the Northwest Passage in 1778, hit yet another dead end and was forced to "turn again." The city got its name because it was the primary "anchorage" for ships bringing materials to build the **Alaska Railroad** in 1915. Anchorage grew as an important military base in World War II and remained significant through the cold war as **Elmendorf Air Force Base** was established to monitor Soviet movements. Today it is the headquarters of the Alaskan NORAD Region and the 11th Air Force Division. The Good Friday Earthquake in 1964 destroyed the downtown business district, but with North Slope oil lease sales on 10 September 1969 bringing in $900 million in seven hours, and a corporate population explosion from 85,000 to 180,000 by the end of the 1970s, the city's economy recovered.

Today Anchorage has a population of over a quarter of a million residents and is the largest and fastest-growing city in the state. It is Alaska's commercial, industrial, and cultural capital, and the only real metropolitan area—complete with skyscrapers and shopping malls. But Anchorage is still a frontier town in spirit, and the starting line for the nearly 1,100-mile Iditarod Trail Sled Dog Race to Nome every March.

Local culinary delights include wild salmon, king crab, and halibut.

- Anchorage Museum of History and Art
- Fourth Avenue Theatre
- Oscar Anderson House and Elderberry Park
- Alaska Experience Theater
- Earthquake Park
- Chugach State Park
- Alaska Arctic and Indian Museum
- Alaska Heritage Museum-Library
- Coastal Trail
- Lake Hood and Alaska Aviation Museum

Bar Harbor, Maine

Mount Desert Island is the lovely backdrop for this town that the English colonists who settled here in 1776 called **Eden.** The island's granite mountains are studded with pines, and its jagged shoreline carved by a pounding **Atlantic** surf is populated by puffins, ospreys, and bald eagles.

Boston Skyline

© VOGEL

The Abenaki Indians had already been living along these shores for many years, subsisting on fish and berries, when Samuel de Champlain set off in 1604 to explore the island. It was part of the Acadian lands granted by France's Henry IV to Sieur de Monts, who had accompanied Champlain. Champlain named it **L'Isle des Monts-déserts** (Mount Desert Island). French Jesuits established a mission here in 1613, which was destroyed by the British in the first of many such conflicts to come. Antoine de la Mothe Cadillac, who was granted title to the island in 1688, stopped here briefly before moving on to found the city of Detroit. The mountain named in his honor is one of the first points in the US to see the sun rise.

Artists and writers from the New York City area discovered this haven in the 1840s and 1850s. The city's high society followed not long after, with such families as the Pulitzers, Rockefellers, Vanderbilts, and Astors erecting enormous summer "cottages" on the island and making Bar Harbor another Newport of sorts. With great foresight, these vacationers acquired 6,000 acres of Mount Desert Island and donated it to the federal government in 1916 as a way to preserve the area for all to enjoy. Thirteen years later Congress created the 35,000-acre **Acadia National Park,** which included 45 miles of lovely carriage roads that Rockefeller had built. Today these byways are used for hiking, biking, and horseback riding. In 1947 a fire swept across the island, destroying all but a handful of houses; some were subsequently repaired, others rebuilt from scratch. Bar Harbor's local population of about 4,500 swells to over 20,000 in summer as visitors flock here to enjoy the island's justifiably famous lobsters and blueberries.

- **Historical Museum**
- **Natural History Museum in College of the Atlantic**
- **Acadia National Park Visitors' Center**
- **Loop Road**
- **Oceanarium and Lobster Hatchery**
- **Afternoon tea at Jordan Pond**
- **Thunder Hole and Otter Cliffs**
- **Cadillac Mountain**
- **Jackson Laboratory**
- **Robert Abbe Museum of Stone Age Antiquities**

Boston, Massachusetts

A band of Puritans from Charlestown across the **Charles River** from Boston, led by John Winthrop, founded Boston in 1630 while searching for drinking water. They succeeded in their mission and prospered despite a harsh first winter. The group even established **Harvard College** six years later. Shipping, ship building, and fishing flourished in Boston's excellent harbor until the mid-18th century when the English Crown began to tighten its grip on the colonists. A series of tough new revenue measures were instigated, cooling relations between the colonies and the motherland and leading up to the famous Boston Tea Party. At this 1773 event, some 60 colonial patriots disguised as Indians hurled 342 crates of the heavily taxed tea into the harbor. This rebellion spurred the American Revolution, and Boston became known as the "Cradle of American Independence."

With a population that included renowned educators, philosophers, poets, abolitionists, and architects,

MARJORIE VOGEL, RHODE ISLAND ORIGINALS

Boston soon became the cultural capital of the United States. By the end of the 18th century, the city had quadrupled in size—marshes were drained, small hills leveled, and landfills created. In later decades, the population swelled with refugees from Ireland's potato famine, augmented by additional waves of Italians, Poles, and Russians. Although the city was hard hit during the Depression, Boston managed to lure back business, cultivating its young student population (there are 71 universities) for jobs in such high-tech industries as electronics and computer research and development. Today over three million people live in Greater Boston—an area covering 1,057 square miles. The city's twisting narrow streets and colonial architecture have been well preserved among the glass and concrete office blocks.

Chowder, lobster, and scrod—as the catch of the day is known—are local dining favorites. Shoppers will be happy browsing at **Faneuil Hall Marketplace** and **Newbury Street** in the **Back Bay.**

- **Boston Common**
- **The Freedom Trail**
- **Beacon Hill**
- **Copley Square and Trinity Church**
- **Hancock Building Observatory**
- **Museum of Fine Arts**
- **Isabella Stewart Gardner Museum**
- **John F. Kennedy Library and Museum**
- **Harvard Yard**
- **Haymarket**

Ft. Lauderdale, Florida

This city was named for Major William Lauderdale who was sent in 1838 to subdue the Seminole Indians and erect a fort on the **New River**'s mosquito-infested swamps. In the 1880s, a railway line was extended south from Palm Beach, the swamps drained, and canals dug, thus creating the plentiful waterfront real estate that exists today.

With 300-plus miles of navigable inland routes along the **Intracoastal Waterway,** which pass palatial estates, citrus groves, and the **Everglades,** Ft. Lauderdale is often called the "Venice of America." It is one of the world's yachting capitals, with thousands of boats of every size and shape converging on the area each winter. Bigger vessels attract more than two million passengers each year, making **Port Everglades** the second-busiest cruise ship port of embarkation after Miami. Ft. Lauderdale's permanent population of about 150,000 swells each winter as snowbirds from the north arrive for the season, and visitors from Asia to Europe fly in for vacations. During spring break, college students from around the country migrate here. Wedged between 23 miles of **Atlantic** coastline and beaches to the east, and the moist green Everglades to the west, Ft. Lauderdale claims to soak up 3,000 hours of rays annually, making it the sunniest city in the continental US.

Culinary delights run the gamut from classic French fare to New American cuisine. Shoppers should steel themselves for **Sawgrass Mills Mall**—the world's largest outlet mall, packed with designer discounters, and the 2,000-vendor **Swap Shop**—the biggest flea market in the south.

- **Hollywood Broadwalk**
- **Museum of Discovery and Science**
- **Hugh Taylor Birch State Park**
- **Las Olas Boulevard**
- **Intracoastal Waterway cruise**
- **Bonnet House**
- **Flamingo Gardens**
- **Stranahan House**
- **Riverwalk**
- **Everglades airboat ride**

Glacier Bay, Alaska

The 12 tidewater glaciers of Glacier Bay line the northern end of Alaska's 1,000-mile long **Inside Passage.** These monumental ice mountains originate from the massive snowfields of the 15,000-foot **Fairweather Range** 72 miles inland and soar hundreds of feet above the bay.

A glacier is created by years of snowfalls that compress into a large and thick ice mass. What makes it unique is that it moves, the glacier's own weight causing it to flow much like a very slow river. The glacier inches forward, taking rock and sediment with it downhill. Entire chunks up to 200 feet high slide into the blue-green waters, creating huge waves and filling the bay's narrow inlets with icebergs. This ongoing action is known as calving.

As recently as 200 years ago, when Captain George Vancouver sailed through the ice-choked waters of **Icy Strait,** what is now Glacier Bay was little more than a dent in the shoreline—it was completely covered by an immense glacier. By 1879, the ice had receded 48 miles when naturalist John Muir visited, and the area was covered by spruce-hemlock forests. By 1916, in the most rapid glacial retreat ever recorded, the ice had withdrawn another 17 miles. Glacier Bay was declared a national monument in 1925 and a national park in 1980. The **West Arm** glaciers are the most popular for viewing: **Lamplugh** is one of the bluest, **Johns Hopkins** one of the most active, and **Margerie** and **Grand Pacific** the largest in the park.

Wildlife thrives here as well. Harbor seals, black blots on the ice floes, slip into the water when a ship approaches. Whales are easily spotted by the noise and spray of their blowholes. Humpbacks especially put on an acrobatic show: They dive deep for krill, then break the surface—their entire 20–30-ton bodies jumping clear of the water—before slamming down, raising a massive spray. Dall and harbor porpoises also visit these waters. On shore bears wander the coast.

Alaska Shopping

One of the few remaining ways that Alaska's Native Americans have been able to preserve their folklore, traditions, and rapidly disappearing way of life is through their handicrafts. Made from a variety of animal and mineral materials, ornamental household items, tools, weapons, and objects used in ceremonial dances and healing rites, as well as clothing and jewelry, are available for sale throughout Alaska. The authenticity of the goods is verified through a state-sanctioned "AUTHENTIC NATIVE HANDCRAFT FROM ALASKA" label.

Inuit—Eskimos—are renowned for their bold wood-carving skills found in totem poles, screens, panels, and masks representing powerfully stylized animal and ancestral figures that are then painted in vibrant reds, blacks, and blues. Ivory is shaped into chess sets; onyx, bone, and soapstone are more commonly used carving materials in the north. Since the early 1800s, Haidas have worked with argillite, a highly polished black shalestone that is fashioned into boxes, ceremonial dishes, and small totem poles that were coveted by the early traders for their high luster.

Aleuts, Inuit, and other assorted Indian cultures each employ a distinct technique in basket weaving, employing fine strands of cedar or spruce bark. Baleen—bonelike material from a whale's mouth—is also used. They are woven in geometric patterns, sometimes so tightly that the baskets are waterproof. Gold nugget jewelry is popular, and artisans use a rainbow of precious and semiprecious stones—jade, coral, garnets, pink quartz, aquamarine, topaz, and hematite—to create adornments.

Fur hats and coats are often less expensive here than in the Lower 48. Scarves, capes, and sweaters made from qiviut, a cashmerelike wool from the musk ox, are in abundance. Chilkat goat hair blankets—intricately patterned colorful shawls—are still worn in Tlingit ceremonies.

Edible items include jams and jellies made from wildberries and salmonberries, as well as canned and smoked salmon.

JENNIFER LEONARD

Haines, Alaska

Straddling the narrow peninsula between the **Chilkoot** and **Chilkat Inlets** at the head of the 1,600-foot-deep **Lynn Canal,** Haines is a quiet town ringed by the 6,500-foot-high **Cathedral Peaks.** The village was originally inhabited by the Tlingit people of the Chilkoot and Chilkat tribes who called it **Deishu** (End of the Trail). The Chilkat are known for the blankets they weave from the wool of mountain goats; they then dye them with natural colorings. These lovely, intricately patterned covers are still worn during dance ceremonies.

White traders and missionaries arrived in the late 19th century and changed the indigenous name to honor Mrs. Haines of the Presbyterian Home Missions Board. During the Klondike Gold Rush in 1898, a shrewd adventurer-businessman named Jack Dalton built a 300-mile road along an old Indian trade route between Haines and the Yukon and charged miners a $150 toll—often collected with the help of a sawed-off shotgun—to use his trail. That old route formed the basis of today's **Haines Highway,** a modern interstate. In 1903 **Fort Seward** was built, and Haines became the US Army's regimental headquarters for Alaska.

Today Haines's population of 1,800 works in fishing, lumber, government, tourism, and the arts. In addition, recent years have brought many types of craftspeople here to work and sell their wares. Haines also attracts as many as 3,500 bald eagles at one time—the earth's largest such gathering—which come to feast on salmon on the **Chilkat River.** Although Haines is quite close to **Glacier Bay,** its weather is temperate because of its protected location, and the area yields a healthy crop of fresh produce every summer.

- Fort Seward complex
- Lookout Park
- Tlingit Park
- Sheldon Museum and Cultural Center
- Chilkat State Park and Seduction Point
- Chilkoot Lake
- Chilkat Bald Eagle Preserve
- Mount Riley Trails
- Chilkat River Float Trip
- Salmon bake at Fort Seward tribal house
- Chilkat Dancers

Juneau, Alaska

This city has the peculiar distinction of being accessible only by boat or plane. Juneau, Alaska's capital, is located along a thin strip of land in the **Gastineau Channel** and is dominated by the 3,576-foot **Mount Juneau** and the 3,819-foot **Mount Roberts.** These mountains help to keep the city's climate mild. Juneau itself is surrounded by the **Tongass National Forest,** and the nearby **Juneau Icefield** produces the **Mendenhall, Taku,** and **Herbert** glaciers.

The Auk Indians, who lived by fishing around creeks, were the original settlers of the area. In 1880, two prospectors, Quebec-born Joseph Juneau and Philadelphian Richard Harris, came to the area to investigate the streams cascading into the Gastineau Channel, which were rumored to harbor gold. With the help of Chief Kowee and the Auk, the pair struck pay dirt in what would become known as **Gold Creek.** This was the beginning of Alaska's multimillion dollar gold rush. In all, 6.7 million ounces of gold were mined from the region. One of the few Alaskan gold-rush towns that didn't burn to the ground in a fire, Juneau retains that era's ambience in its architecture and saloons. Timber, salmon, and halibut have since replaced gold as the city's main sources of income.

Alaska's territorial capital was moved from Sitka to Juneau in 1906, and the city became the state capital in 1959. Today its population of about 30,000 people is spread out over 3,100 square miles, from neighboring **Douglas Island** to right up to the Canadian border.

- ■ Taku Glacier Lodge
- ■ Alaska State Museum
- ■ Red Dog Saloon
- ■ Mendenhall Glacier float trip
- ■ St. Nicholas Orthodox Church
- ■ Auke Bay
- ■ Gold Creek Salmon Bake
- ■ Juneau-Douglas City Museum
- ■ Last Chance Mining Museum
- ■ Gastineau Salmon Hatchery

Ketchikan, Alaska

Billing itself as "the salmon capital of the world," Ketchikan, a sleepy town of about 14,000 that sprawls along the shores of the **Tongass Narrows,** is also "Alaska's First City"—the first stop in the state when approached from the south along the **Inside Passage.** In another dubious honor, it is also one of the rainiest places in the world, getting over 13 feet a year, or an average of a half-inch a day. The Tlingit name Ketchikan ("Wings of An Eagle") refers to the shape of the sandspit at the mouth of the creek as seen from **Deer Mountain,** which looms 3,000 feet above the town.

Ketchikan started out as a Tlingit Indian summer fishing camp along the west coast of **Revillagigedo Island** (named for a one-time viceroy of Mexico). In 1887 Americans from the Lower 48 arrived to set up salmon fisheries. At their peak in the 1930s, the city's 11 canneries churned out nearly two million cases of salmon annually. After World War II, that industry was surpassed by timber and pulp production. Gold was another booming endeavor—Ketchikan was incorporated as a mining town in 1900—with substantial discoveries made in the area and on nearby **Prince of Wales Island.** Ketchikan might be best remembered during those days for its colorful red-light district built on pilings over **Ketchikan Creek.** According to a sign on that infamous street, Ketchikan was "the only place in the world where both the fish and the fishermen went up the stream to spawn."

Nearby on the eastern side of Revillagigedo Island and the adjacent mainland up to the Canadian border is a 3,600-square-mile park whose beauty will be left untouched. Established in 1978, the park is packed with glaciers, rain forests, and rugged mountains, and is famous for its narrow fjords and cliffs soaring 3,000 feet above the sea.

- ■ Creek Street and Dolly's House
- ■ Cable Car to Westmark Cape Fox Lodge
- ■ Frontier Saloon
- ■ Tongass Historical Society Museum
- ■ Totem Heritage Cultural Center
- ■ Totem Bight Historic Site
- ■ Saxman Village
- ■ Deer Mountain Hatchery
- ■ Thomas Basin Boat Harbor
- ■ Misty Fjords National Monument

Key West, Florida

During the late 19th century developer Henry Flagler attempted to establish a "land route" to Cuba by extending his **Florida East Coast Railroad** line to Key West, the United States's most southern community. The final link was going to be a ferry shuttle that would cover the last 90 miles. But when the stock market crashed, and a hurricane destroyed the train tracks, the US government took over and built the **Overseas Highway** along the same circuit. This toll-free road—the world's longest oceangoing thoroughfare—links a 150-mile chain of islands curving westward from the tip of the Florida peninsula to Key West.

Surrounded by an offshore coral reef that is part the **Florida Keys National Marine Sanctuary,** Key West is a 3.5-square-mile subtropical island. The genesis of its name is unclear—one possibility is that it was called **Cayo Oesto** by the discoverer of Florida, Ponce de Leon, who knew the island to be the most westerly of the chain. But for many years it was called **Cayo Hueso** (Bone Island), perhaps because a fierce battle with the Indians in the 18th century left the island littered with corpses. But for all its violent past, Key West remains one of the friendliest towns in Florida.

Descended from London Cockneys who had settled in the Bahamas and Yankee sea captains, the resilient Key West residents were known as conchs (pronounced konks) after the king conchs that cling tenaciously to the undersea rocks offshore. They were a seagoing people who made a living fishing, sailing, and salvaging wrecks off the coast. Today's Key Westers, however, are a mix of Cuban refugees, Caribbean Rastafarians, and artists and writers attracted by the island's relaxed outlook and life-style. Ernest Hemingway, possibly Key West's most renowned resident, wrote many of his novels—including *To Have and Have Not, For Whom the Bell Tolls, Green Hills of Africa,* and his most famous short story, "The Snows of Kilimanjaro"—during the 30 years that he lived here. Other prominent Americans who have spent time in Key West include Harry Truman (who established a "Little White House" here), John James Audubon, Tennessee Williams, John Dos Passos, and Robert Frost. Key West kitchens are famous for their conch chowder and Key lime pie, which is actually yellow, not green.

- ■ Glass bottom boat or snorkeling tour
- ■ Lighthouse Museum
- ■ Audubon House & Gardens
- ■ Wrecker's Museum
- ■ Key West Bight
- ■ Mel Fisher Maritime Heritage Society Museum
- ■ Hemingway's Home
- ■ Harry S Truman Little White House
- ■ Key West Aquarium
- ■ Old City Hall

Los Angeles (Long Beach), California

A Mediterranean climate, frontier attitude, and Hollywood glitter attract the off-beat, the artistic, the glamorous, and the wannabes to this young city with old roots. Sprawled over 467 square miles along sometimes smoggy valleys and a desert plain, across foothills and canyons, Los Angeles is threaded with spaghettilike superhighways where cars creep along at a snail's pace. The Greater Los Angeles area includes such neighborhoods as **Hollywood, Van Nuys,** and **Woodland Hills,** as well as the nearby cities of **Beverly Hills** and **Burbank,** among others. Yet despite its rapid growth, modern architecture, and search for perpetual youth, Los Angeles manages to retain some shreds of its Spanish history.

On 4 September 1781, Don Felipe de Neve, Governor of California, marched to the site of the present-day Los Angeles and with solemn ceremony founded **El Pueblo de Nuestra Señora la Reina de Los Angeles de Porciuncula** (The Town of Our Lady the Queen of Angels of Porciuncula). It remained a quiet pueblo until 1846 when the United States seized the territory and converted it into a frontier community. The Gold Rush of 1849 hastened the place's growth, and the free-for-all town ended up so often on the wrong side of the law that it instead became known as **Los Diablos** (The Devils). Railroads, land and oil booms, and construction of a water line caused the city to expand at an astronomical rate, a growth that only leveled off at the beginning of the 1990s.

Los Angeles is a food and fashion haven. If it's hip, it's here—from the actor-owned eateries all over town to **Rodeo Drive**'s designer boutiques. Asian and Mexican fare also feature prominently on menus around town, as do most any other of the world's cuisines.

- ■ El Pueblo de Los Angeles Historic Monument (Olvera Street)
- ■ Universal Studios Hollywood
- ■ George C. Page Museum of La Brea Discoveries
- ■ Farmers Market
- ■ Queen Mary Seaport

Queen Mary Seaport, Long Beach

- Hollywood Walk of Fame
- Los Angeles County Museum of Art
- J. Paul Getty Museum
- Disneyland
- Catalina Island

Miami, Florida

In 1896 Julia Tuttle bought 640 acres of scrub land on the north bank of the **Miami River,** then got fellow Clevelander Henry Flagler to extend his railroad south from Palm Beach. Now sprawled across 2,054 square miles, Miami is a vast and cosmopolitan city, home to some two million permanent residents. The population swells in the winter months to some five million as the snowbirds flock south to escape nasty weather up north. And as an evolving international trade center, Miami is also the busiest cruise port in the world; over three million passengers board ships here annually for Caribbean cruises.

The former frontier town is also the gateway to Latin America—many of its newer residents are Spanish-speaking refugees from the Caribbean and Central America. Others are affluent Colombians and Venezuelans who spend part of the year here. The Latin American influence is so strong that Spanish is the first language of over 60 percent of Miami's full-time citizens. Each of Greater Miami's neighborhoods has its own distinct personality. **Coral Gables,** one of the most prestigious communities, was designed with Spanish and Italian influences that are still part of its building codes. **Coconut Grove** boasts wealthy winter residents. A former coconut plantation, **Key Biscayne** is lined with expensive high-rises and waterfront estates. **Miami Beach** features some of the most luxurious waterfront homes in the city, while the district with an architectural look of the twenties and thirties attracts musicians, movie stars, and models in droves.

Fresh stone crabs from the Florida waters are a local delicacy, and Miami is a good place to try Cuban food, especially yucca, a starchy staple vegetable.

- Bayside Marketplace
- Little Havana (Eighth Street)
- Art Deco District
- Everglades National Park
- Bass Museum of Art
- Holocaust Memorial
- Villa Vizcaya
- Fairchild Tropical Garden
- Historical Museum of South Florida
- Miami Seaquarium

An easy way to remember which is the starboard (right) side of the ship and which is the port (left) side: The words "port" and "left" both have four letters.

Nantucket, Massachusetts

The Wampanoag Indians who first lived on this flat, scrubby island 30 miles off the Cape Cod coast called it **Nanaticut** ("The Faraway Land"). It was sighted by Englishman Bartholomew Gosnold in 1602 and settled by separatists from Massachusetts in 1659. At their invitation, Ichabod Paddock, an "off islander" from Yarmouth on Cape Cod, came to teach them about hunting whales; from about 1750 to 1840, Nantucket was considered the greatest whaling port in the world. The entire island got caught up in the trade—shipowners, captains, and merchants who built elegant homes with their newfound wealth. Although Nantucket recovered from heavy losses during the Wars of Independence and 1812, the island's fortunes started a downhill slide when ships became too large to navigate the harbor unaided. To make matters worse, a fire swept through town, the Gold Rush took many sailors to California, and the discovery of petroleum in Pennsylvania eliminated the need for whale oil.

For the 7,000 residents who currently live on this 49-square-mile island circled by sandy beach, tourism is the main industry. Summer visitors come here to enjoy the windswept beaches, well-preserved architecture, and ambience of an uncomplicated place harking back to a simpler time.

Nantucket is also a delightful place to try fresh New England clam chowder, lobster, and Nantucket Bay scallops. Traditional handicrafts can be found in galleries and boutiques on **Straight Wharf.** One of the most ubiquitous is scrimshaw—scenes pain-stakingly carved onto whale teeth and bones, a craft that was the sailors' way of passing time between whale sightings. Another art form harking back to sailing days is lightship baskets made from rattan. These were originally designed by sailors who whiled away the hours during their stints on a floating lighthouse.

- Whaling Museum
- Main Street
- Hawden House
- Old Mill
- Fair Street Museum
- Old Gaol
- Nantucket's Oldest House
- Folger Museum
- One of the Three Bricks
- Siasconset

New Orleans, Louisiana

The birthplace of Dixieland jazz and paddlewheelers and the home of Tennessee Williams, "N'awlins" is very much a city defined by its waterways. "Crescent City"—so called for its shape carved by the mighty **Mississippi River** snaking through the metropolis en route to the Gulf of Mexico—is about five feet below sea level. Bridges and causeways leapfrog across the river and the bayous, lakes, and swamps that surround New Orleans. Four parishes—**Orleans, Jefferson, St. Bernard,** and **St. Tammany**—comprise this city of more than 1.3 million people that stretches over an area of 360 square miles.

French Canadian explorer Jean Baptiste Le Moyne founded New Orleans in 1718. The city was a melting pot for more than a century: It was the port where slaves arrived from Africa and the West Indies, German farmers settled, and Acadian (corrupted into "Cajun") trappers and fishermen found a place for their own culture in the swampy bayous. In 1762 Louis XV handed the territory to his cousin, King Charles III, whose Spanish subjects mingled with the French, producing offspring known as Creoles. Fires twice razed the city, leading to a building code of brick, slate, and tile roofs, constructed in the Spanish style of arches and walled courtyards. The late-arriving Anglo-Saxons, who came after the Louisiana Purchase of 1803, were considered "foreigners," but all banded together to repel the British in the 1815 Battle of New Orleans. Sugar from surrounding plantations brought wealth to the city's citizens, and its port became a commercial hub for the South.

The "Big Easy" is a good-time city. Come for the annual extravaganza of Mardi Gras (also brought by the French) or anytime to hear some jazz and enjoy some of New Orleans's famous Cajun and Creole cooking. Sample jambalaya, a cousin of paella made from yellow rice, tomatoes, ham, shrimp, sausage, chicken, celery, onions, and spices; or gumbo, a thick, robust soup. And don't leave without having a coffee and a beignet or two at **Café du Monde.**

- **Aquarium of the Americas**
- **Longue Vue House and Gardens**
- **French Quarter**
- **French Market**
- **Flea Market**
- **Canal Street Ferry**
- **City Park**
- **Garden District**
- **New Orleans Historic Voodoo Museum**
- **St. Charles Avenue Streetcar**

Newport, Rhode Island

In 1639 a group of dissenters from the Bay State Colony (part of what is now Massachusetts) came to what is today Newport in search of a religious haven. Although it soon prospered as a ship-building center, the town also profited from the so-called Triangle Trade: Rum, made from Jamaican molasses in Newport's distilleries, was shipped to Africa in exchange for slaves, who were then traded for more molasses in Jamaica. Newport, which took an active role in the Revolution, was occupied first by the British, then by the French two years later.

Newport's fame as a summer resort of the rich and famous began after the Civil War and peaked during the Gilded Age (1880s-1920s) when such families as the Astors and Vanderbilts built elegant summer homes by the sea and threw outrageous parties. Money was no object until the Depression, two World Wars, and tax law brought reality to roost. Although Newport and its population of 30,000 is still awash in affluence, most mansions—**The Breakers, The Elms, Rosecliff, Marble House, Colonial House,** among others—have become public museums.

Sample the local lobster, oysters, and clams. A sailor's haven, Newport is still famous for its boat builders, and until 1983 hosted the prestigious America's Cup yachting race.

- **Samuel Whitehorne House**
- **Brick Market**
- **White Horse Tavern**
- **Touro Synagogue**
- **Trinity Church**
- **Old Stone Tower**
- **Historic Mansions**
- **International Tennis Hall of Fame**
- **Wanton-Lyman-Hazard House**
- **Cliff Walk**

New York City, New York

Dutchman Peter Minuit bought an island 13.4 miles long and 2.3 miles wide from the Manhattan Indians in 1626 for $24 worth of trinkets and called it **New Amsterdam**. Little did he realize that his real estate deal—a wooded tract of land at the head of one of the world's finest natural harbors—would become one of the Western Hemisphere's most captivating cities. Within this comparatively narrow area bounded by the **East, Hudson,** and **Harlem Rivers,** and **New York Bay** is one of the world's greatest concentrations of wealth and art and the most astonishing variety of humanity.

Italian explorer Giovanni da Verrazano sighted the island in 1524, and Englishman Henry Hudson came along nearly a century later looking for a route to the Orient. The Dutch set up a trading post and called it New Amsterdam. In 1664 the English took the settlement, renaming it for the Duke of York. After the American Revolution, New York served as the country's capital, and George Washington was inaugurated as the first president here; many historical landmarks from that era still stand.

In 1898 **Manhattan** merged with the boroughs of **Brooklyn, the Bronx, Queens,** and **Staten Island** to become a single entity known as Greater New York, accommodating an ever-swelling immigrant work force, most of whom entered through **Ellis Island.** By the turn of the century there were as many Germans in New York as in Hamburg, more than half as many Irish as in Dublin, and almost 2.5 times as many Jews as in Warsaw. Today this multicultural metropolis of over seven million is still one of the world's largest melting pots, offering every variety of ethnic fare to sample and goods to purchase.

- Statue of Liberty and Ellis Island Museum
- Fraunces Tavern
- South Street Seaport
- Greenwich Village
- Times Square
- Empire State Building
- Rockefeller Center
- Museum of Modern Art
- Central Park
- Metropolitan Museum of Art

San Francisco, California

It is love at first sight for just about anyone who visits this city by the bay. Built on 43 precipitous hills and surrounded by hundreds of square miles of water on three sides, San Francisco is the place where almost everyone leaves their heart. Pacific breezes provide a lovely climate that is warm in the winter, cool in the summer, and wrapped in a shroud of romantic fog any time of the year.

In 1776 Juan Bautista de Anza chose the site as a place to dedicate a mission to St. Francis of Assisi. It remained a sleepy port until the 19th century when it evolved into an important trading post. In July 1846 the United States claimed the territory from Mexico and six months later changed the name from **Yerba Buena** to San Francisco. The discovery of gold in Sutter's Mill changed the area forever, transforming the village to a tent city of 20,000. The rush was on, and with the aid of Chinese labor, 2,000 miles of railroad track were quickly laid to join the East Coast to the West. On 18 April 1906 a devastating earthquake, measuring 8.3 on the Richter scale, and ensuing fires destroyed the city and claimed more than 3,000 lives. But San Francisco shook off the dust and rebuilt itself, including the construction of two major connectors to outlying areas— the **San Francisco-Oakland Bay** and **Golden Gate Bridges.**

An important financial and cultural center, San Francisco's population includes people from almost every nation in the world, as well as Americans who relocated here from all over the country. It is also a center of gay and lesbian life. More than 50 periodicals are published here in 13 languages, and every cuisine imaginable is represented in this gourmet's paradise. Don't miss taking one of San Francisco's famous cable cars (the US's only mobile National Historic

Landmark) that crisscross the city in three roller-coaster routes. Shoppers should head for **Pier 39** and **Union Square.**

- Fisherman's Wharf
- Chinatown
- Cable Car Ride
- Golden Gate Park
- San Francisco Museum of Modern Art
- Lombard Street
- Ghirardelli Square
- Alcatraz Island
- Golden Gate Bridge to Sausalito
- Muir Woods National Monument

Seattle, Washington

Famous for coffee, rain, **Mount Rainier,** and **Puget Sound,** Seattle sits on **Elliott Bay** surrounded by fir trees that lead up to the majestic, snowcapped **Olympic** and **Cascade Mountains.** The **Space Needle,** built in 1962 for the World's Fair, is a distinctive shape in the city skyline. It offers wonderful views of the surrounding mountains, and on a clear day Mount St. Helen's (which erupted in 1980) 100 miles to the south is visible from the observation deck.

Golden Gate Bridge

MICHAEL STORRINGS

Few traces remain of the city's rough-and-tumble start in 1851 when Henry Yesler built a sawmill to process timber from the nearby forests. Named for the Suquamish Indian chief Sealth, the young town staggered along under a series of disasters—Indian raids, riots, and fires—until the arrival of the railroad in 1885 brought new fortunes and it became a connecting point for prospectors outfitting themselves for the Alaskan gold rush up north. The city's prosperity increased in the beginning of the 20th century with the completion of the **Lake Washington Canal** in 1918, which connected the inner and outer harbors, and the opening of the Panama Canal in 1914. Although the city was hard hit by the Depression it bounced back during World War II with new industries centered around maritime and aeronautical activity.

Seafood rules Seattle menus, especially Dungeness crab, oysters, clams, and salmon. Dishes are often influenced by this cosmopolitan city's proximity to the Pacific Rim—such flavors as lemongrass, chili, garlic, and ginger are as common as cocktail sauce. Art galleries abound here—collectors can pick up traditional and modern Native American and Eskimo works. Outdoor enthusiasts will find the latest in sports clothing and equipment for mountaineering, camping, fishing, and hunting.

- Pioneer Square and Underground Tour
- International District
- Klondike Gold Rush National Historic Park
- Pike Place Market
- Seattle Art Museum
- Seattle Aquarium
- Pacific Science Center
- Museum of Flight and Northwest Craft Center
- Chittenden Locks
- Burke Memorial Museum

Seward, Alaska

Secretary of State William Henry Seward negotiated with the Russians in 1867 for the purchase of Alaska. The $7.2-million real-estate deal (about two cents an acre) struck most as being so foolish at the time that the entire spread was dubbed Seward's Folly. But 31 years after the statesman's death in 1872, the town of Seward was founded on the ice-free port of **Resurrection Bay** as the starting point for the 470-mile **Alaska Railroad** to Fairbanks.

Wedged between the **Chugach National Forest** and a national park, Seward is surrounded by snow-capped peaks. The icefield nearby has 30-plus glaciers—8 of which are tidewater—that launch enormous chunks of ice into the sea with a thundering roar.

Located 120 miles south of Anchorage, Seward today has replaced Fairbanks in importance as the region's major commercial and transportation hub. Fishing and processing of the fish—mostly halibut—remain important area industries. The 3,600-resident city survived near destruction by an earthquake and a series of tidal waves in 1964.

- Seward Museum
- Seward Library
- Mount Marathon
- Small Boat Harbor
- Seward Marine Educational Center
- Alaska Maritime National Wildlife Refuge
- Caines Head State Recreation Area
- Kenai Fjords National Park
- Exit Glacier
- Harding Icefield

Sitka, Alaska

North America's largest city landwise—sprawling across about 3,000 square miles—Sitka ("this site" in Tlingit) is located on the west coast of **Baranof Island** and faces snow-capped volcano **Mount Edgecumbe** on nearby **Kruzof Island.** It is also quite wet: about eight feet of rain falls here each year.

In 1799 Alexander Baranov and his Russian-American Company founded the settlement of **Michailovsk,** seven miles north of today's Sitka, while searching for sea otter pelts. The Tlingit destroyed the encampment in 1802, and Baranov returned two years later with members of the Russian Navy and rebuilt the town. He called it **New Archangel.** By 1840 Sitka was the capital of Russian America and the center for the fur trade with China. It became the Northwest's most cosmopolitan port and was known as the "Paris of the Pacific" thanks to its wealthy citizens who lived extravagantly. After Alaska became a US territory in 1867, many Russians returned home. Sitka served as Alaska's first state capital (it was moved to Juneau in 1900); during World War II, the city played a major role in the area's defense.

Sitka's 8,500 residents earn their living in the fishing and tourism industries. The Russian influence remains more than a century later: Russian is still spoken on occasion, borscht or piroshki are still served, and Russian folk dances are still performed. In nearby **Sitka National Historic Park,** Tlingit totem poles stand silently amid towering trees.

- St. Michael's Cathedral
- Bishop's House
- Russian Blockhouse
- Castle Hill
- Sheldon Jackson Museum
- Centennial Hall
- Isabel Miller Museum
- Native Cultural Center
- Alaska Raptor Rehabilitation Center
- Kogwantan and Katlian Streets

Skagway, Alaska

The "home of the north wind" is the northernmost town along the **Inside Passage.** It's at the head of the **Lynn Canal,** a fjord named by Captain George Vancouver for his hometown of Kings Lynn, England during an exploratory trip in 1794.

In 1887 pioneer William Moore set up a small cabin here after surveying the **White Pass** route through the Coast Mountains to the Yukon. When gold was struck in the Klondike 10 years later, Skagway became Alaska's largest town overnight. Over 20,000 stampeders (as they became known) flocked to the gateway hamlet to find their fortune 40 mountainous miles away, where $300 million worth of gold was extracted between 1897 and 1900. They went by way of the treacherous White Pass or the shorter and steeper **Chilkoot Pass.**

Skagway became a lawless, rambunctious town packed with con men. Legendary California writer Jack London passed through in 1898 during the height of rush, capturing the local color in his novel *Call of the Wild.* With British backing, Irish-Canadian

Michael Heney masterminded the completion of the 110-mile narrow-gauge railway in 1900. The train carried passengers and freight until metal prices plummeted in 1982. The last of its kind in the country, the railway reopened in 1988 and now transports tourists. Today the town's approximately 800 residents live for the past in this well-preserved pioneer place that resembles a Universal Studios back lot.

- Klondike Goldrush National Historic Park and Visitor Center
- Arctic Brotherhood Hall
- Golden North Hotel
- White Pass & Yukon Railroad
- Lower Dewey Lake
- Trail of '98 Museum
- William Moore Cabin
- Corrington Museum of Alaskan History
- Gold Rush Cemetery
- Lower Reid Falls

See Green

As a day aboard ship draws to an end, many passengers head for the decks and train their eyes to the horizon. They share a common quest: Trying to spot the storied, but elusive, "green flash" in the sky at sunset. The flash—a brilliant, emerald spark—sometimes appears as the last sliver of solar disk seems to melt into the sea.

This natural phenomenon is caused by the refraction, or bending, of the sun's rays as they pass through the thick layers of atmosphere near the horizon. Because blue and green light waves are refracted the most, the setting sun can sometimes

appear to have an emerald sparkle on its top edge as it disappears below the horizon.

The best conditions for seeing the flash are a clear day when the sun shines a brilliant yellow as it sets. It helps if the horizon is sharply defined, which is why the ocean makes an ideal setting. (Never stare into the sun! When seeking the green flash, wait until most of the sun has set.)

But don't be discouraged if the evening sky fails to yield even a hint of green. Some sailors have yet to see the phenomenon despite years of trying.

MICHAEL STORRINGS

Bests

Frank and Elfriede Riley
Travel Writers, Electronic Journalists, Authors, TV/Radio Commentators, Photographers

Among all the "Bests" of our shared cruising experiences these past more than 20 years are many we also remember with a chuckle. Like:

Swimming through the Strait of Magellan: When Portuguese explorer Ferdinand Magellan navigated perilously through the ice and glaciers of this often narrow strait in 1520, he could never have dreamed that cruise passengers of the late 20th century would be swimming through it. Yet that's what two dozen of us out of some 60 passengers were doing aboard the passenger-carrying freighter *Santa Magdalena.* We plunged into the water and swam as glaciers drifted by in the chill moonlight and thereby became members of the **Penguin Club**— an opportunity open to every reasonably able-bodied passenger on a cruise through the strait. All you have to do, as we did, is plunge into the heated swimming pool on deck and swim a few lengths as your cruise ship navigates in the wake of Ferdinand Magellan.

It never happened to Mark Twain: In mid-summer of 1995 we were cruising with some 400 fellow passengers aboard the *Mississippi Queen* paddlewheeler from St. Louis to Mark Twain's boyhood hometown of Hannibal, Missouri. Suddenly our vessel began to edge close to the thick foliage of the Illinois shore for an emergency landing and what our captain was to describe as "the most unusual experience in the history of Mississippi River cruising."

Deck hands wearing lifejackets lowered the gangway into the brush. Then an officer walked carefully down it holding one end of a leash. The other end was attached to the collar of a large and very agitated dog we later learned was Brody, a labrador retriever. The officer disappeared with Brody under the overhanging branches. A few minutes later they emerged from the trees and came back up the gangway. Brody now pranced along with a happy look on his face. We followed him to his stateroom and learned he had come aboard as a trained guide dog for his mistress, a blind schoolteacher. Apparently he had felt too well trained to perform his natural functions anywhere amid the Victorian elegance of the *Mississippi Queen,* with its floral carpeting and chandelier-crowned grand staircase, even though a tucked-away private facility had been prepared for him. After many teeth-gritting hours he was finally relieved by the emergency landing and for the rest of the cruise would allow a uniformed attendant to guide him to his private on-board facility. That evening he was introduced to fellow passengers on the ballroom floor.

Rosemary J. Mosher
General Manager/Property management, Iona Ranch Mobile Home Park

On the **Panama Canal** cruise leaving from Port of **Miami**, **Florida**, one of the ports we visited was **Acapulco.** On the dock we met a woman named Kay traveling alone. She asked us if she could join us on whatever tour we took. We always hire a private taxi. She suggested at the end of the tour we go to **Señor Frog's.** We did, never having heard of it. It turned out to be one of the highlights of our cruise. The manager of **Señor Frog's** opened the restaurant early, to accommodate the passengers of the ship. What we found at the end of our tour was not so many of the ship's passengers, but the crew from the ship. The "Momma Margaritas" were delicious, as were the salsa, homemade tortilla chips, and the chicken fajitas. The staff was friendly and the whole atmosphere "happy."

I would be sorry to neglect including the "fun ship" cruise line, **Carnival,** which we have traveled on eight times. Being a senior couple, we always enjoy meeting so many younger passengers. The pool games on board are always a part we really enjoy, and **Carnival**'s staff go out of their way to make sure we are well taken care of.

Mona Shafer Edwards
Courtroom Artist, *ABC News;* Fashion Illustrator

How golden a childhood I had—blessed to be born to European parents with a penchant for traveling, from sailing to and from Hawaii before it became a state, to six crossings on the decadently splendid *SS France.*

Imagine two children in their own cabin in first class, ordering a bowl of cherries and Champagne at 2AM! From chocolate soufflés (on demand) to marzipan floral bouquets with spun sugar bows, and cups of caviar every night, it was an elegant culinary learning experience for my brother and me. I can still smell those soufflés almost 30 years later!

Having been on many ships since the *France,* I have never lost the passion for cruising the seas—the smell of salt spray; the rich, low sound of a ship's engines; the wet decks in the mornings; and the different colors of each body of water crossed around the world.

The chief officers of five travel-industry organizations were invited to be joint godmothers of Costa Cruise Lines' *CostaAllegra* in 1992, but one missed the ceremony when a snowstorm grounded all flights to Miami (a strange turn of events for a high-powered travel agent).

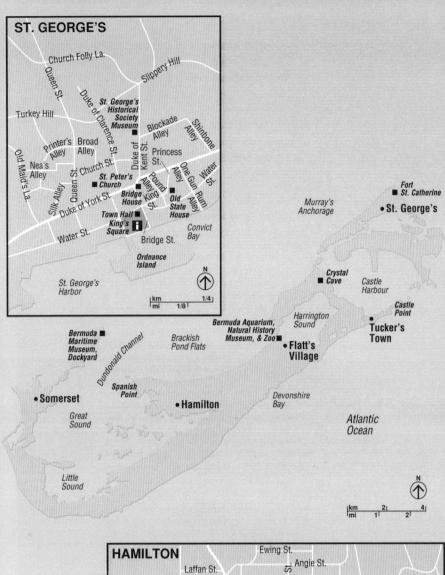
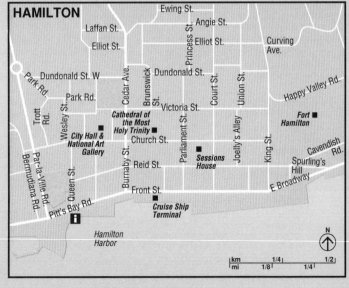

Bermuda

Although a Spaniard, Juan de Bermudez, first sighted (and named) the archipelago in the 16th century, Bermuda was settled in 1609 by the British survivors of the shipwrecked *Sea Venture* bound for Jamestown, Virginia. The 150 passengers declared the town of **St. George's** the capital in honor of their courageous captain (**Hamilton** became the seat of government in 1815). Many more shipwrecks—about 530, some in shallow waters—have occurred since then, creating a paradise for recreational divers and serious treasure hunters. In addition, the fine sheltered harbors and sparkling blue-green waters make it a favorite of sailors.

Located 650 miles east of Cape Hatteras, North Carolina, Bermuda actually consists of about 150 islets; the 6 largest of them are connected by bridges and causeways to form the shape of a fishhook. It boasts a moderate, subtropical climate; rolling green hills tumbling toward a perimeter of pink-sand beaches; a calm iridescent sea; and pastel-colored, white-roofed cottages set among lovely gardens. The 22-square-mile island—easily negotiated by moped—has retained a distinctly proper British atmosphere. Driving is on the left, and cricket matches and high tea are de rigueur. Bermuda is the oldest British colony in the Western Hemisphere, yet it has complete autonomy over local affairs

The island's 60,000 residents are known as "onions" after the sweet type that was its cash crop a century ago. Today over 6,000 international companies—mostly insurance and banking—are based here. Hamilton, a polite town set on **Hamilton Harbor** in the middle of the island, is the chief cruise port, followed by St. George's and **Royal Naval Dockyard.** The best beaches are along the road from Hamilton to **Somerset** on the western tip, and golf is a popular sport. Fish chowder doused with sherry peppers and black rum is probably the island's most popular menu selection. Bermuda onion soup is another favorite, as well as peas and plenty—black-eyed peas cooked with onions and salt pork. Shoppers here snap up such luxury duty-free British goods as cashmere sweaters, Irish linens, bone china, and Scottish tweeds. Local crafts include pottery and woodwork.

Hamilton
- Fort Hamilton
- City Hall, National Art Gallery, and National Society of Arts Gallery
- Sessions House
- Cathedral of the Most Holy Trinity

St. George's
- King's Square
- Town Hall
- Old State House

- Bridge House
- St. Peter's Church
- St. George's Historical Society Museum

Environs
- Fort St. Catherine
- Crystal Cave
- Bermuda Aquarium, Natural History Museum, and Zoo
- Bermuda Maritime Museum, Dockyard

Fort St. Catherine

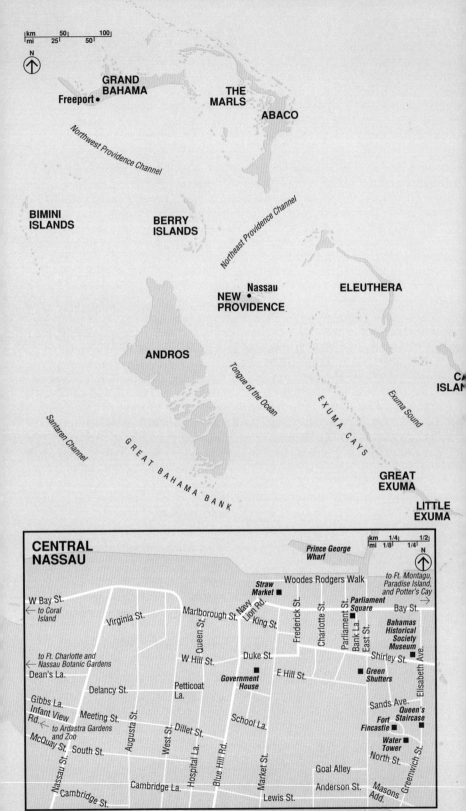

The Bahamas

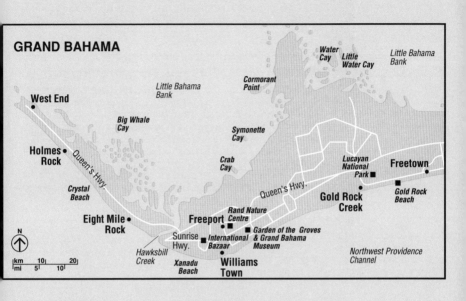

GRAND BAHAMA

West End

Little Bahama Bank

Water Cay

Little Water Cay

Little Bahama Bank

Cormorant Point

Big Whale Cay

Symonette Cay

Holmes Rock

Queen's Hwy.

Crab Cay

Lucayan National Park

Freetown

Crystal Beach

Gold Rock Creek

Gold Rock Beach

Queen's Hwy.

Eight Mile Rock

Freeport

Rand Nature Centre

N

km 10 20
mi 5 10

Sunrise Hwy.

International Bazaar

Garden of the Groves & Grand Bahama Museum

Hawksbill Creek

Xanadu Beach

Williams Town

Northwest Providence Channel

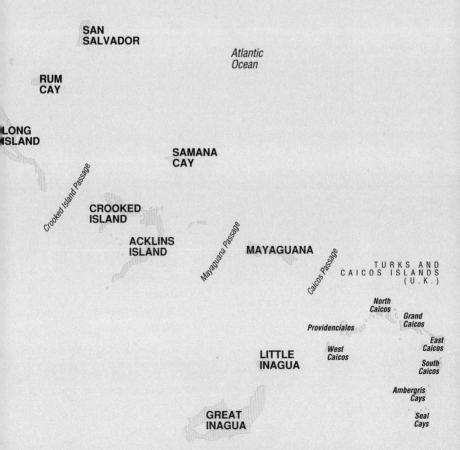

SAN SALVADOR

Atlantic Ocean

RUM CAY

LONG ISLAND

SAMANA CAY

Crooked Island Passage

CROOKED ISLAND

ACKLINS ISLAND

Mayaguana Passage

MAYAGUANA

Caicos Passage

TURKS AND CAICOS ISLANDS (U.K.)

North Caicos

Grand Caicos

Providenciales

East Caicos

West Caicos

South Caicos

LITTLE INAGUA

Ambergris Cays

GREAT INAGUA

Seal Cays

The Bahamas

One of the world's most popular cruise destinations, the Bahamas are an archipelago of over 700 islands and cays that extend 650 miles across the **Atlantic Ocean.** Columbus allegedly made his first landfall in the New World on one of these isles that stretch from the southeast tip of Florida to the edge of the **Caribbean Sea.** Today about 255,000 people of African and Indian descent inhabit roughly 30 of the islands, and each has its own identity and lifestyle—ranging from colonial charm to modern resorts to windswept outer isles.

Freeport, Grand Bahama

The fourth-largest of the Bahama Islands, Grand Bahama's 530 square miles of lush interior is ringed by 57 miles of white-sand beaches that are fringed with a nearly unbroken spectacular reef. Freeport is a tax-free port created by British and American investors in the mid-20th century to bring tourism to the island. Today Grand Bahama is an island of gardens and parks filled with exotic plants and flowers from around the world, set amid waterfalls, streams, ponds, and lush fern gullies. Fishing villages scattered along the coast still impart a small-town feeling; those most accessible from Freeport are on the western part of the island on down. Diving is superb—plenty of wrecks in shallow reefs still yield sunken treasures, and living reefs are home to the rare Atlantic long-nosed butterfly fish.

Grand Bahama was inhabited by the Lucayan before Columbus arrived in 1492. A peaceful Indian tribe, the Lucayan invented the ultimate in relaxation: the hammock. In a very short time the Spanish had decimated the Lucayan, and the island was virtually without inhabitants until the 18th century when loyalists from the American colonies sought refuge on what was by then a British colony. After England abolished slavery in 1834, many of the slaves settled on Grand Bahama as free farmers and fishers. During American Prohibition in the 1920s Grand Bahama was a hub for shipping liquor to the US.

The ubiquitous conch is practically considered a national food, and fresh grouper and lobster are often accompanied by peas and rice and johnnycake (light bread). Shoppers generally head for the **International Bazaar** in downtown Freeport, where there are dozens of shops selling duty-free goods from over 20 countries and four continents.

- Garden of the Groves
- Grand Bahama Museum
- Lucayan National Park
- Underwater Explorers Society and the Dolphin Experience
- Rand Nature Centre
- Gold Rock Beach
- Hawksbill Fish Market
- West End
- North Shore
- Churchill Square

Nassau, New Providence

The island of Nassau has long been prized for its sheltered harbor, ever since the days of the legendary pirate Blackbeard. History is well preserved in this busy hub and capital of the Bahamas (population about 135,000): Victorian mansions, cathedrals, horse-drawn surreys, and cotton candy–colored Georgian buildings. And don't miss Nassau's oldest fort—**Montagu** (1742)—which was seized by the American Navy during the Revolutionary War without a shot being fired.

Nassau boasts excellent dive sites, with shallow reefs, deep-blue holes, old shipwrecks, caves, dramatic drop-offs, and colorful sea gardens. Two James Bond thrillers were filmed in these waters: *Thunderball* and *Never Say Never Again.* Nearby **Paradise Island,** with its famous pink flamingoes and giant swaying palms, is packed with resorts, boutiques, and casinos. At the busy market at **Potter's Cay** beneath the bridge to Paradise Island, local fishers haul in their catch, farmers dispatch fresh produce, and mailboats bring in goods from the **Out Islands,** which include **Abaco, Andros,** the **Berry Islands, Bimini, Cat Island, Crooked Island, Eleuthera,** the **Exumas, Long Island,** and **San Salvador.**

Such old standbys as the 1865 **Green Shutters,** an English-style pub, serve tasty steak-and-kidney pie, along with local favorites like cracked conch and Bahamian crawfish tail. Shoppers head to **Bay Street**'s duty-free stores or to haggle at the **Straw Market** near **Prince George Wharf** for handmade hats, purses, mats, baskets, and other crafts.

- Parliament Square
- Bahamas Historical Society Museum
- Water Tower
- Fort Fincastle
- Queen's Staircase
- Fort Charlotte
- Government House
- Nassau Botanic Gardens
- Ardastra Gardens and Zoo
- Coral Island

The cruise documents sent to all Silversea Cruises passengers arrive in a fine leather case that retails for $65.

Pomp, Circumstance, and Superstition: The Ancient Art of Shipbuilding

Shipbuilding is an ancient industry steeped in ritual and more than a pinch of superstition. This is especially true of cruise ship construction. Many steps of the long process are marked by ceremonies that have grown into public relations events complete with dignitaries and media coverage.

The planning process for a "newbuild" often takes more than five years. First the cruise line commissions a ship design (the superstructure is designed by a team of naval architects, while the public rooms and cabins are designed by one or more "interior" architects), then the design is circulated to various shipyards for their bids. Most modern cruise vessels are built at yards in **Italy, Finland, France, Germany, Norway, Spain,** or **Japan.**

MICHAEL STORRINGS

Once the shipyard is selected, the actual construction process takes about two years. During that time, some or all of the following traditions are observed:

Cutting the first steel Cruise line and shipyard officials are on hand as the first thick slab of steel is sliced like butter with computer-controlled plasma arc cutters.

Laying the keel This formally marks the commencement of construction. The first block of the ship's hull is blessed before being lowered to the construction deck where it remains until "floating out" (see below).

Coin in the keel During this ceremony, shipyard workers, VIPs (shipyard owners, shipyard directors, and the like), and invited guests drop a coin or coins into the keel for good luck.

Coin in the mast Before the mast is affixed to the deck, a coin or coins are placed inside by workers, VIPs, and others in attendance.

Floating out The drydock is flooded with water, and the vessel floats for the first time.

Sea trials The ship is nearing completion. It's steered into open sea where the captain, principal officers, and shipyard representatives test all operational systems and note any problems that need to be corrected.

Delivery The ship is ready to be handed over to the owner. The head of the yard usually presents the completed vessel to the head of the cruise line who, in turn, entrusts the captain with its care.

Christening At this colorful event, a "godmother" names the ship and cracks a bottle of Champagne on its bow. Guests include cruise line, shipyard, and port officials, as well as other VIPs and the media.

Inaugural cruise The ship's first cruise carrying paying passengers is often marked by ceremonies at its first ("maiden") calls in ports.

Bests

John Maxtone-Graham
Marine Historian and Dedicated Passenger

Sea, as opposed to port, days, when the vessel is moving in her element and everybody, passengers and crew alike, is on board.

The activity that never appears in daily programs: Reading a good book in a quiet deck chair within sight of the passing sea before dropping off to sleep.

A drink at sunset in a lounge or bar unassailed by intolerably amplified music.

Leaning on the ship's rail as the vessel arrives in or departs a port: The maritime logistics of buoys, pilotage, tugs, lines, and bollards are fascinating.

A chamber music concert on board. Stringed instruments at sea are timelessly appealing.

A swim in a shipboard pool—outdoors or indoors—when the sea is brisk. Exhilarating and perfectly safe.

A crossing as opposed to a cruise, where everyone on board is going somewhere and a geographical objective—a different continent or hemisphere—awaits.

The combined hilarity and rapidity of shipboard gossip—wildly entertaining and almost always inaccurate.

When the occupants of a cruise ship are referred to as "passengers" rather than the dread hotel-speak, "guests."

The inspiration for Royal Caribbean's trademark Viking Crown Lounges, which circle the funnel of all the original ships in the fleet, was Seattle's most notable architectural lankmark, the Space Needle, built for the 1962 World's Fair. On the newest Royal Caribbean ships, starting with *Grandeur of the Seas* (1996), the Viking Crown Lounge is located atop the Centrum, a multistory atrium.

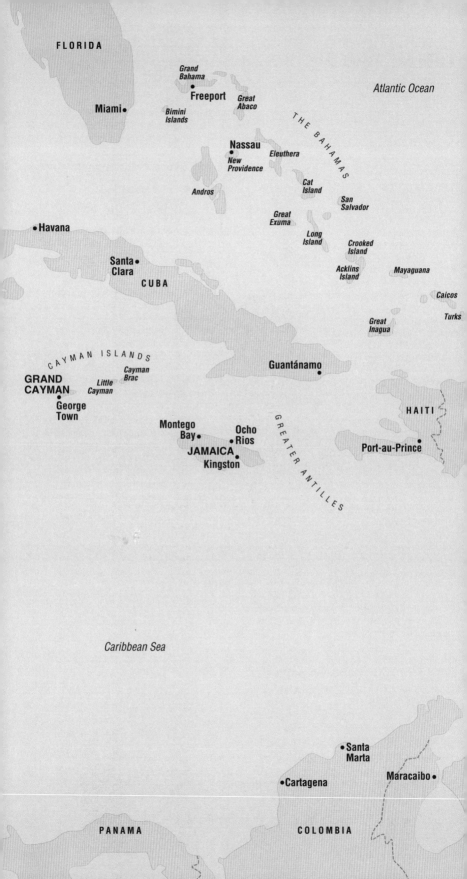

Caribbean

Think palm trees swaying in a tropical breeze, white sandy beaches, and warm turquoise waters teeming with neon-bright fish. Add pastel-colored houses, jungles and volcanic peaks, and exotic flowers. Finally, recall a rich history—colonial conquest, shipwrecks, and the ghosts of indigenous people and African slaves. This is the Caribbean, the world's number-one cruise destination, attracting more than two million vacationers every year.

Situated entirely within the tropics and surrounded by a string of islands that extends from Cuba, off Mexico's Yucatán Peninsula, to **Trinidad**, off the coast of Venezuela, the Caribbean Sea covers an area of about 970,000 square miles. When Christopher Columbus first entered these waters, he thought he had reached the rich East Indies. Today the islands that dot the Caribbean are also called the West Indies, although their "eastern" counterparts are thousands of miles away—to the west.

Antigua

St. John's

Locals like to boast that they have a beach for each day of the year: Indeed, 365 white-sand beaches ring the perimeter of this roughly circular, 108-square-mile island. Shallow reefs, deep coral canyons, caves, and shipwrecks lie just offshore. Nearly half of Antigua's 70,000 citizens live in the capital city of St. John's on the northwest coast.

First inhabited by the Siboney people (artifacts dating to 2400 BC have been unearthed), Antigua became home to a succession of nations: first Arawak and Carib Indians, then French and Spanish settlers, who soon became discouraged by lack of fresh water and constant Indian attacks. In the 17th century, British colonists claimed the island and began clearing tracts of land to create sugar plantations. Soon they imported African slaves to work the fields.

During the 18th and 19th centuries, Antigua's coastline, scalloped with sheltered bays and coves, provided safety for British ships during the numerous wars with other European powers for control of the Caribbean. Admiral Horatio Nelson was stationed in a harbor on the southeast coast. The well-preserved remains of his dockyard are now a national park and one of the most popular tourist destinations on the island.

Antigua, which has been independent since 1981, retains a decidedly English atmosphere, right down to its authentic pubs. But other influences linger as well: Decidedly un-British offerings include saltfish, *funchi* (cornmeal bread or dumplings), and "goat water," or goat stew. In addition to locally produced rum, special Antiguan souvenirs include silk-screened fabrics, straw and shell work, and pottery.

- Museum of Antigua and Barbuda
- St. John's Cathedral
- Redcliffe Quay
- Falmouth
- Nelson's Dockyard and Admiral's House Museum
- English Harbour and Galleon Beach
- Dow's Hill Interpretation Center
- Clarence House
- Shirley Heights Lookout
- Fort George

Aruba

Oranjestad

Aruba is the smallest and most developed of the "ABC Islands" (Aruba, Bonaire, and Curaçao). In fact, it's possible to explore this 70-square-mile island in a day. The flat landscape is intensely dramatic—dotted with twisted divi-divi trees, ancient rock formations, tiny bright red flowers, and an occasional windmill, all ringed by miles of powdery white-sand beaches.

Natural Bridge, Aruba

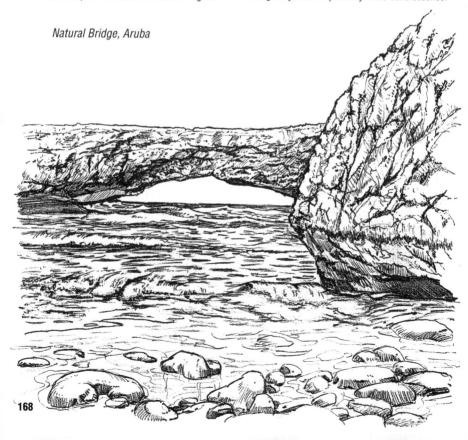

The capital city of Oranjestad, on the west coast, is popular with visitors for its glittering casinos, busy duty-free shops, and picturesque Dutch-style architecture.

In 1499, the island was claimed for Spain by Alonso de Ojeda, but since he deemed the arid, windswept land worthless, the indigenous Arawak people were left relatively undisturbed. In 1636, the Dutch took over, and Aruba remained part of the Netherlands Antilles until 1986. For most of the 20th century, Aruba's largest industry was oil refining; today tourism is number one, thanks in equal part to the island's natural charms and friendly citizens.

Local specialties include Dutch dishes like *erwtensoep* (thick pea soup cooked with pork, ham and sausage); *keri keri* (finely minced fried shark); and *funchi*. As souvenirs, many visitors take home local products like hand-embroidered linens and aloe.

- Wilhelminastraat
- Numismatic Museum
- Fort Zoutman and Historical Museum
- Archaeological Museum
- Seaport Village and Port of Call Marketplace
- Casibari Rock Formation
- Hooiberg (Haystack Hill)
- Natural Bridge
- Arikok National Park
- Reef snorkel or boat trip

Barbados

Bridgetown

The easternmost island in the Caribbean, Barbados is pounded by the **Atlantic Ocean** along its northern and eastern coasts, while calm waters prevail on its protected southern and western shores. The island is ringed by more than 70 square miles of public beaches, their sands ranging from pale pink to purest white. Steady trade winds keep the 166-square-mile island cool and comfortable.

Barbados was given its name by Portuguese sailors who dubbed it *Los Barbados* (bearded men) after the island's distinctive fig trees with beardlike hanging roots. The island was successively inhabited by the Arawak, Carib, and Portuguese; in the 17th century the British claimed it and set about turning jungle into sugarcane. Many of the plantation homes can still be seen today. About 80 percent of the island's 250,000 citizens are descendants of African slaves brought to work the fields.

Nearly one-third of the population lives in Bridgetown, the capital city. Barbados has been independent since 1966, but centuries of uninterrupted British rule have left their imprint—Bridgetown streets are lined with Victorian-style buildings, and cricket is the national pastime; and tea, not coffee, is the beverage of choice. As for island cuisine, flying fish and sea eggs (white sea urchins' roe served deviled or breaded) are among the favorite local delicacies. Other specialties include *cou-cou* (cornmeal and okra); *jug-jug* (a mixture of corn and green peas); *conkies* (Indian corn, coconut, pumpkin, raisins, sweet potatoes, and spices, steamed in a banana leaf); and pepperpot (a spicy meat stew). Barbados produces some of the world's best rum. Popular gifts include native ceramics, leather goods, coral and shell jewelry, woven baskets and wall hangings, and batik and tie-dyed fabrics.

- Carenage and Trafalgar Square
- Old Synagogue
- Barbados Museum
- Gun Hill Signal Station
- Francia Plantation
- Harrison's Cave
- Welshman Hall Gully
- Flower Forest
- Andromeda Gardens
- St. Nicholas Abbey

British Virgin Islands

Road Town, Tortola

Tortola, 12 miles long and just 3 miles wide, is the largest of the more than 50 islands that make up the British Virgin Islands (BVI). Its jagged coastline boasts an abundance of coves, beaches, and bays where crystal clear waters provide excellent snorkeling, fishing, and sailing. Park of the northern coast is protected park; the center of the island is dominated by the 1,710 foot **Mount Sage;** and the rocky southern coast is dry and cactus-covered. The capital city of Road Town, with its pastel pink-and-blue gingerbread houses, is located on the south shore.

Christopher Columbus named the countless Virgin Islands after St. Ursula and her 11,000 female followers. Successive waves of European colonization followed Columbus's landing and eliminated any trace of the native population of Siboney, Arawak, and Carib tribes. Later, Tortola became a safe haven for pirates of the Caribbean, including one Edward Teach, otherwise known as Blackbeard; legends of buried treasure still persist. Actual remains of the past—the sugar plantations that drove the economy in the 18th and 19th centuries—are still scattered about the island.

Today Tortola is a mellow island of about 17,000 inhabitants, relatively unaffected by the mass tourism of most other Caribbean isles. Road Town boasts excellent West Indian cuisine and seafood, such as snapper, dolphinfish, and lobster. **Pusser's,** once the center of rum production for the Royal Navy Pussers (Pursers), is popular for its English pub food. Rum remains a favorite souvenir from the BVI; others include spices, hand-painted furniture, and wood carvings.

- Road Town
- British Virgin Islands Folk Museum
- J.R. O'Neal Botanical Gardens
- Cane Garden Bay
- Callwood Rum Distillery
- Mount Sage National Park
- Brewer's Bay
- Fort Recovery
- Smuggler's Cove
- Long Bay

Cayman Islands

George Town, Grand Cayman

Once remote, swampy, and mosquito-infested, the Cayman Islands were first settled by shipwrecked sailors and pirates. Among the few creatures that thrived here were turtles (Columbus dubbed the islands "Las Tortugas" for the abundant turtles) and a crocodilian species called *caymanas* by the Carib Indians. In the 17th century, the British claimed the island, and it remains a Crown Colony to this day. The accents of its almost 32,000 citizens are a musical mix of English, tinged with Welsh and Scottish overtones and topped off with an island lilt.

The 76-square-mile Grand Cayman, the largest and most populated of the three Cayman Islands, is home to the capital city of George Town. The city is the world's fifth-largest financial center, and a variety of shops and restaurants line the main streets of **Fort Street** and **Cardinal Avenue.** But the main attraction here is the truly spectacular scenery under the sea. Beyond the white-sand beaches, crystal clear turquoise waters teem with colorful corals and reef fish, beckoning scores of divers and snorkelers. It's one of the top five dive destinations in the world. Even nonswimmers can see the reefs and exquisite marine life—including the legendary **Cayman Wall** and its friendly population of southern stingrays—via glass-bottom boats, semisubmersibles, and mini-submarines.

Local fare includes dishes such as spicy Cayman-style snapper, conch fritters and chowder, and turtle steak. Although souvenirs made from turtle and black coral are for sale, items from these endangered species cannot be brought into the US. Instead, opt for jewelry made from shipwreck artifacts, including old gold pieces.

- Cayman Islands National Museum
- Grand Cayman Maritime and Treasure Museum
- Seven Mile Beach
- Cayman Turtle Farm
- Hell
- Pedro St. James Castle
- Queen Elizabeth II Botanic Park
- Stingray City

- Mastic Trail
- Old Homestead

Curaçao

Willemstad

At first this 180-square-mile island 35 miles off the coast of Venezuela might seem like a strange place to see Dutch colonial architecture—gabled buildings splashed with bright paint of many colors, topped off with roofs whose red tiles were brought over as ballast on trade ships. According to local lore, one of Curaçao's first governors thought the strong sun reflecting off the pale buildings was causing his migraines, so he ordered all the houses lining the narrow streets of Willemstad, Curaçao's capital, be painted "anything but white."

The "C" in the ABC islands, 180-square mile Curaçao has been autonomous since 1954 and is the center of government for the Netherlands Antilles. Willemstad, a mix of many worlds—old, new, and funky, inhabited by as many as 50 different nationalities—is divided in two by the narrow **Sint Annabaai** (Santa Anna Bay), which is crossed by the **Koningin Emmabrug** (Queen Emma floating bridge). On the east side are upscale **Punda** ("the point"), the once and future commercial center where everything from electronics to linens and jewelry is sold; and **Scharloo,** the historic Jewish neighborhood filled with elegant Neo-Classical homes and the oldest synagogue in continuous use in the Western Hemisphere. Across the bridge is **Otrobanda** (literally, "the other side") where the old waterfront buildings have been given new life as small shops and restaurants.

Local dishes include *funchi* and *pastechi* (cheese-, fish-, or meat-filled pastries). Curaçao liqueur, which is flavored with orange peel, is made here; Delft pottery and electronics are also popular buys.

- Floating Market
- Mikva Israel Emanuel Synagogue
- Fort Amsterdam
- Landhuis Chobolobo
- Landhuis Brievengat
- Landhuis Knip
- Hato Caves
- Curaçao Seaquarium
- Curaçao National Underwater Marine Park
- Christoffel National Park and Boca Tabla

Among the former owners of Windjammer Barefoot Cruises' *Fantome* is Aristotle Onassis. According to the cruise line, Onassis purchased the schooner as a wedding present for Grace Kelly and Prince Rainier of Monaco. As it turned out, the shipping magnate was not invited to the wedding, so he never sent his gift.

Dominica

Roseau

Rising out of the sea to a height of 4,747 feet in a splendid natural setting of rugged mountains and lush forests, Dominica has not changed much since Columbus sighted it one Sunday in 1493. Though it is one of the poorest countries in the Caribbean, this wild and untamed 290-square-mile island between Guadeloupe and Martinique is certainly rich in natural beauty. It is known as the "Nature Island," and no wonder: It boasts 365 rivers, so much rain it exports water, towering tree-ferns, enormous insects like the 8-inch-long Hercules beetle, and a 17,000-acre national park complete with a boiling volcanic lake.

The Carib Indians arrived on Dominica over a thousand years ago and subdued the indigenous Arawaks. Their aggressive and reportedly cannibalistic society, along with the dauntingly rugged terrain, discouraged European colonization. The French were the first Europeans to arrive, but the British prevailed in a series of battles for control throughout the late 18th century. As Dominica turned into an island of English planters, Creoles, and Catholics, the Carib found themselves boxed into an inhospitable stretch of real estate on the northeastern coast. Dominica became a British colony in 1815 and was granted independence in 1978.

Look out for *crapaud* or "mountain chicken" on menus here—it's really frogs' legs. Handwoven baskets, wood carvings, and spices are good souvenirs.

- Botanical Gardens
- Dawbiney Market Plaza
- Papillote Wilderness Retreat and Nature Sanctuary
- Tritou Gorge and Trafalgar Falls
- Northern Forest Preserve and Morne Diablotin
- Boeri Lake
- Emerald Pool
- Indian River
- Cabrits National Park and Fort Shirley
- Middleham Falls

Grenada

St. George's

Just 21 miles long and 12 miles wide at its widest point, tiny Grenada possesses an incredible variety of terrain: green jungle-covered mountains, racing rivers and streams, waterfalls and lakes, all encircled by lovely beaches. The island features a central mountain range that reaches over 2,000 feet, and banana plantations, sugarcane fields, and coconut groves thrive in the southeast and northwest reaches.

The capital city of St. George's may be one of the Caribbean's most picturesque ports. Its protected inner harbor is lined with pink, ocher, and brick-red buildings and warehouses, many of which date from the 18th century. Behind them, narrow streets and cobblestone alleys climb green hills dotted with red-and-green roofed houses. Wood construction has been forbidden since a number of disastrous fires in the island's earliest days; most structures are made from brick brought over as ballast on British trading ships.

Known as "The Spice Island," Grenada is a source of cinnamon and nutmeg, which is sold with gusto by turbaned women along the waterfront and beaches. Flowers grow here in abundance, and they are used to make other popular souvenirs, including perfume, lotion, potpourri, and tea. The national dish is oil down (breadfruit and salt pork wrapped in dasheen leaves and steamed in coconut milk).

- Carenage
- Market Square Spice Market
- National Museum
- Fort George
- Grande Anse Beach
- Annandale Falls
- Westerhall
- Grand Etang National Park and Lake
- Dougaldston Estate spice factory
- Gouyave Nutmeg Plant

Guadeloupe

Pointe-à-Pitre

The place the Carib people called **Karukéra** ("island of beautiful waters") is part of a 635-square-mile archipelago that is an overseas department of France. Guadeloupe is actually two islands separated by the narrow **Rivière Salée** (Salt River), a four-mile channel flowing between the Caribbean and Atlantic and connected by a drawbridge.

From the air Guadeloupe looks like a butterfly. The western island is mountainous **Basse-Terre,** which is dominated by the lush **Parc National.** The park comprises one-fifth of the country's total land mass and contains more than 300 species of trees and 200 miles of trails. Here also is the 4,813-foot volcano **La Soufrière,** and the capital city (also called **Basse-Terre**), founded in 1643, and still boasting narrow streets and neat squares lined with well-preserved colonial buildings and palm trees. The eastern island is **Grande-Terre,** with flat sugarcane fields, rolling hills, white-sand beaches, and Pointe-à-Pitre. That city was nearly destroyed by an earthquake in 1843 and by a hurricane (Hugo) in 1989. Hot and pulsing, with chic shops and sidewalk cafes interspersed with urban housing and old markets, and a population of 100,000, Pointe-à-Pitre exhibits a decidedly nontouristy attitude.

Guadeloupe is reputed to have the best food in the Caribbean, a combination of classic French and zesty

Creole food with East Indian spices. Specialties include *boudin* (spicy blood sausage), *pâté en pot* (thick Creole soup); *accras* (crispy herb-seasoned codfish fritters), *columbo* (a piquant chicken curry), and crab stuffed with garlic and spices. Good buys include local handicrafts such as madras cotton and carved dolls dressed in madras, straw hats and baskets, and wood carvings.

- Musée Saint-John Perse
- Marché Central (Central Market)
- Musée Schoelcher
- Cathédrale de St-Pierre et St-Paul
- Fort Fleur d'Epée
- Aquarium de la Guadeloupe
- Musée du Rhum (Rum Museum)
- Parc National and La Maison de la Forêt (Forest House)
- Parc des Roches Gravées (Park of Rock Engravings)
- Pointe des Châteaux (Castle Point)

Jamaica

Ocho Rios and Montego Bay

Arawak Indians may have given this island its name—**Xaymaca**—but it appears that the whole world has had a say in Jamaica. From Spain came names like Ocho Rios ("Eight Rivers"); from England, law and language; from Africa, culture; from Portugal, Jewish traditions. More immigrants came from China, India, Syria, Nepal, Scotland, and France. Two Jamaicans talking to each other is a musical mix of English, local patois (a combination of English, African, and Welsh), and unique island language and rhythms.

With 4,411 square miles, Jamaica is the third-largest island in the Caribbean. It has hundreds of miles of coastline in a variety of settings—glorious white-sand beaches, wetlands, and limestone cliffs. Inland, mountains predominate: Nearly half the island is over

1,000 feet in altitude. The **Blue Mountain** range is the source of hundreds of rivers, streams, and waterfalls that keep the island green and lush. More than 200 species of birds twitter among the casuarina, breadfruit, and banyan trees, and orchids and flaming poinsettias bloom in profusion.

Cruise ships dock on the north coast at both Ocho Rios and Montego Bay, 67 miles to the west. The most popular native dish is "jerk" meat—usually chicken or goat. It's marinated in hot peppers, thyme, allspice, scallions, garlic, and nutmeg, then cooked over an outdoor fire, a method brought to the island by African slaves. Saltfish and ackee, a vegetable that looks and tastes like scrambled eggs when cooked, is the national dish. Savvy visitors load up on Tia Maria liqueur, local rum, and Blue Mountain coffee, as well as handmade fabrics (often silk-screened), wood carvings, and paintings.

- Doctor's Cave Beach
- Rockland Wildlife Sanctuary
- Rose Hall Great House
- Greenwood Great House and Antique Museum
- River rafting on Martha Brae
- Dunn's River Falls
- Shaw Park Botanical Gardens
- Fern Gully
- Prospect Plantation
- Brimmer Hall Plantation

Martinique

Fort-de-France

This 425-square-mile island is the southernmost of the French West Indies. Its indigenous people called Martinique the **Island of Flowers,** and with good reason. Its mountainsides are abloom with wild orchids, bougainvillea, magnolia, poinsettia, frangipani, anthurium, and hibiscus; its fields are fertile with pineapple, banana, and sugarcane; its

Rose Hall Great House, Jamaica

trees are heavy with mangoes, papayas, lemons, and limes. Fabulous coral formations, brilliantly colored fish, and more than a dozen shipwrecks make this island an underwater delight as well.

Martinique was colonized by the French for sugarcane plantations; most of the island's almost 360,000 inhabitants are descendants of the African slaves brought to work the fields. Today's economy is still driven by sugar; rum distilling and fruit growing are also significant. An overseas department of France since 1946, Martinique is unmistakably French—from its baguette-filled bakeries and chic boutiques to honking Renaults and topless beaches. In the capital city of Fort-de-France, the narrow city streets are packed with pastel-colored buildings accented with wrought-iron balconies. Josephine, empress of France and wife of Napoleon Bonaparte, was born here.

The island cuisine is a cross between classic French and Creole cooking: *accras* and *lambi* (conch sautéed in oil and seasoned with lemon, garlic, and spices) are two specialties. The typical Martinique souvenir is *Poupée Martiniquaise,* a doll in a Creole madras costume. Rum, straw goods, pottery, and tapestries are also good buys.

- ■ Place de la Savane and Handicraft Market
- ■ Bibliothèque Schoelcher (Schoelcher Library)
- ■ Musée Départemental (Martinique Museum)
- ■ Rue Isambert produce market
- ■ Jardin de Balata (Balata Tropical Park)
- ■ Trois Ilets and Musée de la Pagerie (Josephine Bonaparte's Birthplace)
- ■ Carbet and Centre d'Art Musée Paul Gauguin (Gauguin Museum)
- ■ Saint-Pierre and Musée Vulcanologique (Volcanology Museum)
- ■ Morne Rouge
- ■ Ajoupa-Bouillon and Les Ombrages Botanical Park

Puerto Rico

San Juan

Welcomed by peaceful Taíno Indians in 1493, Christopher Columbus christened the 3,423-square-mile island San Juan, after St. John the Baptist. Soon thereafter, Ponce de Leon founded a settlement on a beautiful bay he called Puerto Rico, or "Rich Port." Somewhere along the way, the two names were exchanged and stayed that way. It was not long before the Spanish subjugated the native population to work the sugarcane fields, imported African slaves, and built immense fortifications to repel attacks from Carib Indians, French pirates, and ambitious Englishmen. By the end of the 19th century, with rebellion brewing, Spain abolished slavery and granted the island autonomy, just before the US took Puerto Rico as the spoils of the Spanish-American War.

Following World War II, the US implemented "Operation Bootstrap" to stimulate economic development and investment in Puerto Rico; today the island enjoys one of the highest standards of living in the Caribbean. A self-governing commonwealth of the US since 1952, with a present-day population of about four million, Puerto Ricans continue to debate what is best for their future— the status quo, US statehood, or independence.

The island's colonial past has been well preserved within the narrow cobblestone streets of **Old San Juan.** This historic area is packed with grand 16th- and 17th-century Spanish architecture and plazas, as well as museums and galleries. On the other side of the timeline in San Juan are **Condado** and **Isla Verde** with their swanky hotels, chic boutiques, and nonstop nightlife.

Island recipes, often based on old Indian dishes, tend to be slightly spicy with overtones of garlic, oregano, and coriander. The most typical Puerto Rican dish is *asopao* (rice stew with chicken, seafood, or peas). Popular gifts include *santos* (small, hand-carved statues of saints), hand-rolled cigars, rum, *guayaberas* (embroidered men's shirts), straw hats, and papier-mâché fruits and vegetables.

- ■ Plaza de Armas (Armament Plaza)
- ■ La Fortaleza (The Fortress)
- ■ Casa Blanca (White House)
- ■ El Morro (El Morro Fort)
- ■ Iglesia de San José (San José Church)
- ■ Convento de los Dominicos (Dominican Convent)
- ■ Museo de Pablo Casals
- ■ Fuerte San Cristóbal (St. Christopher Fort)
- ■ Bacardi Rum Distillery
- ■ El Yunque (Caribbean National Forest)

St-Barthélémy

Gustavia

The island of St-Barthélémy was first settled by French colonists in 1648 and then briefly possessed by the Order of the Knights of Malta. In 1784, Louis XVI ceded what he considered worthless real estate to Sweden in exchange for trading rights. Although the island flourished under its new rulers, hurricanes, fires, piracy, and commercial competition took their toll, and the Swedes sold it back to the French in 1878. Today the island is a dependency of France's overseas department of Guadeloupe.

Ringed by 14 splendid white-sand beaches, most of which are sheltered by both cliff and reef, and surrounded by lush volcanic hillsides, St. Bart's seems more *haute* European than Caribbean. It has become an expensive holiday destination for the rich and famous—from Rockefellers to royalty—who occupy private luxury villas around the eight-square-mile island. About 5,000 people live here; most are Caucasians who are West Indian by birth, but unquestionably French by heritage. In one village elderly women still wear traditional costume, complete with starched white bonnets called *quichenottes;* they cultivate sweet potato patches and weave palm fronds into hats and purses. The economy, formerly based on rum smuggling, today runs on importing liqueurs and perfumes, as well as cattle ranching and lobster trapping.

The capital, Gustavia, named after the 18th-century Swedish king, is a tidy, trendy mix of French, Swedish, and Creole influences, tastefully studded with branches of several well-known designer shops frequented by a young and chic jet-setting crowd. The leading culinary influence is French; *langouste* (clawless lobster) is found on most menus.

- Musée de St-Barthélémy
- Fort Gustave
- Plage des Galets (Shell Beach)
- Corossol
- Inter-Oceans Museum
- Plage de Grand Colombier (Colombier Beach)
- Fort Oscar
- Fort Karl
- Petit Cul-de-Sac
- Ile Tortue

St. Lucia

Castries

At first glance St. Lucia looks like an island right out of *South Pacific,* with its dramatic twin peaks **Gros Piton** (2,619 feet high) and **Petit Piton** (2,438 feet high), seeming to rise right out of the sea. The lush landscape comprises mostly rain forest and some banana plantations. About one-third of the population lives on the northwest coast in the capital city of Castries, whose harbor was once a volcanic crater. On parts of the southwest coast, visitors can hike or even drive into the still-percolating crater of an ancient volcano where an infernal garden of wonders awaits—steaming rock formations, bubbling sulfur springs, and tumbling waterfalls. Louis XVI liked the place enough to build mineral baths here, still a popular soakery.

The island's earliest known inhabitants were the Arawak, who were supplanted by the ferocious Carib, the tribe encountered by European explorers when they made landfall here in 1605. By 1660 the French had gained control of St. Lucia; during the next 150 years the 238-square-mile island changed hands between France and England many times. No matter which flag flew, the Europeans continued to develop sugar plantations worked by West African slaves, from whom most of today's 140,000 St. Lucians are descended. Although St. Lucia has been an independent member of the British Commonwealth since 1979, the island seems more French than British, particularly in the local patois and the names of people and places.

Green figs and saltfish is the national dish; curries, pepperpot stews, and Creole cooking round out the native fare. Dolphinfish and flying fish are favorites, served grilled or sautéed. St. Lucia's best-known products are silk-screened and hand-printed designs and batiks, along with handicrafts such as wood carvings, pottery, and straw hats and baskets.

- Barre de Lisle Trail
- Marigot Bay
- Fort Charlotte and Morne Fortune
- Pigeon Island National Park
- Gros Islet
- Soufrière Village
- Sulphur Springs
- Diamond Falls and Botanical Gardens
- Mineral Baths
- Anse de Pitons

St-Martin/St. Maarten

Philipsburg

You say Saint-Martin, I say Saint Maarten . . . Whatever one calls this 37-square-mile, half-French, half-Dutch island, it most certainly suffers from a delightful case of split personality. It's as popular for its casinos and outstanding duty-free shopping as for its white-sand beaches lapped by aquamarine waters.

The island's inhabitants have included Arawak and Carib people, pirates of all nationalities, and finally, Dutch and French settlers, who began arriving in the 1630s and have lived side by side for over 350 years. When the two nations finally divided the small island (supposedly by a walking contest in which a Dutchman headed off in one direction and a Frenchman went the other) France received 21 square miles, or the northern two-thirds, and Holland took the remaining 16 square miles. Passage between the two sides is incredibly easy, with not so much as a checkpoint between them.

In French St-Martin, the sleepy but sophisticated capital city of **Marigot** features fine French food and designs in chic boutiques. In the more frenetic Dutch capital of **Philipsburg,** West Indian–style cottages with gingerbread trim line *steegjes* (little lanes that open onto courtyards). Although each side speaks its own language, as well as English, some of the island's 60,000-plus residents also speak papiamento, a mélange of English, Spanish, Portuguese, Dutch, and African influences. For a quick meal, locals head for *lolos* (family-run beachfront food stalls) for grilled chicken, sausage, and shrimp. The island does not abound with local crafts; most visitors partake of the duty-free shopping and perhaps guavaberry liqueur, a locally distilled brew of rum and berries.

- ■ Old Street
- ■ Colombier
- ■ Pic Paradis (Paradise Peak)
- ■ Grand Case
- ■ Baie Longue (Long Bay)
- ■ Cupecoy Beach
- ■ Marina Port la Royale
- ■ Guana Bay Point
- ■ Fort St-Louis
- ■ Orléans

Tobago

Scarborough

The southernmost islands in the Caribbean, Trinidad (see below) and Tobago, located just off the Venezuelan coast, are in fact geologically an extension of the South American continent. Tiny Tobago is only 26 miles long by 7 miles wide. It derives its name from tobacco, a crop cultivated by the native Carib. This is a typical Caribbean paradise, a hump of lush mountain greenery surrounded by miles of deserted white beach. Its offshore waters, fed by South America's **Orinoco River,** are punctuated with rocky canyons, tunnels, reefs, and caves, and teeming with dense and diverse marine life. Concern for the island's unique natural resources dates to 1764 when 24,700 acres of rain forest was designated a "protected reserve"—the first protected land in the Western Hemisphere. A wide variety of birds and butterflies inhabits the thickly jungled slopes, and giant leatherback turtles nest on several beaches.

After their sighting by Columbus in 1498, Trinidad and Tobago were the site of exceptionally bloody battles among Spain, England, France, and Holland. Tobago changed hands many times until, in 1877, the British finally consolidated their power. Through the years slaves, laborers, and immigrants arrived from Africa, India, and the Middle East, mostly to work in sugarcane fields. When that industry later went bust, Tobago went down with it, reluctantly becoming a ward of neighboring Trinidad in 1888. Today the economy is fueled largely by tourism. The capital and principal town of Scarborough, located on the southwest coast, is home to 20,000 people; its attractions include carefully preserved historic buildings, including an 18th-century fort.

Island delicacies include crab in curry sauce and *buljol* (saltfish with onions, tomatoes, avocados, and pepper). Local craftspeople produce leather sandals, batik and other fabrics, straw and cane work, wood carvings, carved gourds, handmade jewelry, and steel drums.

- ■ Fort King George
- ■ Fort James
- ■ Buccoo Reef and Coral Gardens
- ■ Pigeon Point
- ■ Adventure Farm and Nature Reserve
- ■ Main Ridge Rain Forest
- ■ Turtle Beach
- ■ Little Tobago Island
- ■ Charlotteville and Pirate's Bay
- ■ Arnos Vale Hotel

Anse de Pitons, St. Lucia

Government House, St. Croix

Trinidad

Port of Spain

Trinidad is 7 miles off the northeast coast of Venezuela and 21 miles from its smaller sister island of Tobago. Much of its 1,864 square miles are covered by tropical forests, but this diverse island also encompasses mountain peaks over 3,000 feet high, two swamps, miles of rich farmland, and both sheltered and windswept coastlines. But it is perhaps most famous for its music—Trinidad is the traditional birthplace of steel-pan and calypso music—and as the home of the Caribbean's most enthusiastic yearly Carnival celebration, complete with parades, balls and bacchanals.

It is not known whether Columbus named Trinidad for the Holy Trinity or for three mountains spied in the distance but in either case, the island soon became another colonial battlefield for the European powers. French Catholic settlers and merchants spread their language and cuisine throughout the island. Spanish settlers created Port of Spain, the capital city, by moving their inland tobacco and cocoa farms to the coast to escape jungle diseases and Indian raids. The British wrested control of the island from Spain during the Napoleonic Wars. In 1962 Trinidad and its ward Tobago achieved independence from Great Britian; in 1976 it became a republic within the British Commonwealth. The discovery of offshore oil deposits in the 1970s led to a prosperity huge by Caribbean standards, but within a decade resources and prices dwindled, a fact often lamented in the country's calypso music.

Trinidad has more than a million citizens, a melting pot of East Indian and African peoples as well as Chinese, Arab, British, French, and native Amerindians. East Indian cuisine prevails, with such dishes as *saheena* (deep-fried patties of spinach, dasheen, split peas, and mango sauce). Popular souvenirs include silk and cotton fabrics, straw and cane work, small steel pans, and locally recorded music.

- National Museum
- Royal Botanical Gardens
- Caroni Bird Sanctuary
- Queen's Park Savannah
- Magnificent Seven Edwardian Mansions
- Fort George Signal Station
- Blanchisseuse Bay
- Asa Wright Nature Preserve
- Maracas National Park
- Nariva Swamp

US Virgin Islands

St. Croix

St. Croix is part of the island chain known as the Lesser Antilles, which loosely defines the border between the Caribbean Sea and the Atlantic Ocean. Columbus landed here at **Salt River Bay** in 1493 and was greeted by flying arrows. After beating a hasty retreat, the Spanish claimed ownership of the islands, but didn't settle them. St. Croix was subsequently occupied by the Dutch, French, British, and the Knights of Malta. In 1733 the Danish bought the islands and oversaw a plantation economy that produced molasses, rum, cotton, and tobacco. In 1917, the US purchased them from Denmark for $25 million, or about $295 an acre, because of the islands' strategic location on the approach to the Panama Canal.

Christiansted, the colorful and compact old Danish capital, boasts buildings and streets constructed with yellow bricks brought over from Denmark as ballast on colonial sailing ships; the entire town has been declared a national historic site. The 850-acre **Buck Island** just off the northern coast is the only underwater national monument in the US; its fantastic coral, drop-offs, and canyons are a diver's delight.

Sprat Hall Plantation, the oldest plantation house in the Virgin Islands, is famous for its interpretation of popular island cuisine—pumpkin fritters, conch in butter sauce, and soursop ice cream. In addition to abundant duty-free shopping, locally made crafts, including jewelry and wood carvings, are for sale.

- ■ **Buck Island Reef National Monument**
- ■ **Cruzan Distillery**
- ■ **Fort Christiansvaern**
- ■ **Fort Frederik**
- ■ **Government House**
- ■ **Rain Forest**
- ■ **Scale House**
- ■ **St. George Village Botanical Garden**
- ■ **Whim Plantation and Museum**
- ■ **Market Place**

St. John

St. John may be only a 20-minute ferry ride from neighboring St. Thomas, but it seems half a world away. The million or so yearly visitors who soak up St. John's scenic wonders know that the island is accessible only by sea. US financier Laurence Rockefeller fell in love with the island in the 1950s and donated the 6,000 acres he owned for the **Virgin Islands National Park.** The park now covers nearly two-thirds of the island and protects another 5,650 acres offshore.

The smallest of the US Virgin Islands, St. John measures a mere 19 square miles. But it is packed with flowers, ferns, butterflies, and birds, which can be observed from any one of the 22 self-guided hiking trails maintained by the Park Service. The coastline is punctuated with more than 40 white-coral sand coves. About 4,500 people live on St.

John, whose capital city of **Cruz Bay** is such a sleepy town that nobody ever bothered to name its streets.

Since this island caters to nature lovers seeking escape, there is not much shopping, although rum is cheaper than water and a popular buy. Food choices lean to American and continental dishes.

- ■ **Trunk Bay**
- ■ **Cinnamon Bay**
- ■ **Maho Bay**
- ■ **Caneel Bay Resort**
- ■ **Mongoose Junction**
- ■ **Annaberg Plantation**
- ■ **Coral Bay Overlook**
- ■ **Hawksnest Bay**
- ■ **Museum Elaine Ione Sprauve**
- ■ **Reef Bay Trail**

St. Thomas

Columbus stumbled upon the 32-square-mile St. Thomas on his second voyage to the New World in 1493. Although the explorer claimed it for Spain, the island was settled—and abandoned—by Dutch and then English colonists; for years it was a pirates' lair, used as a base for plundering treasure-laden Spanish galleons. In 1672, a group of Norwegians and Danes colonized **Charlotte Amalie,** named for the Danish king's consort. The Scandinavians developed a major commercial center here, even as the English struggled to gain control of the island.

Today St. Thomas is one of the world's most popular cruise destinations, primarily because it has one of the world's most beautiful beaches. Heroic efforts erased the ravages of 1995's Hurricane Marilyn and restored Charlotte Amalie to its status as the world's busiest cruise ship port. Shoppers snap up loose gems, gold jewelry, and watches at this duty-free tropical bazaar. Galleries offer wonderful local handicrafts such as basketry, candles, ceramics, dolls, unusual jewelry, paintings, scrimshaw, and sculpture. Exotic jellies, such as tamarind, papaya, and seagrape, and spices are tasty souvenirs.

Conch is a popular ingredient, of course, and appears on most menus, as fritters, in salads, or sautéed with garlic, butter, and herbs, or in callaloo, a West Indian stew made with pork, fish, greens, and garlic.

- ■ **Hotel 1829 and 99 Steps**
- ■ **Blackbeard's Castle**
- ■ **Government House**
- ■ **Frederick Lutheran Church**
- ■ **Fort Christian**
- ■ **Coral World**
- ■ **Drake's Seat**
- ■ **St. Thomas Jewish Synagogue**
- ■ **Estate St. Peter Greathouse and Botanical Gardens**
- ■ **Magen's Bay**

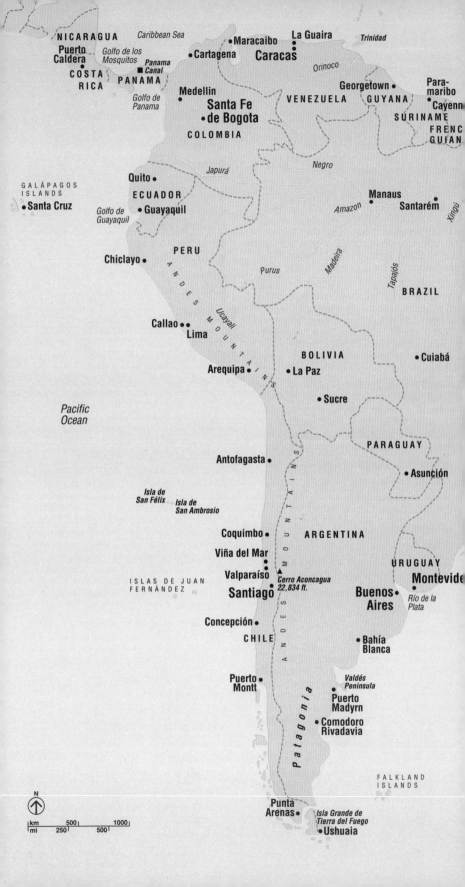

Atlantic
Ocean

• Belém

• São Luís

• Fortaleza

• Teresina

• Recife

• Salvador
da Bahia

Brasília
•

São Francisco

São
Paulo • Rio de
• Janeiro

Atlantic
Ocean

Central/South America

The narrow isthmus of Central America connects continents and hemispheres and separates oceans by mere miles. **Costa Rica**, with its lush cloud forests, democratic traditions, and colonial cities, along with **Panama** and its engineering marvel of a canal, are the most visited nations in that region, especially for cruise ships.

Below Central America is the much larger continent of South America. Extending 4,500 miles from **Colombia** to **Cape Horn**, it is surrounded by the **Atlantic Ocean** on the east, the **Pacific Ocean** to the west, **Drake Passage** on the south, and the **Caribbean Sea** to the north. From the **Amazon** jungle to **Patagonia**'s fjords and glaciers, the beautiful beaches of **Salvador da Bahia** to the marine marvels of the **Galápagos**, South America is filled with natural wonders. It boasts the world's largest rain forest, biggest watershed, widest waterfall, loftiest lake, driest desert, and the **Western Hemisphere**'s tallest mountain. The continent also features two of the planet's most passionate cities—**Buenos Aires**, where tango reigns supreme, and **Rio de Janeiro**, home to Carnival and samba.

First inhabited about 12,500 years ago by various Indian tribes migrating from Asia via the Bering Strait and North America, four main ethnic groups have contributed to South America's present-day population of about 320 million people: pre-Columbian inhabitants; Iberians—Spanish and Portuguese, who explored, conquered, and dominated the continent until the beginning of the 19th century; Africans, imported as slaves by the colonizers; and post-independence immigrants from overseas, mostly Germans and southern Europeans.

South America's 19,000 miles of shoreline is still easily explored by ship, just as those curious navigators did many centuries ago.

Argentina

Buenos Aires

This is a city that feels more like Europe than South America, with its wide jacaranda-lined boulevards, fountain-filled plazas, large green parks, ornate architecture, chic shopping districts, international restaurants and night clubs, and high culture. Indeed, *porteños*—as locals call themselves, taking their name from Buenos Aires's historical importance as a port—like to think of "BA" as the Paris of South America. Today over 11 million people—about one third of Argentina's population—reside in the greater metropolitan area of this 76-square-mile city.

Nuestra Señora de la Santísima Trinidad de los Buenos Aires (Our Lady of the Blessed Trinity of Fair Winds) was first settled by Spaniard Pedro de Mendoza in 1536 at the mouth of the vast brown **Río de la Plata** (Silver River). Continually besieged by the Indians, the Spanish abandoned it in 1541, then later resettled the site in 1580. The Spanish viceroyalty in Lima governed Argentina until 1776 when the separate viceroyalty of **Río de la Plata**—headquartered in Buenos Aires—was formed. The country gained full independence from Spain in 1816, and Buenos Aires became the capital in 1880. The city evolved as an important shipping center from 1880 to 1930. Waves of immigrants from Italy (a large part of the population is of Italian descent), Spain, and Eastern Europe flooded the country during the same period, lured by the government's offer of economic opportunity in a rich new world. Tango music, started by the poor black population at the turn of the century, was adopted by these working-class Europeans, who also helped bring Juan Perón to power in 1946 along with his wildly popular wife Eva ("Evita").

Porteños love to eat (dinner is usually quite late), especially huge slabs of beef, and mostly at *parrillas* (grill restaurants). Nonmeat eaters can opt for *provoleta,* a thick slab of cheese sprinkled with oregano and thrown on the grill. *Confiterías*—the BA equivalent of a French cafe or Italian bar—specialize in sandwiches, *medias lunas* (half moons, a croissantlike pastry), and strong coffee. *Sidra* is a slightly alcoholic cider. *Dulce de leche* is a caramelly concoction found in many dessert selections, including *alfajores* (filled cookies). Buenos Aires is a good place to pick up leather goods—jackets, gloves, boots, bags—and furs, as well as antiques and jewelry.

- ■ Tango show
- ■ Cementerio Recoleta (Recoleta Cemetery)
- ■ Plaza de Mayo (May Plaza)
- ■ La Catedral (Cathedral)
- ■ El Cabildo (Council House)
- ■ Teatro Colón (Colón Theater)
- ■ San Telmo
- ■ Museo José Hernández (José Hernández Museum)
- ■ Museo de Bellas Artes (Museum of Fine Arts)
- ■ Sunday Flea Market, Plaza Dorrego

Puerto Madryn

Love Parry, Baron of Madryn, and 150 Welsh immigrants founded Puerto Madryn on the **Golfo Nuevo** in **Chubut** province in 1886. The original settlers set up a system of irrigation canals, drawing water from the **Chubut River** upstream, which made the brown, scrubby valley bloom. This sparsely populated region is part of **Patagonia,** so named by Europeans, as one story goes, for the indigenous Indians—*patagones* (people with big feet)—who wore thick furs for shoes. The Indians continued to live on the coast until the Indian Wars of 1879-83, when they were mostly exterminated. Today Puerto Madryn is home to about 50,000 people, and although German and Italian immigrants came later, some locals still speak Welsh. Residents earn their living from fishing, aluminum processing, and tourism.

Puerto Madryn is the jumping-off point for wonderful wildlife-viewing expeditions in the region. One hundred miles away is the 50-mile-long **Valdés Peninsula,** which is connected to the mainland by a 3-mile-wide isthmus. Here a confluence of warm ocean waters from Brazil and colder waters from the south brings together two aquatic ecosystems that provide a home to myriad birds and marine mammals. Thousands of sea elephants loll on the beach, Southern Right Whales breed and frolic here, and sea birds nest just to the north on **Isla de los Pájaros.** The world's largest magellanic penguin rookery is south of Puerto Madryn in **Punta Tombo** (*pengwyn* is actually Welsh for "white head"), with more than a million of these birds migrating annually from Antarctica to breed and raise their chicks. Feisty guanacos, llamalike animals, run free as well.

Sample the fresh seafood here, and if possible, *tortas galesas* (black pastries made from a Welsh recipe brought by the colonists), a typical wedding dessert. The people of Chubut like to joke that there are seven sheep for every person in the province. The animal's wool appears in warm sweaters, weavings, and rugs. Gaucho gear, including *bombachas* (trousers), ponchos, and maté gourds and silver *bombillas* (straws), can also be found here.

- ■ Museo Oceanográfico y de Ciencias Naturales (Museum of Natural Sciences and Oceanography)
- ■ Isla de los Pájaros (Bird Island)
- ■ Reserva Faunística Punta Loma (Punta Loma Nature Reserve)
- ■ Valdés Peninsula
- ■ Puerto Pirámide
- ■ Golfo Nuevo
- ■ Trelew
- ■ Gaiman
- ■ Rawson
- ■ Whale-watching cruise

Ushuaia

The southern shores of **Isla Grande de Tierra del Fuego,** an island ringed with waterfalls, glaciers, snow-capped mountains, and great beech forests, is the setting for the southernmost city in the world. Founded in 1870 by Protestant missionaries, Ushuaia still resembles a frontier town of sorts, with corrugated metal buildings interspersed among newer concrete structures. Steep streets overlook the **Beagle Channel,** named after the ship on which naturalist Charles Darwin sailed in 1832. It was on this voyage that Darwin documented the penguins, sea lions, and sea birds that inhabit these waters and developed his theory of evolution. As in other parts of Argentina, most of the indigenous population were driven to extinction; the few remaining Yahgan Indians live in nearby **Parque Nacional Tierra del Fuego.**

Ushuaia's location at 55º latitude south means chilly weather year-round. Some of the hardy residents arrived at the turn of the century in search of rumored gold, while others were lured many years later by government incentives aiming to increase Argentine presence near Antarctic claims. Today most of the city's 50,000 residents earn a living in sheep ranching, timber, fishing, and trapping.

The cold waters yield superb seafood. Some local specialties are *centolla* (king crab) and *cholgas* (giant mussels) prepared in a variety of ways, including as a filling for empanadas. Trout and salmon are found in the island's numerous lakes and rivers. Items carved from *lenga* (wood) make good souvenirs.

- Museo Territorial Fin del Mundo (End of the World Museum)
- Plaza 25 de Mayo (25 May Plaza)
- Casa de Gobierno (Government House)
- Presidio de Ushuaia (Old Prison)
- Cerro Marcial (Martial Hill)
- Beagle Channel cruise
- Estancia Haberton (Haberton Ranch)
- Bahía Lapataia (Lapataia Bay)
- Lago Fagnano (Fagnano Lake)
- Tierra del Fuego

Brazil

Belém

Located about 80 miles from the sea, near the mouth of the mighty **Amazon River,** which supplies one-quarter of the earth's fresh water and its rain forest, plus a third of its oxygen, Belém is a sprawling city of skyscrapers and white colonial buildings. It rains 245 days a year here, downpours that keep the air cool and the jungle plants blooming. Belém has a population of over 1.5 million people.

After Spain and Portugal carved up the New World with the Treaty of Tordesillas in 1494, the Portuguese came to Brazil to stake a claim. They landed in Belém in 1616 and built a fortified city to deter other Europeans who had been making incursions since the

*Mercado Ver-o-Peso
(See the Weight Market),
Belém*

mid-1500s. It was later renamed **Nossa Senhora de Belém do Grão-Pará** (Our Lady of Bethlehem on the Great Pará River). Belém began exporting rubber in the wake of Goodyear's discovery of vulcanization in 1840, and it prospered for almost 40 years. When rubber tree seeds were smuggled out in 1876 by an Englishman, Henry Wickham, and taken to Ceylon and Malaysia, and Asia surpassed Brazil in latex production, a wholesale European exodus caused Belém to sink into decay until the Brazilian government invested in mineral exploration in the area. Today Belém is the largest port on the Amazon and Brazil's commercial hub, with the government sponsoring many large mineral and hydroelectric projects.

Freshwater fish is abundant here. Try pirarucu—a 6-footlong, 200-pound specimen; crabs; and turtle, served every imaginable way. Local specialties include *vatapá* (shrimp, fish, coconut, peanuts, cashews, tomato, onion, hot pepper, ginger, coriander, olive and *dendê*—rich palm oils), *tacacá* (dried shrimp and herbs—reputedly with aphrodisiac powers), and *pato no tucupi* (duck served in a hot sauce made from manioc juice and peppers). Look for such local Indian handicrafts as ceramics, pottery, paintings, wood carvings, intricate wall coverings, basketwork, dolls, sand pictures, shell and bead jewelry, inlaid boxes, and bracelets. Precious stones are also plentiful, and hammocks are a good buy.

- Mercado Ver-o-Peso (See the Weight Market)
- Bosque Rodrigues Alves (Rodrigues Alves Forest)
- Museu Emílio Goeldi (Emílio Goeldi Museum)
- Paraído das Tartarugas (Turtle Paradise)
- Basílica de Nossa Senhora de Nazaré (Our Lady of Nazareth Basilica)
- Forte do Castelo (Castelo Fort)
- Teatro da Paz (Municipal Theater)
- Igreja de Nossa Senhora das Mercês (Church of Our Lady of Mercy)
- Cathedral
- Palácio Lauro Sodré (Lauro Sodré Palace)

Fortaleza

Early Portuguese sailors quickly discovered in the mid-16th century that the region around Fortaleza was ideally suited for sugarcane, although the city wasn't founded until 1612. The Dutch had the same idea, briefly taking control of the area from 1635-54, before the Portuguese powered their way back in to dominate the world sugar market.

Brazilians have been coming to Fortaleza, capital of the state of **Ceará** on the country's northeast coast, for many years to enjoy its fine beaches. But in recent times fewer waters are considered safe for swimming because of the ever-increasing dumping of industrial waste. While sugar is still king here, this port city dotted with many palm-tree–lined *praças* (plazas) and home to two million people, has evolved into an export center for sugar, wax, cotton, castor oil, and salt, along with lobsters (Fortaleza's *jangadeiros*—fishermen—

can still be seen pulling in their catch on **Iracema Beach)** and cashew nuts. The fish—including some of the best lobster in South America—comes fresh from the **Atlantic** and from the **Ceará River.**

Dishes to try include *vatapá* and *empadinhas de camarão* (shrimp patties with olives and hearts of palm). Handmade lace, embroidery, and hammocks are on sale at the **Mercado Central** (Central Market), where bargaining is expected. Visitors can also pick up wood carvings, basketry, clay figures, and cashew nuts.

- Cathedral
- Centro de Turismo (Tourism Center)
- Museu de Arte e Cultura Popular (Museum of Art and Popular Culture)
- Museu Historico e Antropológico do Ceará (Museum of History and Anthropology)
- Forte Nossa Senhora de Assunção (Fort of Our Lady of Assumption)
- Museu de Minerais (Mineral Museum)
- Museu das Secas (Drought Museum)
- Centro de Artesanato Luiza Távora (Artisans' Center)
- Serra de Maranguape
- Praia Combucco (Cumbuco Beach)

Manaus

In 1541, Spaniard Francisco de Orellana, helped and harassed by the indigenous tribes along the way, navigated the **Amazon** from the Andes to the Atlantic. Nearly a century later, Portuguese explorer Pedro Teixeira traversed the route in reverse. Soon thereafter in 1669, the Portuguese established a fort and trading settlement at Manaus, sending ships laden with cacao seeds and turtle oil down river for export. First called **Fortaleza São José da Barra** (Sandbar Fort), after Brazil proclaimed its independence in 1822, the city became Manaus, named for a local Indian tribe. The modern-day history of Manaus, capital of the huge Amazonas state, can be summed up in one word: Rubber. A boom created by demand in North America and Europe generated instant fortunes. Rubber barons built fabulous mansions and a lavish opera house decorated with wrought iron and crystal shipped from Europe. But the boom quickly went bust when the British smuggled out rubber tree seeds and started a crop of their own in Asia.

The heart of the Amazon jungle is the last place you might expect to find a city of over a million people, with high-rise buildings, and a thriving trade center. Today Manaus is a free port and center for the export of Brazil nuts, black pepper, and lumber, and oil from Peru. Although Portuguese is Manaus's official language, Amazonian Indians also speak over 150 tribal dialects. Surrounded by rain forest and waterways, it remains isolated from the rest of Brazil for most of the year because of washed-out roads. The Amazon River, with over 1,100 tributaries—17 of which are more than 1,000 miles long—is its lifeblood. The Manaus harbor is equipped with floating docks to deal with the 46-foot annual rise and fall of the **Rio Negro.**

Notable dishes in Manaus include river fish pirarucu and tucanaré; *tacacá* (a snack made from shrimp, tapioca, and herbs); and *maniçoba* (a stew of pork, calves' feet, animal innards, bacon, sausage fat, vegetables, and beans). Turtles and manatees find their way into some dishes, but beware—they are also finding their way to extinction. Popular souvenirs from the area include such Indian handicrafts as blowpipes, bows and arrows, gourds, woven mats, and beads; as well as stuffed piranha fish; and jewelry with locally mined amethyst, topaz, and aquamarine.

- Teatro Amazonas (Opera House)
- Mercado Municipal (Municipal Market)
- Alfândega (Customs House)
- Museu do Indio (Indian Museum)
- Cathedral
- Museu do Homem do Norte (Anthropological Museum)
- Museu do Porto de Manaus (Harbor Museum)
- Jardim Botânico (Botanic Gardens)
- Meeting of the Waters boat trip
- Rubber baron mansions

Rio de Janeiro

Glamorous and beautiful, but also dirty and dangerous, Rio de Janeiro is in constant contention for that coveted title of "World's Most Beautiful Harbor." The city is divided into three districts: the **North,** impoverished and packed with tiny houses; the busy commercial **Central** section; and the **South,** the high-end quarter full of hotels, restaurants, and beaches. The areas are all connected by 13 tunnels hacked through the mountains to which brightly painted shantytowns called *favelas* cling. Rio boasts 23 beaches, the most famous of which is **Copacabana,** followed by **Ipanema** and **Leblon. Sugar Loaf Mountain**'s 1,230-foot summit was first scaled 150 years ago by a British woman, but most people now reach it by cable car or taxi. **Corcovado**'s 2,310-foot peak is topped with the outstretched arms of 100-foot-high *Christ the Redeemer.*

Portuguese sailors arrived in **Baía de Guanabara** in January 1502 and called the area Rio de Janeiro (River of January), but didn't settle here. The French came in 1555, and after many bloody battles, the Portuguese wrested the region from them in 1567. Though constantly besieged by indigenous Indians, the city prospered, supplanting Salvador as the capital in 1763 until it was moved to Brasilia in 1960. Rio's racially integrated population is composed of a three-fold mix of Portuguese intermarried with both indigenous peoples and the descendants of black slaves. The 20th century brought large immigrations of Eastern Europeans, Italians, and Japanese after both world wars. Rio's six million residents

(cariocas) like to party, especially during its world-famous yearly Carnival celebration. Most of Rio's cuisine was created by slaves in the Bahia province, using seafood, poultry, nuts, fruits, coconuts, and milk. *Feijoada,* the national dish, is made from black beans and pork. Another treat is *xinxim de galinha* (chicken stew cooked with ground dried shrimp, hot spices, and *dendê*). Brazil is the world's top gemstone exporter, and Rio is the place to find the best buys and selection, including jewelry set in 18-karat gold and silver. The Brazilian good-luck *figa* charm (a clenched fist with a raised thumb) is a unique souvenir. Folk art found here includes paintings, tapestries, batik, woodcarvings, and masks. The **Feirarte** (Art Fair) is a good place to find everything from treasures to trinkets.

- Praia de Copacabana (Copacabana Beach)
- Corcovado (Hunchback Mountain)
- Pão de Açúcar (Sugar Loaf Mountain)
- Igreja Nossa Senhora de Candelária (Our Lady of Candelária Church)
- Paço Imperial (Imperial Palace)
- Jardim Botânico (Botanical Gardens)
- Museu do Indio (Indian Museum)
- Museu Histórico Nacional (National Historical Museum)
- Floresta da Tijuca (Tijuca National Forest)
- Mosteiro do São Bento (Monastery of St. Bento)

Salvador da Bahia (Bahia)

Italian explorer Amerigo Vespucci, who sailed under a Portuguese flag, anchored off a sweeping, sandy South American coastline on All Saints Day in 1501 and named the area **Bahia de Todos os Santos**—All Saints Bay. Salvador (often called "Bahia" by Brazilians) was established as the region's capital in 1549, and quickly became the Portuguese Empire's second Lisbon. It was famed for its many gold-filled Baroque churches, ornate mansions, and endless festivals. Over time, the traditional beliefs of the West African slaves brought to work the sugarcane plantations blended with those of the Catholic Portuguese, thus creating a unique carnival culture that still resonates through *capoeira* (foot fighting cleverly disguised as a ritual dance). Salvador prospered anew with the discovery of gold and diamonds in the country's interior in the 18th century, but then stagnated as an antiquated agricultural economy. Only in the 20th century has the city again begun to move forward, with such new, income-producing industries as petroleum, chemicals, and tourism.

The city is divided into **Cidade Alta** (Upper Town), which sits atop a 200-foot cliff, and **Cidade Baixa** (Lower Town), which resides along the waterfront. Bahia is full of crowded markets and pastel colonial mansions in various states of disrepair.

Bahian cuisine is hot and spicy, and many dishes, including *vatapá* and *xinxim,* are made with *dendê.*

Also try *acarajé* (a large, deep-fried fritter made from a batter of dried beans and shrimp, which is split open and filled with a sauce of shrimp, onion, peppers, and ginger). Other specialties include c*amarãos,* fried or stewed in tomato sauce and garlic, and *casquica* (a spicy crab dish). One of Salvador's special products is *pença de balangandà* (a charm-holder pin dating from slave days). Bahian dolls, ceramics, leather goods, jacaranda wood carvings, and lace are also good buys.

- Larceda Elevator Lookout Point
- Forte de São Marcelo
- Igreja de Nossa Senhora da Conceição da Praia(Church of Our Lady of the Immaculate Conception)
- Mercado Modelo (Model Market)
- Feira de São Joaquim (Produce Market)
- Museu de Arte Sacra (Sacred Art Museum)
- Igreja do Pilar (Church of Pilar)
- Sé (Cathedral)
- Igreja de São Francisco (Church of St. Francis)
- Largo do Pelourinho (Pillory Square)

Santarém

This jungle city of 300,000 residents just 2.5° south of the equator sits at the confluence of the **Tapajós** and **Amazon Rivers.** A frontier type of town at a watery crossroads, on some days Santarém's port is jammed with everything from dugout canoes brimming with the catch of the day to oceangoing cargo vessels offloading cars. It serves as a jumping-off point and supply center for miners, gold prospectors, rubber tappers, Brazil nut gatherers as well as those in the jute and timber industries.

The area around Santarém was originally inhabited by Tapuiçu Indians, whom Portuguese explorer Pedro Teixeira encountered on his expedition upriver. It was subsequently settled by Jesuit missionaries in 1661, who christened it after the city of the same name in Portugal. In 1867 Confederates from the US South who had fled their homeland when slavery was abolished, made a failed attempt to settle here.

Fresh river fish, especially pirarucu and filhote, are unloaded at the waterfront daily and find their way into such stews as *caldeirada.* Local crafts include blowguns (that work!) and leather fashioned into knife sheaths and masks.

Mickey Mouse is going to sea. In 1998, Disney Cruise Line launches its first ships, *Disney Magic* and *Disney Wonder,* which will combine a three- or four-day cruise with three or four days at a Walt Disney World resort. The vessels, which promise theme restaurants, extensive children's facilities, and Disney-produced entertainment, will sail from Port Canaveral, Florida.

- Mercado Modelo
- Avenida Tapajós (Tapajós Avenue) and Museu (Museum)
- Docas do Pará (Pará Docks)
- Mercado de Peixes (Fish Market)
- Floating market
- Centro Cultural João Fona (Cultural Center)
- Encontro das Aguas (Meeting of the Waters)
- Pouso das Garças
- Alter do Chão and Indigenous Museum
- Fordlândia and Belterra

Chile

Punta Arenas

Located on the **Straits of Magellan** almost equidistant from the **Pacific** and **Atlantic Oceans,** Punta Arenas ("Sandy Point" in Spanish) is Chile's southernmost city. It's a stark port of about 125,000 people, with some small wooden buildings remaining from the turn of the century, supplemented by concrete and corrugated sheet metal architecture. Punta Arenas is a major sheep-breeding center, exporting wool, skins, and frozen meat worldwide; it also shuttles crude oil and gas between the Straits' oil terminals and refineries in central Chile.

Five Indian tribes inhabited this area at one time when the Europeans colonized the continent in the 16th century: the tall Tehuelche, whose only adornments were guanaco capes draped over their shoulders and red and white bands and charcoal streaks on their faces; the Huash; the Yahgan; the Alcaluf; and the Ona, the last of the tribes, most of whom disappeared only within the past decade. The city was settled in the 19th century by English, Portuguese, and Slavs, who established enormous sheep ranches, and by Salesian monks, an Italian order of missionaries. Punta Arenas boomed before the opening of the Panama Canal, serving as a resupply post for ships rounding **Cape Horn.**

Along with lamb, *centolla* (king crab) is a local delicacy. Empanadas—filled with meat or cheese—are also in abundance. Local buys include leather goods, sheepskins, and chocolate.

- Colegio Salesiano (Salesian College)
- Museo Histórico Regional (Regional History Museum)
- Instituto de la Patagonia (Patagonian Institute)
- Plaza de Armas (Armament Plaza)
- Mirador Cerro de La Cruz (Lookout on Hill of the Cross)
- Catedral (Cathedral)
- Teatro Cervantes (Cervantes Theater)
- Fuerte Bulnes (Fort Bulnes)

■ Reserva Forestal Magallanes (Forest Reserve)

■ Penguin colony at Otway Sound

Puerto Montt

A wonderful assortment of colorful lakes; thick green forests; snow-capped volcanoes; and numerous mountains, valleys, rivers, and waterfalls surround Puerto Montt, the gateway to wild **Patagonia** and a dramatic fjordland to the south. Capital of the **Lake District,** Puerto Montt boasts a panoramic view of **Seno Reloncaví** (Reloncaví Sound), **Tenglo Island,** and **Osorno** (famous for its almost perfect conical shape) and **Calbuco** volcanoes. Wooden Alpine-style homes sport high-pitched roofs, ornate balconies, and shingles well weathered by the region's ever-present drizzle. The Lake District's attractions are of the natural sort—soaking up the scenery or watching the locals haul in the day's catch of brown, brook, and rainbow trout.

The city was founded in 1853 by adventurer Vincente Perez Rosales and a handful of German immigrants, whose ancestors today remain a small but influential percentage of the 150,000 residents. Puerto Montt mushroomed with the arrival of the railroad—the southernmost station in the world— 60 years later.

A regional culinary specialty is *curanto* (a casserole of seafood, chicken, sausages, and potatoes). Puerto Montt is a good place to pick up Mapuche-designed weavings and sweaters, along with silver and lapis lazuli jewelry, and wood carvings.

■ Plaza de Armas (Armament Plaza)

■ Casa del Arte Diego Rivera (Diego Rivera House of Art)

■ Mercado Angelmo (Angelmo Market)

■ Isla Tenglo (Tenglo Island)

■ Puerto Varas and Lago Llanquihue (Lake Llanquihue)

■ Boat ride on Lago Todos Los Santos (All Saints Lake)

■ Parque Nacional Alerce Andino (Andean National Park)

■ Salto de Petrohue (Petrohue Falls)

■ Volcán Osorno (Osorno Volcano)

■ Calbuco, via the old coastal road

Santiago

In 1541 a half-starved Spaniard, Pedro de Valdivia, staggered into a rich fertile valley and founded **Santiago del Nuevo Extremo** in the name of the Spanish crown. The indigenous Mapuche Indians— the Spanish called them *araucanos*—were incensed and burned the settlement down twice; Mother Nature joined in the havoc with a deadly earthquake in 1674. For most of its colonial period, Chile formed part of the viceroyalty of Peru, controlled from Lima, but became separate in 1778. By 1800 Santiago had become a city in its own right. After a seven-year revolt led by patriots Bernardo O'Higgins (from Argentina) and General José de San Martín, Chile declared its full independence from Spain in 1818.

Santiago is located on a plain 2,000 feet above sea level, with the snow-covered **Andes** looming in the distance; the **Río Mapocho**—spanned by several bridges—flows through the city. A modern metropolis bearing few traces of its indigenous past, the capital today is a jumble of colonial architecture mixed among low-rise contemporary buildings, ever conscious of its precarious position along the Pacific Rim's earthquake belt. Today the city is home to nearly five million residents descended from British, German, Slavic, French, and Italian immigrants, together with those of criollo (Spaniards born in Chile) and mestizo ancestry.

Dishes to try here include *caldillo de congrio* (a soup made with conger eel, potatoes, and onions), *cazuela*

Volcán Osorno (Osorno Volcano), Puerto Montt

de ave (chicken stew with potatoes, rice, onions and peppers), *pastel de choclo* (a rich meat casserole topped with a cornmeal mash), as well as the ubiquitous empanadas. World-class wines are grown in the nearby **Maipo Valley.** The deep blue lapis lazuli stone, native only to Chile and Afghanistan, are good buys, along with copper and leather goods.

- Plaza de Armas (Armament Plaza), Museo Histórico Nacional (National History Museum), and Catedral (Cathedral)
- Museo Chileño de Arte Precolombino (Chilean Museum of Pre-Colombian Art)
- Changing of the Guard at Palacio de La Moneda (Presidential Palace)
- Museo Arqueológico de Santiago (Archaeology Museum of Santiago)
- Cerro San Cristóbal (San Cristóbal Hill)
- Iglesia y Convento San Francisco (Church and Convent of St. Francis) y Museo de Arte Colonial (Museum of Colonial Art)
- Mercado Central (Central Market)
- Museo de Artes Decorativos (Museum of Decorative Arts)
- Palacio Cousiño (Cousiño Palace)
- Concha y Toro or Undurraga Winery tour

Valparaíso/Viña del Mar

Chile's principal port and second-largest city (over 400,000 residents), Valparaíso is built in tiers on a circle of *cerros* (hills) in the shadow of the snow-capped **Andean Cordillera.** Narrow winding roads, steep staircases, funiculars, and turn-of-the-century elevators connect the two distinct sections of the city. The business district lines the bay, while the hills above are a jumble of colorful residential shacks built along back alleys with a wonderful view of the action below.

The area around Valparaíso was inhabited by the seafaring Chango Indians when Spaniard Diego de Almagro arrived in the region in 1536. It was a quiet port until English pirates, including Sir Francis Drake, started plundering the South American coast in 1578. The Spanish built the seaside fortress of **San José** for protection, and by 1800 Valparaíso had become Chile's principal international port, as well as a base for British naval operations on South America's west coast. Today little is left of the city's past, particularly after an earthquake devastated it in 1906, followed by another two in 1971 and 1985. Only **El Puerto,** an old colonial area built around the small stucco church **La Matriz,** remains.

Six miles of beaches lead north from Valparaíso to **Viña del Mar,** South America's foremost Pacific coast resort, founded by Jose Vergara in 1878. Set amid a forest, this city of 350,000 people is popular among both well-to-do Chileans and visitors. **Victorias** (horse-drawn carriages) roll along the palm-tree and mansion-lined **Avenida de la Marina.**

Fresh seafood is the order of the day in both cities, with *congrio, corvina* (sea bass), *almejas* (clams), and *cholgas* in plentiful supply. *Sopa de mariscos* (seafood soup) is a popular dish. Woolen weavings and clothing, as well as objects fashioned from lapis lazuli, are found here.

Valparaíso

- Museo del Cielo Abierto (Open Sky Museum)
- Museo Naval (Naval Museum)
- Plaza Sotomayor and Intendencia
- Muelle Prat (Prat Pier)
- Museo de Bellas Artes (Museum of Fine Arts)
- Plaza Echaurren

Viña del Mar

- Palacio Rioja (Rioja Palace)
- Quinta Vergara Gardens and Museo de Bellas Artes (Museum of Fine Arts)
- Centro Cultural (Cultural Center)
- Museo de la Cultura del Mar (Museum of Maritime Culture)

Colombia

Cartagena

The Spanish settled Cartagena in 1533 as a staging ground for the conquest of the entire South American continent. Constant sieges by French and English pirates prompted the construction of a large-scale system of forts and defensive walls. Sir Francis Drake was the most infamous of the lot, pillaging the port in 1586 and making off with 10 million pesos. Cartagena declared its independence from Spain in 1811.

The walled **Ciudad Vieja** (Old City) features warrens of twisting narrow streets. (Be on the alert for modern-day pirates—pickpockets—here.) Within this UNESCO World Heritage Site is **El Centro,** the former aristocratic neighborhood; **San Diego,** which was inhabited by the merchant class; and **Getsamaní,** where artisans once lived in *casas bajas* (one-story houses). Today Cartagena is a sprawling Caribbean metropolis of nearly a million people of European, Indian, and African descent.

The city's cultural diversity is reflected in the local cuisine. Popular dishes include *cazuela de frutas del mar* (similar to bouillabaisse); *viuda de pescado* (fish stew); paella heaped with shrimp and crawfish; and *arepas* (fried cornmeal cakes stuffed with meat or cheese). And don't forget to have a cup of that world famous Colombian coffee. Colombia's famous emeralds can be bought loose here or set in gold jewelry. Other products to shop for include well-made leather, crocodile, and snakeskin goods; pre-Colombian and colonial antiques and reproductions; and such handicrafts as wool rugs, ponchos, hammocks, and basketry.

- Plaza de los Coches (Wagon Plaza) and Torre del Reloj (Clock Tower)

- Convento de San Pedro Claver (Convent of St. Peter Claver)
- Palacio de la Inquisición (Palace of the Inquisition)
- Plaza Bolívar and Catedral (Bolívar Plaza and Cathedral)
- Casa del Marqués de Valdehoyos (House of the Marquis of Valdehoyos)
- Iglesia de Santísima Trinidad (Church of the Holy Trinity)
- Plaza de las Bóvedas
- Castillo de San Felipe de Barajas (St. Philip's Castle)
- Convento de La Popa (Convent of the Stern)
- Museo del Oro y Arqueología (Gold and Archaeology Museum)

Costa Rica

Puerto Caldera

Christopher Columbus sighted what he called "Costa Rica" (rich coast) on his fourth voyage to the New World in 1502. One theory is that he came up with the name not only because of the area's rumored mineral deposits, but its towering mountains; lush valleys thick with coffee, cocoa, and bananas; steaming volcanoes; and white- and black-sand beaches. The Spanish attempted to colonize Costa Rica in 1506 and after several failed attempts founded **Cartago,** the colony's first capital, in 1563. Costa Rica declared its independence in 1821; there were three civil wars in 1917, 1919, and 1948. The army was abolished in 1949, and today Costa Rica has the distinction of being Central America's oldest democracy.

To preserve the country's extraordinary variety of plant and animal life, in the 1960s the government of Costa Rica established a system of national parks and forests, which today occupies 12 percent of the country. Most Costa Ricans, locally known as *ticos,* live up in the mountains because of the intense heat along the coast. The country bridges the **Caribbean Sea** on the east and the **Pacific Ocean** to the west, and is bordered by **Panama** on the south and Nicaragua to the north.

Among the country's dishes are *olla de carne* (beef soup made with plantain, corn, yucca, and two locally grown vegetables—ñampi and chayote) and *gallo pinto* (seasoned black beans and rice). Best buys here include crafts made from wood and leather, such as collapsible rocking chairs; colorful, hand-painted oxcarts—the country's national symbol; pottery; gold and silver ornaments; and pre-Columbian replicas. Coffee beans, macadamia nuts, and coffee liqueur are other popular purchases.

- Green Train
- San José
- Sarchí
- Monteverde Cloud Forest Reserve

- Arenal Volcano and Lake
- La Fortuna
- Tabacon Resort
- Poás Volcano and National Park
- Carara Reserve
- Braulio Carrillo National Park Rain Forest Aerial Tram

Ecuador

Santa Cruz, Galápagos Islands

One of the world's greatest living laboratories, the Galápagos Islands are home to an astonishing variety of unique species of plants and animals—especially reptiles—which adapted themselves to local conditions over a period of thousands of years. The 4,800-square-mile archipelago is located about 600 miles off the South American coast, and consists of 13 small and 6 large islands—5 are inhabited—and dozens of islets from which the peaks of some still-active volcanoes rise nearly 10,000 feet from the **Pacific Ocean** floor. **Santa Cruz** (one of the two main tourist centers with a population of about 10,000 people), **San Cristóbal** (the other tourist center), **Isabela, Fernandina, San Salvador,** and **Santa María** are the larger islands.

Charles Darwin developed his theory of evolution during an 1835 visit aboard the *Beagle* that he later published in his controversial *On the Origin of Species.* Some of the most spectacular species found here include the already rare, giant tortoises called galápagos (from which the islands take their name), along with marine and land iguanas, Galápagos sea lions and fur seals, red- and blue-footed boobies, scarlet crabs, flightless cormorants, and finches. The animals have little instinctive fear of people, who didn't inhabit these isles until 1535 when the Bishop of Panama, Tomás de Berlanga, drifted here by accident. Claimed by Ecuador in 1832, the islands were first populated by exiled soldiers and convicts, pirates, and whalers. In 1959 the entire archipelago was declared a national park, and a large research facility was established in 1960 on Santa Cruz to study the islands' flora and fauna.

A UNESCO World Heritage Site, Galápagos itineraries are regulated by national park authorities in order to evenly distribute human visits; only locally owned-and-operated small vessels are licensed to carry passengers around the islands. Environmentalists continue to discuss the ramifications of rapidly growing tourism and the related migration of mainlanders seeking employment. Illegal harvests of lobster, shark, and sea cucumber for Asian markets also threaten the marine ecosystems.

- Darwin Research Station
- Tortuga Bay
- Puerto Ayora
- Santa Rosa
- Bellavista

■ Media Luna
■ Puntudo
■ Cerro Crocker (Mount Crocker)
■ Chato Tortoise Reserve
■ Lava tubes

Panama

Panama Canal

A simple way of crossing the **Isthmus of Panama** in order to get from the **Caribbean Sea** to the **Pacific Ocean** was sought for centuries. In 1513 Spanish conquistador Balboa walked the distance to catch a glimpse of the Pacific; during the glory days of the Spanish Main, mule trains laden with gold crossed the narrow strip of land to fortresses in the Caribbean. As early as 1524 King Charles V of Spain ordered a survey of the area for construction of a canal. But it wasn't until 1880 that the French Canal Company, led by Ferdinand de Lesseps—builder of the Suez Canal—attempted to erect a sea-level canal to the Pacific.

The financially and emotionally bankrupt French unloaded the enterprise on the United States government for $40 million in 1904. This was one year after Panama revolted from Colombia and was afforded US assistance in return for a 10-mile-wide zone across the isthmus in which to build a canal. President Teddy Roosevelt, along with John F. Stevens and Colonel George W. Goethals, produced a host of engineering miracles. With the largest dam ever built at that time, engineers plugged the wild **Chagres River** four miles from the Caribbean shore, using giant **Gatún Lake** behind it as part of the canal and as a reservoir for lock water. The cost of the canal was about $639 million. The human toll was much higher—an estimated 25,000 died from accidents and diseases from the time the French first started digging to the completion of the canal in 1914. Using American Army doctor Walter Reed's vital 1902 discovery that yellow fever was transmitted by mosquitoes, US doctor Colonel William C. Gorgas finally stemmed the death toll by clearing and draining swamps where mosquitoes bred.

About 52 million gallons of water from Gatún Lake are used for every ship transit through the Panama Canal. In order to raise and lower ships 85 feet up and over the continental divide, three sets of multistep paired locks were built to allow two-way traffic for quick passage—**Gatún** near the Caribbean, and **Pedro Miguel** and **Miraflores** on the Pacific side. Each is 1,000 feet long, 110 feet wide, and 40 feet deep. It takes a ship about nine hours to make the 50-mile canal trip between the two oceans, depending on traffic. (A far cry from the treacherous 8,000-mile journey that ships had to take before the canal was built.) Tolls are charged according to tonnage and cargo: the largest paid was more than $117,000 in 1989 by the *Queen Elizabeth 2,* the smallest—36¢— by a man who swam the canal in 1928. Some 15,000 ships, flying flags of more than 60 countries, pass through the canal yearly with more than 200 million tons of cargo.

Peru

Lima (Callao)

After crushing the Inca empire in 1532 and killing their king, Atahualpa, Spanish conquistador Francisco Pizarro went on to found Lima in 1535 along a river and valley the Indians called **Rimac** (Talking River). The Spanish misheard the name as "Limac," which they shortened to Lima. Pizarro planned the city slightly inland from the port of Callao, midway along Peru's 1,400 mile coast, an area surrounded by wide plains with plenty of space for growth. Lima was Spain's social, commercial, and colonial administrative center in South America until the independence movements swept across the continent in the 19th century, and rivaled many European cities in stature.

Today the population of greater Lima is pushing 10 million, as mountain people make their way to the city looking for jobs, leading to the building of hillside shantytowns, and to domestic discontent. That has been reined in with the submission of the Sendero Luminoso (Shining Path) guerilla movement, but antigovernment groups still exist and commit acts of protest from time to time.

Peru's diverse, rich cuisine has evolved from Inca, Spanish, Italian, and other European cultures, as well as being influenced by African, Chinese, and Japanese immigrants. The food is based on variations of spicy fish, shellfish, stewed meat, tamale, and potato dishes. Popular specialties include *escabeche* (fish with prawns, eggs, onions, hot peppers, olives, cumin, and cheese); *rocoto relleno* (peppers stuffed with meat and rice); *lomo saltado* (spicy beef stew); and *ají de gallina* (spicy creamed chicken). The national drink is a Pisco sour, made with grape brandy, lemon, sugar, egg white, and ice. Silver, gold, leather, and wood, as well as pottery, textiles, tapestries, and rugs and sweaters woven from alpaca wool are great buys. The **Mercado Artesanal** (a group of native markets) sells handicrafts from around the country.

■ Plaza de Armas (Armament Plaza)
■ Catedral (Cathedral)
■ Iglesia y Monasterio de Santo Domingo (Church and Monastery of St. Dominic)
■ Iglesia y Monasterio de San Francisco (Church and Monstery of St. Francis)
■ La Alameda y Convento de los Descalzos (Promenade and Convent of the Shoeless Friars)
■ Museo Nacional de La República (National Museum)
■ Museo de Oro (Gold Museum)
■ Museo de Antropología y Arqueología (Museum of Anthropology and Archaeology)

- Museo Yoshiro Amano (Yoshiro Amano Museum)
- Miraflores

Uruguay

Montevideo

In 1520 one of Magellan's sailors first glimpsed the prominent hill where today's Montevideo sits, and called out, "Monte vide eu"(I see a mountain). Originally inhabited by the Charrúa Indians, Montevideo was founded as a Spanish fortress in 1726 to defend against the Portuguese who had already settled in nearby Colonia del Sacramento. The city changed hands several times, including a brief occupation by the British. Uruguay itself was annexed to Brazil in the 1820s and was populated by gauchos who herded cattle until independence in 1828, when there was an influx of Spanish and Italian immigrants.

Bounded by the **Atlantic** on one side and the **Río de la Plata** on the other, Uruguay's capital affords its nearly 3.5 million residents a life of peace and relative obscurity. Montevideo doesn't seem to suffer the typical crime-and-pollution problems that plague other South American cities. Business is conducted in the **Ciudad Vieja** (Old City), which is located between the

main plaza and the port. Three residential areas surround the city's heart: northern **Prado,** home of enormous 19th-century mansions; **Rambla Pocitos,** the high-rise center to the east; and **Carrasco,** with its beautiful villas and gardens, farther east.

This is beef country: there seems to be a *parillada* (grill) on every corner, and meat is served at almost every meal. *Asado* (barbecued beef) appears in many forms—*de tira* (ribs), *pulpa* (boneless), and *lomo* (steak). Other beef dishes to try include *chivitos* (burgers) and *puchero* (with vegetables, bacon, beans, and sausages). *Morcilla dulce* is a sweet black sausage, made from blood, orange peel, and walnuts. Such gems as amethysts, topaz, agate, and quartz are mined and polished here; antique jewelry can be found in the Ciudad Vieja. Leather and woolen goods

Iglesia y Monasterio de San Francisco (Church and Monastery of St. Francis), Lima

are well-priced, and available at the **Mercado de los Artesanos** (Artisans' Market), or at weekend markets.

- Plaza Independencia (Independence Square)
- Mausoleo de José Gervasio Artigas (Mausoleum of José Gervasio Artigas)
- Cabildo (Town Hall)
- Palacio Legislativo (Legislative Palace)
- Museo de Artes Decorativos (Decorative Arts Museum)
- Museo del Gaucho y de La Moneda (Cowboy and Coin Museum)
- Cerro (Hill)
- Museo Nacional de Antropología (National Museum of Anthropology)
- Mercado del Puerto (Port Market)
- Carrasco

Venezuela

Caracas (La Guaira)

Spanish conquistador Diego de Losada settled Caracas in 1567, naming it after the indigenous tribe he found living along the Caribbean coast. A series of Indian and pirate attacks, earthquakes, and civil unrest took place throughout the years until much-revered native son, Simón Bolívar ("The Liberator"), began the struggle for independence. Under Bolívar's leadership, the colony declared independence from Spain in 1811; it was retaken by the Spaniards a year later, and finally gained independence once again in 1821, and Caracas became Venezuela's capital. The discovery of oil in Lago de Maracaibo in 1914 spurred a boom that attracted over a million immigrants from Italy, Spain, Portugal, as well as other countries in South America.

Keeping Fit Afloat

Calories and cruising are synonymous. The daily caloric intake that comes of multicourse meals augmented by burgers and ice cream at the pool bar, afternoon tea, early evening hors d'oeuvres, and midnight buffets can expand any cruise ship passenger's middle well beyond the last belt hole.

But despite all the temptations, putting on pounds during a shipboard vacation is *not* a given. While cruises have always provided ample opportunities to indulge, today they also make it easy to eat right, feel good, and stay trim, fit, and healthy.

Seagoing chefs now focus more on fresh fruits and vegetables and use a lighter hand with the salt and sauces than they have in the past. Portions are more moderate, and low-fat, low-sodium, and low-calorie dishes have become standard on many menus. Some lines feature vegetarian alternatives or spa cuisine; **American Hawaii Cruises** provides entrées approved by the American Heart Association. In addition, nearly all cruise lines offer healthy snacks like fresh fruit and sugar-free, fat-free frozen yogurt.

Those who do indulge in the dining room will find plenty of places on board to burn off those extra calories. Almost all cruise ships feature fitness centers. No longer confined to a cramped space below decks, they are prominently located, spacious, and bright. Many have floor-to-ceiling windows affording spectacular ocean views. They boast the latest weight machines and free weights, stationary bicycles, Stairmasters, treadmills, and rowing equipment. Aerobics, aquacise, and step classes are led by licensed fitness instructors. Saunas, steam rooms, whirlpools, jogging tracks, and lap pools complete the picture. Some ships even offer body fat analysis, nutrition counseling, and personal training sessions (for a fee).

But passengers need not spend time in the gym to have an active cruise. Deck strolling and shuffleboard are still time-honored shipboard pastimes, but today they're joined by paddle tennis, volleyball, skeet shooting (with biodegradable skeets), golf driving, and putting. A few ships are equipped with fold-out marinas that allow enclosed ocean swimming. In port, some offer water skiing, windsurfing, sea kayaking, and sailing. Golf, tennis, horseback riding, scuba diving, and snorkeling also can be arranged.

Many ships also have onboard spas, where passengers may enjoy Swedish and aromatic oil massages, seaweed wraps, and numerous other exotic treatments as well as hair styling, facials, manicures, and pedicures. These may not help you slim down or shape up, but they will make you feel great—which, after all, is also synonymous with cruising.

Today Venezuela remains one of the world's largest oil producers and exporters, and greater Caracas, still feeling growing pains, is a modern, sprawling city, home to over five million *caraqueños*. **El Centro,** the business district, is flanked by affluent residential areas to the east. Separated from the sea by the 7,083-foot forested peak, **El Avila,** Caracas lies along a narrow 9-mile valley that follows the east-west course of **Río Guaire,** 15 miles from the busy Caribbean port of La Guaira. Caracas's altitude of 3,400 feet affords the city cooler temperatures than are found in most Caribbean climes.

The national dish is *hallaca* (shredded beef, rice, black beans, and fried plantains). Grilled *pargo* (red snapper) is fresh and tasty, and *arepas* are delicious. Venezuela coffee and rum are notable. Look for such handicrafts as weavings by the Guajira Indians, baskets, woolen *ruanas* (ponchos), and the famous painted devil masks worn at the Feast of Corpus Christi. Gold jewelry is also a good buy.

- Plaza Bolívar (Bolívar Plaza)
- Catedral (Cathedral)
- Basílica de Santa Teresa (Basilica of St. Theresa)
- Capitolio Nacional (National Capitol)
- Casa Natal de El Libertador, Museo Bolívar (Birthplace and Museum of Simon Bolívar)
- Iglesia de San Francisco (Church of St. Francis)
- Museo de Arte Colonial (Colonial Art Museum)
- Concejo Municipal (City Hall)
- Paseo Los Próceres
- El Avila (Avila Peak)

For those who are serious about fitness, Carnival Cruise Lines' *Carnival Destiny*, the first cruise ship to top 100,000 gross registered tons, has a two-level, 15,000-square-foot spa.

Bests

Lorraine Arzt
Property Management and Investments, Joachim J. Arzt Inc.

Cruising is unique in that the staff aboard the ships are so diversified that the experience and knowledge from getting to know those who care for your needs is most satisfying and certainly very educating.

Every trip is different but no experience as awesome as sailing into **New York** and passing the **Statue of Liberty** at dawn's early light.

Being on deck as we sail past the glaciers in **Alaska.**

Going through the **Panama Canal**, and understanding what it took in lives lost to complete this amazing accomplishment.

We love the total cruising experience, and I think it would take many pages or perhaps a book to tell all.

Dr. Martin Feldman
Vice President of Marketing, Daniel Products Company

A cruise lets the honeymoon continue—assuming, of course, you had a good time on your honey-moon, even if it was 33 years ago. Our latest cruise was north to **Alaska** on the **Princess Cruise Lines.**

Two side trips (out of many offered) I would strongly recommend for an Alaskan cruise: the helicopter flight and glacier landing (in **Juneau**), and the combination river rafting and flightseeing excursion out of **Skagway.** Each of these trips gives you a different perspective of the terrain and the glaciers.

On the second of these, you're flown from Skagway to **Haines,** Alaska (20 minutes), then bused upstream where you don rubber boots, knit caps, and take off in rubber rafts (10 to 12 people per raft) down a glacial river (no white water, relatively shallow), through the bald eagle preserve. It was a marvelous experience, lasting one and half hours. We saw twenty-plus eagles, and actually floated directly beneath one 15 feet above us.

The flightseeing is incredible. You're flown over and around seven or eight different glaciers in this incredible wilderness setting. Each scene is better than the previous one. Then back to Skagway and your ship.

Cicely and Lew Lawson
Passengers, Royal Cruise Line

Pleasures of cruising:

Stepping on board a cruise ship before an ocean voyage and being greeted by the stewards.

Any time a ship sails out of a port, but especially when the whole **Atlantic** or **Pacific** is in front of you—with many days to enjoy the amenities of your floating hotel.

A port/country/continent that is totally new.

To experience high summer when it is winter at home.

To unpack once.

Bob Clampett
Editor, *Vacationer Magazine;* Writer, Author, Screenwriter

A return to the sea is a homecoming, free of distractions and soothing to the soul. Wherever the destination, ports of call offer intrigue, zest, and mischief.

To enhance any trip on board, bring along any of the marvelous Aubrey-Maturin series of sea tales by the master, Patrick O'Brien.

Antarctica

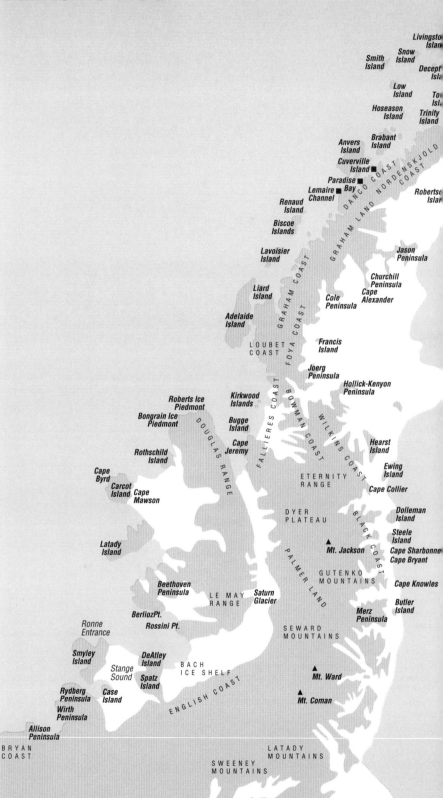

Livingston
Island
Smith   Snow
Island   Island
                              Deception
                              Island
               Low
               Island   To
                                           Isla
        Hoseason
        Island   Trinity
                                   Island
                   Brabant
        Anvers   Island
        Island
        Cuverville
        Island ■
                          Paradise
        Lemaire Bay
        Channel
                                                    Robertson
Renaud   Island
Island

Biscoe   Jason
Islands   Peninsula

Lavoisier   Churchill
Island   Peninsula
                                  Cape
                          Cole   Alexander
        Liard   Peninsula
        Island

Adelaide
Island   Francis
                          Island
LOUBET
COAST   Joerg
                     Peninsula   Hollick-Kenyon
                                   Peninsula
           Kirkwood
           Islands
Roberts Ice
Piedmont   Hearst
Bongrain Ice   Bugge   Island
Piedmont   Island
                                                  Ewing
           Cape   Island
Rothschild Jeremy   Cape Collier
Island
                              ETERNITY
Cape   RANGE   Dolleman
Byrd   Island
Carcot   Cape   DYER
Island   Mawson   PLATEAU   Steele
                                                  Island
                                ▲ Mt. Jackson   Cape Sharbonne
Latady   Cape Bryant
Island

                GUTENKO   Cape Knowles
                MOUNTAINS
Beethoven
Peninsula LE MAY   Saturn   Merz   Butler
           RANGE   Glacier   Peninsula Island
BerliozPt.
           Rossini Pt.   SEWARD
Ronne   MOUNTAINS
Entrance
Smyley
Island   DeAtley
           Island   BACH
Stange   ICE SHELF   ▲ Mt. Ward
Sound   Spatz
Rydberg   Island
Peninsula Case   ▲ Mt. Coman
Wirth   Island   ENGLISH COAST
Peninsula
Allison
Peninsula
BRYAN   LATADY
COAST   MOUNTAINS
              SWEENEY
              MOUNTAINS

Elephant
Island

Clarence
Island

King George
Island

Nelson
Island

South Orkney
Islands

Bransfield Strait

Joinville
Island

Hope
Bay ■ Dundee
Island

Vega
Island

Paulet
Island

James Ross
Island Seymour
Island

Snow Hill
Island

Weddell Sea

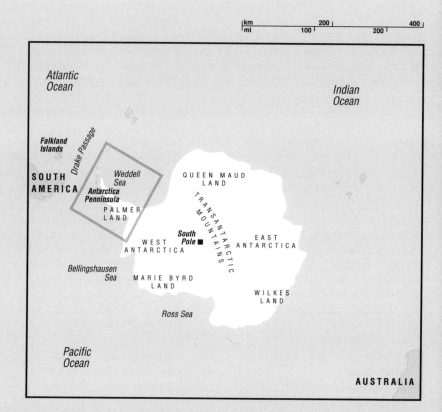

km		200		400
mi	100		200	

Atlantic
Ocean

Indian
Ocean

Falkland
Islands

Drake Passage

Weddell
Sea

QUEEN MAUD
LAND

SOUTH
AMERICA

Antarctica
Penninsula

PALMER
LAND

TRANSANTARCTIC
MOUNTAINS

WEST
ANTARCTICA

South
Pole ■

EAST
ANTARCTICA

Bellingshausen
Sea

MARIE BYRD
LAND

WILKES
LAND

Ross Sea

Pacific
Ocean

AUSTRALIA

Antarctica

This continental land mass of nearly 5.5 million square miles—covered by an ice cap several thousands of feet thick—has only been explored in the last two centuries. Captain James Cook was the first to attempt a scientific exploration of **Terra Australis Incognita** (Unknown Southern Land) in 1773, but he believed the whole area to be a frozen ocean. The mainland was probably first "sighted" in 1820 by an American sea captain, Nathaniel Palmer. Other famed adventurers made subsequent expeditions—Englishmen James Weddell and Robert Scott, Norwegian Roald Amundsen, and American Richard Byrd. Many nations have staked territorial claims to Antarctica over the years, which led to the signing of the Antarctic Treaty in 1959. Under the provisions of this international agreement, Antarctica is to be used only as a special reserve dedicated to peace and science. The Protocol on Environmental Protection to the Antarctic Treaty, signed in 1991, prohibits any mining activity on the continent for at least 50 years. Today more than 40 permanent research stations belonging to nearly 20 different countries conduct scientific investigations south of the 60° latitude.

Today the "Great White Continent" is a unique destination for those wanting to experience the frozen beauty and extraordinary marine life of the earth's lowest latitudes. Visitors will be treated to an array of icebergs that, like clouds, begin to take on shapes and character when looked at long enough. Lichens are the only form of plant life in this barren environment; they grow on ice-free land and exposed rock faces. Antarctica is, however, rich in wildlife. Inhabitants include a wide variety of marine mammals, including whales (blue, fin, humpback, minke, orca, sei, and sperm), dolphins (dusky and hourglass), and seals (crabeater, elephant, fur, leopard, Ross, and Weddell). Birds are also abundant here: sea birds (cormorant, gull, petrel, sheathbill, skua, and tern) and, of course, penguins (Adélie, emperor, Gentoo, king, and rock hopper).

Controlled growth of the number of ships and passengers forging south is an important factor in maintaining the area's integrity and delicate ecosystem. To that end, the International Association of Antarctica Tour Operators has a set of guidelines to minimize visitors' impact. Tourists may not disturb, harass, or interfere with the wildlife; walk on or otherwise damage plants; leave litter; or take anything that may be of historical or scientific value.

The Antarctic cruise season runs from November through early March. In general, operators offering cruises to Antarctica employ smaller, "expedition"-type vessels with reinforced hulls that can plough through icy seas; maintain a flexible itinerary to accommodate quickly changing weather conditions; and utilize a fleet of Zodiac inflatable rafts for scouting shorelines, cruising the face of an iceberg, and transporting passengers ashore. Most vessels have experienced naturalists and scientists on board who offer lectures and assistance with off-ship exploration.

A word of warning: Antarctica is not an easy travel destination. Although operators do everything possible to make modern-day Antarctic exploration as comfortable as possible, passengers should be prepared for wet, cold, and windy weather and a two-day crossing of the often-storm-tossed **Drake Passage**. In addition, a certain amount of agility and mobility is required in order to negotiate in and out of the inflatable rafts and across icy surfaces.

- Cuverville Island
- King George Island
- Hope Bay
- Paradise Bay
- Deception Island
- Lemaire Channel
- Paulet Island
- Petermann Island
- Gerlache Strait
- Neumayer Channel

Behind the Scenes on a Cruise Ship

Cruise ships are sometimes called floating hotels or floating resorts, but they're really more like cities at sea. Beneath the passenger decks and beyond those mysterious doors marked "Crew Only" lie the inner workings of a world that exists purely to serve the guests.

A Seagoing Pantry

One of the largest and most important backstage areas on a ship is the provisions department, where room after room of foodstuffs are stored—refrigerated produce, dairy products, frozen and fresh (sometimes live) seafood, meat lockers, canned and packaged items, and cooking ingredients. This is also where soft drinks, wines, and liquors are kept. The enormous provisions area, usually located below the passenger and crew decks, also contains storage rooms for fresh flowers, dry goods, paper, cleaning products, and other supplies. The butcher may have his headquarters here as well.

Provisions planning is a science. To ensure freshness, foods must be stored at the proper temperature and in the right combinations. Computerized inventories keep track of thousands of items.

When a shipboard department needs something, it's ordered through the provisions master who, in turn, places orders for goods with shoreside offices. In port, goods are loaded onto the ship through huge hatches, usually aboard pallets. Once inside, they're scooped up by forklifts and whisked to their proper storage area.

A Place for Everything

Another below-decks department is the ship's laundry. Here, a massive amount of clothing and linen is primped and pressed, 24 hours a day. The laundry washes or dry cleans and irons crew uniforms, dining room linen, sheets, pillowcases, and towels, towels, towels—used by crew and passengers in their staterooms, at the pool, and in the gym, the beauty salon, and massage rooms. On some cruise lines passengers can arrange for their clothing to be dry cleaned and laundered (usually at an additional charge).

Few seagoing travelers realize that many ships run a full-scale print shop, which churns out menus, wine lists, daily programs, notices, party invitations, and office forms. Also behind the scenes are photographers' darkrooms where passengers' rolls of film are processed, along with the thousands of pictures snapped by the ship's professionals.

There are also rooms for storing stage scenery, costumes, and musical instruments, as well as dressing areas for the performers and lighting and sound booths. The engine room and engine control room (which contains computer equipment and monitors) are also among a ship's "Crew Only" sectors.

Space for Staffers, Too

Crew and officer accommodations also take up a lot of space on cruise ships, some of which have crew-to-passenger ratios as high as 2 to 1. Officers usually get their own cabins with private baths, but most of the rank-and-file crew share accommodations and have to walk down the hall to shower in a communal bathroom.

There are offices for the crew purser, who handles pay, and the crew steward, who supervises food and accommodations. In addition, the crew members have their own cafeterias, day rooms, a crew bar, a crew store (called the "slop chest"), and sometimes a dipping pool, sundeck, and gym.

While a job on a cruise ship may sound cushy, it's not. Crew members work seven days a week and have contracts that usually stretch six months without a break. Very often they don't have time to go ashore in port. To compensate, vacation ashore (unpaid) lasts about two months. Some officers have contracts allowing four months on followed by two months off.

While senior officers may host tables in the passenger dining room and enjoy privileges like attending shows and socializing in public, junior officers often are restricted in their access to passenger areas. And crew members, when off duty, must stick to the crew zones, living in the other world that exists right alongside the passenger's world aboard ship.

MICHAEL STORRINGS

Northern Europe

ICELAND
• Reykjavík

Norwegian Sea

North Atlantic Ocean

• Aberdeen

SCOTLAND

Glasgow
• • Edinburgh

North Sea

NORTHERN
IRELAND

Belfast •

ENGLAND

IRELAND

Irish Sea

Dublin •

Liverpool • • Leeds
Manchester

Cork •

WALES

Amsterdam

The Hague

• Birmingham

Celtic Sea

London •

Rotterdam

Antwerp
BELGIUM

Southampton •

English Channel

Brussels

Bay of Biscay

• Rouen

• Brest

• Paris

Rennes •

Le Mans •

• Orléans

• Nantes

FRANCE

Dijon

Limoges •

Lyon

Clermont-
Ferrand

• Bordeaux

N

| km | | 400 | | 800 |
| mi | 200 | | 400 | |

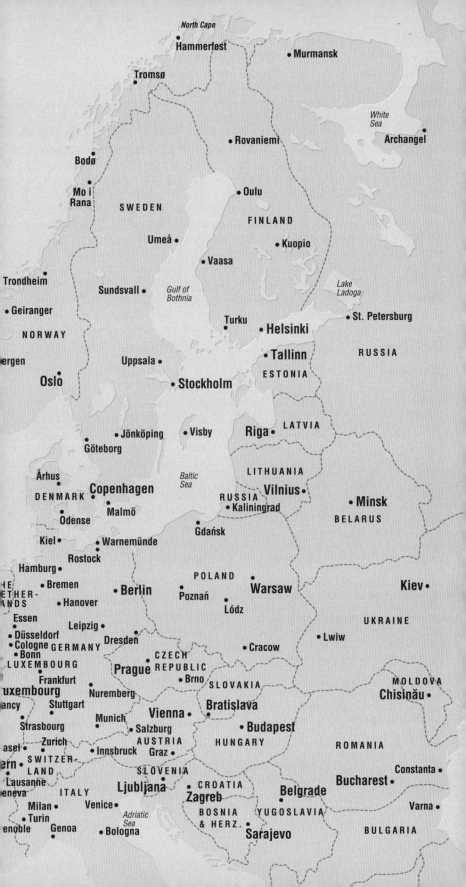

Northern Europe

Touching the American continents to the west and Europe and Africa to the east, the **Atlantic** is second-largest of the earth's oceans, covering about 32 million square miles. For centuries it was the only link between the Old World and New. Most passengers today make the crossing by plane, though many travel by cruise ship to experience this vast ocean, which continues to carry the greatest portion of world shipping.

An arm of the Atlantic Ocean, Northern Europe's **Baltic Sea** borders pristine, fjord-dented **Scandinavia—Sweden, Denmark, Finland,** and also **Norway—** lands of the Midnight Sun whose brave and ferocious Vikings ruled the seas for so long. It also washes up along the coasts of modern-day **Germany, Russia, Poland, Latvia, Lithuania,** and **Estonia,** whose borders continue to shift as history unfolds. Many of these northern European cities were once linked by the powerful 13th-century Hanseatic League. The group's ancient trade routes are today retraced by cruise ships—from megaships to elegant yachtlike vessels—on a wide variety of itineraries packed with lovely harbors, history, culture, and Old World appeal. Fascinating destinations in Norway, **Belgium, The Netherlands, England,** and **Scotland** are found on the **North Sea;** while a cruise along the western shores of the **Irish Sea** introduces the traveler to that mystical, charming Emerald Isle.

Belgium

Antwerp

This city of a half-million inhabitants once was home to Peter Paul Rubens; today it is the world's diamond trade center and boasts the first skyscraper to go up on the Continent. Located along the **River Schelde** 60 miles from the North Sea, Antwerp is one of Europe's largest ports. Its local name, "Antwerpen," is based on the legend immortalized in the *Brabo* statue. Exacting a heavy toll from river boatmen passing his castle, the giant who lived there cut off the hand of anyone who refused payment. To the rescue came Roman soldier Sylvius Brabo, who slew the thug, chopped off its hand, and chucked it into the river; hence the name "hand-werpen," meaning "to throw the hand." Another, less creative, interpretation is suggested by the promontory, or *aanwerp,* reaching into the river, where an early settlement was established. Not far from that site a few centuries later, Charles V built the **Steen Castle,** a city stronghold from the 10th through 16th centuries. The **Steen** was restored in the 1800s and now houses a museum that chronicles the country's history as a seagoing nation.

Antwerp's golden age is well preserved in **Old Town's** narrow alleys and passageways. The first European stock exchange was established here in 1531, and by midcentury Antwerp was the leading port in Europe and one of the richest cities in the world. It also was the center of the great school of Flemish painting. Artists like Bruegel, Rubens, and Van Dyck worked here, and this is where Christopher Plantin set up his great printing press. In addition to dealing in diamonds, today's Belgians are masters of lace and tapestry crafts, as well as artisans in glassware, crystal, and pewter.

A local culinary treat is *paling in het groen* (stewed eel in chervil sauce), a dish that may or may not tempt you. It's impossible, though, to pass up the waffle stands and chocolate shops. Shrimp and mussels also are popular, along with Belgian fries served with a glop of mayonnaise.

- Rubenshuis (Rubens' House)
- Koninklijk Museum voor Schone Kunsten (Royal Museum of Fine Arts)
- National Maritime Museum (Steen)
- Diamond Museum
- Kathedraal (Cathedral)
- Groenplaats (Green Plaza)
- Plantin Moretus Museum
- Grote Markt
- Middelheim
- Brussels

Denmark

Copenhagen

"Wonderful, wonderful Copenhagen," goes the song Danny Kaye made popular about this fairytale-tinged city of cobblestone streets, colorful stuccoed houses, and green copper roofs. It was the home of Hans Christian Andersen, and today his *Little Mermaid* statue continues to delight residents and visitors alike.

Copenhagen started out as a 12th-century fishing village called "Havn" (harbor). Located between the **Baltic** and **North Seas** along medieval Europe's main trading routes, it became an important port and commercial center, changing its name to "Køpmannæhafn" (merchants' harbor) in 1170. Under the 1397 Treaty of Kalmar, Denmark united with its former enemy Norway and later with Sweden, and in the 15th century Copenhagen became the capital of the new kingdom; its position as Denmark's cultural center grew with the founding of its university. The city expanded greatly under King Christian IV (1588-1648), whose passion for building left lasting royal landmarks. The city was severely damaged by two 18th-century fires and was shelled by the British fleet during the Napoleonic Wars in 1801 and 1807. Neutral during World War I, Denmark was occupied by Germany during World War II.

Midmorning coffee is a Danish ritual, although by that time of day most Danes already prefer a glass of Carlsberg or Tuborg beer. Oddly, Danish pastry here is called *Wienerbrød* (Viennese pastry). Herring is high on the menu, served pickled, marinated in wine or sour cream, or fried; and in the summer, *danske rejer* (baby shrimp) are piled high on white bread with mayonnaise, one of the 178 varieties of *smørrebrød* (open sandwiches). Cherry Heering is Denmark's famous cherry liqueur. The country that gave us Lego and Bang and Olufsen is also known for Royal Copenhagen porcelain, Nordic knitware, Georg Jensen silver, and wooden toys. Those items can be found along **Strøget**, the main pedestrian and shopping thoroughfare that started out as a footpath 900 years ago.

- Rosenborg Slot (Rosenborg Palace)
- Runde Taarn (The Round Tower)
- Børse (Stock Exchange)
- Kastellet (Citadel)
- Den Lille Havfrue (Little Mermaid)
- Amalienborg Palace
- Nyhavn (New Harbor)
- Christiansborg Castle
- Ny Carlsberg Glyptotek (Glyptotek Museum)
- Tivoli Gardens

England

Southampton

Situated in a sheltered estuary, protected by the **Isle of Wight** from the choppy waters of the **English Channel**, Southampton has served as a gateway to England since Roman times. Its particular layout of land and sea, combined with unique double tides, provided a perfect harbor for pre–steam era sailing ships. Once Europe's largest port, Southampton has been the staging point for naval battles and shipbuilding activity throughout British history. The Mayflower sailed from Southampton in 1620, carrying pilgrim colonists from Plymouth to Cape Cod Bay. And in 1912 the unsinkable *Titanic* sank on her maiden voyage from here. In the 19th and 20th centuries, Southampton became a major terminus for colonial and transatlantic shipping, and remains the home port today for the likes of the legendary ocean liner *Queen Elizabeth 2*. Like London, Southampton suffered through German bombing during World War II, but British air supremacy over southern England prevented an invasion of any sort.

Southampton is noted for its parks and gardens, and it also is a gateway to the lovely surrounding countryside, including the nearby forests that were once the hunting ground of Norman kings. Much of the city's arcaded medieval wall is still intact, and Southampton is also within reach of ancient monuments and historic cities, including one-time capital of England **Winchester** with its monumental cathedral, and that mysterious, Neolithic-era circle of stones.

Fish and chips, made with cod or plaice, battered, fried, doused with vinegar, and served wrapped in newsprint, is as local as dining gets. Traditional English dishes such as steak and kidney pie, roast beef and Yorkshire pudding, and sticky desserts are also in abundance here. Shoppers will find china and glass with names like Wedgwood, Royal Doulton, and Spode, along with antiques, textiles, and pottery.

- Bargate and History Museum
- Tudor House Museum
- Maritime Museum
- God's House Tower
- Wilton House
- Salisbury Cathedral
- Winchester Cathedral
- New Forest
- Roman Palace at Fishburne
- Stonehenge

Stonehenge

Estonia

Tallinn

The first written reference to Tallinn, Estonia's capital situated between two promontories poking into the **Gulf of Finland**, appeared in the 12th century on Arab maps and charts. Since then Estonia, the northernmost of the three countries on the **Baltic Sea**'s eastern shores, has struggled to maintain its independence in the face of its larger neighbors' imperialist appetites—first Denmark, then Sweden, and finally Russia.

In 1219 the Danes built a castle on the hill that dominates the city. German traders arrived, and the city became a thriving member of the powerful Hanseatic League, trading furs, leather, and seal fat. German knights, along with the bishops, resided up on the hill, while merchants and artisans lived in the walled **Lower Town**, with its narrow cobblestone streets, churches with graceful spires, and merchants' houses and towers with red-tile roofs—today one of the best-preserved medieval towns in northern Europe. The city's fortunes sank into decline as neighboring Sweden, Russia, Poland, and Lithuania fought to carve up the region, with Sweden ruling Tallinn in the 16th and 17th centuries, and Russia controlling it thereafter. Estonia became independent from the former Soviet Union in 1991. Native Estonians are closely linked, both linguistically and culturally, to their Finnish neighbors 50 miles across the gulf, although about 40 percent of the half-million people living in Tallinn are of Russian and Ukrainian descent.

Most local meals start with *seljanka*, a rich meat broth. *Forrell* is smoked trout, usually served with fried bread.

- Toompea
- Raekoja plats (Town Hall Square)
- Linnamuuseum (City Museum)
- Dominiiklaste Klooster (Dominican Monastery)
- Raeapteek (Town Council Pharmacy)
- Pühavaimu Kirik (Holy Spirit Church) and Saia Käik (White Bread Passage)
- Meremuuseum (Maritime Museum)
- Kiek in de Kök (Peek in the Kitchen)
- Tarbekunstimuuseum (Applied Art Museum)
- Kadriorg Park and Palace

The names of all Holland America Line cruise ships end in "dam," following a tradition dating from the company's founding in 1873. The suffix refers to the dams that cross Dutch rivers. The *Maasdam*, for example, is named for the dam on the Maas River. The *Veendam* bears the name of a town in northern Holland where houses were once built with "veen," the Dutch word for peat.

Finland

Helsinki

Although Helsinki's population is only around 600,000, it is one of the most world's most sophisticated capitals. With its carefully planned arrangement of Neo-Classical architecture, Helsinki is graced with many green parks containing some of Finland's outstanding sculptures.

The "Daughter of the Baltic," as the city calls itself, grew up around its harbor to become Finland's commercial and cultural center. Originally founded in 1550 as a small Swedish fishing village called "Helsingfors," Helsinki was frequently a battleground for Sweden and Russia in their long struggle for Finland. Over the years, epidemics, fires, and famine took their toll on the Finnish population. Czar Alexander I moved the Finnish capital from Turku to Helsinki in 1812 and chose German-born architect **Carl Ludwig Engel** to rebuild the city, whose center had been razed by a great fire in 1808. Attempts to "russify" Finland from 1899 to 1917 provoked great popular resistance, and with the fall of the tsarist regime and ensuing Revolution in 1917, Finland declared its independence. Almost immediately thereafter it began a fierce civil war. Although it allied itself with Germany during World War II, Finland has been absolutely neutral ever since.

Finland's history can be savored in its food: From the Scandinavians comes the ubiquitous herring, prepared in traditional ways; from the Samis (Lapps), *poro* (reindeer), served in a cream sauce or smoked; the Russians left their borscht and blinis. *Kahvi* (coffee) is practically the national drink. *Lakka* is a locally produced liqueur made from Arctic cloudberries. On elegant boulevards and in charming markets, shoppers can delight in the Finnish mastery of graphic and industrial design apparent in Marimekko fabrics and in local ceramics and glassware.

- Kauppatori (Market Square)
- Senaatintori (Senate Square)
- Tuomiokirkko (Lutheran Cathedral)
- Kansallismuseo (National Museum)
- Temppeliaukion (Rock Church)
- Helsingin kaupunginmuseo (Helsinki Museum)
- Ateneum (Atheneum Art Museum)
- Esplanadi
- Sibeliuksen puisto (Sibelius Park and Monument)
- Suomenlinna (Fortress of Finland)

France

Bordeaux

Mention of the word "Bordeaux" brings to mind some of the finest wines in the world. The city itself was known as **Burdigala** when it was founded in the third century BC by the Romans, who brought along their grapevines. Bordeaux prospered under later rule by the English, whose fondness for the region's reds (known as claret across the Channel), gave impetus to the local wine industry, which remains the region's most important.

Situated along the **Garonne River,** Bordeaux (population including suburbs is 700,000 people) is a repository of some of the finest 18th-century architecture outside of Paris. It is a city of broad boulevards, parks, museums, monuments, and impressive municipal buildings, thanks largely to Louis XV, who anticipated Bordeaux's rise in commercial and strategic importance and assigned to the region special governors (*intendants*), who imposed a definite Parisian look on the face of the city. Bordeaux is surrounded, naturally, by vineyards, and the name, to most, connotes a region known by a litany of wine labels of renowned chateaux— Margaux, Mouton-Rothschild, Yquem. A 30-minute drive northwest takes visitors to the heart of **Médoc,** known for aristocratic red wines. Forty-five minutes to the east is the medieval village of **St-Emilion,** whose fine red wines can overshadow the charms of the town itself. To the south of Bordeaux (actually in the southern suburbs) are the red and dry whites of **Graves,** while still farther southeast are the fine, sweet wines of **Sauternes** and **Barsac.**

It is said that Bordeaux is the only city where food is chosen to accompany wine. But the regional cuisine can hold its own with local specialties like bordelaise sauce made with red wine, shallots, and beef marrow served over entrecôte steaks. *Cèpes* (wild mushrooms), or *lamproie* (lamprey eels), duck, and foie gras are also popular. Most shoppers head for **Rue Ste-Catherine**, with its many boutiques. Fine wines can be bought here, but it is advisable to ship cases of wine directly from vineyards, if possible.

- **Esplanade des Quinconces (Quinconces Esplanade)**
- **Place de la Comédie (Comedy Square) and Grand Théâtre (Grand Theatre)**

- **Jardin Public (Public Gardens)**
- **Place de la Bourse (Stock Market Square)**
- **Quartier St-Pierre (St. Pierre Quarter)**
- **Cathédrale St-André (St. Andrew Cathedral) and Tour Pey-Berland (Pey-Berland Tower)**
- **Musée des Beaux-Arts (Museum of Fine Arts)**
- **Musée des Arts Décoratifs (Museum of Decorative Arts)**
- **Porte Dijeaux (Dijeaux Gate) and Place Gambetta (Gambetta Square)**
- **Musée du Vin (Wine Museum)**

Germany

Berlin (Warnemünde)

Established around 1200 by fishermen and traders, Berlin became an important center in the Brandenburg Province by the 15th century; the ruling Hohenzollern family made it their official seat in 1470. Despite subsequent occupation, conflagration, and decimation by epidemic, the city prospered, evolving into a trading and manufacturing center where arts, sciences, and large-scale building flourished. A city once compared to Paris, Berlin lay in ruins after World War II; in 1949 it was divided into East and West Berlin. The capitalist western side prospered while its eastern counterpart languished under a communist economy. Unified since 1990, Berlin's east has received much help to assist it in catching up. Construction cranes litter the cityscape; the new Berlin is a building site. The German government is due to complete its move here from the present capital in Bonn at the turn of the century.

The city's rich cultural life has been the constant, even through decades of division, occupation, and radical change, with theaters, opera, and a couple of world-class orchestras. The city of 3.5 million on the **Spree River** never seems to rest, leading many observers to compare Berliners with New Yorkers: brash and brassy, rushed, and renowned for their searing wit and high energy. Sprawling across 342

Brandenburg Gate, Berlin

square miles, Berlin is one of Europe's largest cities, a place of broad boulevards, gardens and parks, and monumental buildings: museums, exhibition halls, stadiums, and opera houses. Portions remain of the wall that cut the city in two on 13 August 1961, a literal and figurative scar since it was dismantled in 1989. The infamous Checkpoint Charlie connecting East with West has since been relegated to museum status.

In addition to the favorite afternoon pastime of *kaffee und kuchen* (coffee and cake), traditional Berlin fare includes *bulette* (a version of the hamburger) with potato salad, a *schrippe* (hard roll), and *rote grütze* (a stew of berries and cherries served with a vanilla custard sauce). A *Berliner* is a jelly doughnut. The **Kurfürstendamm**, universally known as the "Ku'damm," is the main commercial center. Best buys there include cameras, optical goods, china, porcelain, toys, cutlery, and clocks.

- ■ The Wall
- ■ Brandenburg Gate
- ■ Reichstag
- ■ Alte Bibliothek (Old Library)
- ■ Museumsinsel (Museum Island)
- ■ Museum Haus am Checkpoint Charlie
- ■ Unter den Linden and Berliner Dom
- ■ New Synagogue
- ■ Schloss Charlottenburg (Charlottenburg Castle)
- ■ Tiergarten
- ■ Neue Wache (Monument to Victims of Fascism and Militarism)

Hamburg

Hammaburg Fortress was built in the ninth century by Emperor Charlemagne to defend against barbarian attacks and in the Middle Ages the site became a center for the Catholic Church and international trade. In 1189, Frederick Barbarossa granted the city a charter as a free city and port, exempting its ships from paying duty. Hamburg, co-founder in the 13th century of the Hanseatic League, an association of cities that reached as far as Scandinavia and Russia, prospered and grew, evolving into the region's most powerful commercial entity. In the 16th century Hamburg became a cosmopolitan home for English clothiers who had been tossed out of Antwerp, Dutch Protestants fleeing the Spanish, and Jews escaping from Portugal. Hamburg was recognized as an independent city-state in 1618.

Hamburgers always have been extremely proud people. Their home was the birthplace of Brahms and Mendelssohn and today boasts swanky, modern shopping promenades, luxurious lake-studded parks, and dignified museums. For less dignified but perhaps no less popular pursuits, the city also contains a world-infamous **Red Light District**, whose most notable street is the **Reeperbahn**. Pronounced "raper-barn'", it is in fact named for the rope-makers who used to inhabit this once-respectable **St. Pauli**

neighborhood. Germany's largest seaport and second-largest city (after Berlin), Hamburg was all but flattened in Allied bombing raids during World War II. It has rebuilt itself into an elegant and sophisticated metropolis, with the copper-roofed brick architecture so characteristic of northern Germany blending effortlessly with more contemporary buildings. Its port on the **Elbe River**, 70 miles from the North Sea, is one of Europe's largest and continues to grow.

Kaffee und kuchen are served at the **Alsterpavillon** jutting out over the lake. *Aalsuppe* is the local specialty—a sweet-and-sour eel soup made with leeks, carrots, dumplings, dried apricots, prunes, and apples, spiced with sage, thyme, and coriander. German porcelain, cutlery, cameras, optics, and linens can be found in the boutiques around the **Binnenalster**.

- ■ Altstadt (Old Town) and Rathaus (Town Hall)
- ■ Planten un Blomen (Botanical Gardens)
- ■ St. Pauli Fischmarkt (St. Pauli Fishmarket)
- ■ Hamburger Kunsthalle (Art Museum)
- ■ St. Michaeliskirche (St. Michael's Church)
- ■ Museum für Hamburgische Geschichte (Museum of Hamburg History)
- ■ Aussenalster
- ■ Museum für Kunst und Gewerbe (Decorative Arts Museum)
- ■ St. Jakobikirche (St. Jacob's Church)
- ■ Krameramtsstuben (Historic Widows' Quarters)

Iceland

Reykjavík

Studded with steaming geysers, magnificent waterfalls, ancient glaciers, and breathtaking fjords, Iceland is stunning in its primitive beauty. This volcanic island bordering the Arctic Circle is one of the youngest land formations on earth and is still evolving.

Discovered over a thousand years ago by Viking explorers from Norway and Britain, this North Atlantic country is also the oldest republic in the world. Its tradition of democratic government dates back to AD 930 when Iceland established the world's oldest parliament. Ruled by Norwegians from 1262 and the Danes from 1380, Iceland has been independent since 1944.

Icelanders, who number fewer than 300,000, are a hearty mixture of Nordic and Celtic stock with a language, developed from Old Norse, that has changed little over the centuries. One of the world's most literate populations, the country has a rich literary tradition of heroic medieval sagas and poems that are still read by the people today. Perhaps Iceland's most famous citizen was explorer Leif Eriksson, the first European to find North America.

Sometimes called the planet's northernmost metropolis, Reykjavík, which means "Smoky Bay," was first settled by Ingólf Arnarson in 874. What Arnarson saw was actually steam generated from geothermal activity, which, along with hydroelectric power, makes Reykjavik one of the cleanest capitals in the world. Despite its chilly name, Iceland enjoys a relatively temperate climate, due to the North Atlantic Drift's warm currents.

Iceland's clear coastal waters produce deliciously fresh lobster, oysters, and cod, while its chilly rivers yield exceptional trout, salmon, and alpine char. Sheep are raised on its lush green pastures; smoked leg of lamb is a delicacy. Icelandic woolens, with their distinctive designs, make wonderfully warm souvenirs.

- Hallgrímskirkja (Hallgrim's Church)
- Ásmundur Sveinsson Gallery
- Althing (Parliament)
- National Museum and Art Gallery
- Hvalfjördur
- Gullfoss
- Geysir
- The Blue Lagoon
- Thingvellir National Park
- Akranes fishing village

Ireland

Dublin

Just over 50 miles from Britain across the **Irish Sea**, the magical hills and lakes of Ireland for centuries formed the mysterious western fringe of the known world and have been a haven for hermits, rebels, and adventurers. The island, originally inhabited by a short, dark-haired people who migrated from the Mediterranean during the Stone Age, endured wave after wave of invasions by the Celts, Norse, Normans, and English. Ireland's glory days are rooted in the Celtic culture of the Dark Ages, when St. Patrick introduced Christianity, produced superb works of art, and sent religious and cultural missionaries across Europe. The Vikings ravaged the island in the 9th and 10th centuries, followed by the Anglo-Normans in 1167, beginning a long effort at angli-cizing the country, which later led to the separatism of the "six counties." By 1821, Ireland had the highest population density in Europe, leading to food shortages, with millions subsisting on nothing but potatoes. The potato famine of 1845-49 caused widespread starvation, resulting in the migration of more than one million Irish to America, Great Britain, and Australia. A cycle of repression and rebellion of several centuries came to an end when the Republic of Ireland was finally established in 1948.

The name "Dublin" comes from the Irish *dubhlinn* (dark pool). It is also called "Baile Atha Cliath" (the town of the hurdle ford), referring to its selection

centuries ago as a site to cross the **River Liffey** near its exit to the Irish Sea. A city of magnificent Georgian architecture and a lively art and culture scene, Dublin also boasts a remarkable literary tradition. Relative to its size, the Emerald Isle has produced more literary genius than any other country—W. B. Yeats, Jonathan Swift, Oscar Wilde, James Joyce, Bram Stoker, George Bernard Shaw, and Samuel Beckett, among others.

Dublin's menus are stocked with seafood, especially sole, shrimp, and salmon, along with Dublin Coddle, a stew of bacon, sausages, and onions. The Irish drink nearly 500 million pints of beer a year, mostly the creamy dark brown Guinness Stout. Aran sweaters, tweeds, lace, Waterford crystal, and smoked salmon and Irish whiskey are good buys. **DESIGNyard** in the trendy **Temple Bar** district is a converted 19th-century warehouse containing contemporary Irish jewelry, ceramics, glass, furniture, and textiles.

- National Museum and Library
- Dublin Castle
- Dublin Writers Museum and James Joyce Center
- St. Stephen's Green
- Trinity College and Old Library
- Dublin Civic Museum
- Kilmainham Jail
- National Gallery and Merrion Square
- Christ Church and Dublinia
- St. Patrick's Cathedral

Copenhagen really puts out the welcome mat for cruise ship passengers. Since 1993, the Danish capital has operated a hospitality lounge for the exclusive use of travelers who arrive by cruise ship. Visitors can get tips about sightseeing and shopping, leave their parcels for safekeeping, read newspapers and magazines from back home, and enjoy complimentary coffee and snacks. Copenhagen Cruise Lounge is located up-stairs in the Royal Copenhagen House at 6 Amagertorv on Strøget, the pedestrian street. It's open Monday through Saturday whenever cruise ships are in port.

Norwegian Cruise Line is the official cruise line of the National Basketball Association and the National Football League Players Association. Every year, more than 100 professional athletes, Hall of Famers, coaches, and umpires sail on the line's "Sports Afloat" theme cruises, mingling with passengers during demonstrations, workshops, competitions, and autograph sessions.

Netherlands

Amsterdam

Founded as the medieval fishing village **Amstelledamme,** whose inhabitants built a dam to prevent flooding from the **Amstel** and **IJ Rivers,** Amsterdam eventually became a place of Christian pilgrimage and haven for victims of the Spanish Inquisition during the Middle Ages. Already famed for its religious tolerance and cultural life, the city really sprang into full flower in the 17th century, when Rembrandt painted, and the Dutch East Indies Company expanded into a powerful commercial monopoly, establishing trading posts throughout the Far East, Africa, and Australia. Amsterdam and the Netherlands have been independent since 1578; though they were annexed by Napoleon in 1795 and occupied by Germany during World War II.

Today Amsterdam, with a population of 725,000, is Europe's fourth-largest financial center. Despite its modern-day eye for business, however, it is still full of Old World charm and graciousness. Part of that style has to do with its waterways. Amsterdam has 165 canals—more than Venice—spanned by 1,281 bridges. Four main concentric canals ring the city in horseshoe fashion from the IJ River. **Singel** was once the city's fortified boundary. From Singel the town spread outwards in the early 1600s to **Herengracht,** where the wealthiest merchants lived during the Golden Age. **Keizersgracht,** named after Holy Roman Emperor Maximilian, is followed by **Prinsengracht,** where many warehouses remain as they were built, hoisting beams lifting goods from cobbled streets past a series of wooden doorways. Some of these are now used as shops selling Dutch cigars, diamonds, Jenever gin, Delft and Makkum pottery, silver and pewter, and tulip bulbs.

In addition to Dutch culinary specialties such as *erwtensoep* (a pea soup), many restaurants feature Indonesian food, a cuisine embraced during those colonial days. Rijsttafel is made up of dozens of small dishes of curry, satay, skewered meats and peanut sauce, pickled cabbage, raisins and nuts, shrimp chips, coconut, fried bananas, and spicy fish-paste sauces called *sambal.*

- Vincent van Goghmuseum (Van Gogh Museum)
- Rijksmuseum (National Museum)
- Anne Frankhuis (Anne Frank House)
- Rembrandthuis (Rembrandt's House)
- Portugees Synagoge (Portuguese Synagogue)
- Bloemenmarkt (Flower Market)
- Koninklijk Paleis (Royal Palace)
- Stedelijk Museum
- Westerkerk (West Church)
- Amsterdams Historisch Museum (Amsterdam Historical Museum) and Begijnhof (Beguine Court)

Norway

Bergen

The fortunes of Norway's second-largest city, set on a peninsula surrounded by seven mountains, have always been closely linked with the sea. Founded in 1070, Bergen was the country's royal residence; several kings were crowned in the city's cathedral. For four centuries, German merchants of the powerful Hanseatic League developed the city into a major commercial center for trade with continental Europe. Their steep-roofed medieval architecture lines **Bryggen,** the harbor district declared a UNESCO World Heritage site, although over the centuries, devastating fires have several times consumed its wooden structures. Bergen's residents have done their best to restore and preserve the buildings, but none dates before 1702.

The birthplace of the composer Edvard Grieg, Bergen today is a prosperous, culturally minded city with about 220,000 inhabitants and is the administrative and commercial center of the western region. Its shipping industry, the city's biggest business for 900 years, now takes second place.

Seafood here is flopping-fresh off the dock. Salmon—smoked and fresh—halibut, and shrimp are for sale at the city's fish market. Local crafts include hand- and machine-knit sweaters, sealskin slippers, and such embroidered items as tablecloths, pillowcases, and dresses.

- Håkonshallen (Hakon's Hall) and Rosenkrantztårnet (Rosenkrantz Tower)
- Mariakirken (St. Mary's Church) and Schøtstuene (Assembly Rooms)
- Bryggen and Bryggen Museum
- Hanseatic Museum
- Fish Market
- Fløybanen up Mount Fløyen
- Historisk Museum (History Museum)
- Rasmus Meyers Samlinger (Rasmus Meyer's Collection)
- Gamle Bergen and Fantoft Stavkirke (Old Bergen and Fantoft Stave Church)
- Troldhaugen (Grieg's House)

Geiranger

It is no wonder that the word "fjord" is a Norwegian one. **Vestlandet,** Norway's west coast, is punched with literally dozens of these narrow inlets of the sea. Technically speaking, fjords are usually found along mountainous coasts, fingers of the oceans piercing their way into the rocky ridges of mountains, sometimes reaching more than a hundred miles from the sea. Deep at the head and shallow at the entrance, fjords were originally valleys dredged by the weight of advancing glaciers, then filled with water as the Ice Age ended, and sea levels soared.

*Fantoft Stavkirke
(Fantoft Stave Church), Bergen*

The epitome of Norway's fjord country, **Geirangerfjord**, a spectacular slit through towering mountains barely wide enough for passage, is one of Norway's most magnificent sights. Clusters of sod-roofed farm houses line the waterway, which is actually a branch of the **Storfjord**, with its sheer rock cliffs that reflect in glassy calm waters and white-streaked waterfalls that tumble down mountain walls hundreds of feet high. Among the best-known falls are **De Syu Søstre** (The Seven Sisters) and the brooding **Friaren** (The Suitor).

At the very tip of the fjord, Geiranger, the village that gives the fjord its name, nestles in a narrow green valley. A resort area inhabited by families who have lived on their property for centuries, the village has the feel of days both past and present. The most popular—and only—excursion here is a journey up the serpentine road above the fjord, an experience in itself, offering spectacular views. The road climbs to a lookout point, **Flydalsjuvet**, whose view back down to Geiranger and beyond has found its way onto every postcard sold in the country. Several hairpin turns later, at nearly 5,000 feet, the summit of **Dalsnibba Mountain**, poking through the clouds, provides a stunning panorama of mountains, glaciers, and lakes. It continues down the other side to a milky-blue glacial lake called **Djupvatnet**, at 3,335 feet.

North Cape

One of those extreme geographic frontiers that travelers like to add to their been-there-done-that checklists, the North Cape (Nordkapp) is nearly Europe's northernmost point, higher up on the map than Iceland, half of Greenland, and almost all of Alaska. It's found at 71°, 10", 25' north latitude, about 1,250 miles from the North Pole. Just 800 miles north of here, the sea turns to ice and travel proceeds by dogsled. To the east lie the northern reaches of mysterious Siberia. More than 100 miles south, the vast forests give way to an Arctic, sparsely forested, horizon. To the west lies an ocean once explored by Vikings, and 800 miles to the north, Svalbard is still locked in a frozen Arctic grip. Only the Gulf Stream and Midnight Sun keep Norway's coast from freezing over. Officially, the Midnight Sun occurs only north of the Arctic Circle, an area called Haalogaland, or "land of the high flame" by early Norsemen. Caused by the tilting of the earth on its axis (north toward the sun during summer in the Northern Hemisphere, away during the winter), the sun lingers above the horizon continuously at the North Cape from mid-May until the beginning of August. For the summer, at least, it is truly a land where the sun never sets.

British navigator Richard Chancellor named the North Cape in 1553 while looking for the Northeast Passage to the Orient. He failed in his quest, but found instead the northern sea route to Russia, used in Viking days. Atop the cape, which soars 1,017 feet above the sea on **Magerøya Island** ("meager island"), is a monument to King Oscar II who visited in 1873. There is also a visitors' center and restaurant where various mementos, including North Cape certificates, are for sale. Letters mailed from the North Cape are postmarked appropriately and are prized by many collectors. **Honningsvåg**, on the south side of the island, with its population of about 4,000, is the principle town, devoted to the fishing industry.

The Samis (Lapps) are skilled artisans of Arctic survival, traditionally associated with reindeer, although now that two-thirds of Norway's more than 30,000 Sami population have turned to other industries, reindeer play a less important role in Sami culture.

Oslo

Norway's commercial and administrative center, and Scandinavia's oldest capital, Oslo was founded by Viking King Harald Hardråde ("hard ruler," for his exploits as a warrior) along the **Aker River** in 1048. The sturdy medieval **Akershus Fortress**, situated on the river's strategic east bank, was built by one of his successors about 250 years later. The fort-and-castle complex was substantially expanded and renovated by various rulers over the years and with its parklike grounds is still used for royal events. Oslo was leveled by fire in 1624, then rebuilt in brick and renamed Christiania for the Danish king who ruled at the time. It got its name back in 1924. The modern-day city, home to about a half-million people, is a casual mix of architecture old and new.

Located at the head of the dramatic, 60-mile Oslo fjord filled with tiny islands dotted with summer homes, pleasure boats, and ferries, Oslo occupies a higher latitude than Juneau, Alaska. The sprawling 175-square-mile city is surrounded by farmland and packed with numerous parks and wooded areas, making it one of the least urbanized capitals in the world; it is certainly the only one with a ski jump peeking out from pine-tree slopes in plain view. **Karl Johansgate** is a favorite street for strolling and shopping for sportswear, silverware, enamelware, traditional handicrafts, pewter, glass, teak furniture, and stainless steel–crafted items.

Famous for its *smørbrød* (open-faced sandwiches) found across the country, Oslo also offers up seafood delights such as *laks* (salmon), smoked, grilled, or marinated as *gravlaks*; and *reker* (shrimp). For those with no particular affinity for Rudolph, there is *reinsdyrstek* (roasted reindeer).

- Rådhuset (City Hall)
- Akershus Slott (Akershus Castle)
- Frognerparken (Frogner Park) and Vigelandmuseet (Vigeland's Museum)
- Vikingskiphuset (Viking Ship Museum)
- Norsk Folkemusum (Norwegian Folk Museum)
- Kon-Tiki-museet (Kon-Tiki Museum)
- Fram-museet (Fram Museum)
- Munch-museet (Munch Museum)
- Nasjonalgalleriet (National Gallery)
- Holmenkollen and Ski-museet (Ski Museum)

Trondheim

Called "Nidaros" (mouth of the River Nid) when it was founded in 997 by Viking King Olav Tryggvason, Trondheim sits on a peninsula between river and fjord, about 250 miles south of the **Arctic Circle.** Norway's third-largest city, after Oslo and Bergen, Trondheim was the country's first capital and former royal and religious seat, site of Viking assemblies and courts of justice. It was formerly known as the "Royal Town" because Norwegian kings were crowned in the cathedral, which still holds the crown jewels. Built over local patron saint Olav's grave, this cathedral is Trondheim's most famous landmark and one of northern Europe's most beautiful Gothic buildings. It was completed in 1320 after a lengthy period of construction, fell into severe disrepair over the centuries, and underwent an extensive renovation in the 19th century.

The Protestant Reformation in the 16th century resulted in the sacking of many of Trondheim's monasteries and churches. Wars with Sweden and a series of disastrous fires further damaged the city in the 17th century. When the town was rebuilt, extrawide streets were constructed to act as fire breaks, giving the city's center a spacious, sprawling effect. Narrow alleys and pastel-colored wooden waterfront warehouses serve to remind that the city was also an important trading port. About 150,000 residents live in Trondheim, today a lively university town and one of Norway's biggest agricultural communities.

Norwegians love their *gravlaks*, a marinated salmon appetizer, and celebrate with *aquavit*, a powerful drink distilled from potatoes. *Multer med krem* (Arctic cloudberries with cream) is a local treat.

- Nidaros Domkirke (Nidaros Cathedral) and Archbishop's Palace
- Stiftsgården
- Museum of Applied Art
- Trondhjems Kunstforening (Art Museum)
- Ringve Museum of Musical History
- Trondelag Folk Museum
- Waterfront houses and Gamle Bybro (Old Town Bridge)
- Medieval Church ruins at Sparebanken
- Outdoor Market on Torvet (Main Square)
- Kristiansten Fortress

Poland

Gdańsk

The city of Gdańsk grabbed world headlines in 1989 when the Solidarity movement, led by native son Lech Walesa, a former electrician at Gdańsk shipyards, gained ground. The success of this first independent workers' union in Eastern Europe culminated in the democratic rebirth of Poland, the first of many such Communist-led nations to fall.

Settled in the 7th century by Slavs, Poland became known for its prosperity and religious and political tolerance, particularly in the 14th century. It became a haven for many, especially Jews expelled from Western Europe during the Inquisition. Poles, Germans, Tartars, Armenians, and Flemings all lived together peacefully until the country was carved up and crushed, many times over, most heinously during World War II, when the Nazis exterminated six million Poles, including three million Polish Jews.

Situated on the **Baltic** coast at the mouth of the **Wisla River**, Gdansk is Poland's principal port. Its strategic location has made it the target of many a battle over the centuries. It was one of the first Polish cities to undergo a complete overhaul after its destruction in World War II; **Old Town** and its numerous ornate cathedrals, some dating back to the 14th century, were completely rebuilt.

Cuisine plays a big part in Polish tradition: *Golabki* (stuffed cabbage) and *pierogis* (dumplings) with various vegetable, meat, or fruit fillings, are favorite meals. Vodka, such as Wyborowa, is consumed on special occasions.

- **Długi Targ (Long Market)**
- **Ratusz (Town Hall) and Historii Miasta Gdańska (Historical Museum of Gdańsk)**
- **Kościół Najświętszej Marii Panny (St. Mary's Church)**
- **Kościół Sw. Katarzyny (St. Catherine's Church)**
- **Kosciół Sw. Mikolaja (St. Nicholas Church)**
- **Wielkiłyn (Great Mill)**
- **Długie Pobrzeże**
- **Ul. Mariacka (Mariacka Street)**
- **Hala Targowa (Market Hall)**

- **Gdańsk Shipyard Museum and Monument to the Shipyard Workers**

Russia

St. Petersburg

In the early 18th century, Peter the Great captured from Sweden more than a hundred islands at the mouth of the tiny **Neva River** where it flows into the **Gulf of Finland.** Characteristically, his determination to build a strategically situated city on the Baltic outweighed the fact that the site was a swamp along a waterway that often overflowed its banks—when it didn't freeze—almost 400 miles from the imperial and cultural center of Moscow. Europe's best architects designed a city in Baroque and Neo-Classical styles, and in 1712, nine years after its founding, sparkling St. Petersburg became the capital of the Russian Empire and Peter's "Window on the West," in touch with Europe's constantly changing trends. For over two centuries St. Petersburg served as the seat of government from its peak to its difficult end. Russianized to **Petrograd** (Peter's city) during World War I, St. Petersburg was where the Bolsheviks, led by Vladimir Ilyich Lenin, proclaimed a revolution. The city was renamed for Lenin after his death in 1924. More than a million Leningraders died during the brutal two-and-a-half-year siege by the Germans during World War II, and the city suffered extensive damage, though it was able to rebuild following the war. With the fall of the Soviet Union in 1991, Leningrad once again became St. Petersburg. Restoration of historic buildings and the construction of new hotels began the transformation of the city to its former glory.

Russia's largest port and second-largest city, with a population of more than five million, St. Petersburg is

Peterhof/Petrodvorets, St. Petersburg

young by European standards. It is a city of endless squares, parks, boulevards, palaces, and monuments. Situated just a few feet above sea level, it is criss-crossed by rivers and canals and hooked together with hundreds of bridges, much like Venice or Amsterdam. Located in the northern latitude, the city is enveloped in a shimmering twilight during the "White Nights" of summer.

Traditional fare here is caviar spread on blini (light pancakes); borscht (beets, cabbage, and chunks of boiled meat served with sour cream); and *romovaya baba* (cake steeped in rum syrup). Outdoor markets offer *matryoshka* (wooden nesting dolls), amber, caviar, fur hats, lacquered boxes, and vodka.

- Hermitage
- Russky Muzey (Russian Museum)
- Muzey Pushkina (Pushkin Museum)
- Isaakievski Sobor (St. Isaac's Cathedral)
- Peter and Paul Fortress
- Admiralteystvo (Admiralty) and Nevsky Prospekt
- Performance at Mariinsky Teatr
- Summer Palace and Gardens
- Kazanski Sobor (Kazan Cathedral)
- Peterhof/Petrodvorets

Scotland

Edinburgh

Situated on the south coast of the **Firth of Forth**, on the **North Sea**, Edinburgh is the capital and second-largest city of Scotland. Scots, whose heros and history have been depicted in modern-day epic movies such as *Rob Roy* and *Braveheart*, originally came from Ireland in the sixth century, extending their kingdom to its present-day borders in the 11th century. The country united with its long-time enemy England in 1707 to form Great Britain. Scotland was home to the literary trinity of Robert Burns, Sir Walter Scott, and Robert Louis Stevenson.

Edinburgh's history goes back to its castle, built high atop an extinct volcano, with views all the way back to the harbor of Leith. Divided into a medieval **Old Town** and 18th-century **New Town**, Edinburgh is stately and sophisticated, with impressive buildings set in green manicured parks and rolling hills, broad cobblestone streets and narrow passageways, and ancient spires shaping the skyline. The city developed as a cultural center in the 18th and 19th centuries, a tradition it continues by hosting one of Europe's greatest international arts fetes—the Edinburgh International Festival—every summer.

Porridge, kippers, smoked haddock and salmon, shortbread and marmalade are practically national dishes, but perhaps Scotland's most interesting— and of questionable appeal to non-Scots—dish is *haggis*, sheep's innards, oatmeal, suet, onion, and seasoning stuffed into a sheep's stomach bag and boiled. Another local favorite is cock-a-leekie soup,

made with chicken, leeks, and prunes. Although Scotch whisky is no bargain here, rare distillations and malts not available elsewhere are good finds, along with rightly famous woolens such as cashmere, Shetland sweaters, and tweeds.

- Edinburgh Castle
- Royal Mile
- Lady Stair's House
- St. Giles High Church of Scotland
- The Palace of Holyroodhouse and Arthur's Seat
- Princes Street Gardens
- National Gallery of Scotland
- The Georgian House
- Royal Botanic Gardens
- Hopetoun House

Sweden

Stockholm

Sprawling across 14 islands connected by as many as 40 bridges, Stockholm, Sweden's capital since 1634, has been called "a city that floats on water." Geographically, half of the still-growing city of 1.5 million sits on **Lake Mälaren**, the other on **Saltsjön**, leading out to the **Baltic Sea** and a vast archipelago of some 25,000 islands, all different shapes and sizes, scattered across the sea with no discernible pattern. **Gamla Stan**, the **Old Town** packed with narrow alleys and lanes along four islands in the heart of the city, is Stockholm's well-preserved medieval core.

Stockholm was founded in 1250 as a fortress for protection against pirate raids, not long after Swedish Vikings headed east along the Russian rivers to Novgorod, Kiev, and Constantinople, and north to Finland. The original tower was enlarged and called "Tre Kronor" because of its three golden crowns, which today are a national symbol. Sweden was unified with Norway and Denmark in 1397, forming the Kalmar Union. But independent-minded Swedes rebelled for the next two centuries, and in 1523 Gustav Vasa was crowned king, breaking with Rome and adopting Lutheranism. Sweden became one of the great European powers, extending its borders into Poland, Russia, Germany, Denmark, and Norway.

Sweden's most famous culinary attraction is, of course, the *smörgåsbord*, that infamous buffet that can consist of as many as a hundred dishes, including herring prepared innumerable ways, smoked salmon, eel, caviar, shrimp, and smoked reindeer. *Janssons frestelse* is a casserole of potatoes, onions, and cream. Those Swedish meatballs are finished off with *våfflor* (crisp waffles topped with jam and whipped cream). Good buys here include Hasselblad cameras, candles, ceramics, clogs, glassware such as Kosta Boda and Orrefors, silver, stainless steel, and Lapp handicrafts made from reindeer antlers.

- Kungliga Slottet (Royal Palace)
- Storkyrkan (Great Church)
- Riddarholmskyrkan (Church of the Nobility)
- Vasa and Vasamuseet (Vasa and Vasa Museum)
- Djurgården and Skansen (Open Air Museum)
- Stadhuset and View from Tower
- Nationalmuseum (National Museum of Fine Arts)
- Nordiska Museet (Nordic Museum)
- Millesgården (Milles Garden)
- Drottningholm Palace

Visby

The Swedish summer resort island of **Gotland**, situated in the **Baltic Sea** 55 miles off Sweden's southeast coast, is a treasure chest of prehistoric finds, full of burial grounds, building foundations, ancient fortresses, and rock carvings. First inhabited about 7,000 years ago, the country's largest island offers dramatic windswept coastlines whose vertical cliffs and oddly twisted weathered limestone formations, called *raukar*, attract an abundance of birdlife.

Traces of the Vikings, those skillful sailors and warriors who enriched the island with their plunder, are still being uncovered. When they converted to Christianity the Vikings invested part of their amassed wealth in many of the island's nearly 100 churches, some dating from the 12th and 13th centuries. The island is also littered with remains of more than 350 Bronze Age funeral "ships": massive

boulders arranged in the shape of ship hulls, sometimes 150 feet long, within which urns containing cremated remains were deposited.

Visby, also known as "The City of Roses and Ruins," was an important outpost of the powerful and prosperous Hanseatic League. The town's successful citizens also poured their wealth into magnificent churches. Visby has maintained its medieval character with well-preserved ivy-covered stone-and-timber buildings lining narrow alleys and streets; the 12th-century **Ringmuren** (town wall), complete with 40 guard towers, the oldest in Scandinavia, remains virtually intact. Today, Visby's 25,000 villagers cherish their traditions and craftsmanship, such as the creation of candles, pottery, and woodwork. Gotland has its own culinary offering, *gotlandsflundror* (smoked flatfish), in addition to the usual smörgåsbord of Scandinavian specialties.

- Gamla Apotekt (Old Pharmacy)
- Gotlands Fornsal (Historical Museum)
- Almadalen (Old Port of Visby)
- Botanical Gardens
- Kruttornet (Gunpowder Tower)
- Stora Torget (Market Square)
- Domkyrkan Sankt Nicolaus (St. Nicholas Cathedral)
- Domkyrkan Sankta Maria (St. Mary's Cathedral)
- Burmeisterska huset (Burmeister's House)
- Cliffs at Hogklint

Cruising the Coast of Norway

Every summer cruise ships flock to **Norway**, ducking into its picturesque fjords and calling at charming coastal villages en route to the **North Cape,** Europe's northernmost point. But one cruise line plies this route year-round, day in, day out.

Norwegian Coastal Voyages, marketed in the US by New York-based **Bergen Line,** offers 12-day round-trip cruises from **Bergen,** the capital of fjord country, all the way north to Kirkenes on the Russian border. This journey of 2,500 nautical miles takes in 34 ports, ranging from Ålesund, with its Art Nouveau architecture, to the jazz festival town of Molde to the city of Tromsø, the capital of Arctic Norway.

It's billed as "the world's most beautiful voyage," and that's not ad-copy hyperbole. Depending on the season, passengers can glimpse the orangy glow of the midnight sun, virgin snows cooling autumn's crimson blush, the ethereal flickering of the northern lights, or spring's tender green pastures on mountainsides blooming with white cloudberries.

The coastal express—or *Hurtigruten* in Norwegian—was launched a century ago as a means of carrying mail and provisions to

northern communities. But over the decades tourists have become important "cargo" (primarily Europeans, although Americans are often found on board as well). Although the accommodations are not as plush as what you'd find on a cruise ship, with newer, more comfortable, passenger-friendly ships added to the fleet in recent years, the coastal steamers' popularity has blossomed.

For more information, see a travel agent or call **Bergen Line** at 800/323.7436, 800/666.2374 for brochures.

MICHAEL STORRINGS

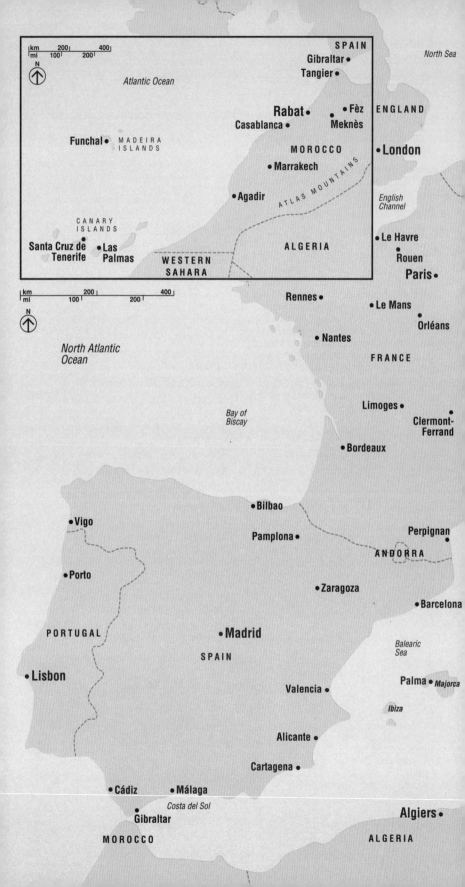

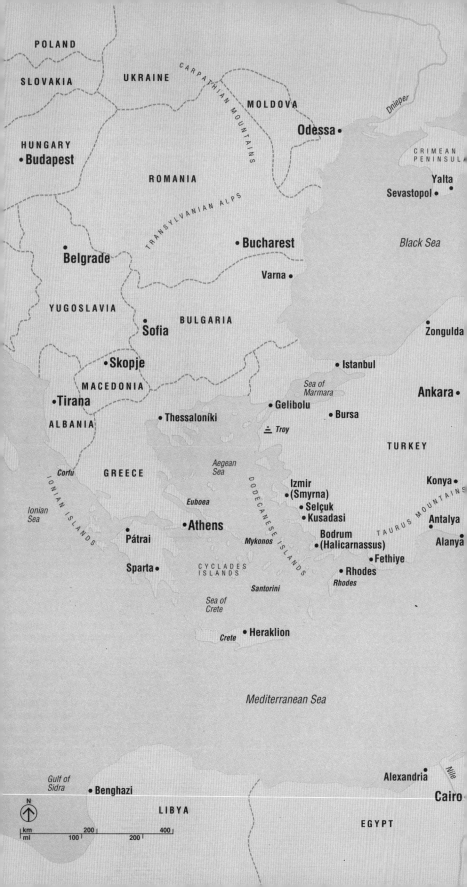

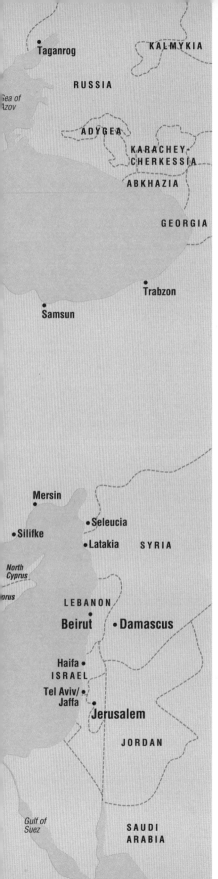

Mediterranean

Odysseus sailed its wine-dark seas; Jason and his Argonauts traversed it in their quest for the Golden Fleece; pirates and warships roamed its waters on missions of plunder and conquest. Today, a much more peaceful place, the Mediterranean has become one of the world's most popular cruise destinations. The Romans bestowed a name—middle of the land in Latin—that was befitting to its strategic importance in the ancient world: The sea bridges the continents of **Europe** and **Africa** and links with the **Atlantic Ocean** and the **Black** and **Red Seas**.

Modern-day Mediterranean voyages revisit many of those ancient sailors' fabled ports of call—albeit in a bit more comfort and style—along what is today **Spain**'s **Costa del Sol**, the **French** and **Italian Rivieras**, **North Africa**, the **Greek Isles**, **Turkey**, **Israel**, and **Egypt**. Some itineraries also include the Black Sea, calling at such historic ports as **Yalta** and **Odessa** in the **Ukraine**.

The Mediterranean is the number-one choice in European cruise routes, accounting for more than 70 percent of the 1,000-plus European sailings that range from three-day Greek samplers to 21-day grand voyages. This almost 2,500-milelong sea is the second-largest cruise market after the Caribbean, offering everything from the exotic port of **Casablanca** to the balmy beaches of **Mykonos**.

Egypt

Alexandria

Five thousand years ago Egypt was the birthplace of one of the world's greatest civilizations; today the country still boasts many largely intact, extraordinary monuments that the pharaohs left. Throughout the centuries Egypt has been ruled by Greeks, Romans, Arabs, and Turks, among others. Alexandria is located on the northwest corner of the **Nile Delta** some 107 miles northwest of Cairo and today is Egypt's chief port, second-largest city, and home to about 5.5 million people. The metropolis is sometimes called "The Pearl of the Mediterranean" because of its long stretches of white sandy beaches.

Alexandria was named for its founder, Alexander the Great, who conquered the region around 300 BC. The city was the capital of Ptolemaic Egypt, a major trade center, and focal point of learning for the entire Mediterranean area. Its ancient library held a half-million books, and the **Pharos** lighthouse was one of the Seven Wonders of the Ancient World. The city remained the capital under Roman rule, which started in 33 BC, but entered a long period of decline after the Arab conquest in AD 641. Napoleon rehabilitated Alexandria at the end of the 18th century, and the city grew as modern Egypt's principal port and conduit at the crossroads of the main trading routes among Asia, Africa and Europe. The 1952 revolution, a military coup that overthrew King Farouk, changed the city's cosmopolitan quality as residents of some of the foreign enclaves began to depart.

Local dishes include fuul and hummus, spreads made with lemon and garlic; the former using fava beans and the latter chickpeas. Falafel is served in pita bread with any of several combinations of salads and tahini, a sesame sauce. Two lamb specialties include *shawarma* (meat roasted on a vertical spit, sliced, and served on pita with vegetables), and kabobs (spicy minced meat pressed onto skewers and charcoal-grilled). Handicrafts found here include gold and silver jewelry—especially hieroglyphic-engraved cartouches, leather, woodwork, basketry, copperware, brassware, ceramics, alabaster, and papyrus paintings. Carpets and cotton textiles in various forms are also popular.

- Ras El Tin Lighthouse and Palace Museum
- Fort of Quaitbey
- Graeco-Roman Museum
- Fine Arts Museum
- Montazah Palace and Gardens
- Mosque of Abu-al-Abbas al-Mursi
- Pompey's Pillar
- Serapeum Temple
- Catacombs of Kom al-Shoqafa
- Roman Amphitheater/Ruins of Kom El-Dekka

France

Ajaccio, Corsica

North of Sardinia and south of mainland France, Corsica is the most mountainous and geographically diverse island in the Mediterranean. It has snowcapped granite peaks, flatland marshes, a national park, uninhabited landscape, and 600 miles of coastline with lovely beaches and villages clinging to mountainsides and nestled in pretty ports. It is a rugged, stunning island that the French appropriately call the Isle of Beauty. The low dense shrub called maquis that covers much of the island finds its way into local cuisine. Corsicans are fiercely independent—they speak a language that is closer to Italian than French (they also speak French) and fly their own flag.

Ajaccio is located on Corsica's western coast between rugged mountains and the **Gulf of Ajaccio** and is a city of spacious squares, tree-lined boulevards, and narrow alleys with pastel-colored buildings. The area has a long history of being colonized by various peoples: Settled by Greeks in the 6th century BC, it passed through the hands of the Vandals, Byzantines, Lombards, Franks, and the papacy. Ajaccio was also ruled by the Romans in the 3rd century and then ceded to Pisa and Genoa in the 11th century. Following a malaria epidemic in 1492 the town was moved 1.5 miles west, and walls were built to ward off pirate attacks. Following a rebellion against Genoa, the French took the city in 1769, the year its most famous native son—Napoleon Bonaparte—was born (every corner features a reminder of this historic event). Ajaccio was colonized by the British during the Napoleonic Wars and became the capital of Corsica in 1811. It remained the capital until 1975 when Corsica was divided into two regions—**Corse-du-Sud** and **Haute-Corse;** Ajaccio is the capital of the former. Germany and Italy both occupied the island during World War II.

Corsicans specialize in terrines and pâtés made of game from the surrounding countryside—blackbird, thrush, and wild boar. A seafood specialty is *soupe de poisson* (fish soup), served with croutons that are topped with a spicy mayonnaise and grated cheese. Handmade pottery, silk, and other textiles are there for shoppers, as are olive-wood items with distinctive textures and patterns.

- Maison Bonaparte (Bonaparte House)
- Musée Napoléonien (Napoleon Museum)
- Musée Fesch (Fesch Museum) and Chapelle Impériale (Imperial Chapel)
- Cathédrale (Cathedral)
- Pointe de la Parata (Parata Point)
- Place Général-de-Gaulle (General de Gaulle Square)
- Vieille Ville (Old City)
- Iles Sanguinaires (Bloody Islands)
- Genoan Watchtowers
- Train ride to Corte

What looks like a big, backwards "C" on the distinctive, winged funnels of all Carnival Cruise Lines ships originated with the company's first vessel, *Mardi Gras*. The ship, formerly the *Empress of Canada*, had a green "CP" logo on its smokestack when Carnival acquired it from Canadian Pacific Railways in 1972. At first, Carnival simply repainted the green letters red, white, and blue. But when Canadian Pacific objected, Carnival altered the "C," creating the current stylized, crescent-shape logo (see page 94).

*Boulevard de la Croisette
(Croisette Boulevard), Cannes*

Cannes

This **French Riviera** town—distinguished from its sister coastal enclaves by sandy, rather than pebble beaches—is famous for its cultural activities and fetes. The May International Film Festival receives top billing, attracting glitterati from around the world for private screenings of movies vying for prestigious awards. Those who miss this annual event can feast their eyes on film stars' handprints and autographs that line the pavement in front of the **Palais des Festivals.** The name Cannes comes from the Latin *canna* (reed), a plant that used to be abundant here. Today the reeds have been replaced by almost 3,000 palm trees and more than 2,000 flower stands, and the seaside promenade of this city of about 75,000 permanent residents is filled with strollers and in-line skaters. Cannes's three casinos and yacht-laden harbors lure the international well-heeled crowd, but the city is less pretentious and exclusive than St-Tropez, its neighbor down the coast.

The Romans settled here in the 2nd century BC, and the town grew along the slopes of **Mount Chevalier** where an 11th-century water tower still stands. It became part of the region of **Provence** in the 14th century. Picasso lived and painted here and in nearby coastal villages and towns. Matisse, who said, "Here light plays the leading role," created his favorite motifs, with his signature sun-drenched colors: lemon golds, wildflower pinks and reds, and bleached pastel blues. Off shore are islands that housed the "Man In the Iron Mask" in the late 17th century—made famous in Alexandre Dumas's novel—and a 5th-century monastery.

Such fresh herbs as rosemary, thyme, and basil, along with olive oil and garlic, are the key ingredients in Provence's regional cuisine. The most famous provençale dish is ratatouille, and *loup de mer* (sea bass) is often prepared with fennel. Shoppers head for the tiny boutiques along **Rue d'Antibes,** where local and international designerwear is on sale. Local pottery, glassware, and items carved from olive wood are also good buys.

- ▓ **Boulevard de la Croisette (Croisette Boulevard)**
- ▓ **Le Suquet and Musée de la Castre (La Castre Museum)**
- ▓ **Vieux Port (Old Port)**
- ▓ **Morning visit to Marché Forville (Forville Market)**
- ▓ **Notre-Dame de l'Espérance (Our Lady of Hope Church)**
- ▓ **Antibes and Musée Picasso**
- ▓ **Biot and Fernand Léger Museum**
- ▓ **St-Paul-de-Vence and Fondation Maeght**
- ▓ **Grasse and Musée Fragonard**
- ▓ **Iles St-Marguerite and St-Honorat**

Nice

Boasting many museums, an Art Deco casino, a legendary Rococo-style hotel, and a four-mile, palm-

215

lined coastal boulevard, Nice is a vibrant, cultural city of almost 517,000 people located on **Baie des Anges**. **Vieille Ville** (Old Town) offers spacious squares, bistros, cafes, and aromatic markets—produce in the morning, flowers in the afternoon. The pastel houses along the quay where fishermen once lived are now filled with restaurants and galleries. Nice is the unofficial capital of the **Côte d'Azur** (the Azure Coast), so named for the sparkling blue Mediterranean Sea along France's southern coast. The **French Riviera,** which stretches from above Marseilles in the west to Menton east of Monaco, is geographically varied, with sheer limestone cliffs, small coves, jutting promontories, wide bays with flat beaches, and the **Maritime Alps** that plunge into the sea.

It was founded by the Greeks in about 500 BC, who thoughtfully brought along their olive trees and grapevines. Ancient Romans developed the region, introducing their legal system and building roads, most notably the spectacular **Grande Corniche** (see "Villefranche-sur-Mer," below), lined with villas and terraced gardens. During the fall of the Roman Empire, barbarians from the north and pirates from North Africa invaded Nice, causing the city's decline. The Counts of Provence brought the city back to its former glory in the 10th century, but in 1388 Nice was wrested from them by the House of Savoy, who retained almost unbroken possession for close to 500 years. In 1860 the region was ceded to France. Throughout history, the coast has been a notable area for painters. The Nice School, strongly influenced by the Italian Renaissance, flourished in the 15th and 16th centuries. The Riviera became a hot spot for 19th-century painters, as the Impressionists sought to capture the subtle effects of light on the Mediterranean landscapes: Morisot at Nice, Monet at Antibes, and Renoir at Cagnes. Signac, a pioneer of pointillism, established his school at St-Tropez. Later, Fauvists, painting brilliant colors in highly personalized styles, used the Riviera as a backdrop.

The birthplace of salade niçoise, Nice is also known for *pissaladière*—onion, olive, and anchovy pizza—and saffron-spiked bouillabaisse. Shoppers will find silk scarves, perfumes, and scented soaps, along with silver, crystal, and haute couture fashions here.

- ■ **Promenade des Anglais (English Promenade)**
- ■ **Marché aux Fleurs (Flower Market)**
- ■ **Parc du Château (Castle Park)**
- ■ **Musée d'Art Moderne et d'Art Contemporain (Modern and Contemporary Art Museum)**
- ■ **Musée Chagall (Chagall Museum)**
- ■ **Musée Matisse (Matisse Museum)**
- ■ **Musée des Beaux-Arts (Fine Arts Museum)**
- ■ **Cathédrale Orthodoxe Russe St-Nicholas (St. Nicholas Russian Orthodox Cathedral)**
- ■ **Monastère de Cimiez and Eglise Gothique (Cimiez Monastery and Gothic Church)**
- ■ **Vieux Port (Old Port)**

Villefranche-sur-Mer

The big, blue bay of **Rade de Villefranche** is the setting for the charming harbor of Villefranche-sur-Mer ("Villefranche" for short). A breath of fresh air in the sometimes frenzied **French Riviera,** Villefranche overlooks **Cap Ferrat,** where an eclectic, treasure-filled Rothschild villa is today a museum. The town itself is a wonderful place for walking, with a jumble of little plazas and narrow streets cut by steps climbing up from the harbor. Yellow, red, and pink pastel stucco houses crawl up and down the hillside, and waterfront cafes line the quay where luxury yachts tie up alongside local fishing boats. Villefranche boasts the oldest street in France (13th century), a covered road lined with tiny houses that are totally protected from the elements.

Villefranche was founded in the early 14th century by Charles II of Anjou, and the Duke of Savoy built a citadel in 1560 along the waterfront. Near the fort is a 14th-century chapel that was decorated by French writer-artist Jean Cocteau in 1957 with drawings of scenes from the life of St. Peter—a longtime favorite of the local fisherfolk.

Its central location on the **Côte d'Azur** makes Villefranche an ideal base from which to tour the area. The *corniches*—three spectacular roads that wind through a magnificent landscape parallel with the coast—connect Villefranche with the rest of the region's sites. Highest is the **Grande Corniche,** built along the Roman **Aurelian Way**; the **Moyenne Corniche,** where medieval villages perch on rocky coastal cliffs; and the **Corniche Inférieure,** which runs along the sea. Bouillabaisse, *soupe au pistou* (soup made with basil), salade niçoise, and aioli are excellent here. A few art galleries and souvenir shops offer gift items.

- ■ **Citadelle (Citadel)**
- ■ **Rue Obscure (Hidden Street)**
- ■ **Chapelle St-Pierre (St. Peter's Chapel)**
- ■ **St-Jean-Cap-Ferrat**
- ■ **Musée Ephrussi de Rothschild (Rothschild Foundation)**
- ■ **Eze**
- ■ **La Turbie**
- ■ **Beaulieu and Villa Kérylos**
- ■ **Nice**
- ■ **Monaco**

Modern cruise ships rarely use tugboats (except when there are high winds or when port regulations demand them). Bow and stern thrusters now do the work that tugs once did. Located beneath the waterline on the sides of the hull, thrusters provide lateral propulsion, increasing maneuverability and enabling a ship to "park" at a pier.

Sea Sagas

Maybe it's the salt air, but cruise ships make spicy settings for romance, adventure, and intrigue—imaginary, as well as real. For a juicy seagoing read, slather on the sun block, order a planter's punch, and curl up in a deck chair with one of these:

A Book of Sea Journeys edited by Ludovic Kennedy (Fontana Paperbacks, 1982) This anthology contains delightful surprises, including accounts of life aboard early ocean liners and the Sylvia Plath poem "On Deck."

Buzz Cut by James W. Hall (Delacorte, 1996) A well-armed psychopath with a grudge hijacks a **Caribbean** cruise liner. The SOS goes out to tough-guy Thorn, author Hall's one-name, South Florida hero.

Crossing & Cruising by John Maxtone-Graham (Charles Scribner's Sons, 1992) Here's the scoop about how the great ocean-liner era spawned contemporary cruising.

Darker Than Amber by John D. MacDonald (Fawcett, 1966) Travis McGee busts a deadly con game; some of the action is set on a Caribbean cruise ship.

Decked by Carol Higgins Clark (Warner, 1992) Private eye Regan Reilly accepts a job as a paid companion for a tippling, accident-prone octogenarian on a transatlantic cruise—then gets caught up in a murder mystery.

Foreign Land by Jonathan Raban (Viking, 1985) An expatriate who leaves **Africa** for retirement in his native England finds only disillusionment and heads out to sea, where he reviews his life—much of which took place aboard ships.

The Innocents Abroad by Mark Twain (Penguin, 1980) First published in 1869 and subtitled *The New Pilgrims Progress*, this is a hilarious satirical account of a group of naive Americans taking a pleasure excursion to **Europe** and the **Holy Land** aboard the steamship *Quaker City*.

Liners to the Sun by John Maxtone-Graham (Macmillan, 1985) Ship buffs will lap up this insider's account of cruising, which touches on everything from shipbuilding personnel to shipboard personalities.

Lusitania by David Butler (Random House, 1982) An epic novel about the doomed liner, rife with romance, thrills, and psychological tension.

A Night to Remember by Walter Lord (Holt, Rinehart and 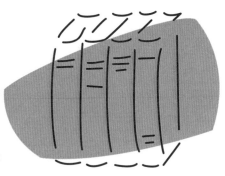 Winston, 1955) A gripping account of the *Titanic* disaster by an esteemed marine historian.

Nothing Can Go Wrong by John D. MacDonald and John H. Kilpack (Fawcett, 1981) Novelist and cruise aficionado MacDonald teamed up with ship captain Kilpack to reveal the behind-the-scenes action on the last long voyage of **Pacific Far East Line's** SS *Mariposa*, sailing from **San Francisco** on 2 May, 1977.

The Only Way to Cross by John Maxtone-Graham (Collier, 1972) The golden era of transatlantic liners, from the *Mauretania* to the *Queen Elizabeth 2*, is captured in this entertaining but scholarly work.

The Poseidon Adventure by Paul Gallico (Coward-McCann Inc., 1969) An ocean liner capsizes, trapping passengers in the hull. Made into a 1972 movie with an all-star cast.

Raise the Titanic! by Clive Cussler (Simon & Schuster, 1976) Cussler's James-Bond-like hero, Dirk Pitt, sets out to recover a valuable ore that went down with the *Titanic*.

Rough Crossing: Freely Adapted from Ferenc Molnar's Play at the Castle by Tom Stoppard (Faber and Faber, 1985) Set on an ocean liner, this is a comedy by the author of the play *Rosencrantz and Guildenstern are Dead*.

Ship of Fools by Katherine Anne Porter (Little, Brown & Co., 1945) In 1933, an unusual group of passengers casts off on an ocean liner from Veracruz, Mexico, bound for Bremerhaven, Germany.

Tremor of Intent by Anthony Burgess (W. W. Norton, 1966) A British agent is assigned to bring back a boyhood friend who has defected to **Russia**. In this suspense novel, the agent's base of operations is a cruise ship loaded with oddball characters.

Gibraltar

The **Rock of Gibraltar** on the **Gibraltar Peninsula,** about 14 miles from the North African coast, dominates the western approach to the Mediterranean. The mountain rises abruptly from low, flat ground at the north front in a fine granite wall to a height of 1,398 feet. In summer the levanter (east wind) blows through the **Strait of Gibraltar,** causing a damp cloud to hang over the Rock. The small colony of Barbary macaques that lives here is almost as famous as the mountain itself. Legend has it that when these primates (which are actually North African monkeys) disappear from Gibraltar, so will the British.

British forces have controlled access to the Mediterranean from this heavily fortified point for more than two centuries, surviving blockade, submarine attack, and aerial bombardment during the two world wars. Gibraltar was one of the **Pillars of Hercules** in the ancient world (the other is Jabal Musa on the Moroccan shore across the strait). Its modern name is derived from the Arabic *Jebel-al-Tarik* (Tarik's Mount) for the Moorish conqueror who captured and fortified the Rock in AD 711. The Moors largely ruled until 1462 when the Spanish took control of the Rock. More than two hundred years later, British and Dutch forces wrested Gibraltar from Spain, and in 1713 the Treaty of Utrecht gave Britain full ownership in perpetuity.

The town of Gibraltar, with its Victorian architecture and streets with such names as **Parliament Lane**, resembles an English seaside resort, complete with corner pubs and blue-suited bobbies. Most of the 2.5-square-mile colony's 31,000 inhabitants are a mixture of many nationalities, including British, Genoese, Maltese, Portuguese, and Spanish, and speak both Spanish and English. Gibraltar is a duty-free port—**Main Street** is a good place to shop for electronic goods, Lladro porcelain, perfumes, and watches. Homesick Brits and Anglophiles can indulge in fish and chips, pints of ale, and afternoon tea. Such Spanish delights as tapas, paella, and sangria are also available.

- ▇ Cable Car to Top of the Rock
- ▇ Ape's Den and Nature Reserve
- ▇ St. Michael's Cave
- ▇ Princess Caroline's Battery
- ▇ Upper Galleries
- ▇ Gibraltar Museum
- ▇ Trafalgar Cemetery
- ▇ Moorish Castle
- ▇ Alameda Gardens
- ▇ Europa Point

On average, it takes a ship eight hours to pass through the Panama Canal.

Greece

Athens (Piraeus)

Located four miles from the sea and the port of Piraeus, Athens is in a strategic position—it is bordered on the southwest by the **Attica Peninsula** and surrounded by mountains on the other three. It overlooks the **Aegean Sea** and the **Saronic Gulf** and was built across eight hills. The city currently is home to over four million residents and what seems like as many automobiles. In an effort to reduce traffic and pollution, in 1995 the government set in motion a $3-billion plan that will eventually replace motor vehicles with minibuses and trolleys. Today Athens is far from its glory days, when the city was the pride of the classical world and the foundation for modern civilization. Still, the visitor who leaves the main streets behind and seeks out the maze of narrow side streets overflowing with tavernas, shops, and bouzouki music will be rewarded with a trip back in time.

Athens reached its political peak after the Persian Wars of the 5th century BC, when it led the Delian League, a confederacy of Greek states formed to protect Aegean cities from further Persian aggression. Under the auspices of such scholars as Sophocles, Euripides, Socrates, and Plato, Athens became a major center of art, architecture, philosophy, and drama. The city-state lost its supremacy to Sparta in the Peloponnesian War (also in the 5th century), and later came under the rule of Macedon and Rome. Capital of modern Greece since 1834, Athens today is once again a center of commercial, political, cultural, and administrative activity.

A typical taverna meal might include *tzatziki* (a cucumber, yogurt, and garlic dip), *soupa avgolemono* (chicken soup with an egg-and-lemon sauce), *salata choriatiki* (salad of sliced vegetables, feta cheese, and olives), dolmades, and moussaka. Souvlaki, spanakopita (spinach-and-cheese pie), and *tiropita* (cheese pie) are favorite snack foods. The flea market at **Monastiraki** features *flokati* (sheep's-wool rugs), often priced by the kilo, icons and folk art, gold and silver jewelry, and furniture.

- ▇ Acropolis
- ▇ Plaka
- ▇ Syntagma Square and Parliament
- ▇ National Archaeological Museum
- ▇ Kapnikarea Church
- ▇ National Picture Gallery/Alexander Soustos Museum
- ▇ Ancient Agora
- ▇ Lickabetus Hill
- ▇ Benaki Museum
- ▇ Monastiraki

Corfu

According to legend Corfu is the island of Scheria where Odysseus was washed ashore and met the beautiful Princess Nausicaa. Located off the north-western shore of Greece along the border with Albania in the **Ionian Sea,** Corfu is the second-largest of the six **Ionian Islands.** Corfu (Kerkyra in Greek) is covered with gently rolling green hills and valleys bursting with cyprus and olive trees and ringed with sparkling beaches. **Corfu Town,** the island's main city and capital and home to 100,000 permanent residents, is between two fortresses on a peninsula on the east coast. Pastel-colored buildings with balconies adorned with flowers line narrow alleyways that open onto little market-filled plazas.

Corfu's history dates from 733 BC, when the Corinthians established the colony of **Corcyra** here. It became part of the Roman empire in 229 BC and in AD 336 became part of the Byzantine Empire. Subsequent conquerors included the Venetians, Turks, and British. Corfu was united with independent Greece in 1864.

Bourdetto (a spicy white fish in olive oil and hot red pepper) is a Corfu specialty. In addition to the usual array of dips, snacks, and spreads, *kalamarakia* (battered and deep-fried baby squid) is also a favorite. Local handicrafts include bowls and trays made from olive wood; such textiles as *tagari* (a colorful woolen shoulder bag), small rugs, floor mats, shawls, bedspreads, and sweaters; and Venetian-designed silver.

- Archeologiko Mousio (Archaeological Museum)
- Spianada (Esplanade)
- Liston
- Palace of St. Michael and St. George
- Old Town
- Agios Spiridon (Church of St. Spiridon)
- Mitropoli
- Palaio Frourio (Old Fort)
- Church of Sts. Joseph and Sosipatros
- Paleokastritsa and Panagia Theotokos

Heraklion, Crete

Mountainous, fertile Crete at the southern end of the **Aegean Sea** is the largest (about 3,189 square miles) of the Greek Islands. It was the birthplace of the Minoan culture—Europe's earliest civilization—which peaked from 2000 to 1400 BC. The palace at **Knossos**, associated with the mythical King Minos, features over five acres of halls and ceremonial rooms adorned with magnificent frescoes. An advanced sanitation system and many luxurious amenities were also part of the palace system. Most of the island was destroyed in a tidal wave resulting from a volcanic eruption on Santorini (Thíra in Greek) around 1500 BC.

Parthenon, Acropolis, Athens

Almost equidistant from Europe, Asia, and Africa, Crete has been fought over and occupied by countries from all three continents because of its strategic location. Forts, churches, and mosques of varying architectural styles were left behind by the Romans, Byzantines, Arabs, Venetians, and Turks, and heavy ramparts bear testimony to fierce battles fought. The capital of Heraklion—known as **Candia** until the 17th century—on the island's developed north coast is surrounded by massive 15th-century walls, in some places up to 45 feet thick. Under the Venetians Crete became a refuge for artists, writers, and philosophers who fled Constantinople after the Turkish conquest. Native son El Greco was inspired by the Venetians to move to Italy and study under the great Titian before making Spain his home. Greece's best-known writer, Nikos Kazantzakis, is buried under a wooden cross bearing a quotation from his famous novel, *Zorba the Greek*. Today Crete is home to over a half-million people.

Dolmades, *soupa avgolemono,* and *taramosalata* (a fish roe and olive oil dip) are standard fare here, as is *loukoumades* (deep-fried dough doused with honey). *Pasimatia* (wheat toast soaked in olive oil and served with a basil-tomato sauce) is a Cretan specialty and is usually accompanied by raki, the Greek spirit. Tangerines grow in profusion all over the island; Mandarini, a liqueur made from the fruit, is produced here. Crete is considered one of the best places in Greece to buy high-quality, inexpensive leather goods. It is also known for handwoven fabrics, embroidery, wood carvings, and jewelry.

- ■ **Church of San Marco**
- ■ **City Hall and Loggia**
- ■ **Platia Venizelou**
- ■ **Agios Titos**
- ■ **Agia Ekaterini (Church of St. Catherine)**
- ■ **Archaeological Museum**
- ■ **Historical Museum of Crete**
- ■ **Koules (Venetian Castle)**
- ■ **Kazantzakis' Tomb along Wall**
- ■ **Phaestos**

Cunard's *Queen Elizabeth 2* employs 239 waiters, 139 kitchen workers, 50 beverage staffers, 14 bartenders, 16 bakers, 18 wine stewards, 13 croupiers, eight carpenters, five exercise specialists, four printers, two doctors, two nannies, one dentist, one disc jockey, one librarian, and 90 stewards/stewardesses.

During World War II, Windjammer Barefoot Cruises' *Flying Cloud* (then named the *Oiseau des Isles*) was used for spying by the Allied forces.

Mykonos/Delos

One of the most popular Greek Islands, Mykonos boasts beautiful beaches, whitewashed sugar-cube houses, brightly painted wooden balconies bedecked with geraniums and bougainvillea, chic boutiques, and a rousing nightlife. The rocky 33-square-mile island is also dotted with windmills, small churches, and chapels. The twisting, narrow lanes of **Mykonos Town** were deliberately designed to confuse and ward off ravaging 18th-century pirates. Artists from around the world are lured here by the island's beauty; many frequent the **Skholi Kalon Tekhnon,** a branch of the Athens School of Fine Art.

It is said that the island's rocks are the bodies of giants conquered by Hercules, which he petrified with the help of Zeus. The Carians from southwest Asia Minor were the first to settle the island during the Bronze Age (around 2500 BC). Egyptians, Phoenicians, Cretans, Ionians, Romans, Venetians, and Turks followed. A fiercely proud people, the Mikonites were the first to raise the flag of revolution when the Greek war of independence broke out in 1821.

The neighboring island of Delos was an important religious and commercial center during ancient times, reaching its peak during the 5th century BC, but it was inhabited only until the early Christian era. It was the birthplace of Apollo, god of light, poetry, music, and prophecy; and his sister Artemis, the huntress. Today the uninhabited island and its ruins can be visited only on day trips.

All the culinary Greek standbys, including *mezedhes* (appetizer plate of dips and spreads), souvlaki, and *kalamarakia* are on taverna menus. Wonderful watercolors painted by artists from the Skholi Kalon Tekhnon, folk art, and woven fabric bags are available throughout the island, as are gold and silver jewelry and ceramics.

- ■ **Waterfront Fish Market**
- ■ **Folklore Museum**
- ■ **Archaeological Museum**
- ■ **Paraportiani**
- ■ **Alefkandhra (Little Venice)**
- ■ **Windmills at Kato Myli**
- ■ **Psarou Beach**
- ■ **Paradise Beach**
- ■ **Mitropoleos**
- ■ **Ano Mera**

Rhodes

The sun god Helios chose Rhodes as his bride, according to legend, giving her light, warmth, and vegetation—even today the island is abundant in grains, grapes, figs, pomegranates, and oranges. Two columns on either side of the harbor mark the supposed site of one of the Seven Wonders of the Ancient World, the *Colossus of Rhodes.* This enormous statue of Helios straddled the harbor, and allowed boats to pass beneath its huge legs. The giant was felled by an earthquake in 224 BC.

Rhodes has been conquered, plundered, fortified, and settled by Minoans, Dorians, Romans, Persians, Arabs, Crusaders, Turks, and Italians since its founding in the Bronze Age (about 2500 BC). All these civilizations prized the island's beauty and critical position at the end of the **Aegean Sea,** 10 miles off the Turkish coast. During the classical age, oratory (Julius Caesar, Cato, and Lucretius frequented Rhodes's famed school), painting, and sculpture flourished here.

Rhodes is the largest of the **Dodecanese Islands** (around 545 square miles) and has a population of 47,000 people. In addition to being known for the *Colossus,* the island is famous for its unequaled medieval architecture, impressive ancient ruins, and rocky coves. The city of Rhodes is divided into two sections. The Italian-built **New Town** boasts a market, government buildings, national theater, and handsome churches. **Old Town** is surrounded by walls built by the Knights of St. John who fled from Jerusalem in the 14th century. Inside are narrow cobblestone alleys, plazas filled with medieval and Ottoman architecture, and mellow stone archways covered in clinging flowering vines. Local folk art includes brightly colored plates painted with patterns of fish, ships, and flowers.

- **Mandraki Harbor windmills**
- **Archaeological Museum**
- **Palace of the Grand Masters**
- **Odhos Ippoton (Street of the Knights)**
- **Platia ton Evreon Martiron (Square of The Jewish Martyrs)**
- **Folk Art Museum**
- **Süleyman Mosque**
- **Citadel of Ialiassos**
- **Kameiros and Valley of the Butterflies**
- **Acropolis of Lindos**

Santorini

First settled by Bronze Age peoples about 5,000 years ago, Santorini evolved into a sophisticated outpost of Minoan civilization by 2000 BC. In 1430 BC a massive volcanic eruption buried the island under millions of tons of lava and pumice, some say triggering a tidal wave large enough to eradicate most of the Minoan civilization that was centered on Crete 70 miles to the south. The center of Santorini sank into the sea, producing its modern-day characteristic crescent shape, along with the largest caldera on earth, today a tranquil, shimmering bay. Many speculate that Santorini may be the legendary lost continent of Atlantis, the "Happy Isles Submerged by the Sea" described by Plato and Solon. After the great eruption, some believe that Santorini remained uninhabited until the Phoenicians arrived 500 years later, and was subsequently settled by Dorians. Over the years, various waves of

Egyptians, Romans, Venetians, and Turks have also called the island home.

Although Santorini is officially known as "Thíra," after the Theban hero Thiras who settled on the island in the 8th century BC, most visitors use the name honoring the island's patron saint—St. Irene of Thessaloniki, who died here in exile in AD 304. The island's main town of **Fíra** features whitewashed, cubelike buildings that cling to brown, black, gray, and red layered cliffs that hang 1,000 feet above the sea. Fíra can only be reached by climbing 566 zigzagging steps—on foot or donkey—or by cable car.

Fava bean soup made with oregano, onions, lemon, and olive oil is Santorini's most famous dish. *Pseftokeftedes* ("false meatballs"), finely chopped vegetables and flour batter, are served as a snack. Handicrafts here include gold and silver jewelry, glassware and pottery, along with handwoven bags, rugs, fabrics, and leather goods.

- **Ruins at Akrotiri**
- **Archaeological Museum**
- **Skala Fira**
- **Ancient Thíra**
- **Profitis Ilias Monastery**
- **Imerovigli**
- **Oía**
- **Nea Kameni**
- **Winery visit**
- **Megaron Gyzi Museum**

Israel

Haifa

The city of Haifa has been a shipping center and active port since the time of the Phoenicians. During the Middle Ages, Arabs and Jews defended the coastline against the crusaders' seaborne invasion in 1100 and subsequent Turkish occupation. Its recent history dates back to the end of the 19th century when Zionist immigrants settled the region. Haifa was one of the gateways for the flood of Jewish immigrants who arrived fresh from the horrors of post-World War II Europe to start a new life in the "land of milk and honey." Today it is Israel's third-largest metropolis.

The new city that developed during the British Mandate prior to independence in 1948 boasts broad and imposing thoroughfares that give way to side streets bearing the unmistakable Middle Eastern atmosphere of Arab bazaars. A maze of hairpin roads connect the lower town with the hotels, homes, and university atop **Mount Carmel.** Many of the city's 436,500 hard-working residents are involved in the high-tech industries based here.

With its advanced irrigation technology that helped turn a desert into a hothouse, Israel produces a wide range of vegetables and fruits. Sabra, the nickname for native-born Israelis, comes from the cactus fruit—

tough and prickly on the outside, soft and sweet on the inside; it also the name of an orange-and-chocolate liqueur. Falafel served with vegetables in pita bread can be found all over the city. Olive wood and mother-of-pearl find their way into local handicrafts.

- ■ **Haifa Museums**
- ■ **Baha'i Shrine and Gardens**
- ■ **Clandestine Immigration and Naval Museum**
- ■ **Chagall Artists' House**
- ■ **Carmelite Monastery**
- ■ **Monorail ride to Carmel Center**
- ■ **Old Akko**
- ■ **Nazareth**
- ■ **Meggido**
- ■ **Caesarea**

Tel Aviv/Jaffa

Just a century ago Tel Aviv (Hill of Spring) was a series of sand dunes; today it is the heart of Israel's second-largest metropolitan area, home to nearly two million people. It is also the country's financial, business, and entertainment center, boasting skyscrapers that soar along the coastline, and relatively few monuments and ruins. **Sheinkin** and **Dizengoff Streets** and the shorefront **Tayelet** are Tel Aviv's prime spots for people watching, cafe sitting, and window shopping.

By contrast, Jaffa—now considered part of cosmopolitan Tel Aviv—is one of the oldest cities in the world. According to the *Old Testament,* Noah's son Japheth settled here after the flood. He named it after himself, giving rise to the Hebrew word *yafo* (beautiful). Jaffa was subsequently inhabited by Egyptians, Philistines, Israelites, Persians, Syrians, Maccabees, Romans, Muslims, Crusaders, Turks, and the British. Today **Old Jaffa** has a decidedly Eastern ambience. In addition to a stunning view of the harbor, there's a mix of old and new—winding streets and back alleys, chic boutiques and galleries.

Tel Aviv's culinary scene is international, in part because of the influence of the Jews who emigrated

Baha'i Shrine and Gardens, Haifa

here from around the world and brought their traditions with them. **Shuk Betzalel** features an entire street of falafel vendors and the largest salad selection this side of the Mediterranean. Leather jackets and gold jewelry are some of the articles on sale throughout the city.

- Eretz Israel Museum (Land of Israel Museum)
- Bet Hatfutsot (Museum of the Jewish Diaspora)
- Tel Aviv Museum of Art
- Bet Bialik (Bialik House)
- Diamond Museum
- Shuk Ha Carmel (Carmel Market)
- Newe Tzedek
- Kerem Ha Temanim (Yemenite Quarter)
- Museum of Antiquities of Tel Aviv–Jaffa
- Kikkar Kedumim

Italy

Florence (Livorno)

Originally settled by the Etruscans between the 9th and 8th centuries BC, Florence became a thriving trading center during Roman times because of its critical location along the **Arno River.** This changed after the fall of the Roman Empire, and it wasn't until the Middle Ages that the *comune* (city-state) prospered anew with an increase in commercial and banking activities. The republic flourished under the patronage of the powerful Medici family and was Europe's undisputed capital of art, architecture, and science. Such notables as Dante, Machiavelli, Donatello, Brunelleschi, Michelangelo, and Botticelli lived and worked here in the birthplace of the Italian Renaissance.

Florence today (population almost 400,000) features many vestiges of the past, with the 14th-century pink, white, and green marble **Duomo** (cathedral) dominating the skyline. The view from its **Campanile** (bell tower) features a panorama of red-tile rooftops sprawling in all directions and rolling hills covered in olive trees and grapevines and fields of sunflowers. Florence boasts some of the world's greatest art treasures and museums, which have survived shelling during World War II, devastating floods, and a recent terrorist attack.

Crostini (toasted bread rounds sometimes spread with a chicken liver pâté) and bruschetta (toasted bread rubbed with garlic and drizzled with olive oil, and often topped with tomatoes) are typical antipasti. Other specialties include *bistecca alla fiorentina* (a thick slab of steak grilled over charcoal with olive oil, salt, and pepper, and served rare), *trippa alla fiorentina* (tripe stewed with tomatoes), and *vitello arrosto* (roasted veal). Gold jewelry is displayed in the many shops on the **Ponte Vecchio,** and leather goods and straw items are offered in both the **Mercato di San Lorenzo** (San Lorenzo Market) and the **Mercato Nuovo** (New Market). Designer fashion

boutiques can be found among imposing 15th-century palazzi on **Via dei Tornabuoni.**

- Convento di San Marco (Monastery of San Marco)
- Galleria dell'Accademia (Academy Gallery)
- Chiesa di San Lorenzo and Cappelle Medicee (Medici Chapels)
- Chiesa di Santa Maria Novella
- Battistero (Baptistry)
- Palazzo Bargello and Museo Nazionale
- Piazza della Signoria and Palazzo Vecchio
- Galleria degli Uffizi (Uffizi Gallery)
- Palazzo Pitti
- Forte di Belvedere

Naples

The magnificent **Bay of Naples** has long been lauded by its many illustrious visitors for its gently curving shoreline, beautiful seaport, palm-lined seaside avenues, mild climate, and romantic isles. But Naples has always had a darker side. Brooding **Mount Vesuvius,** hovering over the city to the southeast, buried neighboring **Pompeii** and **Herculaneum** with ash and lava when it erupted in AD 79 at the height of the Roman Empire. More recently the earthquake that devastated southern Italy in 1980 took a tragic toll in Naples, adding yet another problem to the city's permanent ills of unemployment, crime, and traffic congestion.

Naples was settled as a Greek colony in about 1000 BC, and was once occupied by Napoleon, who made his brother Joseph ruler. Today it is Italy's third-largest city (over one million inhabitants) and a major seaport and manufacturing center. Naples also has its share of ornate churches, grand palazzi, and art and archaeology museums. A massive Norman yellow-brick fortress stands on a promontory that divides the bay in two. Across the Bay of Naples is the **Isle of Capri,** with soaring cliffs, bougainvillea-draped balconies, and the fabled **Grotta Azzurra** (Blue Grotto). Ruins of villas built by Roman emperors are another of the island's attractions.

The city gave the world Enrico Caruso and *pizza margherita,* prepared here with fresh tomatoes, oregano, basil, and garlic. Many menus feature *frittura del golfo* (tiny fried fish) and *sfogliatelle* (a flaky ricotta-filled pastry). Naples is located in the Campania region in southern Italy, and its rich volcanic soil is well suited to the art of wine making—white Lacrima Christi is one of the better-known varieties. **Via Roma** is Naples's main shopping street, where such goods as locally produced fine porcelain, pottery, and terracotta; coral jewelry; handmade lace and embroidery; copper and wrought-iron work; stone sculptures; wood carvings; and nativity puppets can be found.

- Piazza del Gesù Nuovo and Chiesa del Gesù Nuovo
- Duomo

- Via Tribunali and Port' Alba
- Palazzo Reale (Royal Palace)
- Teatro San Carlo
- Museo Nazionale Archeologico
- Museo di Capodimonte
- Funicular to Vomero and Certosa di San Martino (Carthusian Monastery and National Museum of St. Martin)
- Pompeii and Herculaneum
- Anacapri

Rome (Civitavecchia)

The **Tiber River** curves gracefully through Rome; most of the ancient city's attractions are found on one bank, while **Vatican City** lies on the other. Although Italy's capital and largest city (about 2.5 million residents) can be quite chaotic, Rome still offers quiet little piazzas tucked away at the end of narrow lanes. And even the simplest square is accented with the sculpture and architecture for which the Eternal City is so famous—magnificent churches, palaces, fountains, and statuary.

According to legend Rome was founded in 753 BC by Romulus and Remus, twin sons of Roman god of war Mars, who were raised by a she-wolf after being abandoned on the banks of the Tiber River. Romulus killed his brother while arguing over which one would rule, then established the city on the **Palatine**—one of the city's **Seven Hills.** As the center of the most powerful empire of the ancient world, Rome provided Western civilization with advanced forms of government, architecture, literature, and other arts and sciences. It was also the birthplace of organized Christianity, and today is still the center of the world's largest Christian denomination—the Roman Catholic Church. Rome was an important hub during the Renaissance and Baroque periods; its legacy of art and architecture is visible throughout the city.

Classic Roman cuisine includes *spaghetti alla carbonara* (with eggs, pancetta, and cheese), *saltimbocca alla romana* (rolled veal fillets stuffed with ham and sage), *carciofi alla giudia* (flattened whole artichokes fried in oil), and *supplì* (battered, deep-fried rice balls filled with mozzarella). Shoppers here snap up designer clothing and leather goods, as well as fabrics and jewelry. Paintings and antiques are also plentiful.

- Colosseum and the Arch of Constantine
- Roman Forum
- Fontana di Trevi (Trevi Fountain)
- Pantheon
- Piazza Navona
- Galleria Nazionale d'Arte Antica (National Gallery of Ancient Art)
- Piazza di Spagna and the Spanish Steps
- Villa Borghese and Museo e Galleria Borghese (Borghese Museum and Gallery)
- Basilica di San Pietro (St. Peter's Basilica)
- Vatican Museums

Venice

Despite flooding, industrial pollution, and lagoon dredging that have caused Venice to start sinking, the city's fairy-tale magic endures. This archipelago of 118 islands, 400 bridges, and more than 100 canals built on piles sunk deep into the mud in the

Ponte dei Sospiri (Bridge of Sighs), Venice

northwest corner of the **Adriatic Sea**, has caused such writers as Casanova, Goethe, Byron, Browning, Dickens, Twain, James, Proust, Mann, and Hemingway to wax poetic about its watery charms.

Venice was originally inhabited by fishermen and sailors in AD 400, followed by refugees from the mainland of Italy who were driven south to Venice's marshlands, islands, and lagoons by the Lombard invasion in 568. In about 800 Venice started its illustrious millennium as a maritime republic (La Serenissima), becoming one of the greatest commercial and seafaring powers in history. Venetian native Marco Polo opened a trade route to China in 1275, the first step in establishing a commercial exchange with the Far East. During the Crusades Venice acquired over half of the Byzantine empire, including its wealth of art treasures and traditions. Ruled by doges until Napoleon Bonaparte conquered Italy and dissolved the republic in 1797, Venice passed through periods of French and Austrian control before joining the Kingdom of Italy in 1866.

The Venetians gave the world gambling casinos, the glass mirror, Vivaldi, and the city was home to Monteverdi. While a gondola ride is a romantic splurge, a trip on a *vaporetto* (water bus) may well be one of the world's great transportation bargains. Risotto is often prepared with *seppie* (squid), sometimes in its own ink (*nero).* Another rice first course is *risi e bisi* (with peas). Seafood and fish entrées are in abundance—*baccalà alla veneziana* (salted codfish with anchovies and onions) and *branzino bollito* (sea bass simmered in white wine, onions, carrots, and herbs). Carnivores can feast on *fegato alla veneziana* (sautéed calves' liver and onions). Polenta is served with nearly every meal. Shoppers can find Venetian glass, Carnival masks, and marbled paper, along with clothing and leatherwear.

- ◾ **Canal Grande (Grand Canal) and Ponte di Rialto (Rialto Bridge)**
- ◾ **Piazza San Marco (St. Mark's Square) and Basilica di San Marco (St. Mark's Basilica)**
- ◾ **Palazzo Ducale (Doges' Palace) and Ponte dei Sospiri (Bridge of Sighs)**
- ◾ **Collezione Peggy Guggenheim (Peggy Guggenheim Collection)**
- ◾ **Galleria dell'Accademia (Academy of Fine Arts)**
- ◾ **Scuola Grande Arciconfraternità di San Rocco**
- ◾ **Campo San Polo**
- ◾ **San Giorgio Maggiore**
- ◾ **Murano**
- ◾ **Burano**

Costa Cruise Lines lives up to its motto, "Cruising Italian Style." In addition to dishing up homemade pasta, the line hosts a wacky Roman bacchanal—complete with togas made with bedsheets—on every Caribbean cruise.

Malta
Valletta

The three-island archipelago of Malta, almost 60 miles south of Sicily and strategically located in the middle of the Mediterranean, has many excellent natural harbors. As a result, it has been occupied over the years by Phoenicians, Carthaginians, Romans, Byzantines, Moslems, Normans, Castilians, French, and British until it became an independent country in 1964. The Neolithic farmers who first settled Malta some 5,000 years ago left behind Stonehengelike temples. The Knights of Malta also bestowed a unique imprint on the archipelago after their arrival in 1530—under their fortified watch, trade, commerce, culture, architecture, and the arts flourished.

The capital Valletta is one of the earliest examples of a planned city. Named in honor of Jean de la Vallette, the Grand Master leader of the Knights of Malta, it was built on the grid system by the best European engineers and artists of the time. Valletta's magnificent palaces and other treasures led Sir Walter Scott to describe it as "the city built by gentlemen for gentlemen."

Islanders speak Maltese, a melange of Arabic, Italian, and French. They are intensely Catholic and are constantly celebrating some festival. Island restaurants offer a variety of fresh seafood, including lampuki, a fish unique to Malta. Stewed *fenek* (rabbit), usually served with spaghetti, is a national dish. The Maltese are known for glassware, jewelry, brown-and-blue glazed ceramics, and wrought ironwork, as well as knit and crocheted textiles and lace.

- ◾ **St. John's Co-Cathedral and Museum**
- ◾ **Manoel Theater**
- ◾ **Palace of the Grand Masters and Armory of the Knights**
- ◾ **Upper Barracca Gardens**
- ◾ **National Museum of Archaeology**
- ◾ **National Museum of Fine Arts**
- ◾ **Auberge de Castille de Leon**
- ◾ **Fort St. Elmo**
- ◾ **Walk along the Fortifications**
- ◾ **Mdina**

Monaco
Monte Carlo

A luscious playground for the world's rich and famous, Monaco is the queen of the **Côte d'Azur.** This less-than-one-square mile sovereign state comprises four districts—Monte Carlo with its yacht-lined port is probably the country's best-known area. Perched high atop **Le Rocher** (the Rock) is **Monaco-Ville** where the **Vieille Ville** (Old Town)—with medieval, vaulted passageways—is located. Le Rocher is crowned by the **Palais Princier** (Prince's

Palace), home to Prince Rainier and the ruling Grimaldi family—one of Europe's oldest reigning dynasties. The district of Monte Carlo boasts the **Casino de Monte Carlo**, built in 1878 by Paris Opera House architect **Charles Garnier.**

The building drips with Rococco turrets, green copper cupolas, onyx columns, red velvet, and gold chandeliers. Entry fees are worth the wander through the ornate gaming rooms; if not to take a chance, then to watch others do so—in huge denominations. The **Salle Garnier** (Garnier Room) inside the casino attracts audiences as well, though here opera and ballet are the draw.

Monaco was probably first inhabited by the Phoenicians in about 700 BC. It has been ruled by the Genovese House of Grimaldi since 1297 when François Grimaldi snuck in with his troops disguised as monks. The Grimaldis were dethroned during the French Revolution but reinstated in 1814. The country first declared its independence from France in 1489, but it wasn't until 1861, when Charles III negotiated a treaty with France, that the sovereignty of Monaco was guaranteed.

Charming restaurants in Vieille Ville or seaside outdoor cafes feature Monégasque cuisine. Regional specialties include *barbagiuan* (pastry stuffed with spinach, rice, eggs, and herbs) and *l'estocaficada* (an aromatic fish stew of smoked haddock with garlic, onion, tomatoes, peppers, new potatoes, and olives). Haute couture and such luxury items as precious jewelry and perfume are found throughout the city.

- **Musée Océanographique (Oceanographic Museum)**
- **Museé Napoléonien et des Archives Monégasques (Museum of Napoleonic Souvenirs)**
- **Cathédrale du Monaco (Monaco Cathedral)**
- **Musée d'Anthropologie Préhistorique (Museum of Prehistoric Anthropology)**
- **Palais Garnier**
- **Musée National (National Museum) at Villa Sauber**
- **Prince of Monaco's Private Collection of Classic Cars**
- **Jardin Japonais (Japanese Gardens)**
- **Jardin Exotique (Exotic Gardens)**
- **Market at Place d'Armes**

Morocco

Casablanca

Not a single scene from the movie *Casablanca* was filmed here, yet **Rick's Cafe** immediately comes to everyone's mind when the place is mentioned. An estimated four million residents live in Morocco's biggest city (Dar el Beida in Arabic) and Africa's second-largest urban area. It is Morocco's center of trade, industry, and finance. Casablanca's wide boulevards are a remainder from the French colonial period in the 20th century, and its large white buildings feature a blend of French and Moroccan styles. The city boasts the world's largest mosque, complete with a retractable roof.

Once known as **Anfa,** capital of an ancient Berber state, the small village that would become known as Casablanca was conquered by the Arab Almohads in 1188, who developed it as a port, famous for both trade and piracy. Casablanca was a safe haven for Jews who fled the Spanish Inquisition in the 15th century—a large Jewish population lived in the medina, the old part of the city noted for curving alleys. The Portuguese came here in the 15th and 16th centuries and twice destroyed their own enclave that pirates had seized. They reestablished themselves in the late 16th century and named the city **Casa Branca** (white house). The city was destroyed by an earthquake in 1755 and rebuilt by Sultan Sidi Mohammed Ben Abdellah later in the 18th century. After the French arrived in the 20th century and built an artificial harbor, the city grew rapidly. The country has been independent since 1956.

Arabic is the official language, although French and some English are also spoken. A typical Moroccan meal features *harira* (a filling soup made with chickpeas); couscous; and kebabs of beef or lamb, washed down with mint tea. *Tagine* (a meat and vegetable stew with potatoes, olives, lemon, prunes, and/or spices) is cooked in a conical ceramic dish. Traditionally the best bargains and the most authentic shopping experience are in the souk, where haggling for leather goods, pottery, metal and wood objects, and jewelry is de rigueur. Textile arts from basic rugs to silk carpets reflect regional traditions.

- **Place des Nations Unies**
- **Cathedral de Sacré Coeur**
- **Hassan II Mosque**
- **Corniche**
- **Quartier Habous**
- **Marabout of Sidi Abderrahman**
- **Aïn Diab**
- **Souk**
- **Rabat**
- **Oualiega Oyster (Farm/Pearl Factory)**

Delta Queen Steamboat Co.'s *Delta Queen* was built in 1927 and is the world's only authentic, fully restored, overnight steamboat. It was designated a National Historic Landmark in 1989. The boat still boasts its original hardwood paneling, stained-glass and diamond-cut windows, and dramatic grand staircase, crowned by a Tiffany crystal chandelier.

Portugal

Lisbon

With its fine harbor along the **Tagus River,** Lisbon ("Lisboa" in Portuguese) was most likely developed around 1200 BC as a Phoenician trading post. (Legend also claims that the city was founded by Odysseus during his travels.) It was an important port of call for ships sailing between the Mediterranean and Northern Europe and was conquered in succession by the Greeks, Carthaginians, Romans, Visigoths, and Moors. Under the rule of Prince Henry the Navigator in the 15th century, Portugal entered an era of conquest and discovery when such famous explorers as Vasco da Gama and Bartolomeu Dias set off from Lisbon to discover new trade routes. A vast empire was created during these golden years that at its peak extended to India and the Far East, Brazil, and Africa.

Lisbon remains a vital seaport and export center for many of Portugal's goods. Although it is just a few miles from the Atlantic Ocean, the city looks and feels Mediterranean, with pastel facades, red-tile rooftops, tree-lined boulevards, narrow cobblestone streets, and hand-painted wall tiles. There is also a Moorish feel to some of Lisbon's architecture. The city today is the westernmost capital on the European mainland and has a population of over two million people. At press time Lisbon's historic neighborhoods and waterfront were undergoing a massive facelift in preparation for **Expo '98** and the 500th anniversary of Vasco da Gama's voyage to India, which kicked off the Age of Discovery.

Fado (fate) is the music of Portugal. Songs of longing and lament, tragedy and despair, they are to Portugal what the tango is to Argentina. The singer, usually dressed in black, is accompanied by two guitars. Small fado clubs can be found in the **Alfama** or **Bairro Alto** districts. *Açorda de marisco* (spicy garlic-scented pudding made with seafood, bread, and eggs) is a favorite local dish, along with *bacalhau cozido com grão* (cod with chickpeas and potatoes). Local handicrafts to look for include embroidery from Madeira, shawls, knitwear, pottery, rugs, *azulejos* (hand-painted tiles), filigree, and wickerwork.

- Alfama and Largo de Santa Luzia
- Castelo de São Jorge (St. George's Castle)
- Sé (Cathedral)
- Mosteiro dos Jerónimos (Jerónimos Monastery)
- Museu dos Coches (Coach Museum)
- Padrão dos Descobrimentos (Monument of the Discoveries)
- Torre de Belém (Belém Tower)
- Museu do Azulejo (Tile Museum)
- Museu Calouste Gulbenkian (Gulbenkian Museum)
- Sintra

Funchal, Madeira

The Portuguese island of Madeira boasts dazzling flowers, lush greenery, majestic cliffs, and soaring,

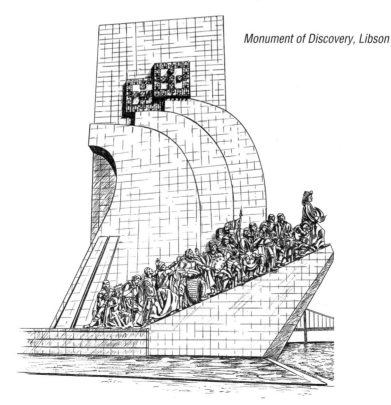

Monument of Discovery, Libson

mist-shrouded mountains dotted with white houses. Located on the island's south side, the capital city of Funchal (about 130,000 residents) is sheltered from the north by mountain ridges 4,000 feet high and boasts an armada of fishing boats in the harbor. Funchal offers several novel means of transportation. One is the bullock car—a canopied ox-drawn four-seat sled that was introduced to the island in 1848. Another more thrilling form of conveyance is the *carro de cesto,* a wicker toboggan guided by pairs of white-clad men who run alongside. Walkers and hikers enjoy exploring the *levadas*—an extensive network of irrigation channels carrying water from the mountains to the terraced fields and villages below.

Located about 560 miles southwest of the Portuguese mainland, Madeira was first sighted by explorer João Gonçalves Zarco in 1419. The 286-square-mile volcanic island later became a way station for British army officers and their families on long sea voyages to and from colonies in Africa and India.

Wine making in Madeira dates back to the 15th century when Prince Henry the Navigator planted vines from Cyprus and Crete and sugarcane from Sicily here. The four types of Madeira wines are dry Sercials, semidry Verdelhos, semisweet Buals, and sweet Malmseys. Fishing is also a big industry for the islanders—the mild, sweet *espada* (black scabbard fish), prepared in a variety of ways, is plentiful, as is tuna. A typical Madeiran meat dish is *espetada* (skewered, charcoal-grilled beef cubes with laurel and garlic). Local artisans produce much sought-after embroidery, glassware, marquetry, straw hats, tapestry, and wickerware.

- ■ Adega de São Francisco (St. Francis Wine Lodge)
- ■ Mercado dos Lavrodores (Workers' Market)
- ■ Convento de Santa Clara (Convent of St. Clare)
- ■ Jardim Botânico (Botanical Gardens)
- ■ Sé (Cathedral)
- ■ Museu Quinta das Cruzes (Mansion of the Crosses)
- ■ Museu de Cidade (City Museum)
- ■ Rua da Carreira
- ■ Museu Frederico de Freitas (Frederico de Freitas Museum)
- ■ Monte

Porto

Porto (Oporto in Portuguese) is probably best known for the wine to which it lends its name. The manufacture of the sweet, usually red wine fortified with brandy and aged in enormous oak barrels still fuels the city's economy. Many of the 80 *adegas* (wine lodges) offer both tours and tastings of their products. Porto is located on Portugal's north-western coast, along a gorge cut by the **Douro River** on its cross-country course to the Atlantic. It is Portugal's second-largest city with a population of about 350,000 people, and the north's industrial and

commercial center. The river splits Porto in two: the city center and its medieval churches and museums lie on the north side, and **Vila Nova da Gaia**—where the port wine lodges are found—is on the south bank.

The city's prime location has always made it attractive to traders and settlers. The Phoenicians, drawn by the region's metal deposits, came to the mouth of the Douro to trade. The Romans fortified it when they arrived in the third century and named it **Portus.** Subsequent invaders included the Visigoths, Moors, Spanish, French, and British.

Tripas à modo do Porto (tripe with chopped bits of pig's ear and snout, bacon, sausages, white beans, onions, carrots, parsley, and herbs, and served over rice) commemorates Prince Henry the Navigator's 1415 invasion of Morocco when residents slaughtered all their cattle, gave the meat to the fleet, and kept the entrails for themselves. Other culinary delights include *bacalhau* (codfish), cooked in any number of ways, and *caldo verde* (a spicy soup of green cabbage, puréed potatoes, and sausage). Embroidery, linen, textiles and tapestry work, jewelry and filigree, ceramics, pottery, works in wood, leather, copper, wrought iron, and wicker are some of the best local handicrafts.

- ■ Palacio da Bolsa (Stock Exchange)
- ■ Igreja de São Francisco (Church of San Francisco)
- ■ Torre dos Clérigos (Tower of Clerics)
- ■ Sé (Cathedral)
- ■ Ribeira (Esplanade)
- ■ Casa de Serralves/Museu de Arte Moderna (Modern Art Museum)
- ■ Solar do Vinho do Porto
- ■ Mercado de Bolhão
- ■ Museu Nacional Soares dos Reis (Soares dos Reis National Museum)
- ■ Port Wine Lodge Tour

Spain

Barcelona

The history of Barcelona dates back to 218 BC, when Carthaginian Hamilcar Barca (Hannibal's father) founded a settlement here named **Barcino**. The Romans developed the town, and the Visigoths fought over it in the 5th century AD, followed by the Moors in the 8th century. Charlemagne conquered Barcelona in 801, and after uniting with Aragon in 1137 it was the commercially and intellectually prosperous capital of Catalonia, extending its reach across the Mediterranean through the 16th century. At the end of the 15th century Barcelona assimilated into the new Spain of Ferdinand and Isabella, but Catalan autonomy remains an issue to today.

With a population of three million, Barcelona is Spain's second-largest city after Madrid, although the Catalan people, for whom Barcelona is the capital, might argue that it is number one. Fiercely proud and independent, they take great pride in their own culture, continuing to speak Catalan and using the language in newspapers, on the radio, and on stage. Architect **Antoni Gaudí** created many of his master-pieces in Barcelona during the 19th and 20th centuries, combining stone, iron, and ceramics in a masterful fashion. Thanks to his efforts, Barcelona has one of the richest collections of Modernist buildings in the world. Native son Joan Miró's abstract art adorns city museums and public spaces, while museums house vast collections of Pablo Picasso and Salvador Dalí.

A Catalan culinary high point is *zarzuela* (a seafood and fish stew). *Xató de Sitges* is a salad made from anchovies, tuna, olive oil, vinegar, hot red pepper, garlic, and ground almonds. Locally produced crafts include ceramics, glassware, leather goods, embroidery, lacework, and woven products. Filigree jewelry is popular, as are antiques, including old maps, books, and furniture.

- Barrio Gótico (Gothic Quarter)
- Catedral de Santa Eulalia and Museum
- Mercat San Josep/La Boquería (St. Joseph Market/Covered Market)
- Las Ramblas (Promenade)
- Monument a Colom (Monument to Columbus)
- Sagrada Familia (Sacred Family)
- Parc Güell (Güell Park)
- Museu Picasso (Picasso Museum)
- Montjuïc and Fondacio Joan Miró
- Museu d'Art de Catalunya (Museum of Art of Catalunya)

Las Palmas, Gran Canaria, Canary Islands

Although canaries do live in the Canaries, the archipelago's name comes from another source. Pliny wrote of an expedition sent to these legendary isles by the African king, Juba. The explorers returned with huge, wild dogs; hence the name **Canarias,** from the Latin *canis* (dog). The Spanish conquered the Canary Islands in 1483, taking them from the Guanche cave dwellers—the original inhabitants—and Columbus stopped here a decade later on his way to the New World.

These volcanic islands are located 65 miles off the northwest coast of Africa. Gran Canaria is the third-largest of the islands—the 600-square-mile isle is often called a miniature continent because of its diverse topo-graphy. It is a place of stark granite mountains scored by deep ravines, arid desert and lush vegetation, where plants from Europe, Africa, and the Americas grow—pine forests, lime trees,

vineyards, coffee, palms, bananas, almonds, sugarcane, tomatoes—all surrounded by miles of coastline featuring dramatic cliffs and golden beaches. The capital, Las Palmas, on the northeast corner of the island is the largest city in the archipelago, home to a half-million inhabitants. Today it is both a historical center of stately homes with quiet courtyards and wrought-iron balconies facing narrow streets and sheltered squares, and a cosmopolitan resort, attracting planeloads of pale Northern European tourists year-round.

In addition to every sort of seafood imaginable and *gofio* (a roasted mixture of wheat, maize, or barley that is sometimes eaten instead of bread), Canary Islanders love *cabrito asado* (roasted kid goat),

*Sagrada Familia
(Sacred Family), Barcelona*

papas viudas, ("widows' potatoes," made from roasted potatoes, carrots, peas, ham, onions, green peppers, and olives), and *papas arrugadas* ("wrinkled potatoes," baked in salt and eaten with *mojo*—the red or green piquant sauce made from hot peppers). The Canary Islands are best known for their embroidery—delicate needlework adorning bedspreads, napkins, tablecloths, and hand towels. Ceramics, carvings, baskets, and cigars are also noteworthy.

- ■ Vegueta
- ■ Old City and Cathedral
- ■ Casa de Colón (House of Columbus)
- ■ Museo Canario (Canary Museum)
- ■ Catedral de Santa Ana (St. Ann Cathedral)
- ■ Arucas
- ■ Teror
- ■ Cruz de Tejada (Cross of Tejada)
- ■ Caldera de Bandama (Bandama Crater)
- ■ Gáldar

Palma de Majorca, Majorca, Balearic Islands

The first visitors nearly 4,000 years ago of the Balearic Islands off Spain's eastern shore were Iberians from North Africa and Celts from Northern Europe. Carthaginians, Romans, Goths, and Moors subsequently occupied the islands; at other times they were also independent Muslim and Christian kingdoms. After rejoining the Spanish Empire in the 14th century, Majorca prospered, becoming an artistic and cultural center, until the 16th century when the Spanish turned toward Latin American conquests. Today Northern Europeans invade Majorca every summer in search of sand, sun, and fun.

Majorca is the largest of the four inhabited Balearic Islands (there are a total of seven)—60 miles long, it covers 1,405 square miles off Spain's eastern shore. Palma, the islands' provincial capital and largest city, is named for the palm trees introduced from Africa during the long Arab occupation. Narrow streets snake through centuries-old Arab and Gothic quarters.

Island specialties include *lechón* (roasted suckling pig), *sopa mallorquína* (a thick soup made from bread, green vegetables, onions, and garlic), *tumbet* (eggplant, peppers, potatoes, and tomatoes sauteed in olive oil), and *ensaimadas* (fluffy, spiral-shaped pastry). Majorca features leather clothing and shoes, glassware, and high-quality artificial pearls, coated with a substance made from fish scales.

- ■ Palacio de la Almudaina (Almudaina Palace) and Es Born
- ■ Seo (Cathedral)
- ■ Barrio Portella and Baños Arabes (Arab Baths)
- ■ Palacio Vivot (Vivot Palace)
- ■ Convento de San Francisco (Convent of St. Francis)
- ■ Paseo Marítimo (Seaside Promenade)
- ■ La Lonja (Commodity Exchange) and Museum of Art
- ■ Castillo de Bellver (Bellver Castle)
- ■ El Consejo Interinsular de Baleares (Inter-Island Balaeric Council)
- ■ Fundació Joan Miró (Joan Miró Foundation)

Santa Cruz de Tenerife, Tenerife, Canary Islands

Largest of the Canary Islands at 793 square miles, the triangle-shaped Tenerife off the Moroccan coast boasts a spectacular, sometimes lunar landscape. It is crowned by the highest mountain in Spain, the 12,198-foot-high volcano **Pico de Teide** that is covered with snow in the winter. The island's name is said to come from a Guanche word (for more on the history of the Canary Islands, see "Las Palmas," above) meaning snow-capped mountain. The climate here is pleasantly dry, with warm trade winds. Over 2,000 species of flowering plants grow on the rich volcanic soil of "The Island of Eternal Spring"; many of them are unique to the Canary Islands.

Santa Cruz, a sunny, garden-filled city of 250,000 and the capital of the island and province, sits on the peak's lower, pine-covered slopes facing a large bay. It is Spain's busiest port because of its strategic location.

Traditional dishes served here include *sancocho canario* (salted sea bass, potatoes, and *mojo*), *conejo salmorejo* (spicy rabbit), and *gofio*. Bananas and tomatoes are a major source of income for the islands and find their way into various recipes, as do avocado and papaya. The island's craftspeople are known for their brilliantly colored embroidery, pottery, palm-leaf basketry, wickerwork, wood carvings, and goldsmithing.

- ■ El Cabildo Insular (Island government building and Archaeology Museum)
- ■ Palacio Carta (Carta Palace)
- ■ Iglesia La Concepción (Conception Church)
- ■ Plaza El Principe and Municipal Museum of Paintings and Sculpture
- ■ Paso Alto Castle
- ■ Monte La Esperanza (Mount La Esperanza)
- ■ Las Cañadas del Teide
- ■ Taganana
- ■ Forest of Aguamansa
- ■ La Orotava and Casas de las Balcones

Actually heard on board:

"What time is the midnight buffet?"

Tunisia

Tunis (La Goulette)

The 7th-century Arab invasion and final destruction of neighboring Carthage—home of Hannibal— brought prosperity to the city of Tunis, but it wasn't until the Hafside Dynasty in the 13th century that it evolved into a religious and intellectual center. Tunis was occupied by the Ottoman Empire in the 16th century and subsequently became a center for pirate ships plying the Mediterranean. An influx of Spanish Moors at the beginning of the 17th century brought craftsmen who made *chechias* (little red hats) that were exported throughout the Mediterranean for three centuries. The city was colonized by the French in 1881, invaded by Germany during World War II, and became independent in 1956.

Situated on the shores of **Lake of Tunis,** the city is linked by a narrow entrance to the sea at La Goulette ("The Gullet"). Tunis (population 1.5 million) imparts a distinctly European air as a result of the French occupation, with wide boulevards and cafes in the newer section. Palaces, mosques, and markets line the winding alleyways of the **Old Town**—a UNESCO cultural heritage site. Arabic is the official language, but French and some English are also spoken.

Fish—especially mullet—is the specialty along the coast here. Other dishes include *brik* (deep-fried pastry filled with a runny egg and any one of a variety of other ingredients, including chopped tuna, ground beef, or vegetables), *chakchouka* (ratatouille with chickpeas, tomatoes, peppers, garlic, onions, and a poached egg), and couscous. The markets are packed with perfumes, precious stones, jewelry, carpets, blankets, leather, and brass.

- ■ **Dar Ben Abdallah Palace and Museum of Popular Arts and Traditions**
- ■ **Bardo Museum**
- ■ **Medina**
- ■ **Roman Ruins at Dougga**
- ■ **Carthage**
- ■ **Great Mosque Ez-Zitouna**
- ■ **Souks el Attarine (Perfume), el Kumach (Cloth) and el Birka (Jewelry)**
- ■ **Dar Hussein**
- ■ **Medersa Mouradia**
- ■ **Tourbet el Bey**

Turkey

Istanbul

The only city in the world straddling two continents, Istanbul is a teeming crossroads of Europe and Asia. It is linked by a bridge spanning the **Bosphorus Strait** at the northeastern corner of the **Sea of Marmara.** Its skyline of slender minarets, domed mosques, and

Sultanahmet Camii
(Mosque of Sultan Ahmet or Blue Mosque), Istanbul

turreted palaces is an unforgettable sight, especially when approaching the city by sea at any hour of the day.

Greek settlers with instructions from the Oracle at Delphi founded the city in the 7th century BC, naming it **Byzantium** after their leader, Byzas. Prosperity brought plunderers, however, and a long history of attacks on the city soon began. Over the course of 2,500 years, Persians, Spartans, Macedonians, Thracians, Romans, Bithynians, Gauls, Persians, Slavs, Saracens, and crusaders have all controlled or fought over it. Emperor Constantine made the city the capital of the Eastern Roman (Byzantine) Empire in AD 330 and renamed it Constantinople for himself. Immense city walls—15 feet thick and 49 feet high—and 96 towers kept a series of invaders at bay until crusaders sacked the city in 1204. They cleaned out the churches, shipped out the art, and melted down the gold. In 1453 Mehmet II ("the Conqueror") brought an end to the Byzantine Empire, marching his troops into the city's most famous church, and converting it into a mosque. The city was rebuilt anew as capital of the Ottoman Empire. When the Turkish Republic was proclaimed in 1923, the capital was moved to Ankara. The city's name was changed in 1930, and Istanbul is today a sprawling city of 14 million that remains the country's center of business, finance, and culture.

Local dishes include *sis kebap* (shish kebab) and *dolma* (grape leaves stuffed with a meat and/or rice mixture). *Imam bayaldi* (literally "the priest fainted") is a knee-weakening meal of eggplant stuffed with ground lamb, tomatoes, onions, and garlic. *Börekler* are among the oldest and most important elements of traditional Turkish cuisine—phyllo dough wrapped around a meat, cheese, or vegetable filling—as is baklava (a sweet pastry). The city's many markets offer an opportunity to bargain for gold and silver jewelry, leatherware, brass and copperware, kilims, and spices.

Royal Caribbean's *Sovereign of the Seas*, the world's largest passenger ship when it debuted in 1988, was christened with one of the world's largest bottles of Champagne. Fourteen over-size bottles of Taittinger Champagne were hand blown in Italy especially for the christening ceremony.

Royal Caribbean called the bottles "sovereigns" in honor of the new ship but also as a nod to the tradition of naming large Champagne bottles after Old Testament kings (Nebuchadnezzar, Balthasar, etc.). The bottles are more than three feet tall, hold 26 liters of bubbly (equivalent to 34 regular bottles), weigh 77 pounds, and have a diameter of just over one foot. Royal Caribbean has used sovereigns for every subsequent ship christening.

- Topkapi Palace
- Dolmabahçe Ciragan Palace
- Hagia Sophia (Church of the Holy Wisdom)
- Sultanahmet Camii (Mosque of Sultan Ahmet or Blue Mosque)
- Atmeydani (Hippodrome)
- Ibrahim Pasha Palace (Museum of Turkish and Islamic Arts)
- Kapali Carsi (Grand Bazaar)
- Süleymanuye Mosque Complex
- Galata Tower
- Arkeoloji Müzeleri

Kusadasi

The island of Kusadasi (Bird Island) was once a sleepy fishing village midway down Turkey's **Aegean** coast. Today it is a coastal resort and favorite call for cruise ships. More significantly, however, it is the jumping-off spot for some of the most extensive and impressive Ionian archaeological ruins in the world, namely **Ephesus.**

Colonized by Ionian Greeks in the 10th century BC, Ephesus was one of the greatest ancient cities, surviving Persian and Roman rule, eclipsed in the East only by Alexandria. At its height, after the Romans took control in 133, Ephesus had a population of over 250,000 people and was the unofficial capital of Asia. Renamed for the Amazonian queen Ephesia, the city was a meeting place of merchant caravans with exotic treasures from the East and served as a major port until the harbor silted up and dried out in the fifth century. The worship of the fertility goddess Cybele flourished, and it later became a center for early Christianity. Earthquakes and invasions gradually destroyed Ephesus by the 12th century. The first excavations were begun here in the early 1860s, and marble streets, arches, and columns, facilities for hot and cold running water, and mosaic sidewalks, all built 2,000 years earlier, were uncovered. Today more *tels* (hills) remain unexcavated.

The nearby **Temple of Artemis** (or Diana), with 127 columns—each 60 feet tall—was one of the Seven Wonders of Ancient World. The Virgin Mary is said to have lived her last years close by in **Selçuk.**

Dolma, grilled local fish, *sis kebap, imam bayaldi,* and *börekler* are found on menus throughout Kusadasi. The island's narrow, pedestrian streets strung with lights are lined with stores selling gold and silver jewelry; wares of leather, brass, and copper; kilims; and carpets.

Ephesus

- Ampitheater
- Vedius Gymnasium
- Arcadian Street
- Temple of Hadrian

- Celsus Library
- Marble Way
- Fountain of Trajan

Selçuk

- Basilica of St. John
- Meryemana (House of Mary)
- Ephesus Museum

Ukraine Republic

Odessa

The temperate climate (average 250 sunny days a year) and wide sandy beaches of Odessa make it a favorite resort city for Eastern Europeans, who also come to partake of the therapeutic mud baths. A major port on the **Black Sea**, Odessa has wide avenues and boulevards climbing up and down the hills surrounding **Odessa Bay** and many gardens and parks. Poet Alexander Pushkin lived here for a while, and **Teatr Opery ta Baletu**—its Baroque opera house—was designed by the architects of the Vienna Opera House. Odessa today has over one million residents and remains a cultural and educational center. Film director Sergei Eisenstein immortalized the city's **Potiomkinski Skhody** (Potemkin Stairs)—a monumental stairway connecting the central city with the waterfront—in his epic 1925 film, *Battleship Potemkin.*

The site of today's Odessa was settled in prehistoric and early historic times by various ancient tribes. In 1415 the Ottoman Turks founded a colony here that they named **Khachybe.** The city received its current appellation in 1795 when Russians mistakenly named the port Odessa, believing it to be the ancient Greek colony of Odessos. It was occupied by the Romanians and heavily damaged by the Germans during World War II; over a quarter of a million of its citizens—most of them Jews—were either massacred or deported at that time.

This is the land of fresh beet-and-vegetable borscht. Shop here for painted wooden boxes, plates, and spoons; earthenware; embroidered cloth; and woolen rugs.

- Primorski Boulevard
- Catacombs
- Palace of Prince Vorontsov
- Flower Market
- Arkheolohichny Mucei (Odessa Archaeological Museum)
- Uspensky (Assumption) Cathedral
- Mucei Moroskoho Flotu (Museum of the Black Sea Fleet)
- Museum of Western and Oriental Art
- Privoz Market
- Deribasivska

Yalta

Ukrainian history spans eleven centuries, from the ancient Russian state of **Kievan Rus** in the mid-9th century to the independent country of today. The cradle of three Slavic peoples—Russians, Ukrainians, and the Belarusans—Ukraine was annexed by the former USSR in 1922. It was a founding member of the United Nations (even though it was part of the USSR), and because of its active participation in international politics and policy-making, Ukraine was able to declare its independence in 1991 with the recognition of over 100 countries.

Yalta is on the **Black Sea,** along the southern shore of the **Crimean Peninsula.** The Russian royal family chose Yalta as a summer residence, and dachas still dot the forested hillsides surrounding the city. After the revolution, it became the holiday region for Communist Party VIPs. It is the site of the famous battleground where Britain, France, Turkey, and Sardinia battled Russia over Sebastopol in the 1850s, inspiring Tennyson to write "The Charge of the Light Brigade." Today home to over 88,000 people, Yalta is probably best remembered for the conference in 1945 among Stalin, Roosevelt, and Churchill, when they finalized postwar territorial claims. (The actual meeting took place at the Great Palace—Nicholas II's ornate summer home in nearby Livadii.)

In addition to the ubiquitous borscht, many local restaurants offer *pilmeny* (dumplings) served by the plate. The famous Crimean wine is available both in restaurants and shops.

- Prymorsky Park Gagarina
- Chekhov's House and Museum
- Hlastivchyne Hnizdo (Swallow's Nest)
- Armenian Church
- Polukorsky Hill
- Villa of Kichkine
- Hurzuf and Pushkin Museum
- Livadii and Great Palace
- Uchansu Waterfall
- Alupka and Palatsa Vorontsova

"My experience of ships is that on them one makes an interesting discovery about the world. One finds one can do without it completely."

Dr. Jochum, in *Stepping Westward*, by Malcolm Bradbury

The sail cruiser *Sea Cloud* was commissioned as a private yacht for financier E.F. Hutton and heiress Marjorie Merriweather Post. Christened *Hussar* in 1931, the cruiser carried such famous guests as Franklin D. Roosevelt and the Duke and Duchess of Windsor.

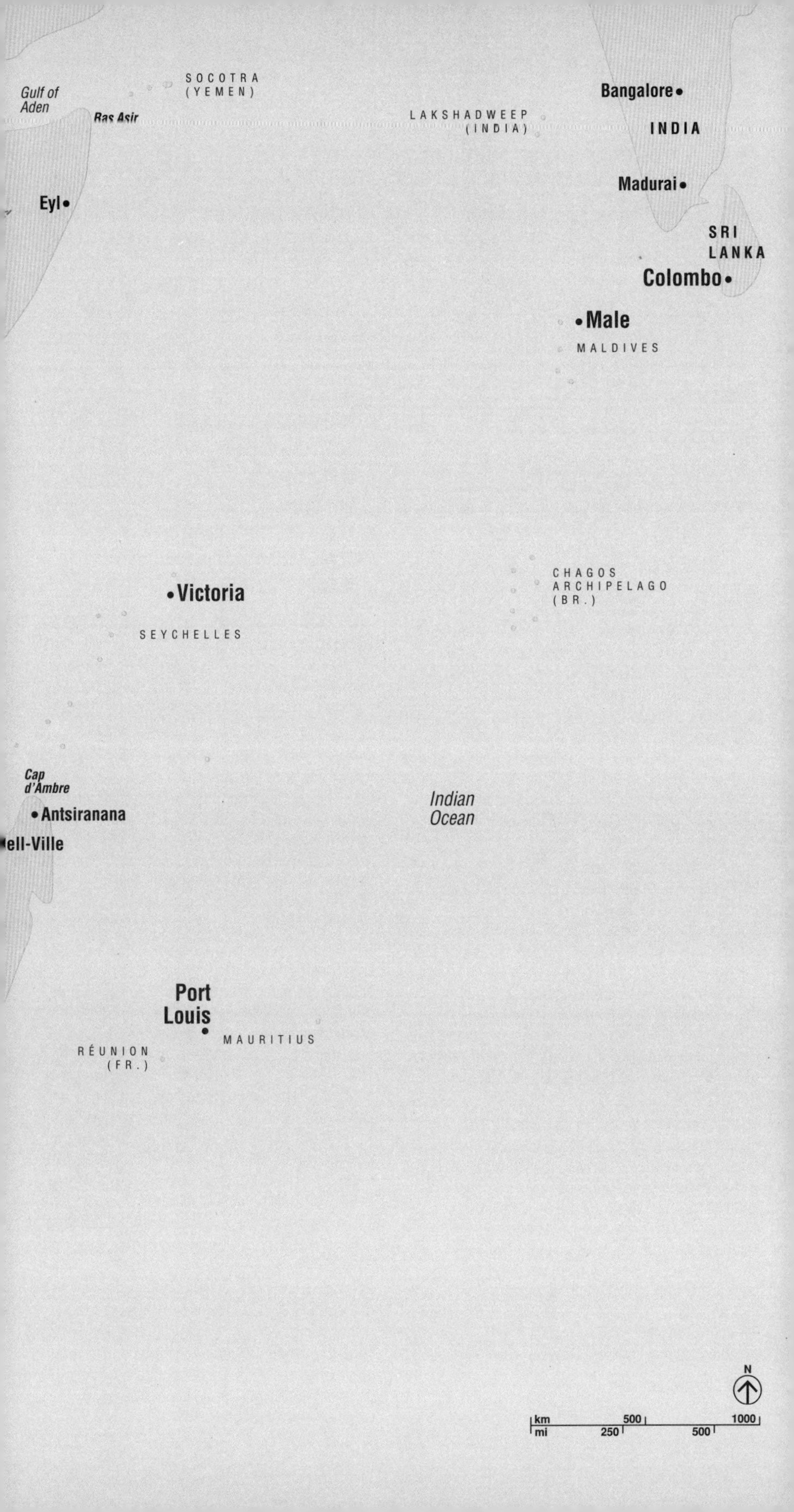

Gulf of
Aden

SOCOTRA
(YEMEN)

Ras Asir

LAKSHADWEEP
(INDIA)

Bangalore•

INDIA

Madurai•

SRI
LANKA

Colombo•

Eyl•

•Male

MALDIVES

•Victoria

SEYCHELLES

CHAGOS
ARCHIPELAGO
(BR.)

*Cap
d'Ambre*

•Antsiranana

Indian
Ocean

Hell-Ville

Port
Louis
•

MAURITIUS

RÉUNION
(FR.)

N

| km | | 500 | | 1000 |
| mi | 250 | | 500 | |

Indian Ocean

The Indian Ocean, south of Asia and bordered by Africa, Australia, and Antarctica, offers a kaleidoscope of cultures, wildlife, and dramatic scenery. The world's third-largest ocean, covering nearly 30 million square miles, laps along Africa's eastern and southern shores and encompasses hundreds of exotic isolated islands, including **Madagascar** and the **Seychelles**.

To the visitor, East Africa offers the legendary spice-laden ports of **Zanzibar** and **Mombasa**, both on offshore islands. And **South Africa**, where African, Asian, and European cultures cautiously merge in a fresh spirit of equality, is attracting more visitors than ever. The highlight of any African trip may well be an inland safari where the opportunity to observe elephants, giraffes, and lions in their natural environment provides a once-in-a-lifetime experience.

Kenya

Mombasa

Located on a 20-square-mile island linked to the mainland by causeway, bridge, and ferry, Mombasa is Kenya's second-largest city. It's also the country's most important port with **Mombasa Harbour**, used by *dhows* (lateen-rigged boats) from the Persian Gulf, and **Kilindini Harbour,** filled with commercial container vessels. The city's population of 600,000 is a blend of the great cultures of Africa, Arabia, and Europe, and home to Kenya's largest concentration of Muslims, as evidenced by the more than 100 mosques on the island. Modern-day Mombasa is a mystical mix of old and new. The older parts are a labyrinth of narrow streets and lanes crammed with crumbling colonial homes and broad shady verandas. From open-fronted shops waft the pungent aromas of exotic spices. The *dhow* harbor is dominated by a 16th-century fort, and coral reefs and white-sand beaches stretch north and south along the coast.

A center of the spice trade for nearly 2,000 years, Mombasa was razed, rebuilt, and ruled by the Portuguese in the 16th and 17th centuries. The Portuguese were expelled by the Omanis, highly active slave traders, who in turn were tossed out by the British in 1887. While they governed, the British established a rail link from the coast to Uganda, thereby turning Mombasa into the gateway to East Africa. The former British crown colony achieved independence in 1963 with Jomo Kenyatta, a leader of the infamous Mau Mau uprising of 1952, as its first president.

The menu in Mombasa can be a wildlife lover's nightmare, with offerings like zebra, ostrich, and giraffe. Fried tilapia (fish with spicy tomato sauce) and *ugali* (dried corn porridge) are local favorites, and coconut and tamarind are used liberally. Local handicrafts include baskets and bags made from sisal, *kangas* (brightly colored cloth squares), soapstone sculptures, wooden carvings, beaded necklaces, and traditional tribal weapons and musical instruments. While English is the official language, Swahili is the national language of Kenya. The simple greeting "Jambo" means "How are you?"

- City Market
- Fort Jesus and Museum
- Old Town
- Leven House and Steps
- Old Law Court
- Mbaraki Pillar
- Kizingo
- Shimba Hills National Reserve
- Moi Avenue and Elephant Tusks
- Tsavo National Park

Madagascar

Nosy-Be

Off the northwest coast of Madagascar lies the 115-square-mile island of Nosy-Be (*Nosy* means island, and *Be* means great). It is often called the "Perfume Island" because the abundant rainfall and sunshine here produce exotic plants, yielding fragrant ylang-ylang, patchouli, lemon grass, and vanilla beans, all staples of the perfume industry. Nosy-Be's volcanic hills contain deep turquoise-blue crater lakes, home to the area's crocodile population. The main town, a sleepy colonial sort of place called **Hell-Ville,** is on the south coast.

The Malagasy people are descendants of Africans and Indonesians; the latter crossed the Indian Ocean in huge outrigger canoes about 1,500 years ago, bringing along their language (an ancient member of the Malayo-Polynesian family), crops (taro, sugarcane, bananas, and coconuts), and customs. The northern tip of Madagascar was always an Arab outpost for the Indian Ocean trade, dealing in gold and silver mined from the interior and slave traffic with East Africa. In the 16th century it became an important provisioning port for Portuguese ships en route to the East. Following the Franco-Malagasy War of 1883, Madagascar became a French colony, settled by planters. Independent since 1958, most of Madagascar's 12 million people continue to live in rural conditions.

Hena ritra (beef stew with tomato, garlic, and hearts of palm) is a typical Malagasy dish, as is *achard* (tomatoes, soy beans, shallots, and pickled onions). Local souvenirs include *lamba* (traditional clothing made of woven lengths of cotton or silk), Antaimoro paper, herbs and spices, wickerwork, wood carvings, and coral objects.

- Hell-Ville Market
- Andilana Beach
- Indian Cemetery
- Palm Beach
- Mont Passot
- Oceanographic Institute
- Andokombe Volcano
- Anbatoloaka village
- Ambanoro village
- Nosy-Komba

Seychelle Islands

Victoria, Mahé

Comprising 92 scattered islands about 1,000 miles east of Kenya, the Seychelles are a luscious mixture of low-lying coral atolls and mountainous granite, blanketed with luxuriant foliage, circled by sandy white beaches studded with bays and lagoons and ringed by coral reefs crowned with white foam. A mountainous island 17 miles long by 5 miles wide, **Mahé,** where 90 percent of the country's inhabitants live, lies just four degrees south of the equator. **Victoria,** the business center and only town to speak of, is one of the world's smallest capital cities. Its main streets are lined with Indian and Chinese shops with wide verandas and tin roofs.

Uninhabited until the French arrived in 1770, the Seychelle Islands changed hands several times during the Napoleonic Wars, until they were finally ceded to Britain in 1814 under the Treaty of Paris. They became a British Crown Colony in 1903 and achieved independence in 1976. The Seychellois people, numbering just over 100,000, are mostly mixed descendants of early French settlers, Asians, and African slaves freed from British navy ships. Residents also include Indians, Chinese, British, and French from Mauritius. The native language is Creole, a French-based patois with English, Arabic, and African influences.

French cuisine predominates; fresh fish, lobster, octopus, coconuts, and tropical fruits round out menus. Local items to look for include handicrafts made from shark's teeth, mother-of-pearl, fish scales, and coral. Coco-de-Mer palms, which grow only on the islands of **Praslin** and **Curieuse,** can live up to 800 years; their nuts—which take 25 years to mature and 7 years to ripen—are polished and halved to make bowls.

- Handicraft Market
- Big Ben
- State House
- Tea Plantation
- Snorkeling/Glass-bottom boat ride
- L'Islette
- Morne Seychellois National Park
- Grand Anse
- Anse Boileau
- Beau Vallon

La Pigue, Seychelle Islands

South Africa

Cape Town

At the southernmost tip of Africa, bounded by Namibia, Botswana, and the Indian and Atlantic Oceans, **Cape Province**—the region where Cape Town is located—is a place of soaring mountains, tumbling rivers, and broad sandy beaches punctuated by rocky promontories, coves, deltas, and lagoons. Sitting in the shadow of 3,566-foot, flat-topped **Table Mountain,** Cape Town is South Africa's oldest, and some say most beautiful city. Its mix of Edwardian, Victorian, and Cape Dutch architectural styles have been well preserved, and the historic waterfront area has been refurbished and restored. The cobblestone streets, mosques, and flat-roofed pastel-colored homes of the city's **Malay Quarter** lend an eastern air.

Although charted by Portuguese navigators as early as the 15th century, when Dutchman Jan van Riebeeck arrived here in 1652, the area was occupied only by nomadic Bushmen. The Dutch established a settlement at Cape Town (Kaapstad in Afrikaans) to resupply the ships of the Dutch East India Company with fresh food. The British battled the Boers—a hardy people of Dutch-Germanic descent—for control of Cape Town; the British won, and Cape Town became an English colony until 1910 when it became a federal union.

There are 11 official languages of South Africa's 40 million residents, whose rich multicultural heritage is reflected in its menus, most notably traditional Cape Malay and Indian. Typical shopping might include antiques of the Cape Dutch, Victorian, and Georgian styles; traditional African crafts such as bold batiks, ceramics, and beadwork; as well as silk saris and spices from the Indian markets.

- ■ Table Mountain
- ■ Botanical Gardens of Kirstenbosch
- ■ Victoria and Alfred Waterfront
- ■ South African Maritime Museum
- ■ Castle of Good Hope
- ■ South African Museum
- ■ Jewish Museum
- ■ Stellenbosch
- ■ Somerset West and Vergelegen Estate
- ■ Cape of Good Hope Nature Reserve

Durban

It's hard to believe that only 150 years ago hippos wallowed among the reeds in Durban's harbor, and elephants strolled through forests along these shores on Africa's southeast coast. Today Durban, named after colonial governor Benjamin D'Urban, is the largest city in **Kwazulu-Natal Province,** and its harbor on **Natal Bay** is one of the world's busiest. Durban is also South Africa's playground by the sea, complete with its stretch of luxury hotel–studded beaches lining the warm Indian Ocean. An intriguing blend of Eastern, Western, and African influences, here you'll find Zulu women selling baubles along the beach, rickshaw drivers weaving in and out of traffic, and mosques, temples, and bazaars filling the air with spice and incense.

Durban was first visited by Portuguese navigator Vasco da Gama in 1497; Zulu King Shaka and his warriors inhabited the Zululand hills when the first British settlers arrived in 1824 to set up a base for ivory trade. Many Boers migrated here from Cape Town toward the end of the next decade. They subdued the Zulu and in the 1850s established the republics of the Orange Free State and the Transvaal. Indentured Indian laborers began arriving by the boatload in 1860 to work the sugar plantations. A majority of the region's population by 1900, Indians' rights were almost nonexistent until fought for by a young lawyer named Mohandas Gandhi.

The English left little in the way of a culinary legacy. Cape cuisine, which is a marriage of Malay and Dutch tastes, offers the best eating. Dishes include *bredie* (a lamb-and-vegetable stew) and *snoek* (a Cape fish served smoked, salted, or curried). Popular souvenirs include such tribal crafts as traditional carvings, beadwork, and jewelry.

- ■ Da Gama Clock
- ■ City Hall
- ■ Local History Museum
- ■ African Art Center
- ■ Old House Museum
- ■ Victoria Market
- ■ Africana Museum
- ■ Beachfront Promenade
- ■ Golden Mile Beach
- ■ Valley of 1,000 Hills

Tanzania

Zanzibar

Exotic Zanzibar, 22 miles off the coast of Tanzania, has a long tradition of visitors. First were eighth-century Arab traders who brought Islam, which remains the island's dominant religion and culture. In 1841 the Sultan of Oman moved his capital here, built several palaces, and promoted the production of palm oil and cloves. Gold, ivory, and rhino horns were traded for guns, textiles, and beads. Once the world's largest supplier of cloves, Zanzibar is most infamous for its role in the former African slave trade to the Middle East. While slavery was abolished in 1873, the practice continued illegally into the 20th century, with slaves hidden in underground tunnels and caves until they could be shipped out secretly. Zanzibar was designated a British protectorate in 1890 and has been independent since 1963; its minority Arab population has suffered badly in massacres, riots, and exile. The island's most famous citizen may be the late Freddie Mercury, of the British rock group Queen, who was born Farokh Bulsara.

Persians, Egyptians, Indians, and Chinese traders left their mark in the oldest parts of the town's narrow winding alleys, overhanging balconies, and ornately carved doors.

Influenced by Arabic and borrowing from English, Swahili is still the spoken language. *Mishkaki* (grilled beef kabobs) and roast corn are local taste treats.

- ■ Old Stone Town
- ■ Central Market

- ■ National Mueseum
- ■ Anglican Church of Christ
- ■ Beit al-Sahel (People's Palace)
- ■ Hamamni Persian Baths
- ■ Beit-el-Ajaib (House of Wonders)
- ■ Dhow Harbor
- ■ Fort
- ■ City Hall

Precious Cargo: Traveling on a Freighter

Imagine being among just a handful of adventure-minded passengers aboard a ship carrying cargo to an array of exotic ports. Just such an experience awaits those who book passage on a freighter.

For the intrepid traveler, freighter travel has much to recommend it. Passengers have the run of the vessel and may even dine with the officers. Freighter accommodations are usually equal to or better than the standard cruise ship cabin, the food is hearty and plentiful, and the atmosphere is casual. Time in port may vary from a few hours to as long as four or more days. In terms of price, freighters usually undercut cruise ships.

But this type of travel is not for everyone. Voyages tend to run long—three or four weeks or more is not uncommon—and, because cargo takes priority over guests, sailing schedules may be altered on short notice. Passengers are pretty much left to their own devices; entertainment options include diving into a stack of novels, tackling crossword puzzles, playing cards, or checking out the latest films in the video library. In addition, the ship may dock in a remote place, making it difficult or costly to venture ashore, and, because of limited space, bookings must be made well in advance.

Furthermore, freighters carrying fewer than a dozen passengers don't sail with a physician—something to keep in mind if you're not in tip-top health. (A doctor is present on larger freighters.) Some ships have a passenger age limit (79 or 80 is typical), and many require a doctor's certificate of good health.

An exception to some of these rules about freighter travel is **Ivaran Lines'** *Americana*. Billed as "the most luxurious cargo vessel ever built," it offers elegantly appointed cabins, a gym with saunas and massage, a pool and Jacuzzi, slot machines, a hairdresser, light entertainment, a gift shop, and shore excursions. *Americana* cruises from **New Orleans** to **South America,** carrying up to 88 passengers. The staff includes a cruise director/purser and a doctor and nurse.

The **Ivaran** fleet also includes the 1994-built *San Antonio*, which sails to **South America** from Port Elizabeth, New Jersey, and **Miami** with up to a dozen travelers on board. Although the facilities are more limited and accommodations are not quite as plush as on the *Americana*, cabins come equipped with mini-refrigerators and VCRs, and there's a pool, gym, sauna, and gift shop. **Ivaran** also offers fly/sail programs and pre- or post-cruise hotel stays. Contact **Ivaran Agencies, Inc.** (800/451.1639).

Other big names in freighter travel include **Bank Line, Blue Star, Columbus Line, Lykes Line,** and **Mediterranean Shipping Co.,** but scores of freighters around the world welcome passengers. For information on all types of freighter travel or to book passage, contact **TravLtips Cruise and Freighter Association** (800/872.8584). This travel agency/membership organization publishes a bimonthly magazine with ship reviews and a listing of available sailings. Another travel agency dedicated to freighter cruising is **Freighter World Cruises** (818/449.3106).

MICHAEL STORRINGS

Pacific Ocean

Na Pali
Coast
Waimea ■
Canyon
Waialeale
Hanalei
Valley
▲
Opaekaa
■ Falls
KAUAI ●Lihue
NIIHAU
Kaulakahi
Channel
Spouting
Horn
Kauai
Channel

Polynesian ■
Cultural Center
OAHU
Nuuanu Pali
Lookout
■
Waipahu Cultural ■
Garden Park
●Honolulu
Pearl
Harbor
Diamond
Head

Hawaiian Islands

An exotic beauty and an ideal climate have made the Hawaiian Islands a
popular destination ever since Captain James Cook cruised these shores in
1778. This archipelago of islands, islets, reefs, and rocks stretches 1,500 miles
across the central **Pacific Ocean** and is the result of volcanic eruptions
through a plate crack in the ocean floor 25 million years ago. The most
frequently visited islands of **Oahu**, the **Big Island of Hawaii, Maui**, and
Kauai offer an abundance of lush rain forests, volcanoes—both dormant and
active—frolicking whales, pounding surf, and sandy beaches, as well as a
Hawaiian culture rich in royalty, art, history, music, and dance.

In Captain Cook's day, the islands were inhabited by warring Polynesian
chiefdoms. Captain Cook was considered a god when he arrived on the
islands, but he met his end on the Big Island's western coast after an
argument over a stolen boat (he took the local chief hostage). By 1791 King
Kamehameha the Great had unified the islands, around the same time
American trading ships had begun stopping here to load sandalwood to trade
in China. Christian missionaries followed in 1820 and set about westernizing
the islands. Then came the whalers, which at their peak numbered nearly 600
vessels a year. This in turn gave way to sugarcane plantations that attracted
laborers from China, Japan, and other Asian countries. The United States
annexed the islands at the turn of the century, and there created its huge
Pacific naval headquarters. The famous Japanese attack on the base pulled the
country into World War II. Hawaii became the 50th state of the US in 1959.

In culinary terms, the state might be most famous for the luau. This
traditional Hawaiian feast features a pig roasted for hours in an imu, an
earthenware, in-ground oven; poi made from taro roots; *laulau* (a
combination of pork, fish, and taro leaves wrapped together and steamed);
lomilomi (salted salmon with tomatoes and onions); and *ulu* (breadfruit).

Pacific Ocean

km   40   80
mi   20   40

N

Kaiwi Channel

MOLOKAI

Kalohi Channel

Whalers Village
Whaling Museum

Lahaina   **Kahului**

LANAI   *Auau Channel*   Iao Valley   **MAUI**   Hana Hwy.

Haleakala ▲   **Hana**

Kealaikahiki Channel   Haleakala National Park   ■ Oheo Gulch & Seven Pools

KAHOOLAWE

Alalakeiki Channel   *Alenuihaha Channel*

Waipio Valley Lookout

Puukohola Heiau
National Historic Site   ■ Parker Ranch   *Hamakua Coast*

Hapuna ■
Beach

Mauna Kea
13,796 ft. ▲   Akaka
Falls ■   Hawaii Tropical
Botanical Gardens

Kailua   **HAWAII
(THE BIG ISLAND)**   **Hilo**●

Puuhonua
O Honaunau
(Place of Refuge) ■   Mauna Loa
13,678 ft. ▲   Hawaii Volcanoes
National Park

*Kona
Coast*   ▲ Kilauea

Honolulu, Oahu

Although the once-primitive beauty Robert Louis Stevenson, Mark Twain, Jack London, and James Michener found on Oahu has been eclipsed by waves of change and development, there's still magic in the air. Dramatic high cliffs stretching inland provide stunning velvety green backdrops to many of the island's long white beaches and aqua bays.

Oahu is the third-largest (597 square miles) of the Hawaiian Islands and home to nearly a million people—over three-fourths of the state's population. Honolulu ("sheltered bay" in Hawaiian), is Hawaii's biggest city and only real metropolis. It grew as a stopover for ships using its deepwater harbor, and today is the center of Hawaii's state government, commerce, and industry. Famous **Waikiki Beach,** the curving strip of white sand lined with palm trees and high-rise hotels that was once swampy wetlands, now attracts tourists from around the world.

Shoppers will find resortwear, in addition to such traditional handicrafts as *tikis* (gods) of wood or lava; coral jewelry; and woven mats, hats, and baskets.

- Waikiki Aquarium
- Diamond Head
- Mission Houses Museum
- Iolani Palace and Grounds
- Pearl Harbor/USS Arizona
- Bishop Museum
- Hanauma Bay
- Nuuanu Pali Lookout
- Polynesian Cultural Center
- Plantation Village at Waipahu Cultural Garden Park

Kailua, The Big Island

Commonly called the "Big Island," Hawaii is nearly twice the size of the rest of the state combined. Its 4,037-square-mile landscape has been shaped by the many vast black lava flows that continue to cover much of the island's surface. Likened to a mini-continent for its varied geography and climate, the Big Island boasts the highest peak in the Pacific—the 13,796-foot **Mauna Kea,** the world's deepest crater—the 13,678-foot **Mauna Loa,** and the world's most active volcano—**Kilauea.** Hawaii's goddess of fire, Pele, makes her home here. Black and white sand beaches ring the isle, while macadamia trees and coffee plants cover the lush coastal valleys and verdant slopes.

The Big Island was the historic and cultural center of all the Hawaiian Islands until the establishment of the US military base at Pearl Harbor shifted the focus to Oahu. Kailua was a retreat for Hawaiian royalty in the 19th century. The dry, sunny west **Kona Coast** (leeward in Hawaiian) is the world's number-one spot to snag a Pacific blue marlin, with some catches topping a thousand pounds. **Hilo,** Hawaii's principal city, is located on the island's rainy eastern side, where orchid and anthurium plants thrive in nurseries and parks.

Kona coffee and macadamia nuts are popular items to purchase, as are koa (a native wood) bowls and handwoven baskets.

- Hawaii Volcanoes National Park and Kilauea Crater
- Mauna Kea Observatory
- Hamakua Coast, Akaka Falls, and Hawaii Tropical Botanical Gardens
- Waipio Valley Lookout
- Parker Ranch
- Puukohola Heiau National Historic Site
- King Kamehameha's Kona Beach Hotel
- Hulihee Palace
- Hapuna Beach
- Puuhonua O Honaunau (Place of Refuge)

Lahaina, Maui

The charming capital of Maui almost looks like a New England fishing port, with waterfront pine buildings, wide verandas, and a three-masted schooner moored in the harbor. Wedged between mountain and sea, Lahaina was an ancient royal court for Maui chiefs, where missionaries and whalers attempted to coexist. The whalers are gone, but the whales—giant humpbacks—still come after summering in Alaska, to mate, calve, and frolic in the waters just off this town of about 10,000 people. In recent years, over a thousand whales have been sighted each season between November and May.

Ashore, Maui is landscaped with deep valleys filled with tropical flowers and ferns, idyllic beaches, and reefs. The island's exquisite beauty inspired aviator Charles Lindbergh to spend his final years here, his tomb aptly inscribed: "If I take the wings of the morning and dwell in the uttermost parts of the sea…" According to island lore, the mighty volcano **Haleakala** (House of the Sun) is where Maui, a Polynesian Prometheus of sorts, caught the sun as it passed over the crater and made it promise to cross more slowly so people would have longer to fish and cultivate crops. Its 10,023-foot summit is one of Maui's most popular—and most spectacular—places for visitors to watch the sun rise. Haleakala is the world's largest dormant volcano.

The reconstructed wooden houses and shops at **Whaler's Market Place** on historic **Front Street** sell ceramics, jewelry, and scrimshaw. The **Old Lahaina Cafe** offers what many consider the most authentic re-creation of the Hawaiian luau, complete with story-telling, music, and hula dancing.

- Oheo Gulch and Seven Pools
- Hana Highway Drive
- Haleakala National Park and Kalahaku Overlook
- Front Street and Pioneer Inn
- Baldwin House and Masters' Reading Room
- Whalers Village Whaling Museum
- Kaanapali Beach/Black Rock

- Black Gorge and Iao Valley
- Waikapu Valley and Maui Tropical Plantation
- Whale-watching Trip

Lihue, Kauai

The oldest and most geographically diverse of the Hawaiian Islands, Kauai's wrinkled, weathered topography is most obvious in the colorful 2,857-foot-deep **Waimea Canyon,** called by some "The Grand Canyon of the Pacific." The reds and browns of its exposed volcanic rock contrast with the intense greenery blanketing the rest of "The Garden Isle." And viewed from **Kalalau Lookout** approximately 4,000 feet above, the northwest **Na Pali Coast** is creased with velvety valleys and fragrant wildflowers.

Kauai was formed by the now dormant **Waialeale** volcano, which rises through the center of the island. Its summit is supposedly the wettest point on earth—an average of 440 inches of rain fall here yearly—feeding Hawaii's only navigable river, the **Wailua.** Polynesians migrated here from the Marquesas Islands around AD 500, and in 1778

Captain Cook made his first landfall in the Hawaiian Islands in **Waimea Bay.**

Throughout the years, directors have chosen this green island with lovely white-sand beaches for their films. The most famous are: *South Pacific, Raiders of The Lost Ark,* and *Jurassic Park.* Despite the $1.6-billion damage the island sustained as a result of Hurricane Iniki in 1992, at press time Kauai was mostly recovered and rebuilt. Shop here for leis made of shells, woven baskets, and batik clothing.

- Kauai Museum
- Spouting Horn
- Waimea Canyon
- Kalalau Valley Lookout
- Hanalei Valley and Bay
- Na Pali Coast State Park
- Waialeale Crater
- Opaekaa Falls
- Wailua River to Fern Grotto
- Kilohana Plantation

Iao Valley, Maui

South Pacific

Explorers, drifters, artists, and writers have long been enchanted by the South Pacific, and today's adventurers who ply these waters in cruise ships are likely to fall under the spell of the same charms—turquoise seas, crystal-white sands, coral-ringed islands rising to volcanic peaks, and, at every port of call, a friendly welcome.

American Samoa

Pago Pago

American Samoa, spread over seven islands, is the only inhabited US territory south of the equator. The main port of call is Pago Pago (pronounced Pango Pango), where ships set anchor in one of the most breathtaking harbors in the South Pacific—the crater of a long-extinct volcano backed by the steep peaks of **Matafao Peak** and **Mount Alava.** The only trouble a traveler is likely to encounter in this paradise is in the form of precipitation: Pago Pago and the surrounding jungles are drenched by more than 100 inches of rain a year, a meteorological phenomenon that Somerset Maugham romanticized in his short story "Rain."

Polynesians have inhabited these islands since 600 BC, and it wasn't until the 18th century that Dutch, French, and British explorers and missionaries began to arrive. The foreigners most in evidence today are American sailors stationed at bases that served as important resupply depots during the two world wars. Despite the presence of air strips and American-style roads, Polynesian life continues as it has for many centuries—an extended family clan system is the dominant force of society.

Even on a short stop visitors can find some traces of local ways at markets where islanders sell hand-woven mats and other handicrafts, or at *fia-fias*, traditional feasts where a meal of roast pig and breadfruit is accompanied by dancing.

- ◼ Cablecar ride up Mount Alava
- ◼ World War II Cannons
- ◼ Old Courthouse
- ◼ Jean P.Haydon Museum
- ◼ Public Market
- ◼ Governor's House
- ◼ Samoan Village at Pago Pago Park
- ◼ Massacre Bay
- ◼ Afono Mountain Pass
- ◼ Fagiatua Burial Grounds

Chile

Easter Island

What puts this easternmost Polynesian island, about 2,000 miles west of Chile, on the map are the hundreds of colossal stone statues, called *moais*,

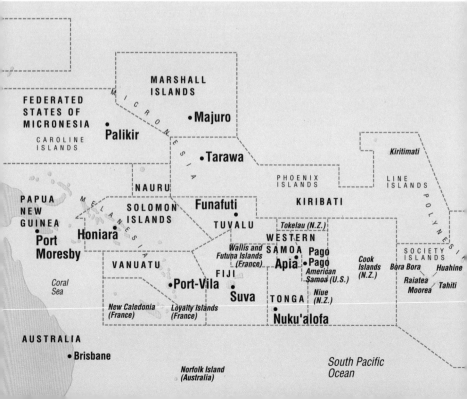

that litter the grassy hillsides. It has never been determined who carved the statues and placed them atop *ahus* (burial altars)—Norwegian anthropologist Thor Heyerdahl surmised that they are the burial monuments of early inhabitants who arrived from South America in the fourth century; others have theorized that these intriguing figures evolved from the traditional Polynesian *marae* (temples) found elsewhere across the Pacific.

Dutch admiral Jacob Roggeveen gave the island its name when he landed on Easter Sunday 1722. Though the admiral sailed away peacefully, other explorers have not been as kind. In 1862, the captain and crew of a fleet of Peruvian slave ships kidnapped the king and about one thousand other Easter Islanders. Some of them were sent home after much international protest, but smallpox destroyed most of the people, leaving only a few hundred survivors. Annexed by Chile in 1888, today Easter Island is home to about 2,000 inhabitants.

Most ships anchor off an area where there is a small museum and no shortage of guides eager to lead visitors to the slopes of a nearby mountain, which is strewn with more than a hundred statues.

- Hanga Roa
- Archaeological Museum
- Rano Raraku Volcano
- Ahu Tahai
- Ahu Tepeu
- Ahu Akivi
- Punapau Crater
- Ahu Vinapu

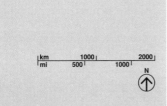

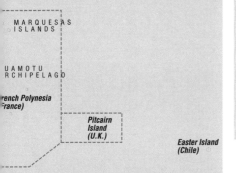

km 1000 2000
mi 500 1000

N

South Pacific Ocean

MARQUESAS ISLANDS

UAMOTU RCHIPELAGO

rench Polynesia France)

Pitcairn Island (U.K.)

Easter Island (Chile)

- Orongo
- Ahu Tongariki

Fiji

Suva

Fiji comprises more than 800 volcanic and coral islands spread out over about a million square miles just west of the International Date Line. Only about a hundred of these beautiful islands are permanently inhabited, and the largest of these is **Viti Levu,** or Great Fiji, where ships dock at the capital city of Suva. As you pull into port and see this bustling city of 70,000 inhabitants it might take a stretch of the imagination to recall that only a century ago the islands were still known as the **Cannibal Islands.**

Once a British colony and independent since 1970, Fiji today reflects the diversity of the peoples who have settled the islands at different times over the past 2,500 years—Polynesians, dark-skinned Melanesians, Caucasian progeny of sailors and convicts escaping from Australia, and Indian laborers brought in 1880, whose descendants today outnumber native Fijians.

Many visitors partake of a *meke,* the traditional Fijian feast of reef fish and whole pig cooked over hot stones in an earth oven known as a *lovo.* Yaqona, a mildly numbing, muddy-looking mixture made from the root of the pepper plant, is the drink of choice and has inspired many visitors to stand up and join in the traditional dances. Shops throughout the islands sell native crafts: tapa cloth stamped with rhythmic geometric designs in natural red and black dyes, woven mats and baskets, shell ornaments, and native wood carvings.

- Fiji Museum
- Tholoisuva Forest Park
- Orchid Island
- Albert Park
- Grand Pacific Hotel
- Thurston Botanical Gardens
- Fiji Museum
- Suva Market
- Wailoku Falls
- Raft trip through Waingga Gorge

Actress Grace Kelly sailed from New York to her 19 April 1956 wedding in Monaco aboard the *Constitution* with four steamer trunks, 36 pieces of luggage, 20 hat boxes, and a multitude of wedding gifts. Later Prince Rainier and Princess Grace made several transatlantic crossings on the *Constitution* (which was retired in 1995) and on her sister ship, the *Independence.*

French Polynesia

Bora Bora

With their flower-clad mountain peaks, coral atolls, and lagoons where tropical fish dart through clear waters, the 130 islands that comprise French Polynesia epitomize the South Pacific. The administrative center and main port of call is **Vaitape** on the island of Bora Bora, home to more than 4,000 people.

James Michener called Bora Bora, 150 miles northwest of Tahiti, the most beautiful island in the world, and few visitors would disagree. Reefs and sandy beaches ring the island, and the interior climbs the craggy volcanic peaks of **Mount Taimanu** and **Mount Pahia** in a profusion of palms, hibiscus, and bougainvillea. From the wharves in Vaitape, visitors can set off on motorbikes or jeeps to explore the island on the 17-mile-long ring road. There is little else to do in this paradise, home to 2,500 permanent residents, except linger on a sandy beach, snorkel, or visit a few ancient *marae* (temples).

- **Hotel Bora Bora**
- **Hotel Sofitel Marara**
- **Bloody Mary's Restaurant**
- **Matira Beach**
- **Naval Cannons and Bunkers**
- **Faanui Bay**
- **Marae Aehautai**
- **Fareopu Marae**
- **Marotetini Marae**
- **Reef trip**

Huahine

A quiet island of about 4,500 inhabitants who fish and farm for a living, Huahine is slowly becoming as well known as more-visited ports of call in the South Seas. Huahine's volcanic peaks tower 2,000 feet over dense jungles of chestnut trees and vanilla vines, and white-sand beaches and pretty lagoons dotted with little islets called *motu* ring the 20 miles of shoreline. But the attractions of Huahine—which is actually two islands, **Huahine Nui** (Great Huahine) and **Huahine Iti** (Little Huahine) that form the image of a reclining woman when seen from the sea—extend beyond physical beauty. First inhabited over 1,300 years ago, Huahine has many two-tiered ancient temples called *marae;* in fact, the village of **Maeva** is one of the most important archaeological sites in French Polynesia. There is much to see here: the village is surrounded by *marae* strewn along the shores of **Lake Fauna Nui** and the slopes of the nearby hills; a *fare pote'e,* a 15th–16th-century round-ended communal house, was completely rebuilt in 1974; stone walls, built to ward off invaders from Bora Bora, still stand; and ancient stone fish traps are still in use in the waters just off shore. Ships dock nearby in the main town, a pleasant little place, with a palm-tree lined boulevard along the waterfront and a scattering of shops.

- **Fare**
- **Fare Pote'e**
- **Maeva**
- **Maeva defensive walls**
- **Marae Te Ava**
- **Marae Paepae Ofata**
- **Marae Matairea Rahi**

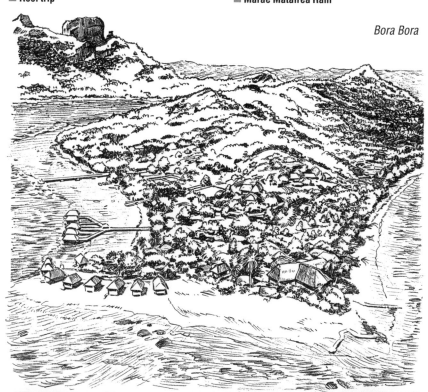

Bora Bora

- Marae Manunu
- Marae Anini
- Port Bourayne

Moorea

This paradise in French Polynesia may look familiar to visitors—the musical *South Pacific* was filmed here (Moorea was the enchanted island of Bali H'ai) and so was the 1983 version of *The Bounty,* which depicts the mutiny against Captain Bligh that unfolded in these very waters. In 1777, the more benevolent Captain Cook and his crew were the first Englishmen to set foot here.

About 8,000 people live on this butterfly-shaped island, just 11 miles across the water from the traffic jams of Papeete on neighboring Tahiti. Hibiscus, bougainvillea, and tropical fruit trees grow wild on the steep slopes of jagged-peaked mountains, and 35 miles of sandy beaches ring the shoreline.

Hotels put on *tamaaraa*—typical island feasts of breadfruit, taro, *fei* (mountain bananas), and roast pork wrapped in banana leaves, all prepared in a pit over layers of wood, volcanic stones, branches, and cloth. Wood carvings, *tikis,* tapa cloth, black pearls, mother-of-pearl products, and shell and coral jewelry are the souvenirs of choice.

- Opunohu Valley
- Cook's Bay
- Opunohu Bay
- Lagoon snorkel trip/Glass-bottom boat ride
- Fruit Juice Factory
- Tropical Aquarium
- Moorea Pearls Center
- Papetoai Church
- Marae Titiroa and Belvedere Lookout
- Afareaitu settlement

Raiatea

Raiatea, some 120 miles northwest of Tahiti, was at one time an important religious center, and the ruins of the great temple of **Marae Taputapuatea** stand as testimony to the days when elaborate rituals were held beneath cloud-shrouded **Mount Temehani.** It was also from here that ancient Polynesians launched voyages to New Zealand and Hawaii; today the island is a popular base for sailboats cruising the South Seas.

The island is dominated by 3,337-foot Mount Toomaru and ringed by a wild, broken shoreline. The sleepy town of **Uturoa** is Eastern Polynesia's second-largest "city" and the administrative center of the **Leeward Islands.** Across the lagoon, neighboring **Tahaa,** half the size of Raiatea, is 15 miles around, with a population of about 4,000. According to popular mythology, the two islands were split by an eel.

- Uturoa
- Mount Tapioi
- Faaroa Bay
- Marae Taputapuatea
- Marae Tainuu
- Tevaitoa Church
- Fetuna village
- Mount Temehani
- Tahaa
- Lagoon trip to motu

Papeete, Tahiti

Gauguin painted the island; Robert Louis Stevenson and James Michener wrote about it. Indeed, no paradise is more fabled than Tahiti. The first European to stumble upon and be seduced by Tahiti's exotic charms, in 1767, was Captain Samuel Wallis, who staked a claim for Britain while his sailors enthusiastically removed nails, spikes, and other metal parts from the ship to give to the lovely island women in exchange for favors. French explorer Bougainville took possession of the island the following year for France, and Tahiti and the 130 islands that comprise French Polynesia have been an official French Overseas Territory since 1959.

In the capital of Papeete, verdant volcanic peaks loom over a mix of colonial buildings and modern shops selling Tahiti's most sought-after souvenirs: the South Seas black pearls and tapa cloth. Restaurants serve the tasty Polynesian, French, and Chinese mélange that constitutes Tahitian cuisine: *Poisson cru* (raw fresh fish marinated in coconut milk with chopped onion, tomatoes, and hot pepper), *mahi-mahi au fafa* (boiled or grilled white fish served with a spinachlike taro-leaf puree prepared with coconut), and *pahua au curry* (clams in curry sauce).

- Papeete Market
- Royal Tombs at Arue
- Point Venus
- Museum of Tahiti
- Arahoho Blowhole
- Faaruumai Waterfalls
- Gauguin Museum and Botanical Gardens
- Maraa Fern Grotto
- Marae of Arahurahu
- Vaiufaufa Viewpoint

Who's the cruise industry's most visible and vocal spokesperson? It has to be Kathie Lee Gifford, who's been shilling for Carnival Cruise Lines since 1984.

Child's Play

As more and more parents bring the kids along on seagoing vacations, more and more cruise lines are responding to the trend with kid-friendly facilities, services, and activities. These days, many ships offer age-specific children's activity programs, youth counselors, kid's menus, teen discos and video arcades, baby-sitting services, and extra-roomy family cabins. Besides these basics, some lines provide extra-special attractions and amenities for young passengers. Here's a sampling:

1 **Disney Cruise Line,** which starts sailing in 1998, will pair a cruise with a stay at **Walt Disney World.** The line's first ship, *Disney Magic*, promises theme restaurants, a family/children's pool, and a family lounge.

2 Bugs Bunny, Tweety Bird, Road Runner, and other Warner Brothers Looney Tunes characters have the run of *The Big Red Boat* **(Premier Cruise Lines),** making surprise appearances at children's parties and other events. They're also available (for a fee) to tuck in the kiddies at bedtime and to join them for breakfasts that combine pancakes, eggs, and cereal with singing, dancing, and souvenirs.

3 A two-deck-high, indoor/outdoor **Camp Carnival** play area and a winding, three-deck-high water slide are kid-pleasing features of the world's largest cruise ship, **Carnival Cruise Lines'** *Carnival Destiny.*

4 **Mad Science** is the name of **Royal Caribbean International'**s children's program. Youth staff members mix up bubbling potions, create pyro-effects, demonstrate how to brew "slime," and lead other activities aimed at making science fun. Youngsters build rockets to launch from the line's private **Caribbean** island.

5 **Norwegian Cruise Line's Kid's Crew** activities include autograph sessions with **National Football League** and **National Basketball Association** stars and visits to the bridge. **NCL'**s **Circus at Sea** program teaches children juggling, clown acts, and other circus routines that they perform for adults at the end of the voyage.

6 Children sailing on **Princess Cruises'** ships can take part in the **Save Our Seas** environmental awareness program, which offers fun-filled projects that teach kids about caring for the oceans and marine life.

7 On **Alaska** cruises, **Holland America Line** offers tours specifically designed for two age groups: kids ages 6 to 12 and teens. Participants learn how totem poles are carved, hike through a rain forest, join an Alaska treasure hunt, or zip along the rugged coast outside **Ketchikan** on a jet boat.

8 On **American Hawaii Cruises,** a kumu (Hawaiian teacher) teaches island culture and traditions while regaling youngsters with Hawaiian legends and ghost stories.

9 Lounges equipped with video games and high-tech children's playrooms with interactive computers are found on the newest ships in **Celebrity Cruises'** fleet.

10 **Costa Cruise Lines** gives the grownups in the family a break during its Caribbean sailings with "Parents' Night Out." On these evenings, kiddies sup at their own buffet and are cared for by baby-sitters, freeing the folks to dress up and enjoy a romantic, adults-only formal dinner

Tonga

Nuku'alofa

Captain James Cook dubbed these 170 volcanic and coral islands scattered across 100,000 square miles the "Friendly Islands" after exceptionally warm receptions during his visits, the first in 1773. Legend has it that the islanders actually intended to cook Cook, but the captain's gift of a Galapagos turtle, who lived for another nearly 200 years, removed him from the dinner list.

Tonga is the only kingdom in Polynesia never brought under foreign rule (although it was a British protectorate from 1900 to 1970). The missionaries who arrived in the 1820s helped end bloody tribal wars and left a devout Methodist population, but long-standing island traditions are still much in evidence: Many men and women continue to dress in the *ta'ovala,* a woven skirt that is worn as a sign of respect for elders and the royal family.

The capital of the island kingdom is Nuku'alofa (which means "love dwelling"), a city of pastel-colored Victorian houses on the flat, coral island of **Tongatapu.** Here and elsewhere in Tonga the coconut provides the flavoring for many foods: *Lu feke* is octopus with coconut milk, and *lu moa* is chicken cooked in coconut leaves. Tapa cloth is of exceptional quality in Tonga and easy to come by in Nuku'alofa. Shops in Nuku'alofa also sell baskets, wood carvings, and coral and shell jewelry.

- Royal Palace
- Royal Tombs
- Talamahu Market
- Houma Blowholes and Hufangalupe
- Kolovai
- Captain Cook's Landing
- Ha'amonga'a Maui
- Stalactite Caves
- Langi at Mu'a
- Langa Fonua Handicraft Center

Western Samoa

Apia

It seems unlikely that a tubercular Scot would be a Polynesian national hero, but novelist Robert Louis Stevenson may well have been Western Samoa's most memorable, and longest-staying, visitor. Samoans call him *Tusitala,* the teller of tales, and his tomb overlooking the busy waterfront capital of Apia is practically a national shrine. Writers Rupert Brooke, Somerset Maugham, and James Michener have also found inspiration here, among lush green highlands dotted with clear lakes, tumbling waterfalls, and fragrant flowers.

Apia, where colonial wooden buildings have wide verandas shaded by palm trees, is on the north coast of **Upolu,** one of the nation's four inhabited islands. Europeans arrived on the scene in 1722, when Dutchman Jacob Roggeveen sighted the islands. English missionary settlers and German colonists followed, and in their wake came whalers and sealers. In 1899 Samoa was divided between the US and Germany; New Zealand seized German-held Western Samoa in 1914 and ruled until independence in 1962. The islanders remain intensely traditional—they wear wrap-around skirts called *lavalava,* submit to extensive tattooing, and live with large, extended families in open-air dwellings, called *fale.*

The local culinary specialty is Samoan-style *palusami* (thick coconut cream wrapped in a leaf then cooked on hot stones and served on slices of baked taro). Other dishes include *suafa'ai* (ripe bananas with coconut cream), and *oka* (raw fish marinated in coconut milk, lemon juice, and onions). Shops are piled high with the Samoan *siapo* (tapa cloth made from mulberry bark and painted with natural dyes); woven mats and baskets, hand-carved bowls, shell jewelry, and bright native prints are also popular souvenirs.

- Vailima (Stevenson's home)
- Sliding Rocks at Papaseea
- Felafa Village and Falls
- Piula Cave Pool
- Royal Tombs
- Mulivai Beach
- O Le Pupu-Pu'e National Park and Togitogiga Falls
- Mafa Pass and Fuipisia Falls
- Apia Market
- Nu'usafe'e Island

In just one week, Carnival Cruise Lines' Destiny will serve its 3,400 passengers 2,800 pounds of prime rib, 6,000 pounds of chicken, 1,200 Cornish game hens, 800 whole ducks, 22,000 shrimp, 800 pounds of veal, 5,200 hot dogs, 6,800 hamburgers, 1,200 pounds of ham, 600 pounds of salmon, and 300 pounds of smoked salmon.

When it comes to shipboard tipping, King Saud is probably the last of the big-time spenders. After a nine-day trip from from Naples to New York aboard the *Constitution,* the Saudi ruler handed out an estimated $20,000 worth of tips and gifts, including gold watches for his cabin steward and the ship's captain.

Celebrity Cruises' three newest ships, *Century, Galaxy,* and *Mercury,* offer special refuges for cigar aficionados. The intimate, wood-paneled Michael's Clubs are styled after 19th-century gentlemen's smoking rooms and feature hand-rolled Havanas.

Whangarei

Auckland

Bay of
Plenty

Hamilton
*North
Island*

Tauranga

Waitomo
Caves

Rotorua

Lake
Taupo

Urewera
National
Park

*Tasman
Sea*

New
Plymouth

Hawke
Bay

South
Taranaki Bight

Wanganui

Palmerston
North

Karamea
Bight

Porirua

Lower Hutt

Nelson

Cook Strait

Blenheim

Wellington

Nelson Lakes
National Park

Arthur Pass
National Park

Mount Cook
National Park

Christchurch

Port
Lyttelton

SOUTHERN ALPS

Mount Aspiring
National Park

Canterbury
Bight

*South Pacific
Ocean*

Milford
Sound

▲ Mt. Tukoto
9,042 ft.

Timaru

Mitre Peak ▲
5,551 ft.

*South
Island*

Fiordland

Lake
Wakatipu

Lake
Te Anau

Doubtful
Sound

Lake
Manapouri

Dunedin

Invercargill

Foveaux Strait

Stewart
Island

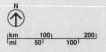

N

km   100   200
mi   50   100

New Zealand

Divided into two separate land masses, New Zealand's **North Island** offers rolling green hills and velvety volcanoes, while **South Island** boasts snow-covered glacial peaks and stunning fjords. In addition to its spectacular natural beauty, this delightful nation in the middle of the South Pacific has British-toned cities such as **Auckland, Wellington,** and **Christchurch,** while incorporating its rich native Maori culture. A bit provincial compared to its Australian neighbors across the **Tasman Sea** to the west, this country's oft-quoted claim to fame is that it is home to more sheep than people—there are nearly 3.5 million inhabitants; no one's managed to count the sheep yet. Cruises to this "other" Down Under nation are usually offered in conjunction with Australia on 14- and 21-day itineraries.

Auckland

Dutch navigator Abel Tasman anchored off New Zealand briefly in 1642, and although mapmakers named Tasman's discovery after a Dutch province, *Nieuw Zeeland,* it was England, in the form of Captain James Cook, that claimed the islands in 1769. European whalers, traders, and missionaries began arriving at the turn of the century, snapping up the 3,000 acres of verdant pastureland and forested hills that is present-day Auckland. Named *Tamaki makau-rau* (Battle of a Hundred Lovers) in Maori, Auckland's highly desirable location was fought over for centuries. The city is built over and around 60 volcanoes on an isthmus that overlooks the **Pacific Ocean** on one side and the **Tasman Sea** on the other.

Located on **North Island,** Auckland is New Zealand's commercial center and largest city with more than 800,000 inhabitants. It is also the largest Polynesian city in the world, populated by Pacific islanders who come seeking education and employment. Although the city has a definite British flavor, Maori culture persists in language, crafts, music, and dance. The Maori are particularly proud of their world-famous opera star Kiri te Kanawa.

Local fish sport exotic names like terakihi and hapuka; a pale green chowder is made from a clam called toheroa. Pavlova is a creamy meringue dessert named for the ballerina. For shoppers, greenstone (also called "New Zealand jade" or nephrite) comes in a variety of shades and prices. Paua shell products, sheepskin items, and handknit woolens are good buys. Known as "The City of Sails" long before New Zealand walked away with the America's Cup, today Auckland is spiffing up for the future: plans are under way for city improvements in anticipation of the cup's defense at the turn of the century (1999 or 2000).

- ■ Customs House
- ■ Auckland Domain and Museum
- ■ Mount Eden
- ■ One Tree Hill
- ■ Victoria Park Market
- ■ Parnell Village and Rose Garden
- ■ Devonport
- ■ Rangitoto Island
- ■ New Zealand National Maritime Museum
- ■ Waitomo Caves

Christchurch

Often called "more English than England," Christchurch is filled with old stone buildings, Victorian Gothic architecture, and manicured gardens. It's also known as "the Garden City," and even has a willow-lined meandering **Avon River.** Like American descendants of *Mayflower* passengers, Christchurch citizens proudly trace their ancestry back to the "Canterbury Pilgrims" who arrived on the "First Four Ships" in 1850. These settlers were selected by the Anglican Church to establish a model agricultural community, built around the cathedral there.

Today Christchurch is New Zealand's third-largest city. **Port Lyttelton,** seven miles to the south, is a natural deep-water harbor and the chief gateway to **South Island.** Inland, the majestic **Southern Alps** form a snowcapped backbone that runs the length of the island, making it apparent why the ancient Maori called New Zealand *Aotearoa*—"Land of the Long White Cloud."

Canterbury Plain, the fertile field on which Christchurch sits, is famous for lamb and dairy products. Crayfish, local fish such as terakihi and hapuka, and bluff oysters (raw or fried) are popular foods. Many visitors take home Maori-made souvenirs such as *tikis,* tiny ritual objects with their tongues sticking out.

- ■ Christchurch Cathedral
- ■ Cathedral Square
- ■ Provincial Council Buildings
- ■ Canterbury Museum
- ■ McDougall Art Gallery
- ■ Botanical Gardens
- ■ Mona Vale
- ■ Sign of the Takahe Mansion
- ■ Summit Road Drive and Port Hills
- ■ Mount Cook National Park

Cunard's *Queen Elizabeth 2* is the world's fastest passenger ship still in service, with a zippy top cruising speed of 32.5 knots.

Mount Cook, New Zealand

Milford Sound

Milford Sound, one of many indentations along **South Island's** spectacular west coast, is one of New Zealand's most memorable sites. It is part of **Fiordland,** a 3-million-acre preserve, one of the world's largest national parks. Too mountainous and remote for much development, its trails, alpine lakes, and rain forests attract hikers and sightseers from around the world.

Stretching 10 miles from the open ocean to its head, Milford Sound was created thousands of years ago by great glaciers that gouged out the granite and formed a deep basin, which was later filled by the sea when the ice receded. Milford Sound is 1.5 miles wide at its broadest point, and 1,280 feet deep. At its narrowest passage, **Dale Point,** only about 450 yards separate the two sheer walls of granite on either side. Because it receives about 300 inches of rainfall a year (sometimes a foot a day), a lush carpet of ferns and small trees cling to the otherwise bare vertical walls that rise several thousand feet into the air. Several waterfalls—notably the 480-foot-high **Stirling Falls** and 562-foot-high **Bowen Falls,** near the entrance—cascade down the cliffs into the calm waters.

The view from the head of the fjord looking back toward the sea is breathtaking, with triangular 5,551-foot **Mitre Peak** and glacier-strewn 6,710-foot **Pembroke Peak** reflected onto the dark waters of the fjord. Aside from a small lodge marking the end of the **Milford Track,** the famous wilderness trail between **Lake Te Anau** and Milford Sound, there are, blissfully no artificial blights upon the landscape.

- **Doubtful Sound**
- **Sinbad Gully**
- **Copper Point**
- **Fairy Falls**
- **St. Anne Point**
- **Seal Point**
- **Harrison Cove**
- **Milford Sound Underwater Observatory**
- **Glowworm Cave**
- **Lake Manapouri**

Wellington

Situated on the **Miramar Peninsula** at the southwest tip of New Zealand's **North Island,** Wellington looks across **Cook Strait** to South Island only 20 miles away. Named after the Duke of Wellington (of Waterloo fame), New Zealand's capital is also known as the "Windy City," blown by a fresh sea breeze that keeps it free from pollution. Local lore says that you can always tell a Wellingtonian because he clutches his hat as he rounds a corner. Wellington's wonderful harbor is surrounded by steep hills, crosshatched by long staircases and alleys leading to gabled wooden cottages and homes, prompting some visitors to compare it with San Francisco and Hong Kong. Unfortunately, glass and concrete are slowly replacing the city's original colonial character. New Zealand's second-largest city, Wellington has 350,000 inhabitants.

Local menus list seafood patés, including crayfish and smoked eel, and a popular raw fish appetizer of terakihi (a firm-fleshed sea-fish) marinated in lemon juice and served in coconut milk. Lamb is a local favorite, cooked with garlic and served with mint sauce on the side.

Along with greenstone, local craftspeople fashion New Zealand timber into a variety of wooden articles and children's toys and puzzles. Small items, especially vases, are made from *ponga* (fernwood).

- Lambton Quay
- Botanic Gardens and Lady Norwood Rose Garden
- Alexander Turnbull Library
- Parliament Buildings
- Funicular up to Kelburn Lookout
- Old Government Building
- Old St. Paul's Cathedral
- National Museum and Art Gallery
- Marine Drive and Mount Victoria Lookout
- Tramway Museum

Who's Who on Board

The uniforms worn by ship officers are more than a means of making them look dashing (although they do that, too). You can figure out an officer's position by the way he or she is dressed—specifically, by their epaulets or the stripes on their sleeves.

The captain and department heads are "four stripers." The big boss is the captain. Directly beneath him are the heads of the ship's three departments: the staff captain of the deck department, whose officers handle navigation and safety; the chief engineer, who leads the engine department, which handles everything from the main and auxiliary engines to the generators, electrical, cooling, plumbing, and ventilation systems; and the hotel manager, who oversees the hotel division. The latter is the largest of the three departments and includes the chef and galley staff, maître d' and dining room waiters, food and beverage personnel, the purser's office, the cruise director and the social staff, the entertainers, and "concessionaires" such as beauticians, masseurs, casino dealers, gift shop personnel, and the like. Positions denoted by three stripes, two stripes, and one stripe vary from ship to ship.

While stripes denote rank, an officer's epaulets also indicate his or her department. Some cruise companies use different colors to distinguish between departments, while others use symbols such as propellers for the engine staff and diamonds for the deck.

Here's a brief rundown of some key shipboard personnel and what they do:

Captain Master of the entire ship. Commands the officers and crew from the bridge.

Staff Captain Second in command to the captain, can assume control in an emergency. Oversees the deck department and is in charge of safety, maintenance, and discipline.

Chief Engineer Head of the engine department. Supervises the operation and maintenance of all engines and motors.

MICHAEL STORRINGS

Hotel Manager Oversees the ship's hotel operations, including cabin, dining, and entertainment facilities. The person to see about any unresolved problems in these areas, after more immediate channels have been exhausted.

Cruise Director Plans and runs all the activities and entertainment. Acts as emcee.

Chief Purser In charge of the ship's information center/reception desk. Handles all financial and cabin-related matters for passengers.

Chef de Cuisine Plans and executes all menus.

Food & Beverage Manager Supervises matters related to food and bars.

Maître d'Hotel In charge of the dining room. Assigns passenger tables and oversees the waiters, sommeliers, and busboys.

Bar Manager Leads the bar staff. The person to see about setting up private cocktail parties.

Housekeeper Supervises cleaning in the staterooms and the public rooms. Oversees cabin stewards and stewardesses.

Concierge Assists passengers with special needs such as planning private parties, obtaining theater tickets, and the like. Usually only found on luxury ships.

Australia

Timor Sea

Melville
Island
Bathurst   Van Diem[...]
Island   Gulf
Beagle
Gulf   ●Darwin

Kaka[...]
Nation[...]
Pa[...]

Indian
Ocean

Cape   Joseph
Londonderry   Bonaparte
Cape   Gulf
Bougainville
●
Kalumburu

Gregory
National
Park

Rowley
Shoals

●**Pender
Bay**

THE
KIMBERLEY

TANAMI
DESERT

Roebuck
Bay   ●**Broome**

●**Port
Hedland**

Rudall River
National Park

Lake
Mackay

MACDONNEL[...]

North West
Cape

THE
PILBARA

●**Newman**

GIBSON DESERT

Gibson Desert
National Park

Uluru ■
(Ayers Rock-
Mt. Olga)

●**Carnarvon**

Shark
Bay

WESTERN
AUSTRALIA

●**Meekatharra**

Conservation
Park

●**Geraldton**

Great Victoria
Desert National
Park

Nullarbor
Regional
Reserve

Yellab[...]
Region[...]
Reserv[...]

●**Kalgoorlie**

Eucla
●

Yalata

●**Perth**

Nuytsland Nature
Reserve

Great Australian
Bight

●**Bunbury**

Cape
Naturaliste

●**Esperance**

Point
D'Entrecasteaux

●**Albany**

Southern
Ocean

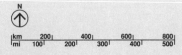

N

km	200	400	600	800
mi	100	200	300	400	500

Aboriginal Lands

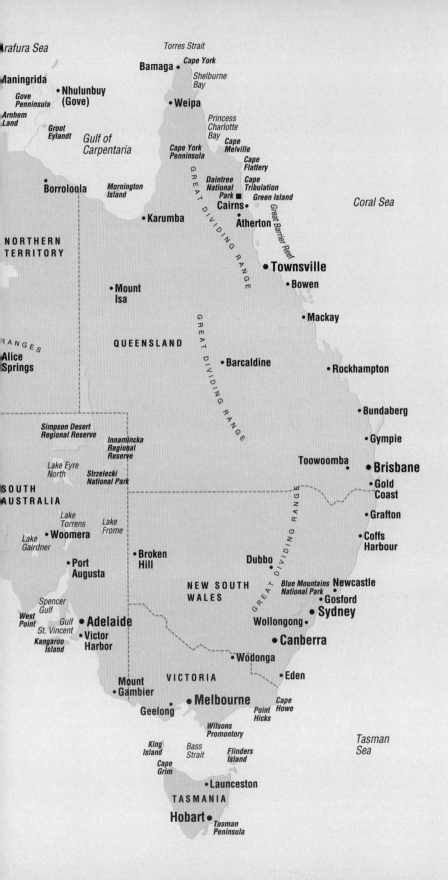

Australia

Packed with both sophisticated cities and rugged natural wonders, Australia beckons. Located entirely in the southern hemisphere (that's why it's called "Down Under"), this island-nation is surrounded by the **Timor, Arafura** and **Tasman Seas,** the **Coral Sea,** and the **Indian Ocean.** Covering a continent of nearly 3 million square miles, Australia luckily boasts an abundance of attractions near the coast. Cruises take in the popular east coast ports of **Sydney, Hobart, Melbourne, Cairns,** and the world's largest living organism—the **Great Barrier Reef**—on itineraries ranging from 14 to 21 days. Cruises to the Land of Oz, as it's affectionately known, also offer safe surroundings, friendly hosts, and a chance to hear the most colorful interpretation of the English language ever.

Cairns, Queensland

Closer to Papua, New Guinea than it is to most Australian cities, Cairns (pronounced Cans) is a tropical town with a frontier attitude. It is located on **Trinity Bay** on the northeast coast, surrounded by a range of purple mountains, rain forests, palm trees, and plantations bursting with macadamias, pineapple, and sugarcane.

Today some 70,000 people live in this city of colonial-style homes, broad avenues planted with giant bougainvilleas, and a pretty esplanade radiating from the wharf area. Cairns is perhaps most famous as a gateway to the amazing **Great Barrier Reef,** 20 miles offshore in the turquoise **Coral Sea.** High-speed catamarans, floatplanes, and helicopters whisk visitors to the 1,240-mile long reef—the world's largest living organism—for glass-bottom boat rides, snorkeling, and scuba trips. Often called the eighth wonder of the world, the reef is home to an incredible variety of tropical fish and crustaceans, sponges, starfish, sharks, turtles, giant clams, and sea cows.

The region is also renowned for its sportfishing, especially black marlin, which can weigh in at more than 1,000 pounds. Inland, the rivers and rain forests of **Daintree, Kuranda,** and the **Atherton Tablelands** are attracting a new wave of visitors. Weekend markets feature regional crafts and jewelry as well as aboriginal art and products from New Guinea. Mud crabs are a local favorite dish.

- Cairns Museum and Art Gallery
- Kuranda Railway
- Tjapukai Aboriginal Dance Theatre (Kuranda)
- Mission Beach
- Great Barrier Reef Trip
- Atherton Tablelands
- Daintree Rainforest
- Cape Tribulation
- Cape York Peninsula
- Green Island

Hobart, Tasmania

A heart-shaped island off Australia's southeast coast, Tasmania was sighted by Dutch navigator Abel Tasman in 1642, who named it Van Diemen's Land after the governor-general of the Dutch East Indies. Tasmania, which is about the size of Ireland, is greener and more mountainous than the mainland. Originally inhabited by Aborigines, its first European settlement was founded near present-day Hobart in 1803. In a tragic chapter in Australian history, the Aboriginal population, which had already been decimated by disease and battle, were shipped to **Flinders Island** in the **Bass Strait** where the last full-blooded Tasmanian Aborigine died in 1876.

From 1830 on Tasmania served as a penal settlement for repeat-offender convicts deemed "most dangerous." The main prison was located in **Port Arthur,** southeast of Hobart. Today about a sixth of Tasmania's half-million inhabitants can trace their ancestry to those convicts. After transportation (as it was called) ended, Hobart prospered as a whaling port, and the rugged interior of the island opened up to farming, forestry, and mining.

Hobart, Australia's smallest state capital, stretches out along the **Derwent River,** beneath the sometimes snowy and always windy **Mount Wellington.** Colonial homes and warehouses are neatly preserved around **Sullivan's Cove** and other areas. Local products and a wide range of handicrafts including woolen goods, hand-turned pine products, pottery, antiques, and honey from leatherwood tree blossoms can be found at **Salamanca Place,** where shops and stalls set up in a festive Saturday morning market.

- Mount Wellington
- Salamanca Place
- Battery Point
- Constitution Dock
- Port Arthur Penal Settlement and Tasman Peninsula
- Richmond Village
- Botanical Gardens
- Mount Field National Park (Tall Trees Walk and Russell Falls)
- Tasmanian Museum and Art Gallery
- Van Diemen's Land Folk Museum

A mechanized Champagne-sipping lady in a bathtub toasts slot machine jackpot winners in the casino on board Norwegian Cruise Line's *Leeward.*

Coping with Mal de Mer

On a moving ship, the brain receives conflicting information from the body's senses of sight, balance, and position. This clash can lead to headache, nausea, and vomiting—the distinctively unpleasant malady known as seasickness.

Who's susceptible? Some people fall ill only occasionally; some never seem to get seasick; others claim they "always" do. A scientific study of midshipmen revealed a possible psychological aspect. Those who were told they could expect to fall ill often did; those who were continually reinforced with the message "You won't get seasick" seldom succumbed.

Fear of *mal de mer* preoccupies many prospective cruisers, but experienced sailors know that there's little to dread. Today's ships steer a course for tranquil waters and are equipped with stabilizers that steady the vessel in high seas.

In rare instances of rocking and rolling, several remedies are effective. First, prevention. A few days before cruising, cut out heavy, fatty, hard-to-digest foods such as meat, gravy, and cheese. Avoid alcohol, which can aggravate symptoms, and try to get plenty of rest.

On board ship, continue light eating and keep active. It's best to avoid indoor activities that demand concentration such as reading, writing, or working puzzles. A walk on deck in the fresh air is a better choice if you're feeling peaked. Many people find it helps to focus on the steady horizon.

Some sailors recommend munching saltines, sipping ginger ale, or popping ginger capsules. Another very popular folk remedy is wearing elastic bands that apply pressure to the wrists. Marketed under names like "SeaBands," these are sold in drugstores as well as in many shipboard shops.

A new antiseasickness product is also worn on the wrist. The battery-powered ReliefBand generates mild electric impulses that are thought to modulate nerve activity. Originally developed to relieve pain, the band also proved effective against nausea in clinical tests. It must be prescribed by a physician.

Several nonprescription drugs also can help, but to be most effective they should be taken before the symptoms occur. The best known are dimenhydrinate (Dramamine), meclizine (Bonine), and diphenhydramine (Benadryl). They're often sold in the ship's shop or are available, usually for free, at the purser's office or reception desk. Drowsiness is a common side effect; if you can't stay awake, try reducing the dosage.

Prescription drugs are another option. Promethazine (Phenergan) and ephedrine taken together have proven effective without causing drowsiness. Scopolamine, administered in the form of a behind-the-ear skin patch called Transderm Scop, is controversial. After being pulled from the US market by its manufacturer, the drug was expected to be available again as this book went to press. Some ship passengers swear by "the patch" and suffer no side effects; others have experienced a dry mouth, visual disturbances, confusion, and worse. Patients with heart conditions should not use Scopolamine.

If the weather turns miserable, you're really suffering, and none of these remedies work, the ship's doctor can administer an injection or prescribe suppositories. These magic bullets do the trick for most people.

Melbourne, Victoria

In 1835 John Batman of Tasmania bought 700,000 acres of land on **Port Phillip Bay** and around the mouth of the **Yarra River** from local Aborigines in exchange for several hundred wool blankets, mirrors, and axes. Although Batman intended "Bearbrass," as it was originally called, to be an agricultural settlement, the colony's population exploded during the gold rushes of the mid-19th century when "diggers" arrived from all over the country. Still a busy port, Melbourne was Australia's capital until the 1950s when the government resettled itself in **Canberra.**

Sometimes suffering a "second city" complex in relation to the better-known and bigger Sydney, Melbourne has a style all its own. This dignified city of Victorian mansions, working turn-of-the-century trams, and numerous gardens and parks, has evolved into Australia's multicultural metropolis, and a center for fashion, finance, theater, and fine arts. The tastes of its ethnically diverse population of three million favor Asian and Mediterranean infusions of garlic, soy sauce, lemongrass, and olive oil, over meat pies and fish and chips.

Boutiques and galleries around town, especially along elegant **Collins Street,** feature Aboriginal art; stylish ceramics, jewelry, and stained glass; and leather and sheepskin products; as well as the traditional opals and antiques. More adventurous shoppers should head to the raucous trash-to-treasure **Queen Victoria Market.**

- ■ **Old Melbourne Gaol**
- ■ **King's Domain and Royal Botanical Gardens**
- ■ **National Gallery of Victoria**
- ■ **Rippon Lea**
- ■ **National Museum of Victoria**
- ■ **Tram Ride to Collins Street**
- ■ **Government House**
- ■ **Fitzroy Gardens**
- ■ **Phillip Island and Penguin Parade**
- ■ **Puffing Billy Steam Train and Dandenongs**

Sydney, New South Wales

Blessed with a sunny climate, fabulous beaches, and one of the most beautiful harbors in the world, Sydney is Australia's oldest, largest, and most sophisticated city. Its sail-like **Opera House** billowing out over the bay and the **Harbour Bridge** (dubbed "The Coathanger") have become international icons, their images splashed on postcards, T-shirts, tote bags, and just about anything else you can name.

Opera House, Sydney

In 1788 Great Britain established a penal colony here to relieve its notorious overcrowded jails; by 1868 nearly 170,000 convicts had been transported to Sydney to serve time for petty crimes. In the 19th century, the discovery of gold brought another huge wave of immigration, along with an outbreak of the plague, which led to razing and rebuilding entire sections of the decaying city about the time of Australian independence in 1901. The city is now home to more than 4 million of country's 18 million residents.

Sydney's menus reflect the city's growth as a world-class metropolis. Local fish, such as John Dory or whiting, might be served with lemongrass sauce, grilled with red peppers and olive oil, sliced sushi-style, or coated in coconut and chili paste. Grilled barramundi filled with fresh herbs, Moreton Bay bugs (sand lobsters), and Sydney rock oysters are longtime favorites, all washed down with frosty Foster's Ale or delicious wines from nearby **Hunter Valley** vineyards. Shoppers should look for wool products from sheep; opals; outback wear such as oilskin coats, moleskin trousers, and Akubra hats; beach and resortwear by designers like Ken Done; and Aboriginal artwork.

- **Circular Quay**
- **The Rocks**
- **Taronga Zoo**
- **Centrepoint Tower**
- **Darling Harbour**
- **Sydney Aquarium**
- **Powerhouse Museum**
- **Australian Maritime Museum**
- **Art Gallery of New South Wales**
- **Blue Mountains**

Bests

Bruce Good
Director of Cruise Product, Royal Cruise Line

Amsterdam, Netherlands

In the **Rijksmuseum**, while your tour group are all craning over each others' shoulders to see Rembrandt's wall-sized *Night Watch*, sneak away to view the two small Vermeers on the same floor. They are absolute gems of glowing color and light, and (sadly) usually not crowded at all.

Belém, Brazil

In this trading town near the mouth of the **Amazon**, don't miss the public market. There's an entire section of stalls selling supplies for *curandeiros* (something between an herbalist and a witch doctor). Fascinating bundles and batches of every form of plant and animal life from the forests upriver. Mummified sloths, dramatic toothy "saws" from the snout of sawfish, whole anaconda skins, as well as myriad barks, leaves, essences and oils, plus garish candles in the shape of saints both Catholic and Candomble. Very photogenic.

Copenhagen, Denmark

After you've seen the *Little Mermaid* statue and **Tivoli**, don't miss the **Ny Carlsberg Glyptotek** (Glyptotek Museum). Founded by the Carlsberg brewers, it has lots of surprising treasures, including many paintings sent by Paul Gauguin from Tahiti to his long-suffering Danish wife, some deliciously erotic sculptures by Rodin, and a collection of miniature sculptures hand modeled by Degas after he lost his sight. The **Canal Boat Tour** is also great, inexpensive fun. You get to see the city from a different angle, and the talented young guides do the whole tour in three or four languages, depending on who's on board.

Dominica, West Indies

The capital of **Roseau** is practically a time-capsule of old-fashioned Caribbean life. No strip malls of duty-free shops or casinos. Lots of ornately gingerbreaded overhanging balconies along the narrow streets. In the supermarkets, look for Blow's brand herbal teas, the freshest, most full-flavored I've ever had. Also locally produced bay rum lotion, made by hand in wood-fired stills outside town. Elsewhere on Dominica, the last surviving descendants of the indigenous Carib Indians weave wonderful straw crafts, tinted with natural dyes.

Cruising:

Don't miss entries and exits of harbors. These often occur early morning or dinner time, but you'll find it well worthwhile to be on deck as your ship cruises into port or departs. (Incidentally, the "arrival" listed in your daily program usually means the scheduled docking time. Ask the bridge for an estimated time of entry into the harbor, and get up early!) For the most part, the harbor of a city is the historic heart of the place, and you'll be seeing the city for the first time just as people have for centuries. Morning and evening light will add to the magic, and even nighttime departures have a glittery glamour all their own. There's an excitement of anticipation on arrival, and after a day spent in a new place, there's also a bittersweet thrill to departing as the engines thrum and the great ship slowly picks up speed and the skyline sinks into the wake behind. Time for a toast to today's adventures, and tomorrow's, too.

Marilyn Monroe draped in hot pink satin and a cigarette-smoking Humphrey Bogart are among 24 movie star mannequins dotting the corridors and public rooms of Carnival Cruise Lines' *Fascination*, a ship glittering with Hollywood glamour.

Radisson Seven Sea's *Radisson Diamond* is both the largest twin-hull ship ever constructed and the only cruise ship designated *SSC* (semisubmersible craft). It is equipped with struts attached to a pair of submerged hulls that lift the vessel above the water. This design offers greater stability than conventional hulls.

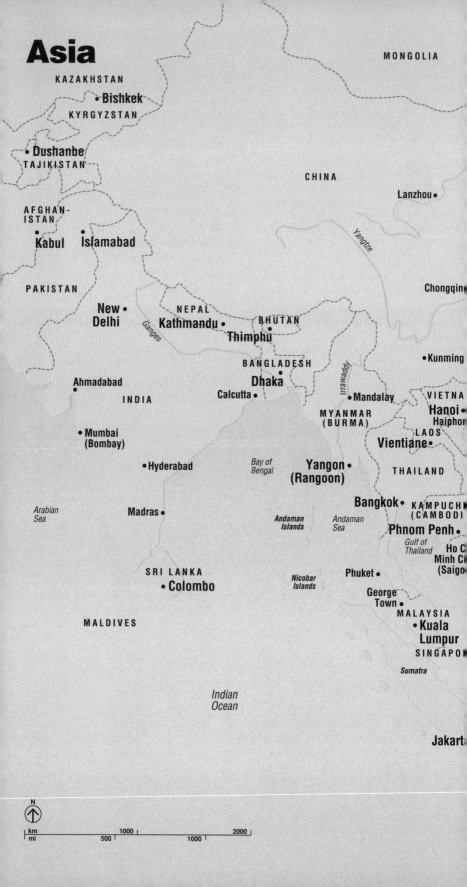

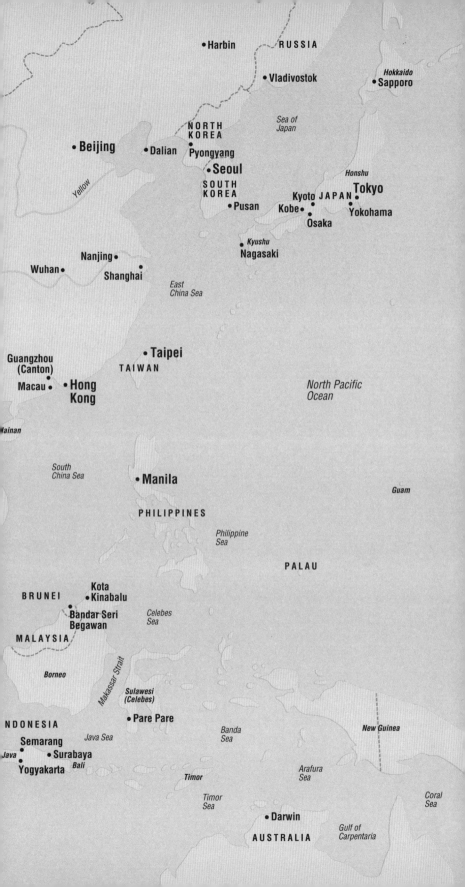

Asia

Lands of vine-twisted jungles and rain forests, rice paddies terraced up and down volcanic mountains active and extinct, exquisite underwater life, the scent of spice and incense, long houses, junks, pagodas, village festivals—it is easy to see why writers like Maugham, Hesse, Conrad, and Kipling were so mesmerized by Asia.

Asia covers over 17 million square miles ringing the **Pacific Rim.** The continent's history, with its shifting national boundaries, is complex and often dramatic, with mystical religions, ruling dynasties, colonial empires, and vast networks of trade routes still vital to modern-day business and government. The drama and change that make Asia exciting also make it a continent that defies general description. A region with some of the world's most ancient cultures, Asia is also one of the fastest changing, transformed by still-shifting borders, leaders, and economic policies. Cities are now mushrooming around once tranquil temples in the countryside, and energy formerly devoted to agrarian-intensive economies now goes to supplying goods across the globe. Long sealed, some nations are opening their doors to the world, allowing a peek at a well-preserved past.

Western seafarers began sailing the **Arabian Sea, Indian Ocean, South China Sea,** and the vast **Pacific Ocean** five centuries ago; modern travelers have found that cruising these waters offers a familiar, comfortable home base from which to sightsee their fascinating shores, allowing numerous exotic destinations in a single vacation on itineraries ranging from 10 to 14 days.

China

Beijing

Since Peking Man first set up house over a half-million years ago, Beijing (which means "northern capital") has evolved into one of the 10 largest metropolitan areas on earth. Located on the northern edge of the great **North China Plain,** China's capital of more than 11 million is packed with thousands of years of history—an ancient city in the midst of modernization. Only in in the past 20 years has the city swung the gates open to admit foreigners.

What began as a small market town was conquered in 221 BC by the first Qin ruler, Shi Huang Di, who unified the empire and joined existing walls built in the north to form what is perhaps the world's most famous wall. This attempt to secure Chinese borders against invaders unfortunately bankrupted the empire. Succeeding dynasties—Han, Tang, Song—continued to change the face of the city until Ghenghis Khan's Mongols conquered Beijing in the 13th century. His grandson Kublai Khan rebuilt it as the capital of the Yuan dynasty and named the city **Khanbalik.** Fifteenth-century Ming rulers, who erected the opulent, imperial **Forbidden City** and reconstructed much of China's famous wall that we see today, were overthrown by the Manchus in the 17th century. Imperial China began its death throes with the Opium Wars in 1860 and the Taiping Rebellion of 1864-66, culminating in the Boxer Rebellion of 1900. In 1911, the last imperial dynasty fell, and a year later Sun Yat-sen formed and led a new republic. Internal struggles, as well a war with Japan, continued under Chiang Kai-shek until 1949 when Mao Zedong proclaimed the Communist

People's Republic of China, and Beijing once again became the country's capital. Internal events, from Mao's Cultural Revolution in the mid-1960s through pro-democracy demonstrations in 1989, caught world attention. But only following Mao's death have capital and country slowly begun the slow and painful process of becoming a major player on the world scene while retaining a basic Communist framework. But modernity aside, Beijing is still a place of jingling bicycles and wide boulevards, walled imperial palaces, and narrow back alleys called *hutongs*, a city that fascinates visitors today as much as it did explorer Marco Polo centuries ago.

Several regional cooking styles are represented in Beijing, most of which are stir-fried and scooped up with chopsticks; rice and noodles are staples. Beijing is probably most famous for Peking duck rolled in pancakes with green onions and plum sauce; Muslim barbecue features lamb kabobs called *shashlik*. Items from across the country are available in Beijing at government Friendship Stores, markets, and small shops. Good buys include down jackets, stationery items such as hand-carved seals called "chops," brushes and ink, prints, silk, antiques, cloisonné, furniture, ginseng, ivory (prohibited for import by US Customs), jade, rugs, scroll paintings, tea, and woodblock prints.

- ■ **Tiananmen Guangchang (Tiananmen Square)**
- ■ **Zijincheng (Forbidden City)**
- ■ **Beihai Gongyuan (Beihai Park)**
- ■ **Tiantan Park (Temple of Heaven)**
- ■ **Yonghegong (Lama Temple)**
- ■ **Di Xia Cheng (Underground City)**

- ■ Xiangshan Gongyuan (Fragrant Hills Park)
- ■ Yiheyuan (Summer Palace)
- ■ Wanli Changcheng (Great Wall)
- ■ Ming Ling (Ming Tombs)

Dalian

Wedged between green hills and the sea at the southern tip of the **Liaodong Peninsula** in northeast China, Dalian suffers from an identity problem of sorts, its eclectic personality evolving over a century of occupation that shifted among three different countries. Long coveted for its location and status as an ice-free port, it has been known by a jumble of names—**Dalien, Dairen, Dalny,** and **Luda.** Three years after Japan snagged the peninsula in 1895, Russia's Tsar Nicholas II signed a lease expanding the existing Chinese naval base and developing a new commercial port, a move that gave Russia control. Japan retook the region in 1905, completing the port facilities in 1930. The Soviets reoccupied Dalian as part of the Yalta Agreement from 1945 until 1954. Dalian, which means "great junction," continues to be China's northernmost major port, although it retains vestiges of its past occupations. It is a city of wide avenues and spacious squares, onion-dome churches, Soviet-style government buildings, and until recently, bilingual signs in Chinese and Russian.

Dalian's over 2.5 million residents work in shipbuilding, petroleum refining, food processing, chemical, glass and textile industries, fishing, and agriculture (mainly apple-growing). It is also a resort area, with many Chinese visiting to partake of the city's sandy beaches and parks.

Known for its seafood, Dalian hauls in more than a hundred kinds of fish in its local catch, along with such shellfish as shrimp, scallops, abalone, and sea cucumber. Intricate shell pictures, as well as crystal and glassware, can be seen in production at factory tours and found alongside other typical Chinese goods at the local Friendship Store.

- ■ Sidalin Guangchang (Stalin Square)
- ■ Zhongshan Guangchang (Sun Yat-sen Square)
- ■ Ziran Bowuguan (Natural History Museum)
- ■ Shell-carving Factory
- ■ Glass Works
- ■ Underground Tunnels
- ■ Xinghai Gongyuan (Starry Sea Park)
- ■ Laodong Gongyuan (Laodong Park)
- ■ Fujiazhuang Haishui Yuchang (Fujiazhuang Beach)
- ■ Laohutan Gongyuan (Tiger Beach Park)

Shanghai

The city of Shanghai (which means "up from the sea") started out as an obscure fishing village on mud flats near the mouth of the **Yangtze River** a thousand years ago. Largely ignored by the rest of the world for several centuries, it kept to itself until the Opium War's Treaty of Nanking opened the city to foreigners in 1842. Europeans and Americans living and working in separate settlements called "concessions," exempt from Chinese law, prospered in the boom town, firing the revolutionary movement among the Chinese, who were reaping none of the benefits. The Chinese Communist Party, which formed here in 1921, seized the city in 1949.

But even after the Communist Revolution, Shanghai's entrepreneurial spirit has persisted and its European ambience never was completely eradicated. Dominated by the **Huangpu River**, a wide stretch of brown water packed with both oceangoing vessels and small boats, today Shanghai is one of the world's top 10 cargo-handling ports. It is China's most important industrial, commercial, and trade center, with about half of all the country's exports passing through. With more than 12 million people jammed into one of the most crowded urban areas in the world, the air is sometimes yellow with smog, and the streets always clogged with cars. Nonetheless, Shanghai retains a sophisticated air of nostalgia harking back to a time of intrigue and adventure.

Shanghai's style of cooking emphasizes seafood and fresh river fish, especially steamed freshwater crabs, honey-fired eel, and braised yellowfish. Meats are often marinated and then braised in a soy, wine, and sugar sauce. Breadlike buns, steamed dumplings, and noodles are sometimes eaten, although rice is the staple. In addition to the ubiquitous Friendship Stores, **Nanjing Road**'s department stores are packed with such goods as antiques, ivory carvings (illegal to import to the US), jackets, chops (Chinese signature seals), silk, and tea.

- ■ Wai Tan (The Bund)
- ■ Nanjing Donglu (Nanjing Road East)
- ■ Yuyuan Shangchang (Mandarin Gardens Bazaar)
- ■ Yufo Si (Jade Buddha Temple)
- ■ Gongyi Meishupin Yanjiusuo (Arts and Crafts Research Institute)
- ■ Shanghai Bowuguan (Shanghai Museum)
- ■ Shanghai acrobatics performance
- ■ Faguo Zujie (French Concession)
- ■ Suzhou via Grand Canal
- ■ Wuxi via Grand Canal

Since the founding of Holland America Line in 1872, the fleet's flagship has been christened *Rotterdam*, in honor of the great Dutch seaport that was the company's original home. The current *Rotterdam*, launched in September 1997, is the sixth ship to bear the name.

Princess Cruises' *Sun Princess* must have an enormous linen closet. The ship, which carries 1,950 passengers, stocks 64,000 bed sheets, 51,000 towels, and 7,400 bathrobes.

Mary Anne Shula christened Carnival Cruise Lines' *Inspiration* in 1996, one season after her husband, Don, retired from coaching the Miami Dolphins.

Victoria Peak Tram, Hong Kong

Hong Kong

Ceded to the British after the first Opium Wars (1839-49), Hong Kong (which means "fragrant harbor") reverted to Chinese rule on 1 July 1997. The almost 400-square-mile former Crown Colony of Hong Kong consists of **Hong Kong Island**; **Kowloon,** where cruise ships dock at the labyrinthine **Ocean Terminal**; and the **New Territories,** farmland reaching up to the border. Hong Kong's tiny size belies its influence on international finance, manufacturing, and trade. **Victoria Harbour,** one of the world's most spectacular sea arms, has been the conduit that connects China with the rest of the world. On any day, the harbor might be jammed with bat-winged junks leaning into the wind, a visiting aircraft carrier, Scandinavian container ships, Japanese car carriers, luxury cruise liners, tiny sampans, yachts, and tugs.

More than six million people live and work amid the soaring skyscrapers perched precariously along shores and clinging to the hillsides of Hong Kong Island. The city is heavily populated by refugees from mainland China's 20th-century political upheavals. Smoky temples and raucous outdoor markets of the romantic old Hong Kong coexist comfortably within a few steps of gleaming office buildings and modern luxury hotels of the new Hong Kong. Cantonese is the local dialect, although English is widely spoken.

One of the world's most sophisticated culinary capitals, Hong Kong offers classical and regional Chinese food, predominantly Cantonese, along with an astounding array of global options. Dim sum—a centuries-old tradition—is a meal comprised of multiple servings of small portions of shrimp dumplings, steamed pork buns, spring rolls, and other delicacies.

Hong Kong's staggering selection of merchandise can stun even veteran shoppers. Antiques, Chinese art, cameras, electronic equipment, eyeglasses, rugs and carpets, designer clothing, custom-made clothing, ceramics and porcelain, cosmetics and toiletries, hand-carved furniture, pearl and jade jewelry, watches, and leather goods only begin the list of items available at Hong Kong's famous malls, hotel arcades, department stores, boutiques, and street markets. It is advisable to shop at stores that carry the Hong Kong Tourist Association insignia.

- Li Yuen Street
- Ladder Street and Man Mo Temple
- Hollywood Road
- Victoria Peak Tram
- Star Ferry
- Jade Market
- Temple Street Night Market in Kowloon
- Sampan ride in Aberdeen
- Yau Ma Tei neighborhood (Typhoon shelter)
- Lantau Island

"The Love Boat" and Beyond: Cruising on the Small Screen

Say "cruise ship," and the first words that pop into the minds of many American are "The Love Boat." The long-running television series, which aired from 1977 to 1986, provided millions of viewers with their first (albeit idealized) glimpse of shipboard life, making **Princess Cruises** a household name and giving the entire cruise industry a boost.

The popular show was the brainchild of producer Douglas Cramer, creator of "Love American Style," who decided to transplant the premise of that hit comedy series to a cruise ship. **Princess Cruises'** *Pacific Princess* was chosen as the set (shows were taped on board both the *Pacific Princess* and her sister ship, the *Island Princess*), and the rest is TV history. To this day, "The Love Boat," with its laughably implausible plots and always-happy endings, lives on in the popular imagination (and in reruns). Capitalizing on the show's lasting appeal, **Princess Cruises** continues to use Gavin McLeod, who played Captain Stubing, as the line's official spokesman.

But the *Pacific Princess* isn't the only cruise ship to have played a role on the small screen. Years before "The Love Boat" was launched, Lucille Ball dropped onto the deck of the *Constitution* from a helicopter in a 1956 episode of "I Love Lucy." Actually, the sequence, along with scenes of Lucy Ricardo dancing in the ship's lounge and getting stuck in a porthole, was shot in a Hollywood studio. Only the exterior footage was authentic.

On a more highbrow note, **Cunard**'s *Queen Elizabeth 2* appeared in the PBS-TV series "Brideshead Revisited" and also was the subject of a National Geographic film on great ocean liners.

More recently, television star Fran Drescher and the cast of "The Nanny" taped a 1996 episode on board **Celebrity Cruises'** *Century.* Some of the ship's passengers participated as walk-ons and extras, while several *Century* staff members and officers netted speaking roles, including Captain Iakavos Korres, who played himself.

And the *Titanic* was recently the subject of a made-for-TV movie and a National Geographic special. But perhaps the less said about the *Titanic* the better.

MICHAEL STORRINGS

India

Mumbai

Formerly known as **Bombay,** Mumbai is a place that grabs guests by the nose. It seethes with more than 12 million people and exudes an aroma that mingles exhaust, heat, overpopulation, spices, and salty sea air. Situated on India's west coast on the **Arabian Sea,** separated from the rest of the country by the **Western Ghats** range, the city has a long history of Arab and European influence. The Portuguese sailed into the harbor in the early 16th century, calling it "Bom Bahia" (good bay). The British acquired the region as part of a marriage dowry when Charles II wed Catherine of Braganza, daughter of Portugal's king, in 1662. It was then a marshy area, consisting of seven islands occupied by Koli fishermen. The British built forts, reclaimed lands, and linked islands with bridges, forming the thin isthmus on which the city now stands. It evolved into a cosmopolitan trade center, prospering from its shipyards. The construction of a railway and the opening of the Suez Canal contributed to even greater growth, especially in cotton exports.

Today, multinational companies and financial services are headquartered in Mumbai, and it produces more movies than any other city in the world, with more than 300 flicks filmed here yearly. The city's architecture is an extravagant mix of Victorian-Gothic and Indian influence, and many remnants of the Raj still stand, including the city's symbol, an archway built to commemorate the 1911 visit of King George V and Queen Mary. Mumbai, capital of the state of **Maharashtra,** has never been able to keep its services up with its population, almost one-third of which still lives in makeshift sidewalk dwellings. India, which gained its independence in 1947 with help of a lawyer named Mohandas Gandhi, is today bursting at the seams, with a population of nearly one billion and growing.

Most Westerners think of curry when they think of Indian cuisine. In reality, the country offers a staggering selection and variety of dishes, with each region adding its own signature spice. Rice is the staple, and because 80 percent of the country is Hindu, vegetarian choices are endless. A *thali* is a complete meal traditionally served on a banana leaf, although today, more often than not, it comes on a stainless steel tray. It consists of a couple of curries, *chapati* (grilled or fried whole-wheat flatbread), *dal* (lentil-based gravy), and *pappadum (*a roasted or deep-fried paper-thin round). Best buys here are silver and gold jewelry by weight, antiques, silks and saris, wood carvings, brassware, and textiles.

- Gateway of India
- Mani Bhavan (Gandhi Museum)
- Hanging Gardens and Towers of Silence
- Victoria and Albert Museum
- Prince of Wales Museum
- Mahatma Jyotibal Bhule Market (Crawford Market)
- Chor Bazar
- Town Hall
- Victoria Terminus
- Walkeshwar Temple

Indonesia

Bali

Mystical, mysterious, and enchanting. It is said that Dutch soldiers passing Bali in the 17th century leapt overboard in their eagerness to reach the island, never to be seen again. Bali lies eight degrees south of the equator, between the **Java Sea** and the **Indian Ocean.** More than three million people live here, among rice paddies terraced up the slopes of 10,308-foot **Mount Agung,** a verdant volcano. The Balinese believe that the volcano is home to the gods, whom they spend a greater part of the day pacifying with gifts and offerings at more than 20,000 temples scattered across the island. Bali's rice fields are the most sophisticated in Indonesia, with an elaborate irrigation system consisting of dams, canals, and underground tunnels.

Indian traders and Hindu and Buddhist monks introduced Indian culture to Bali by the ninth century. When Islam arrived in Indonesia 600 years later,

Kintimani Temple, Bali

Hindu faithful found refuge here, developing a unique ritualistic culture. Balinese often express themselves through dance. The *Legong,* with young women dressed in silk sarongs and flower headdresses, tells the story of a wicked king who tried to force his attentions upon a princess. The *Kecak* (Monkey Dance), performed at night by a group that includes about 150 men who play monkeys, recounts an episode from the Hindu epic *Ramayana.* The *Barong* dance tells the story of the good-natured mythical beast resembling a lion who battles the wicked queen of witches.

An exception to Indonesia's Muslim majority, Bali makes the most of pork. *Babi guling* is stuffed, spit-roasted suckling pig seasoned with herbs and spices, while *babi kecap* is pork cooked in a sweet soy sauce. Balinese coffee is aromatic and robust. The lush hills are dotted with villages, some devoted to single crafts. One is home to many of Bali's best painters; in another, woodcarvers use teak, coconut, ebony, and hibiscus to create characters and animals from their religious myths. In **Celuk,** craftsmen delicately transform gold and silver into jewelry.

- Celuk
- Mas
- Ubud
- Tenganan

- Pura Besakih (Besakih Temple)
- Rafting on Ayung River
- Kintimani and Lake Batur
- Bali Museum in Denpasar
- Kerta Gosa (Hall of Justice) in Klungklung
- Pura Kehen (Kehen Temple) in Bangli

Jakarta, Java

Located on the northwest coast of Java, Jakarta is the hot, sprawling capital of Indonesia. A city of more than 10 million people, it draws on the diverse traditions of migrants from all corners of Indonesia, which itself has more than 300 ethnic groups who inhabit the over 70,000 islands lying along the **Pacific Ocean**'s volcanic "Ring of Fire." Java is an island of contrasts—more than 100 million people live in an approximately 50,000-square-mile area where the landscape ranges from rain forests and rice paddies to crowded cities. Jakarta is Indonesia's cultural and governmental center and the largest city in the country's far-flung archipelago. It is a smoggy metropolis, with insane traffic made worse by the heat. Although a decade of frenetic construction has transformed the city into a slick commercial hub, it is still possible to return to the colonial past in neighborhoods like **Kota** (Old Batavia), as well as the old harbor town that thrived from the 12th to 16th centuries, where traditional Makassar schooners still tie up.

Jakarta was originally a Hindu-ruled settlement called **Sunda Kelapa;** it was renamed **Jayakarta** ("city of victory") by a conquering Muslim prince in the 16th century. The Dutch and their East India Company took the city in 1619, renamed it **Batavia**, and ruled for over 300 years. Japan occupied the city during World War II, during which time the name reverted to Jakarta; Indonesian independence was declared in 1945, but not recognized by the Dutch until four years later.

As in the rest of Asia, the Indonesian diet is based on rice. *Nasi goreng* (fried rice, often with an egg on top) could be called the national dish. *Gado gado* is steamed vegetables topped with peanut sauce and prawn crackers. Satay, grilled skewers of meat or chicken with peanut sauce, is also a favorite. A Dutch feast known as rijsttafel is offered at most hotels. Handicrafts from across Indonesia can be found in Jakarta, including silverwork and *wayang golek* (three-dimensional shadow puppets). Batik, one of Indonesia's best-known crafts, is produced by covering material with a wax design, dyeing it, then scraping off the wax. Repeated waxing and dyeing can produce colorful and complex designs. Batik fabric is a good buy here.

- Medan Merdeka (Merdeka Square) and Monas National Monument
- Sunda Kelapa (Old Harbor)
- Glodok (Chinatown)
- Pasar Ikan (Fish Market)
- Museum Bahari (Maritime Museum)

- Wayang Museum (Puppet Museum)
- Gedung Gajah (National Museum)
- Textile Museum
- Taman Ismail Marzuki (Jakarta Cultural Center)
- Taman Mini Indonesia Indah (Mini Indonesia Cultural Park)

Semarang, Java

Originally inhabited by Java Man about 40,000 years ago, Java was later populated by Malay people who arrived from the Southeast Asian mainland. The culture grew under Indian influence, and many kingdoms rose and fell, notably the Shailendra kingdom of **Central Java,** which saw the building of the massive Buddhist temple of **Borobudur** in the ninth century, only rediscovered in 1814 by Sir Stamford Raffles. Muslims settled in large numbers in the 15th century, followed by the Portuguese in the 16th, then the Dutch, who ruled for over 300 years until independence in 1949.

Semarang, one of the oldest cities in the Indonesian archipelago, first grew as an important gateway over a thousand years ago. A busy fishing port situated on the northern coast of central Java, it shows obvious Islamic and Chinese influences in architecture and customs. The oldest mosque in Central Java is here, and southwest of the city some of Java's oldest Hindu temples still stand. Semarang was at one time a Dutch administrative and trading center and remains the commercial hub of the region. Its 1.2 million residents include a sizeable Chinese population. It was known as the "Red City" after Communists set up camp here in the 1920s; Japanese soldiers were first welcomed as liberators during World War II, but later despised as occupiers.

Standard Indonesian fare is found in Semarang, including *nasi goreng, bak mie goreng* (fried noodles), *gado gado* (lightly cooked vegetables with peanut sauce), and satay. Semarang's own local specialty is *masrochan,* a banana fritter of sorts. Batik fabric, clothing, and paintings are sold here. Gold and silver jewelry, as well as leather, ceramics, wood carvings, and *wayang golek* can be found at the **Pasar Johar** market.

- Gedong Batu (Stone Building or Sam Po Kong Temple)
- Chinatown
- Gereja Belanda or (Gereja Blenduk) Church
- Dutch East India Company fortress ruins
- Candi
- Cog Railway from Ambarawa to Bedono
- Demak village
- Mount Merapi (Fire Mountain)
- Borobudur
- Dieng Plateau temples

Initial Explanation

The initials that sometimes appear before a ship's name (MS *Hanseatic*, SSC *Radisson Diamond*, SS *Independence*, MV *CostaRomantica*, TSS *Stella Solaris,* etc.) are abbreviations that indicate the type of vessel. These terms usually are related to the way the ship is powered.

The following are the most common such prefixes:

IB ice breaker

MS motor ship

MTS motor twin screw or motor turbine ship

MV motor vessel

MSY motor sailing yacht

SS steamship

SSC semisubmersible craft

TSS turbine steamship

YS yacht ship

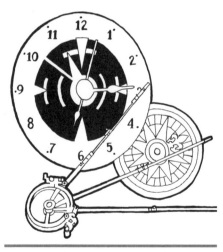

Abercrombie & Kent's *Explorer,* designed expressly for polar cruising, was commissioned by the Swedish travel pioneer Lars Eric Lindblad in 1969. Originally named the *Lindblad Explorer*, it was the first passenger vessel to sail to Antarctica. It still cruises to the White Continent every austral summer.

Pare Pare, Sulawesi

Formerly known as the **Celebes**, the mountainous Indonesian island of Sulawesi straddles the equator, just east of **Borneo,** between the **Banda Sea** and **Makassar Strait.** Its strange shape spreads out in four arms like a sea creature. The island of 13 million people is terraced with rice paddies and has deep valleys, swift rivers, and many active volcanoes. Wild orchids thrive.

Bugis and Makassarese trading kingdoms first took hold here along the southern coastal region. By the 17th century Dutch, English, Arab, Malay, Chinese, and Indian seafarers were doing a brisk business in spices, sandalwood, birds' nests, and slaves. The Bugis, coastal pirates renowned across Southeast Asia since the 16th century for their Vikinglike fearlessness on the high seas, are still famous for their schooners—handmade without nails—found throughout Indonesia. Up in the cool highlands, **South Sulawesi** is renowned for the Torajan culture up in the cool highlands, with its striking architecture and elaborate funeral ceremonies and burial practices.

Pare Pare, Sulawesi's second-largest city, is a narrow enclave that spreads out along the coast with a population of more than 100,000. Nearby **Sengkang** is a center for silk production, where weavers create traditional Buginese designs in plaids, checks, and stripes , along with distinctive warp *ikat* blankets in black, red, and blue, used by the Torajan to bury their dead.

- **Monumen Rakyat Pejuang**
- **La Bangenge Museum**
- **Jalan Hasanuddin Mosque**
- **Sengkang**
- **Lake Tempe**
- **Ke'te Kesu'**
- **Londa**
- **Lemo**
- **Suaya**
- **Tampangallo**

Surabaya, Java

Hot, smoggy Surabaya, Indonesia's second-largest—and perhaps fastest-growing—city, is also an important industrial and commercial center. Home to more than three million people, it is situated on the **Kali Mas River** on the north coast of **East Java. Tanjung Perak Harbor** is one of the most important conduits for exports to Europe, Asia, and the Western Hemisphere. Surabaya itself contains few cultural and historical sites, but does serve as a gateway to other attractions in the area, such as the neighboring island, where bull races called *kera pan sapi,* accompanied by much merrymaking by both locals and visitors, are run from August through October.

Surabaya emerged as an important port in the 14th century. The Dutch subsequently established a trading post here, which moved rice, salt, sugar, and bronze throughout the region. The city later rebelled against the Dutch, and there followed six years of bloody conflict. Its resistance against foreign rule over the centuries earned Surabaya the title "City of Heroes."

Indonesian cuisine, based on rice, noodles, chilies, lemongrass, and garlic, is found here, along with Chinese food. Stock up in Surabaya on handicrafts, batik, *wayang* puppets, silver, and wood carvings, which come from Java's **Yogyakarta,** the cultural capital of the country.

- **Kalimas wharf**
- **Kampung Arab (Arab Quarter) and Ampel Mosque**
- **Jalan Kayum Flower Market**
- **Grahadi (Government House)**
- **Chinatown**
- **Tretes hill station**
- **Bull races on Madura Island**
- **Mount Bromo and Bromo-Tengger-Semeru National Park**
- **Candi Jawa**
- **Trowulan**

Japan

Kobe

As is often and unfortunately the case with unfamiliar places, most Westerners got their first look at Kobe when catastrophe struck—when their TVs broadcast terrifying images of the devastating earthquake of 1995. With typical industriousness, Kobe dusted itself off and quickly got down to the business of rebuilding from the bottom up. Situated on the southwest coast of **Honshu** on **Osaka Bay,** Kobe is a cosmopolitan city wedged between the densely forested **Rokko Mountains** and the **Inland Sea.** Kobe was virtually flattened in World War II and was rebuilt on reclaimed land, including **Port Island,** an industrial, residential, and commercial district linked to the mainland by a train.

The city has been a port since the 13th century. Today Kobe, translated as "God's door," has an international population of more than 1.5 million residents and more than 1,200 parks. It is the country's second-largest port, serving as many as 10,000 ships a year and is also a gateway to the imperial cities of **Osaka** and **Kyoto.**

Westerners will associate the name Kobe with its famous hand-massaged beef, renowned for its buttery texture and taste, and served in classic dishes such as *shabu shabu.* Sukiyaki (beef, vegetables, tofu, onions, and soy sauce cooked in a broth in an iron pot) is also a popular item on the menu. Kobe has been a center for the production of *sake* (rice wine served hot or cold) for over 600 years. Kobe's stores, many of which are found on its popular shopping street, **Motomachi,** are well stocked with Japanese-made stereo equipment, cameras, watches, electronic goods, ceramics, cloisonné, porcelain, pearls, bone china, lacquerware, prints, paintings, kimonos, and artistic paper products. In addition to the usual merchandise, Japanese department stores offer everything from art exhibitions to food emporia and children's playlands.

- **Kobe City Museum**
- **Ikuta Jinja (Ikuta Shrine)**
- **Kitano Cho**
- **Chouéké Yashiki (Chouéké Mansion)**
- **Kazami Dori no Yakata (Weathercock House)**
- **Hakutsuru Art Museum**
- **Nunobiki-no-taki Falls**
- **Kikumasamune Shuzou Shiryo Kinenkan (Sake Museum)**
- **Mount Rokko**
- **Arima Onsen (Arima's Hot Springs Resort)**

Kyoto

Although less than an hour from **Kobe** across **Honshu** by bullet train, Kyoto and its 2,000 temples and shrines, quiet back alleys, and tea shops are a world away. To wander this city is to travel back through time and experience a tranquillity rarely found in the middle of the modern world. Kyoto was the capital of Japan from the eighth century until 1868, when Tokyo replaced it. The city was spared the bombs of World War II, leaving its ancient architecture intact. But tradition is inevitably eroding as the city of more than about 1,400,000 inhabitants has slowly evolved into a major industrial center where electrical equipment, cameras, chemicals, silk, and porcelain are manufactured.

Especially lovely during spring cherry blossoms or fall foliage and accompanying festivals, Kyoto is a wonderful city to walk through, its early Chinese influence evident in its gridded street system. It remains the center of Japanese culture and civilization, and the emperor still visits the palace of the emperors on his birthday.

Buddhism, which predominates in Kyoto, has strongly influenced its cuisine. The region is famous for *kyo-ryori,* a type of cooking close to *kaiseki,* a formal method of food preparation and dining that evolved from the traditions of Buddhist monks. Temple-restaurants often feature *shojin ryori,* vegetarian cuisine centered around tofu and beautifully presented, introduced from China.

Still a center for traditional arts and crafts, Kyoto probably offers the best selection of handicrafts in Japan. Especially famous for its silk, dyed according to ancient methods, it is also known for bamboo crafts, lacquerware, ritual fans, textile weaving, and a damascene technique that involves laying pure silver and gold onto figures engraved on prints, screens, and scrolls.

- ■ **Kyoto Gosho (Imperial Palace)**
- ■ **Nijo-Jo Castle**
- ■ **Nishi-Honganji Temple**
- ■ **Ryoanji Temple**
- ■ **Nanzenji Temple**
- ■ **Tetsugaku-no-Michi (Path of Philosophy) and Zenrinji Temple**
- ■ **Kiyomizu-Dera Temple**
- ■ **Okyoto Kokuritsu Hakubutsukan (Kyoto National Museum)**
- ■ **Higashi-Honganji Temple and Kikokutei Shosei-en Garden**
- ■ **Kinkakuji Temple**

Nagasaki

Clinging to steep green hills wrapped around a deep bay on **Kyushu**'s west coast, Nagasaki has long been a conduit for Japan's contact with the rest of the world, first with China and Korea in the 12th and 13th centuries, then with the Portuguese and Dutch in the 16th and 17th. In 1549 Saint Francis Xavier was the first of many missionaries to visit the city. Even after 17th-century shoguns (military governors) expelled all missionaries and Christian traders, and Japan slammed its doors shut for over 200 years, Nagasaki still provided an open window to the Western world through its continued contact with Dutch traders. Traces of foreign influence remain throughout the city. Chinese culture is reflected in major temple compounds, while the Dutch legacy can be seen in the city's brick buildings, canals, and winding cobblestone streets.

Standing in the lovely gardens overlooking the bay, the setting for Puccini's opera *Madama Butterfly,* it is hard to envision the effects of the atomic bomb that in 1945 leveled the city, chosen as a target in part because of its shipbuilding activity. Today Nagasaki, home to 450,000 people, remains one of the world's largest shipbuilding centers.

Nagasaki's cuisine has been shaped by its Chinese and European history as well. In addition to the usual array of such beautifully prepared typical Japanese dishes as sushi, sashimi, tempura, yakitori, and sukiyaki, local specialties include *champon,* a thick Chinese noodle served as a soup dish. *Kasutera,* a sponge cake of sorts introduced by Portuguese sailors centuries ago, is most often found gift-wrapped to go. Items made with mother-of-pearl, porcelain, and tortoise shell (banned for import to the US) can be found here, in addition to the usual selection of cameras and electronics.

Kinkakuji Temple, Kyoto

- Glover House and Gardens
- Jorokuban-kan Mansion
- Oura Catholic Church
- Dejima and Orandazaka (The Holland Slope)
- 26 Martyrs Memorial
- Sofukuji Temple
- Kofukuji Temple
- Heiwa-Koen (Peace Park) and International Culture Hall
- Nagasaki Park and Suwa Shrine
- Mount Inasa

Tokyo

Originally named **Edo** (Gate of the Estuary) for its location at the mouth of the **Sumida River,** Tokyo dates from the end of the 12th century. In 1603 Tokugawa Ieyasu established his shogunate (military government) here, and after imperial rule was restored in 1868, Emperor Meiji moved the country's capital from Kyoto in 1873 and renamed the city Tokyo (eastern capital).

Flattened by a devastating earthquake in 1923 and bombings during World War II, Tokyo was rebuilt out instead of up. Today Greater Tokyo goes from **Mount Fuji** in the west, through **Nikko** in the north, down to the southeast through **Narita** and the **Boso Peninsula,** across **Tokyo Bay** to **Yokohama** and the **Miura** and **Izu Peninsulas** on the southwest. Its over 7.5 million residents live in one of the world's biggest—and most expensive—cities. Tokyo itself comprises numerous districts, each with its own particular atmosphere and character, which radiate outward from the **Imperial Palace** at the core of the city. To the east lie the business, shopping, and entertainment districts of **Hibiya, Marunouchi, Yurakucho, Nihombashi, Ginza,** and **Shimbashi.** The political hub—**Kasumigaseki**—lies south of the palace, and industrial districts sprawl along Tokyo's waterfront. North of the palace are **Kanda,** which includes a number of universities; **Asakusa,** noted for its amusement areas; **Roppongi,** renowned for its international cuisine ; **Akasaka,** with its rolling hills and sophisticated entertainment; and the fashionable residential neighborhoods of **Aoyama** and **Azabu.**

One is never far from the sea in Japan, and the menu features plenty of fish, served raw as sushi or sashimi, deep-fried as tempura, or grilled as *yakizakana.* Sukiyaki is probably Japan's most popular dish for festive occasions. *Teppanyaki* (seafood, beef, and vegetables) is sometimes cooked tableside; yakitori is available in both meat and vegetable versions. Rice or noodles always round out the menu. Sake served hot or cold is a national drink. The shopping possibilities are as elegant and varied as the food. **Ginza** is one of the most famous and expensive shopping streets in the world. Cameras and electronic goods are abundant, but not necessarily available at bargain prices. Collectible souvenirs from around the country include pearls and such handicrafts as lacquerware,

ceramics, cloisonné, *netsuke* (ivory charms), metalwork, fans, and handmade paper.

- Edo-Tokyo Museum
- Imperial Palace and Gardens
- National Museum of Modern Art
- Tokyo National Museum
- Ueno Park
- Asakusa and Senso-ji Temple
- Pentax Gallery
- Harajuku and Meiji-jingu Shrine
- Koraku-en Gardens
- Tsukiji Fish Market

Macau

This Portuguese enclave approximately 70 miles south of **Guangzhou** (Canton) is filled with pastel-colored villas, decaying palaces, and Baroque churches, a crumbling monument to European colonialism. The tiny territory is caught in a time warp dating back to 1513, when Portuguese navigator Jorge Alvares sailed to southern China. Macau, which some translate as "City of the name of God," soon was established as Europe's most important center for trade and Christianity in the Far East and for two centuries was the one of the richest cities in the world. Legend has it that in 1557 China swapped the six-square-mile territory, consisting of a peninsula of China's Guangdong province along with two quiet islands—one joined by a I.5-mile bridge and the other by causeway—in exchange for Portuguese protection from pirates.

Visiting Macau, with its half-million residents, is an international adventure. Remnants of its glory days are evident in street signs of typical blue and white ceramic tile, written in Portuguese and Chinese, and the Lisbon-like cobblestone streets that lead up to the steps of a Buddhist temple. Casinos are filled with chain-smoking day-trippers from neighboring Hong Kong. Chinese and Portuguese are the official languages, but English is widely spoken. Macau is due to revert to Chinese rule in 1999.

Local menus might contain *caldo verde* (a vegetable soup), *bacalhau* (codfish), Brazilian *feijoada* (a heavy stew of pork, potatoes, cabbage, and beans, served with rice), spicy African chicken, dim sum, or Macau sole, all washed down with superb Portuguese wines. Available here are such Chinese products as hand-carved furniture, traditional arts and crafts, including items of brass, lacquer, bronze, handwoven rugs and carpets, jade and other jewelry, silk, gold, and coral.

Carnival Cruise Lines' chairman, Mickey Arison, is a hoops fanatic. He owns the Natonal Basketball Association franchise Miami Heat and seldom misses a home game.

- Church of São Paulo
- Monte Fort
- Guia Fortress and Lighthouse
- Kun Iam Temple (Goddess of Mercy)
- Leal Senado (Loyal Senate)
- Church of São Domingos
- Lou Lim Ieoc Gardens
- A-Ma Temple
- Macau Maritime Museum
- Taipa and Colôane

- Signal Hill
- Waterfront markets
- Masjid Sabah (State Mosque)
- Sabah State Museum
- Tanjung Aru Beach
- Kinabalu National Park
- Penampang
- Tamparuli footbridge and market
- Mengkabong stilt village
- Sunday Market at Kota Belud

Malaysia

Kota Kinabalu

Sailors who survived voyages on the sometimes stormy **South China Sea** named the island south of the typhoon belt "The Land Below The Wind," or **Sabah.** Once part of the Brunei empire, Sabah was long avoided for its pirates who looted and torched Kota Kinabalu so often that the city became known as **Api Api** (fire fire). The capital of the Malaysian state of Sabah gets its name from *kota* (fort) and **Kinabalu,** the nearby mountain, at 2.5 miles high one of the loftiest in Asia. Today it is known locally as "KK."

In 1888 North Borneo, along with Brunei and **Sarawak,** became a British protectorate. Kota Kinabalu, then known as "Jesselton" after Sir Charles Jessel, the British ruler of Borneo, was completely destroyed during World War II. By 1963 Malaysia became an independent federation, comprising **West Malaysia** on the Malay Peninsula and—about 400 miles away across the **South China Sea—East Malaysia,** formed by Sabah and **Sarawak** on the island of **Borneo.** The country has a population of over 19 million, spread out over 129,000 square miles.

The country's society is multiracial; in Kota Kinabalu Chinese are the largest single group. Nearly half of Sabah's 13 million inhabitants are Malay and other indigenous peoples, including the various Kadazan headhunting tribes; Baju, best known as seafarers, but who now are farmers and ranchers; and Murut, who still hunt with blowpipes.

Their handicrafts, such as batik, baskets, mats, beadwork, pottery, tribal swords, knives, and blowpipes (which may be considered lethal weapons at customs!) are all sought-after souvenirs. Satay may as well be the national dish. Tasty offerings also include *sambal udang* (curried prawns spiced with hot chili peppers and red onions) and *sop kambing* (mutton soup cooked with cauliflower, onions, carrots, ginger, and cloves).

Cunard's *Queen Elizabeth 2* was pressed into military service during the 1982 Falklands War. It took two weeks to convert the liner into a troop ship, but two months to refit her for passenger service.

Kuala Lumpur (Port Kelang)

Chinese miners discovered tin at the junction of the **Kelang** and **Gombek Rivers** on **Peninsular Malaysia,** a long finger of land stretching down from the Thai border to **Singapore,** at the place named "Kuala Lumpur" (muddy river mouth) by the Malay people. From 1858 the city—today called "KL"—grew on tin and rubber exploitation. Malaysia continues to be one of the world's leading suppliers of both resources; neat rows of high-yield rubber trees dot much of Peninsular Malaysia's western coastal plain.

Kuala Lumpur, situated in the state of **Selangor,** is the capital and largest city. With more than two million residents, it is one of the most progressive and modern cities in Southeast Asia, serving as the commercial, educational, and cultural center of Malaysia. KL's **Petronas Tower** looms over temples, colonial mansions, and a Chinatown that never sleeps; at 1,477 feet it eclipses the Sears Tower in Chicago as the world's tallest building. Malaysia and its capital—a multicultural society of Malays, Chinese, Indians, Arabs, Asians, and Europeans—are predominantly Muslim. This heritage dates back to the 15th century, when the Maharaja of Malacca converted to Islam, and Arab merchant ships brought Muslim missionaries via what is today Port Kelang and Malacca. Buddhism and Hinduism have followers as well.

Malaysian dishes are built around a rice-based diet. Local fare includes satay, along with Chinese and Indian cuisine. Batik, bamboo walking sticks, *kain songket* cloth, Malaysian kites, wood carvings, wicker, and silverwork can be found at the **Central Market, Karyaneka Handicraft Village,** and **Kampung Baru Saturday Night/Sunday Market.**

- Masjid Jame
- Sultan Abdul Samad Building
- Balai Seni Lukis Negara (National Art Gallery)
- Central Market
- Chinatown
- Sri Mahamariamman Temple
- Masjid Negara (National Mosque)
- Muzium Negara (National Museum)
- Lake Gardens
- Batu Caves

George Town, Penang

Captain Francis Light found the uninhabited Penang at the end of the 18th century, 2.5 miles off the **Malay Peninsula,** and acquired it from the Sultan of Kedah. It was the first British settlement in **Malaya.** The approximately 108-square-mile island, whose name means "betelnut," was once a hideout for pirates preying on ships laden with goods from Malacca. Light called it **Prince of Wales Island** and declared it a free port. Immigrants, mainly Chinese, soon started to arrive. George Town, situated on the northeast point of the island, close to the mainland, prospered with the ensuing tin and rubber booms.

Referred to by locals simply as "Penang," George Town is the capital of Penang state, a region inhabited by more than a million people. It is the island's cultural and educational center, and because its development was overtaken by Singapore, many of its original colonial buildings have been preserved in what is the largest prewar collection in Southeast Asia. George Town is small enough to get around on foot, with crowded streets that are fascinating to wander, where shoppers will find antiques, basketware, and batik. The island

of Penang, called the "Pearl of the Orient" for its beautiful beaches, is known locally as "Pulau Pinang."

Although fish, crabs, and prawns are popular, Penang is particularly famed for its soupy noodle dishes. *Laksa assam* (a sour fish soup flavored with *assam*—tamarind—paste) is served with white noodles; *laksa lemak* is the same idea, flavored with coconut milk. Chinese and Indian influences are found in the popular *murtabak* (a thin pancake stuffed with egg, vegetables, and meat).

- **Fort Cornwallis**
- **Clock Tower**
- **Penang Museum and Art Gallery**
- **St. George's Church**
- **Kuan Yin Teng (Goddess of Mercy Temple)**
- **Sri Mariamman Temple**
- **Khoo Kongsi (Chinese Clan House)**
- **Botanical Gardens**
- **Kek Lok Si Temple**
- **Penang Hill via funicular**

*Kek Lok Si Temple,,
George Town, Penang*

Sex at Sea

They don't call it "The Love Boat" for nothing. Respondents to a *Cosmopolitan* magazine survey rated cruises "extremely or very romantic" compared to land-based vacations. *Cosmo* handled the topic of sex at sea with characteristic delicacy by conducting a no-holds-barred poll of 2,000 passengers sailing not on the actual Love Boat fleet (that's **Princess Cruises**) but on the ships of **Royal Caribbean International**.

The findings? **Royal Caribbean** could make **Princess** blush. Making love on board was, in *Cosmo's* words, "a preferred activity," with almost half the cruisers saying they indulged up to six times on vacation compared to their usual once or twice a week at home. A full 80 percent said they felt more amorous at sea.

Not leaving anything to chance, most passengers admitted making some romantic preparations. Seventy-nine percent said they packed sexy lingerie or underwear; one in three brought body lotions or massage oils. Even the men—73 percent—confessed they toted along special underwear, and they outnumbered women when it came to arriving equipped with romantic accouterments such as massage oils, sexy toys, and novelty condoms.

With love in the air, the **Royal Caribbean** cruisers let their imaginations run wild in choosing shipboard locations for hanky-panky. Asked where they would have sex if given the chance, *Cosmo* survey participants listed their preferences as follows:

1. a whirlpool
2. the **Royal Suite**
3. an elevator
4. a lifeboat
5. the bridge

When asked to cite the most romantic shipboard activities, **Royal Caribbean** passengers showed a somewhat more conventional streak. *Cosmo* reports that the Top 10, in order of preference, were:

1. strolling in the moonlight
2. kissing
3. dancing
4. sharing a romantic dinner
5. star gazing
6. watching the sunset
7. drinking Champagne
8. giving each other a massage
9. having breakfast in bed
10. indulging in such aphrodisiacs as artichokes or chocolate

Myanmar

Yangon

The very notion of **Burma**, a colonial relic on the **Bay of Bengal** bordering **Bangladesh, India, China, Laos,** and **Thailand,** conjures up magical visions captured in the writings of Rudyard Kipling and Somerset Maugham—along with mixed emotions about a modern-day government's iron-fisted rule. The Union of Myanmar, as Burma is now officially called, has been ravaged since the ninth century by natural disaster, years of war, and infighting, especially between the Burmese and Mon kingdoms. The country has been gradually opening its tightly closed doors to foreigners after a 20-year restrictive tourism policy. The present regime's repressive policies contrast with its people's gentle, gracious nature and their devotion to Buddhism, with its countless golden-domed pagodas encrusted with precious stones. In 1989 the government officially changed the country's name from Burma. Now they are working hard to change their image: In 1995 they released Daw Aung San Su Kyi, the pro-democracy leader and Nobel Peace Prize winner whom they had placed under house arrest six years earlier.

Rangoon, now named Yangon, which means "the end of strife," originally was a trading village called **Dagon** at the mouth of the **Irrawaddy River,** which flows nearly 1,400 miles down from the **Himalayas.** After a series of wars, the British annexed Burma as part of their Indian empire. When they captured the city in 1852, they developed it as a modern metropolis, built on a grid system with wide boulevards and tree-lined streets. In a country rich in rice, oil, and teak that attracted Malays, Indians, Chinese, Thais, and Europeans, Rangoon was a cosmopolitan city (it became independent in 1948) until a military coup in 1962 led to a long period of seclusion that was just recently starting to come to an end. Today four million people, a conglomeration of more than 135 ethnic groups, live in the capital of Yangon.

The Burmese diet is based on rice and noodles, like most Asian cuisine. *Hingo* (soup, often sweet and sour) is served with most meals; *hin* (curry) is milder than its Indian cousin; *ngapiye* (fermented fish) or *balachung* (shrimp paste) usually accompanies dishes. Yangon is an important textile center; local products include embroidery with geometric designs, *kalaga* (appliqué in gold and sequins), and *acheik* (horizontal-weave patterned silk). Lacquerware is abundant, along with objects made from silver, and precious stones (which will be confiscated without the proper documentation upon departure).

- Sule Pagoda
- Bogyoke Zay (Scott Market)
- Strand Hotel
- Botataung Pagoda
- National Museum
- Buddhist Art Museum
- Kandawgyi Lakes
- Shwedagon Pagoda
- Martyrs' Mausoleum
- Kaba Aye Pagoda

Negara Brunei Darussalam (Brunei)
Bandar Seri Begawan

Tiny, tropical Brunei (which means "abode of peace"), a 500-year-old sultanate, is the remnant of a once great empire that stretched across the **South China Sea** as far as the **Philippines,** amassed by the 16th-century sultan Bolkiah. Situated on the northwest coast of **Borneo**, the third-largest island in the world, Brunei defended itself over the centuries against successive attacks by European powers including the Portuguese, Spanish, and Dutch. In the 19th century it became a British protectorate under the "white rajahs" in exchange for a promise to end the piracy problem along the coast.

The oil discovered at **Seria** in 1929 changed the face of Brunei forever. Today, compact Bandar Seri Begawan, named in 1970 after the current sultan's father, is stocked with modern Moorish buildings, new cars, and a glittering gold-domed mosque; though it is still surrounded by an ancient stilt village where almost 30,000 people live in wooden houses over the **Brunei River.** Scattered tribes of indigenous Iban and Punan, who once worshipped spirits and hunted with blowguns and poison darts, still live in the hilly interior. The country has been independent since 1984; the ruling sultan, 29th in the line, is one of the richest men in the world. There is free education, medical care, and pensions, and no income tax for the country's population of 267,800, mainly people of Malay and some of Chinese descent. English is widely spoken.

Malay, Chinese, and Indian dishes are sold at the outdoor food stalls near the river; such fruits as cassava, pineapple, and bananas are plentiful. Brunei is a strict Muslim country, and alcohol consumption and sales are strictly prohibited here. Traditional crafts made from silver, brass, and bronze, as well as sarongs, woven mats, and baskets, can be found at the **Arts and Handicrafts Centre** overlooking **Kampong Ayer.**

- Omar Ali Saifuddin Mosque
- Kampong Ayer

- Churchill Memorial Museum
- Brunei Museum
- Kota Batu (Stone Fort)
- Sultan's Palace
- Lapau (Royal Ceremony Hall)
- Dewan Majlis (Legislative Building)
- Temburong Long House
- Tomb of Sultan Bolkiah

Philippines
Manila

The hectic, tropical capital of the 7,100-island archipelago that makes up the Philippines, Manila is home to more than eight million people. The islands originally were inhabited by Malays from Indonesia, then traders from India, Arabia, and China, who, along with their goods, brought the practice of Islam. In 1571 Spanish conquistadores came here, named the islands after King Philip II of Spain, and established their colonial capital at present-day Manila. The Philippines were ceded to the US after the Spanish-American War of 1898. Manila was occupied by Japanese forces in World War II, but was recovered by General Douglas MacArthur's forces, although the city was virtually destroyed in battle. Their legacy, "jeepneys"—US Army jeeps turned into wildly decorated mini-buses—constitute a large part of Manila's chaotic traffic.

The city in southwest **Luzon** is the Philippines' political, cultural, and economic center. Asia's only Catholic capital, it abounds in churches and festivals and has a population visibly divided into haves and have-nots. Former President Ferdinand and First Lady Imelda Marcos made headlines by helping themselves to the national treasury (remember the famous shoe collection?) and establishing martial law. The official languages are English and Filipino, of which Tagalog is one of more than 87 dialects.

Spanish influence remains in such popular dishes as paella. Local Filipino food includes *adobo* (stewed chicken and pork in a soy, vinegar, garlic, and peppercorn sauce), *mami* (noodle soup), *pangsit* (dumplings), *lumpia shanghai* (spring rolls), and *gulay* (a vegetable dish, sometimes simmered in coconut milk). Among Manila's shopping districts is **Ermita,** where rattan, macrame, baskets, beads, and other handicrafts are sold. Local specialties include the *barong tagalog*, a festive embroidered men's shirt; and *santos,* originals and replicas of Spanish angels and saints created by 19th-century woodcarvers for churches and home shrines.

- Intramuros
- Church of San Augustin
- Fort Santiago
- Manila Hotel
- Jose Rizal Park

- Manila Cathedral
- Malacañang Palace
- Corregidor Island
- Pagsanjan Falls
- Tagaytay (Taal Volcano)

Singapore

Strategically located between the **South China Sea** and **Indian Ocean**, Singapore was visited by various Chinese groups from the 3rd century through the 14th. British colonialist and historian Sir Stamford Raffles selected Singapore as a British port in 1819, and the enclave prospered through its free-trade policy in Chinese tea, opium, and Malay rubber and tin. British rule continued until 1963, when Singapore entered a short-lived federation with Malaysia, which it left two years later to declare its independence.

The closest metropolis to the equator, Singapore, which means "lion city" (symbolized by its famous merlion statue), is a city-state of three million citizens. The people are a mix of Chinese, Malay, Indian, and Eurasian descent who live together peaceably on a 225-square-mile island in a region where multiethnic coexistence isn't always so congenial. Just a generation ago Singapore was an impoverished, politically unstable colony. Since then it has become one of the safest, cleanest, wealthiest places in the world, albeit largely through force of an iron will. Strict laws and harsh punishments have contributed to its evolution; not only are handguns severely restricted, chewing gum is outlawed. High-rises, marble shopping malls, businessmen toting cellular phones, and a port full of container ships are all signs of Singapore's rapidly expanding economy.

Singapore offers Chinese food from every province, Indian curries, and Malay satays. Hawker centers are clusters of food stalls that stir fry or grill delicious fresh seafood for a song (the food is safe, due to the country's high health standards). The exotic fruit selection includes rambutan, mangosteen, starfruit, and the noxious-smelling durian. **Orchard Road** is famous for electronics, jewelry, and watches. Antiques, batik, curios, orchids, and silk are found throughout the city.

- Chinatown
- Sri Mariamman Temple
- Telok Ayer Street and Thian Hock Keng Temple
- National Museum and Art Gallery
- Raffles Hotel
- Arab Street and Kampong Glam
- Little India
- Singapore Botanic Gardens
- Jurong Bird Park
- Mandai Orchid Gardens

South Korea
Seoul (Inchon)

A country of more than 45 million people, South Korea has remained resilient over the years, maintaining its own culture and heritage despite invasions, wars, and colonial rule. The **Korean Peninsula**, which stretches 600 miles south from Asia, was divided at the 38th parallel into North and South Korea after the Korean War (1950-53). Today South Korea is the world's largest supplier of semiconductor chips and the fifth-largest shipbuilder.

Seoul, also known as the "City of Kings," was established in 1392 as the seat of a dynasty ruled by 27 successive kings. Situated midway down the Korean peninsula, it once was enclosed by a 10-mile-long city wall with many gates, five of which still stand. Inchon, the modern deep-water port for the city, was the famous landing site of General Douglas MacArthur in 1950. Seoul was completely flattened in the war but has risen from ashes to reinvent itself as a modern, high-rise metropolis of more than 12 million people. Despite the city's pulsating modernity, however, throughout the countryside, Buddhist monks wander the streets for alms, children bow to their grandparents, fortune-tellers offer advice, and families head for the mountains to honor their ancestors and the beauty of their surroundings.

Kimchee (cabbage fermented in red pepper and garlic) might well be called Korea's national dish. Other favorites include *bulgogi* (beef strips marinated in a soy, garlic, onion, sesame seed, oil sauce and charcoal grilled at the table), *dakchim* (steamed chicken marinated in a host of spices), *jabgokbab* (rice with black beans, dried fruit, and chestnuts), and *kujolpan* (pancakes) that are wrapped around a selection of meat and vegetables. Local products to look for include silks, brocades, knitwear, leather, gold jewelry, jade, topaz, amethyst, amber, silver, ginseng, brassware, laquerware, wood carvings, painted screens, musical instruments, and wooden furniture. Shops in **Insadong** (Mary's Alley) sell antiques.

- Changdok Palace
- Chongmyo Shrine (Royal Shrine)
- National Museum (under renovation at press time)
- Kyongbok Palace and National Folk Museum
- Chogye-sa (Buddhist Temple)
- Toksugung Palace and Museum of Contemporary Art
- Tongdae-mun (Great East Gate) and Namdae-mun (Great Southern Gate)
- South Gate Market
- Nam-san (South Mountain)
- Kumgok-nung (Royal Tombs)

Sri Lanka

Colombo

It has been known officially since 1972 as Sri Lanka ("Resplendent Land"), but most people remember this pear-shaped Indian Ocean island as Ceylon. Sri Lanka is rich in tropical vegetation; such resources as rubber and famous Ceylon tea; and precious gems including rubies, sapphires, and garnets. Sri Lanka originally was inhabited by Sinhalese, who came to the island from northern India in the sixth century BC and who now form the bulk of the current population of about 19 million. They founded their capital at **Anuradhapura,** which became a major center of Buddhist religion and culture in the third century BC. Invasions by the Hindu Tamils from southern India forced the Sinhalese into the southwestern portion of the island. In the 12th century, Arab traders appeared, and some say that in the 14th, the Chinese carried away a Sinhalese king into captivity. Settled successively by Portuguese, who named it **Ceilao,** the Dutch, who dubbed it **Ceilon,** and the British, Sri Lanka became independent in 1948.

The capital city of Colombo still exudes tinges of colonial charm left from its days as an outpost of the British Empire. Already an important spice trading center when the Portuguese arrived in 1505, it is still a center of commerce, with a busy bazaar area and central business district. Here batik handicrafts, along with leatherwork and gemstones, are popular purchases.

Local Sinhalese dishes resemble those of India, with lots of spicy curries. *Lumprice* is a rice and curry dish baked in a banana-leaf wrapper. *Hoppers* are a popular snack, served either as a plain pancake, with an egg fried onto the top, or as a tangled circle of noodles. For the brave there is also *arrack,* a powerful native alcohol made from coconut flowers.

■ Galle Face Green
■ The Fort District
■ Pettah Bazaar
■ Clock Tower
■ President's Residence
■ National Museum
■ Art Gallery
■ City Museum
■ Kandy and Dalada Maligawa (Temple of the Tooth)
■ Pinnawala Elephant Orphanage

Taiwan

Taipei (Keelung)

One hundred miles off the coast of **China,** Taiwan, which means "terraced bay," has suffered a bit of an identity crisis ever since the Portuguese arrived in the 1500s and named the island **Ilha Formosa** (beautiful island) for its forests, lakes, rice paddies, and butterfly-filled valleys. The Dutch established a colony here in 1624, and Spanish settlers attempted to do the same soon after; but a Ming loyalist from the mainland tossed everyone out by 1661, banning Europeans until the French occupied the north part of the island over an Indochina dispute. In 1886 Taiwan fell under Chinese control and remained so until it was ceded to the Japanese in 1895 in a dispute over Korea. It reverted to Chinese rule after the World War II Japanese surrender. Four years later, after Communist forces in mainland China gained control of a civil war, the nationalist government under Chiang Kai-shek—and about 1.25 million Chinese—crossed over to Taiwan. The island is now home to over 21 million people, approximately 370,000 of whom are members of ten main aboriginal nationalities.

Zhongzheng Ji Nian Tang
(Chiang Kai-shek Memorial Hall), Taipei

The port of Keelung once was known as "Santissima Trinidad." The second-largest of the five international seaports in Taiwan, it is situated on Taiwan's north coast overlooking the **East China Sea,** guarded by a 74-foot-high statue of *Guan Yin,* Goddess of Mercy. It is one of the wettest cities in the world, with 214 days of rain a year keeping the city soggy and green. About a half-hour drive away, on the **Tanshui River,** is Taipei, designated as the "provisional capital of the Republic of China" by the Chinese nationalists in 1949. Not long ago Taipei was home mostly to farmers; today, with nearly three million people, it is Taiwan's center of commerce, government, and culture—a sprawling city of modern buildings and back alleys.

Taiwan's cuisine—featuring exotic seafood, dumplings, and Beijing duck—reflects a variety of regional Chinese styles. Street markets, state-run stores, and department stores offer opportunities to pick up antiques, chops (Chinese signature seals), coral jewelry, teak furniture, jade, marble, paintings and scrolls, porcelain, tea, and toys.

- Zhongzheng Ji Nian Tang (Chiang Kai-shek Memorial Hall)
- Kongzi Miao (Confucius Temple)
- Grand Hotel
- Longshan Si (Dragon Mountain Temple)
- Huaxi Jie (Snake Alley)
- Yangmingshan
- Shung Ye Museum of Formosan Aborigines
- Zhong Lie Ci (Martyrs' Shrine)
- Gugong Bowu Yuan (National Palace Museum)
- Chinese Opera performance

Thailand

Bangkok

Better known to the world as **Siam**, some theorize that Thailand was first inhabited by migrants from southern **China** in the 11th century, who set up several kingdoms that are possibly today's **Laos, Myanmar, Kampuchea** (Cambodia), and **Malaysia.** Thailand prospered until the 18th century, when it gave up some territory to—but was never colonized by—the British and French. It was 19th-century ruler King Mongkut (Rama IV) whom Yul Brynner portrayed in the musical and movie *The King and I.*

Bangkok, whose official name "Krungthep" means "city of angels," has been the capital of Thailand since 1782. The sprawling metropolis is home to more than six million people, or about one-tenth of the country's population, including a large Chinese minority. It is a city both royal and religious, exotic and erotic, with golden-spired temples and palaces that line the banks of the **Chao Phraya River,** whose *klongs* (canals) are packed with tiny boats carrying goods and people to neighborhoods along the waterways. As Bangkok has grown, many of the

klongs have been filled in and paved with roads; but a river taxi is still often the quickest—and most pleasant—way to get from one place to another in the steamy city, jammed with open-air triwheel motorcycle taxis called *tuk-tuks.* Over 90 percent of Thais are Buddhists, whose inner peace prevails over a sometimes manic metropolis, where 400 *wats* (temple-monasteries), along with thousands of tiny spirit houses, dominate the cityscape. Early risers can see the city at its calmest, when saffron-robed monks quietly pad about accepting offerings of rice.

Thai food can pack quite a kick, courtesy of red hot chili peppers. Basil, coconut milk, coriander, cinnamon, lemongrass, and lime juice are prevalent. Fresh seafood can be selected, along with vegetables, and cooked to order at some restaurants. *Khow pad* (fried rice, sometimes topped with cucumber, fried egg, and hot peppers) is something of a national dish. *Pad thai* is stir-fried noodles, bean sprouts, crushed peanuts, egg, chilis, and prawns. Local items to look for include Thai silks, cottons, precious and semiprecious stones, jewelry, antiques, rattan, bamboo, wood carvings, pottery, teak furniture, lacquerware, bronzeware, and decorative silver items. Arcades, malls, and markets sell everything from antiques to orchids.

- National Museum
- Wat Phra Keo (Temple of Emerald Buddha) and Grand Palace
- Wat Pho (Temple of Reclining Buddha)
- Wat Arun (Temple of Dawn)
- Ride on Chao Phraya River
- Wat Benchamabophit (Marble Temple)
- Jim Thompson's House
- Suan Pakkard Palace
- Vimanmek Palace
- Damnoen Saduak (Floating Market)

Phuket

Called "Pearl of Thailand" for its shape, Phuket, at about 360 square miles, is Thailand's largest island. It is situated off the west coast of **Kra Isthmus,** which separates the **Gulf of Thailand** and the **Andaman Sea,** and is connected to the mainland by causeway. The name is derived from the Malay word *bukit,* meaning "hill," and Phuket is indeed very hilly. The island is lined with palm-fringed beaches and coral reefs; the wild elephants, rhinos, and tigers that once roamed the island are long gone, replaced with sun-seeking Europeans whose forebears first arrived as 16th-century traders in search of rubber, pearls, and ivory. The Portuguese and Spanish left their mark in the architecture of **Phuket Town,** the island's provincial capital.

Phuket originally was inhabited by "sea gypsies," indigenous, ocean-going people; today, in addition to Thais, the population of almost 208,000 is made up of Malays, Chinese, and Indians. The Chinese and

Indians arrived before the 18th century; the Malays during the tin boom at the turn of the century. The island remains a major tin center, but tourism has surpassed mining in importance. **Patong Beach,** although far from peaceful, is the most developed and main resort area. **Nai Harn,** 11 miles southwest of **Phuket Town**, is one of the island's loveliest locations, complete with spectacular views and sunsets. Phuket is surrounded by many smaller satellite islands, most notably **Phi Phi,** for those seeking a quieter, gentler tropical Thai experience.

Along with fresh seafood and Chinese cuisine, specialties on Phuket include *khao niaw mamuang* (sticky rice, mango, and grilled bananas) and *kuaytiaw naom* (a noodle soup). The usual array of Thai handicrafts is available on the island, but the best buys here are pearls and gold jewelry.

- Panwa House Restaurant
- Marine Biological Research Center and Aquarium
- Wat Chalong
- Nai Harn and Promtuep Cape
- Thalang National Museum and Wat Phranang Sang
- Khao Phra Thaeo Wildlife Park
- Bang Pae Waterfall
- Naka Noi Island and Pearl Farm
- Phi Phi Islands
- Phangnga Bay

Vietnam

Ho Chi Minh City

Vietnam, for many, brings back war-torn memories of battlefront footage on the nightly news. A new generation, however, is discovering that the country, a thousand miles long on the east coast of the **Indochinese Peninsula,** offers a spectacular landscape of rugged mountains, fertile valleys, and white-sand beaches. The strife-ridden region has a long history of occupation and conquest by a lengthy list of peoples and dynasties, most notably and frequently the Chinese. And it has long fought within itself, with warring kingdoms battling along north-south lines. The French found their way past Vietnam's borders in the late 1800s, ruling until the country was partitioned in 1945. Bordered by **Cambodia, Laos, China,** and the **Gulf of Thailand,** the unified Socialist Republic of Vietnam was declared in 1976.

Known in the past as **Saigon,** capital of the former South Vietnam, Ho Chi Minh City was renamed again in 1975 when American troops withdrew. Today, however, most of the five million locals, many friendly and eager to learn once-frowned-upon Western ways, still call the industrial, commercial, and cultural center of Vietnam "Saigon." The city also was once called "Paris of the East" for its French colonial architecture,

sidewalk cafes, and tree-lined streets. Ho Chi Minh City still exudes an air of its bygone era with rickshaws (called "cyclos"), persistent street vendors, and boisterous markets. More than 40 markets are scattered across the city, where such sought-after souvenirs as silk, embroidered items, and silverwork are sold. These attest to the country's new flirtation with free enterprise, now making a comeback, along with tourism.

Pho might be the most famous Vietnamese dish: a meat-based soup with beef or chicken, rice noodles, *nuoc mam* (fish sauce), chiles, mint, bean sprouts, and lemon. *Bana* is a cold salad of lettuce, cucumbers, carrots, rice noodles, and grilled meat, topped off with peanuts and the ubiquitous fish sauce.

- Historical Museum
- War Crimes Museum
- Thong Nhat (Reunification Palace)
- Cholon (Chinatown) and Thien Hau Temple
- Quan Am Pagoda
- General Post Office
- Binh Tay Market
- Rex Hotel
- Notre Dame Cathedral
- Cu Chi tunnels

Bests

Karl W. Helft
Writer and Producer of military history documentaries for German television

A floating five-star hotel with unending culinary delights, around the clock whisking you to (sometimes) interesting ports offering tempting purchases.

Entertainment and other personal activities to bore no one.

The ship, if the right one to suit your own pace, can be a quiet and secluded escape from the pressure of every day living or, if you wish, a launching platform for hyperactivity, if that's what you want.

A set of inaccurate bathroom scales are necessary for your return home.

Marty Leshner
Writer

What I love most about cruising: Sail-aways at sunset, whitecaps, deck buffets, jogging up on the **Sun Deck,** midnight buffets, elaborate production shows, verandas, dressing up on "formal" nights, a cheerful can-do crew, dolphins playing off the starboard bow, meeting new people, cozy bars, first-rate housekeeping, first-run movies, the prospect of the next port, the peace and quiet, international buffets, making new friends, reunions with old ones, pampering, unpacking once, a sense that the sea renews, "team trivia," and did I mention buffets?

Index

A

Abercrombie & Kent **92**
Acapulco, Mexico **144**
Accessibility for the disabled **7, 35, 38**
Account settlement **62**
Active tours **54**
Activities, shipboard **17, 50**
Adventure cruises **9**
Adventurer, Clipper **102**
Air deviations **37**
Airfare, free or reduced **28**
Air/sea packages **25, 37**
Air upgrades **28**
Ajaccio, Corsica, France **214**
Alaska Shopping **151**
Alaska, US **148, 150, 151, 152, 157, 158**
Alexandria, Egypt **213**
Allegra, Costa **103**
Alternative dining **52**
Alumni discounts **30, 31**
American Canadian Caribbean Line **93**
American Hawaii Cruises **93**
American Samoa **244**
American West Steamboat Co. **147**
Amsterdam, Netherlands **204**
Anchorage, Alaska, US **148**
Annual promotions **29**
Antarctica **2** (map), **192** (chapter and map)
Antigua **168**
Antwerp, Belgium **198**
Apia, Western Samoa **249**
Argentina **180**
Aruba **168**
Arzt, Lorraine **191** (bests)
Ashore, going **53**
Asia **260** (chapter and map)
Athens (Piraeus), Greece **218**
Auckland, New Zealand **251**
Australia **254** (chapter and map)

B

Baggage **63**
The Bahamas **162** (chapter and map)
Bahia (Salvador da Bahia), Brazil **183**
Balearic Islands, Spain **230**
Bali, Indonesia **266**
Bandar Seri Begawan, Negara Brunei Darussalam (Brunei) **275**
Bangkok, Thailand **278**
Bank Line **239**
Barbados **169**
Barcelona, Spain **228**
Barge cruises **9, 83**
Barging Through Europe **83**
Bar Harbor, Maine, US **148**
Behind the Scenes on a Cruise Ship **195**

Beijing, China **262**
Belém, Brazil **181**
Belgium **198**
Bergen Line **209**
Bergen, Norway **204**
Berlin (Warnemünde), Germany **201**
Bermuda **160** (chapter and map)
The Big Island, Hawaiian Islands **242**
Blue Star **239**
Bon Voyage! **46** (chapter)
Booking cruises **31**
Books **217**
Bora Bora, French Polynesia **246**
Bordeaux, France **200**
Boston, Massachusetts, US **149**
Brazil **181**
Bridgetown, Barbados **169**
British Columbia, Canada **143, 144**
British Virgin Islands **169**
Brochures, comparing fares **23**
Brochures, examining deck plans **23**
Brochures, how to read **22, 23, 24**
Brunei (Negara Brunei Darussalam) **275**
Buenos Aires, Argentina **180**

C

Cabins, checking upon arrival **47**
Cabins, choice of **34**
Cabins for physically challenged passengers **35**
Cabins, location **36**
Cabins, number of people in **34, 35**
Cabins, ocean-view or inside? **35**
Cabins, standard or deluxe? **35**
Cabo San Lucas, Mexico **145**
Cairns, Queensland, Australia **256**
California, US **153, 156**
Callao (Lima), Peru **188**
Canada **142**
Canary Islands, Spain **229, 230**
Cancellations **40**
Cancún/Cozumel, Mexico **145**
Cannes, France **215**
Cape Town, South Africa **238**
The Captain's Table **111**
Captain's table, dining at **52, 111**
Caracas (La Guaira), Venezuela **190**
Caribbean **166** (chapter and map)
Caribbean Prince $★ **93**
Carnival Cruise Lines **94**
Carnival Destiny $$★★★★ **94**
Cartagena, Colombia **186**
Casablanca, Morocco **226**
Castries, St. Lucia **174**
Cayman Islands **170**
Celebration $★★★ **95**
Celebrity Cruises **66, 100**
Central Nassau, The Bahamas **162** (map)

Central/South America **178** (chapter and map)
Century $$$★★★★★ **66, 100**
Checking in **46**
A Checklist for Honeymooners **42**
Children, free or discounted fare **28**
Children, making friends **59**
Children's excursions **54**
Children's progams **248**
Children, travelers with **38**
Child's Play **248**
Chile **184, 244**
China **262**
Choosing a cruise **20**
Choosing a travel agency **32**
Choosing the right cabin **34**
Christchurch, New Zealand **251**
Christening ceremony **77**
Civitavecchia (Rome), Italy **224**
Clampett, Bob **191** (bests)
Classica, Costa **68, 104**
CLIA-affiliated agencies **32**
CLIA (Cruise Lines International Association) **21**
Clipper Adventurer **102**
Clipper Cruise Line **102**
Clothing **43**
Club Med Cruises **102**
Club Med 1 $$$★★★★ **102**
Club Med 2 $$$★★★★ **102**
Cocktails **52**
Color coding *see inside front cover*
Colombia **186**
Colombo, Sri Lanka **277**
Columbus Line **239**
Commemorating a special date **39**
Comment cards **62**
Copenhagen, Denmark **198**
Coping with Mal de Mer **257**
Corfu, Greece **218**
Corsica, France **214**
CostaAllegra $$★★★★ **103**
CostaClassica $$★★★★★ **68, 104**
Costa Cruise Lines **68, 103**
CostaMarina $$★★★★ **103**
CostaOlympia **104**
Costa Rica **187**
CostaRomantica $$★★★★★ **68, 104**
CostaVictoria $$★★★★★ **68, 104**
Cozumel/Cancún, Mexico **145**
Credit card perks **28**
Credit line, shipboard **48**
Crete, Greece **219**
Crew, making friends with **59**
Crew, who's who **253**
Crown Majesty $$★★ **113**
Crown Princess $$$★★★★★ **76, 120**
Cruise combos **27**
Cruise discounts **27**

Cruise, end of **61**
Cruise Lines and Cruise Ships **65**
  (chapter)
Cruise Lines International
  Association (CLIA) **21**
Cruise nights **22**
Cruise-only agencies **32**
Cruise-only packages **26, 37**
Cruises, duration **14**
Cruise ship, checking in **46**
A Cruise Ship Directory **92** (chapter)
Cruise ship, getting to **46**
Cruise Ship Superlatives **69**
Cruises, how sold **31**
Cruises, how to choose **20**
Cruises, pricing **26**
Cruises, reasons people choose **5**
The Cruise that Changed History **15**
Cruising, environmental concerns **16**
Cruising European Waterways **122**
Cruising off peak **13**
Cruising safely **15**
Cruising styles **8**
Cruising the Coast of Norway **209**
Crystal Cruises **70, 105**
Crystal Harmony $$$$★★★★★★★
  70, 105
Crystal Symphony
  $$$$★★★★★★★ **70, 105**
Cultural differences, respect for **55**
Cunard **72, 74, 105**
Curaçao **170**
Customs forms **63**

D

Daily program of activities **50**
Dalian, China **263**
Dawn Princess $$★★★★★ **78, 120**
Days of Wine and Roses: Extras for
  Newlyweds and Other Happy
  Couples **101**
Debarkation **63**
Debarkation, preparing for **61**
Debarkation talk **62**
Delos/Mykonos, Greece **220**
Delta Queen Steamboat Co. **147**
Deluxe cabins **35**
Denmark **198**
Deposit **39**
Destinations **139** (chapter)
Destiny, Carnival **94**
Diamond, Radisson **126**
Dietary requirements, special **38**
Diller, Phyllis **45** (bests)
Dining **51**
Dining alternatives **52**
Dining arrangements **48**
Dining at captain's table **52, 111**
Dining hours **51**
Dining in port **56**
Dining-room seating **37**

Disabled travelers **7, 35, 38**
Discounts **27**
Discounts, credit card companies **28**
Discounts, early-booking **27**
Discounts for additional passengers
  28
Discounts for advance payment **27**
Discounts for "alumni" **30, 31**
Discounts for children **28**
Discounts for groups **29**
Discounts for onboard future
  bookings **30**
Discounts for organizations **29**
Discounts for seniors **30**
Discounts for singles **30**
Discounts, "free days" **28**
Discounts, introductory **29**
Discounts, last-minute **29**
Discounts, promotions **29, 30**
Discounts, standby **30**
Discounts, two-for-one **28**
Discounts, value-added **30**
Disney Cruise Line **109**
Disney Cruises: Magic and Wonder
  at Sea **109**
Disney Magic **109**
Disney Wonder **109**
Documents, travel **41**
Dolphin Cruise Line **107**
Dominica **171**
Double cabins **34**
Dreamward $$$★★★ **114**
Drills, fire/lifeboat **49**
Drinks **52**
Dublin, Ireland **203**
Durban, South Africa **238**

E

Early-booking discounts **27**
Easter Island, Chile **244**
Eating and drinking ashore **56**
Ecstasy $★★★ **96**
Ecuador **187**
Edinburgh, Scotland **208**
Edwards, Mona Shafer **159** (bests)
Egypt **213**
Elation **97**
Emergency evacuation **41**
Emergency medical assistance **16**
Enchantment **127**
End of the cruise **61**
Engel, Carl Ludwig **200**
England **199**
Enjoying life at sea **59**
Entry requirements **41**
Environment, and cruising **16**
Ephesus, Turkey **232**
Estonia **200**
Etiquette, shipboard **53**
EuroCruises **122**
European-style cruising **12**

Evacuation, emergency **41**
Excursions for children **54**
Excursions, shore **38**
Expedition cruises **9**
Explorer $$$$★★★ **92**

F

Families **6**
Fantasy $★★★ **96**
Fantome $★★ **138**
Farcus, Joe **94, 96, 97**
Fares *see inside front cover*, **6, 26**
Fascination $★★★ **96**
Feldman, Martin, Dr. **191** (bests)
Fiji **245**
Final payment **40**
Finding your way around the ship **48**
Finland **200**
Fire drill **49**
Fitness programs and facilities **190**
Flag state **15**
Flat rates **28**
Florence (Livorno), Italy **223**
Florida, US **150, 152, 154**
Flying Cloud $★★ **138**
Fortaleza, Brazil **182**
Fort-de-France, Martinique **172**
France **200, 214**
Free days **28**
Free or reduced air **28**
Freeport, Grand Bahama, The
  Bahamas **164**
Freighter cruises **239**
French Polynesia **246**
Ft. Lauderdale, Florida, US **150**
Funchal, Madeira, Portugal **227**

G

Galápagos Islands, Ecuador **187**
Galaxy $$$★★★★★ **66, 100**
Garnier, Charles **226**
Gaudí, Antoni **229**
Gays **7**
Gdańsk, Poland **206**
Geiranger, Norway **204**
Gentleman hosts **121**
George Town, Grand Cayman,
  Cayman Islands **170**
George Town, Penang, Malaysia
  273
Germany **201**
Getting Hitched at Sea **108**
Getting the best value **26**
Getting to the ship **46**
Gibraltar **218**
Glacier Bay, Alaska, US **150**
The Godmother **77**
Going ashore **53**
Golf **119**
Good, Bruce **259** (bests)
Grace, Oceanic **117**

Index

Gran Canaria, Canary Islands, Spain **229**
Grand Bahama, The Bahamas **163** (map), **164**
Grand Cayman, Cayman Islands **170**
Grande Caribe $★ **93**
Grandeur of the Seas $$★★★★ **127**
Grand Princess **120**
Greece **218**
"Green flash" **158**
Grenada **171**
Gross registered tons (GRT) **13**
Group rates **29**
Groups **5**
Guadeloupe **171**
Gustavia, St-Barthélémy **173**

H

Haifa, Israel **221**
Haines, Alaska, US **151**
Halifax, Nova Scotia, Canada **142**
Hamburg, Germany **202**
Hamilton, Bermuda **160** (map)
Hanseatic $$$★★★★ **125**
Harmony, Crystal **70**, **105**
Hawaiian Islands **240** (chapter and map)
Health **16**
Helft, Karl W. **279** (bests)
Helsinki, Finland **200**
Heraklion, Crete, Greece **219**
History of cruising **4**
Hobart, Tasmania, Australia **256**
Ho Chi Minh City, Vietnam **279**
Holiday $★★★ **95**
Holland America Line **109**
Hollywood Sets Sail **99**
Honeymooners **7, 38, 42, 101, 108**
Hong Kong, China **264**
Honolulu, Oahu, Hawaiian Islands **242**
Horizon $$$★★★★ **100**
Hours, dining **51**
How cruises are sold **31**
How to choose a cruise **20**
Huahine, French Polynesia **246**

I

Iceland **202**
Identification papers **41**
Imagination $★★★★ **97**
Immigration forms **63**
IMO (International Maritime Organization's) regulations **15**
Inchon (Seoul), South Korea **276**
Independence $★★ **93**
India **265**
Indian Ocean **234** (chapter and map)
Indonesia **266**
Infants, travelers with **38**
Initial Explanation **268**

Inoculations **41**
Inside cabins **35**
Inspiration $★★★★ **97**
Insurance **40**
Insurance, trip cancellation and interruption **40**
International Maritime Organization's (IMO) regulations **15**
Internet **21**
In the cabin **47**
Introduction to Cruising **2** (chapter)
Introductory discounts **29**
Ireland **203**
Island Princess $$$★★★★ **121**
Israel **221**
Istanbul, Turkey **231**
Italy **223**
Itineraries, analyzing **23**
Ivaran Lines **239**
Ixtapa/Zihuatanejo, Mexico **147**

J

Jaffa/Tel Aviv, Israel **222**
Jakarta, Java, Indonesia **267**
Jamaica **172**
Japan **269**
Java, Indonesia **267, 268**
Jubilee $★★★ **95**
Juneau, Alaska, US **151**

K

Kailua, The Big Island, Hawaiian Islands **242**
Kauai, Hawaiian Islands **243**
KD River Cruises **122**
Keelung (Taipei), Taiwan **277**
Keeping Fit Afloat **190**
Kenya **236**
Ketchikan, Alaska, US **152**
Key West, Florida, US **152**
Kobe, Japan **269**
Kota Kinabalu, Malaysia **272**
Kuala Lumpur (Port Kelang), Malaysia **272**
Kusadasi, Turkey **232**
Kyoto, Japan **269**

L

La Goulette (Tunis), Tunisia **231**
La Guaira (Caracas), Venezuela **190**
Lahaina, Maui, Hawaiian Islands **242**
Las Palmas, Gran Canaria, Canary Islands, Spain **229**
Last-minute discounts **29**
Lawson, Cicely and Lew **191** (bests)
Leeward $$★★★ **115**
A Legendary Liner **10**
Legend of the Seas $$$★★★★ **128**
Legend, Seabourn **84**
Length of cruises **14**

Lesbians **7**
Leshner, Marty **279** (bests)
Lifeboat drill **49**
Lihue, Kauai, Hawaiian Islands **243**
Lima (Callao), Peru **188**
Lisbon, Portugal **227**
Livorno (Florence), Italy **223**
Location, of cabins **36**
Los Angeles (Long Beach), California, US **153**
Louisiana, US **154**
"The Love Boat" and Beyond: Cruising on the Small Screen **265**
Lusitania **15**
Lykes Line **239**

M

Maasdam $$$$★★★★ **109**
Macau **271**
Madagascar **236**
Madeira, Portugal **227**
Magic, Disney **109**
Mahé, Seychelle Islands **237**
Maine, US **148**
Majesty Cruise Line **113**
Majesty of the Seas $$★★★ **129**
Majorca, Balearic Islands, Spain **230**
Making a reservation **34**
Making friends on board **58, 59**
Making the most of your cruise **49**
Malaysia **272**
Malta **225**
Manaus, Brazil **182**
Mandalay $★★ **138**
Manila, Philippines **275**
Map Key *see inside front cover*
Marco Polo $$$★★★★ **118**
Marina, Costa **103**
Martinique **172**
Massachusetts, US **149, 154**
Maui, Hawaiian Islands **242**
Maxtone-Graham, John **165** (bests)
Mayan Prince $★ **93**
Mazatlán, Mexico **146**
Meals **51**
Medical care at sea **16**
Medical, inoculations **41**
Medical protection **41**
Medical requirements **38**
Medication **44**
Mediterranean **210** (chapter and map)
Mediterranean Shipping Co. **239**
Megaships **8**
Melbourne, Victoria, Australia **258**
Mercury **101**
Mermoz $$★★★★**104**
Mexico **144**
Miami, Florida, US **154**

Mileage programs 27
Milford Sound, New Zealand 252
Minerva $$$★★★ 137
Mombasa, Kenya 236
Monaco 225
Monarch of the Seas $$★★★ 129
Money 45
Monte Carlo, Monaco 225
Montego Bay, Jamaica 172
Montevideo, Uruguay 189
Montreal, Quebec, Canada 142
Moorea, French Polynesia 247
Morocco 226
Mosher, Rosemary J. 159 (bests)
Movies 99
Mumbai, India 265
Murphy, Karen 45 (bests)
Myanmar 274
Mykonos/Delos, Greece 220

N

Nagasaki, Japan 270
Nantucket Clipper $$$★★★ 102
Nantucket, Massachusetts, US 154
Naples, Italy 223
Nassau, New Providence, The
    Bahamas 164
Nature cruises 9
Nautical terms 57
Negara Brunei Darussalam (Brunei)
    275
Netherlands 204
Newlyweds 42, 101, 108
New Orleans, Louisiana, US 154
Newport, Rhode Island, US 155
New Providence, The Bahamas
    164
Newsletters 21
New South Wales, Australia 258
New York City, New York, US 155
New Zealand 250 (chapter and map)
Niagara Prince $★ 93
Nice, France 215
Nieuw Amsterdam $$★★★ 110
Noordam $$★★★ 110
Nordic Empress $$$★★★ 131
North America 140 (chapter and
    map)
North Cape, Norway 205
Northern Europe 196 (chapter and
    map)
Norway 204
Norway $$$★★★★ 10, 115
Norway, coastal cruises 209
Norwegian Coastal Voyages 209
Norwegian Star $$$★★★★ 117
Norwegian Cruise Line 114
Nosy-Be, Madagascar 236
Nova Scotia, Canada 142
Nuku'alofa, Tonga 249
Number of people in the cabin 34, 35

O

Oahu, Hawaiian Islands 242
OceanBreeze $$★★ 107
Oceanic Cruises 117
Oceanic Grace $$$$★★★★ 117
Oceanic, Star/Ship 120
Ocean-view cabins 35
Ocho Rios, Jamaica 172
Odessa, Ukraine Republic 233
Odysseus $$★★ 132
Off-peak cruising 13
Olympia, Costa 104
Olympic $$★★ 134
Onboard booking discounts 30
Option 40
Oranjestad, Aruba 168
Organization discounts 29
Oriana $$$★★★ 122
Orient Lines 118
Orpheus $$★★ 134
Oslo, Norway 206

P

Pacific Princess $$$★★★★ 121
Packages, air/sea 25, 37
Packages, cruise only 26, 37
Packages, pre-/post-cruise 39
Packaging of cruises 24
Packing for a cruise 43, 44
Packing for debarkation 63
Packing, medication 44
Pago Pago, American Samoa 244
Palma de Majorca, Majorca,
    Balearic Islands, Spain 230
Panama Canal, Panama 188
Papeete, Tahiti, French Polynesia 247
Paradise 97
Pare Pare, Sulawesi, Indonesia 268
Passenger questionnaires 62
Passport 41
Paul Gaugin 125
Payment 39
Penang, Malaysia 273
People with special interests 8
Perfect Gentlemen 121
Perks, credit card 28
Perks for Cruise Line Alumni 31
Personnel, ship 253
Peru 188
Peter Deilmann EuropAmerica
    Cruises 122
Philippines 275
Philipsburg, St-Martin/St. Maarten
    174
Phuket, Thailand 278
Physically challenged travelers 7,
    35, 38
Piano, Renzo 76
Piraeus (Athens), Greece 218
Plying the Exotic Rivers of the
    World 130

Pointe-à-Pitre, Guadeloupe 171
Poland 206
Polaris $$$$★★ 136
Polynesia $★★ 138
Pomp, Circumstance, and
    Superstition: The Ancient Art of
    Shipbuilding 165
Port Kelang (Kuala Lumpur),
    Malaysia 272
Port of Spain, Trinidad 176
Porto, Portugal 228
Ports, debarking 54
Ports, preparing for 53
Port state rules 15
Ports, touring 53
Portugal 227
Post-cruise packages 39
Pre-booking shore excursions 38
Precious Cargo: Traveling on a
    Freighter 239
Pre-cruise packages 39
Premier Cruise Lines 120
Preparing to Cruise 20 (chapter)
Preparing to go ashore 53
Pricing 24
Pricing, by number of people in
    cabin 24
Pricing, by season 24
Pricing, cruise only 26
Pride, Seabourn 84
Princess Cruises 76, 78, 120
Private balconies 36
Problems, dealing with 60
Promotions, annual 29
Promotions, special or offbeat 30
Publications 20
Puerto Caldera, Costa Rica 187
Puerto Madryn, Argentina 180
Puerto Montt, Chile 185
Puerto Rico 173
Puerto Vallarta, Mexico 146
Punta Arenas, Chile 184

Q

Quebec, Canada 142, 143
Quebec City, Quebec, Canada 143
Queen Elizabeth 2 (QE2)
    $$$$★★★★ (Grill Class);
    $$$$★★★ (Caronia Class);
    $$$$★ (Mauretania Class) 105
Queensland, Australia 256

R

Radisson Diamond $$$$★★★★★
    126
Radisson Seven Seas Cruise Line
    80, 125
Raiatea, French Polynesia 247
Range of meals 51
Rating the ships *see inside front
    cover*

Index

Reading brochures **22**
Rebates **30**
Regal Princess $$$★★★★★ **76, 120**
Renaissance Cruises **126**
Renaissance V $$$★★★ **126**
Renaissance VI $$$★★★ **126**
Renaissance VII $$$★★★ **126**
Renaissance VIII $$$★★★ **126**
Reservations **34**
Resources **20**
Respecting other cultures **55**
Reykjavík, Iceland **202**
Rhapsody of the Seas **131**
Rhode Island, US **155**
Rhodes, Greece **220**
Riley, Frank and Elfriede **159** (bests)
Rio de Janeiro, Brazil **183**
River cruises **9, 122, 130, 147**
Road Town, Tortola, British Virgin Islands **169**
Rollin' on the River **147**
Romantica, Costa **68, 104**
Rome (Civitavecchia), Italy **224**
R1 **126**
Roseau, Dominica **171**
Rotterdam VI **112**
Royal Caribbean International **127**
Royal Majesty $$★★★ **113**
Royal Olympic Cruises **132**
Royal Princess $$$★★★★ **123**
Royal Viking Sun $$$$★★★★★★ **72, 106**
R2 **126**
Rules, governing ships **15**
Russia **207**
Ryndam $$$★★★★ **109**

S

Safety on shore **55**
Safety regulations **15**
Sail cruises **10**
Sailor Speak: A Guide to Shipboard Lingo **57**
St-Barthélémy **173**
St. Croix, US Virgin Islands **177**
St. George's, Bermuda **160** (map)
St. George's, Grenada **171**
St. John's, Antigua **168**
St. John, US Virgin Islands **177**
St. Lucia **174**
St-Martin/St. Maarten **174**
St. Petersburg, Russia **207**
St. Thomas, US Virgin Islands **177**
Salvador da Bahia (Bahia), Brazil **183**
Samoa, American **244**
Samoa, Western **249**
San Francisco, California, US **156**
Sanitation **16**
San Juan, Puerto Rico **173**
Santa Cruz de Tenerife, Tenerife, Canary Islands, Spain **230**

Santa Cruz, Galápagos Islands, Ecuador **187**
Santarém, Brazil **184**
Santiago, Chile **185**
Santorini, Greece **221**
Scarborough, Tobago **175**
Scotland **208**
Sea Bird $$$★★ **137**
Seabourn Cruise Line **84, 135**
Seabourn Legend $$$$★★★★★★ **84**
Seabourn Pride $$$$★★★★★★ **84**
Seabourn Spirit $$$$★★★★★★ **84**
SeaBreeze $$★★ **108**
Sea Cloud $$$$★★★★ **135**
Sea Cloud, Inc. **135**
Sea Cloud Kreuzfahrten **122**
Sea Goddess I $$$$★★★★★★ **74, 106**
Sea Goddess II $$$$★★★★★★ **74, 106**
Sea Lion $$$★★ **137**
Sea Princess **78**
Sea Sagas **217**
Seasickness **257**
Seasonal differences in pricing and packaging **24**
Seating, dining times and **37**
Seattle, Washington, US **156**
Security **15**
See Green **158**
Selçuk, Turkey **233**
Semarang, Java, Indonesia **267**
Seniors **7**
Seniors' discounts **30**
Sensation $★★★ **96**
Seoul (Inchon), South Korea **276**
Setting sail **49**
Seven Seas Cruise Line, Radisson **80, 125**
Seward, Alaska, US **157**
Sex at Sea **274**
Seychelle Islands **237**
Shanghai, China **263**
Shipboard activities **17, 50**
Shipboard credit line **48**
Shipboard etiquette **53**
Shipbuilding **165**
Ship facilities **195**
Ship layout **48**
Ship names **268**
Ship personnel **253**
Ship size **13**
Ships, rating *see inside front cover*
Ships' rules **15**
Shopping **56, 151**
Shore excursions **53**
Shore excursions, pre-booking **38**
Silver Cloud $$$$★★★★★★ **86, 136**
Silversea Cruises **86, 136**
Silver Wind $$$$★★★★★★ **86, 136**

Singapore **276**
Singles **6**
Singles, cabins for **35**
Singles' discounts **30**
Sitka, Alaska, US **157**
Sizing Things Up **13**
Skagway, Alaska, US **158**
Sky Princess $$$★★★★ **124**
Sloane, Barbara **91** (bests)
Small ships **8**
Smoking **52**
Song of America $$★★★ **131**
Song of Flower $$$$★★★★★★ **82, 126**
South Africa **238**
Southampton, England **199**
South/Central America **178** (chapter and map)
South Korea **276**
South Pacific **244** (chapter and map)
Sovereign of the Seas $$★★★ **132**
Spain **228**
Special diets **38**
Special Expeditions **136**
Special interests **8**
Special-interest Sailing: Selecting a Theme Cruise **33**
Special needs, travelers with **38**
Special occasions **39**
Special or offbeat promotions **30**
Spirit, Seabourn **84**
Splendour of the Seas $$$★★★★ **128**
Sri Lanka **277**
Standard cabins **35**
Standby rates **30**
Star Clipper $$★★★★★ **88, 137**
Star Clippers **88, 137**
Star Flyer $$★★★★★ **88, 137**
Star Princess **124**
Star/Ship Oceanic $$★★ **120**
Statendam $$$★★★★ **109**
Stateroom upgrades **29**
Stella Oceanis $$★ **133**
Stella Solaris $$$★★★ **133**
Stockholm, Sweden **208**
Suites **36**
Sulawesi, Indonesia **268**
Sun Princess $$★★★★★ **78, 120**
Surabaya, Java, Indonesia **268**
Suva, Fiji **245**
Swan Hellenic Cruises **137**
Sweden **208**
Sydney, New South Wales, Australia **258**
Symbols *see inside front cover*
Symphony, Crystal **70, 105**

T

Tahiti, French Polynesia **247**
Taipei (Keelung), Taiwan **277**
Taiwan **277**

Taking a shore excursion 53
Talk About a Water Hazard!: Golf on the High Seas 119
Tallinn, Estonia 200
Tanzania 238
Tasmania, Australia 256
Teens, making friends 59
Tel Aviv/Jaffa, Israel 222
Television 265
Tenerife, Canary Islands 230
Terms, nautical 57
Thailand 278
Theme cruises 33
Third/fourth passenger, free or discounted fare 28
Tipping 61
Tobago 175
Today's ships 5
Tokyo, Japan 271
Tonga 249
Top Ships 66 (chapter)
Tortola, British Virgin Islands 169
Tours, active 54
Tours, port 53
Traditional cruising 8
Travel agencies 31
Travel agency newsletters 21
Travel documents 41
Travelers with special needs 38
Trinidad 176
Trip cancellation and interruption insurance 40
Triples/quads, cabins 35
Trondheim, Norway 206
Troubleshooting 60
Tunisia 231
Tunis (La Goulette), Tunisia 231
Turkey 231
Two-for-one discounts 28
A Typical Day on a Caribbean Cruise 17
Typical seasons 12

U

Ukraine Republic 233
Ultraluxury cruises 11
United States 148
Upgrades, air 28
Upgrades, stateroom 29
Uruguay 189
Ushuaia, Argentina 181
US Virgin Islands 177

V

Valletta, Malta 225
Valparaíso/Viña del Mar, Chile 186
Value-added discounts 30
Value, getting the best 26
Vancouver, British Columbia, Canada 143
Veendam $$$★★★★ 109
Venezuela 190

Venice, Italy 224
Victoria, Australia 258
Victoria, British Columbia, Canada 144
Victoria, Costa 68, 104
Victoria, Mahé, Seychelle Islands 237
Vietnam 279
Villefranche-sur-Mer, France 216
Viña del Mar/Valparaíso, Chile 186
Visas 41
Visby, Sweden 209
Vision of the Seas 132
Visitors on board 46
Vistafjord $$$$★★★★ 106

W

Wait list 40
Warnemünde (Berlin), Germany 201
Washington, US 156
Web sites 21
Weddings at sea 108
Welcome aboard! 47
Wellington, New Zealand 252
Westerdam $$★★★ 112
Western Samoa 249
Wheelchair accessibility 7, 35
When to cruise 12
Who are today's cruisers? 6
Wholesalers 32
Who's Who on Board 253
Why cruise? 5
Willemstad, Curaçao 170
Windjammer Barefoot Cruises 138
Wind Song $$$★★★★★ 90, 138
Wind Spirit $$$★★★★★ 90, 138
Wind Star $$$★★★★★ 90, 138
Windstar Cruises 90, 138
Windward $$$★★★ 114
Wines 52
Wonder, Disney 109
The World 2 (map)
World Wide Web 21

Y

Yalta, Ukraine Republic 233
Yangon, Myanmar 274
Yankee Clipper $★★ 138
Yorktown Clipper $$$★★★ 102
Young children, travelers with 38

Z

Zanzibar, Tanzania 238
Zenith $$$★★★★ 100
Zihuatanejo/Ixtapa, Mexico 147

Ships Index

Only ships with star ratings are listed below. All ships are listed alphabetically in the main (preceding) index. Price categories reflect the fare per passenger per day for a mid-category cabin (or suite on an all suite ship) during the peak season.

★★★★★★ As good as it gets
★★★★★ Exceptional
★★★★ Excellent
★★★ Very Good
★★ Good
★ Seaworthy

$$$$ Big Bucks ($500-$1,000)
$$$ Expensive ($300-$450)
$$ Reasonable ($200-$300)
$ The Price Is Right ($100-$200)

★★★★★★

Crystal Harmony $$$$ 70, 105
Crystal Symphony $$$$ 70, 105
Royal Viking Sun $$$$ 72, 106
Seabourn Legend $$$$ 84
Seabourn Pride $$$$ 84
Seabourn Spirit $$$$ 84
Sea Goddess I $$$$ 74, 106
Sea Goddess II $$$$ 74, 106
Silver Cloud $$$$ 86, 136
Silver Wind $$$$ 86, 136
Song of Flower $$$$ 82, 126

★★★★★

Century $$$ 66, 100
CostaClassica $$ 68, 104
CostaRomantica $$ 68, 104
CostaVictoria $$ 68, 104
Crown Princess $$$ 76, 120
Dawn Princess $$ 78, 120
Galaxy $$$ 66, 100
Radisson Diamond $$$$ 126
Regal Princess $$$ 76, 120
Star Clipper $$ 88, 137
Star Flyer $$ 88, 137
Wind Song $$$ 90, 138
Wind Spirit $$$ 90, 138
Wind Star $$$ 90, 138

★★★★

Carnival Destiny $$ 94
Club Med 1 $$$ 102
Club Med 2 $$$ 102
CostaAllegra $$ 103
CostaMarina $$ 103
Grandeur of the Seas $$ 127
Hanseatic $$$$ 125
Horizon $$$ 100
Imagination $ 97
Inspiration $ 97
Island Princess $$$ 121
Legend of the Seas $$$ 128
Marco Polo $$$ 118
Norway $$$ 10, 115
Norwegian Crown $$$ 117

Oceanic Grace $$$$ **117**
Pacific Princess $$$ **121**
Queen Elizabeth 2 (QE2), Grill
   Class $$$$ **105**
Royal Princess $$$ **123**
Ryndam $$$ **109**
Sea Cloud $$$$ **135**
Sky Princess $$$ **124**
Splendour of the Seas $$$ **128**
Statendam $$$ **109**
Veendam $$$ **109**
Vistafjord $$$$ **106**
Zenith $$$ **100**

★★★

Celebration $ **95**
Dreamward $$$ **114**
Ecstasy $ **96**
Explorer $$$$ **92**
Fantasy $ **96**
Fascination $ **96**
Holiday $ **95**
Jubilee $ **95**
Leeward $$ **115**
Majesty of the Seas $$ **129**
Minerva $$$ **137**
Monarch of the Seas $$ **129**
Nantucket Clipper $$$ **102**
Nieuw Amsterdam $$ **110**
Noordam $$ **110**
Nordic Empress $$$ **131**
Oriana $$$ **122**
Queen Elizabeth 2 (QE2), Caronia
   Class $$$$ **105**
Renaissance V $$$ **126**
Renaissance VI $$$ **126**
Renaissance VII $$$ **126**
Renaissance VIII $$$ **126**
Sensation $ **96**
Song of America $$ **131**
Sovereign of the Seas $$ **132**
Stella Solaris $$$ **133**
Westerdam $$ **112**
Windward $$$ **114**
Yorktown Clipper $$$ **102**

★★

Crown Majesty $$ **113**
Fantome $ **138**
Flying Cloud $ **138**
Independence $ **93**
Mandalay $ **138**
OceanBreeze $$ **107**
Odysseus $$ **132**
Olympic $$ **134**
Orpheus $$ **134**
Polaris $$$$ **136**
Polynesia $ **138**
Royal Majesty $$ **113**
Sea Bird $$$ **137**
SeaBreeze $$ **108**
Sea Lion $$$ **137**

Star/Ship Oceanic $$ **120**
Yankee Clipper $ **138**

★

Caribbean Prince $ **93**
Grande Caribe $ **93**
Mayan Prince $ **93**
Niagara Prince $ **93**
Queen Elizabeth 2 (QE2),
   Mauretania Class $$$$ **105**
Stella Oceanis $$ **133**

Features

Alaska Shopping **151**
Barging Through Europe **83**
Behind the Scenes on a Cruise Ship
   195
The Captain's Table **111**
A Checklist for Honeymooners **42**
Child's Play **248**
Coping with Mal de Mer **257**
Cruise Ship Superlatives **69**
The Cruise that Changed History **15**
Cruising European Waterways **122**
Cruising the Coast of Norway **209**
Days of Wine and Roses: Extras for
   Newlyweds and Other Happy
   Couples **101**
Disney Cruises: Magic and Wonder
   at Sea **109**
Getting Hitched at Sea **108**
The Godmother **77**
Hollywood Sets Sail **99**
Initial Explanation **268**
Keeping Fit Afloat **190**
A Legendary Liner **10**
"The Love Boat" and Beyond:
   Cruising on the Small Screen **265**
Perfect Gentlemen **121**
Perks for Cruise Line Alumni **31**
Plying the Exotic Rivers of the
   World **130**
Pomp, Circumstance, and
   Superstition: The Ancient Art of
   Shipbuilding **165**
Precious Cargo: Traveling on a
   Freighter **239**
Rollin' on the River **147**
Sailor Speak: A Guide to Shipboard
   Lingo **57**
Sea Sagas **217**
See Green **158**
Sex at Sea **274**
Sizing Things Up **13**
Special-interest Sailing: Selecting a
   Theme Cruise **33**
Talk About a Water Hazard!: Golf on
   the High Seas **119**
A Typical Day on a Caribbean Cruise
   17
Who's Who on Board **253**

Bests

Arzt, Lorraine (Property Manage-
   ment and Investments, Joachim
   J. Arzt Inc.) **191**
Clampett, Bob (Editor, *Vacationer
   Magazine;* Writer, Author,
   Screenwriter) **191**
Diller, Phyllis (Entertainer) **45**
Edwards, Mona Shafer (Courtroom
   Artist, *ABC News;* Fashion
   Illustrator) **159**
Feldman, Martin, Dr. (Vice
   President of Marketing, Daniel
   Products Company) **191**
Good, Bruce (Director of Cruise
   Product, Royal Cruise Line) **259**
Helft, Karl. W. (Writer and Producer
   of military history documentaries
   for German television) **279**
Lawson, Cicely and Lew (Passen-
   gers, Royal Cruise Line) **191**
Leshner, Marty (Writer) **279**
Maxtone-Graham, John (Marine
   Historian and Dedicated
   Passenger) **165**
Mosher, Rosemary J. (General
   Manager/Property management,
   Iona Ranch Mobile Home Park)
   159
Murphy, Karen (President,
   Murphy/O'Brien
   Communications) **45**
Riley, Frank and Elfriede (Travel
   Writers, Electronic Journalists,
   Authors, TV/Radio Commentators,
   Photographers) **159**
Sloane, Barbara (Personal
   Assistant, Writer, Proofreader) **91**

Maps

Antarctica **2**, **192**
Asia **260**
Australia **254**
The Bahamas **162**
Bermuda **160**
Caribbean **166**
Central America **178**
Central Nassau **162**
Grand Bahama, The Bahamas **163**
Hamilton, Bermuda **160**
Hawaiian Islands **240**
Indian Ocean **234**
Map Key *see inside front cover*
Mediterranean **210**
New Zealand **250**
North America **140**
Northern Europe **196**
St. George's, Bermuda **160**
South America **178**
South Pacific **244**
The World **2**

ACCESS® Guides

Order by phone, toll-free: 1-800-331-3761

Travel: Promo # R00111

Name _____ Phone _____

Address _____

City _____ State _____ Zip _____

Please send me the following ACCESS® Guides:

☐ **ATLANTA** ACCESS® $18.50
0-06-277156-6

☐ **BARCELONA** ACCESS® $17.00
0-06-277000-4

☐ **BOSTON** ACCESS® $18.50
0-06-277197-3

☐ **BUDGET** EUROPE ACCESS® $18.50
0-06-277171-X

☐ **CAPE COD, MARTHA'S VINEYARD, & NANTUCKET** ACCESS® $18.50
0-06-277159-0

☐ **CARIBBEAN** ACCESS® $20.00
0-06-277165-5

☐ **CHICAGO** ACCESS® $18.50
0-06-277196-5

☐ **CRUISE** ACCESS® $20.00
0-06-277190-6

☐ **FLORENCE/VENICE/MILAN** ACCESS® $18.50
0-06-277170-1

☐ **HAWAII** ACCESS® $18.50
0-06-277223-6

☐ **LAS VEGAS** ACCESS® $18.50
0-06-277224-4

☐ **LONDON** ACCESS® $18.50
0-06-277161-2

☐ **LOS ANGELES** ACCESS® $18.50
0-06-277167-1

☐ **MEXICO** ACCESS® $18.50
0-06-277166-3

☐ **MIAMI & SOUTH FLORIDA** ACCESS® $18.50
0-06-277226-0

☐ **MONTREAL & QUEBEC CITY** ACCESS® $18.50
0-06-277160-4

☐ **NEW ORLEANS** ACCESS® $18.50
0-06-277227-9

☐ **NEW YORK CITY** ACCESS® $18.50
0-06-277162-0

☐ **NEW YORK RESTAURANTS** ACCESS®
$13.00 0-06-277218-X

☐ **ORLANDO & CENTRAL FLORIDA** ACCESS®
$18.50
0-06-277228-7

☐ **PARIS** ACCESS® $18.50
0-06-277163-9

☐ **PHILADELPHIA** ACCESS® $18.50
0-06-277155-8

☐ **ROME** ACCESS® $18.50
0-06-277195-7

☐ **SAN DIEGO** ACCESS® $18.50
0-06-277185-X

☐ **SAN FRANCISCO** ACCESS® $18.50
0-06-277169-8

☐ **SAN FRANCISCO RESTAURANTS** ACCESS®
$13.00
0-06-277219-8

☐ **SANTA FE/TAOS/ALBUQUERQUE** ACCESS®
$18.50
0-06-277194-9

☐ **SEATTLE** ACCESS® $18.50
0-06-277198-1

☐ **SKI COUNTRY** ACCESS®
Eastern United States $18.50
0-06-277174-4

☐ **SKI COUNTRY** ACCESS®
Western United States $18.50
0-06-277174-4

☐ **WASHINGTON DC** ACCESS® $18.50
0-06-277158-2

☐ **WINE COUNTRY** ACCESS® France $18.50
0-06-277193-0

☐ **WINE COUNTRY** ACCESS®
Northern California $18.50
0-06-277164-7

Prices subject to change without notice.

Total for **ACCESS**® Guides:	$
Please add applicable sales tax:	
Add $4.00 for first book S&H, $1.00 per additional book:	
Total payment:	$

☐ Check or Money Order enclosed. Offer valid in the United States only. Please make payable to HarperCollins*Publishers*.

☐ Charge my credit card ☐ American Express ☐ Visa ☐ MasterCard

Card no. _____ Exp. date _____

Signature _____

Send orders to: HarperCollins*Publishers*
P.O. Box 588
Dunmore, PA 18512-0588